STATE AND SOCIETY

STATE AND SOCIETY

A Reader in
Comparative Political Sociology

EDITED BY
REINHARD BENDIX
University of California, Berkeley

IN COLLABORATION WITH

COENRAAD BRAND
RANDALL COLLINS
ROBERT G. MICHELS
HANS-EBERHARD MUELLER
GAIL OMVEDT
ELIEZER ROSENSTEIN
JEAN-GUY VAILLANCOURT
R. STEPHEN WARNER

University of California Press
Berkeley, Los Angeles, London

UNIVERSITY OF CALIFORNIA PRESS
BERKELEY AND LOS ANGELES, CALIFORNIA
UNIVERSITY OF CALIFORNIA PRESS, LTD.
LONDON, ENGLAND

COPYRIGHT © 1968, BY LITTLE, BROWN AND COMPANY (INC.)

FIRST CALIFORNIA EDITION, 1973
CALIFORNIA PAPERBACK EDITION, 1973
ISBN: 0–520–02490–7 (PAPER-BOUND)
    0–520–02421–4 (CLOTH-BOUND)
LIBRARY OF CONGRESS CATALOG CARD NUMBER 73–76270

PRINTED IN THE UNITED STATES OF AMERICA

Contents

v

SECTION E
THE WESTERN EXPERIENCE:
POLITICS OF THE MODERN STATE

E 1 / Social Groups Considered Politically

E 2 / Structure of Authority

E 3 / Aspects of Legitimacy

INTRODUCTION

In the *Communist Manifesto*, Marx and Engels celebrated the revolutionizing role of the bourgeoisie in the development and spread of modern civilization:

> The bourgeoisie, wherever it has got the upper hand, has put an end to all feudal, patriarchal, idyllic relations. It has pitilessly torn asunder the motley feudal ties that bound man to his "natural superiors," and has left no other bond between man and man than naked self-interest, than callous "cash payment." . . . It has accomplished wonders for surpassing Egyptian pyramids, Roman aqueducts, and Gothic cathedrals. . . . The bourgeoisie, by the rapid improvement of all instruments of production, by the immensely facilitated means of communication, draws all nations, even the most barbarian, into civilisation. . . . It compels all nations, on pain of extinction, to adopt the bourgeois mode of production; it compels them to introduce what it calls civilisation into their midst, *i.e.*, to become bourgeois themselves. In a word, it creates a world after its own image.[1]

Greatly influenced by this image of the bourgeois revolution against feudal society and its worldwide repercussions, economic history and comparative economics have been focused on the questions "How did modern industrial society come to be?" and "How can its achievements be realized elsewhere?"

This volume is devoted to the analysis of related transformations in the political sphere: the emergence in Western Europe of the modern nation-state and the impact of that state on societies around the world. In this case too, there was a revolutionary agent of change which tore asunder the political ties of feudalism. This agent was the absolute monarch and his "royal servants" in the 16th, 17th, and 18th centuries. The autonomous jurisdictions and private armies of feudal society were replaced by a centralized administration and a standing army of mercenaries. "The whole process," writes Max Weber,

> is a complete parallel to the development of the capitalist enterprise through the gradual expropriation of the independent producers. In the end, the modern state controls the total means of political organization, which actually come together under a single head.[2]

This centralization of the functions of government was a many-sided process, variously related to the commercial expansion of Europe since the end of the 15th century. Eventually, the modern state, as it developed in Europe, also coordinated the commercial outposts overseas through colonial regimes which put their own stamp on the spread of European civilization around the world.

This reader contains articles analyzing this phenomenon. The articles have been selected with a particular "comparative political sociology" in mind. The introduction indicates what meaning we have given to this field of study.

[1] *The Communist Manifesto* (New York: International Publishers, 1948), pp. 11–13.
[2] *From Max Weber: Essays in Sociology*, ed. H. H. Gerth and C. Wright Mills (New York: Oxford University Press, 1946), p. 82.

II

Today comparative studies are quite fashionable. Academics are enjoined to make their research proposals "comparative" in scope. Training grants to students make comparative studies an attractive area of specialization. Articles, journals, books, and readers with the adjective "comparative" in the title are appearing in increasing number. This reader is an instance of this trend.

There are many reasons for this interest. The introduction of European social theory to America in the 1930's did much to break up the parochialism of American sociology. Alongside the older sociological concerns of the family, crime, social disorganization, and social psychology rose the interest, stimulated by the study of Marx, Weber, and Durkheim, in understanding the distinctiveness of modern society in comparison with its historical predecessors. Also, in reaction to academic overspecialization, interdisciplinary groups of all sorts have been set up, encouraging a broadening of interests. Still more important than the inherent development of intellectual interests has been the direct impact of World War II. Irrevocably, the United States, having important military and economic interests all over the world, has been drawn into the international arena. As a result, research on social processes beyond the confines of American society has been stimulated greatly. In addition, there is surely need for such research, where — as in the new nations — planned social and economic development has become the hallmark of policy.

There is a danger, however, that in this drive toward exploration beyond the borders of his country and his discipline, the student and researcher may forget where he came from and where he is going. What, after all, is the intellectual justification for a concern with "comparative analysis"? All inquiry into causes is comparative insofar as it uses a pure or approximate experimental method. Two similar units are subjected to different experiences; any differences in results are then interpreted as the "effect" of the different, experimentally produced experiences. Yet "comparative studies" seems to imply more than this experimental procedure. A brief review of earlier approaches is in order.

The oldest of these is the study of comparative constitutions, which goes back to ancient Greece. Aristotle and the students in his Lyceum collected and classified the constitutions of more than a hundred Greek city-states. Their purpose was to define the characteristics of the best possible political structure, given the conditions of economic organization and of human nature. Continuing through a series of classical, medieval, and modern writers such as Montesquieu, Bryce, and Mosca, this tradition has been fundamentally *normative* in approach. It asks what kind of government is best for the maximization of certain values, whether these be justice, freedom, or stability. Lipset's paper on party systems (below, Section E1) is partly an exercise in this tradition of comparative constitutions.[3]

---

[3] This is not to ignore the considerable normative content of much contemporary comparative work. It is merely to point out one of the historically distinctive bases of comparative concerns.

Another old tradition, again finding its roots in ancient Greece, is the theory of *social evolution*. In the 19th century, Auguste Comte adopted a particular version of this theory. According to Comte's use of the "comparative method," all societies presently existing could be arranged on an evolutionary scale from primitive and metaphysical to modern and scientific. Such "comparison" consisted in an assessment of intellectual modernity. Once this was done, all existing societies could be arranged on the scale, irrespective of time and place. At best this was merely a way of classifying societies; no actual comparison leading to a verified theory of social evolution was presented. Some recent attempts at a theory of social change by functionalist sociologists have revived this earlier interest in a fusion of evolutionary and comparative interests.[4]

Cross-societal comparison is also used, and rightly used, as a *pedagogic device*. Every beginning sociology student is warned against the pitfalls of ethnocentrism. Let him not think that the way he finds his social life ordered is the only way things can be done. Thus he learns that in many societies the husband-wife-children group is not the basic social unit; that many societies do not use money; that social regulations are more often understood than written and codified; that not all societies have governments. In the same process, he also learns to appreciate the distinctiveness of his own society. This kind of learning experience is not our primary aim in this reader, but we hope that it will be used in this manner as well.

The comparative studies of such writers as Marx, Weber, and Tocqueville have a related, but distinctive, objective. Marx and Weber were both interested in *specifying the distinctiveness* of modern society, which for Marx was characterized by bourgeois relations of production and for Weber by rationalized social organization. Marx undertook studies of the ancient world and of China and India partly to understand in what ways these societies differed from his own. He maintained that the absence of private property in Asia and the existence of communal property in ancient Greece were the key features separating them from modern society. For Weber, property relations were one aspect rather than the basic determinant of social structures. He focused attention upon the interrelation between material interests and the beliefs of status-groups in order to study societies comparatively.[5] Tocqueville, in his anxiety over the future of France, wanted to understand what the new social order called "democracy" involved. His studies of America provided him with an opportunity to observe the implications of equality where equality had become accepted and hence to assess the possibilities and dangers which lay in store for the more inequalitarian societies of Europe. The articles by

---

[4] Cf. Talcott Parsons, *Societies: Evolutionary and Comparative Perspectives* (Englewood Cliffs, N.J.: Prentice-Hall, 1966). It should be noted, however, that Parsons avoids the major problem of Comte's theory: the failure to specify a mechanism of social change.

[5] See Randall Collins, "A Comparative Approach to Political Sociology" (*infra*), for a discussion of Weber's comparative methodology.

Dahrendorf, Huntington, Neustadt, and Pekelis, reprinted below, have in part such specifications as their object. Although they do not attain the goal of a scientific test of an empirical proposition — which, after all, is an ideal not often attained — such efforts are an indispensable beginning. For without being clear what is distinctive about the cases we are concerned with, we may find ourselves explaining the wrong thing. For instance, Pekelis tells us that it is not individualism which is peculiar to England and the United States but rather the power of the small collectivity. Thus it is with the latter, not the former, that we must deal.

Perhaps the most important issue of comparative studies today is the development and application of a *suitable conceptual language*. Comparative studies must contend with the fact that the same process, from the point of view of sociological analysis, takes on different names in different societies; or different processes may have the same name. As Neustadt points out below, the term "cabinet officer" as applied to officials both in England and the United States, obscures more than it reveals. Here again we are faced with the problem of identifying what it is we are trying to explain. Thus political scientists led by David Easton and Gabriel Almond have developed elaborate classificatory systems in order to pave the way for comparative analysis.[6] Properly considered, these schemes are the beginning of comparative studies, but to date they have been used largely as labeling devices. Thus someone will write a statement on Indian politics using the new language; another on Japan; another on Ghana; and in this way the opportunity for comparative analysis is missed.

Each of these approaches has something to be said for it, and particularly the last two — specification and classification — are indispensable. Yet the goal of comparative studies toward which we may realistically strive is still something else. It involves a return to the logic scientific procedure and to the art of asking "why." Tocqueville's analysis of the causes of the French Revolution is a case in point. Here we have the basic ingredients of a scientific puzzle: of several countries of similar feudal backgrounds only one had experienced the revolution. Why? Tocqueville finds that in comparison to Germany, France had experienced a decline of feudal institutions. More peasants owned land. Feudal lords were no longer performing their traditional functions though they were still enjoying their traditional privileges. Administration was more centralized. Moreover, within Germany, it was in the provinces along the Rhine, most like France, that revolutionary zeal was experienced. By means of comparison, therefore, Tocqueville is able to delineate the true causes of the revolution. Wertheim's discussion of corruption in South-East Asia similarly shows how we can separate out actual from spurious casual relations. Rather than attributing corruption to an "inscrutable Asiatic personality," he maintains that corruption can only be identified as a problem upon the introduction of Napoleonic administrative reforms. It is only on the basis of

[6] For a recent statement, see Gabriel A. Almond and G. Bingham Powell, Jr., *Comparative Politics: A Developmental Approach* (Boston: Little, Brown and Co., 1966).

these or similar reforms that one can speak of a separation between public and private spheres of life, and without such separation the term "corruption" lacks clear meaning. Thus Western Europe, and not Asia, is seen as historically exceptional.

Ideally, comparative studies should be used to test empirical propositions of universal applicability. But in the present state of knowledge, close comparative analyses of a few cases may be more fruitful than constructions and illustrations of elaborate typologies.[7]

III

This approach, however, does not and cannot avoid a minimum of conceptual considerations. After all, we have a certain topic in mind, namely, "political sociology." What do we mean by "political"? There is no easy answer. We may confine ourselves to that which is conventionally defined as political. This strategy will restrict the scope of our comparisons to societies that are similar in their explicit recognition of a "political sphere" and, therefore, in much else besides. On the other hand, if we define the political without regard to socially defined institutions — for instance, if we analyze the "political" aspect of the family or the business corporation — the scope of our comparison may become so large that nothing can be legitimately excluded from our consideration and we are left without analytic guidelines. In his discussion of types of domination Weber discarded the concept of "power" for analogous reasons, because the applicability of the term to *all* social relationships made its meaning amorphous and scientifically useless.[8]

The answer we have adopted for this volume reflects this dilemma. We recognize that basic ingredients of "politics" occur in every society: social inequality, group conflict, decision-making, the use of force. The articles we have included in the section on "Pre-Modern Politics" analyze some of these processes in societies in which "politics" is not explicitly recognized as such. The reason is that in these societies political actions occur among several competing, equally legitimate, centers of authority. We maintain that in speaking of "politics" today we implicitly recognize a "separate sphere," because actions become "political" in a special sense when they pertain to the state as the single legitimate center of authority. The institution of the state is a distinctive invention of the modern world. One should add that as a historical phenomenon the state should be distinguished from the "Politics" of the Pre-Modern World, and that it may also have to be distinguished from an as yet ill-understood "Politics" of the Post-Modern World.

Accordingly, we have decided to use the term "political" in a restricted rather than a universal sense. Though "political functions" like leadership, conflict, adjudication, decision-making, or the legitimate application of force may

---

[7] This is however a matter of choice and also of division of scientific labor. Ours is hardly the only legitimate approach.

[8] Max Weber, *Wirtschaft und Gesellschaft*, ed. Johannes Winckelmann (Koeln: Kiepenheuer and Witsch, 1964), Vol. II, p. 692.

occur in all societies, we wish to distinguish those societies in which these functions are performed by some group or organization specifically authorized for this purpose. The governments of modern nation-states perform this authenticating function, even if actual implementation is delegated to subordinate agents or agencies. We note that attempts to avoid reference to such *socially defined institutions* and instead identify and discuss *analytically defined processes* find themselves in the end dealing with these concrete institutions all the same. If, for example, the political aspect of society is defined as "those interactions which affect the use or threat of use of legitimate physical coercion," the empirical problem still comes down to the analysis of group-impacts upon the state and the response of the state's administration.[9]

It is for this reason that in the title of this volume we refer to the traditional institutional distinction of state and society rather than to the more recent analytical distinction of political and social systems. On the Continent the distinction between state and society is considered a major, if controversial, perspective for an understanding of the nation-state. By contrast, in the Anglo-Saxon tradition, the distinction is considered artificial and more or less inapplicable. A proximate reason for this difference is historical, related to the timing and degree of governmental centralization. Crudely put, in many continental countries absolute monarchy developed an administrative corps of its own, which constituted a socially and politically distinct group. In England, however, monarchy depended upon a society governed since the Norman Conquest by a socially and economically preeminent gentry at the local level, and since the late 17th century at the national level as well. One consequence has been that in England high rank in status and wealth has been associated with the administrative implementation of political rule, an association which made the distinction between society and the state difficult to perceive. Such obstacles to perception did not exist to the same extent on the Continent. But these historical and perceptual distinctions (which are merely hinted at by these remarks) are not hard and fast. There is a state apparatus with its hierarchic structure in Anglo-Saxon countries, and an effect of social groups on that state apparatus on the Continent. Aware of this historical and intellectual background, we have chosen *State and Society* as our title in the belief that at a conceptual level the distinction can be put to good use.

In the modern world the state is the dominant political institution; and it is with this state — its forging, its use, its maintenance, and its problems — that these articles deal. Thus, we do not define "politics" analytically as a universal phenomenon, cutting across all socially defined institutions. Nor, even, do we define the political as a function that is contingent upon the growth of a society to a certain size or complexity.[10] We are not concerned whether the appearance of the state was a matter of evolutionary "emergence" — some-

[9] Cf. Almond and Powell, *op. cit.*, pp. 17–18.

[10] Cf. Walter Goldschmidt, *Comparative Functionalism: An Essay in Anthropological Theory* (Berkeley and Los Angeles: University of California Press, 1966), pp. 106–117.

thing, that is, which was "natural" in the course of development. On the contrary, to speak of politics today is to refer to a historically developed pattern of institutions. Since its creation by European princes in the last centuries of the feudal era, the state has proved to be an effective means of using and holding power, which has been forced upon, adopted by, or at least emulated by leaders of societies all over the world. Recourse to this historical development in order to understand the conditions under which states can be made and maintained appears to us more promising than to pretend that historical events and international imitation and penetration have not played a decisive role (see Sections D and F). That does not imply exclusive concentration on the European experience and a disregard of the conditions obtaining in the non-Western world. On the contrary, we feel that those theorists who disregard the conditions under which the modern state developed and expanded are most likely to universalize a "political process" and hence to underestimate the differentiating effects of the historical legacies and institutional structures of non-Western societies.[11]

It is not enough, however, to say that we are concentrating on the comparative analysis of the state. This, too, is a diffuse topic requiring further specification. What sort of specification? In the discussion leading to the preparation of this volume, two approaches were suggested. One was the general historical outline much as it was finally adopted. The other was an emphasis on common analytical problems of political life, such as the organization of power, the handling of grievances, the articulation of demands, the maintenance of a claim to rule, and so on. At first, the historical and the analytical approaches were presented as mutually exclusive alternatives. We decided, however, that this need not be so.

In the first place, a crude conceptualization is involved in the organization of the volume, as follows:

PRE-MODERN POLITICS
THE WESTERN EXPERIENCE: POLITICS OF TRANSITION
                            POLITICS OF THE MODERN STATE

POLITICS OF MODERNIZATION: WESTERN IMPACT AND NATIVE RESPONSE
                            SEARCH FOR A NEW ORDER

This outline makes explicit the assumptions on which our approach is based. Since "the state" originated in the era of absolute monarchies, we should become aware of three dimensions: the type of politics characteristic of societies that are not organized as "states"; some of the transitional processes that went into the formation of the "modern state"; and some of the political problems characteristic of that state as an operating institutional framework. At the same time we recognize the fact that this political structure of Western societies has had international repercussions, at first through European commercial expan-

---

[11] See also Charles C. Moskos, Jr., and Wendell Bell, "Emerging Nations and Ideologies of American Social Scientists," *American Sociologist*, Vol. II (May 1967), pp. 67–72.

sion and subsequently through the development of colonialism. Societies around the world have come under the sway of Western expansion, whether or not they were conquered. These societies have experienced crises of legitimacy as a result of the Western impact and have attempted to establish a political order of their own, especially after World War II when a large number of dependent or colonial territories gained their independence. Here again it seems appropriate to distinguish — however crudely — between a period of transition, i.e., the early repercussions of the Western impact, and a period of proximate political consolidation. We would emphasize the uncertainties not only of the outcome of that attempted consolidation but also of the "politics of the modern state" as we know it in the West. A historically delimited term like the "state" implies not only a transition in the early modern period but sooner or later a transition to new and as yet unrealized or unrecognized institutional patterns in the future.

In the second place, there are problems more or less common to the modern state as it has developed in the West and diffused to other parts of the world. These common problems should be approached at a general, analytic level, and we decided to do so by selecting three areas on which we wish to comment briefly. The first of these areas, "social groups considered politically," involves the following problems: How do groups become politically relevant? How are the members of various groups brought into the political arena? What are the effects of different kinds of cleavages between groups? How do these groups make known their political demands? The basic orientation of these sections (E1 and G1) is the fact that the political organization of any society is based upon concrete groups and their interests, not upon the characteristics of the people taken as a homogeneous mass. This is at once the basis of political life as well as the source of many of the day-to-day worries of the political leader.

The second problem area is called "the structure of authority." It asks the questions: How do leaders handle power? How do they attempt, successfully or unsuccessfully, to secure the prerogatives of their power against the tendency of their subordinates to arrogate power to themselves? What are the conditions under which the making of political decisions can be isolated from the administration of those decisions? The articles in these sections (E2 and G2) are all based on the awareness that the use of political power involves organization and delegation of authority and hence dependence of the holder of power on other individuals. Organization is thus at once necessary and problematic.

The third problem area, which we have called "aspects of legitimacy," focuses on the maintenance of political authority vis à vis those who are subjected to it. How is the fact of holding power transformed into a right? What are some of the promises made by political leaders to the people, and what are the effects of these promises? What are considered to be the legitimate issues for political controversy and conflict? We begin in these sections with the idea that political leaders attempt to justify their positions by transforming the fact of their power into a right, often through promises to "deliver the goods." This again is a dilemma, for justifications have a way of becoming constraints on those who have made them.

These focal concerns are not exhaustive of the problems facing the modern and the modernizing state. Our outline can only be suggestive in this respect. Yet we do maintain that the problem-areas chosen are important from the standpoints both of policies of development and of sociological analysis.

IV

What, finally, do we take to be a "sociological approach"? In our search for selections we went well beyond the sociological journals or even the journals of the other social sciences. Our own experiences and the subject as we had defined it suggested rather a wide variety of substantive and disciplinary areas. The diversity of the selections in this volume reflects this orientation. Fustel de Coulanges, Hintze, Pirenne, and von Laue are historians; Fallers and Despres are anthropologists; Huntington, Neustadt, Ehrmann, Rudolph, Kling, and Weiner are political scientists; the selection on "The Rise of National Feeling in Western Europe" is by an interdisciplinary committee; and Tocqueville, though we sociologists like to claim him, defies classification. We are not embarrassed by this variety. Political sociology is a hybrid field existing at the intersection of several disciplines. We venture to think that the materials here presented may serve as teaching aids in courses dealing with the relationships between state and society, whether these be taught in history, sociology, political science, or anthropology.

Despite this lack of disciplinary definition, the articles reprinted in this volume share something of a common approach to the analysis of social life. That approach may not be the dominant one in present-day American sociology, but it is one from a distinguished tradition and, moreover, one which fits in closely with the actual experience of social life. The logic of this approach is developed at length in the article by Collins below; let us here mention three of its salient features.

First, the unit most useful for the analysis of social life is not society-as-a-system but rather the existing social group or organization. Eberhard speaks of layers; Despres of plural ethnic groups. Fei analyzes peasants and gentry; Fustel de Coulanges, patricians and clients and plebs. The utility of this approach becomes clear when we deal with the pluralistic social orders discussed by Furnivall and Despres, where "society" exists at best as an unsteady imposition of the colonial ruler. More generally, the point is to emphasize that, whether or not a society is (or is usefully regarded as) a "system" is problematic. This approach faces the issue, often ignored by functionalists, that social integration is always a matter of degree, that some societies are more integrated than others, and that this variation remains to be explained.

Secondly, and related to this emphasis on the group and organization as units of analysis, there is the institutional approach to social analysis as opposed to another aspect of the organicist approach. Let us explain this distinction. Some theorists have maintained that in comparative analysis we should disregard the labels conventionally applied to human activities and look instead to the effects of these activities upon the whole of society.[12] Such a view usually insists that we get beyond the "merely formal" aspects of society — such as laws, administrative structures, and constitutional procedures — and look instead to the "informal" interactions among men in society through which these institutions actually work. We, on the other hand, hold that social life is structured — not exclusively of course, but structured nonetheless — by just those formal institutional mechanisms. To disregard such structures at least implies the belief that social reality is essentially amorphous. This does not mean that institutions work as they are intended to work; it does mean that they have an effect. Weber, for instance, treats the act of delegating administrative authority as having important consequences; it means that the superordinate — the "political" leader — becomes to some extent dependent on his subordinate — the "administrative" officer. Thus the working of the formal structure makes precarious the also formally defined distinction between politics and administration. For political sociology as we see it, the most useful view is that which comprehends formal institutions as important structural bases to which patterns of interaction should be related. We call this approach "sociological," but we do not insist on the label. Lipset makes this particular point a guiding theme of his article, "Party Systems and the Representation of Social Groups." He writes (below, pp. 280–281):

> Concern with formal constitutional provisions has generally been outside the province of political sociology. Sociologists tend to see party cleavages as reflections of an underlying structure, and hence, wittingly or not, frown on efforts to present the enacted rules of the game as key *causal* elements of a social structure. The sociologist's image of a social system, all of whose parts are interdependent, is at odds with the view of many political scientists, who believe that such seemingly minor differences in systems as variations in the way in which officials are elected can lead to stability or instability. An examination of comparative politics suggests that the political scientists are right, in that electoral laws determine the nature of the party system as much as any other structural variable.

The third feature of the approach here adopted is its emphasis on history. By this we mean three things. Social structures change; their backgrounds differ in important respects; and — most important of all — *the way things are today is in part explained by how they have come to be.* Huntington's article comparing American and European development is an excellent example. He finds that the American political structure represents, so to speak, an arrested case. Its decentralization, its profusion of autonomous jurisdictions, is accounted for, Huntington says, not by the pluralism of an industrial society but by the political structure of the Tudor constitution from which it derives. Thus well beyond the conventionally noted difficulties of constructing a similar system in the new

[12] E.g., Neil J. Smelser, "Notes on the Methodology of Comparative Analysis of Economic Activity," *Transactions of the Sixth World Congress of Sociology.*

states stands the problem that this decentralized system is not at all in harmony with the requirements of a modernizing society. As well as providing a source of pessimism as regards the prospects of American-style democracy in the new states, Huntington thus demonstrates the necessity of taking history into account.

V

In the above explication of what we understand comparative political sociology to be, we have developed the logic of the organization of this volume. Let us summarize it briefly. We begin with a section entitled "Perspectives" in which two approaches to comparative analysis are presented and evaluated. In "Pre-Modern Politics" we present articles illustrating both the presence of political processes such as conflict, decision, and control, and the absence of a modern state structure. Section D discusses the growth of that structure — a single authority holding sway by means of a rationalized administration over the population in a defined territory — as it first came to be in Western Europe. In Section F, the impact of that invention — colonialism and international emulation — is examined. Sections E and G are organized around the three problem areas — the handling of groups, the organization of power, and the securing of legitimacy — discussed above (p. 9). By separating the "Western Experience" from the "Politics of Modernization" we emphatically do not imply that the emergence of the Western state is a final model of development or that it is in any way the "natural" goal toward which development tends.[13] Rather, we want to draw attention to the fact that it is the Western state that has brought, to paraphrase Marx, all nations into its orbit of civilization. For better or worse, it has attempted to create a world after its own image, and we are witnessing today some of the repercussions of that attempt.

A word on the criteria we used for the selection of articles. We did not strive for a nice regional balance, such as four articles on Asia, four on Africa, and so on, for our purpose is analysis of political processes rather than illustration of variety. Instead we selected articles that were internally comparative (dealing with two or more cases or confronting one empirical case with a theory derived from another) or those that could be clearly juxtaposed with another article, the comparative implications to be drawn by the section introductions or by the reader.

Finally, we should point out that the nine editors share equally in the responsibility for this volume. The project was initiated in a graduate seminar, held during the Fall Quarter, 1966, in the Department of Sociology at the University of California, Berkeley. Work on the project continued throughout the academic year, 1966–1967, and the intellectual orientation set forth in this Introduction and elaborated in the article written by Randall Collins was "hammered out" in the course of our meetings. The senior editor expresses appreciation to his collaborators for their dedication to standards of scholarly

[13] For further remarks on this point, see Wilbert E. Moore, *Social Change* (Englewood Cliffs, N.J.: Prentice-Hall, 1963), p. 106.

excellence evident throughout. We are grateful for financial assistance in the preparation of this volume to the Research and Training Program for Comparative Developmental Studies, under a grant from the Carnegie Corporation, administered by the Institutes of Industrial Relations and International Studies at the University of California, Berkeley.

Senior Editor:
  Reinhard Bendix
Collaborating Editors:
  Coenraad Brand
  Randall Collins
  Robert G. Michels
  Hans-Eberhard Mueller
  Gail Omvedt
  Eliezer Rosenstein
  Jean-Guy Vaillancourt
  R. Stephen Warner

SECTION B

PERSPECTIVES

Problems of
Historical Sociology

WOLFRAM EBERHARD

SOCIAL SYSTEM AND MULTIPLE SOCIETY

An historical sociologist, especially one whose field of research is outside the U.S., encounters, to say the least, a number of difficulties in communication with those of his colleagues who are studying present-day society. These difficulties are most acute with respect to the new school of comparative sociologists, and they result in part from the fact that certain sociological concepts such as "social system," developed by analysts of American society, are not applicable to non-Western societies; in fact, their general usefulness seems to be doubtful. On the other hand, the concept "multiple society," which is usually thought to be the novelty par excellence in America, appears to be better suited to describe Asian social conditions.

"Social system," one of the most common, all-embracing concepts of American functionalists, has been used as an analytical tool for the study of any given society. This concept implies two assumptions. One assumption is that in such a system each unit, often called a sub-system, has a function in terms of all other units and thus interacts with these other units. While it is true that in a modern society any sub-system, especially one concerning activities, has some and often quite close interactions with many or all other units in the field of economics, it is usually implied that there is also social interaction between the units. The second assumption, although usually not mentioned, is that a social system implies a political-geographical area with clear-cut

From Wolfram Eberhard, *Conquerors and Rulers: Social Forces in Medieval China* (Leiden: E. J. Brill, 1965), pp. 1–17. Reprinted by permission of the author and publisher.

WOLFRAM EBERHARD is Professor of Sociology, University of California, Berkeley. A specialist in Asian societies, he is the author of numerous works including A *History of China* (1950), *Social Mobility in Traditional China* (1962), and most recently *Guilt and Sin in Traditional China* (1967).

borders, so that, for instance, the social system of the U.S. implicitly covers the area within the political boundaries of the U.S. In contemporary sociology, although with many exceptions, this concept of "social system" may be of some usefulness, but the historical sociologist immediately faces its limitations, to say the least.

First, concerning the area, can we speak, for example, of an "Indian social system" or even of an "India" in 1000 A.D.? A number of scholars do so. But others reject this approach on the grounds that in 1000 A.D. there was no political-geographical unit in the area now called India, which in those days consisted of a number of states. These states were separate units insofar as the states regarded themselves as independent. Each one differed from the other in a number of respects: in social stratification, economic organization, religious cults and material culture. Each state, therefore, represented a society of its own. Yet, undoubtedly, the historian who studies these states finds traits which all had in common.

Or — to change the perspective — can we speak of a Chinese social system, for example, around 1700 A.D.? Scholars usually do so and go on to describe the different social units such as government, bureaucracy, nobility, lower classes, guilds, family, etc., covering a field which they regard as China proper. If we look more closely, the "China" treated with this approach covered only a small part of the area that a Chinese official around 1700 would have regarded as the land of the Chinese. For a Chinese in early times, there existed only one society on earth. In its center there was the capital which was more highly developed culturally and better organized politically and socially than areas outside the center; and the greater the distance from the center, the lower the cultural level, the looser the political cohesion. On the outer periphery were those aborigines who, though a part of this society in Chinese opinion, were not aware of that fact and behaved and acted as if they were a society of their own, independent of China. The Chinese around 1700 certainly included Tibet, Burma and Korea in their concept of China, because these countries were, although in different ways, connected with China. This connection was stronger in the case of Tibet, and quite loose in the case of Burma; it was mainly political, but not at all exclusively so. Even a present-day analyst would certainly include in his definition of "China" those several millions of non-Chinese tribesmen who in 1700, and partly still today, inhabited large areas in South China, though the tribes regarded themselves as independent, self-ruled and self-contained, though they were continuously harassed by Chinese administrators and individuals who proclaimed that these aborigines were a part of Chinese society. Western historians have tended to reject the concept of "China" shared by all Chinese politicians of their time and have interpreted China in terms of our Western concepts of a state. It is O. Lattimore's merit to have shown that there were no "borders" in the early and pre-modern Far East, but only "frontiers," large zones of transition, which in some historical periods were claimed by one organized state, in other periods by another one, but which were never a part of a "social system" of any one state. There was always interaction between certain social units on both sides. Therefore, for example, sometimes people in such areas have been referred to as "Mongols," and sometimes the same people were called "Chinese."

Secondly, concerning "functional interrelations," the historical sociologist is confronted with even greater difficulties. For example, a functionalist would readily ascribe a number of "functions" to these tribes, and discuss in detail the social "interaction" between the tribes or members of the tribes, and China or individual Chinese. But if we look into descriptions of this kind, we find that normally they deal with economic and not social interactions. Or, where social interactions occur, they are of the type that is common between foreign or even hostile nations. If, in these cases, we insist on speaking of a "Chinese social system," we block the way to understanding.

As a second example: when the Dutch began their contacts with the Japanese and questioned citizens about the form of government, it took them a long time to learn that the shogun was not the emperor of Japan, but that Japan had an emperor and a shogun. Their Japanese informants had had no knowledge of their emperor, which demonstrates the absence of an all-Japanese system of social interaction. In the same vein, the ordinary Korean or Tibetan around 1700 did not know that he was regarded as a part of Chinese society; nor did the ordinary Indian farmer under Moghul rule regard the Moghuls as belonging to his own society, despite the fact that the Moghuls were quite an important segment of the population at large. The Indian farmer did not understand the language of these Moghuls, nor their customs or religion. The social institutions such as family, customs and laws, were all quite different from his own institutions. The only thing he knew — and knew well — was that from time to time strangers came to his village asking for some "tribute" that the stranger called "taxes"; if they had orders to collect a certain quota of tax from each farmer, the farmer did not know this, but in any event he had to comply. When we analyze the farmer's tax payments, we find that the farmer paid much more than his quota. The Moghuls among themselves justified their action, if they felt need to do so, by saying that the tax served to protect the farmer against greedy enemies who, if not restrained by the military power of the strangers, would rob the farmers. If the farmers had known that they were paying a price for protection, they would have asked to be left alone, because no robber would have taken more than these strangers.

Misguided by a habit of thinking in economic terms, and by a mental set concerning the oneness of societies, people speak, for example, of "Moghul society" in spite of the above-mentioned circumstances. It has been assumed that the political boundaries of Moghul India can be compared with boundaries as we have them now; it has been implicitly concluded that since there was economic interaction, and since the farmer had an economic function for the Moghuls, there was social interaction as well. In short: because economic relations were found, a "social system" was constructed.

The basic fault of this approach had its origin in the lack of attempts to determine the actual intensity and character of the ties which, to take another example, connected the Chinese farmer in the fifth century with the T'o-pa ruling class. In terms of structural analysis, this farmer had a definite place near the bottom of the structure. But this "social structure" is abstracted from the point of view of the T'o-pa rulers, and we cannot accept it as an existing reality. If we would compare the contacts of the Chinese farmer, let us say in Ho-nan province, with all other units of the so-called "T'o-pa social system," we would find that the farmer in Ho-nan did not live in the same social world as did the T'o-pa. First, most of his contacts, including the most intimate and intense associations, were with members of his nuclear and extended family. Many villages consisted only of lineage members — and this has often remained so down to almost the present time. Even the fields were situated so that the farmer hardly met other people than his own lineage members when he worked on the land. His contacts with neighboring villages were less intense. Often, they may not have amounted to more than two or three visits per year. In these neighboring villages there lived the families of the wives of the farmers. The next level was the market place, either in a place between villages or in a town. At this level, his contacts would already be of quite low intensity and numerically restricted. But here, he would also have some contacts with men from other social classes. He would meet craftsmen and artisans on the market place, and he might also have to have some contact with the state administration by meeting an official of low rank to whom he had to pay some fee which the man called a "tax." In his own village and environment, he would probably never meet a T'o-pa; his contact with the rulers, represented by officials, was normally restricted to the occasional visit of a low official of Chinese, not T'o-pa origin, whom he and his co-villagers would try to satisfy when he asked for deliveries of grain and cloth. Other contacts with the ruling bureaucracy might be dangerous and best were avoided. They could mean being called to court, being led to prison or forced into the army.

The political borders of the T'o-pa state did not coincide with the boundaries for the Chinese farmer. During all of the T'o-pa time we find that farmers had relatives belonging to their own clan or to their wives' clans on the other side of the border, in the Southern States. Even if a farmer did not have such contacts, when he met a farmer from the other side, a fugitive or visitor, he would regard him as one of his own people and not as a stranger from a different state. But when he met a man from the Kan-su province in the Northwest of the T'o-pa state, he would regard him as an utter stranger, even if that man also worked on his fields; probably such a man at that time hardly spoke Chinese but either a Mongolian or a Tibetan dialect; besides, he was dressed differently and had different social institutions and customs. That man, on the other side, would feel quite at home in Central Asia and in Tibet proper. He may not even have been aware that he was a "citizen" of the T'o-pa empire, and that the farmers in Ho-nan were his "co-citizens." It makes little sense to take both as parts of a Chinese "social system" and as members of "the lower class."

The Buddhist priests of the time were in the same position, if we leave aside those few who were directly appointed by the T'o-pa aristocracy to serve in the official temples. They lived in their monasteries and their world was a community which stretched from India and Central Asia down to the South of China and Korea. In their monasteries, there were people of the most divergent origin: Iranians, Indians, Chinese, all united by their interest in religion, philosophy, service. They read books which nobody else could understand; they travelled from one area to the other, crossing state borders without hesitation or limitation, serving rulers whenever rulers wanted them, serving people wherever they needed them. At one time, we might find them as "subjects" of the T'o-pa and then again a few years later as "subjects" of the South Chinese empire. But for them, there was no boundary to restrain them.

Similar to them were the literati of the time. They, too, had their contacts and friendships all over the Far East, disregarding the borders of the T'o-pa state; most of them even had close clan relatives on the other side of the border. Many of them served the T'o-pa as bureaucrats, and we know that in time these Chinese officials, in fact, became the rulers. But if one of them left the service of the T'o-pa state and went to serve the Southern state, his contemporaries did not regard him as a deserter or traitor. Within his own layer, he changed his position — that was all.

We are accustomed to regard a colonial system, as we find it in the 19th and early 20th centuries in Asia or Africa, as an anomaly, as something unjust. From our mid-20th century value system, this might be so. But the idea that a society should be integrated, that there should be, if possible, only one race, one language, one culture in a state, and that all or almost all people within political borders should have a right to determine what should be done — all this is new, the result of 19th century Western thinking. In earlier societies it did not matter of which race, religion, culture the rulers were. They lived their own life in their palaces and cities. They did not interfere with the life of other groups, communities, classes, layers, except that they forced them to make contributions to their support — for which they promised "protection." And the members of the lower layers, too, did not care who ruled them, nor did they care what people in the other layers did, how they looked, which language they spoke. Each layer had its own social life, lived its own way, avoided getting into trouble with other layers, and paid "taxes" as a necessity to live in peace, as long as they were able to pay.

In summary, when we study earlier societies we can fairly easily describe certain social groups, be they classes, strata or occupational groups. Any of these groups can be characterized by group consciousness of its members and by numerous and intimate contacts, often across considerable distances, whenever time and geographical conditions allowed. We can, further, describe geographically the extension of these groups on the map of the world. In addition, in most cases, we can arrange these groups in an hierarchical order, one above the other, always to some degree, but almost never completely overlapping. In some cases, what we call a "layer" may coincide with what others have called a "community," and in such cases, a layer may even be stratified in itself. This is true, for instance, with the Chinese immigrant into California or into Singapore in the 19th century. He believed that he lived in "China," and that the part of San Francisco or Singapore in which he lived truly belonged to a much larger unit comprising villages in Kuang-tung province in China, among others. He would have admitted that he and his friends were occasionally harassed by white people who claimed to have certain rights, although they often came much later than the Chinese. But it took some time until he understood that he was claimed as a part of American or British society.

Similarly, the Arab community in T'ang-time Canton was a "community" with stratification inside China, if the study is restricted to Canton and ignores the rest of the Arab world. But according to our view, one should regard the Arab community in Canton as one section of a layer which in T'ang time covered wide areas of the Far East, South-East Asia, South Asia and the Near East, perhaps even parts of Europe. True, the Chinese administration included these Arabs in Canton to some degree in their political and economic system, for example, by creating offices to control the foreigners, by recognizing some Arabs as leaders of the group, by exacting payments from them. But it is significant that on the other hand the Chinese government granted them what we now call "extraterritoriality," regarding them as a segment of another, non-Chinese society.

Between all these layers social interaction may or may not exist. It is a subject of study in each individual case to determine the strength and the character of the ties connecting one such layer to the other(s).

A factor of high importance in such a task is the density of population. In countries with a low density, such as in pre-modern Burma, interaction between different strata was minimal outside the capital and the court, and even between different rural settlements. Groups varying widely in language, customs, social organization and material culture could live side by side for hundreds of years without any degree of assimilation.

If one uses concepts such as "Moghul social system" or "Chinese social system," one cuts through these layers in a more or less arbitrary way. In the case of "big merchants," for instance, one may barely hit this layer at all in a "Moghul social system," because a very small part of this layer would geographically be inside the Moghul state borders. The big merchant only partly belonged to Moghul society, but he was a full member of a larger social unit which stretched over the whole subcontinent and the whole Near East; only if we study this entire area and the merchants' social relations in it can we understand the function of the big trader. Regarding a "Moghul social system" as a unit of analysis and discussing the functions of one group with regard to the other groups leads to a distortion of true social conditions, and to the construction of "ideal" pictures that have little correspondence with reality. The same applies to many other categories of people.

The priest in Moghul India was in fact only a peripheral part of that society, but he was a true member of a large unit covering the whole subcontinent. Only within this larger unit had the priest his true function; only if we study him in this framework can we understand him and his role.

To a certain extent, sociologists have been aware of similar complexities in contemporary America, and they have tried to solve the problem by introducing the concept of a "plural" or "multiple" society. This concept has been used to explain the co-existence of different value and behavior patterns in "American society," with the concept of "American society" being preserved.

One can certainly maintain that the term "multiple society" might be equally or even more applicable to Asian societies, particularly where no social or cultural assimilation occurred. Certainly the Ottoman Empire before 1918 was a "multiple society" in the sense that it was a political unit under the rule of a dynasty which had its origin in a minority of Turkish-speaking, once nomadic, people, and among whose subjects there were Armenians, Greeks, Bulgars, Arabs, Kurds and many others. All of these units spoke their own languages, had their own value systems, often their own religion or denomination, and their own customs and institutions. It was the political rule that kept them together as servants or subjects of the dynasty. Only in talking with people outside the Ottoman Empire they probably designated themselves, or were called by outsiders, "Ottoman Turks." Each group engaged in minimal or no interaction with the other groups. Let us take a second example from China. In the 19th century we find in Yün-nan Province a political rule of a bureaucracy which was controlled by Peking and represented the "Chinese" government; there were villages and cities in the plains, inhabited by other Chinese who interacted with the government representatives and to some degree identified with that government. But on the slopes of the mountains there were other groups, in theory also subjects of China, yet living their own life — as far as they were allowed, and having their own values and institutions, even their own economic system. Interaction with the valley-living Chinese was minimal and restricted to the sale of fire-wood and buying of salt or textiles. Finally, there was often a third group on the top of the mountains, again with its own institutions, language, values, religion. We can, if we like, bypass such conditions by calling these people "minorities." Yet the earlier the periods we study, the more such apparent minorities were truly self-contained societies, linked sometimes loosely by economic ties, and by occasional interaction; the relationship of such a society to the ruling power was typically that of subject to conqueror at the end of a war, with contacts held to a minimum from both sides.

Thus, first in the same geographical area several "societies" can exist side by side without functional social relations and without acculturation or assimilation. Political rule may in some way be superimposed upon all of them, upon some of them or only upon some parts of them. Political boundaries, even linguistic boundaries, do not delimit such societies.

Secondly, another type of "society," such as the merchants, consists of members widely scattered over large distances who share values and behavior and belong socially only peripherally to their actual environment. Neither of these two types can be properly called "minority," because of their social and cultural independence. Nor can they be called "sub-cultures," because they cannot be seen as subordinate with respect to social interrelations and values.

It would seem that a model depicting multiple social units in this sense, such as, for example, the co-existing Indian farmers and the merchants in Moghul India who were in part geographically overlaid by other units, would consist of more than four or five such layers, each, as a rule, hierarchically structured. Such a model would facilitate the formation of an historical theory of social change — a problem that, as many of us feel, functionalists have not been able to study successfully. Only an historical theory of change could conceive that innovations are born and spread inside one of these layers, and that this same layer carries them easily across political borders and sometimes even continents (overseas merchants). For example, merchants from Central Asia may have learned business methods such as credit and loan arrangements from their friends in the Near East and carried them to Central Asia and farther to China; they may also have carried with them the latest jokes or songs which they learned when they stayed in the same caravanseray or the same tea house with their Near Eastern friends. Technical innovations such as the compass, or organizational innovations such as trade companies (*ortaq*), have thus been carried over whole continents and often without leaving any trace in between two places, simply because the merchants did not touch these places or did not find men of their "social circle" in these localities. We should not be astonished to find certain folk-tales in the whole Near East, in some parts of South Asia and, finally, on the Fu-kien coast of China, while we do not find them in the Philippines or on Hainan Island. Miao tribes in Kui-chou for centuries preserved their own customs, beliefs and tales in spite of Chinese settlements only a few miles away in which other customs, beliefs and tales were propagated. Miao and Chinese in such places did not interact, as a rule, except in the fields of economic exploitation or military aggression. But the Miao in Kui-chou might have had the same customs as Miao in Viet-nam because — as we can often prove — some contacts were maintained even over long distances and long periods.

However, things are more complicated than all that. It is quite a different question whether or not an innovation which spread within one layer from one area to another area will also be accepted by another layer in the new area. A folk-tale of typical trade-city character (*Decamerone* type) might never spread into the villages surrounding the trade city, because it would be told only in tea houses or houses of prostitution; scholars in the trade city might hear it but might not like it because it might be too strongly in conflict with their own values. Songs may spread over continents more easily through tea houses and geisha girls because scholars and officials who, like traders, visit these entertainers and their establishments may like the melodies, and they can easily compose texts which do not violate social or religious values. Pieces of dress may quickly spread because a prestige factor may be assigned to them. For example, Western male clothing — although in no way superior to Chinese clothes — was quickly adopted by the upper classes after they first saw it in the trade cities, because it became the symbol of wealth, status and power. Once an innovation has been accepted by the upper class and has thus been assigned social prestige, the processes of "trickling down" (H. Naumann's theory of "gesunkenes Kulturgut") begin to operate: the lower classes want to imitate the higher classes to raise their status; the higher classes first try to prevent this (often by sumptuary or other laws), but then try to find another "innovation" which is adopted in order to set off the upper class again from the other classes. The bound feet of the Chinese women are a good example of this process. They were at first limited to women of the highest classes, but in the last century even farm women had adopted this custom while women of the upper classes had already begun to give it up in favor of Western hosiery and shoes. Incidentally, it seems quite probable that the bound feet were first introduced to China by Central Asian dancing girls, imported by merchants into China. The girls danced like ballet dancers on carpets with designs symbolizing lotos and other flowers of religious significance.

As an historical sociologist I feel I should go no further than to advocate the use of the layer model for studies in all societies, including contemporary Western ones. Only as a demonstration of one possible starting point for an analysis along this line, I should like to ask the contemporary sociologist whether, for example, the role of the scientist in modern Western society can readily be understood if we study him only in his relation to industry, government, family, social clubs, etc., inside the borders of any given state. Is the scientist not close to his colleagues beyond the borders? Do his contacts with these colleagues not mean more to him than contacts with people in other occupational groups in his neighborhood? He may even be organizationally tied to these colleagues beyond the border, for example, by membership in international scholarly societies. And the approach he uses in his work, the ideology he accepts, down to the organization of his daily routine and his family life, may be more influenced by that large "community of scholars" to which he feels he belongs than by middle class standards of his neighborhood, or by any other frame of reference derived from the country of his residence.

Or to shift back about 200 years: do we really have to assume that the whole of English society was permeated by a "Protestant ethic" and that only in such an atmosphere could the industrial revolution succeed? I think we could show that there were different layers, for example, of scholars, of scientists, of businessmen, of technicians and of craftsmen, that the men in these layers had their closest contacts with their colleagues in Flanders, Holland, France, Germany and Italy, and that none of these layers covered all of England. A few of these men lived in a few cities in England, in more similar cities on the continent. The "fusion" which eventually produced the industrial revolution happened in one or two places in cities in England. It spread at first within the same layers to other cities in England; then quickly invaded other layers, with the result of engulfing the English farmers and villages; soon it began spreading, within the original layers, to cities on the continent, where it also led to engulfing the continental farmers and villages; at the present time the same process is still spreading all over the world, engulfing and, in its first period, exploiting more and more people in more and more layers. The ways in which industrialization transformed the life of the farmers around the places where the first industries in England came into being may be comparable to the ways industrialization a century later spread into other areas of the world — with some important reservations which we will make immediately. But once we free ourselves from the limitations of political boundaries we may arrive at a better understanding of developments. For example, from this point of view, 19th century imperialism and colonialism might appear as temporary concomitants of the expansion of new forms of technology and organization. We may even come to think of the industrial revolution not as a product of English society but as a product of human development. A consequence, then, of our "layer theory" seems to be that there are no local "social systems." There is only humanity as such: the social world of man. Processes such as industrialization in the 19th century or the development of the city millennia before the Christian era should be regarded as processes of mankind and not as processes of England or Sumer. For reasons of practicality, the study of any subject might be restricted to a particular area, whether we define this area in geographical terms or in terms of political borders. But any analysis of large historical processes must eventually reach beyond such restrictions. However, within large processes, such as industrialization, the specific processes of social or other change which develop in one layer and then are carried to other layers, followed by either acceptance, rejection, modification or the birth of something new, have to be studied separately. There is little reason to assume that conditions in far-apart corners of the world are alike or mean the same even if they look alike and belong theoretically to the same layer.

WORLD TIME

An historical sociologist today has still other grave reservations concerning current sociological research. To say the least he feels uneasy when presented with studies in which, for example, the labor movement of Japan around 1960 is compared to the labor movement of England around 1860, especially if such studies conclude with generalizations and new theories. As long as two series of events are compared simply for the purpose of classification into classes or types of event sequences, no objections need be raised. But as soon as processes are compared in order to discover general ways of behavior or attitude, the matter becomes serious. It seems that some comparative sociologists have made a false analogy to the natural sciences. It would not be the first such false analogy, one of whose faults is the disregard of time. If, for example, an experiment with certain kinds of bacteria was first made in Brussels in 1860 and was repeated in Chicago in 1960, for all practical purposes the results would be directly comparable, as far as one knows today. Time — or what might be called "world time" — seems to play no significant role in scientific experimentation, although there have been some contra-indications recently. In any event, a *social* process such as the English labor movement in 1860 cannot be directly compared with a similar-looking process of 1960 simply because of the passage of time, even if there were not the additional complication that the first event occurred in England and the second in Japan. "World time" is the crucial factor here. Leaving completely aside all other differences between Japanese and English societies (although, of course, one should never do this), the intellectual climate of any country in the world in 1860 was radically different from the climate in 1960. While the year 1860 fell at the beginning of a period of evolutionist and early Marxist thinking, by 1960 evolutionist and Marxist ideas, as well as many ideas and experiences in between, had been integrated in one way or another into the thought-systems of all contemporary persons, particularly leaders. This is also true for Japan since it does not exist on another planet. In accordance with our model, which was described in the preceding section, several social layers inside the borders of Japan belonged to groups which extended far over the borders, deeply into Western society. Many developments in Japan around 1960 were therefore determined, in part, by what happened internationally since 1860, and consequently cannot be compared with events of 1860 in a simple fashion.

Let me illustrate the case of "world time" by yet another example. When discussing the industrialization of developing nations, Japan is often set up as a model case. Japan is the only Asian country which successfully changed and became a modern nation without any "foreign aid." If the case of Japan is analyzed, two important reasons for its success seem to be: 1) no promise was given to the common man that his own personal standard of living would soon become better; 2) the innovations and changes were introduced from above by an élite which was largely the old élite of pre-industrial times. The authority pattern did not break down until modernization was well advanced. We restrict ourselves here to these two factors only. The first factor clearly shows the influence of "world time": with the spread of ideas of individualism, rights of the individual, private enterprise and socialistic ideas, all of which began to cover Europe and the U.S. beginning with the early 20th century, no reformer today could ask his common population, his poor farmers, to work harder, to work more, without the promise of more rewards. All nations now have rising expectations for the individual — yet modernization can be successful only if as much as possible of the profits is invested and not consumed. The second factor also shows the influence of world time: new ideas about democracy of Western or Soviet form have undermined the position of any old élite in any part of Asia so much by now that no élite anywhere could today ask its citizens of the lower classes to work harder and to obey. What could be done in Japan was possible only in the 19th century in combination with unquestioned ideas of nationalism while ideas about democracy, individualism and private capitalism were not yet fully known. We could add another point here: Japan could adopt a pattern which England and Europe had used, namely to draw surplus rural population into the cities where the new industries needed them, and thus relieve the pressure upon the land. Again, no modernizing country today can copy this pattern. Modern industry does not need millions of unskilled workers, it needs thousands of very highly skilled technicians. Yet modernization cannot be fully effective if 80% of the population remains farmers on the land. Japan's case is unique; it will not have parallels in the 20th century.

However, these considerations do not render comparisons impossible or meaningless. I do not think that sociology must be content being "verstehende Soziologie" in the restrictive sense of the study and explanation of differences, although this may be a necessary first step in an analysis. But these considerations are meant to warn people who naively compare "processes," disregarding time, that they may compare phantoms and not societies. Behavior patterns or action patterns may look alike, but the similarity may be so superficial that comparison does not lead to insight, since the actors on the new scene are no more the same kind of human beings. Man of 1860 was different from man in the same place in 1960 because of the difference in "world time," which was long enough to produce feedback in many areas of thought and attitudes. Therefore, one has to be careful in comparing similar-looking processes at different times even in the same country. The same attention needs to be given to this factor of "world time" in cross-cultural studies.

Those who operate with the concept of "traditional society" in contrast to modern or industrial society, may object by saying that, while the time factor admittedly plays a great role in modern industrial development, traditional societies are characterized by being "timeless," in that change is slow and imperceptible. Therefore, according to that view, the time factor in comparisons can be left aside. An historical sociologist must object on two grounds.

It is true that everyone feels that our society is changing rapidly, almost visibly, from year to year. Looking backwards, one feels that at the time of one's father changes were quite slow, and farther back, one perceives no changes worth mentioning. But if we read historical documents of a bygone time, we find to our surprise that, for example, Chinese authors of the 15th century complained about all the changes which went on in their lifetime. Implicitly, they seem to have felt that in still earlier times changes were slow. The first reason, then, why the historical sociologist objects to the neglect of the time factor in comparisons involving traditional societies is that the feeling of the unchangeability of "traditional societies" is an error based on ethnocentric thinking. It means little to point out, as many do, that statistical analysis has shown that in this or that field of science or technology more inventions have been made in the last 20 years than in the 1,000 years before 1940: changes occurring, for example, between 1640 and 1660 are essentially statistically incomparable to changes between 1940 and 1960. Questions as to what constitutes a "change" would immediately block the investigation. What seems important is that people *felt* there were changes going on all during their lifetime, even when we regard such societies as "traditional" or stationary. Secondly, the historical sociologist of today knows how quickly many crucial inventions spread over the whole old world, even in very early times. For example, after the first domestication of the horse the whole old world was changed — not only Mesopotamia, because the domesticated horse transformed all societies all the way to China. From this moment on, not only new forms of military organization became possible, but also new social classes and political domination over large areas. After the domestication of the horse somewhere in Western Asia, the whole world simply could never be the same. "World time" thus played an important role even in 2000 B.C., not only now.

But what, then, are "traditional societies"? For example, China before 1948 is commonly called a traditional society. But in that country processes of selection of people for government according to certain well-defined, objective qualifications were already developed in the third century B.C., and constantly refined up to the 19th century. These processes were intended as means of reducing or removing the importance of ascribed status. Western society developed similar processes only in the early 19th century (and, it seems, under a direct stimulus from China), i.e., at a time when at least England was normally already called a "modern" society. There is no doubt that at least in this field of the recruitment of the governmental élite, Chinese society for many centuries cannot well be called a "traditional" society. This would put China on a level with, let us say, Congolese society, where quite different "traditional" processes of selection of leaders were practised until almost the present day. We could name a number of other areas where it would be difficult to maintain that China was a "traditional" society. Rational thinking, for instance, as opposed to irrational or magical thinking, was prevalent certainly among the élite in China in the 11th or 12th century to at least the degree that it was in the 19th-century "modern" Western societies. And when sociologists make their comparisons, they tend to repeat Levy-Bruhl's mistake: they compare the educated élite of the modern West with the common lower classes of the "traditional" society. If they would compare lower classes in both cases, their results would be surprising!

And one more remark. If, as is common practice, the term "traditional society" means nothing but "non-industrialized" society, we classify all societies into two classes on the basis of a single criterion — a procedure which is scientifically untenable. Social scientists in the distant future might even regard the development of industries as only one, and not even the most important, factor in the total changes of mankind between 1000 and 2000 A.D. . . .

Political Systems
and Political Change

GABRIEL A. ALMOND

Concern with the problem of political development and change has acquired a new impetus in recent decades. This is primarily a response to the emergence in the contemporary world of the new nations, and the efforts of many of the older ones to modernize themselves. Students of politics seeking to explain and order these phenomena have found little help in the concepts and insights of political theory. This is not to say that political theorists have neglected the theme of political change.

From *American Behavioral Scientist*, Vol. VI, No. 6 (June 1963), pp. 3–10. Reprinted by permission of the author and publisher.

GABRIEL A. ALMOND is Professor of Political Science, Stanford University. His publications include *The American People and Foreign Policy* (1950), *The Appeals of Communism* (1954), and *The Civic Culture* (with S. Verba, 1963). He is co-editor with James Coleman of *The Politics of the Developing Areas* (1960).

CONCEPTS OF POLITICAL CHANGE IN
POLITICAL HISTORY

Plato and Aristotle placed political stability and change at the very center of their theories. Their conception of the three pure forms of government — aristocracy, monarchy, and democracy — the principles embodied in these forms, the causes of the perversion, and the sequences of change which they are alleged to undergo, has been one of the most influential conceptual schemes in the history of political theory. These ideas are to be found repeated, elaborated, and modified in Polybius, Cicero, Machiavelli, Bodin, Locke, Montesquieu, and the Federalist Papers.[1] Similarly, Aristotle's and Polybius' formula for obtaining the best and most stable form of government by mixing the pure forms, elaborated in a more modern context and with variations by Montesquieu, was one of the chief theoretical tools employed by the Founding Fathers in framing the American Constitution.

In this conception of political development as it was formulated in the Enlightenment, change was seen as inevitably progressive, as political institutions became more congruent with man's nature as a reasoning, choosing being with inalienable rights. The more conservative Enlightenment tradition took a more qualified view of man's nature and stressed the importance of institutional arrangements which would mitigate the impact of transient popular passions on institutions and public policy. The Radical tradition in England and the Populist tendency in America rejected these qualifications, unequivocally favored popular participation in governmental processes, and postulated a trend of political change in which these principles would imminently be realized. Whether in its qualified or extreme form, the Enlightenment theory of political change was a unilinear evolutionary theory of progress toward more popular government.

A variant of this Enlightenment approach to political change was manifested in the continental European social revolutionary movements of the nineteenth century, and particularly in Marxism. Marxism was pre-eminently a theory of economic-social and political change, in which the latter was assumed to follow upon the former. Quite in contrast with Radicalism and Populism, which assumed that equitable distribution and social justice would follow upon popular political participation, Marxism assumed that the revolutionary elimination of economic privilege was the inevitable precursor and the only possible avenue to genuine democratic participation.

Thus, the theme of political change is a very central concern of political theory; and yet the contemporary student of politics finds these conceptions unsuitable for the explanation and ordering of the problems and patterns of change in the modern world.

There are perhaps two aspects of the traditional theories which create these problems. In the first place, the Enlightenment theories were conceived, and in

[1] See W. A. Dunning, *A History of Political Theories: Ancient and Medieval* (New York: Macmillan, 1923), Chapters II, III, IV; Dunning, *Political Theories from Luther to Montesquieu*, Chapters III, X, XII; and C. E. Merriam, *American Political Theories* (New York: Macmillan, 1920), Chapter III.

general applied, within the Western world with its common Christian and
Greco-Roman culture, and with the nation-state as the dominant political
form. Hence its conception of the starting point of political change was culture-
bound, so to speak. The starting point of political change in the contemporary
world is immensely varied in both culture and structure. A contemporary theory of political change must explain not only Western patterns, but those of a
Japan, an Indonesia, an India, a Yemen, and a Uganda.

In the second place, the concepts of change in political theory assume an
inevitable and unilinear course of development. When Western political scientists, in the Enlightenment tradition, view the variety and instability of political systems in the modern world, they may retain their faith in or hope for
such an outcome but they can hardly believe with conviction in the general
triumph of effective democracy in the foreseeable future.

INTERPRETATION OF EUROPEAN
POLITICAL SYSTEMS

We are searching for a theory of change more sober in spirit, more open in
concept, and more versatile in its explanatory capacity than those made available to us in traditional political theory. One way of approaching the problem
stems from the body of knowledge and interpretation dealing with the political
systems of Europe and particularly continental Europe. Events in the analyses
of the political histories and processes of France, Germany, and Italy — countries in the very center of the Greco-Roman-Christian tradition — have raised
the most serious question about the Enlightenment theory of democratic progress. How explain the instability of French politics, or the failures of the democratic systems of Germany and Italy, in contrast with the steady consolidation
of democracy in Britain, the United States, and the Old Commonwealth? In
France a whole series of historians and political scientists including Siegfried,
Thomson, Micaud, Philip Williams, Luethy, and others have concerned themselves with this problem.[2]

In one form or another, these students of French politics have pointed out
that French political movements and ideologies since the French Revolution
have been fragmented along two lines of cleavage. The first of these is the
classic French revolutionary cleavage between left and right — the first republican, democratic, and rational-anticlerical in spirit; the second royalist, aristocratic, and traditional-clerical in tendency. The second line of cleavage, based
on demands for an equitable distribution of economic and social values and
opportunities, emerged before consensus and stable institutions were established in response to the first challenge. Thus, France in the nineteenth and
twentieth centuries has been seeking to solve two basic problems of growth

[2] See André Siegfried, *France: A Study in Nationality* (New Haven: Yale University
Press, 1933); David Thomson, *Democracy in France* (Oxford University Press, 1958);
Charles Micaud, "The Bases of Communist Strength in France," *World Politics*,
September 1955, pp. 354 ff.; Micaud, "French Intellectuals and Communists," *Social
Research*, Autumn 1954, pp. 286 ff.; Philip Williams, *Politics in Post-War France* (Lon-
don: Longmans, 1958); Herbert Luethy, *France Against Herself* (New York: Praeger,
1955).

simultaneously, that of political participation and that of socio-economic distribution. French immobilism and constitutional instability is explained in terms of political structure and culture incapable of producing positive and stable majority coalitions. An anti-clerical left consisting of Communists, Socialists, and radicals polarizes a clerical conservative right consisting of working and middle and upper class Catholics, and the economically conservative middle and upper classes fearful of social revolution. The left, collectivist and social welfare-oriented, loses its middle class republican allies and polarizes a coalition of the conservative middle and upper classes and peasantry.

This pattern of political culture and infrastructure explains the classic sequence of French political history — the immobilist, heterogeneous center coalitions incapable of decisive action in either the constitutional or social policy direction, followed by "crisis-liquidation" cabinets such as the *Union-Sacrée* of World War I or the brief Mendès-France interlude in the 1950's, when a grave national emergency creates a temporary consensus. It also explains the latent "Caesarism" and authoritarianism of French politics. Immobilism and cabinet instability create a widespread cynicism toward democratic politics. From the French Revolution right on through MacMahon, Boulanger, and de Gaulle, the alternative of national unity, authority, dignity, and order consistent with the glorious Napoleonic and monarchic past has exerted great attraction not only among French traditionalists, but among disillusioned democrats. The fragility and ineffectiveness of French politics becomes especially manifest in periods when the French political process has been loaded with fateful problems of national accommodation, as in the present period of decolonization. The pathetic life and the sudden and almost voluntary death of the Fourth Republic was a consequence of the impact of three grave problems which that Republic was unable to solve — the problems of participation and governmental organization, welfare distribution, and international accommodation.

The introduction of the international problem turns our attention to the experience of Germany and Italy, for in a special degree — in a degree far greater than in the case of France — Germany and Italy were hit by problems both of international accommodation and integration at the same time that they were seeking solutions to the problems of political participation and welfare distribution. Indeed, Fascism and Nazism as the manifestation of Italian and German authoritarianism, in contrast with the more moderate and traditional authoritarianism of France, may in part be explained by the special impact of the problem of national accommodation and integration on the politics of those countries. At the same time both Germany and Italy were seeking solutions to the problems of political participation and social distribution, they were confronted in the very basic sense by the problems of establishing national identities through the integration of their parochial components and through accommodation in an international political system, already well established and not providing much freedom of maneuver vis-à-vis the older great powers.

Here again we are not saying anything new but simply explicating, as an analytical tool, explanations of political system characteristics and performance which are to be found in the literature dealing with German and Italian politics.[3] Thus, the late arrival of the German Reich at nationhood has often been viewed as an explanation of the failure of the German middle classes to carry through a participation revolution and as an explanation of the special virulence and sensitivity of German nationalism. The failure of the German Reich to democratize itself has been offered as an explanation of the radicalization of the German left. The strength of Marxism in Germany is attributed to pessimism regarding the responsiveness of German political institutions to popular demands for democracy and social welfare. The rise and popularity of National Socialism is attributed in part to the political fragmentation of the Weimar Republic along traditional authoritarian and democratic lines, religious lines, socialist-antisocialist, and nationalist-cosmopolitan lines. The national humiliation of the Weimar Republic, its political instability and fragmentation, and its related failures to solve the distribution and welfare problems of the inflation and depression are the chief situational reasons cited for the rise of National Socialism.

The German and Italian patterns of political development, similar though they were in some respects, may be explained in terms of the different impacts of these unsolved problems. Germany came into the period of national unification with its largest constituent unit, Prussia, thoroughly integrated in the sense of national identity and penetration of parochial, regional, and pluralistic status groups. Indeed, the breaking of the civic will of the German middle classes had begun long before the national unification which followed the Franco-Prussian War. As one writer put it, the Prussian middle classes had begun to be infeudated by the aristocratic and bureaucratic-authoritarian regime in the course of the eighteenth and first part of the nineteenth centuries.[4] At the time of national unification, it was the culture and socio-political structure of Prussia which was quickly imprinted on the whole of Germany. Thus Germany began its career as a nation as a "disziplin-volk," as Max Weber expressed it, and with a widespread, though insecure, sense of national identity. To be sure there were separatist and pluralist tendencies, but the dominant model for German integration was that of Prussia.

In Italy, national unification was superficial in both a structural and cultural sense. The historic particularities of Italy, and especially the Church, retained substantial autonomy, and while Fascism sought to break through these autonomies and create an aggressive sense of national identity, it was only partially successful at best. Thus, Italian Fascism was dilettantish in its efforts to mobilize Italian resources and to create an aggressive nationalism, by comparison with the gruesome pedantry and demonic aggressiveness of National Socialism.

If we contrast British political experience in recent centuries with that of

---

[3] See, for example, K. S. Pinson, *Modern Germany* (New York: Macmillan, 1954); Sigmund Neumann, "Germany: Changing Patterns and Lasting Problems" in Neumann (ed.), *Modern Political Parties* (University of Chicago Press, 1956), pp. 354 ff.; Joseph LaPalombara, *Pressure Groups and Bureaucracy in Italy*, forthcoming, Chapter 1.

[4] See Hans Rosenberg, *Bureaucracy, Autocracy, and Aristocracy*.

France, Germany, and Italy, it is evident that we are dealing with a radically different historic pattern. With the exception of the problem of Ireland, which was to plague Britain and disrupt its political process in the last decades of the nineteenth century and the first decades of the twentieth, Britain had attained a stable integration of its constituent parts by the early seventeenth century. Its sense of national identity was well established and widely distributed early as the Elizabethan era, was sustained by success in the international political system in the whole of the modern era, and now seems to be adapting to a radical lessening and restructuring of its international position without significant disruptive political consequences. Its problem of political participation was solved incrementally in a historical process beginning in the thirteenth century and continuing step by step into the post-World War II period, with only one discontinuous episode. Its problem of social distribution, though in part solved in the same incremental, continuous manner, is still in many respects unsolved. This issue of the distribution of social opportunity in Britain and accommodation to its new international position are the chief unsolved problems of contemporary British politics. The probability that they will be dealt with without radically altering the British political system is high, in view of the widespread and secure sense of national identity and the general acceptance among Britons of the legitimacy of their political system.

A DEFINITION OF POLITICAL CHANGE

This body of historical interpretations of European political systems suggests a theoretical insight: a conception of political change which may be formulated in terms of the performance capabilities of political systems. The British pattern of political change was one in which these fundamental problems of system adaptation were solved with appropriate structural and cultural adaptations, so that the system "grew," so to speak, from monarchy to aristocratic oligarchy, from aristocratic oligarchy to a welfare democracy. In France by contrast, the problem of political participation was not solved but rather continued through the nineteenth and twentieth centuries as a basically unsolved problem of system adaptation. France was fixated, so to speak, in a state of fragmented political culture and structure, a fragmentation which was compounded in the nineteenth and twentieth centuries by her inability to solve the problem of social distribution. Thus, France became neither a stable democracy nor a welfare democracy, but was caught in conflicting impulses to carry through these systemic changes, or to suppress them; became, in other words, an immobilist, unstable, democratic-authoritarian system. The immobility and instability of Germany and Italy, on the other hand, were compounded by the fact that these two countries were unable to solve satisfactorily the problems of national integration and national identity, in other words, were ambivalent in the national sense. How else can we explain the contrast between the intense nationalism of National Socialism and Fascism, and the apparent absence of national feeling in contemporary Germany and Italy? We may say of France, Germany, and Italy in the last century that they were caught in the grips of cumulative revolutions, unable to solve any one of them through appropriate systemic adaptations, in considerable part *because of the simultaneity* of their impact.[5]

It should be clear that we are defining political change in a special sense. We are not using it here to refer to the general phenomenon of change, the sense in which all political systems undergo change. We mean by political change the acquisition by a political system of some new capability. For example, we may say that when a tribal elite develops an officialdom capable of penetrating the tribal villages, extracting tribute and manpower, the tribe develops an integration and mobilization capability, and has changed systemically from its earlier essentially kinship and religious cohesion to a specifically political cohesion. If such a tribal political system uses the resources which it now can mobilize as a means of accommodating itself in its relations to other political systems in the international arena (whether by regular military defense or aggression or by diplomatic negotiation), we may say that it has acquired an *international accommodative capability*. It has changed systematically. It has acquired the familiar attributes of the nation-state: effective internal political integration, territorial boundaries, and more or less regularized exchanges with other nation-states. If such a political system develops a culture and a structure which enable its population or a substantial part of it to participate in the recruitment of elites and formulation of public policy, we can say that it has acquired a *participation capability*. It has changed from some sub-species of authoritarian state to a participant, or democratic, one. Similarly, if such a political system develops a capability of penetrating the economy and social structure in such a way as to respond regularly or recurrently to demands for the distribution of the social product, we may say that it has acquired a *welfare* or a *distribution capability*.

We call each one of these changes "systemic" changes because the acquisition of the new capability is associated with fundamental changes in political culture and structure. Thus, the development of the integrative capability is accompanied by the development of a sense of national identity and the emergence of a specialized central bureaucracy. The development of an international accommodative capability is associated with the development of a more open, cosmopolitan culture supportive of regular exchanges across national boundaries, and the further development of bureaucracy — foreign offices, diplomats, armed services. The development of a participation capability is associated with the development and spread of a political culture of civic obligation and competence, and the elaboration of the various components of the democratic infrastructure — political parties, associational interest groups,

---

[5] I am indebted for this concept of the simultaneity or cumulativeness of revolutions to Sigmund Neumann, "Toward a Comparative Study of Political Parties," in *Modern Political Parties*, but more particularly to his oral presentation of this concept on a number of occasions. In applying this analysis in the non-Western world, let me acknowledge my debt to Lucian Pye's *Politics, Personality, and Nation Building* (New Haven: Yale University Press, 1962), and in particular to his concept of role conflict and the identity crises in the new nations.

and autonomous media of communication. The development of a distribution capability is associated with the development and widespread dissemination of a welfare culture; further special bureaucratic changes; and emergence of a pattern of accommodation between the political structure and process, and the social structure and process.

THE PROBLEM OF UNILINEARITY

Stated in this simple way, we seem to be falling victim to the same unilinear evolutionary theory, from which we are seeking to escape. But this is not the import nor the intention of this concept of change. In the first place, political systems may not encounter these problems or may not encounter them in the same order, form, or intensity, or having encountered them in some special way, they may solve them differently. What we are arguing is that the systemic characteristics of political systems — their structural, cultural, and performance properties — are determined by the way in which these problems or challenges are encountered and experienced. The sources of tendencies toward political system change are either indigenous or from the international environment, or both. The kind of impulses which emerge from these sources, their order, and intensity are capable of great variation.

If we focus for a moment on man's historical experience with political systems prior to the Renaissance and the emergence into international dominance of the Western state system, the impact of these problems and their solution in various parts of the world was relatively compartmented and independent. Thus, what happened in Japan was independent of what happened in India or in Africa. Furthermore, political systems acquired and lost capabilities and their associated cultural, structural, and performance characteristics in anything but a unilinear, evolutionary way. Within the confines of the Greek city states, Aristotle and Plato could respond to the patterns of political change which they observed only by positing a cyclical theory of political change, and Machiavelli, observing the Italian principalities and city states, was drawn to a similar model. In ancient and even recent Asia and Africa, nations and empires formed in response to these challenges, then reverted to the closure and parochialism of less versatile political systems, and then formed up again into larger and more capable systems without any apparent regularity or order.

But we have to argue that since the Renaissance, the Enlightenment, and the industrial revolution some of the independence of man's political experiments has been lost, that the course of recent history supports the idea of the emergence of world culture.[6] We would argue that recent centuries have seen a fundamental change in the world historical process. In a sense political systems have increasingly been losing their uniqueness with respect to the kinds

6 See C. P. Snow, *The Two Cultures and the Scientific Revolution* (New York: Cambridge University Press, 1961), pp. 47 ff.; and as applied in the specific context of the theory of political development, Lucian Pye, *op. cit.*, pp. 10 ff.; and *The Political Context of National Development*, unpublished ms. (Center for International Studies, MIT, Cambridge, Mass., 1962).

of problems they encounter, and in the ways in which they may solve these problems. The technological and communications revolutions have fundamentally changed the speed and the direction of cultural diffusion. Communication, industrialization, and urbanization force the problems of national integration, international accommodation, political participation, and welfare distribution on the new nations and the traditional older ones. They are confronted inescapably with the simultaneous or cumulative revolutions of which Neumann speaks, and which Lucian Pye has analyzed so cogently in his Burmese study. The structure, culture, and performance characteristics of the new nations and the rapidly changing older ones will be determined by the way they encounter these four problems and the way in which they seek to solve them. However, the implications of this modification in the patterns of cultural diffusion and cultural change are far from unilinear. We still begin with the enormous variety of cultural and structural starting points in the emerging nations, and even though they are confronted with all four problems of political growth simultaneously, the dosages of each vary from case to case, and the responses of elites to these challenges differ from one country to the next. Thus, while we can say that there will be *some common content* in the outcomes of these processes of change, this is far from arguing that there will be *one common outcome*.

TYPES OF POLITICAL SYSTEMS
AND POLITICAL CHANGE

We have suggested that political systems change, in the sense in which we have defined the term, when they acquire new capabilities in relation to their social and international environments. This in turn suggests an approach to political classification in terms of such a concept of political change. Differences among political systems may be put in terms of their acquisition of capabilities, their failure to have developed these capabilities, or their having become fixated in the process of acquiring them. But first several points must be made, regarding the nature of political capabilities, the relations between capabilities and the structural and cultural aspects of political systems, and the interrelationships among capabilities.

The difference between simple and complex political systems is not that the latter possess capabilities and the former lack them. In both a functional and a structural sense all the capabilities present in "modern" political systems are present in primitive ones. The sole exception would be the international accommodative capability in those cases of genuine isolation as in oceanic island communities, and even here the evidence would seem to suggest that complete isolation over long periods of time is very rare. Aside from this possible exception, we may say that all political systems somehow cope with the problems of international accommodation, internal integration, and resource mobilization, participation, and distribution. At the other extreme, we have to say that no political system ever develops its capabilities to the point where they become fully stabilized at optimum levels of performance. The best-ordered and most stable political system may be shaken or destroyed by a change in the structure of the international environment, or some internal disruptive development. Thus, most if not all contemporary traditional systems — some of them stable for centuries — are undergoing rapid internal transformation as a consequence of their efforts to accommodate and respond to the international environment. A Britain having served for a century as the leading power in the international political system now has to respond to a fundamentally changed international political system, and cannot escape the internal systemic strains resulting from it.

The integrative, accommodative, participant, and distribution capabilities of political systems, even when we can speak of them as being "developed," still confront "issues" and undergo structural and cultural change. What do we mean then by the acquisition of a performance capability? We mean that the new performance capability is expressed in a specialized structure and related differentiated psychological orientations or culture. The capability acquires a kind of autonomy. The political system now can respond to problems of integration, accommodation, participation, or distribution in their own terms. Thus, one way of explaining the instabilities of the ancient empires of the Near East is to point out that most of them failed to differentiate accommodative capabilities from their integrative capabilities. They were neither structurally nor culturally capable of coping with other nations in the international environment in accommodative terms. They sought rather for unlimited empire by integrating other nations into their own political systems.

In more recent times nations such as Japan, Germany, and Russia have had similar problems in adjusting to participation in the international political system, *i.e.*, in developing a specialized accommodative structure and the relatively open culture which stable membership in the international political system requires. The criterion of political change, then, is the acquisition of a new capability, in the sense of a specialized role structure and differentiated orientations which together give a political system the possibility of responding efficiently, and more or less autonomously, to a new range of problems.

The order in which political systems encounter particular problems of change, and the way in which they solve them greatly limits their freedom in responding to and solving problems which arise later. Thus, Germany and Japan, late arrivals in the international political system, concentrated on integration and resource mobilization, and finding a satisfactory place in the international political system, and responded by subordinating their participation capabilities, or better, repressing their tendencies to acquire an autonomous culture and structure. An America, on the periphery of the international political system and under little pressure to integrate and mobilize its resources, developed a participation capability which limited its capacity for integration and resource mobilization, a pattern of growth almost the converse of that which occurred in Japan and Germany. But this question of the relations among capabilities may be treated more systematically by examining a variety of different types of political systems.

Let us take seven classes of political systems which have been suggested in the recent literature.[7] These seven broad classes include:

(1) Traditional Systems
(2) Modernizing Authoritarian Systems
(3) Tutelary Democracies
(4) Immobilist Democracies
(5) Conservative Authoritarian Systems
(6) Totalitarian Systems
(7) Stable Democracies

Traditional Systems. This class contains an enormous variety of political systems ranging all the way from the primitive band to systems as complex as the Ottoman Empire. Coleman sub-classifies the traditional systems of the Sub-Saharan African area into four categories: (1) large-scale states, (2) centralized chiefdoms, (3) dispersed tribal societies, (4) small autonomous local communities.[8] What they would all appear to have in common, in contrast with non-traditional systems is a comparative lack of structural differentiation, although the range in this respect among Coleman's four classes is enormous.

As examples of traditional systems we will take the small-scale autonomous local community at the one extreme, and the large and complex traditional empire at the other. We have already suggested that small-scale political systems have all four of our performance capabilities, but they are expressed in intermittent structures (i.e., without fully specialized roles) and relatively diffuse orientations. Such a political system may mobilize its resources, carry on warfare and negotiate with other political systems, and provide for participation in political decisions and the distribution of the social product. But each one of these capabilities is limited in the adaptive or problem-solving sense. Its integrative and accommodative capabilities are not flexible enough to withstand pressure from more integrated and specialized political systems. Thus, in warfare a professional army, other things being equal, will overpower a levy of age sets; in negotiation, an officialdom will out-maneuver a headman, or council of elders. Similarly its participation structure will take the form of an intermittent aspect of its integration structure, which limits its versatility in coping with either the integration or the participation problems. This arrangement may be quite stable until such a system encounters more specialized systems either by being included in a modernizing state, or through cultural diffusion. The relative inefficiency of intermittent structure and diffuse culture comes out clearly when these systems come into contact with specialized bureaucracies on the one hand, and political parties and interest groups on the other.

At the other extreme, the large-scale traditional empire becomes such an empire because it is able to develop an integrative capability superior to that of

---

[7] For the sources of this classification see Edward Shils, *Political Development in the New States* (The Hague: Mouton, 1962); James Coleman in Almond and Coleman (eds.), *The Politics of the Developing Areas* (Princeton: Princeton University Press, 1960), pp. 532 ff.; and G. A. Almond, "Comparative Political Systems," *Journal of Politics*, August 1956, pp. 395 ff.

[8] James Coleman in Almond and Coleman, *op. cit.*, pp. 254 ff.

surrounding political systems. But even though by comparison with other political systems it has acquired such an integrative capability, the empires that we usually call traditional have not developed genuinely penetrative bureaucracies and supportive national political cultures on the one hand, or specialized international accommodative capabilities on the other. Hans Speier once referred to pre-Communist China as "governments and armies afloat on a sea of people." Though traditional China and the Ottoman Empire at times were able to integrate enormous populations, and mobilize large resources for the support of a specialized officialdom, they both foundered and disintegrated in contact with smaller political systems with more versatile capabilities. What accounts for this, and what leads us to refer to these quite elaborate systems as traditional is that they tended to be closed political systems and only partially integrated ones. They tended to conceive of the environing world in closed terms, counterposing sacredness and cultural perfection on the one hand with the infidel and the barbarian world on the other. Given such cultural closure a genuine diplomacy of accommodation could not develop. Even in its most cohesive condition, the integrative capability of the Ottoman Empire involved an extractive rather than a penetrative relationship between central authority and local units. Persisting parochial loyalties stood in the way of developing national loyalties, and the force of custom stood in the way of an effective and legitimate system of resource allocation which might have enabled it to resist the new forces of the nineteenth and twentieth centuries. In competition with more thoroughly nationalized and integrated political systems which had more versatile diplomatic capabilities, political systems such as the Ottoman Empire are caught with international commitments that extend them far beyond their integrative and mobilizing capacities.

Modernizing Authoritarian Systems. Under this classification, we include such countries as Ghana, Egypt, and Pakistan — political systems which are not far along in the development of specialized capabilities. What differentiates them from other kinds of modernizing systems is their suppression of the participation and distribution capabilities, or rather their assimilation to the integration and mobilization capability. Confronted with models of more efficient political systems, and exposed to the fragmenting and disruptive impact of the "four-fold revolution," they have opted for integration and the capacity for mobilization of resources that it brings. The examples of this type of system which we have cited differ in a number of respects. Thus, Ghana has gone farthest in assimilating its participation capability — in the form of a monopoly party — to its integration capability. Egypt is in process of developing a monopoly party as a means of more effective mobilization of resources. Pakistan appears to be caught in the dilemma of permitting a participation capability to develop autonomously or of using it as an instrumentality for integration. What they all have in common are relatively undifferentiated capabilities. Their elites confront predominantly parochial cultures, and traditional tribal or local structures, and they are striving to attain cultural and structural integration. In their brief histories as independent nations they have sought to escape the disintegrative consequences attendant upon simultaneous exposure to the four capability requirements by focusing on integration or "nation-building" in its simplest sense. In the cases of Egypt and Ghana, partly in an effort to create a national mentality and enlarge the resource base of their countries, they pursue aggressive and expansionist foreign policies. This does not represent the development of an autonomous international accommodative capability, since these aggressive foreign policies are primarily serving integrative needs.

Tutelary Democracies. By tutelary democracies we mean those new or rapidly changing nations which, at least in the formal sense, confront all four of the capability requirements simultaneously and openly. India and Mexico represent rather stable examples of this class of political systems, while Burma represents an unstable one. It is of interest that both India and Mexico, though formally permitting the development of an autonomous participation and distribution capability, have in fact subordinated these capabilities to their needs for integration and resource mobilization. This is accomplished by the existence of a single dominant political party (despite freedom of party organization and competition) and by the overlap between the top levels of the dominant party with the bureaucracy. In this way the party may be used as a means of creating a sense of national identity and of mobilizing resources in support of efforts at economic and social development.

The chief difference between these political systems and the modernizing authoritarian ones is the successful combination by the tutelary democracies of the integrative and participation capabilities within a formally free framework. Were this condition not present it is difficult to see how India and Mexico could avoid going the way of a Burma or a Pakistan, shifting uneasily from authoritarian suppression to ineffective formal freedom. The important point to be made here is that the four-fold impact of capability requirements forces new political systems into very similar though not identical patterns.

Immobilist Democracies. The chief differences between the immobilist democracies and the tutelary democracies is that we are dealing in the former case with older nations more integrated in the cultural and structural sense, and more advanced in the sense of industrialization, urbanization, and education than the new tutelary democracies. However, we have already seen that the problem of integration was by no means solved in any stable sense in Germany and Italy, and that it was this and the unsolved accommodative problems which further complicated their efforts to solve the participation and distribution problems. But the peculiar property of immobilist systems is the fragmentation, both in a cultural and structural sense, resulting from the cumulative impact of the participation and distribution revolutions. Without having developed a consensus on governmental structure and process, these political systems had to confront the challenges of industrializing societies with their new class structures and social institutions. The emergence of socialist revolutionary ideologies in these countries is the ideological counterpart of the structural cultural fragmentation, a fusion of participation and distribution ideology, while in Britain democratic ideology could develop incrementally from political participation demands to welfare distribution demands.

Conservative Authoritarian Systems. The discussion of immobilist democracies leads logically to the analysis of conservative authoritarian systems. These authoritarian forms have emerged in the socially and economically more developed West, and in political systems fragmented by the simultaneous impact of multiple capability requirements. Thus, Spain and Portugal developed in a conservative authoritarian direction as a consequence of the simultaneous impact of the participation and distribution revolutions. In these two countries, the traditional forces of the Church, bureaucracy, officer corps, and the large landowners were able to take power and suppress the participation and distribution revolutions. Being ruled by conservative-traditional coalitions concerned with the maintenance of an existing social order, these systems, while focusing on integration, have not been particularly concerned with the mobilization of resources for aggressive foreign policies. Hence the participation capability has been permitted a limited autonomy. Thus, business interest groups, professional groups, and various political tendencies in the Church appear to influence and to bargain in the policy-making process.

Totalitarian Systems. Totalitarian systems on the other hand are dominated by revolutionary elites arising in disintegrated, fragmented, and immobilist political systems. They have in common the assimilation of the participation capability by the integrative capability, and the partial assimilation of the international accommodative capability by the integrative capability. That is, their foreign policies tend to be expansionistic and integrative rather than accommodative.

The Communist variety of totalitarianism differs from the Fascist type in that the concentration on integration is greater. It is a fascinating problem of contemporary Soviet politics to trace the gradual and tentative emergence of participation and distribution capabilities into autonomous structures and cultures. Russia's successful economic and social modernization has produced an educated population, and highly skilled professional and technical groups. Educated youth, managers and technicians, artists and writers, and even workers and peasants are in process of acquiring a bargaining capability which has implications for the possible future emergence of relatively autonomous participation and distribution capabilities in the Soviet Union.

Stable Democracies. One sub-class includes Britain, the United States, and the countries of the Old Commonwealth, and another one the stable multiparty democracies of the European continent — the Scandinavian and Low Countries and Switzerland. At an earlier point we compared the historical development of British and American democracy with that of France, Germany, and Italy in terms of capability requirements and structural and cultural characteristics. The point made was that a special set of historical circumstances enabled Britain and the United States to solve their problems of political change incrementally, and that as a consequence they were able to develop autonomous integrative, accommodative, participant, and distributive capabilities with their specialized structures and cultures.

What this seems to suggest is that the stable democratic systems are more versatile in their performance capabilities than other political systems. The structural and cultural autonomy of their capabilities enables them to cope with the variety of political system problems with relative efficiency and without disruptive systemic changes. Stable democratic systems do not have as efficient and as penetrative a mobilization capability as do the totalitarian systems. They have opted — or perhaps historical and geographic circumstances have made it possible for them to opt — for a more balanced development of capabilities, for an overall optimization of political capability. They cannot solve some problems as well as totalitarian systems, but they have some capability for solving the whole variety of problems which political systems encounter. Totalitarian systems have a kind of rigidity. They solve some kinds of problems with enormous efficiency, but other problems such as elite recruitment and succession, popular participation in decision-making, or competing demands for the distribution of the social product, they can only solve inefficiently, *i.e.*, with unstable consequences or by suppressing these capabilities.

A Comparative Approach to Political Sociology *

RANDALL COLLINS

The comparative method is an important means of generating and testing theory. By comparing the conditions under which similar activities and institutions appear, the social scientist can approximate the advantages of the experimental method of research. His aim is to generalize his explanations beyond particular instances, to reject unsound inferences, and to refine his explanations to take account of complex processes. Comparative politics, therefore, should not be viewed as a peripheral specialization within the study of politics but as a crucial set of materials for developing our understanding of politics everywhere.

In the recent revival of interest in comparative politics, the principal theoretical approaches have been varieties of structural-functional analysis borrowed from general sociological theory. Nevertheless, structural-functionalism is not a good theory of politics. It involves several conceptual difficulties, and its usefulness for empirical research has not yet been convincingly demon-

This article was written especially for this volume and is used by permission of the author. Copyright 1968 by Randall Collins.

RANDALL COLLINS is Acting Instructor in Sociology, University of California, Berkeley. He is co-author with Joseph Ben-David of a number of articles in the sociology of science and is currently working on his Ph.D. dissertation.

* I am indebted to my co-editors for their suggestions in the preparation of this article, and especially to Professor Bendix, to whom I owe many of the ideas contained herein.

strated. At a minimum, it is clear that functionalism has not remedied the serious lack that exists in the area of a general theory of politics.[1] We have few sound generalizations as to what determines the form of political institutions; some work has been done on the determinants of one overall form of government — democracy — but as will be shown below, much of the theorizing in this one area is not empirically valid. We have virtually nothing in the way of general explanations of what kinds of political movements and parties will develop under what conditions; the Communist and Fascist movements of the 20th century caught political theorists off guard, and while theorists have been engaged in after-the-fact explanations of these past movements, they have put forward no general theory that offers some insight into the present and future. Nor has much attention been given to the conditions under which different types of movements, parties, groups, or individuals are able to win various measures of power, except for analyses of a few spectacular revolutions. The main empirically-tested theories of politics have been devoted to the analysis of the determinants of the attitudes and behaviors of the rank-and-file voter; and even these theories tend to be specific to the institutional contexts provided by a few modern industrial democracies.

In short, there is a large gap in the area of social science that should be filled by an explanation of political events, institutions, and behavior. Structural-functionalism has the merit of being a general theory of society, but it is inadequate to fill this gap. An alternative approach is available, which has remained largely inaccessible to the American social scientists who are doing the principal theoretical and empirical work in comparative politics today. This alternative may be found in a European tradition of comparative studies of an earlier period. For the sake of convenience, I shall refer to this as the "historical sociology" approach; its most notable figure is Max Weber. In the following sections, I shall present the main points of structural-functionalism as it has developed historically, and as it has been recently applied to political analysis; the bulk of this paper will develop the "historical sociology" approach at some length, with numerous comparisons between the two approaches. My purpose is to show that the approach to comparative politics represented by Weber provides a basis for a general theory of politics, capable of explaining political institutions and processes across the entire range of human societies.

STRUCTURAL-FUNCTIONALISM

The basic principles of structural-functionalism can be summarized under five headings:

1. Society is a *system* of interdependent parts. Events taking place in one part of the system have repercussions throughout the system; hence, relations of cause and effect involve circular processes, and statements concerning these processes are extremely complex.

---

[1] Scott Greer and Peter Orleans, "Political Sociology," in R. E. L. Faris (ed.), *Handbook of Modern Sociology* (Chicago: Rand McNally & Co., 1964); Seymour Martin Lipset, *Political Man* (Garden City, N.Y.: Doubleday & Co., 1960), pp. 12–24.

2. Most parts of the system serve *functions* enabling the system to survive. This idea is based on an organic model of society going back to classical writers like Plato; in medieval political theory, the principal analogy compared the king to the head of the social body, with soldiers as its arms, peasants as its feet, and so forth. The ancient Hindu theory of the origins of castes uses a similar analogy. Thus, the dominance of the ruler was explained and justified by his functional importance for society.

3. There is a *division of labor* among the parts of the system, so that the several parts exchange the particular services in which each of them specializes. This idea, implicit in the medieval model, was developed in the 18th century by Adam Ferguson and Adam Smith; they shifted emphasis from the political to the economic aspect of society, which they maintained could regulate itself automatically, without government control. The significant idea introduced was that the parts of the social body could carry on their mutually advantageous exchanges without the constant supervision of the head. This idea led to the 19th-century attempts to downgrade or deny entirely the functional importance of the state for society.

4. Social systems tend toward a state of order or *integration*; despite disturbances in the orderly exchange among the parts, the system will usually return (if not strained beyond a certain limit) to an equilibrium at which the necessary exchanges for the survival of the system are reestablished. This system integration has been explained in a number of ways. One answer, made explicit among 19th-century "social organicists," [2] but also still traceable among contemporary functionalists, is to reify the organic analogy and assert that society tends toward integration simply because it is a functional system. Another answer is that functionally integrating institutions have simply evolved, by the trial and error of individuals or by natural selection among societies; this position was classically expressed by William Graham Sumner. A third answer points to the rational self-interest of individuals and the "invisible hand" of the market as the basis of social integration. It was Durkheim's attack on this utilitarian position that got modern functionalism under way. Durkheim argued that a system of exchanges based upon the division of labor can take place only if the individuals involved trust each other to adhere to the rules of exchange. In order that rational self-interest can come into play in the market place, there must be a pre-contractual social solidarity allowing the market to be established. This solidarity Durkheim found in a "collective conscience," which he based on the psychological premise that similar attitudes held by large numbers of individuals reinforce each other and thereby acquire great strength and a supra-individual, imperative force in directing the activities of individual members of society.[3]

Talcott Parsons' contributions to modern functionalism have built upon the problems and formulations of Durkheim. These contributions are: (a) to

---

[2] Schäffle, Lilenfeld, Fouillée, Worms, and to some extent their predecessor, Comte.

[3] Emile Durkheim, *The Division of Labor in Society* (New York: The Free Press of Glencoe, 1933), pp. 96–103, 200–229, 275–280.

rename the "collective conscience" as the "value system" and to replace Durkheim's archaic psychological underpinnings with a neo-Freudian theory of value-internalization in the individual through childhood socialization; [4] (b) to categorize the various functions that must be performed in a social system, thus making it possible to analyze social structures in terms of the functions that they serve; (c) to add a "social action" perspective, i.e., to view the system from the point of view of the individual's orientations, using categories taken from Toennies and Weber.

5. Since it is based on an organic analogy, the functionalist model has always been implicitly concerned with *change*, as an analogue to growth. The appropriate category for describing such change is *differentiation*, the process of increasing the division of labor within the system.[5] The categories for describing and comparing societies, therefore, are the relative states of differentiatedness, or the polar types on this continuum, "traditional" and "modern." Differentiation also has universal concomitants or effects: it frees social energy and makes possible a more efficient use of resources, thus increasing the output of the system (just as the evolution of specialized organs in living organisms makes possible greater mobility, greater sensitivity, and more selective response); it also creates problems for integrating the newly-specialized parts.[6]

This model also raises the question of the causes of differentiation, of which the following have been suggested: (a) imperfect socialization of individuals into the prevailing values may give rise to innovators, including "charismatic" leaders, who act to change the system; [7] (b) the imperfect integration of the parts of the system may cause strains — between conflicting values, conflicting structures, or between values and structures — which result in attempts to overcome these strains, and thus may lead to unexpected changes; [8] (c) the system may change as a reaction to changed conditions in the "external" environment, either natural conditions or the influences of other societies; [9] (d) change may be built into the system itself, which may take the form of a "moving equilibrium;" concrete examples of such change are the built-in effects of institutionalized scientific and technological innovation; [10] (e) change

[4] Talcott Parsons, *The Social System* (New York: The Free Press of Glencoe, 1951), especially Chapter VI.

[5] To counter any evolutionary bias in this position, sophisticated functionalists have pointed out that change may also be de-differentiation, in which specialized units recover lost functions and decrease their exchange with other units. See S. N. Eisenstadt, "Institutionalization and Change," *American Sociological Review*, Vol. XXIX (1964), pp. 235–247.

[6] S. N. Eisenstadt, *The Political Systems of Empires* (New York: The Free Press of Glencoe, 1963), especially pp. 94–112; Neil Smelser, "Mechanisms of Change and Adjustment to Change," in Bert F. Hoselitz and Wilbert Moore (eds.), *Industrialization and Society* (The Hague: Mouton, 1963), Chapter 2.

[7] Wilbert E. Moore, *Social Change* (Englewood Cliffs, N.J.: Prentice-Hall, 1963), Chapter 1.

[8] Neil J. Smelser, *Theory of Collective Behavior* (New York: The Free Press of Glencoe, 1963), pp. 47–66.

[9] Moore, *loc. cit.*

[10] Parsons, *op. cit.*, pp. 505–520; Francesca Cancian, "Functional Analysis of Change," *American Sociological Review*, Vol. XXV (1960), pp. 818–26.

in the cultural system — i.e., in the values around which society is integrated — will result in change in the social system; thus, religious movements have been important in major historical changes.[11]

The functional model has been applied to politics, most notably by Gabriel Almond, in the form of categorizations of political functions and analyses of the various structures that may fulfill them, and in the concern for "political socialization" and "political culture." [12] More generally, the functionalist viewpoint pervades many theoretical discussions of politics, which share the following assumptions: [13] (1) The unit of analysis is taken to be a social system, and the politics of that system (in practice, usually identified as a nation-state) is interdependently related to other aspects of that society, such as its economy, its system of stratification, its family system, and its culture-bearing institutions such as churches and schools. (2) The polity provides certain functions for society, and (3) exchanges its services for support from the other institutions of the society, thus taking part in the social division of labor. (4) Individuals are integrated politically, as in other respects, by internalizing the basic values and rules of the political process and by developing loyalty to the system. (5) Finally, political change is bound up with changes in the rest of the social system. In general, politics is a dependent variable; for example, most theories view some form of democracy — i.e., pluralistic and participant politics — as functionally related to economic development. Politics is also recognized to be a source of change, as in the transformations wrought by colonial domination or in the government programs of the "modernizing" nations; but the original forms of the political institutions, in these cases, are treated as arbitrary, as starting points only, not as subjects to be explained by the theory.

There is a tendency among functionalist writers on comparative politics to assert that structural-functional analysis is the only adequate way of dealing systematically with both Western and non-Western politics. Outside of the modern Western nations, the argument goes, the social setting of government becomes all-important; indeed, in the absence of many of the recognizable Western structures, certain parts of the process of government must be picked

[11] Talcott Parsons, *Societies: Evolutionary and Comparative Perspectives* (Englewood Cliffs, N.J.: Prentice-Hall, 1966).

[12] Gabriel A. Almond, "Introduction: A Functional Approach to Comparative Politics," in Gabriel A. Almond and James S. Coleman (eds.), *The Politics of the Developing Areas* (Princeton: Princeton University Press, 1960), pp. 3–64.

[13] See, for example, Talcott Parsons, "Evolutionary Universals in Society," *American Sociological Review*, Vol. XXIX (1964), pp. 353–356; Lucian W. Pye (ed.), *Communications and Political Development* (Princeton: Princeton University Press, 1963); S. N. Eisenstadt, "Bureaucracy and Political Development," in Joseph La Palombara (ed.), *Bureaucracy and Political Development* (Princeton: Princeton University Press, 1963); Gabriel Almond and Sidney Verba, *The Civic Culture* (Princeton: Princeton University Press, 1963); Edward Shils, *Political Development in the New States* (The Hague: Mouton, 1962); Clark Kerr, John T. Dunlop, Frederick Harbison, and Charles A. Myers, *Industrialism and Industrial Man* (Cambridge, Mass.: Harvard University Press, 1960); Seymour Martin Lipset, *Political Man* (Garden City, N.Y.: Doubleday & Co., 1960); Daniel Lerner, *The Passing of Traditional Society* (Glencoe, Ill.: The Free Press, 1958).

out as functions of non-specialized, non-government structures. The alternative viewpoints, as seen for example by Eckstein, are either the formal-legal, institutional approach of traditional political science or the relatively limited-range theories based only upon direct empirical inductions. These approaches are held to be inadequate; the former because of its lack of concern with non-government institutions and the latter because of its lack of a generalizing, analytical frame of reference.[14]

Nevertheless, there is another major approach to comparative studies; this is the tradition of historical and comparative sociology found in some very well-known (but not always well-understood) European writers — Weber and Tocqueville — as well as in some less known figures — Fustel de Coulanges and Otto Hintze.[15] The neglect of this tradition is largely due to a failure to recognize that it is in fact a distinct approach to comparative politics. This failure is particularly acute in regard to Max Weber, the most important figure of this group. The misunderstanding of so famous a theorist as Weber is due to a number of causes: the difficult nature of his writings; the rather checkered publishing history of his works in English translation, so that various parts of his exceedingly complex analysis of the rise of modern society have been torn out of context and thus subjected to one-sided interpretations; [16] and his use of analytical as well as descriptive concepts. But perhaps the most influential source of misunderstanding of Weber's views on politics is the assertion of Talcott Parsons that there is a "convergence" in the basic ideas of Durkheim and Weber.[17] As noted above, Durkheim is the legitimate father of modern structural-functional analysis; in his elaboration of Durkheim, Parsons added a social-action dimension, which was based in part on some of Weber's conceptualizations. In addition, Parsons has drawn on Weber's sub-

---

[14] Harry Eckstein, "A Perspective on Comparative Politics, Past and Present," in Harry Eckstein and David E. Apter (eds.), *Comparative Politics* (New York: Free Press of Glencoe, 1963), pp. 26–29.

[15] Hintze has not yet been translated into English, with the exception of a piece printed in this volume for the first time; a translation of his most important writings, contained in *Staat und Verfassung*, is currently in process in England.

[16] For example, Weber has been accused of a one-sided religious determinism in the rise of modern capitalism, on the basis of one of his earliest translated works, *The Protestant Ethic and the Spirit of Capitalism* (1930). The comparative studies on the world religions, which fill in some of the social-structural side of the process, appeared over twenty years later, after the original erroneous impression had gained wide currency; these works are *The Religion of China* (1951), *Ancient Judaism* (1952), and *The Religion of India* (1958). Weber's critics might have been warned by footnotes in *The Protestant Ethic*, as well as by the brief but comprehensive analysis in Part 4 of his *General Economic History*, which appeared in English in 1927. The fullest exposition of Weber's views on the rise of capitalism, however, contained in *Wirtschaft und Gesellschaft*, still remains untranslated as a whole; the first complete translation, by Guenther Roth, is scheduled to be published in the near future.

[17] Talcott Parsons, *The Structure of Social Action* (New York: The Free Press of Glencoe, 1937). In this work, Parsons does not so much directly misinterpret Weber's political sociology as to overlook it, by almost totally ignoring Part 3 of *Wirtschaft und Gesellschaft*. Parsons constructs a system based principally on Weber's discussion of religion, which Parsons then assimilates to a framework already developed in his discussions of Marshall, Pareto, and Durkheim.

stantive work on the world-religions for an interpretation of world history.[18] Nevertheless, Parsons has borrowed only rather selectively from Weber's work, and although a part has been found capable of being grafted onto a Durkheimian framework, the basic principles are fundamentally different.

In a sense, then, the following exposition of an alternative to functionalism will describe the difference between Weber and Durkheim. It will draw heavily on ideas presented a half century and more ago, not because they are the final truth, but rather because they are still very good ideas. It is because of the widespread misunderstanding and neglect of this tradition by American social science that its formulations still define a forefront of research; with more widespread application, they may undoubtedly be modified and improved upon.[19]

INTERNAL DYNAMICS [20]

Weber's formulations provide a fairly comprehensive model for analyzing the internal processes of a unit of political organization. An important difference from the structural-functional approach already appears in the preceding sentence: the processes to be analyzed take place within quite concrete organizations, not in a social "system" (a concept which Weber did not employ). Weber's approach makes no assumptions about the interdependence of the parts in any social unit; that is a matter for empirical investigation.[21]

The primary analytical concepts of the Weberian approach are the material and ideal interests of individuals, and the group and organizational structures developed by individuals to further these interests. Since many of these interests are directed toward "goods" which are scarce relative to the demand for them, there is a struggle among individuals, and among groups, for these goods. Individuals or groups are coordinated on two analytically distinct principles, which correspond to the spheres of "society" and "state." In the sphere of "society," groups are formed as "constellations of interests," in which the parties act together voluntarily for what they feel is their mutual benefit. Such groups are formed on two bases: coincidence of interests in the economic market, and feelings of identity with others who hold a

[18] Talcott Parsons, "Christianity and Modern Industrial Society," in Edward Tiryakian (ed.), *Sociological Theory, Values and Sociocultural Change* (New York: The Free Press of Glencoe, 1963); also, *Societies: Evolutionary and Comparative Perspectives.*

[19] See, for example, the works of Reinhard Bendix and Wolfram Eberhard, cited below, for developments of important ideas from this tradition.

[20] This section is based on Max Weber, *Wirtschaft und Gesellschaft*, 2nd edition (Tübingen: J. C. B. Mohr, 1925), especially Part III; and on the analysis of Reinhard Bendix, *Max Weber, An Intellectual Portrait* (Garden City, N.Y.: Doubleday & Co., 1962), pp. 257–281, 285–456.

[21] Weber regarded functional analysis as serving for a preliminary orientation to show how various forms of action contribute to the survival of groups and institutions, but he stressed that the main task of sociology is to explain behavior and institutions in terms of the action of individuals and warned against invoking a reified whole to explain the behavior of the parts. See Max Weber, *The Theory of Social and Economic Organization* (New York: Oxford University Press, 1947), pp. 101–104, 106–107.

common culture or ideal. In the sphere of the "state," coordination is based on dominance, in which one individual or group is placed in a position to enforce his will on the others. Such coordination is based on an organizational apparatus of domination and on some kind of principles of legitimacy. In both of these spheres of action, there is a struggle for advantage: for a favored position of "life chances" in the realm of exchange, and for the upper position in dominance relationships. Individuals struggle for advantage within organizations, and organizations struggle with each other.

In this view, the polity is first of all (both historically and analytically) an organization through which particular individuals or groups attempt to achieve their interests. This approach differs from the structural-functional approach by explaining most characteristics of the political process, not by how they meet the interests of society as a whole, but rather by how they reflect the interests of specific groups or individuals fighting for control of the political organization. The polity is first of all an apparatus of domination.[22]

This analysis applies to democratic as well as autocratic polities; for to say that the state is an apparatus of domination does not mean that it necessarily dominates very widely, or is controlled by a dictatorial group or individual. A stalemate may arise among contending power groups, and the resulting limitations of power on all sides may be institutionalized; the competing elites may appeal for support to groups not previously participating in the power struggle and, as a result, dissipate their power further to the point of becoming representatives of these lower classes. (This, in fact, is a capsule history of democratic institutions.) The fact that, under the conditions of such an internal balance of power, the state apparatus may provide services for all members of society should not obscure the continual struggle of individuals and groups to push the compromise in the direction of their own interests.

This approach takes into account the main phenomena stressed by the Marxist and by the elitist views (such as those of Pareto, Mosca, and Michels) of politics, but does not reduce to either. The crucial difference is that the political and economic spheres (or "state" and "society") are viewed here as independent but interacting orders; even when they coincide in the same concrete organizations they should be kept analytically distinct, because the principles of action in each sphere are not contingent on those in the other. That is, there is a struggle over economic resources and exchange opportunities

[22] Weber notes that the polity has historically been used for every conceivable purpose, but that there is no single purpose for which *all* states have been used. For this reason, he argues that the polity can be basically characterized only by its means, its ultimate ability to use force. (*Theory of Social and Economic Organization*, p. 155.) This view contrasts with Parsons' treatment of power as a "generalized symbolic medium" in the political system, which is treated as an exchange system parallel to the economic exchange system. See Talcott Parsons, "On the Concept of Political Power," in Reinhard Bendix and S. M. Lipset (eds.), *Class, Status and Power*, 2nd edition (New York: The Free Press of Glencoe, 1966), pp. 240–265. Weber, however, had argued that the concept of "power" is too diffuse to be useful; one may impose one's will over others by a variety of circumstances. Weber therefore emphasized the *imperative* nature of *authority*, which ties power to a specific context of domination. (*Theory*, pp. 152–153.)

in the market, and there is a struggle over control of the apparatus of domination. But the outcome or even the alignments in the political struggle are not solely or preponderantly determined by the relationship of groups to the economic structure, as in the Marxist theory; on the other hand, the organization of economic interests and resources cannot be dropped out of the analysis, as in the elite theories. The contending groups, resources and interests in both the economic and political spheres must be taken into account.

Ideals and Political Order. In the Weberian approach, values and ideals, along with forms of organization, are prime resources of the political sphere of action. Values are seen as defining goals and facilitating social coordination, as in the functionalist approach. But values do not form a *system*; rather, disparate values and ideas are found in a society, based upon different groups and organizations. Expressions of these ideals enter into the political struggle in at least two ways.

Firstly, to uphold certain ideals may be goals in themselves for individuals and groups. This is the primary meaning of Weber's statement that individuals have both material *and ideal* interests. This fact can be recognized without necessarily explaining it, which would involve speculative forays into psychology. Ideals are not necessarily cloaks for material interests; not all expressions of ideals are ideology, although they may be this as well. The clearest examples are religious values, but political ideals may also be quite sincerely held, without contamination by material interests. However — and this is the crucial point — ideals are nevertheless *interests*. One man's (or one group's) ideal interests are not the same as another's; even within a particular culture, as Weber pointed out, every status group has its own ideals, reflecting a lifestyle that it attempts to enhance. Although such status groups may not be so prominent in the more culturally homogeneous modern societies as in previous eras, similar processes continue to operate; organized groups of various kinds (businesses, labor unions, government agencies, voluntary associations) develop their own ideals — often in explicit contrast to the ideals of competing groups.[23] Even at the level of whatever agreement on abstract ideals may be found in a society, there is disagreement over how to put ideals into practice. Everyone agrees on such values as "loyalty," "altruism," and "achievement," for example; but there are great disagreements over *what* to be loyal to, or whether altruism should prevail over individual achievement in particular cases. Moreover, individuals fight for domination in order to fulfill their ideal interests quite as much as for their material interests; despite the ideal nature of these interests, domination — and hence struggle — is often necessary to achieve them.

Secondly, individuals may use ideals as weapons in the political struggle. They may put forward rationalizations for their conduct; for example, a ruler defending his rule may claim he is serving the will of God or the good of the people. Groups may defend their privileged positions as being appropriate to

[23] Philip Selznick, *Leadership in Administration* (Evanston, Ill.: Row, Peterson & Co., 1957).

their very high ideals; an aristocracy justifies its privileges by building a code of honor (in a similar way, a modern profession justifies its freedom by elaborating a code of ethics). Clearly, ideal appeals are useful as political weapons only if some other persons are convinced by them. But this consideration need not lead back to the view that all members of society share a common value-system or that such a value-system is needed to integrate society.

How, then, is social integration possible in this inherently divisive social universe? Weber did not concern himself with this question in the large, as Durkheim did; but he showed a great deal of concern for the stable coordination of human activities through particular groups and organizations. The answer to the question is implied in these two facts. A society, as *an aggregate of individuals*, is *not* integrated; common values do not operate to hold them all together. Rather, individuals form groups and organizations on the bases of the mutual accommodation of their interests — material and ideal — and of the domination of some individuals over others. Groups and organizations, in turn, may act together on the bases of common interests or by the domination of some organized groups over others. What we call a society is nothing more than a shifting network of groups and organizations, held together by one or both of these two principles — coalitions of interests, or dominance and submission.

But in what way are interests coordinated, and how is domination possible, especially since it is admitted that ideal justifications of dominance are important means of maintaining political control? Must there not be some common value-agreement, as Parsons (following Durkheim) argued, to avoid the Hobbesian problem of "war of all against all"? The answer involves, first of all, separating the question of stable coordination *within* groups, from coordination *between* groups. Members of the same status group or organization, for example, may share common values, but the emotional solidarity found within such groups is not needed to assure "social integration" between groups. Clearly, it is possible for an organized group, especially one with great *force*, to dominate other groups without the groups sharing common values. The fact that some kinds of understandings and expectations may grow up between ruling and ruled groups may contribute to the stability of their relationship, but force is still the basis of domination.

Nevertheless, the value-appeals of a ruling group may have an effect on the subordinate group.[24] There are two reasons for this effect. The primary reason is that the ideals expressed by rulers to justify their authority give information that is valuable to the ruled; it tells them what the rulers can be expected to do and what sort of "deals" he is making with those around him. Even quite subordinate individuals can turn these official pronouncements to their own

[24] However, political elites vary in their emphasis on such appeals. The traditional conqueror did not spent much effort justifying himself to conquered peasants but only made known the brute force of his armies. Elites appeal to values more in dealing with those on whom they depend for their power — in dealing with their own administrative and military staffs, in autocracies, or with the public, in democracies.

advantage; individuals who are on a more nearly equal plane with the person in authority, whose support is fairly strongly desired by him, have even better reason to take note of these official ideals. An individual can dominate others over any extended period of time only by organizing a network of mutual expectations among them. Thus, certain "bargaining" relationships between the ruler and his immediate staff, his allies, his supporters, and sometimes even his subjects are summarized under some general ideals: "loyalty," "protection," "nation." The ideal sets, in a general way, the terms of the bargain, however one-sided it may be. Since even the strongest ruler, as an individual, depends on others to carry out his orders, he must ensure the continuity of the principles that govern his relationships with those on whom he depends for power, whether they be a small group of military retainers, a series of quasi-independent feudal allies, a large administrative or party bureaucracy, or millions of voters. Thus, by an ironic twist, values become particularly crucial in political struggles: those who appeal to values, whether as ends in themselves or as ideological cover for their material interests, become constrained by these very values. The idealist must live up to his ideals, and the ideologist may be caught in his own ideology.

The above analysis emphasizes how cold-blooded calculations of power arrangements may depend on orientation to publicly stated values. It should be noted that these are not disembodied values, floating in the "political culture"; individuals will orient to them only if they know that other persons, and especially the most powerful persons, are also oriented to them. Hence, the important values are those that are publicly *expressed* by individuals who clearly occupy places in dominant political institutions.[25] Secondarily, individuals may become *emotionally* committed to supporting the ideals that play such a role in political coordination; they may "internalize" the values to a degree that approximates the value-commitment that functionalists posit as the basis of political order. Nevertheless, this psychological commitment is derived from *participating* in the coalitions and struggles around the center of power, and although this commitment may *add* stability to a political order, that order is not itself based on psychological commitments. An autocratic regime is based on the fact that an individual or group is able to gain a central position in the cold-blooded bargaining for power, playing everyone off against everyone else; a democratic regime is based on a condition of continuing stalemate between contending power groups. Over a period of time, the populace may build up loyalty to the autocracy or a respect for the principles of de-

[25] Weber did not pursue this issue of the acceptance of legitimating principles, but an analysis may follow the lines of an informational model of social behavior; see Thomas C. Schelling, *The Strategy of Conflict* (Cambridge, Mass.: Harvard University Press, 1963), pp. 89–92. For an interpretation of norms as those principles that individuals know *each other* are oriented toward, see Thomas J. Scheff, "Toward a Sociological Model of Consensus," *American Sociological Review*, Vol. XXXII (1967), pp. 32–45. For an example of the importance of communication in an extreme situation of dominance, see Paul Kecskemeti, "Totalitarian Communications as a Means of Control," *Public Opinion Quarterly*, Vol. XIV (1950), pp. 224–234.

mocracy, in these respective situations.[26] But when the basic political bargaining positions change, the power arrangement is likely to shift also, no matter what the value-commitments of the populace are. A regime that is backed up only by sentiment is in a precarious position.[27]

The Dynamics of Authority. Weber devoted much attention to the ways in which rulers are limited by various principles of legitimating their authority. It should be noted that these principles are ideal types, which may be found in various combinations, particularly as participants in the political struggle attempt to shift the grounds of legitimation to their own advantage. The ruler who gains support on the basis of *tradition* occupies a secure place in the center of a network of stable expectancies; however, his personal freedom of action is hindered by the fact that traditions are binding upon him, as well as upon his subjects. As a traditional ruler, he is expected to show a certain amount of personal arbitrariness; but there are limits to the kinds of actions he may take, especially in tampering with traditional institutions. To increase his own power, he tends to threaten the basis of his own legitimacy. Thus, he may break traditional restraints and demand increased subjugation on the grounds of his unique, personal qualities (*charisma*). But there are great dangers in using the charismatic justification of authority; it erodes traditional principles, and thereby fosters ambitions on the part of individuals who might otherwise acquiesce in their traditional positions. Even more importantly, to base authority on one's personal qualities chains the ruler to the consequences of this claim; he must be able to live up to the extraordinary standards he has claimed to exemplify. Although the traditional ruler needs no extraordinary talents, the charismatic ruler must be prepared to show such talents at appropriate times, under penalty of undermining his own support.[28]

---

[26] Thus, we may expect that even anti-democratic traditionalist groups, e.g., in Indian politics, may eventually develop a commitment to democratic rules, not because they believe in these values, but because they can be politically active in a balance-of-power situation only by adhering to the rules of the political struggle.

[27] Emotional commitments adapt to reality. When it is impossible to overthrow the government, individuals will eventually not even want to try. But their loyalty is based on two conditions: that the current government arrangement meets at least some of their interests and that it appears impossible for them to change the form of government. Under such circumstances, the best chances for the individual to advance his interests is to identify with existing arrangements and to strive for the best position within them. Thus, the structural situation can engender genuine loyalty and even idealism. But if the balance of power shifts for any extended period of time, the form of government will change. The emotional commitments of individuals may lag behind for a while after the institutional arrangements that supported them have changed, but in the long run they are displaced by value-commitments to the new regime. Thus, loyalty alone is not enough to keep military officers from overthrowing a democratic government; they can always appeal to other ideals to justify their actions, if the balance of power among institutions does not make it appear impossible for them to succeed in a revolt.

[28] The dynamics of legitimacy are made even more complex by the fact that the *ruled* may vary in their demands for the ruler to live up to the promises implicit in his principle of legitimacy. In times of crisis, subjects or followers may call for a "sign" of

The ruler may seek to extend his power by appealing to yet another principle of legitimacy: he may attempt to bring his staff under the sway of a set of comprehensive procedural rules, while retaining his own control over the setting of goals. By setting down codified, rational principles, the ruler can attempt to maintain the regular expectancies that are the basis of a power apparatus, while avoiding the total regulation of both means and ends set down by tradition. But even here, the ruler becomes bound by his principles of legitimation; having established a *rational-legal* order, he must obey the rules. Having established generalized procedures, he cannot abrogate them in particular cases, particularly when they are used to make claims against him; for to violate his own laws is to disturb the sense of regularity in the networks of mutual expectancies that support his power. Although any particular violation of a principle of legitimacy may have no untoward consequences, a series of such violations can result in the loss of power.

A look at these phenomena from the other side will show exactly what the danger is. Even when a particular ruler appears to be firmly in power, there is at least a latent struggle among his subjects and supporters. Should the *traditional* ruler break tradition in his efforts to extend his personal sway, there are always potential contenders ready to seize upon the event and use it as a bargaining point in luring members of the ruling apparatus into revolt. The *charismatic* leader is surrounded by other would-be leaders, ready to put forward their own charismatic or traditional claims, should he falter. And in a *rational-legal* order, too much arbitrariness generates opposition: in a democracy, at the polls; in an autocracy, in plots or revolutionary movements. Principles of legitimacy, like other ideal appeals, contain implicit promises of at least minimal benefits or protections in return for acquiescence; when promises are broken, the political bargains tend to break down, and change occurs until some new bargains are struck.[29]

---

the power or "grace" of their leader. The ruler tends to reject such demands as indicating lack of respect for his prerogatives to do as he please. Nevertheless, if he cannot maintain belief in his powers by acting appropriately, either in times of crisis or in circumstances of his own choosing, he undermines his support. Modern totalitarian regimes have developed elaborate means of avoiding responsibility for failure to live up to their self-expressed standards, as the ruler may place the blame on administrative agencies who carry out his decisions, and the agencies in turn avoid blame by referring to their obedience to orders from above. See Reinhard Bendix, "Max Weber's Sociology Today," *International Social Science Journal*, Vol. XVII (1965), pp. 19–22; also, Reinhard Bendix, "Reflections on Charisma," in this volume.

29 See Reinhard Bendix, *Work and Authority in Industry* (New York: John Wiley & Sons, 1956), for an application of this approach to the history of industrial relations. Bendix has suggested, in an unpublished lecture, that the dynamics of Weber's treatment of religion are analogous to the dynamics of political legitimacy. In any society with a religious orthodoxy, variants and heresies inevitably appear. There are two reasons for this continual struggle in the field of religion. Among the religious elite, the specialists in ritual and doctrine, there is a continual temptation to follow out the inherent logic of various points of doctrine to their ultimate conclusions; but this strain to intellectual consistency clashes with the *organizational* needs for reconciling opposing principles. That is, the intellectually committed "theologians" strive for consistency, and may

Thus, there is an internal principle of change in political structures. The dynamic factor is the (latent or manifest) struggle of individuals and groups, based upon divergences of interest, material and ideal. This is the source of energy; its release into action is guaranteed by the basic instability of power arrangements. These arrangements have two aspects: the principles by which the ruler attempts to legitimate his power and the organizational apparatus through which he attempts to dominate. Both of these are inherently unstable. As noted above, the bases of legitimacy supporting particular arrangements of power are liable to be undermined in the struggle of individuals to gain or extend power: the principle of charisma is too demanding for rulers to continually live up to; tradition restrains rulers more than they are willing to be restrained; and a rational-legal order tends to make particular individuals, including rulers, quite dispensable.[30]

But there is also an instability in the organizational apparatus of domination. It is impossible for an individual ruler to exercise direct, central control over large numbers of subjects scattered over a wide territory, especially under conditions of poor transportation and communication. However, if the central ruler delegates his authority, he tends to lose it; his agents develop their own areas of autonomy, based upon their superior knowledge of specialized or local conditions, geographical distance, and the ruler's reliance upon them. To reassert central control, the ruler must use more agents to check up on the other agents, either in the field or in a central information-gathering apparatus; but this in turn creates more enclaves of expert — and hence somewhat autonomous — jurisdiction. The ruler may control any particular individuals

---

arrive at extreme statements of mysticism, asceticism, pantheism, or other attempts to overcome doctrinal contradictions; but the leaders of the religious organization must compromise logical consistency for the sake of bolstering their organization's position in the world. A second level of struggle goes on between the religious elite and the masses of believers. The religious doctrine, like a principle of legitimacy, holds out certain promises to the faithful. To be sure, the promises for salvation in another world cannot be assessed very well by the living, except when they feel that the *entire church* is in jeopardy because of the corruption of its leaders. (The Protestant Reformation may be interpreted as the result of just such a problem of loss of legitimacy by the church; see Reinhard Bendix, "A Case Study in Cultural and Educational Mobility: Japan and the Protestant Ethic," in Neil J. Smelser and Seymour Martin Lipset [eds.], *Social Structure and Mobility in Economic Development* [Chicago: Aldine Publishing Co., 1966], pp. 262–279.) But as Weber continually stressed, the higher teachings of any religion are most important for the religious elite; the masses of believers expect some worldly as well as otherworldly benefits, ranging from emotional comfort to miraculous (or magic) intervention in worldly affairs. The religious elite may resist the calls for a miracle, as showing a lack of faith, just as the charismatic or traditional ruler may reject the calls of his subjects for a sign of his extraordinary powers or beneficence, as showing a lack of the sense of duty or of faith in him. Nevertheless, if the political ruler remains inactive too often in times of hardship among his people, his legitimacy is undermined, and contenders for his authority may arise. Similarly, the religion that cannot produce occasional evidence of worldly benefits also loses its authority and promotes the rise of competing doctrines.

[30] This dispensability may be institutionalized in the democratic form of a rational-legal order.

by a divide-and-conquer technique of fostering mutual suspicions among his staff, but this technique only reduces the efficiency of his apparatus in dealing with external threats, and in any case it perpetuates the *overall* situation of the dissipation of central power.[31]

This dilemma continues despite changes in organizational forms, even changes designed to overcome it. Hintze, following up the lines of Weber's analysis, has shown how European rulers created rationalized bureaucracies in order to counter the dissipation of authority as patrimonial officials turned themselves into feudal lords.[32] But the new organizational form resulted in a new dissipation of authority, in this case not spatially into territorial fiefs, but into the specialized bureaucracy itself.[33]

This view of social change contrasts with that of the functionalists, outlined above. Imperfect socialization into prevailing values or other failures of integration in the system need not be invoked to account for change; in fact, such concepts cannot be used here. The very terminology of functionalism assumes that a state of perfect value-integration is logically *possible*, whether it actually occurs or not; such a concept of a system in equilibrium is the ideal type, the basic model against which all deviations are measured. But the Weberian approach is based on the principle that individual interests diverge; hence, a situation in which the material and ideal "goods" are so divided, or individuals are so socialized that no one would try to change things more to their advantage, is impossible. Hence, the political struggle is itself a continual basis for political change. Not only do individuals and groups replace each other in holding power, but also political institutions and political ideals change, as groups try to mold them to their advantage.[34]

[31] The history of the Imperial Chinese bureaucracy provides a good example of these processes as well as of the way a ruler can become a virtual prisoner of his traditional legitimation.

[32] Otto Hintze, "Der Commissarius und seine Bedeutung in der allgemeinen Verwaltungsgeschichte," *Staat und Verfassung* (Goettingen: Vandenhoeck & Ruprecht, 1962), pp. 242–274; see also Weber, *Wirtschaft und Gesellschaft*, Part 3, for the basis of such an analysis. As discussed above, the same development can be analyzed on the level of principles of legitimacy, as traditional and charismatic principles are replaced by rational-legal principles.

[33] In the modern Western state, the government encounters the dilemma in a new form. As its administrative agencies attempt to regulate the functioning of more and more social groups, it finds that its authority dissipates into the groups to be regulated. Just as the patrimonial ruler had to rely on agents who could build up local strongholds and hence gain autonomy from him as feudal lords, the government agencies rely on the technical expertise and cooperation of the groups they are regulating and serving and hence lose much control to them. See Henry W. Ehrmann, "Interest Groups and the Bureaucracy in Western Democracies," *Revue Française de Science Politique*, Vol. XI (1961), pp. 541–568; reprinted in this volume.

[34] Ralf Dahrendorf, *Class and Class Conflict in Industrial Society* (Stanford: Stanford University Press, 1959), and P. L. Van den Berghe, "Dialectic and Functionalism," *American Sociological Review*, Vol. XXXVIII (1963), pp. 695–705, have attempted to graft versions of the Marxist struggle onto the functionalist model. The interpretation of Weber presented here, however, is not intended as a supplement to functionalism, but as an alternative to all social-system models, be they functionalist, Marxist, or a combination of the two.

EXTERNAL PERSPECTIVES

A second difference between the approach presented here and the functionalist one is in the conceptualization of external perspectives. As indicated above, the reference for "external" is to a concrete political organization, not a "system," although operationally, functionalists also point to concrete political boundaries when giving examples of "systems." The two approaches thus agree in practice on the unit of analysis, in many cases; nevertheless, there are two important disagreements.

Layer Societies. Firstly, functionalists have derived their conceptual model of a "system" from two typical examples: the primitive village described in the anthropological literature and the modern nation-state. Both of these units have relatively distinct boundaries and a functional division of labor among their parts. However, these models are extended to cases in which these characteristics are absent. For example, functionalists may talk of Imperial China as a "system," but as Eberhard has pointed out, its boundaries were far from clear: starting from a center of strong political control and cultural solidarity, the Chinese empire stretched out into areas of progressively weaker control and greater cultural diffuseness. At the outer fringes, it was difficult to draw the line between temporary tributaries and actual enemies. Nor can the boundaries be drawn on economic or cultural lines: economic exchanges functioned over far greater distances than even the tributary relationships, whereas extreme cultural diversity could be found almost at the heart of the Empire.[35]

These characteristics are not peculiar to historical China; one can argue that they come near to describing virtually all political units between the isolated primitive village and the modern nation-state. An appropriate model for such arrangements is of more than historical interest, for most of the "modernizing" nations of today are undeniably closer to the model of superficial government control over culturally and economically isolated groups than to the model of an internally organized nation-state. Eberhard has suggested the image of "layers" for such historical societies: at the bottom, relatively self-contained peasant villages; at the top, a ruling military and administrative group. The two layers are culturally distinct; not only are their ways of life different, but often the rulers are culturally alien invaders, speaking a different language and worshipping different gods. The ruling layer may be displaced by another, of totally different culture and internal organization, without it making any difference to the life of the villagers, except to vary somewhat the degree of their hardships. There are also layers of specialists of various kinds — merchants, priests, entertainers — who may have networks of cultural contact and economic exchanges spreading across continents.

To call the relationship between the rulers and the villagers "functional" is to impute a degree of interdependence that does not exist. There is no economic division of labor and consequent exchange between rulers and peasantry, nor is it clarifying to say that the villagers exchange their economic produce

[35] Wolfram Eberhard, *Conquerors and Rulers,* 2nd edition (Leiden: E. J. Brill, 1965), pp. 2–17; reprinted in this volume.

for protection from thieves and despoilers; from the villagers' point of view, the rulers *are* the very despoilers they are supposedly protecting against.[36] A more reasonable usage would be to reserve "functional" terms for cases in which actual *exchange* relationships exist and to recognize *dominance* relationships where they exist (as emphasized in the previous section). In this way, it is possible to see the sharp difference that arises when formerly isolated groups begin to come into economic exchange relationships with each other — i.e., in the commercial and industrial revolutions — and when the fragmented lower layer first comes into the nationwide political bargaining process formerly carried on only *within* the ruling layers — i.e., in the "democratic" revolution, the spread of citizenship.[37]

Internal and External Determinants of Politics. Secondly, even in the modern nation-state, there is a danger in taking the boundaries too seriously or in confining attention too closely to an "internal" model of change. As noted above, the functionalist perspective is to see change as analogous to growth, as a process of "differentiation." It should be kept in mind that this term is a modern synonym for "the division of labor," and despite the abstractness with which it is frequently used, it often refers to just what Adam Smith had in mind: the development of *economic* specialization and exchange. If one looks beyond the terminology to the concrete reference, one finds that functionalists tend to view economic developments as the major dynamic of political change, at least in the modern world.[38] In general outlines, the functionalists' view of political change is similar to that of their not-so-distant intellectual cousins, the Marxists, who also developed from the 19th-century

[36] *Ibid.*

[37] The parallel between these historical "layer" societies and many of the new nations, especially in Africa, is striking. Similarly, Furnivall has emphasized the dual nature of colonial societies, which are particularly good examples of an international layer — e.g., the British or the Dutch colonial governments — ruling over large numbers of separate "native" groups. See J. S. Furnivall, "The Political Economy of the Tropical Far East," *Journal of the Royal Asiatic Society*, Vol. XXIX (1942); reprinted in this volume. Finally, even in more modern societies, elements of the "layer" structure may continue to be important. For example, the attitude of the peasants of rural Greece toward the modern government in Athens, or of southern Italy (Calabria and Sicily, the home of the Mafia — a pre-modern, patrimonial "government," developed in the "underground" in opposition to the formal government systems imposed by outsiders during the last several centuries) toward the government situated in the North, continues to be like the attitude of Eberhard's Chinese villagers toward the tax-collectors of whoever happened to be in power.

[38] The economic determinism is often hidden under the general label of "modernization," but it is clear that virtually all of the nonpolitical features of modernization, which in turn are cited as bases of political development — decline of local ascriptive ties, mobilization, urbanization, exposure to mass media, rising income, and increasing income equality — are considered to be concomitants of industrialization. See the sources cited in footnote 13; some of these (Kerr *et al.*; Lipset, Chapter 2) explicitly cite industrialization as the basis for "political development," which usually means some form of democracy. Such a functionalist theorist as Eisenstadt, writing on the pre-modern empires, also gives economic development a crucial role, although hiding it under the abstract term "structural differentiation." S. N. Eisenstadt, *The Political Systems of Empires* (New York: Free Press of Glencoe, 1963), pp. 3–112.

tradition of utilitarian economics. This economic bias will be further discussed below in relation to the concepts of tradition and modernity.

This viewpoint is particularly limiting in the study of political change, for it directs attention away from explicitly political factors. One of these, the internal power struggle, has been dealt with in the previous section; this section will focus on the external political relationships of states, which are obscured by an emphasis on internal economic factors. Firstly, it should be noted that particular states are usually *constituted* by the interaction of several polities. All presently existing states are the organizational heirs, modified by revolution, secession, or unification, of forms resulting from military conquest. A glance at a historical atlas will reveal that the nature of political units themselves is heavily determined by an external struggle among organized forces; and although it is harder to see the process during the short time span of our present, a look backward through twenty-five years shows that this determinant is still at work.

Even short of the overwhelming force of conquest, the external relations among polities may be important determinants of their internal structures. No one should have to be reminded, in this day of international ideological movements, aggressive diplomacy (both overt and covert), and actual military interventions, that the political structures of states can be crucially affected by the activities of alien states. Yet there is a dearth of theory construction in this area; in all that has been written on political development in the new nations, virtually nowhere is there a treatment of such international factors. As a result, there is an air of unreality about the predictions of most social scientists concerning political development in the Third World. This great gap in theory may be due to ideological bias, since most social scientists are citizens of the United States, one of the major contenders in the struggle to determine the form of these states.

But the theoretical bias goes deeper than the ideological one. As Kenneth Bock has shown, theorists who view societies through an organic analogy have always tended to divide social phenomena into the regular and the accidental.[39] Particular historical events are held to be unique, nonrecurring, and hence not amenable to any generalized explanation; the social scientist, then, must concentrate on the nonhistorical regularities, the *forms* of organic interrelationship and growth specified by his theoretical model. But as Bock points out, the dichotomy is a false one, for the materials of any empirically relevant theory are of only one kind: events occurring in historical time and space. Any theoretical regularities that are not purely conceptual must involve some kind of induction from these events. Modern social science, as heir to concepts deriving from the organic analogy, has tended to adopt this dichotomy between the regular and the accidental, in practice, although not necessarily in theory. Thus, theorists of politics look for regularities only *within* the theoretically designated "system" and treat the external impingements as accidental. But the fact that little theoretically significant regularity is apparent among the external relations

[39] Kenneth E. Bock, *The Acceptance of Histories* (Berkeley and Los Angeles: University of California Press, 1956).

of states is a fault of the conceptual scheme rather than of the data. As an area in which to search for determinants of political structure and behavior, it is almost untouched.

Widening the Framework of Analysis. Nevertheless, a few significant generalizations can be made already, and a coherent theoretical perspective can be built up if these generalizations are set in the proper context. For example, we may note that even without direct interference, the external relations of a state may affect the strategies and the needs of the contending groups in internal power struggles. External defeats may cause a crisis in legitimacy for a ruling group or at least weaken its specific claims to leadership; the outbreaks of coup d'etat and revolution after defeat in war are well known. Another generalization is that large-scale wars, in which the entire population is mobilized, bring about increased democratization — in the sense of increased mass participation in the political process.[40] War has been an important determinant of many features of modern politics, from the demand for the extension of the franchise that developed with the introduction of universal military service on the Continent, to the Negro movement in the United States following the all-out national effort in the Second World War. Wars also increase centralized government control and hence the possibility of authoritarian regimes.[41] There is no paradox here: the compatibility of mass democracy and centralized dictatorship was noted long ago by Tocqueville in viewing French political development, although he did not note the possibility that the wars France fought throughout the 18th century may have influenced both of these developments.[42]

External relations may affect internal structure in yet another way: through the diffusion of ideas and goals. This process may be looked on as a variety of the cultural diffusion with which a school of anthropologists has long been concerned, but it has an important *political* dimension. A significant example can be found in the process of modernization. As Bendix has argued, modernization is most accurately described, not as a universal evolution of societies from a state of tradition to a state of modernity due to their own internal developments, but as a process of international emulation.[43] Political and economic changes in France and England around the turn of the 19th century put those nations in a condition of superiority over other nations; the French and English, for whatever reasons, had developed political or economic structures that important groups within other nations envied. The reasons for the envy are obvious: the rulers of states, in a setting of international struggles, could hardly be unresponsive to developments that increased the political and economic strength of competing states; the contending groups in the *internal* power struggles were also quite capable of seizing upon foreign innovations

[40] Stanislaw Andrzejewski, *Military Organization and Society* (London: Routledge & Kegan Paul, 1954), especially Chapter 2.

[41] *Ibid.*, pp. 92–95.

[42] Alexis de Tocqueville, *The Old Regime and the French Revolution* (Garden City, N.Y.: Doubleday & Co., 1955), Part 2.

[43] Reinhard Bendix, "Tradition and Modernity Reconsidered," *Comparative Studies in Society and History*, Vol. IX (April 1967), pp. 292–346.

that offered them opportunities to better their positions. Thus, rulers especially wanted to borrow England's economic power, and subordinate groups wanted to borrow French popular democratic institutions.

The diffusion of elements of "modernity" has been a process of active *borrowing* by various groups from their "reference states" — usually the states by which the rulers feel most directly threatened, or which non-ruling groups see as providing the best pattern for their own interests. The *process* of modernization in each nation, then, is formed by the nature of the international threat and by the condition of the power struggle among its internal groups. The combination of elements in each nation's policy of modernization is the result of the mixture of the aims of these contending parties. In this struggle over the incorporation of foreign innovations, certain groups which are the focus of external contacts — such as the intellectuals and the military — play crucial roles. Eberhard has suggested that cross-national "layers" (such as merchants' networks or chains of monasteries) have been the basis for rapid cultural transmission in traditional societies; [44] following this suggestion, one might also look at the organized structure of similar transmission belts in the process of modernization. [45]

HISTORICAL CONTINUITIES

A third major perspective, the historical, must be added to the internal and external perspectives in explaining political structures and events. The significance of such a perspective can be grasped by examining the concepts of "tradition" and "modernity." A dichotomy between concepts of this sort is common in most theories of social change: Gemeinschaft and Gesellschaft, mechanical and organic solidarity, sacred and secular societies, the small town and the mass society, and so forth. Such contrasts go as far back as the 18th-century critics of commercialization, as do the basic themes of the contrast: old authority vs. new freedom, or old belongingness vs. new alienation. [46] For our purposes, the crucial fact is that many of modern social science concepts derive from various formulations of the contrast: [47] primary and secondary group relations, ascribed and achieved status, particularistic and universalistic standards, diffuse and specific obligations, and other pairs of contrasting concepts.

[44] Eberhard, *loc. cit.*

[45] One might ask: How can we go beyond treating such external factors as arbitrary, "accidental" starting points for internal processes, in the way that functionalists take colonialism as a starting point for the analysis of political development in the new states? The solution is to shift the context of analysis and focus on whatever *group* of political units are in any significant contact with each other. Etzioni has attempted to make this shift of focus in his analysis of international unification, although he uses a form of functionalist analysis which differs widely from the perspective used here. See Amitai Etzioni, "The Epigenesis of Political Communities at the International Level," *American Journal of Sociology*, Vol. LXVIII (1963), pp. 407–421.

[46] Bendix, "Tradition and Modernity Reconsidered."

[47] For example, Parsons has stated that his pattern variables derive from Toennies' contrast of Gemeinschaft and Gesellschaft. Talcott Parsons, "Comments on the State of the General Theory of Action," *American Sociological Review*, Vol. XVIII (1953), pp. 618–631.

The validity of these concepts does not depend on their intellectual ancestry, of course; it is with their use that problems arise. There is a tendency among social scientists — although not based on any logical imperative — to attempt to describe social change as the movement of an entire society from a position near one end of a continuum involving *all* of these dichotomies, toward the other end of the continuum, where the other sides of the dichotomies are grouped. That is, societies change from a state of tradition — characterized by a predominance of primary groups (the prototype being the family), ascribed statuses (low social mobility), particularistic standards (the precedence of persons over laws) — to a state of modernity, in which something close to the opposite obtains — predominance of formal organizations, high social mobility, the rule of abstract law, limited contractual agreements, and so forth. The various elements at both ends of the continuum are seen as making up an ideal type — a society characterized completely by ascription, particularism, and so on, or by achievement, universalism, and the rest. As Bendix has shown, social change is then viewed as the movement of societies along the continuum from one type to the other.[48]

The foregoing is a way of conceptualizing social change, not a way of explaining it, hence it cannot be criticized on grounds of its empirical truth or falsity. However, one may question whether this is the most useful way of conceptualizing the process of modernization, whether these concepts direct one to the key causal factors. A previous section of this article has suggested where the dynamics of modernization are to be found — in processes of international emulation among nations, interacting with internal competition among the social groups within each nation. These central dynamics can be described without the use of the above dichotomies; these dichotomies may be of use in describing the results of such change, although even here, concepts referring to concrete organizational structures may be more useful. But if dichotomous concepts deriving from the contrast between tradition and modernity are to be used, it must be with considerable care, for elements of the past make up crucial parts of the present. This is true in two senses.

Analytical and Descriptive Concepts. First, analytical concepts should not be confused with concepts for the immediate description of reality. An analogy to concepts relating to the physical world may help make this clear: we can directly describe objects by their shapes — round, square, octagonal — and we can also analyze them into the unseen molecules which compose them and give them their characteristic properties — combustibility, weight, and so forth. The shapes are readily identifiable, for an object must have one shape or another, never several; the molecular composition, however, can generally be discovered only by experimentation, because the molecules are usually mixed. But the nature of the component molecules is the crucial item of information, for the molecular makeup determines most of the behavior of the object, whereas the superficial shape is generally useful only for a preliminary classification.

---

[48] Bendix, "Tradition and Modernity Reconsidered."

Explanatory concepts in the social sciences are almost always analytical rather than descriptive; they refer to structures or processes that are usually latent within the phenomena to be explained, and must be analyzed out with the aid of empirical indicators. The empirical reality is almost always a resultant of several processes tending in different directions, fostering different social structures at the same time. To understand social reality, we try first to examine the various processes in isolation — by efforts at abstraction, attempting to hold other, disturbing processes "constant," at least in imagination; only after having grasped something of the dynamics of each process, do we put them back together and view them interacting in the complex reality we are trying to explain.

The most useful concepts, then, are those which can be used analytically, to point out the various processes going on simultaneously in social phenomena. Weber designed his ideal types for this purpose: to come to grips with the great complexities of social reality in such a way that generalized explanations could still be made, and to formulate ways of looking at reality so that it could be researched.[49] But in order for such concepts to be useful, they must refer to dynamic processes or to the structures resulting from such processes, and they must be capable of being seen in combination with other processes designated by other analytical concepts. Hence, to use such concepts as mere dichotomies to classify descriptive materials is to waste them. Sets of concepts based on a contrast between tradition and modernity are useful in explaining change only if the concepts are allowed to vary independently of each other, not if they are treated as bundles of attributes that go together to make up an ideal type of an entire society. The dynamic can be seen only by looking at the separate processes occurring in various institutions and groups, and at the resulting conflicts among them.[50]

Nor is it useful to treat every contrasting pair of concepts as having a reciprocal relationship — the more of one, the less of the other. One of the concept-pairs often used to contrast traditional and modern governments is "particularism vs. universalism." To put this in somewhat more popular terms, the contrast is between the personal rule of aristocrats and the operations of an impersonal modern bureaucracy; in Weberian terms, one may contrast patri-

---

[49] See Max Weber, *The Methodology of the Social Sciences* (Glencoe, Ill.: The Free Press, 1941), pp. 89–94, 99–101, and especially Weber's actual use of such concepts as bureaucratic and patrimonial administration, and the types of legitimacy. It should be noted that Weber, in the essay cited here, was concerned primarily with the use of generalized causal explanations, not for their own sake, but for their help in explaining unique configurations of historical events; my emphasis here, rather, has been on the use of ideal types for theory construction as an end in itself. See also Reinhard Bendix and Bennett Berger, "Images of Society and Problems of Concept Formation in Sociology," in Llewellyn Cross (ed.), *Symposium on Sociological Theory* (Evanston, Ill.: Row, Peterson & Co., 1959), pp. 92–118.

[50] See Samuel P. Huntington, "Political Development and Political Decay," *World Politics*, Vol. XVII (1965), pp. 386–430, for a similar critique of the prevailing tendency to identify political development with a general process of social modernization rather than to view them as separate, and sometimes antithetical, processes.

monial and bureaucratic administration. If these concepts are used dichoto-
mously, then we may describe a change from the former to the latter, perhaps
with slips back; but the concepts themselves are not dynamic; they explain
nothing. But as mentioned above, Weber's concept of bureaucracy is nothing
if not dynamic; it refers to one structural solution of a major problem of a ruler
(be he individual autocrat or representative of some constituency): to maintain control over his administrative agents. It can be properly understood only
if one is aware of the other major solution: the ruler may attempt to surround
himself with personally loyal allies, who can be used on special missions, to
check up on his other agents and to muster personal support. This solution is
somewhat contradictory to the first one; the personally loyal agents must be
able to circumvent routine regulations in carrying out their tasks for their
leader, but the leader needs the enforcement of that routine if his entire
administrative apparatus is to be kept under control. Yet both solutions are
almost always attempted to some degree at once. As Roth points out, patrimonial elements in modern polities do not disappear; the complex phenomena
of modern political behavior and political structure can be understood only by
viewing both strategies of control at work.[51]

Social reality is exceedingly complex, and chains of cause and effect are hard
to disentangle. The functionalists attempt to deal with this complexity, as
noted at the beginning of this essay, through the idea of a "system" of interdependent parts. Since events in one place have repercussions elsewhere, often
reacting back upon the starting point, functionalists have some justification for
building a model of complete interdependence, which they then apply to entire
societies. The payoff of this strategy is that the functionalist does not have to
disentangle the network of cause and effect; since these are assumed to flow in
a circle, it is the overall forms of the system that are crucial to discern.

The validity of the functionalist model depends on the assumption that
most of the important characteristics of any society are interdependent; its
persuasiveness rests on the additional argument that describing the form of a
system is the only way to find much regularity in complex social phenomena.
The approach outlined here disputes both of these claims. Not only is there
good reason to believe that the various persons and institutions of a society
are considerably autonomous from each other, but there is a method of finding
regularity amid the complexity, by analyzing out *competing* processes. As in
the functionalist approach, the Weberian approach attempts to find "universals" applicable across many particular historical events. But the most useful
"universals" are not those which give static descriptions of a few types of societies but those which explain the changing surface by showing the competing
processes at work within.

The Survival of Institutions: Democracy. The past remains in the present in
another sense: in the survival of institutions as well as in the continuing relevance of old processes and concepts with which to analyze them. Contrary to

[51] Guenther Roth, "Personal Rulership, Patrimonialism and Empire-Building in the
New States," in this volume.

the image suggested by a concept of tradition as a set of logically related elements and modernity as another set of the opposite elements, also logically related, the institutions that make up a society may be quite independent of one another. The most striking examples are the representative institutions of democracy and the bureaucratic institutions of the modern state. As Tocqueville and Hintze have shown, modern representative democracy is based on the survival of feudal institutions which arose to represent corporate groups: the institutions, mostly judicial, of the Ständestaat.[52] These came into existence as the result of a period of relative stalemate in the power struggle between the central ruler and the independent aristocracy, before the decentralizing weaknesses of patrimonial administration began to be shored up by the introduction of rationalized bureaucratic techniques.

From this point on, two distinct processes came into play. On the one hand, the ruler attempted to undermine independent centers of power, to weaken or crush the representative institutions, and to build up a centralized bureaucracy. On the other hand, commercialization and industrialization began to throw increasing numbers of previously localized, politically disengaged subjects into the national political life. It has been the interaction of these two processes that has determined the subsequent success of democracy in various nations. Where the centralizing activities of the ruler had had the least success, the lower classes were mobilized into participation in the old, decentralized feudal institutions of legislature and judiciary; pluralistic politics prevailed in the modern era from the outset, and revolutionary goals among the lower classes were weak. But where the ruler had been successful in reducing the privileges of the aristocracy, especially in destroying the independence of the judiciary and eliminating administration by local notables, the political mobilization of the lower classes resulted in the mass politics of fragmented interests and plebiscitarian, revolutionary appeals.[53] As Tocqueville put it, contrasting Britain and France, the "levelling-up" of the masses into participation in aristocratic privileges laid the basis for an orderly democracy of public responsibility and private rights; but the levelling-down of the aristocracy by the central power left all rights and immunities precarious, and the danger of mass-style tyranny always present.[54]

We are fortunate that institutions are not functionally integrated so that all elements of a traditional or a modern society hang together; viable democracy is an unusual thing, not the automatic characteristic of all modern societies. Indeed, one might suspect that the centralized state, with its tendency to level individual rights and privileges, is more logically related to the structure of modern society than the decentralized institutions which make democracy possible. As Huntington has pointed out, America's democracy is based on the

[52] Tocqueville, op. cit. (see selections in this volume); Hintze, Staat und Verfassung.

[53] Reinhard Bendix, "Social Stratification and the Political Community," in Reinhard Bendix and S. M. Lipset (eds.), Class, Status and Power, 2nd edition (New York: Free Press of Glencoe, 1966), pp. 73–86.

[54] Tocqueville, op. cit.

most archaic political forms still in existence, having a direct continuity from decentralized Tudor institutions transplanted into the early colonies.[55]

Thus, this presentation of an approach to comparative politics may end by shedding some light on one of the most serious political questions of today: the prospects for democracy, especially in the Communist states and the Third World. Many theories of modernization founder on misconceptions as to the original rise of democracy in the West: holding a "social system" perspective, with its content generally filled in by the single case of Britain, the first modernizing nation, they see democracy as the political correlate of industrialization.[56] But this view confuses several processes that become distinct in comparative perspective: the mobilization of the masses into political participation, which *does* go along with economic development, and the form of that political participation, which does not. The forms of political participation that make up a stable democracy are based upon supporting institutions that uphold the personal immunities and procedural rights that make real political participation possible.[57] These institutions — independent judiciary systems and locally responsible political bodies — can make possible the network of political associations that mediate between the individual and the central state; thus they provide both a check on central power and a basis for cooperation between individual interests without it being necessary for the central state to intervene to prevent fragmentation.

But these institutions will not follow along automatically from economic development, with or without a "strong middle class," nor will they follow merely from attempts to inculcate democratic *values*. As noted above (footnote 27), democracy can be institutionalized only by institutionalizing a real balance of power; if at least a few different social groups do not have real autonomy, it is illusory to think that democracy can be built merely on the good will of a ruling group. Wishful thinking aside, the prospects for democracy in the Third World do not appear good; the basis of the decentralized institutions found in some Western countries — a viable feudal heritage — does not exist in most of these nations. However, we know very little as yet as to what substitute bases of such pluralism may exist; Lloyd Rudolph's analysis of the transformation of Indian castes into political associations shows one type of possibility.[58] This

[55] Samuel P. Huntington, "Political Modernization: America vs. Europe," *World Politics*, Vol. XVIII (1966), pp. 379–413; reprinted in this volume. Tocqueville himself noted this continuity. In describing the local representative government forms of small medieval communities, before they were brought under the centralized power of the French government, he mentions how strikingly they resembled the townships of New England he had seen on his American tour. Tocqueville then corrects his previous belief (expressed in *Democracy in America*) that these features were the image of the future, and notes that the New England township was but the rural parish of the feudal era, transferred to America. *The Old Regime and the French Revolution*, p. 48.

[56] See footnote 13 above.

[57] T. H. Marshall, "Citizenship and Social Class," *Class, Citizenship, and Social Development* (Garden City, N.Y.: Doubleday & Co., 1964), Chapter 4.

[58] Lloyd I. Rudolph, "The Modernity of Tradition: The Democratic Incarnation of Caste in India," *American Political Science Review*, Vol. LIX (1965), pp. 975–989; reprinted in this volume. See also Charles C. Moskos, Jr., and Wendell Bell, "Emerging Nations and Ideologies of American Social Scientists," *American Sociologist*, Vol.

problem has hardly begun to be explored, although we might expect one general principle to emerge: the bases of democratic pluralism will be found in institutions embodying traditional group autonomies, transformed to include formerly unprivileged groups of individuals, rather than in the destruction of all local powers because of their dominance by privileged traditional groups.

CONCLUSION

The main points of the historical sociology approach to politics may be summarized under the following headings, parallel to the summary of functionalism given at the outset of this article.

1. The basic unit of analysis is the *group*, or *organization*, viewed in relation to other organizations and groups with which it has contact. We may focus on narrower or wider contexts of interaction among organizations, for the purpose of analyzing one set of processes at a time; thus, we may examine the groups within the territory of a particular government or the interrelations among all the states in the world that interact with each other. The organizations existing at any particular time may include those formed in the entirely different context of an earlier historical period; there is no necessary trend toward uniformity of type among institutions in any particular era. This unit of analysis contrasts with the functionalist *system of interdependent parts*.

2. and 3. The basic process that takes place in and among these units is the *struggle* of individuals and organizations to further their material and ideal interests. The emphasis is on the *action* of human beings; ideals and organizational forms are to be interpreted as the creations of human actors, as individuals try out various strategies to gain the collaboration or the subordination of others. This process may be contrasted with the functionalist emphasis on behavior and institutions as performing *functions* in the *division of labor* within a system.

4. The bases of stable coordination of human activities are *constellations of interests*, especially in solidary groups, and the *dominance* of certain groups over others. This explanation of social integration contrasts with the functionalist emphasis on the individual *internalization* of a society-wide set of *values*.

5. Political change is explained by the *struggle* for political advantage, both within and between states, made continual by the *instabilities and dilemmas* of legitimatizing principles and of arrangements of domination. This explanation of change may be contrasted with the functionalist emphasis on *system strains*, *cultural changes*, and *system evolution*.

II (1967), pp. 67–72. Moskos and Bell argue for a number of neglected considerations in the literature on modernization, including the independence of democracy from economic modernization, and point out the fallacy of expecting democracy to evolve from single-party regimes or military dictatorships.

SECTION C

PRE-MODERN POLITICS

Introduction

The use of the term "Pre-Modern Politics" as title to this section has two implications: first, that there are political processes in all societies of which we have knowledge; second, that there is, however, a qualitative distinction in the configuration of political processes between societies that are not governed by modern states and those that are.

The basic ingredients of politics are inherent in social life. Groups differ in what they conceive their interests to be. Some of these differences necessarily involve conflicts of purpose, as when the means available for the realization of such interests are limited or when two or more groups are joined in a social body which can pursue only one of the proposed policies. Furthermore, some groups are more able, by reason of greater resources, to gain their ends than are others. Conflicts there will be, and decisions will be made even when they are evaded. Yet it is not enough that some decision-making, or conflict adjudication, center, as some theorists conceive the "political" order to be, is recognized. For the very recognition of a political structure itself raises new problems. Who is to participate? What kinds of issues are to be handled? What are to be the boundaries?

To speak of universal political processes is not to imply that the "political" can be identified as an "objective" function. The substance of the political in any society is not objectively defined. On the contrary, in each of the societies here analyzed, there is a structured political life which is given its force and its meaning by the members of the society themselves. Though we consider social conflict, decision, and coordination to be political, we cannot tell a society *what* its conflicts and *who* its decision-makers and coordinators are to be. From the outside, the observer may easily identify in a society latent conflicts which have not become "political" to the members of that society. Only such conflicts as are pressed by interested groups against the decision-makers, or by decision-makers against groups, create *political* problems demanding *political* responses. One must, therefore, have recourse to the way social life is structured by members of a society in order to determine how politics works in that society. Thus, even in the primitive systems of tribal Africa, there is, as Fallers points out, a kind of political theory which specifies the role in conflict and decision of a particular social structure, the kinship group.

All of the societies discussed here lack that crucial aspect of modern social structure, the nation-state. For this reason, not because of any evolutionary assumption, we designate them as pre-modern. There is no centralization of power and political loyalty, and no mobilization of the populace into a citizenry. (For the development of these features of the modern state, see the articles by Tocqueville, the Royal Institute of International Affairs, and Bendix in Sections E1 and E2 below.) In these pre-modern polities, there is no direct relation of authority from "government" to "subject." Instead authority is mediated through the gentry-official (China), the village-headman (India), the patrician (ancient Greece), or the nobility (feudal Europe). Administration is intermittent rather than regularized. Power is dispersed, and boundaries are ill-defined. There is no single set of laws for all subjects. Whatever may be the divergences of some contemporary states from the model of the centralized modern state, we cannot imagine, for instance, an American municipality having diplomatic relations with a foreign power as is the case of the Indian villages described by Frykenberg. What is missing in these pre-modern polities is the continuous and direct penetration of a settled community by a single authority.

The creation of such a central authority is not, however, a matter of an inherent or an inevitable development. It is a process which must be explained by reference to external as well as internal developments. The special and significant history of the making of the modern state in Europe is discussed in the following section. We wish to indicate some of the political precursors to that story.

The pre-modern polities treated here are typically characterized by one of two conditions: the presence of either a relatively homogeneous and integrated society without a continuous political administration or a militarily superior empire without an integrated society or penetrating administration.

The tribal societies discussed by Fallers have indeed a recognized "political theory" which specifies how disputes are to be handled. This theory is based on the accepted legitimacy of the kinship group. The political order comes into contingent activity when a dispute occurs between kinship lineages. The probability of its success is based on a precarious balance between lineages. Such a system, fragile though it may be, is not inherently self-destructive. It is, however, vulnerable, and when it comes into contact with the world-historical civilizations, as Hintze puts it (Section D), it is destroyed or transformed. This process of the collision of pre-modern societies with militarily, politically, and economically more powerful societies is discussed specifically with reference to the Western impact in Section F.

In the second selection, taken from his classic *The Ancient City*, Fustel de Coulanges discusses a more dynamic process. Beginning with the family as the first form of society, he shows the further growth of society to the form of the city-state and the destruction of that in turn by the Empire. The city-state was perhaps the closest approximation in the pre-modern world to the modern state (although Fustel warns us against attributing to the ancients a modern idea of freedom unknown to them). There, by reason of the organization of society on the basis of a political religion, self-sufficiency — the relative coincidence of political, economic, religious, and social organization — was possible. Yet the very source of the cohesion of the society — its parochial religion — was also a source of weakness insofar as it precluded wider forms of social organization than the city-state. Thus the Greek states could fight one another instead of uniting against the imperial threats of Macedonia and Rome. Thus also Rome, when it had conquered, could not expand its political constitution to the extent that it had expanded its military power. Finally, as Fustel shows, the conditions of government were changed when Christianity, following Stoicism, declared that religion and society were no longer one.

The Empire and the religious revolution had destroyed the self-sufficiency of the city-state but had put little in its place. Whereas the polis, like the modern state, had, in Hintze's terms, an intensive form of organization, the Empire was extensive. Its administrative capacity, loosely and superficially centralized, was not equal to its military capacity. These weaknesses of the politics of empire are discussed in the succeeding two selections by Frykenberg on India and Fei on pre-revolutionary China. The Indian village keeps the central government at arm's length. The central ruler depends administratively on local leaders, who, by means of their command of local information and contacts, are able to subvert the dictates of the center. In China, according to Fei, organizational power is held by the land-holding gentry. They organize to protect their economic privilege and provide political protection to the peasantry against the imperial administration. Here again the state's penetration of the society is effectively limited by the power of intermediary authorities.

The final selection, Pirenne's treatment of feudal Europe, discusses the political victory of the locality over the Empire. Wider forms of political regime — the Empire, the Church, and the kingdoms — remained, but effective power passed into the hands of the territorial princes, who "were in touch with reality." On the basis of changed economic conditions — the breakdown of the imperial economy and the rise of the manorial system — the territorial princes could organize effective local sovereignty and military power even as they continued to pay homage to their kings. Here, in contrast to India and China, the localities did not merely keep the central authority at arm's length, they effectively began to reorganize the political life of Europe. This, however, leads us into the next part of our story, the transition to the modern state.

Locality against center, weak and intermittent administration, multiple authorities, lack of coincidence of political, military, economic, and social capacities — these are the hallmarks of pre-modern politics. Yet, although the distinction between pre-modern and modern politics is a qualitative one, there are lessons to be learned from these analyses for today's world of modern and modernizing states. We shall mention five. First, as patrician stood between city and client, as gentry between emperor and peasant, and as prince between king and subject, so today mediating authorities may continue to play an im-

portant political role. Pekelis (Section E3), in his contrast of the civil law
and common law traditions, shows how the latter depends to a great extent on
the power of the local community standing between individual and state.
Second, centralization of power, while it has proceeded in the modern world
far beyond the achievements of the British in India, the emperor in China, and
the kings of feudal Europe, is still a variable. Huntington (Section D) makes
clear that power has never been as centralized in the United States as in modern Europe. Third, the infusion of politics by administration has been a continuing phenomenon in the pre-modern, modern, and modernizing worlds. The
problems of this infusion discussed by Fallers, Frykenberg, and Fei are mitigated, not resolved, by the construction of a rationalized bureaucracy, as Weber
(Section E2) demonstrates. Fourth, the political mobilization of a populace, a
general condition of modern, as contrasted to pre-modern, polities, is also a variable. The contrast between England and the United States drawn by Shils
(Section E2) shows that the state may be more or less of a focus of popular
interest. The Englishman is far more politically mobilized than the South
Indian villager or the Chinese peasant, but he is, Shils tells us, less so than the
American. Finally, though administrative capacities have been expanded, they
are still outdistanced by military and political ambitions. A modern state may
itself be the seat of empire. Thus in a world dominated by modern states —
England, France, Germany, and Japan in the past, the United States, the
Soviet Union, and China today — the politics of empire persist.

Political Sociology and the
Anthropological Study of
African Polities

LLOYD FALLERS

During the past twenty years a concern with political institutions has been a
dominant theme in the work of English-speaking social anthropologists in
Africa. Combining the intensive fieldwork methods of Malinowski with the
functional sociological perspective of Durkheim and Radcliffe-Brown, they
have produced a body of comparative material on non-modern politics of unparalleled range and depth. Beginning with the publication of *African Political
Systems* and with the fuller monographic accounts produced by the authors of

Reprinted by permission, in an abridged form, from the *European Journal of
Sociology*, Vol. IV, No. 2 (1963), pp. 311–325.

LLOYD FALLERS is Professor of Anthropology, University of Chicago. He is the author of *The King's Men* (1964), *Bantu Bureaucracy* (1956), and numerous articles
dealing with African societies. Currently he is dividing his time between field work in
Turkey and completion of a study on African law.

that volume, there has accumulated, particularly since World War II, a massive collection of "tribal" studies and, more recently, works of comparative analysis.* I do not intend to attempt here a full-scale evaluation of this work — even an annotated bibliography would fill many pages, and in any case Easton has recently reviewed much of it[1] — but I should like to consider briefly the following questions: First, what ideas of relevance to a general, comparative political sociology have emerged from this work? And, second, how far do these studies, principally concerned as they have been with the pre-colonial and colonial politics of the traditional African political communities, help us to understand the political life of the "new nations" of post-colonial Africa?

I

The most basic question to which this work draws our attention is, quite simply: what is "the political"? The problem is of more than definitional interest, for only by means of some generally applicable conception of the political field can systems of widely varying kinds be made commensurable — be brought within range of comparative analysis. Faced with an extraordinarily wide variety of polities, from the great kingdoms of the Western Sudan and the interlacustrine region to the tiny autonomous kinship groups of the Khalahari Bushmen, anthropologists working in Africa have sought to define a field of comparative political study which would encompass them all. Clearly the former have kinds of political apparatus that the latter have not — hence the common practice of terming the latter "stateless" or "acephalous." But this need not mean that the less differentiated societies lack politics or political systems of any sort.

* John A. Barnes, *Politics in a Changing Society* (London: Oxford University Press, 1954); Paul J. Bohannan, *Justice and Judgement among the Tiv* (London: Oxford University Press, 1957); K. Busia, *The Position of the Chief in the Modern Political System of Ashanti* (London: Oxford University Press, 1951); M. Fortes and E. E. Evans-Pritchard, *African Political Systems* (London: Oxford University Press, 1940); E. E. Evans-Pritchard, *The Nuer* (Oxford: Clarendon Press, 1940); M. Fortes, *The Dynamics of Clanship among the Tallensi* (London: Oxford University Press, 1945); Lloyd A. Fallers, *Bantu Bureaucracy* (Cambridge: W. Heffer, 1956); Max Gluckman, *The Judicial Process among the Barotse* (Manchester: Manchester University Press, 1955); Max Gluckman, *Custom and Conflict in Africa* (Oxford: Blackwell, 1955); H. Kuper, *An African Aristocracy* (London: Oxford University Press, 1947); Lucy P. Mair, *Primitive Government* (Baltimore: Penguin Books, 1962); J. Middleton and D. Tait, *Tribes Without Rulers* (London: Routledge and Kegan Paul, 1958); S. F. Nadel, *A Black Byzantium* (London: Oxford University Press, 1942); A. I. Richards (ed.), *East African Chiefs* (London: Faber and Faber, 1959); I. Schapera, *Government and Politics in Tribal Societies* (London: Watts, 1956); M. G. Smith, *Government in Zazzau* (London: Oxford University Press, 1960); A. W. Southall, *Alur Society* (Cambridge: W. Heffer, 1954); V. W. Turner, *Schism and Continuity in African Society* (Manchester: Manchester University Press, 1957); Edward A. Winter, *Bwamba: A Structural-Functional Analysis of a Patrilineal Society* (Cambridge: W. Heffer, 1956). I have listed here only books in which political structure is the major theme. In addition, of course, there have been many monographs partly devoted to the subject and a very large number of journal articles, particularly in *Africa*, *African Studies* and the *Papers* and *Journal* of the Rhodes-Livingstone Institute.

[1] David Easton, "Political Anthropology," in B. Siegel (ed.), *Biennial Review of Anthropology* (Stanford: Stanford University Press, 1959).

The solution to which social anthropologists concerned with African polities have tended in their search for a universal conception of the political — and in this their thinking has converged with that of many sociologists and political scientists — involves considering the polity and its major constituent elements as analytical, functional concepts. As in the work of Parsons, Levy, Easton and others, the polity or political system is viewed, not as a concretely distinct part of the social system, but rather as a functional aspect of the whole social system: that aspect concerned with making and carrying out decisions regarding public policy, by whatever institutional means.[2] Of course the political system operates through actual social groups and relations, but these need not be specialized "governmental" or "state" organizations. Just as political scientists have increasingly come to the view that in modern Western societies the political system cannot be adequately understood if attention is confined to the formal organization of government, so social anthropologists working in Africa have concluded that the absence of such organization is not most profitably interpreted as an absence of political institutions and processes as such. And just as political scientists and political sociologists have been led to examine the political functions of classes, occupational groups, religious communities and "non-political" associations, so social anthropologists have found polities, where none seemed to exist, by examining the activities of multi-functional social groups — particularly the unilineal descent groups, or lineages, which are so common in Africa. Even where over-arching state organization, consisting of rulers and their subordinates, does not exist, they have concluded, decisions regarding public policy are made and carried out through the activities of such groups.[3] Of course the fact that political organization in such societies is not clearly differentiated from, say, that of economics and religion — the fact that the people who are together concerned with the formation and execution of public policy are the same as those who work and worship together — has important consequences for the nature of the political process in such societies. It restricts the degree to which the policy, as distinct from the religious and economic fields, can be elaborated and made the focus of continuous attention. It does not, however, mean that political systems and political processes cannot exist.

As both Easton and Mair have pointed out, a further common consequence of this "embedding" of the polity in multi-functional social groups (or, to describe the same phenomenon from the opposite point of view, the lack of specialized political organization) is to render problematical and situational the boundaries of the "public" on behalf of which policy decisions are made and carried out.[4] In situations where the village or the band encampment is fully autonomous politically and where, consequently, its relations with other such

[2] David Easton, *The Political System: An Inquiry into the State of Political Science* (New York: Alfred A. Knopf, 1953); Marion J. Levy, *The Structure of Society* (Princeton: Princeton University Press, 1952); Talcott Parsons, *The Social System* (Glencoe, Ill.: The Free Press, 1951).

[3] Perhaps the best single analysis of this process is L. Bohannan's essay: "Political Aspects of Tiv Social Organization," in Middleton and Tait, *op. cit.*

[4] Mair, *op. cit.*, chap. II; Easton, 1959, *op. cit.*

groups may be viewed as essentially "foreign relations," there may be little difficulty in defining the boundaries of the polity. In such situations, the boundaries of local community and polity are the same.[5] But in many parts of Africa one finds societies without specialized political organization in which, nevertheless, a wider, multi-community political order is capable of operating in particular situations to produce decisions applying to a field wider than that of the local community. Such societies — too thoroughly knit together politically to be regarded as congeries of autonomous communities but yet too discontinuously united to be called "states" — have been objects of particular interest to social anthropologists.

The best-known examples are the so-called "segmentary societies," in which political relations are viewed as resting upon a widely-ramifying unilineal (patrilineal or matrilineal) system of genealogical relations. In such societies, the local community is thought of, for political purposes, as forming a single corporate lineage, but the genealogical system stretches beyond the local community; increasingly more extensive territorial units are viewed as comprising an ever-widening series of more inclusive unilineal descent groups so that, in extreme cases, the whole society may appear to its members as a single lineage whose constituent units, down to the local community, are lineage segments of varying scale. In this way, the Nuer of the Sudan and the Tiv of central Nigeria, for example, are able, without rulers or officials, to order political relations among hundreds of local communities and tens of thousands of persons.[6]

It is important to stress here the point that the genealogical framework that unites the several local communities in such societies is a *cultural* system, a system of *ideas* — in fact a kind of *political theory* — which may have rather little to do with "biological reality." It is a way of thinking and talking about community and trans-community political relations in the idiom of kinship and in terms of this idiom persons of the most diverse biological origins may, by means of "legal fictions," be treated for political purposes as if they were members of a single unilineal descent group.[7] In most such societies persons ordinarily become members of their local communities through unilineal descent and the several local communities which form a wider territorial unit are often composed in the main of descendants of a common ancestor, but it is not the rigid following of rules of unilineal descent for affiliating individuals to groups that is essential to the political functioning of such societies. What is important for political purposes is rather the fact that community and trans-community territorial units are treated *as if* they were lineages. And this fictional, "as-if" character of the system is quite clearly recognized by the people themselves; they explicitly make use of the genealogical idiom to manipulate their political relations.

I have said, however, that the political order that results is of a problemati-

[5] This is essentially the situation among the !Kung Bushmen of the Khalahari, described by L. Marshall in "!Kung Bushman Bands," *Africa*, XXX (1960).

[6] L. Bohannan, *op. cit.*; Evans-Pritchard, *op. cit.*

[7] M. Fortes, "The Structure of Unilineal Descent Groups," *American Anthropologist*, LV (1953); L. Bohannan, *op. cit.*; G. Lienhardt, "The Western Dinka," in Middleton and Tait, *op. cit.*

cal, situational character and it is when one examines the nature of decision-making processes within such an order that this becomes most clear. A problem requiring decision may arise, for example, in the form of a dispute between communities, or between individual members of different communities, concerning the possession of territory for grazing or agriculture. In such situations, since there is no chief or council to exercize continuous, society-wide authority, decisions must be arrived at by *ad hoc* gatherings of representatives of the groups concerned or through arbitration by neutral parties. Such conciliation or arbitration is usually successful, however, only when the groups concerned are roughly equivalent in size and when they are in a position of what Fortes has called "complementary opposition" in the genealogical scheme; since there is no superordinate authority able to impose a solution, an effective decision must represent a high degree of consensus and must be supported by a substantial balance of power.[8] Groups related to those immediately concerned tend to be drawn into the dispute until larger groups, of equivalent scale and complementary genealogical position, are engaged, at which point accommodation becomes possible.

A simple illustration will perhaps help the reader to visualize the way in which the genealogical scheme of political theory is used in making decisions:

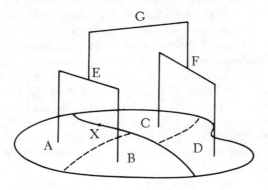

In the diagram, A, B, C and D are local communities, each associated with a unilineal descent group. In the lineage political theory, A and B are thought of as fraternal segments within the larger lineage E; similarly, C and D are considered fraternal segments within lineage F. In turn, E and F are territorial units within the larger unit G and are thought of as fraternal segments within the total lineage associated with all of G. If, now, a dispute arises at point X along the border between E and F, which at this point is also the border between A and C, how can it be resolved? The initial dispute will likely involve only a few persons on either side of the border. All members of A and C, the local communities involved, will be obliged to go to the aid of their respective

[8] L. Bohannan, *op. cit.*; Fortes, 1953, *op. cit.*

fellows. But, even if A and C are units of roughly equal size and power, it will not be possible for them to settle it by themselves, for A and C are not in "complementary opposition" — are not groups which, at the next level in the genealogical system of political theory, are fraternal segments within a larger lineage. They are incapable, by themselves, of forming a consensual community. Only after B comes to the aid of A and D to the aid of C is this condition fulfilled. When this happens, E and F, groups in complementary opposition within the still larger unit G, are engaged; in terms of the genealogical political theory, an institutional framework which "encloses" the disputing parties, enabling them to form a consensual community, comes into being and a settlement becomes possible. We may note that, had the dispute arisen on the border between A and B, the mobilization of a different, less extensive, part of the genealogical system would have sufficed. Since A and B are in complementary opposition within E, F and its constituent segments would have remained uninvolved.

It seems reasonable to describe what takes place here as "decision-making regarding public policy," despite the transitory character of the polity: a particular distribution of territory, with its accompanying resources, among the groups concerned, is defined and legitimated. To this extent there is in operation here a genuine political system. The proceedings are more than a matter of diplomatic negotiation among essentially sovereign powers, for the trans-community genealogical scheme provides a wider institutional system into which the several local communities may fit as constituent parts. But most of the time this wider institutional system is merely potential; the decision-making machinery comes into being only with the appearance of the policy problem — the dispute. There are no chiefs or officials to represent its continued existence. When there are no problems, it is in abeyance. And the boundaries of the polity — the "public" on behalf of which policy is made — also vary with the policy problem. Only such groups as are necessary to resolve the particular problem at hand become involved. Thus the political system is, in Easton's useful phrase, a "contingent political system," as contrasted, we may say, with a continuous one.

The contingent political system would seem to be a necessary consequence of the absence of specialized, continuously functioning political roles and institutions in terms of whose jurisdiction fixed boundaries for the polity might be defined. As I have noted, the phenomenon has been discussed most frequently in connection with the "segmentary societies," in which the relations that obtain among territorial communities are thought of in a unilineal genealogical idiom. Indeed, as Easton has pointed out, the social anthropologists who have studied these matters in the field have tended to interest themselves primarily in the structures of unilineal descent which give form to polities in these societies rather than in the nature of the polities themselves; they have studied lineage politics more from the point of view of lineages than from the point of view of politics and it is perhaps for this reason that it was left to a political scientist, commenting upon the social anthropological literature, to formulate the concept "contingent" to conceptualize the phenomenon in a more general way. In fact, however, the contingent political system is probably a feature of "stateless" societies generally, wherever local communities are not entirely "sovereign," as they probably seldom are. We may therefore expect to find a variety of contingent polities, making use of kinds of political theory other than the genealogical one.

The Baamba of the middle Uganda-Congo border area lack the trans-community genealogical framework characteristic of the segmentary societies, though their villages are organized internally along lineage lines, each village consisting mainly of men of a single lineage, together with their wives and children.[9] Internally, the village and its dominant lineage are segmented in terms of a genealogical framework, but quite different principles are made use of in the field of inter-community relations. These the Baamba order by means of alliances between village lineages. Just how these alliances are established is not entirely clear, but they are not, apparently, conceived of genealogically. Each lineage and its associated village is allied to a series of other lineages and villages and within the alliance group both marriage and warfare are pro-hibited. Each community's total group of alliances, however, is unique; each is allied with certain other communities with which its allies are not allied. Thus, when a dispute arises and allies come to the aid of the disputing communities, a point is ultimately reached at which some community is allied with both disputants. At this point accommodation becomes possible: a contingent polity capable of reaching a policy decision binding upon a unit which embraces the disputing communities comes into being, however fleetingly.

There are no doubt still other types of contingent policy with other kinds of political theory for manipulating relations among acephalous territorial units; but the usefulness of the concept of the contingent political system is not limited to the analysis of relations among semi-autonomous village com-munities. It may also shed a certain light upon the political systems of the larger, more differentiated and more clearly-bounded polities. Perhaps the most general way of setting forth the concept is to say that it draws our attention to all those non-continuous polities that function wherever the political system is not characterized by absolute sovereignty, either on the community or some higher level. To the extent to which there is sovereignty, there is continuous authority within the unit and war and diplomacy without. But, despite the fascination with which Western political philosophers have regarded the con-cept of sovereignty, its more extreme manifestations are probably rare and its existence in pure form impossible. Jouvenel tells us that even in the West its prominence is quite recent.[10] Probably much more common are polities in which society-wide authority is limited, both within and without, leaving room for contingent political arrangements both among societies, in the form of institutions which go beyond diplomacy, and within societies, in the shape of the many processes of policy-making that take place in spheres lying beyond

[9] E. A. Winter, "The Aboriginal Political Structure of Bwamba," in Middleton and Tait, op. cit.

[10] Bertrand de Jouvenel, Sovereignty: An Inquiry into the Political Good (Chicago: University of Chicago Press, 1957), chap. X.

the authority of the state. These arrangements, like those we have seen at work in the segmentary societies, are no doubt similarly dependent upon consensus and balance for their successful operation. To the extent to which such phenomena do appear within and among the more differentiated polities, the more markedly contingent political systems of Africa are not something exotic — something limited to traditional African and other non-literate societies — but rather represent a particularly marked development of an element common, in some degree, to all or most of the world's political systems.

II

As I have indicated, social anthropologists working in Africa have given a great deal of attention to the sociology of unilineal descent groups — in part, of course, simply because such groups are so extremely common and important in African societies. Lineages are to sub-Saharan Africa what caste is to South Asia: a pervasive structural theme tending to appear, with variations, throughout the area. In the "acephalous" or "stateless" segmentary societies, lineages, as we have seen, provide the framework for "contingent polities." But of course not all African societies are of this kind; many have specialized political roles and institutions which serve to define more continuously-functioning polities and these societies, too, very often contain unilineal descent groups. Just as the detailed study of the structure and functioning of lineages in the segmentary societies has produced ideas relevant beyond the range of these particular societies, so analyses of the role of lineages in the more continuously-functioning polities of Africa are also proving to have a wider relevance. In particular, they promise to contribute usefully to the discussion of the limits and determinants of the centralization of power and authority. Just as, that is to say, a study of lineages in segmentary societies has taught us something about the conditions for the functioning of any stateless, trans-community polity, so also a study of their role in African kingdoms teaches us something about the distribution of power and authority in any state.

As I noted when discussing the work on segmentary societies, social anthropologists have tended to approach these phenomena with a primary interest in institutional particularities, such as lineages and chiefship, rather than in their political functions in a wider comparative perspective, and this has sometimes delayed the recognition of the different functions that may be performed by similar institutions in polities of different types. In their famous introduction to *African Political Systems* — a statement which has been the point of departure for most anthropological studies of political systems since its publication — Fortes and Evans-Pritchard classified the societies described in the volume into two types: "centralized primitive states," with specialized administrative and judicial institutions; and lineage-based "stateless societies," which lacked such institutions.[11] It was immediately apparent that there were difficulties with this classification: it rather implied that politically important lineages and specialized political roles and institutions were mutually exclusive, though the authors cannot have meant this, for among the societies described

[11] Fortes and Evans-Pritchard, *op. cit.*, pp. 5–7.

in the book were some, like the Zulu for example, in which both were obviously present. At any rate, the classification served to raise the question: if, in the segmentary societies, the function of the lineage system was to order trans-community political relations in the absence of specialized political institutions and roles — the functioning of what Easton was later to call the "contingent political system" was by this time quite well understood, for in addition to the brief accounts of such societies published in *African Political Systems*, Evans-Pritchard had at about the same time published his first full monograph on the Nuer [12] — what then were the functions of lineages in the states that possessed such specialized political institutions?

In the years following World War II there appeared, in answer to this question, a series of excellent monographs, among which perhaps the most important were Barnes' study of the Ngoni of Northern Rhodesia and Nyasaland, Southall's of the Alur of northwestern Uganda, and Busia's of the Ashanti of Ghana.[13] All were clearly what Southall termed "segmentary states": polities having specialized political institutions in the form of hereditary rulers, with at least rudimentary administrative staffs, as well as politically significant lineages.[14]

I should perhaps pause here to explain what "politically significant" means in this context. A unilineal descent group is, in its minimal sense, simply a group formed by the descendants, in either the male or the female line, of a common ancestor.[15] It may have many or few, important or trivial, functions. In the segmentary societies, lineages, or territorial units based upon lineages in terms of a political theory, are the sole political units, as we have seen. The complementary opposition of such lineage-based units provides the sole institutional framework for decision-making. "Citizenship" means membership by descent, actual or fictional, in such a unit, or series of progressively more inclusive units. In some African societies, on the other hand, such as Buganda and the other interlacustrine states, lineages hold property rights but are not the basic building-blocks of the polity at large: its territorial sub-units are not in any sense lineage-based and citizenship means primarily membership in the national state through loyalty to the king.

The segmentary states — clearly a common political form in Africa — illustrate an intermediate situation. They are "states" in the sense that they have hereditary rulers, around whom gather councillors and retainers, forming a (more or less) continuously-functioning body capable of taking decisions on behalf of a (more or less) clearly bounded polity. But they are also "segmentary" in the sense that (a) the subdivisions of the polity, which are the primary units for citizenship, are formed around unilineal descent groups, and (b) each of these subdivisions is part of a hierarchy of more or less inclusive units of the same segmentary type, ranging from the local community to the

[12] Evans-Pritchard, *op. cit.*
[13] Barnes, *op. cit.*; Busia, *op. cit.*; Southall, *op. cit.*
[14] *Ibid.*, chap. IX.
[15] Corporate bilateral descent groups also exist, but have not been reported from Africa.

whole state. What makes it possible for them to be segmentary states instead
of segmentary stateless societies is the presence within each unit in the hierarchy of some principle of seniority by which, at each level, a chiefly line is
distinguished, making possible in turn hereditary rulership. But, as in the
segmentary stateless society, the boundaries of the polity as a whole remain
problematical to a degree (though to a lesser degree than in the former case).
A local community's membership in the state as a whole, like that of an individual, is not direct but rather is mediated by that of the next most inclusive
unit. As in the segmentary society, units can only be mobilized for policy decisions in order of inclusiveness. Each unit's primary loyalty is to the next most
inclusive unit, not to the whole polity.

Thus, such polities tend to be loose and often rather fragile. They are, as
Fortes has noted, essentially "federal" in nature.[16] The polity as a whole has
a less shadowy existence than that of the segmentary society, for there is a
hierarchy of chiefs to symbolize its continuity and mobilize it for decision-
making. But the authority of the paramount ruler tends to be limited, since
each subordinate unit exercizes a good deal of autonomy, and problematical,
since each, possessing its own hereditary ruler, is potentially autonomous. The
authority of the paramount over the whole state depends upon his ability to
maintain a balance of power among the subordinate units.

If we return to the diagram of the segmentary society above, we may, by
visualizing within each lineage at each level a senior line, bearing an hereditary
chief, use it to represent the segmentary state. The paramount, G, does not
rule A, B, C and D directly, but only through and by virtue of his authority
over E and F. Neither does the paramount appoint any of these subordinate
chiefs; rather, they are chosen, according to some hereditary principle, through
processes taking place within their respective segments.[17] G possesses little
military force of his own; he is, in one sense, simply another lineage head,
although the most senior. His authority over F depends, ultimately, upon the
willingness of E to support him against F, thus maintaining a polity,
capable of decision-making, which includes both E and F. If he proves incapable of maintaining this balance, the state may split. Thus, the principle of
"complementary opposition," which in segmentary societies is necessary to
bring a larger polity into occasional operation, is, in the segmentary state, necessary to maintain its existence. The segmentary state might perhaps be characterized as a contingent polity manipulated by chiefs.

Both the stateless segmentary society and the segmentary state are, of
course, "ideal type" concepts and one finds, among the actual societies of
Africa, a range of intermediate cases in which the chiefship element is present,
but relatively little developed.[18] Similarly, there are numerous cases in Africa
in which segmentary states have moved in the direction of more unitary ones,
producing a similar series of intermediate cases in the opposite direction. These

---

[16] Fortes, *op. cit.*, 1953.

[17] These processes may vary from quite rigid rules of seniority to relatively open
election from among the members of a lineage.

[18] Several such intermediate cases are described in Middleton and Tait, *op. cit.*

latter seem typically to have resulted from the efforts of paramount chiefs to lessen their dependence upon the loyalty of lineage heads by building up central administrative staffs, particularly on the military side. The Asantehene, paramount chief of the Ashanti Confederacy, built up within his own chiefdom of Kumasi an appointive administrative staff with both civil and military functions. This organization to some extent superseded the lineage-based political structure and enabled the Asantehene to assert within the confederacy as a whole a position amounting to rather more than that of a *primus inter pares*.[19] Similarly, Shaka, the early nineteenth-century Zulu paramount, was able for a time to exert, through control over the military age-regiments which he organized, a strongly centralized authority over what had formerly been a much more segmentary polity.[20] Neither of these efforts was, ultimately, entirely successful, though both states were for a time capable of formidable military operations. Our interest in these cases, however, lies less in their particular histories than in the light they throw upon the political process in segmentary states.

As we have seen, the limited authority of the ruler in the ideal-typical segmentary state, like the rulerless political order of the segmentary society, depends for its existence upon the complementary opposition of subordinate units. It is the paramount's ability to confront a rebellious segment with the juxtaposed power of another, more loyal, segment that enables him to maintain such limited authority as he enjoys. But the same lineage solidarity that underlies this order-through-complementary-opposition also stands in the way of a ruler's attempts to increase the scope of his authority. Viewed from the vantage point of the segmentary society, the lineage structure in the hands of a segmentary state-type ruler supports a somewhat more "solid," less contingent, polity; from the point of view of a more unitary state, however, the same lineage structure appears divisive, productive of a more limited, more problematical, polity. From this latter point of view, lineages are the commonest sources of political pluralism in African kingdoms — the commonest sources of political sub-structure capable of limiting the authority of rulers and of providing media of political expression for social sub-groups.

Our understanding of the functional significance of this lineage-based pluralism in African society has recently been greatly enhanced by the writings of M. G. Smith, growing out of his studies of the political system of the Hausa-Fulani emirate of Zazzau (Zaria) in Northern Nigeria.[21] Within every political system, Smith suggests, it is useful to distinguish analytically between "politics" and "administration." (Smith uses the term "government" to mean what I have termed the "political system" or "polity" — the overall system of which politics and administration are analytical aspects. I prefer not to follow him in this, though I attach little importance to the choice of terms.) As in our everyday use of these words, "politics" is the exercize of power — the process of struggle or competition through which decisions regarding public policy are

---

[19] Busia, *op. cit.*
[20] M. Gluckman, "The Rise of a Zulu Empire," *Scientific American*, CCII (1960).
[21] Smith, *op. cit.*

arrived at — while "administration" is the exercize of authority — the process through which such decisions are carried out. Of course our use of these terms in common speech is associated historically with the separation in modern Western polities of parliaments and parties on the one hand from administrative bureaucracies on the other; but Smith argues, convincingly, that, even where such separation does not exist, the analytical distinction is worth making because an analysis of the degrees and kinds of fusion and differentiation between administration and politics helps us to understand the ways in which different kinds of polities function.

The lineage-based polities, he suggests, represent situations in which administration and politics are most completely fused; both lodge in the same units — the lineage-based territorial segments. In the segmentary societies (to extrapolate from his rather brief remarks on such societies), the lineage-based units which, through complementary opposition, come to policy decisions, are also the units by which the decisions are carried out. More concretely: since there are no administrators or policemen, the person whose right to certain benefits is legitimated by a gathering of lineage representatives is left, with the support of public opinion, to take appropriate action — a process which has been called "self-help justice." In the segmentary states, though their polities are more continuously-functioning, politics and administration are also fused; the chiefs who are the heads of lineage-based segments are both politicians and administrators *vis-à-vis* their paramount. The latter can come to a policy decision only with their concurrence and through a process in which they are the political contenders on behalf of the territorial units of which they are heads; he then depends upon them, in their capacity as administrators, to carry out the policy decision. And of course if the system is multi-tiered the same processes are repeated at all levels. It is essentially the mixed administrative-political character of the chiefly hierarchy in such societies that makes the centralization of authority difficult. The paramount cannot exercize purely administrative authority through subordinates who are at the same time the legitimate political representatives of the major sub-units of the society.

It is only when administrative units are more differentiated from the political sub-units of the society that higher degrees of concentration of administrative authority become possible. Over the large parts of Africa where unilineal descent groups are the most prominent elements in the sub-structure of society and thus the commonest bases for the formation of political groups, this means separation of administration from the lineage system. Examples of societies in which this has occurred are the kingdom of Buganda in southern Uganda and the Nigerian emirate of Zazzau, studied by Smith.[22] In both cases the territory of the state proper was mainly administered by officials appointed by, and responsible to, the hereditary ruler. The central areas were administered much more closely and continuously than is possible in any segmentary state — a fact perhaps best exemplified by the regular systems of taxation that prevailed — though in each case, to be sure, there was a penumbra of tributary

[22] Smith, *op. cit.*; Lucy P. Mair, *An African People in the Twentieth Century* (London: G. Routledge and Sons, Ltd., 1934).

vassal states, under their own hereditary rulers, which was much more loosely controlled. Since within the state territory proper officials were not, at the same time, the political representatives of the groups they were responsible for administering, administration in the true sense of the handing down of orders supported by legitimate authority was possible to a degree to which it is not in segmentary states. Every administrative act was not, as it tends to be segmentary states, simultaneously a process of political negotiation.

What then becomes of politics in such societies? Policy, Smith tells us, is formed by the competition of political groups; if it does not, as in the segmentary states, lodge in lineage-based territorial segments which are simultaneously administrative and political groups, where then is it to be found? There is, of course, no electoral system of popular representation of the sort found in modern Western societies — no differentiated legislature where politicians, representing the interests of diverse groups, may contend over a policy which, when arrived at, may be handed to a set of civil servants who are insulated from politics. In such traditional bureaucratic (or, to use Max Weber's term, "patrimonial") states, politics tends to lodge in the hierarchy of administrative officials itself and their groups of supporters. It is one of Smith's most important insights which, if not original with him, has at any rate been stated by him with a new force and clarity, that political power cannot be monopolized by a ruler, however despotic.[23] However dependent his officials may be upon him, he is also dependent upon them and hence they are in a position to contend among themselves for influence upon his policy decisions, including decisions regarding appointments to office. When he dies they, being in possession of the administrative apparatus, may contend for the role of king-maker, with all its attendant rewards in the form of enhanced political weight in future policy struggles.

Thus it would be inaccurate to say that politics and administration are completely differentiated in such politics. (Nor, Smith suggests, can they ever be; the most purely bureaucratic administrative systems, as we know, always develop systems of internal politics. And the relatively high degrees of differentiation of administration and politics found in modern Western societies are probably limited to those societies.) But the two are differentiated in Buganda and Zazzau in a sense in which they are not in segmentary states, and this kind of differentiation makes possible higher degrees of centralization of authority. Administrators in these states are perhaps always also politicians, but the units over which they are administrators are not the units on behalf of which they act as politicians. The former are the territorial and functional divisions of the state; the latter are kinsmen, clients and colleagues distributed through the administrative hierarchy. Thus, as factions or rudimentary parties lineages and other kinship groups may play an important political role in such societies, indeed their role is now much more specifically political in Smith's sense, for they are no longer administrative units as well. It is this breaking of the direct link between administrator and administered — the loss by the ad-

[23] See also H. Goldhammer and E. A. Shils, "Types of Power and Status," *American Journal of Sociology*, XLV (1939).

ministrator of his role as political representative of the administered — that makes possible both the centralization of authority and elite politics — the concentration of high politics within a relatively restricted social circle.

It is, of course, easy to over-emphasize the degree of concentration of power and authority which may result from this. On the one hand, the dilution of authority by politics brought about by the ruler's dependence upon his subordinates is repeated at lower levels in the administrative hierarchy. On the other hand, widespread networks of political allegiance may draw large numbers of persons into the political process. Administrative centralization and political autocracy, furthermore, are distinct, and not always co-variant, phenomena. Nevertheless, there remains an important difference between a state each of whose servants is the legitimate political representative of the people he governs and one in which the official is chosen through processes distinct from his unit of administrative responsibility, however political these processes may be.

The possibilities for fruitful comparative study suggested by Smith's ideas concerning the relationship between administration and politics are obviously extensive. Their relevance for contemporary political scientists' and political sociologists' preoccupation with "pluralism" and "group theory" in the study of highly differentiated modern polities, as well as for historical studies of the dévelopment of Western political systems from decentralized "feudal" to centralized "patrimonial" ones, is apparent.[24] By restating in terms of a general conception of the polity and its analytic elements ideas which other social anthropologists have tended to express in terms of the structural peculiarities of African societies, Smith has, I believe, helped to make possible a fruitful dialogue between the rich corpus of research on African political systems and other bodies of thought concerning comparative politics.

[24] T. F. Tout, *Chapters in the Administrative History of Medieval England* (Manchester: The University Press, 1920–33); M. Weber, *Wirtschaft und Gesellschaft* (Tübingen: J. C. B. Mohr, 1947), pp. 679–752.

Selections from
The Ancient City

N. D. FUSTEL DE COULANGES

The Family (Gens) was at first the only Form of Society.

. . . Let us place ourselves, in thought, in the midst of those ancient generations whose traces have not been entirely effaced, and who delegated their beliefs and their laws to subsequent ages. Each family has its religion, its gods,
its priesthood. Religious isolation is a law with it; its ceremonies are secret.
In death even, or in the existence that follows it, families do not mingle; each
one continues to live apart in the tomb, from which the stranger is excluded.
Every family has also its property, that is to say, its lot of land, which is inseparably attached to it by its religion; its gods — *Termini* — guard the en-
closure, and its Manes keep it in their care. Isolation of property is so
obligatory that two domains cannot be contiguous, but a band of soil must be
left between them, which must be neutral ground, and must remain inviolable.
Finally, every family has its chief, as a nation would have its king. It has its
laws, which, doubtless, are unwritten, but which religious faith engraves in
the heart of every man. It has its court of justice, above which there is no
other that one can appeal to. Whatever man really needs for his material or
moral life the family possesses within itself. It needs nothing from without; it
is an organized state, a society that suffices for itself.

But this family of the ancient ages is not reduced to the proportions of the
modern family. In larger societies the family separates and decreases. But in
the absence of every other social organization, it extends, develops, and rami-
fies without becoming divided. Several younger branches remain grouped
around an older one, near the one sacred fire and the common tomb.

Still another element entered into the composition of this antique family.
The reciprocal need which the poor has of the rich, and the rich has of the
poor, makes servants. But in this sort of patriarchal regime servant and slave
were one. We can see, indeed, that the principle of a free and voluntary service, ceasing at the will of the servant, would ill accord with a social state in
which a family lived isolated. Besides, the domestic religion did not permit
strangers to be admitted into a family. By some means, then, the servant must
become a member and an integrant part of the family. This was effected by a
sort of initiation of the new comer into the domestic worship.

A curious usage, that subsisted for a long time in Athenian houses, shows us
how the slave entered the family. They made him approach the fire, placed
him in the presence of the domestic divinity, and poured lustral water upon

From N. D. Fustel de Coulanges, *The Ancient City* (Garden City, N.Y.: Doubleday Anchor Books, 1956), pp. 112–116, 126–133, 219–223, 374–380, 389–396.

N. D. FUSTEL DE COULANGES (1830–1889) was Professor of History at Strasbourg
and at the Sorbonne in Paris. His *The Ancient City*, published in 1864, was a pioneering
analysis of the role of religion in classical antiquity. The author of a number of other
works on institutional history, Fustel de Coulanges' ideas influenced a number of
French sociologists and anthropologists, among them Emile Durkheim, who was his
student at the École Normale Supérieure.

his head. He then shared with the family some cakes and fruit.[1] This ceremony bore a certain analogy to those of marriage and adoption. It doubtless
signified that the new comer, a stranger the day before, should henceforth be a
member of the family, and share in its religion. And thus the slave joined in
the prayers, and took part in the festivals.[2] The fire protected him; the religion
of the Lares belonged to him as well as to his master. This is why the slave was
buried in the burial-place of the family.[3]

But by the very act of acquiring this worship, and the right to pray, he lost
his liberty. Religion was a chain that held him. He was bound to the family
for his whole life and after his death.

His master could raise him from his base servitude, and treat him as a free
man. But the servant did not on this account quit the family. As he was
bound to it by his worship, he could not, without impiety, separate from it.
Under the name of *freedman*, or that of *client*, he continued to recognize the
authority of the chief or patron, to be under obligations to him. He did not
marry without the consent of the master, and his children continued to obey
this master.

There was thus formed in the midst of the great family a certain number
of small families of clients and subordinates. The Romans attributed the establishment of clientship to Romulus, as if an institution of this nature could
have been the work of a man. Clientship is older than Romulus. Besides, it has
existed in other countries, in Greece as well as in all Italy. It was not the cities
that established and regulated it; they, on the contrary, as we shall presently
see, weakened and destroyed it by degrees. Clientship is an institution of the
domestic law, and existed in families before there were cities.

We are not to judge of the clientship of earlier ages from the clients that
we see in Horace's time. The client, it is clear, was for a long time a servant
attached to a patron. But there was then something to give him dignity; he had
a part in the worship, and was associated in the religion of the family. He had
the same sacred fire, the same festivals, the same *sacra* as his patron. At
Rome, in sign of this religious community, he took the name of the family.
He was considered as a member of it by adoption. Hence the close bond
and reciprocity of duties between the patron and the client. Listen to the old
Roman law: "If a patron has done his client wrong, let him be accused, *sacer
esto*, — let him die." The patron was obliged to protect his client by all the
means and with all the power of which he was master; by his prayers as a
priest, by his lance as a warrior, by his law as a judge. Later, when the client
was called before the city tribunal, it was the patron's duty to defend him. It
was his duty even to reveal to him the mysterious formulas of the law that
would enable him to gain his cause. One might testify in court against a cog-

---

[1] Demosthenes, *in Stephanum*, I. 74. Aristophanes, *Plutus*, 768. These two writers
clearly indicate a ceremony, but do not describe it. The scholiast of Aristophanes adds
a few details.

[2] *Ferias in famulis habento*, Cicero, *De Legib.*, II. 8; II. 12.

[3] *Quum dominis, tum famulis religio Larum*. Cicero, *De Legib.*, II. 11. Comp. Æsch.,
Agam., 1035–1038. The slave could even perform a religious act in the name of his
master. Cato, *De Re Rust.*, 83.

nate, but not against a client; and men continued long to consider their duties towards clients as far above those towards cognates.[4] Why? Because a cognate, connected solely through women, was not a relative, and had no part in the family religion. The client, on the contrary, had a community of worship; he had, inferior though he was, a real relationship, which consisted, according to the expression of Plato, in adoring the same domestic gods.

Clientship was a sacred bond which religion had formed, and which nothing could break. Once the client of a family, one could never be separated from it. Clientship was even hereditary.

From all this we see that the family, in the earliest times, with its oldest branch and its younger branches, its servants and its clients, might comprise a very numerous body of men. A family that by its religion maintained its unity, by its private law rendered itself indivisible, and through the laws of clientship retained its servants, came to form, in the course of time, a very extensive organization, having its hereditary chief. The Aryan race appears to have been composed of an indefinite number of societies of this nature, during a long succession of ages. These thousands of little groups lived isolated, having little to do with each other, having no need of one another, united by no bond religious or political, having each its domain, each its internal government, each its gods.

. . .

THE CITY FORMED

. . . It is of little account to seek the cause which determined several neighboring tribes to unite. Sometimes it was voluntary; sometimes it was imposed by the superior force of a tribe, or by the powerful will of a man. What is certain is, that the bond of the new association was still a religion. The tribes that united to form a city never failed to light a sacred fire, and to adopt a common religion.

Thus human society, in this race, did not enlarge like a circle, which increases on all sides, gaining little by little. There were, on the contrary, small groups, which, having been long established, were finally joined together in larger ones. Several families formed the phratry, several phratries the tribe, several tribes the city. Family, phratry, tribe, city, were, moreover, societies exactly similar to each other, which were formed one after the other by a series of federations.

We must remark, also, that when the different groups became thus associated, none of them lost its individuality, or its independence. Although several families were united in a phratry, each one of them remained constituted just as it had been when separate. Nothing was changed in it, neither worship nor priesthood, nor property nor internal justice. Curies afterwards became associated, but each retained its worship, its assemblies, its festivals, its chief. From the tribe men passed to the city; but the tribe was not dissolved on that account, and each of them continued to form a body, very much as

---

[4] Cato, in Aulus Gellius, V. 3; XXI. 1.

if the city had not existed. In religion there subsisted a multitude of sub-ordinate worships, above which was established one common to all; in politics, numerous little governments continued to act, while above them a common government was founded.

The city was a confederation. Hence it was obliged, at least for several centuries, to respect the religious and civil independence of the tribes, curies, and families, and had not the right, at first, to interfere in the private affairs of each of these little bodies. It had nothing to do in the interior of a family; it was not the judge of what passed there; it left to the father the right and duty of judging his wife, his son, and his client. It is for this reason that private law, which had been fixed at the time when families were isolated, could subsist in the city, and was modified only at a very late period.

The mode of founding ancient cities is attested by usages which continued for a very long time.

If we examine the army of the city in primitive times, we find it distributed into tribes, curies, and families,[5] "in such a way," says one of the ancients, "that the warrior has for a neighbor in the combat one with whom, in time of peace, he has offered the libation and sacrifice at the same altar." If we look at the people when assembled, in the early ages of Rome, we see them voting by curies and by *gentes*.[6] If we look at the worship, we see at Rome six Vestals, two for each tribe. At Athens, the archon offers the sacrifice in the name of the entire city, but he has in the religious part of the ceremony as many assistants as there are tribes.

Thus the city was not an assemblage of individuals; it was a confederation of several groups, which were established before it, and which it permitted to remain. We see, in the Athenian orators, that every Athenian formed a portion of four distinct societies at the same time; he was a member of a family, of a phratry, of a tribe, and of a city. He did not enter at the same time and the same day into all these four, like a Frenchman, who at the moment of his birth belongs at once to a family, a commune, a department, and a country. The phratry and the tribe are not administrative divisions. A man enters at different times into these four societies, and ascends, so to speak, from one to the other. First, the child is admitted into the family by the religious ceremony, which takes place six days after his birth. Some years later he enters the phratry by a new ceremony, which we have already described. Finally, at the age of sixteen or eighteen, he is presented for admission into the city. On that day, in the presence of an altar, and before the smoking flesh of a victim, he pronounces an oath, by which he binds himself, among other things, always to respect the religion of the city. From that day he is initiated into the public worship, and becomes a citizen.[7] If we observe this young Athenian rising, step by step, from worship to worship, we have a symbol of the degrees through which

---

[5] Homer, *Iliad*, II. 362. Varro, *De Ling. Lat.*, V. 89. Isæus, II. 42.

[6] Aulus Gellius, XV. 27.

[7] Demosthenes, *in Eubul.* Isæus. VII. IX. Lycurgus, I. 76. Schol., *in Demosth.*, p. 438. Pollux, VIII. 105. Stobæus, *De Repub.*

human association has passed. The course which this young man is constrained to follow is that which society first followed.

An example will make this truth clearer. There have remained to us in the antiquities of Athens traditions and traces enough to enable us to see quite clearly how the Athenian city was formed. At first, says Plutarch, Attica was divided by families.[8] Some of these families of the primitive period, like the Eumolpidæ, the Cecropidæ, the Gephræi, the Phytalidæ, and the Lakiadæ, were perpetuated to the following ages. At that time the city did not exist; but every family, surrounded by its younger branches and its clients, occupied a canton, and lived there in absolute independence. Each had its own religion; the Eumolpidæ, fixed at Eleusis, adored Demeter; the Cecropidæ, who inhabited the rocks where Athens was afterwards built, had Poseidon and Athene for protecting divinities. Near by, on the little hill of the Areopagus, the protecting god was Ares. At Marathon it was Hercules; at Prasiæ an Apollo, another Apollo at Phlius, the Dioscuri at Cephalus, and thus of all the other cantons.[9]

Every family has its god and its altar, had also its chief. When Pausanias visited Attica, he found in the little villages ancient traditions which had been perpetuated with the worship; and these traditions informed him that every little burgh had had its king before the time when Cecrops reigned at Athens. Was not this a memorial of a distant age, when the great patriarchal families, like the Celtic clans, had each its hereditary chief, who was at the same time priest and judge? Some hundred little societies then lived isolated in the country, recognizing no political or religious bond among them, having each its territory, often at war, and living so completely separated that marriage between them was not always permitted.[10]

But their needs or their sentiments brought them together. Insensibly they joined in little groups of four, five or six. Thus we find in the traditions that the four villages of Marathon united to adore the same Delphian Apollo; the men of the Piræus, Phalerum, and two neighboring burghs, united and built a temple to Hercules.[11] In the course of time these many little states were reduced to twelve confederations. This change, by which the people passed from the patriarchal family state to a society somewhat more extensive, was attributed by tradition to the efforts of Cecrops: we are merely to understand by this, that it was not accomplished until the time at which they place this personage — that is to say, towards the sixteenth century before our era. We see, moreover, that this Cecrops reigned over only one of these twelve associations, that which afterwards became Athens; the other eleven were completely independent; each had its tutelary diety, its altar, its sacred fire, and its chief.[12]

[8] κατα γενη, Plutarch, *Theseus*, 24, 13.
[9] Pausanias, I. 15; 31, 37, II. 18.
[10] Plutarch, *Theseus*, 13.
[11] Id., *ibid.*, 14. Pollux, VI. 105. Stephen of Byzantium, εχελιδαι.
[12] Philochorus, quoted by Strabo, IX. Thucydides, II. 16. Pollux, VIII. 111.

Several centuries passed, during which the Cecropidæ insensibly acquired greater importance. Of this period there remains the tradition of a bloody struggle sustained by them against the Eumolpidæ of Eleusis, the result of which was, that the latter submitted, with the single reservation that they should preserve the hereditary priesthood of their divinity.[13] There were doubtless other struggles and other conquests, of which no memorial has been preserved. The rock of the Cecropidæ, on which was developed, by degrees, the worship of Athene, and which finally adopted the name of their principal divinity, acquired the supremacy over the other eleven states. Then appeared Theseus, the heir of the Cecropidæ. All the traditions agree in declaring that he united the twelve groups into one city. He succeeded, indeed, in bringing all Attica to adopt the worship of Athene Polias, so that thenceforth the whole country celebrated the sacrifice of the Panathenæa in common. Before him, every burgh had its sacred fire and its prytany. He wished to make the prytany of Athens the religious centre of all Attica.[14] From that time Athenian unity was established. In religion every canton preserved its ancient worship, but adopted one that was common to all. Politically, each preserved its chiefs, its judges, its right of assembling; but above all these local governments, there was the central government of the city.[15]

From these precise memorials and traditions, which Athens preserved so religiously, there seem to us to be two truths equally manifest: the one is, that the city was a confederation of groups that had been established before it; and the other is, that society developed only so fast as religion enlarged its sphere. We cannot, indeed, say that religious progress brought social progress; but what is certain is, that they were both produced at the same time, and in remarkable accord.

We should not lose sight of the excessive difficulty which, in primitive times, opposed the foundation of regular societies. The social tie was not easy to

[13] Pausanias, I. 38.

[14] Thucydides, II. 15. Plutarch. *Theseus,* 24. Pausanias, I. 26; VIII. 2.

[15] According to Plutarch and Thucydides, Theseus destroyed the local prytanies, and abolished the magistracies of the burghs. If he attempted this, he certainly did not succeed; for a long while after him we will still find the local worships, the assemblies, and the *kings of tribes.* Boeckh, *Corp. Inscrip.,* 82, 85. Demosthenes, *in Theocrinem.* Pollux, VIII. 111. We put aside the legend of Ion, to which several modern historians seem to us to have given too much importance, by presenting it as an indication of a foreign invasion of Attica. This invasion is indicated by no tradition. If Attica had been conquered by these Ionians of the Peloponnesus, it is not probable that the Athenians would have so religiously preserved their names of Cecropidæ and Erechtheidæ, and that they would have been ashamed of the name of Ionians. (Hdts, I. 143.) We can also reply to those who believe in this invasion, and that the nobility of the Eupatrids is due to it, that most of the great families of Athens go back to a date much earlier than that given for the arrival of Ion in Attica. The Athenians certainly belong to the Ionic branch of the Hellenic race. Strabo tells us that, in the earliest times, Attica was called *Ionia* and *Ias.* But it is a mistake to make the son of Xuthus, the legendary hero of Euripides, the parent stock of these Ionians; they are long anterior to Ion, and their name is perhaps much more ancient than that of Hellenes. It is wrong to make all the Eupatrids descendants of this Ion, and to present this class of men as conquerors who oppressed a conquered people. There is no ancient testimony to support this opinion.

establish between those human beings who were so diverse, so free, so inconstant. To bring them under the rules of a community, to institute commandments and insure obedience, to cause passion to give way to reason, and individual right to public right, there certainly was something necessary, stronger than material force, more respectable than interest, surer than a philosophical theory, more unchangeable than a convention; something that should dwell equally in all hearts, and should be all-powerful there.

This power was a belief. Nothing has more power over the soul. A belief is the work of our mind, but we are not on that account free to modify it at will. It is our own creation, but we do not know it. It is human, and we believe it a god. It is the effect of our power, and is stronger than we are. It is in us; it does not quit us: it speaks to us at every moment. If it tells us to obey, we obey; if it traces duties for us, we submit. Man may, indeed, subdue nature, but he is subdued by his own thoughts.

Now, an ancient belief commanded a man to honor his ancestor; the worship of the ancestor grouped a family around an altar. Thus arose the first religion, the first prayers, the first ideas of duty, and of morals. Thus, too, was the right of property established, and the order of succession fixed. Thus, in fine, arose all private law, and all the rules of domestic organization. Later the belief grew, and human society grew at the same time. When men begin to perceive that there are common divinities for them, they unite in larger groups. The same rules, invented and established for the family, are applied successively to the phratry, the tribe, and the city.

Let us take in at a glance the road over which man has passed. In the beginning the family lived isolated, and man knew only the domestic gods — θεοι πατρωοι, *dii gentiles.* Above the family was formed the phratry with its god — θεος φρατριος, *Juno curialis.* Then came the tribe, and the god of the tribe — θεος φυλιος. Finally came the city, and men conceived a god whose providence embraced this entire city — θεος πολιευς, *penates publici;* a hierarchy of creeds, and a hierarchy of association. The religious idea was, among the ancients, the inspiring breath and organizer of society.

The traditions of the Hindus, of the Greeks, and of the Etruscans, relate that the gods revealed social laws to man. Under this legendary form there is a truth. Social laws were the work of the gods; but those gods, so powerful and beneficent, were nothing else than the beliefs of men.

Such was the origin of cities among the ancients. This study was necessary to give us a correct idea of the nature and institutions of the city. But here we must make a reservation. If the first cities were formed of a confederation of little societies previously established, this is not saying that all the cities known to us were formed in the same manner. The municipal organization once discovered, it was not necessary for each new city to pass over the same long and difficult route. It might often happen that they followed the inverse order. When a chief, quitting a city already organized, went to found another, he took with him commonly only a small number of his fellow-citizens. He associated with them a multitude of other men who came from different parts, and might even belong to different races. But this chief never failed to organize the new state after the model of the one he had just quitted. Consequently he divided his people into tribes and phratries. Each of these little associations had an altar, sacrifices, and festivals; each even invented an ancient hero, whom it honored with its worship, and from whom, with the lapse of time, it believed itself to have been descended.

It often happened, too, that the men of some country lived without laws and without order, either because no one had ever been able to establish a social organization there, as in Arcadia, or because it had been corrupted and dissolved by too rapid revolutions, as at Cyrene and Thurii. If a legislator undertook to establish order among these men, he never failed to commence by dividing them into tribes and phratries, as if this were the only type of society. In each of these organizations he named an eponymous hero, established sacrifices, and inaugurated traditions. This was always the manner of commencing, if he wished to found a regular society.[16] Thus Plato did when he imagined a model city.

· · ·

THE OMNIPOTENCE OF THE STATE. THE ANCIENTS KNEW NOTHING OF INDIVIDUAL LIBERTY

The city had been founded upon a religion, and constituted like a church. Hence its strength; hence, also, its omnipotence and the absolute empire which it exercised over its members. In a society established on such principles, individual liberty could not exist. The citizen was subordinate in everything, and without any reserve, to the city; he belonged to it body and soul. The religion which had produced the state, and the state which supported the religion, sustained each other, and made but one; these two powers, associated and confounded, formed a power almost superhuman, to which the soul and the body were equally enslaved.

There was nothing independent in man; his body belonged to the state, and was devoted to its defence. At Rome military service was due till a man was fifty years old, at Athens till he was sixty, at Sparta always. His fortune was always at the disposal of the state. If the city had need of money, it could order the women to deliver up their jewels, the creditors to give up their claims, and the owners of olive trees to turn over gratuitously the oil which they had made.[17]

Private life did not escape this omnipotence of the state. The Athenian law, in the name of religion, forbade man to remain single.[18] Sparta punished not only those who remained single, but those who married late. At Athens the state could prescribe labor, and at Sparta idleness. It exercised its tyranny even in the smallest things; at Locri the laws forbade men to drink pure wine; at Rome, Miletus, and Marseilles wine was forbidden to women.[19] It was a com-

[16] Herodotus, IV. 161. Cf. Plato, *Laws*, V. 738; VI. 771.
[17] Aristotle, *Econom.*, II.
[18] Pollux, VIII. 40. Plutarch, *Lysander*, 30.
[19] Athenæus, X. 33. Ælian, *V. H.*, II. 37.

mon thing for the kind of dress to be invariably fixed by each city; the legislation of Sparta regulated the head-dress of women and that of Athens forbade them to take with them on a journey more than three dresses.[20] At Rhodes and Byzantium the law forbade men to shave the beard.[21]

The state was under no obligation to suffer any of its citizens to be deformed. It therefore commanded a father to whom such a son was born, to have him put to death. This law is found in the ancient codes of Sparta and of Rome. We do not know that it existed at Athens; we know only that Aristotle and Plato incorporated it into their ideal codes.

There is, in the history of Sparta, one trait which Plutarch and Rousseau greatly admired. Sparta had just suffered a defeat at Leuctra, and many of its citizens had perished. On the receipt of this news, the relatives of the dead had to show themselves in public with gay countenances. The mother who learned that her son had escaped, and that she should see him again, appeared afflicted and wept. Another, who knew that she should never again see her son, appeared joyous, and went round to the temple to thank the gods. What, then, was the power of the state that could thus order the reversal of the natural sentiments, and be obeyed?

The state allowed no man to be indifferent to its interests; the philosopher or the studious man had no right to live apart. He was obliged to vote in the assembly, and be magistrate in his turn. At a time when discords were frequent, the Athenian law permitted no one to remain neutral; he must take sides with one or the other party. Against one who attempted to remain indifferent, and not side with either faction, and to appear calm, the law pronounced the punishment of exile with confiscation of property.

Education was far from being free among the Greeks. On the contrary, there was nothing over which the state had greater control. At Sparta the father could have nothing to do with the education of his son. The law appears to have been less rigorous at Athens; still the state managed to have education in the hands of masters of its own choosing. Aristophanes, in an eloquent passage, shows the Athenian children on their way to school; in order, distributed according to their district, they march in serried ranks, through rain, snow, or scorching heat. These children seem already to understand that they are performing a public duty.[22] The state wished alone to control education, and Plato gives the motive for this: [23] "Parents ought not to be free to send or not to send their children to the masters whom the city has chosen; for the children belong less to their parents than to the city."

The state considered the mind and the body of every citizen as belonging to it; and wished, therefore, to fashion this body and mind in a manner that would enable it to draw the greatest advantage from them. Children were

---

[20] *Fragm. Hist. Græc.* Didot. t. II. pp. 129, 211. Plutarch, *Solon*, 21.

[21] Athenæus, XIII. Plutarch, *Cleomenes*, 9.

"The Romans thought that no marriage, or rearing of children, nay, no feast or drinking bout, ought to be permitted according to every one's appetite or fancy, without being examined and inquired into." Plutarch, *Cato the Elder*, 23.

[22] Aristophanes, *Clouds*, 960–965.

[23] Plato, *Laws*, VII.

taught gymnastics, because the body of a man was an arm for the city, and it was best that this arm should be as strong and as skilful as possible. They were also taught religious songs and hymns, and the sacred dances, because this knowledge was necessary to the correct performance of the sacrifices and festivals of the city.[24]

It was admitted that the state had a right to prevent free instruction by the side of its own. One day Athens made a law forbidding the instruction of young people without authority from the magistrates, and another, which specially forbade the teaching of philosophy.[25]

A man had no chance to choose his belief. He must believe and submit to the religion of the city. He could hate and despise the gods of the neighboring city. As to the divinities of a general and universal character, like Jupiter, or Cybele, or Juno, he was free to believe or not to believe in them; but it would not do to entertain doubts about Athene Polias, or Erechtheus, or Cecrops. That would have been grave impiety, which would have endangered religion and the state at the same time, and which the state would have severely punished. Socrates was put to death for this crime. Liberty of thought in regard to the state religion was absolutely unknown among the ancients. Men had to conform to all the rules of worship, figure in all the processions, and take part in the sacred repasts. Athenian legislation punished those by a fine who failed religiously to celebrate a national festival.[26]

The ancients, therefore, knew neither liberty in private life, liberty in education, nor religious liberty. The human person counted for very little against that holy and almost divine authority which was called country or the state. The state had not only, as we have in our modern societies, a right to administer justice to the citizens; it could strike when one was not guilty, and simply for its own interest. Aristides assuredly had committed no crime, and was not even suspected; but the city had the right to drive him from its territory, for the simple reason that he had acquired by his virtues too much influence, and might become dangerous, if he desired to be. This was called *ostracism*; this institution was not peculiar to Athens; it was found at Argos, at Megara, at Syracuse, and we may believe that it existed in all the Greek cities.[27]

Now, *ostracism* was not a chastisement; it was a precaution which the city took against a citizen whom it suspected of having the power to injure it at any time. At Athens a man could be put on trial and condemned for incivism — that is to say, for the want of affection towards the state. A man's life was guaranteed by nothing so soon as the interest of the state was at stake. Rome made a law by which it was permitted to kill any man who might have the intention of becoming king.[28] The dangerous maxim that the safety of the state

[24] Aristophanes, *Clouds*, 966–968.
[25] Xenophon, *Memor.*, I. 2. Diogenes Laertius, *Theophr.* These two laws did not continue a long time; but they do not the less prove the omnipotence that was conceded to the state in matters of instruction.
[26] Pollux, VIII. 46. Ulpian, *Schol. in Demosthenes; in Meidiam.*
[27] Aristotle, *Pol.*, VIII. 2, 5. Scholiast on Aristoph., *Knights*, 851.
[28] Plutarch, *Publicola*, 12.

is the supreme law, was the work of antiquity.[29] It was then thought that law, justice, morals, everything should give way before the interests of the country.

It is a singular error, therefore, among all human errors, to believe that in the ancient cities men enjoyed liberty. They had not even the idea of it. They did not believe that there could exist any right as against the city and its gods. We shall see, farther on, that the government changed form several times, while the nature of the state remained nearly the same, and its omnipotence was little diminished. The government was called by turns monarchy, aristocracy, democracy; but none of these revolutions gave man true liberty, individual liberty. To have political rights, to vote, to name magistrates, to have the privilege of being archon, — this was called liberty; but man was not the less enslaved to the state. The ancients, especially the Greeks, always exaggerated the importance, and above all, the rights of society; this was largely due, doubtless, to the sacred and religious character with which society was clothed in the beginning.

. . .

Rome everywhere destroys the Municipal System.

The institutions of the ancient city had been weakened, and almost exhausted, by a series of revolutions. One of the first results of the Roman dominion was to complete their destruction, and to efface what still remained of them. This we can see by observing the condition into which the nations fell as they became subject to Rome.

We must first banish from our minds all the customs of modern politics, and not picture to ourselves the nations entering the Roman state, one after another, as in our day provinces are annexed to a kingdom, which, on receiving these new members, extends its boundaries. The Roman state (*civitas Romana*) was not enlarged by conquests; it never included any families except those that figured in the religious ceremony of the census. The Roman territory (*ager Romanus*) never increased. It remained enclosed within the immutable limits which the kings had traced for it, and which the ceremony of the *Ambarvalia* sanctified every year. What increased with every conquest was the dominion of Rome (*imperium Romanum*).

So long as the republic lasted, it never entered the mind of any one that the Romans and the other peoples could form a single nation. Rome might, indeed, receive a few of the conquered, allow them to live within her walls, and transform them, in the course of time, into Romans; but she could not assimilate a whole foreign people to her people, an entire territory to her territory. Still this was not peculiar to the policy of Rome, but a principle that held through all antiquity; it was a principle from which Rome would sooner have departed than any other city, but from which she could not entirely free herself. Whenever, therefore, a people was conquered, it did not enter the Roman state; it entered only the Roman dominion. It was not united to Rome, as provinces

[29] Cicero, *De Legib.*, III. 3.

are to-day united to a capital; between other nations and itself Rome knew only two kinds of connection — subjection or alliance.

From this it would seem that municipal institutions must have subsisted among the conquered, and that the world must have been an assemblage of cities distinct from each other, and having at their head a ruling city. But it was nothing of the kind. The effect of the Roman conquest was to work in every city a complete transformation.

On one side were the subjects *deditii*, or those who, having pronounced the formula of the *deditio*, had delivered to the Roman people "their persons, their walls, their lands, their waters, their houses, their temples, and their gods."

They had therefore renounced, not only their municipal government, but all that appertained to it among the ancients, — that is to say, their religion and their private law. From that moment these men no longer formed a political body among themselves; nothing that goes to make up a regular society remained to them. Their city (*urbs*) might remain standing, but the state (*civitas*) had perished. If they continued to live together, they lived without institutions, laws, or magistrates. The arbitrary authority of a *præfectus* sent by Rome maintained material order among them.[30] On the other hand were the allies — *fœderati*, or *socii*. They were less cruelly treated. The day on which they entered the Roman dominion, it had been stipulated that they should preserve their municipal government, and should remain organized into cities. They therefore continued to have in every city a constitution, magistracies, a senate, a prytaneum, laws, and judges. The city was supposed to be independent, and seemed to have no other relations with Rome than those of an ally with its ally. Still, in the terms of the treaty which had been drawn up at the time of the conquest, Rome had been careful to insert these words: *Majestatem populi Romani comiter conservato*.[31] These terms established the dependence of the allied city upon the metropolitan city, and as they were very vague, it happened that the measure of this dependence was always in accordance with the will of the stronger. These cities, which were called free, received orders from Rome, obeyed proconsuls, and paid taxes to the collectors of the revenue. Their magistrates rendered their accounts to the governor of the province, who also heard the appeals from the judges.[32] Now, such was the nature of the municipal system among the ancients that it needed complete independence, or it ceased to exist. Between the maintenance of the institutions of the city and their subordination to a foreign power, there was a contradiction which perhaps does not clearly appear to the eyes of the moderns, but which must have struck every man of that period. Municipal liberty and the government of Rome were irreconcilable; the first could be only an appearance, a falsehood, an amusement calculated to divert the minds of men. Each of those cities sent, almost every year, a deputation to Rome, and its most minute and most private affairs were

[30] Livy, I. 38; VII. 31; IX. 20; XXVI. 16; XXVIII. 34. Cicero, *De Lege Agr.*, I. 6; II. 32. Festus, v. *Præfecturæ*.

[31] Cicero, *Pro Balbo*, 16.

[32] Livy, XLV. 18. Cicero, *ad Attic.*, VI. 1, 2. Appian, *Civil Wars*, I. 102. Tacitus, XV. 45.

regulated by the senate. They still had their municipal magistrates, their archons, and their strategi, freely elected by themselves; but the archon no longer had any other duty than to inscribe his name on the registers for the purpose of marking the year, and the strategus, in earlier times the chief of the army and of the state, now had no other care than to keep the streets in order, and inspect the markets.[33]

Municipal institutions, therefore, perished among the nations that were called allies as well as among those that bore the name of subjects; there was only this difference, that the first preserved the exterior forms. Indeed, the city, as antiquity had understood it, was no longer seen anywhere, except within the walls of Rome.

Then, too, the Romans, while everywhere destroying the municipal system, substituted nothing in its place. To the people whose institutions they took away, they did not give their own instead. The Romans never thought of creating new institutions for their use; they never made a constitution for the people of their empire, and did not understand how to establish fixed rules for their government. Even the authority which Rome exercised over the cities had no regularity. As they made no part of her state, or of her city, she had no legal power over them. Her subjects were strangers to her — a reason why she exercised this irregular and unlimited power which ancient municipal law allowed citizens to exercise towards foreigners and enemies. It was on this principle that the Roman administration was a long time regulated, and this is the manner in which it was carried on.

Rome sent one of her citizens into a country. She made that country the *province* of this man, — that is to say, his charge, his own care, his personal affair; this was the sense of the word *provincia*. At the same time she conferred upon this citizen the *imperium*; this signified that she gave up in his favor, for a determined time, the sovereignty which she held over the country. From that time this citizen represented in his person all the rights of the republic, and by this means he was an absolute master. He fixed the amount of taxes; he exercised the military power, and administered justice. His relations with the subjects, or the allies, were limited by no constitution. When he sat in his judgment-seat, he pronounced decisions according to his own will; no law controlled him, neither the provincial laws, as he was a Roman, nor the Roman laws, as he passed judgment upon provincials. If there were laws between him and those that he governed, he had to make them himself, for he alone could bind himself. Therefore the *imperium* with which he was clothed included the legislative power; and thus it happened that the governors had the right, and established the custom, on entering the provinces, of publishing a code of laws, which they called their Edict, and to which they morally promised to conform. But as the governors were changed annually, these codes changed every year, for the reason that the law had its source only in the will of the man who was for the time invested with the *imperium*. This principle was so rigorously applied that, when a judgment had been pronounced by a governor, but had not been

---

[33] Philostratus, *Lives of the Sophists*, I. 23. Boeckh., *Corp. Inscr.*, passim.

entirely executed at the time of his departure from the province, the arrival of his successor completely annulled this judgment, and the proceedings were recommenced.[34]

Such was the omnipotence of the governor. He was the living law. As to invoking the justice of Rome against his acts of violence or his crimes, the provincials could not do this unless they could find a Roman citizen who would act as their patron,[35] for, as to themselves, they had no right to demand the protection of the laws of the city, or to appeal to its courts. They were foreigners; the judicial and official language called them *peregrini*; all that the law said of the *hostis* continued to be applied to them.

The legal situation of the inhabitants of the empire appears clearly in the writings of the Roman jurisconsults. We there see that the people are considered as no longer having their own laws, and as not yet having those of Rome. For them, therefore, the law did not exist in any manner. In the eyes of the Roman jurisconsult, a provincial was neither husband nor father, — that is to say, the law recognized neither his marital nor his paternal authority. For him property did not exist. It was a double impossibility for him to become a proprietor; it was impossible by reason of his personal condition, because he was not a Roman citizen, and impossible by reason of the condition of the land, because it was not Roman territory, and the law admitted the complete right of ownership only within the limits of the *ager Romanus*. For the lawyers taught that the land in the provinces was never private property, and that men could have only the possession and usufruct thereof.[36] Now, what they said in the second century of our era of the provincial territory had been equally true of the Italian soil before Italy obtained the Roman franchise, as we shall presently see.

It is certain, then, that the people, as fast as they entered the Roman empire, lost their municipal religion, their government, and their private law. We can easily believe that Rome softened in practice whatever was destructive in this subjection. We see, indeed, that, though the Roman laws did not recognize the paternal authority in the subject, they allowed this authority still to subsist in practice. If they did not permit a certain man to call himself a proprietor of the soil, they still allowed him the possession of it; he cultivated his land, sold it, and devised it by will. It was not said that this land was his, but they said it was as good as his, *pro suo*. It was not his property, *dominium*, but it was among his goods, *in bonis*.[37] Rome thus invented for the benefit of the subject a multitude of turns and artifices of language. Indeed, the Roman genius, if its municipal traditions prevented it from making laws for the conquered, could not suffer society to fall into dissolution. In principle the provincials were placed outside the laws, while in fact they lived as if they had them; but with the exception of this, and the tolerance of the conquerors, all the institutions of the vanquished and all their laws were allowed to disappear.

[34] Gaius, IV. 103, 105.
[35] Cicero, *De Orat.*, I. 9.
[36] Gaius, II. 7. Cicero, *Pro Flacco*, 32.
[37] Gaius, I. 52; II. 5, 6, 7.

The Roman empire presented, for several generations, this singular spectacle: A single city remained intact, preserving its institutions and its laws, while all the rest — that is to say, more than a hundred millions of souls — either had no kind of laws, or had such as were not recognized by the ruling city. The world then was not precisely in a state of chaos, but force, arbitrary rule, and convention, in default of laws and principles, alone sustained society.

Such was the effect of the Roman conquest on the nations that successively became its prey. Of the city everything went to ruin; religion first, then the government, and finally private law. All the municipal institutions, already for a long time shaken, were finally overthrown and destroyed; but no regular society, no system of government, replaced at once what had disappeared. There was a period of stagnation between the moment when men saw the municipal governments dissolve and that in which another form of society appeared. The nation did not at once succeed the city, for the Roman empire in no wise resembled a nation. It was a confused multitude, where there was real order only in one central point, and where all the rest enjoyed only a factitious and transitory order, and obtained this only at the price of obedience.

. . . .

CHRISTIANITY CHANGES
THE CONDITIONS OF GOVERNMENT

The victory of Christianity marks the end of ancient society. With the new religion this social transformation, which we saw begun six or seven centuries earlier, was completed.

To understand how much the principles and the essential rules of politics were then changed, we need only recollect that ancient society had been established by an old religion whose principal dogma was that every god protected exclusively a single family or a single city, and existed only for that. This was the time of the domestic gods and the city-protecting divinities. This religion had produced laws; the relations among men — property, inheritance, legal proceedings — all were regulated, not by the principles of natural equity, but by the dogmas of this religion, and with a view to the requirements of its worship. It was this religion that had established a government among men; that of the father in the family; that of the king or magistrate in the city. All had come from religion, — that is to say, from the opinion that man had entertained of the divinity. Religion, law, and government were confounded, and had been but a single thing under three different aspects.

We have sought to place in a clear light this social system of the ancients, where religion was absolute master, both in public and private life; where the state was a religious community, the king a pontiff, the magistrate a priest, and the law a sacred formula; where patriotism was piety, and exile excommunication; where individual liberty was unknown; where man was enslaved to the state through his soul, his body, and his property; where the notions of law and of duty, of justice and of affection, were bounded within the limits of the city; where human association was necessarily confined within a certain circumference around a prytaneum; and where men saw no possibility of founding larger societies. Such were the characteristic traits of the Greek and Italian cities during the first period of their history.

But little by little, as we have seen, society became modified. Changes took place in government and in laws at the same time as in religious ideas. Already, in the fifth century which preceded Christianity, the alliance was no longer so close between religion on the one hand and law and politics on the other. The efforts of the oppressed classes, the overthrow of the sacerdotal class, the labors of philosophers, the progress of thought, had unsettled the ancient principles of human association. Men had made incessant efforts to free themselves from the thraldom of this old religion, in which they could no longer believe; law and politics, as well as morals, in the course of time were freed from its fetters.

But this species of divorce came from the disappearance of the ancient religion; if law and politics began to be a little more independent, it was because men ceased to have religious beliefs. If society was no longer governed by religion, it was especially because this religion no longer had any power. But there came a day when the religious sentiment recovered life and vigor, and when, under the Christian form, belief regained its empire over the soul. Were men not then destined to see the reappearance of the ancient confusion of government and the priesthood, of faith and the law?

With Christianity not only was the religious sentiment revived, but it assumed a higher and less material expression. Whilst previously men had made for themselves gods of the human soul, or of the great forces of nature, they now began to look upon God as really foreign by his essence, from human nature on the one hand, and from the world on the other. The divine Being was placed outside and above physical nature. Whilst previously every man had made a god for himself, and there were as many of them as there were families and cities, God now appeared as a unique, immense, universal being, alone animating the worlds, alone able to supply the need of adoration that is in man. Religion, instead of being, as formerly among the nations of Greece and Italy, little more than an assemblage of practices, a series of rites which men repeated without having any idea of them, a succession of formulas which often were no longer understood because the language had grown old, a tradition which had been transmitted from age to age, and which owed its sacred character to its antiquity alone, — was now a collection of doctrines, and a great object proposed to faith. It was no longer exterior; it took up its abode especially in the thoughts of man. It was no longer matter; it became spirit. Christianity changed the nature and the form of adoration. Man no longer offered God food and drink. Prayer was no longer a form of incantation; it was an act of faith and a humble petition. The soul sustained another relation with the divinity; the fear of the gods was replaced by the love of God.

Christianity introduced other new ideas. It was not the domestic religion of any family, the national religion of any city, or of any race. It belonged neither to a caste nor to a corporation. From its first appearance it called to itself the whole human race. Christ said to his disciples, "Go ye into all the world, and preach the gospel to every creature."

This principle was so extraordinary, and so unexpected, that the first disciples hesitated for a moment; we may see in the Acts of the Apostles that several of them refused at first to propagate the new doctrine outside the nation with which it had originated. These disciples thought, like the ancient Jews, that the God of the Jews would not accept adoration from foreigners; like the Romans and the Greeks of ancient times, they believed that every race had its god, that to propagate the name and worship of this god was to give up one's own good and special protector, and that such a work was contrary at the same time to duty and to interest. But Peter replied to these disciples, "God gave the gentiles the like gift as He did unto us." St. Paul loved to repeat this grand principle on all occasions, and in every kind of form. "God had opened the door of faith unto the gentiles." "Is he the God of the Jews, only? Is he not also of the gentiles?" "We are all baptized into one body, whether we be Jews or gentiles."

In all this there was something quite new. For, everywhere, in the first ages of humanity, the divinity had been imagined as attaching himself especially to one race. The Jews had believed in the God of the Jews; the Athenians in the Athenian Pallas; the Romans in Jupiter Capitolinus. The right to practise a worship had been a privilege.

The foreigner had been repulsed from the temple; one not a Jew could not enter the temple of the Jews; the Lacedæmonian had not the right to invoke the Athenian Pallas. It is just to say, that, in the five centuries which preceded Christianity, all who thought were struggling against these narrow rules. Philosophy had often taught, since Anaxagoras, that the god of the universe received the homage of all men, without distinction. The religion of Eleusis had admitted the initiated from all cities. The religion of Cybele, of Serapis, and some others, had accepted, without distinction, worshippers from all nations. The Jews had begun to admit the foreigner to their religion; the Greeks and the Romans had admitted him into their cities. Christianity, coming after all this progress in thought and institutions, presented to the adoration of all men a single God, a universal God, a God who belonged to all, who had no chosen people, and who made no distinction in races, families, or states.

For this God there were no longer strangers. The stranger no longer profaned the temple, no longer tainted the sacrifice by his presence. The temple was open to all who believed in God. The priesthood ceased to be hereditary, because religion was no longer a patrimony. The worship was no longer kept secret; the rites, the prayers, the dogmas were no longer concealed. On the contrary, there was thenceforth religious instruction, which was not only given, but which was offered, which was carried to those who were the farthest away, and which sought out the most indifferent. The spirit of propagandism replaced the law of exclusion.

From this great consequences flowed, as well for the relations between nations as for the government of states.

Between nations religion no longer commanded hatred; it no longer made it the citizen's duty to detest the foreigner; its very essence, on the contrary, was to teach him that towards the stranger, towards the enemy, he owed the duties of justice, and even of benevolence. The barriers between nations or races were thus thrown down; the *pomœrium* disappeared. "Christ," says the apostle, "hath broken down the middle wall of partition between us." "But now are they many members," he also says, "yet but one body." "There is neither Greek nor Jew, circumcision nor uncircumcision, Barbarian, Scythian, bond nor free: but Christ is all, and in all."

The people were also taught that they were all descended from the same common father. With the unity of God, the unity of the human race also appeared to men's minds; and it was thenceforth a religious necessity to forbid men to hate each other.

As to the government of the state, we cannot say that Christianity essentially altered that, precisely because it did not occupy itself with the state. In the ancient ages, religion and the state made but one; every people adored its own god, and every god governed his own people; the same code regulated the relations among men, and their duties towards the gods of the city. Religion then governed the state, and designated its chiefs by the voice of the lot, or by that of the auspices. The state, in its turn, interfered with the domain of the conscience, and punished every infraction of the rites and the worship of the city. Instead of this, Christ teaches that his kingdom is not of this world. He separates religion from government. Religion, being no longer of the earth, now interferes the least possible in terrestrial affairs. Christ adds, "Render to Cæsar the things that are Cæsar's, and to God the things that are God's." It is the first time that God and the state are so clearly distinguished. For Cæsar at that period was still the *pontifex maximus*, the chief and the principal organ of the Roman religion; he was the guardian and the interpreter of beliefs. He held the worship and the dogmas in his hands. Even his person was sacred and divine, for it was a peculiarity of the policy of the emperors that, wishing to recover the attributes of ancient royalty, they were careful not to forget the divine character which antiquity had attached to the king-pontiffs and to the priest-founders. But now Christ breaks the alliance which paganism and the empire wished to renew. He proclaims that religion is no longer the state, and that to obey Cæsar is no longer the same thing as to obey God.

Christianity completes the overthrow of the local worship; it extinguishes the prytanea, and completely destroys the city-protecting divinities. It does more; it refuses to assume the empire which these worships had exercised over civil society. It professes that between the state and itself there is nothing in common. It separates what all antiquity had confounded. We may remark, moreover, that during three centuries the new religion lived entirely beyond the action of the state; it knew how to dispense with state protection, and even to struggle against it. These three centuries established an abyss between the domain of the government and the domain of religion; and, as the recollection of this period could not be effaced, it followed that this distinction became a plain and incontestable truth, which the efforts even of a part of the clergy could not eradicate.

This principle was fertile in great results. On one hand, politics became definitively freed from the strict rules which the ancient religion had traced, and could govern men without having to bend to sacred usages, without consulting the auspices or the oracles, without conforming all acts to the beliefs and requirements of a worship. Political action was freer; no other authority than that of the moral law now impeded it. On the other hand, if the state was more completely master in certain things, its action was also more limited. A complete half of man had been freed from its control. Christianity taught that only a part of man belonged to society; that he was bound to it by his body and by his material interests; that when subject to a tyrant, it was his duty to submit; that as a citizen of a republic, he ought to give his life for it, but that, in what related to his soul, he was free, and was bound only to God.

Stoicism had already marked this separation; it had restored man to himself, and had founded liberty of conscience. But that which was merely the effort of the energy of a courageous sect, Christianity made a universal and unchangeable rule for succeeding generations; what was only the consolation of a few, it made the common good of humanity.

If, now, we recollect what has been said above on the omnipotence of the states among the ancients, — if we bear in mind how far the city, in the name of its sacred character and of religion, which was inherent in it, exercised an absolute empire, — we shall see that this new principle was the source whence individual liberty flowed.

The mind once freed, the greatest difficulty was overcome, and liberty was compatible with social order.

Sentiments and manners, as well as politics, were then changed. The idea which men had of the duties of the citizen were modified. The first duty no longer consisted in giving one's time, one's strength, one's life to the state. Politics and war were no longer the whole of man; all the virtues were no longer comprised in patriotism, for the soul no longer had a country. Man felt that he had other obligations besides that of living and dying for the city. Christianity distinguished the private from the public virtues. By giving less honor to the latter, it elevated the former; it placed God, the family, the human individual above country, the neighbor above the city.

Law was also changed in its nature. Among all ancient nations law had been subject to, and had received all its rules from, religion. Among the Persians, the Hindus, the Jews, the Greeks, the Italians, and the Gauls, the law had been contained in the sacred books or in religious traditions, and thus every religion had made laws after its own image. Christianity is the first religion that did not claim to be the source of law. It occupied itself with the duties of men, not with their interests. Men saw it regulate neither the laws of property, nor the order of succession, nor obligations, nor legal proceedings. It placed itself outside the law, and outside all things purely terrestrial. Law was independent; it could draw its rules from nature, from the human conscience, from the powerful idea of the just that is in men's minds. It could develop in complete liberty; could be reformed and improved without obstacle; could follow the progress of morals, and could conform itself to the interests and social needs of every generation.

The happy influence of the new idea is easily seen in the history of Roman law. During several centuries preceding the triumph of Christianity, Roman law had already been striving to disengage itself from religion, and to approach natural equity; but it proceeded only by shifts and devices, which enervated and enfeebled its moral authority. The work of regenerating legislation, announced by the Stoic philosophers, pursued by the noble efforts of Roman jurisconsults, outlined by the artifices and expedients of the pretor, could not completely succeed except by favor of the independence which the new religion allowed to the law. We can see, as Christianity gained ground, that the Roman codes admitted new rules no longer by subterfuges, but openly and without hesitation. The domestic penates having been overthrown, and the sacred fires extinguished, the ancient constitution of the family disappeared forever, and with it the rules that had flowed from this source. The father had lost the absolute authority which his priesthood had formerly given him, and preserved only that which nature itself had conferred upon him for the good of the child. The wife, whom the old religion placed in a position inferior to the husband, became morally his equal. The laws of property were essentially altered; the sacred landmarks disappeared from the fields; the right of property no longer flowed from religion, but from labor; its acquisition became easier, and the formalities of the ancient law were definitively abolished.

Thus, by the single fact that the family no longer had its domestic religion, its constitution and its laws were transformed; so, too, from the single fact that the state no longer had its official religion, the rules for the government of men were forever changed.

Our study must end at this limit, which separates ancient from modern polities. We have written the history of a belief. It was established, and human society was constituted. It was modified, and society underwent a series of revolutions. It disappeared, and society changed its character. Such was the law of ancient times.

Traditional Processes of Power
in South India:
An Historical Analysis
of Local Influence

ROBERT ERIC FRYKENBERG

Normally, in the West, a concentration of political power into one control system has been distinguished from the administrative apparatus through which that power was exercised. This has been especially apparent in modern and more than nominally democratic and constitutional systems, wherein power components have been elaborately organized and equipped with corrective checks, functional channels, and legitimizing symbols to prevent breakdown or misgovernment. Such neat distinctions are more difficult to apply to political institutions which existed in pre-modern India.[1]

Few dissent from the general view that political behavior within the social order of pre-modern India was by tradition primarily administrative in character, both as to its structure and its functions. By this we mean that political energies, which were motivated by acquisitive and predatory aspirations of various elite groups competing for advantage within a highly complex and communally segmented social structure, found expression in the elements and operations of military and financial organization. In short, a power system could expand and prosper only by employing its forces in warlike action (and in diplomacy based upon its war potential); moreover, that system could nourish itself only by efficiently extracting revenue. Essentially administrative functions were involved; and these functions of control were hierarchically and territorially interlocked with the variable intricacies of the social order.

It is not enough, therefore, simply to trace the rise and fall of dynastic kingdoms and principalities in terms of their military prowess, ascendency, or decline. What is required is a more fundamental appreciation of internal structures and changing interrelations between socio-political entities within a far wider mosaic of potentially dysfunctional or eufunctional parts (or of mechanisms of parts within parts). Such an appreciation of intrinsically administrative processes demands more than two-dimensional studies of superficial breadth and chronological length. Historical light must be thrown deeper into local affairs, illuminating the springs from which traditional influences have flowed.

For this reason, one area of South India has been selected and the development of local influences within it studied intensively. A comparative analysis

From the *Indian Economic and Social History Review*, Vol. I, No. 2 (October–December 1963), pp. 122–142. Reprinted by permission of the author and publisher.
ROBERT ERIC FRYKENBERG is Associate Professor of History, University of Wisconsin. An expert on the history of South India, he is the author of *Guntur District, 1788–1848* (1965), and numerous articles in professional journals.

[1] Precise conceptual tools for describing either political processes or entities which, when observed closely, manifest themselves in bewildering patterns (now feudal, then tribal, again imperial, now regal, or patrimonial, or communal, in seemingly endless permutation and variety) has yet to be discovered.

of the history of Guntur District [2] under the rule of Company Bahadur with reference to other localities, other times, and other regimes should provide grounds for generalization upon the strength of localizing tendencies and traditions.

I

There is evidence to show that certain local elite groups and institutions of the Krishna-Godavari Deltas have survived the intrusions of exogenous forces through many centuries. While leading warrior castes can be traced into the mists of antiquity, these communities did not leave many records concerning their early history. As might be expected, those who did leave clear records of the past were the literate castes; and, quite naturally, those castes which carried on these written records made claims of their own preponderant influence in local affairs. Without a doubt, the oldest seats of continuous local leadership about which we can have some certainty were those of the *Karnams* or Village Accountants.

The possibility that Karnams may originally have been appointed as local representatives of extra-village power, although this cannot automatically be presumed, does not minimize their potential for exercising local influence. Indeed, the enduring strength of these remarkable leaders arose out of their control of all the bookwork necessary for administering village finances and for rendering any demands imposed by forces outside the village. Karnams prepared and preserved financial accounts. They signed and registered receipts; they inscribed official letters and documents; they announced orders and decrees; and they recorded village expenditures for superior systems of power, if necessary. To a large degree, if village government had evidences of continuity productivity or of past productivity, these were due to the persons who preserved that knowledge. It was very difficult for any exogenous, centralized system of power (e.g. some form of state) to extract revenues sufficient to maintain power enough to control villages, much less to wage war, without cooperation from Karnams. Because of this, it became the object of every strongly centralized dynastic power to bring these local functionaries tightly under control.

Understandably, local positions became focal points for controversy, manipulation, and patronage. But the skills and techniques of local, administrative scribes were closely guarded sacred-secrets, often the strictly preserved monopoly of one family or caste in each village. Family or caste combinations, however, could be developed and networks of influence extended over wider localities. Such combinations could sometimes become increasingly sophisticated and organized strongly enough to resist, to corrupt and infiltrate, and finally to permeate and undermine progressively higher levels and wider areas of political and administrative authority. Such combinations could be very difficult to discover, much less control. Violence was no answer. A few Karnams might be eliminated or replaced. One or two villages might be crushed. Yet the functions of Karnams were altogether too valuable and their skills too rare. Drastic,

----

[2] The area of Guntur District is now listed as 5,795 square miles. Its population in 1847 was listed at 411,599, and in 1961 at 3,009,997.

wholesale eradication was not feasible unless large groups of dependable replacements were available. But, even when systematic substitutions from the top of an administrative hierarchy downward were made, there was usually and eventually a silent recurrence of combining local influences to the corrupting of central power.

The earliest Karnams, of which we know, were Aravas (Goldsmiths), Buddhists, and Jains. The resurgence of medieval Hinduism brought about repeated efforts to displace these groups. Successive kingdoms sought to introduce small groups of military and financial officers into the administrative hierarchies and areas under their control. Family elements of these loyal groups would be given dominant positions in carefully selected and strategically important villages. On successive occasions under different regimes, therefore, we know that Benares Brahmans, Hoysala Brahmans, Patrulu Brahmans, Badagal Brahmans, Nandavarika (or Yagnavalkya) Brahmans, (Ayyar or Iengar) Tamil Brahmans, Kanakapillais, Lingayats, Linga or Gazulu Balijas, and Kayasthas, were introduced into various positions of administrative power within Guntur District, or Kondavidu Sima as it was known in pre-Muslim times. But since these groups were numerically small, they retained only isolated pockets of influence in widely scattered villages once their dynastic regimes were superseded.[3]

The most significant Brahman group to grow strong in Telugu country have been the Niyogis. There are various legends about how this administrative elite originated and how it became predominant in Karnamships. Undoubtedly, Niyogis were locally influential by the middle of the 12th century; moreover, despite many stories about the *Aruvelu-Niyogilu* and *Murduvelu-Niyogilu* ("6000 Niyogis" and "3000 Niyogis"), it is doubtful whether either Brahminical or Niyogi power triumphed very suddenly.[4] The last Kakatiya king of Warangal is reported to have "crushed Jains in oil mills" and the Reddi kings of Kondavidu also dealt harshly with non-Hindu groups. Not until Vijayangara power extended across in the peninsula in the early 16th century did Niyogis reach their greatest power.[5]

It is necessary at this point to consider how local systems of power were structured, both as to military and revenue functions, at the village level and at extra-village levels of power. Functionally, as has already been indicated,

[3] Elliot Mss., *Local History I*, "On the Origin of Village Accountants" (India Office Library, abbr. IOL: Mss. Eur. F. 46), pp. 93–97; and *Local History III*, "Historical Memoir of Chebrolu" (IOL: Mss. Eur F. 48), pp. 91–104. Note: Translations of stone and copper inscriptions, together with writings on *cadjan* leaves, show how elite groups regarded their past, cf. *South Indian Inscriptions: Volume X* (Madras: 1948). Collected between 1788 and 1817 and then translated into Marathi and English by servants of Col. Colin Mackenzie, the village histories of Guntur in the Elliot Collection are enhanced by the fact that they come from important and old villages. These mixtures of fact, folklore and precept permit insights into tradition.

[4] *Ibid.*, *Local History I*, "Translation of Dandakaville by Vadhamundi Kamaraz, Curnum of Peturu Village in Repalle Talook, Zillah Guntur," p. 106.

[5] Gordon Mackenzie, *A Manual of Kistna District* (Madras: Government of Madras, 1883), pp. 1–50. *Op. cit.*, *Local History I*, "*Condavid Country*, or Guntoor," pp. 103–105. K. A. Nilakantha Sastri, *A History of South India* (Madras: Oxford University Press, 1955), pp. 271–287.

some leadership communities specialized in skills of the pen. Hierarchically and geographically, depending upon the strength and sophistication of exogenous organizations of power above and beyond the limits of village systems of power, there usually would be different but socially homogenous communities performing military and clerical functions on behalf of those extended families which represented or collectively embodied a supreme regal or imperial authority.

It would be erroneous to suppose that all village systems of power were alike. As clusters of human settlement, villages represented no flat uniformity of economic or cultural achievement nor of any social or demographic distribution.[6] Some villages were very large while others, very small. Some villages were very old while others were newly born. Some were very rich, powerful, and domineering while others were mere abjectly subservient hamlets (*pallems*) tottering on the brink of extinction. Market conditions, wealth and productivity differentials, socio-political, cultural or religious attractions, and plain geographic (if not climatic) conveniences made village influence highly unequal. For example, certain deltic and coastal villages depended entirely upon maritime trade, overland traffic, salt productions, fishing, textile weaving, stone working, metal smelting, rice cultivation, or garden crops, to name just a few instances. Other villages were entirely parasitic or enjoyed special privileges, such as *agraharams, devasthanams, samasthanams,* or various other kinds of *inams (maniams, savarams,* or *shrotriams)* which might be controlled by local elite communities or granted by fiat from some extra-local power. Likewise, in various villages, different local Brahman castes (chiefly Niyogis) tended to monopolize positions requiring clerical skill while local warrior castes such as Rajus, Kammas, Velamas, Kapus, and Telagas dominated military occupations. Below these castes were ranged the trading, artisan, and lesser cultivating castes. More than a score of castes were to be found at the bottom of the social order. The lowest of the low who loathed each other were the Madigas and Malas. Outside necessary economic or patrimonial relationships, communities shunned contact with each other, each often cordially despising the rest. Rituals, marriage, eating, dress, conversation, and other social actions were closely circumscribed by family, gotram, subcaste, and caste rules.[7]

Thus, it is understandable that there were concentric circles of exceedingly complicated competition between elite groups possessing the specialized skills indicated above, between sword-holders and pen-holders at each level and in each area, to say nothing of the larger, extra-village or territorial arenas of political competition. Larger and more sophisticated systems of territorial power developed out of these arenas of competition.

[6] Useful analytical tools are found in the ideas of Karl Deutsch, *Nationalism and Social Communication* (Cambridge, Mass.: Technology Press of MIT & John Wiley & Sons, 1953).

[7] Boswell, J. A. C., *A Manual of Nellore District* (Madras: Government of Madras, 1873), pp. 202–260. Norton, J. B., *A Letter to Lowe on the Condition of the Madras Presidency* (Madras: Pharaoh and Co., 1854), p. 206. See recent sociological and anthropological studies for greater elaboration.

II

The consolidation and rise of the last and perhaps the greatest Hindu system of dynastic power was that which centered in Vijayanagara. This particular concentration of power originated in certain warrior and clerical families of Telugu-Kannada areas, most notably the Reddis and Niyogis. In the wake of Muslim provocations culminating in the incursion of Muhammad Tughluq, there followed a furious bubbling of local power which erupted and spewed tidal waves of regal and then of imperial power across South India. These tides carried Telugu warrior and clerical communities with them, first for extension of power and then for administration; moreover, when these tides finally began to recede, more than two centuries later (after the battle of Talikota in 1565), they left a residue in the form of small, widely scattered social enclaves extending across the land to the very periphery of the tidal expansion. As Vijayanagara power crumbled, the *Nayaks* of Tanjore, Mysore, Madura, and Ramnad and the *Poliyagars* of Anantapur, Cuddapah, and Salem were but a few of the many warrior families which vainly tried to assume high titles and dignities and to retain ever larger revenues and powers. Likewise also, Niyogi families of former generals, ministers, and lesser officers stubbornly clung to steadily dwindling resources and many managed to preserve local strong-holds of power in scattered villages of the south.[8]

Perhaps the next really significant and immediately premodern rise of locally originated, socio-political forces was that of the Marathas. The spread of Maratha influence can conveniently be seen as having occurred in three successive waves: initially, in service to the Deccani Sultanantes; then, in bids for regal and imperial hegemony; and finally, in service to the British Company. Ultimately, this movement of social forces was altogether too diffused and decentralized in origin to achieve political hegemony. Lacking in dynastic centrality and control, Maratha groups were, on the whole, more successful as servants than as masters; moreover, it is in their role as servants that they are of particular interest here.

The very origins of Bahmani power appear to have been linked with support from local, Deccani leadership. Maratha officers and soldiers contributed substantially to the military strength of the kingdom. Revenue management remained in local hands and was conducted in vernacular languages. There is reason to believe that Mahmud Gawan's greatness as an administrator was due to his sagacious employment of groups of Maratha Brahmans who were known as Desasthas. The breakup of Bahmani authority following the senseless execution of this able *Diwan* in 1481 led to increasing dependence upon the services of these Desasthas by the Sultans of Bijapur, Golkonda, and Ahmednagar. Then, as Muslim power expanded southward over the remains of Vijayanagar

<hr/>

[8] R. Sewell, A *Forgotten Empire* (London: Swan Sonnenschein & Co., 1924) is still a minor classic; but I am particularly indebted to the ideas expressed by K. A. Nilakantha Sastri. Also to be consulted are R. Sathianatha Aiyar, *History of the Nayaks of Madura* (Oxford: Oxford University Press, 1924) and *Tamilaham in the 17th Century* (Madras: 1956), together with the works of T. V. Mahalingam, B. A. Saletore, N. Venkataramanayya, and V. Vriddhagirisan. District Manuals are especially helpful sources of social history.

principalities in the last 16th and early 17th centuries, this ascendency brought predictable changes in administrative personnel, changes which were very beneficial for Maratha Brahmans.[9]

On the south bank of the Krishna, the name of the present Guntur District was changed from Kondavidu Sima to Murtazanagar Circar. Desastha (Maratha Brahman) families and families of Golkonda Vyaparis, to whom they were related, were put in control of the financial administration of the area. Niyogis and Velamas were very harshly treated — many being put to the sword — and Kammas were raised to higher military positions in the district.[10]

But as the hegemony of the Qutb Shahis of Golkonda weakened during the century of their ostensible sway, local combinations of power in Guntur became more and more strong. Since political selection was rooted in caste and nourished by nepotism (through kinship), these local combinations silently gained inner and decentralized control, finding nourishment within the state structure without disturbing or causing the collapse of that structure. Khasa Raya Rao retained financial control of the district while his Muslim co-rulers were repeatedly replaced. Neither Raya Rao nor his Desastha successors moved to halt increasing incursions by Mughals and Marathas. Golkonda's power gradually vanished and local autonomy became virtually complete.[11] The Brahman ministers of the last Golkonda king, Akanna and Madanna Pantulu, "governed by means of the inhabitants of the country." [12] This mild and orderly rule by local Brahmans, while smacking of heresy to Sunni fanatics, inspired folklore, songs and legends which still survive." [13]

The houses of Timur and Asaf Jah did not do better in Guntur than the House of Qutb Shah had done. During 65 years, from 1687 to 1752, forty-two Muslim officers (hakims) were appointed to Murtazanagar.[14] But, while these Amildars (Collectors) gave themselves to the entertainments, wars, and intrigues of Hyderabad, James Grant concludes that:

> A certain class of Hindus . . . relieved their ignorant voluptuous Mussalman rulers from the intricate details of internal police and the management of mofussil collections.[15]

[9] M. G. Ranade, *Rise of the Maratha Power and Other Essays* (Bombay: University of Bombay, 1961), pp. 1:19. R. Sathianatha Aiyar, *Tamilaham in the 17th Century.* (Madras: 1956).

[10] Elliot Mss., *op. cit.*, "Origin of Village Accountants," p. 101; and "Translations of Dandakavile at Condavid Village by Vinnacotta Venkanah," pp. 331 ff.; and Volume III, "Historical Memoir of Chebrole in the Districts of Chintapilly," p. 100, translated from Telugu into Marathi and from Marathi into English by Venkata Rao in 1817.

[11] *Ibid.*, vol. I, p. 332.

[12] *Ibid.*, pp. 333–34. Read parallel accounts in Mackenzie, *op. cit.*, pp. 35–38, and H. Morris, *A Descriptive and Historical Account of the Godavery District* (London: Trubner & Co., 1878), pp. 167–76. *Note:* Tanisha, the last king, probably had good practical reasons for keeping local Hindu bureaucracies. Firmans indicate that these Shia kings developed a sophisticated state cult in which their kingship was deified.

[13] Elliot Mss., vol. I, *op. cit.*, p. 101. Mackenzie, *op. cit.*, p. 38.

[14] *Ibid.*, vol. II, "Lists of Hakims or Officers Administering the Gontoor and Ellore Circars," pp. 62–71.

[15] James Grant, "Political Survey of the Northern Circars." Cf. W. K. Firminger (ed.), *The Fifth Report*, vol. III (Calcutta: R. Cambray & Co., 1918), p. 26.

The ancient administrative machinery of the district, "merely an extension of village institutions in circles of villages," [16] remained largely undisturbed. Only the district administrative titles changed, *Desmukh* (Executive), *Despandi* (Accountant-Registrar), and *Mannavar* (Head of Police) being Marathi and *Mazmudar* (Auditor) and *Sarrishtadar* (Chief Secretary) being Persian in origin.

III

These hereditary district officers, acting as buffers between local inhabitants and foreign intruders and as cementing agents between opposed cultures, religions, customs, and languages, were at the time indiscriminately labelled and perhaps mislabelled *Zamindars* by Hyderabad officials.[17] The semi-feudal chieftains and ancient Gajapati lords of Ganjam and Vizagapatam, the appointed Desasthas, Kammas, and other elites of the Godavari-Krishna Doab, the Poliyagars and other robber chiefs of the Carnatic, and the Nayaks of the south all came under this common label. Nevertheless, although these Zamindars possessed distinct functions and powers and although, in Guntur, each was chosen from a different caste — the sword-holders being Kammas, Telegas, and Velamas while the pen-holders were Desasthas [18] — the Hyderabad regime failed to prevent the silent combination of local power systems in its districts. In the words of Walter Elliot:

> . . . a continual struggle was carried on between the *Sir Subah* and the Hyderabad Sirkar on the one hand, and the *Sir Subah* and the Zamindars on the other: while these had a similar game to play with village officers and Ryots. The whole gave rise to a general system of evasion and deceit.[19]

As Hyderabad power relaxed, Zamindari power grew stronger.

But, while they walked like gods, upon the earth, playing off Mughal, Maratha, British, and French power to greatest advantage, the Zamindars themselves in turn fell prey to the same inner pressures, which were besetting Hyderabad, and were themselves devoured by corrosive influences arising out of the villages. In their little "states," they isolated themselves by mutual distrust; they cut themselves off from the assistance which a superior system of power might have afforded; and they lost the support of their own servants in turn. Being propped up later by the British merely prolonged the collapse of institutions which were already dead husks, monuments of defunct power systems.

[16] Walter Elliot (Report on Guntur District) to Government of Madras (para. 99), April 17, 1846: *Madras Revenue Proceedings and Consultations* (IOL: range 3281 vol. 20), December 6, 1847.

[17] Great Britain. House of Commons. *The Fifth Report of 1812, Appendix 13.* James Grant, "Political Survey of the Northern Circars" (IOL: Parliamentary Collection No. 56, pp. 631–32).

[18] There were four Zamindaris in Guntur: i.e. the Kammavaru Vasireddy family of Chintapalli and Amaravati, the Telegavaru Malrazu family of Navasaraopet, the Vellemavaru Manika Rao family of Repali, and the Desastha Manur Rao families of Chilkalurpet and Sattanapalli.

[19] Walter Elliot's Report to Government of Madras (para. 13), *op. cit.*

The Great Vasireddy, Venkatadri Naidu, was the last great Zamindar of Guntur. In collusion with local leaders, he deceived the British to the real resources of over five hundred villages under his authority. He scrupulously paid his tribute to the British. He kept a retinue of several thousand men, 300 horses, 80 elephants, 50 camels, and uncounted bullock carts. The magnificence of his palaces at Amaravati, Chebrolu, and Chintapelli, and his town-house in Guntur became subjects of folklore. He built temples and repaired the lofty *gopuram* (temple gate) at Mangalagiri. Over a 100 richly gilt brass pillars, 30 feet high, were erected in his name at various shrines. Daily he fed hundreds of *purohits* (priests) and employed them to pray for him day and night. Often he distributed shawls, gold, and jewels among learned sadhus. The sums he spent on festivals, sacrifices, fire offerings, and marriages became legendary. Several times he divided his own weight in gold or silver among Brahmans. At great feasts and on "auspicious" occasions, he gave clothing and gifts to village leaders and their wives. On pilgrimage in Benares, he delivered rich gifts to the ex-Peshwa, Baji Rao; and on his way home from Ramesvaram, he paid the Nizam a *nazar* (gifts) of a lakh of pagodas just for the empty title of "Manur Sultan." [20]

The Zamindars of Guntur vied with each other to keep up this brilliant ostentation, indulging in every vanity and fancy to such a degree that their annual spending would have supported "13 battalions of Native Infantry." [21] Such extravagance led to rapid decay, the old story of dynastic decline occurring in miniature. Instead of zanana poisons, rebellions, and wars, family members and servants conspired and intrigued against each other. Supervision was relaxed for the sake of pleasure. Death resulted in disputed inheritance. Debts accumulated. Power was entrusted to Diwans bent on quick gains. Even though they reached lower and lower into the villages for needed funds, revenues failed to materialize.[22]

Again using the Vasireddy Zamindari as an example, when Venkatadri Naidu died in 1816, a struggle of baffling complexity ensued. Liquid assets of 5.5 million pounds of sterling disappeared within two years, insomuch that gold and silver had to be peeled off pillars and copper off the roofs of palaces in order to pay *saukars* (bankers). Litigation over the disputed succession lasted thirty years.[23] Two Diwans (who were friends) pursued the litigation, hired pandits, bribed witnesses, bought mantrams, furnished entertainments, and

[20] Elliot Report (para. 7), *ibid.*, John Goldingham to C. R. Cotton (paras. 13–17, 30), December 13, 1839; *Madras Revenue Proceedings & Consultations* (range 380: vol. 7: pp. 2470–74), No. 30 of April 16, 1841. The Goldingham Report is a lengthy study of the social and economic conditions of Guntur.

[21] Elliot Report (para. 7).

[22] Goldingham Report (paras. 46, 38), *op. cit.* In the case of Guntur Zamindars, the Permanent Settlement was set at an amount far below what was recommended by either Collector or Zamindars; moreover, roughly 90 lakhs of rupees in public and private debts were cancelled and full revenue payments were deferred eight years. Even so, in 1837, the Zamindars were worse off than they had been in 1802, when the settlement was made.

[23] Goldingham Report (para. 30); Elliot Report (paras. 7, 16), *op. cit.*

finally provided loans for the young heirs (who were also friends). How this case moved by intricate turns through a tangled maze of English procedures, Hindu laws, and a court hierarchy is a story of 115 pages.[24] When the decision was finally handed down from the Privy Council in London, the issue no longer mattered; for the fortune was gone, the Zamindari was gone; many disputants were dead; and two Desastha families were known to be the wealthiest in that part of the country.[25]

If the Zamindars were betrayed by their own family members and servants, they also engaged in a disastrous tug-of-war with village leaders. Financial pressure brought them into collision with Karnams and Ryots who themselves sought to keep back as much as possible. Both sides used every trick of deception and artifice of ingenuity.

The best hope of a Zamindar lay in cracking the shell of village solidarity. By dividing a village against itself and driving a wedge between leading communities or factions, he could play upon discord to pry out what he wanted. While one group of village leaders would grow fat, the rest would be picked clean. The favoured would attend *darbars, tamashas,* and *melas* would be flattered with gifts of cloth and jewels, advances for seed, and loans for special need. The recalcitrant would be coerced with ingenious instruments, imaginative tortures, and frightening invocations of evil spirits. There were countless methods of exaction.[26]

Villages, however, were not unequal to such struggles. So long as their respective leaders remained united and were able to form silent combinations, they could present a tight phalanx. Secrecy was their shield and bribery their sword. Operating silently, they encroached on Zamindars with unremitting pressure, deceiving inspectors, bribing eyes until they closed, hiding true records, spiriting crops away by night, and burying wealth in secret places. At every turn, with disarming submissiveness and apparent poverty, these leaders matched wits with the Zamindars and their servants.[27]

---

[24] E. F. Moore (ed.), *Reports of Cases Heard and Determined by the Committee of the Privy Council on Appeal from the Supreme and Sudder Dewanny Court in the East Indies, Vol. IV: 1846–50* (London: 1930), pp. 1–113. Governor Munro found the heirs tired of the suit and willing to stop; but the Diwans prevented this. Cf. A. J. Arbuthnot, *Selections from . . . Writings of Sir Thomas Munro* (Madras: Higginbotham & Co., for Madras University, 1886), p. 196.

[25] Gordon Mackenzie, *op. cit.*, p. 314.

[26] Elliot Report (para. 16), *op. cit.*, examples of chants and spells are found in Elliot's note books. Cf. R. Sewell, *Sir Walter Elliot of Welfelee* (Edinburgh: 1896). Arzi (Deposition) of S. V. R. Rao on conditions in Guntur Zillah, Appendix A of Goldingham Report, *op. cit.* P. B. Smollet, *Civil Administration of Madras* (London: Richardson Bros., 1858), pp. 1–34. J. B. Norton, *A Letter . . . on the Condition of the Presidency of Madras,* p. 206. *The Torture Commission Report* (Madras: Government of Madras, 1855), pp. 14, 17, 36–47, reveals methods of exaction which were customary.

[27] Daniel Smith to Board of Revenue, June 21, 1806 Extract in Elliot Report (paras. 82–83), *op. cit.* Knowledgeable village leaders were by no means blind to the impunity afforded to themselves by Regulation XXX of 1802. Cf. F. R. Hemingway, *Godavery District Gazetteer* (Madras: 1907), pp. 164 ff.

IV

The new bureaucracy which came into influence with the emergence of British rule owed its origin to an early start and near monopoly in language, the English language. European traders in India required the services of go-betweens or interpreters. Depending upon caste or function, these go-betweens were variously called *Dubashis, Banyas, Diwans,* or in later times, *Babus.*[28]

A small compact group of Desastha Brahmans who knew English and who, by beating competitors and by jealously guarding and transmitting their secret skills through family apprenticeships, monopolized this knowledge of English, became entrenched in Guntur before the turn of the 19th century.[29] The key officer and leader of this elite of district officers was the Huzur Sheristadar, the go-between of go-betweens. This elite group had family links with the Manur Rao, Desastha Zamindars within the district, and with other Maratha Brahman families throughout South India.[30] At times, the group became so strong that it dominated the administration, resisted Government policies, and either thwarted or else sought to corrupt and even ruin successive British officers. Whenever control from Madras became weak, their power grew strong. Each growth of Maratha strength awoke internal factional strife, in which one group was supported by the Manur Rao while the other was supported by the Vasireddy.[31]

A serious disturbance of this kind occurred in 1811.[32] Twenty years of control by two stronger Collectors followed; but another six years of weakness, in which fourteen British officers migrated through the Collectorship like wandering strangers and a third of the population was swept away by famine and pestilence, more than sufficed to bring submerged enmities to the surface.[33] In

[28] We have already noted how such groups entered Guntur in the Golkonda period. M. Ruthnaswamy, *Some Influences that Made the British Administrative System in India* (London: Luzac & Co., 1939), pp. 87, 293.

[29] A fascinating account of how English was learned under the old system of education is found in: V. V. Gopal Row, *The Life of Vennelacunty Soob Row, Native of Ongole, Translator and Interpreter to the Late Surdr Court, Madras, from 1815 to 1829.* (Madras: Government of Madras, 1873).

[30] *Ibid.,* pp. 1–30, 62–70. Soob Row, in visiting other districts, had an uncle, a cousin, a wife's brother, etc. who was Huzur Sheristadar, Head Munshi, Head English Accountant and so on. See also: J. A. B. Dykes, *Salem: An Indian Collectorate* (London: 1852), pp. 332, 327, E. H. Aitken, *Behind the Bungalow* (Calcutta: Thackeray, Spink & Co., 1889), p. 75.

[31] For details see: R. E. Frykenberg, *The Administration of Guntur District with Special Reference to Local Influences on Revenue Policy: 1837–1848* (London: Unpublished Thesis, 1961), chaps. 3 and 4.

[32] F. W. Robertson to Board of Revenue, February 21, 25, April 15, May 19, June 15, July 1, August 20, 1811: *Guntur District Records* (vol. 385: pp. 23–39, 44–50, 66–74, 211–223; . . . 303–320). Many of these letters are found in Appendix C of Elliot Report, *op. cit.*

[33] Elliot Report (para. 96), *ibid.,* "Chart of Officers appointed Acting or Permanent to the Office of Collector." Mackenzie, *op. cit.,* pp. 113, 358. A graphic description of the great Guntur Famine was made by Col. Walter Campbell, *My Indian Journal* (Edinburgh: Edmonston & Douglas, 1864), p. 424.

1837, a struggle between the contending forces in the district broke out and the new Collector was caught in the middle.

John Goldingham found that "the district had suffered greatly because of irregularities" and that both the governmental structure and the people were threatened. Without first "removing those who had brought about this state of things, who by their commanding influence in the Huzur [were] organizing instead of checking corruption," he could see no remedy.[34] Ready assistance was offered by the faction which had been trying for thirty years to displace the ruling oligarchy. Sabnavis Venkata Krishna Rao was made Huzur Sheristadar by the Collector; and he promptly began to fill the administration with his own men.[35]

The metal of the old leaders, however, had yet to be put to the test. Under the leadership of Nyapati Shashagiri Rao, a veteran with more than thirty years experience, the entrenched were able to turn back every assault upon their position. In this they were solidly supported by the Madras Board of Revenue. Time after time, Shashagiri Rao went over the head of the Collector. Krishna Rao's appointment was disallowed; and Shashagiri Rao was forced upon the Collector. Each time Goldingham dismissed him, invariably the Board insisted that he be reinstated as Huzur Sheristadar. After each contest of strength, the Sheristadar's prestige went up while that of the Collector went down. All Goldingham's careful reports were rejected and his pleadings were unavailing insomuch that, after five years of this, he begged the Governor to send him to another district. The rival faction was defeated and the old leaders prevailed.[36]

The crowning exhibition of local power was Shashagiri Rao's scheme to discredit the new Collector, to increase the power of his group, and to conciliate village leaders, all at one blow. For over three years, Huddleston Stokes was unaware that:

> . . . the whole of his servants were in league against him and that they made common cause with the people, both parties participating in the advantages to be gained at the expense of the revenue.[37]

Suspicions which he voiced and mild suggestions for improving efficiency were quashed. The Board of Revenue held it wrong to go against the judgment of so old and trusted a servant as Shashagiri Rao, even on simple and valid points.[38] By the time Stokes realized the full nature of the conspiracy against

---

[34] John Goldingham to Board of Revenue (paras. 2–14), January 5, 1839; *Guntur District Records* (vol. 5397: 1–24).

[35] Board of Revenue to Goldingham, November 9, 1837: *Guntur District Records* (vol. 5368: p. 281); and Goldingham to Board of Revenue, November 24, 1837: *Guntur District Records* (vol. 5393: pp. 222–227).

[36] Elliot Report (paras. 55–58), *op. cit.* Daniel White (Report) to Board of Revenue (paras. 39–42, 61), July 10, 1845; *Guntur District Records* (No. 58 in vol. 5404; pp. 79:139).

[37] Elliot Report (para. 50), *ibid.*

[38] Board of Revenue Proceedings, November 10, 1842; *Guntur District Records* (vol.

himself and against the State, his health had broken and he was forced to go to the Cape on sick leave.

The new Acting Collector, a young and inexperienced officer named Lockhart, was no match for the wily old Sheristadar and was completely taken in. By this time, however, people in Madras were beginning to suspect that something was drastically wrong in the Northern Circars and particularly in Guntur. Although the economy had recovered from the great famine of 1833, district revenues had dropped from 12.2 lakhs to an all-time low of 5.5 lakhs. Henry Montgomery's report on Rajahmundry pointed to a silent and subversive conspiracy as the root of that district's troubles. A district-wide network of officers had been diverting revenues from the treasury to themselves.[39]

Walter Elliot, one of the most experienced and able Civilians in Madras, and Appa Rao, one of the best Maratha Brahmans in the Presidency, were sent to Guntur. These officers plunged immediately to the root of the trouble. Karnams of a hundred villages were ordered to appear and show their records. These village leaders dutifully presented themselves but, when asked about their records, could only make appropriate sounds and gestures of sorrow. "Without exception, they declared that no such accounts existed." [40] Zamindars had taken their accounts into custody. Fire had destroyed. Thieves had broken in. Storms and floods had come. White ants and silver fish had eaten. Misplaced books disappeared and became lost. Brother or uncle who normally kept books was away on pilgrimage, was sick unto death, was no more — and who could tell what *he* knew? The Commissioner and his Sheristadar, however, knew where and how to poke and probe. The records of Takkalapadu (Village) were ferreted out and severe examples of punishment were made; and suddenly, many remembered where their records were kept. Amid more gestures and sounds of sorrow, much extortion and bribery were confessed.

At this, the district officers took alarm. Acting as a group, they bent every effort to stifle the investigation and counter the Commission's work. Obstacles of every sort, small and big, were thrown up. As the first effects of Elliot's presence wore off, and as they were bolstered up by promises, bribes, and threats, many of the Karnams rallied and resisted with every device of their imaginations. Elliot soon became convinced that he was confronting something more than just ordinary corruption. As he put it, "a general and well organized combination of the Collector's establishment — was able at once to act with

---

5373: pp. 431–457), dealing with Stokes' letter of October 25, 1842. How Guntur affairs looked from Madras on the eve of Stokes' departure may be found in the Board's Proceedings on the Jamabandi Report for Fasli 1252, August 26, 1844: *Guntur District Records* (vol. 5373: pp. 297–337).

[39] Sir Henry Montgomery to George Drury (Madras Government Chief Secretary), March 18, 1844: *Madras Records Proceedings and Consultations* (range 280: vols. 48, 49: pp. 2090–2292), No. 8 of May 28, 1844. The records of this period were filled with heated controversy on how to deal with the Guntur problem. A bitter fight occurred between Governor Tweeddale and Henry Chamier, the First Member in Council. See Nos. 42–48 of September 10, 1844, *Madras Revenue Proceedings & Consultations* (range 280: vol. 52).

[40] Elliot Report (para. 24), *op. cit.*

vigor and concert throughout every part of the district." [41] Nevertheless, while Shashagiri Rao held court and sent messengers from his house in Guntur, Elliot and Appa Rao moved relentlessly from village to village.

Affairs in most of the major villages of the district were investigated.[42] Almost invariably, after original village accounts were separated from those which were spurious — there were often three sets: one for the Zamindar, one for the State, and the true one, — years of unauthorized collections, extortionate rack-renting, and extensive bribery would be uncovered. Attempts to palm off fabricated accounts were the rule. Some false accounts had been written and kept ready for years, ready to be shown on the right occasion. True accounts were found in wells or tanks, torn up or burned, buried, hidden in grain, or otherwise disposed of when an inspector came too near. Once, a whole house was set ablaze to destroy damning records. The inspector got out. The records didn't.[43]

Elliot's report on Guntur came as a shock to British authorities in Madras and London. In less than twelve years Madras had lost over 74 lakhs, more than six times the annual revenue from the district.[44] Disclosures from other districts soon revealed that Guntur was no isolated case.

V

It is clear that, just as district officers undermined central authority, they in turn were undermined by village leaders. As soon as a subordinate officer accepted village money, he was vulnerable (or responsible) only until he brought his superior into the transaction. By passing blame to his superior, he shielded himself from the wrath to come. The higher corrupting influence of villages spread into the hierarchy of power, the more shields there were between village leaders and eventual retribution. Level by level, superiors became prisoners to those below them and risked exposure and discipline from those above them. Power became caught and tangled in the webs of village, caste, and family influence. The strength of Madras Presidency was tied to the earth by countless tiny threads and was made captive to Lilliputian systems of power.

The Huzur Sheristadar was most vulnerable. Blame stopped with him. When revenues failed, he had to supply reasons. Bad climate, disease, and low prices served as excuses for only so long. The gullibility, inefficiency, wrong judgment, or laziness of the British Government had limits. Then the blow would fall and vacancies would occur in the upper cadres. But the Guntur leaders were accustomed to this; and indeed, they had gone through the process several times without their re-entry into district service being jeopardized. Their very uncertain tenure, combined with their preferred status and their nepotistic hold on

[41] Elliot Report (para. 25), *ibid.*
[42] Elliot Report (paras. 27–28, 43–48), *ibid.*
[43] Elliot Report (para. 27), *ibid.*
[44] Court of Directors to Government of Madras (paras. 29–31), January 31, 1849: *Madras Despatches* (vol. 111: pp. 455–530), No. 1 of 1849. A summary of reactions at each level may be obtained in the *Board's Collections*, Nos. 116, 221, Vol. 2272 (i.e. Board of Control) in the India Office Library.

the high positions, encouraged them to make the most of their moments in power. Family and caste loyalty — Shashagiri Rao alone had 74 family members in district service within Guntur — and steady pressure from lower levels tended to compel collusive operations.[45]

In light of such circumstances, the question as to whether systematic collusion and corruption originated and were organized by Desasthas at the top or village leaders at the bottom of the district hierarchy is hard to answer. But basic orientation of segmented social values being such that primary loyalties were directed to family (or caste) and village (or patrimonial) interests and obligations, rather than loyalties to any general population, wider "public," or centralized system of political power, it is not difficult to presume that propensities for such behaviour to originate could be found at every level. Once such behaviour began or corrupting operations reached a more advanced stage, however, Desasthas would do all possible to organize and control the process in their own interests. But again, in this they would have to match wits with village leaders of other castes.

Over the long run, the British were able to devise some very thorough and lasting solutions to stem localizing power processes, perhaps more thorough and lasting than had ever been done before. They combined a growing awareness of problems with a realistically self-critical, self-corrective, and analytical faculty which was being carried along in the main stream of the growing and modernizing technological age. British resources and persistence had a relentless, almost machine-like, quality so that, while wheels turned slowly, they were able to make steady progress.

It was realized that local forces were able to blunt government measures because of their facility in forming silent combinations and thereby in controlling channels of communication. By hiding or fabricating vital information, local leaders kept rulers in ignorance or worse, in partial ignorance. Remedies were devised. Regularly appointed and paid Village Headmen (called *Munsifs*) were installed as a counterpoise to the Karnams. Marathi as a medium of exchange between Telugu and English was abolished. Record offices, which had been kept in such purposeful muddles that an estimated six years were needed to set them in order were eventually reorganized completely.[46] English schools admitting members from all communities were established during the 1840's and 1850's; and these broke the Maratha Brahman monopoly on the higher administrative positions. Shortly thereafter, in 1861, the doors to the Indian Civil Service were opened to Indians, thus providing an escape valve for the

[45] Elliot Report (para. 58), *op. cit.* A detailed report on the activities of this remarkable Sheristadar was made by Daniel White to the Board of Revenue, July 10, 1845: *Guntur District Records* (vol. 5405: pp. 79–139).

[46] A detailed list of recommendations for Guntur which were slowly carried out during the next 20 years is contained in paras. 82–105 of the Elliot Report. Complaints about Marathi were made by J. D. Bourdillon, in his *Remarks on the Ryotwar System of Land Revenue as It Exists in the Presidency of Madras* (Madras: 1853) and by J. B. Norton, *A Letter . . . on the Condition of the Presidency of Madras*, p. 136.

energies of the Desasthas and other groups who soon would follow them.[47] Finally, regulations were passed at about the same time which forbade any two members of the same family from serving in the same district and any two members of the same caste from sharing the two top positions in the District Headquarters (*Huzur Cutcherry*).[48] Successful implementation of these policies released a sequence of revolutionary social changes which are still continuing today.

VI

Our analysis of the history of Guntur has revealed that from generation to generation local interests sought to resist interference and non-local interests sought to interefere in the affairs of a deltic area. Localizing forces arising from villages struggled with each other but combined to thwart the actions of predatory forces from outside. Centralizing agents tried to enforce compliance from local leaders. Localizing energies tried to corrupt and undermine "foreign" agencies. Clashes of sword and pen occurred within the intermediate institutions and areas between the villages and the cities where regal power centered. Struggle revolved around the corruptibility or loyalty of go-betweens. In the days of the Company Bahadur, as in former days, localizing and centralizing forces collided in the actual day-to-day politics and functions of government; moreover, they left marks in degrees of disorganization or organization, in channels and blockades, in staff selections and reshuffles, in black ink and red-tape, and in countless decisions and forms set up to control or obstruct political machinery. The side which most thoroughly controlled this machinery saw its interests advance.

It should be apparent by now that, in seeking to understand exceedingly complex processes of power, deliberate care has been taken to avoid confusing or indiscriminate use of the term "state." This Western concept, though increasingly refined and broken down into various categories by political theorists, so far largely fails to fit the circumstances of institutionalized systems of power which prevailed in pre-modern India. By state we usually mean an entity defining a condition of political existence with processes which have at least certain minimum attributes. Such a system of power must be organized so as to have exclusive and formal (or legitimate) authority enabling it to exercise supreme force (or sanctions) within a definite and integrated territory over an indefinite but continuous period of time. But the existence of a formal, territorially expanding, organizationally sophisticating, and administratively centralizing accretion of power called "state" poses questions as to whether less formal if not

[47] A. Howell, *Education in India prior to 1854 and in 1871* (Calcutta: 1872), is most useful on this subject. For a view of what happened at the local level, see John Nobel, *A Memoir of the Rev. Robert T. Noble, Missionary to the Telugu People of India* (London: Seeley, Jackson & Halliday, 1867), pp. 266–71, 190, 292, 296, 350. See also: A. J. Arbuthnot, *Papers Relating to Public Instruction in Madras* (Madras: 1855).

[48] T. G. K. Pillay, *The Revenue Compendium of Madras Presidency*, Volume 1 (Madras: Basel Mission Press, 1873), pp. 120–123.

clandestine, ever simplifying and fragmenting systems of power can, as shadow forms of power, be so constituted that they inadvertently act to negate state power.

Search for new analytical concepts adequate for dealing with baffling political forms and processes in the non-Western world must lead at times to some almost bizarre new approach. It is helpful in some such cases to construct a mock-up to serve as a working model; and in this we can perhaps learn from the physical or biological sciences. Drawing a parallel from concepts of "anti-matter" and "anti-body," I have fabricated a mock-up concept and called it "anti-state." [49] "Anti-state," as used here, denotes a kind of political system which, residing within a state, disperses its power and proliferates itself to the detriment of the State and acts in such a way that it not only naturally opposes but actually prevents the State from functioning properly. In this sense, by covert or overt antagonism to any exogenous or "foreign" system of power, "anti-state" types of power cannot be anything but antigenic and antidotal to the normal processes and tendencies of state power, as defined above. Thus, if state is conceived to be a positive element, anti-state is negative (or vice versa). But, in either case, although their processes may be characteristically different — the one centralizing and the other localizing — , both are conceived essentially as being systems of power.

In other terms, it is significant that historical sources for pre-modern India have very little to show in the way of maps and very little to say about boundaries between larger systems of power.[50] Certainly great kings liked to note the number and size of their provinces, districts, and villages; but these notes were either vague or otherwise abstract. Indeed, with the exception of occasional boundary disputes between villages, we know virtually nothing about the boundaries of dynastic systems. Even villages have shown a distinct aversion to fixity of boundary markers. Of great cities where power was centralized and its splendor made apparent, such as Tanjore, Vijayanagara, Hyderabad, and Poona, we can be sure. But of frontiers, we can only grope in blind uncertainty. Furthermore, we read of annual forays by the armies of each power in which opposing forces crossed and re-crossed what we would normally feel to be the lands of other dynastic systems with impunity and with little regard for the niceties of territorial integrity. If this were not enough, different centralized powers seem to have ruled congruently over the same territories, to have shared the same intermediate agencies and administrative apparatus, and to have laid claim to revenues from the same villages. (The Peshwas of Poona and the Nizam of Hyderabad did this in the 18th century, to name just one example.) What the British found when they came to Guntur in 1788 serves as a prize example of indeterminate and diffused power. Roughly a thousand villages were so intermingled among the four great zamindari families that "the Zamindars

---

[49] "Counter-state" has also been suggested by one helpful critic, as an alternate term.

[50] I am aware of some references to boundaries in the chronicles of the time and of the existence of boundary stones, hedges, etc., but this does not affect the point I am making about the political reality of the boundaries.

might have done just as well if they had drawn their villages by lot" — some villages were actually shared by two or three Zamindars.[51]

In his *Twilight of the Mughals*, Percival Spear drew a parallel between conditions of North India, where the State regarded sturdy villagers as bandits and local lords regarded the State as a robber, and Augustine's incisive observation — "The State is a great robber band, for robber bands, what are they but little states?" [52] The same parallel might be drawn with pre-modern South India. Only what seems to emerge from our analysis of South India are "box-within-box" congeries of robber bands within robber bands, composite systems of power within power with varying amounts of state and anti-state properties. Moreover, the larger and more regal or imperial was a traditional system of power, the less it retained of the accepted properties of a state, by Western standards. Shortages of loyal and dependable manpower, which could only come from the limited resources of family and caste, became more apparent as power grew to imperial strength. But the smaller and more local was a system, the more it took on the properties of a state. The Sword and Pen of Hyderabad was far less indivisible than that of Chebrole.

Largest (if not only) degrees of political homogeneity seem to have existed in a bewildering variety of very local patrimonial systems (of extended families and villages) which were often territorially dispersed by other intervening, "foreign," but local systems. These local systems, all interlocked within larger structures and wider areas, functioned with reference to each other as tiny states and with reference to regal or imperial forces as anti-states — giving signs of submission in forms of compliance and tokens of revenue but reserving as much substance as possible for themselves. One can find no broad bedrock of ultimate loyalty beyond family, caste, and village and beyond patrimonial relationships surrounding an intricate complexity of local lords and lordlings of the soil.

VII

So far the primary emphasis of this study has been on one area. We have made an intensive and comparative examination of events in one district of South India. But we should not delude ourselves by thinking that our findings pertain only to an exceptional, isolated case or that the phenomena described do not have broader applicability. Indeed, evidences of political processes such as those observed in Guntur can be found in the history of virtually every part of South India.

Instances of localizing influence in various parts of the peninsula have been too numerous even to catalogue. A few cases where sword or pen was so exercised may be cited, however, simply to show the wider prevalence of the processes in question. During the 1830's alone, when Company power was at its zenith, the Purla-Kimedi and Gumsur rebellions led to costly jungle cam-

[51] Gordon Mackenzie, *Manual of Kistna District* (Madras: 1883), p. 345.
[52] Spear, Percival, *Twilight of the Mughals* (Cambridge: University Press, 1952), p. 126.

paigns; [53] there was a rising of the Moplahs in Malabar,[54] an insurrection in Canara,[55] and an outbreak among the Khond tribes; [56] the Nawab of Kurnool was implicated in the Wahabi conspiracy; [57] and a threat of revolt in Mysore had to be investigated.[58] S. R. Chaudhri's *Civil Disturbances during the British Rule in India: 1756–1857* (Calcutta: 1955) serves to list the more violent incidents. The history of recurring mutiny within the British-Indian army in India is well enough established not to warrant repetition here.[59] In the sphere of collusion and subversion, perhaps the most notorious case in the Madras Presidency was that of Casee Chetty, the Coimbatore Treasurer whose ingenious fabrications and daring embezzlements became so extensive that he came to regard the administration as his shop and the district as his commodity for trade. For a decade he used British power for his own purposes and reaped enormous profits. His dismissal in 1817 was based upon known embezzlements amounting to 418,316 pagodas.[60] Subversive combinations prompted the British to take over the administration of Mysore in 1830.[61] During the decade between 1840 and 1850, serious administrative deterioration in Vellore, South Arcot, Madura, Rajahmundry, Bellary, Tinnevelly, and Masulipatam, successively provoked the Madras authorities into appointing special commissions of enquiry.[62] Henry Ricketts, the Commissioner appointed to investigate administrative organization throughout India, wrote concerning South India:

> . . . in every district, in a greater or lesser degree, the whole body of public servants form a combination, bound together by strong ties of interest (not only out of hope of gain but out of fear of injury) and often of family or caste connection, to maintain abuses.[63]

[53] Russell, G. E., *Report on the Disturbances in Purla Kimedy, Vizapapatam and Goomsoor in 1832–36* (Madras: Government of Madras, 1856); Selections from Records series.

[54] Innes and Evans, *Malabar District Gazetteer* (Madras: Government of Madras, 1908), pp. 83–89.

[55] Letters on Canara Insurrection: *Elphinstone Collection* (IOL: Eur. Mss. F. 87), Box 3–C, Nos. 8–13.

[56] T. J. Maltby, *A Manual of Ganjam District* (Madras: W. H. Moore, 1882), pp. 154–59.

[57] N. G. Chetty, *A Manual of Kurnool District* (Madras: Government of Madras, 1886), p. 41.

[58] Shashagherry Row to Commissioner, October 15, 1838; Elphinstone Collection, *op. cit.*, No. 39.

[59] Ruthnaswamy, M., *Some Influences that Made the British Administrative System in India*, pp. 220–227.

[60] Ruthnaswamy, *op. cit.*, pp. 303–306. *Selections of Papers from the Records of the East India Company* (London: 1820–26), Vol. I, 1820. It was Sir Thomas Munro who finally unveiled the work of Casee Chetty.

[61] Venkatasubha Sastri, K. N., *The Administration of Mysore Under Sir Mark Cubbon* (London: G. Allen & Unwin, Ltd., 1932), pp. 1–31.

[62] Although District Manuals will mention these cases, full treatment is only to be found by consulting respective series of district records.

[63] Ricketts, H., *Report of the Commissioner for the Revision of Civil Salaries and Establishments* (Calcutta: John Grey, "Bengal Harkuru" Press, 1858), part I, p. 343.

He reckoned the average siphoning of revenues into the pockets of Desastha officers at a minimum of 70 lakhs of rupees a year for Madras Presidency.[64]

Finally, taking a longer view of traditional processes which have been shown clearly to have existed during the days of the Company, there seems to be little doubt that localizing tendencies have played a dominant role in the history of South India. The comparatively small proportions of time in which greatly centralized powers have held sway in local areas, the indirect and delegated and socially segmented (or insulated) quality of central power under great kingdoms and empires, and the narrowly constricted and compartmentalized nature of socially "civic" or "public" spirit and political consensus in pre-modern times were probably the chief contributing factors behind this tradition.

[64] *Ibid.*, p. 346.

Peasantry and Gentry:
An Interpretation of Chinese Social Structure and Its Changes

HSIAO-TUNG FEI

The polarization of the rich and the poor gives birth to a social dichotomy common in many advanced communities. Benjamin Disraeli used "The Two Nations" as the alternative title for his *Sybil*, a story describing the social life in nineteenth-century England. That describes our traditional China equally well. Probably more than 80 per cent of the Chinese are peasants. They are poor but they are economically productive. In a country in which industry and commerce are not yet fully developed, the peasants are the sole producers. Those who stay at the peak of the social pyramid are the leisure class — the gentry — a minority who live on rent collected from the peasants. Wealth and poverty create not only an economic difference which separates the rich from the poor but a social gulf between the two classes as well. The people thus separated carry on their lives differently. The upper class live in a more elaborate structure of social relations and are more sophisticated and more articulate. They are usually considered as the cultured group, while the majority of the population,

From the *American Journal of Sociology*, Vol. LII, No. 1 (July 1946), pp. 1–12, 17, by permission of The University of Chicago Press. Copyright 1946 by The University of Chicago.

HSIAO-TUNG FEI is presently retired and living in China. He was Professor of Sociology at Yunnan University, China. A student of Malinowski, Park, and Radcliffe-Brown, he obtained his doctorate from the University of London. He is the author of *Peasant Life in China* (1939), *Earthbound China* (1945), *Chinese Gentry* (1953), and other writings.

engaged in the hard work of production, leaves little impression on observers and little trace in historical documents. When the historians exalt or condemn the Greeks or the Romans, they have in mind only the warriors and the philosophers. Is it not also true that China has been praised and criticized according to that China which is found in Western museums, exhibited in art galleries, and described by writers of best-sellers? The China so represented comprises only the minority, the leisured gentry. A fair view of China, however, should include both the poor and the rich and the relation between them.

I

Peasantry, the key toward understanding China, is a way of living, a complex of formal organization, individual behavior, and social attitudes, closely knit together for the purpose of husbanding land with simple tools and human labor. Peasants are settled and sedentary. Growth of population on limited resources puts the law of diminishing returns in effective operation. Cultivation of land tends to be intensified. Minute care of the soil and delicate application of human labor hinder the utilization of improved tools. Standard of living lowers as population increases. Animal labor becomes uneconomical. Highly developed application of human skill in handling soil and crops yields a return only sufficient for a bare existence. When work is mainly done by hands and feet, the advantage of division of work is reduced. Extensive organization in such enterprises gives no appreciable profit but rather complicates human relations. This accounts for the fact that among the peasant society the basic group is usually small.

The smallness of the co-operative group is characteristic of peasantry. Peasants, unlike nomads, live in settled communities. They are nonaggressive because, on the one hand, extension of land beyond the ability of cultivation means little to them, and, on the other, living in a rural environment, they face no immediate threat of innovation or invasion. Security is a matter of course. There seems to be no necessity for any militant organization on a large scale.

This is perhaps one reason why the family is so predominant in the structure of social organization in a peasant community. The family in a peasant community is a sufficient unit to provide the necessary and minimum social co-operation in everyday economic pursuits. Such co-operation is maintained by, or rather an extension of, another main task of the human race, that of reproduction. The mutual reinforcement of the related functions of life achieves a strong solidarity.

The small size of the basic social unit seems quite contrary to the popular conception of the Chinese social structure. It is often believed that in China the family unit is large. There are big houses in which a large number of kin live together, but this is found only in the gentry. Among Chinese peasants, the basic social unit is numerically small and is mainly composed of parents and children. Evidences from various studies in rural China show no exception. The average varies from four to six persons. However, from the point of view of structure, the basic group among the Chinese peasants is more than a family, as defined by anthropologists. It sometimes includes children who have grown up and married. I have called it the "expanded family." [1] If the principle of expansion carries far, the result will be a clanlike big house, as seen among the gentry; but among peasants such expansion is limited. As a rule, lateral expansion — brothers continuing to live together after marriage — is rare and unstable. The usual practice is that the aged parents stay with one of the married sons. Without any social provision for the old, it seems very natural that the parents should be taken care of by their son.

In a mobile community, nomadic or industrial, an individual has his own locus. He moves about by himself and acquires his social status on his own behalf. But for a settled peasant, it seems that all his activities are bound to the group. The family is a self-sufficient and self-supporting group, in which he maintains his existence and perpetuates his kind. It is the center from which his relations, kinship, local, and professional, ramify. The singularism in extension of social relations differs in principle from the pluralism in modern society. Individuals in such a structure are counted only as members of a certain family.

The traditional ideology in China suppresses individualism in favor of familism. The meaning, or value, of the individual's existence is defined by its being a link in the chain of social continuity which is concretely conceived in terms of descent. The most important task of a man is to continue the family line. Of the three traditional charges against an undutiful son, the failure in giving offspring comes first. The interest of the group is paramount even in such affairs as in modern society are strictly private. The collective responsibility of family members in social contributions or offenses has only recently been abolished by law, though it still persists in practice. Fathers will be held responsible for the crime committed by their children. Wives and sons are often killed solely because their husbands and fathers are revolutionists. Even now district (county) jails are full of prisoners who have committed no crime other than the fact that some of their family members happen to be deserters from the army. I am not certain whether such imprisonment is lawful, but this is the practice and no legitimate protests have been made. For the present purpose, I am taking it as a living evidence of the collectiveness of the family group and the nonrecognition of the individual as such in social responsibility.

The same principle is found in the part played by the family in wider organizations. In community organization the family, not the individual, is the unit. In practice the basic constituents of a local government are families. Local assemblies are represented by family heads; local taxes are collected from families. The family thus is a civic unit. Few have questioned the validity of the family basis of civic society, although democracy in the modern sense is essentially a recognition of equal rights among individuals. Thus in Western democracies individuals enter the civic society directly and the family has no place in the political structure. It is interesting to note that, when modern civic structure is introduced to China, the traditional form persists. The family still supersedes the individual.

[1] *Peasant Life in China: A Field Study of Country Life in the Yangtze Valley* (New York: E. P. Dutton & Co., 1939).

The family is thus the basic unit in the social structure of rural China. From this basis larger organizations are formed, but on the whole these are not strong. The peasants recognize kinship. They gather on ceremonial occasions and help each other when they are in need. But it is rare to find wider kinship organizations of a permanent nature among the peasants, and even mutual obligations among the relatives are not pronounced. In local organizations, neighborhood is universal. But as I have seen in the villages near Lake Tai, each house counts five families on either side of it as its neighbors. In Yunnan, however, neighborhood forms a permanent group and possesses a common temple. The function of the neighborhood is limited to ceremonial assistance and recreation. When we come to the village organization, we find that it is not organized by the peasants alone but by the gentry as well. It is, in fact, a rule of the gentry over the peasants. As far as the peasants are concerned, social organization stops at the loosely organized neighborhood. In the traditional structure, peasants live in small cells, which are the families, without strong ties between the cells. They carry on productive work in this kind of small co-operative group. They maintain their own subsistence and at the same time support the living of those who occupy higher positions in the social structure.

II

The chief occupation of the Chinese people as a nation is agriculture, and they depend on land for their living. As population increases, less fertile land can be utilized. Gradually there emerges a class of landowners who can afford to live without working on the land while they still enjoy the benefits of the land on account of their privileges as owners. This can be done either by employing farm laborers to work for them or by renting the land to tenants. The rise of a nonlaboring rentier class is an important step in the evolution of an agrarian community.

Farm work under primitive technique is drudgery. It is quite conceivable that those who can afford to live without being engaged in hard work will do so even at the expense of their standard of living. It seems that there are two ways of reducing the painful experience in productive pursuits: either to improve tools and utilize animal and natural power or to shift the burden to others. The first is exploitation of nature and the second is exploitation of man. In an agrarian community, when the population has increased to such a huge size as in China, the cost of human labor becomes even lower than animal labor. Under such circumstances, the first way is blockaded. It is small surprise to see that the tools used by the Chinese peasants of today are very much similar to those excavated from ancient archeological sites. Wooden wheels, an old invention, can be seen in their most primitive form on village roads, and even these are not extensively used. Loads are carried on human shoulders with the assistance of a pole. Exploitation of man is the only choice that one can make to avoid physical toil in getting a living.

I venture to think that the indulgence in physical comfort in the form of avoiding any sort of labor, which finds its highest expression in opium-smoking, is a reaction of the peasantry against hardship. Sharp contrasts of this kind are often observed in all cultures. Among the starving mass, the value of food is always exalted; the most extravagant cookery and exotic recipes are always found in poverty-stricken nations; the reckless and lavish maharajas vie with each other in gastronomical display in a famished India. Under the most strict code of sexual relations, periodic license is customary. When a long-suppressed desire becomes realizable, it drives the fortunate few unscrupulous. An unduly heightened value usually arises from the negation of the popular practice and normal discipline. The elevation from the common order becomes the goal of the common people. The hard-working Chinese peasant looks toward leisure and comfort with unusual eagerness. The denial by the laboring class of its own importance is expressed in the generally accepted popular saying, as first epigrammatically pronounced by Mencius: "Those who earn their living by labor are destined to be ruled." The self-abdication of the laboring class as the master of their own destiny is the foundation of a social dichotomy — a leisure class on top of hard-working peasants.

There is a social necessity for the gentry to develop a more elaborate social structure for themselves. The economic basis for their class is rent. It is a privilege which has to be protected by political power. Mencius' dictum has to be read in the sense that, in a community essentially agrarian, unless those who do not earn their living by labor can rule the peasants, their position is not secure. It is because an economically unproductive class living upon privileges is politically vulnerable. For the sake of security, the gentry has to be better organized. Better organization spells power. Gentry as a class differs from peasantry both in kinship and in local organizations.

I have said that among the peasants the basic social co-operative group is small. Among the gentry it is different. Big kinship groups are found. Peasants earn their living mainly by their own efforts. They work and they live. The sense of independence is strong. Although the Chinese peasants usually live with their parents who are too old to work and depend on the younger generation for support, the rule of the old is not deep-rooted. An adult son who tills the land and brings back necessities for the household is not living under the thumb of his father. But when a person does not earn his living by his own labor but depends on rent, the situation is different. An absentee landowner needs political power for his protection. In holding their privilege, the gentry are militant, as they must be. To be politically powerful and influential, the organization of the gentry has to be big and strong. Division of the household and independence of the young, as very frequently seen among the peasants, are definitely disintegrative forces and will weaken the group solidarity. In the town where I was reared, I was familiar with a number of big houses, each a colony of a number of dependent families, under the rule of a powerful and centralized authority. The head of the house holds the power in financial and social matters, maintaining the discipline of the members and enforcing the family laws. Some of them even have their own law courts. Patriarchy works out in its full strength. The son refers to his father before others as "the terrible old one," which he literally is. He enjoys no intimacy with his father, who seldom laughs in front of his children. A good description of the patriarchal relation is found in the novel *The Dream of the Red Chamber*.

A big house is an empire by itself. The members, like subjects, live under the rule and whim of the patriarch. They know no independence until they themselves are promoted to the position of a ruler. They depend upon their house for their living; their career is determined by the house; for whatever they are worth the house is solely responsible. By such a strong kinship organization, the political power of the house in the larger community is secured. The members, even the servants, of the house enter the power structure of the nation with facility. The position they hold in the government in turn supports the privilege of the house, and their economic basis is thus guaranteed.

As the size of the house grows, generation after generation (the idea being that five generations should live under the same roof), the tension within the organization grows, too. Once an emperor questioned a patriarch by what means he ruled his house successfully. The latter answered by writing three characters: forbearance, forbearance, and forbearance. Yet forbearance has its limits. Houses disperse. But to maintain close relationship among the kin is necessary for the gentry. Then clan appears. A clan is a disintegrated house; the individual family in the clan gains a certain amount of independence, while kinship unity is preserved for the common interest.

I think that both the big-family (or the house) system and the clan are the gentry's organizations. Sometimes among the peasants, the clan is found, but it is of another kind. In Yunnan, for instance, I have seen that in villages local organization is formed in terms of clan which includes even members of different surnames. Functionally these are not strictly kinship groups. I shall leave the question open as to the nature of the so-called clan-village. I rather suspect that such an organization among the peasants is a local organization, not a kinship organization. But I am sure that the clan is not universal in China, and the most effective and elaborate clans are found in the gentry. A clan organization among the landless or even petty owners is superfluous. Take my own clan, for instance. When the need for protecting our joint interest in landholding disappeared, our clan faded away. What is left now is only a name.

For a clan to be effective, it must possess some common property — invariably land. A piece of land is usually contributed to the organization by a member who is a government official, the ostensible pretext being that the products of the land may cover the expenses necessary in the keeping-up of the ancestors' tombs and regular sacrifices. But, in fact, this common property is a common security with which the position of the clan may be maintained in the wider power structure of the community. It finances the education of the young members so that they may be able to enter the scholar class and attain high official positions and protect the interests of their kinsmen. Members of the same clan are under obligation to help each other when help is called for. The clan organization, furthermore, has the authority to set up sanctions against any alienation of land. As is widely observed, individual contract in land transaction is not valid unless it is signed by clan members of the seller. This shows how closely the clan organization is linked up with land rights.

Clan organization, which defines the propinquity among unilateral kin, regulates the inheritance of land in order to prevent any disruption caused by a confusion in the line of descent and to enforce the solidarity of the group. This is known as the *tsung fa* in China, the system of descent. It is of little account when no problem of inheriting large estates is involved. In the villages of petty owners, as I have seen in Yunnan, the spirit of the *tsung fa* is weak. In other words, the people there do not observe strictly the rule of inheritance according to patrilineal descent. What the peasants in general care for most is the maintenance of the working efficiency of the basic group. It has been the custom that, when a married son dies, a substitute will be found to take the place of the deceased, and, when the substitute becomes a widower, he will take another wife. As a result the family unit is bound by no biological relations at all. However, the basic working group achieves its continuity, and life carries on. This will not happen among the sophisticated gentry. The gentry who live on land rights have reasons to adhere to orderliness and discipline in order to hold the property.

The solidarity of the big house and the clan is only one aspect of the strategy of the propertied class. To be powerful and to achieve security, big houses have to be aligned. This is done through an extension of affinal relations. Marriage has been regarded as a family affair and has been customarily defined as an alliance of houses. Choice of mate is made on the ground of family status. Through marriage a number of big houses are confederated into a powerful group. But if we turn to the peasants, we shall see that the main consideration in matchmaking is the working ability of the girl.

It is true that in China kinship is the key to social organization, but it would be wrong to think that kinship is itself so dear to the people. Kinship is only a means by which social groups are organized for different purposes. I do not think that kinship possesses any force of extension by itself and is valued as such. Procreation can be carried on without extensive recognition of kinship ties. It is so recognized because such ties can be used to organize social groups for definite purposes. In China it is the gentry who find it necessary, in order to be powerfully organized, to employ the principle of kinship extensively.

III

The peasantry and the gentry can further be contrasted by showing their ecological positions. To understand the rural economy of China, one has to bear in mind the fact that, with a very small farm under cultivation, land is closed to ambition. The average farm in China is only a few acres. (In Yunnan a good-sized farm is only about one acre.) Small farming makes accumulation of capital impossible. Villagers put it neatly: "Land breeds no land." In a community in which industry and commerce are not developed, in which land has already done its best, and in which the pressure of increasing population is felt, ambitious people have to seek their fortune not through ordinary economic enterprises but through acquiring power legally or illegally. Just the same they must leave their village for good. When they obtain wealth, they may come back to their village to acquire land, but if they retire to live in the village, the pressure of population will be borne upon them and soon wear them out — and after a few generations the big house will break down into a number of petty owners again. Therefore, it is essential for the rich to keep away from the village. The place where they can maintain their power and wealth is the town.

Towns in traditional China are not founded on manufacturing or commerce. In China the chief industries, such as textiles, are mainly peasant occupations. Owing to the smallness of the farm, the peasants cannot live entirely upon the land. It is a matter of necessity to have some additional income. Moreover, since agriculture cannot give full employment to the peasants, they have plenty of time to carry on industrial jobs in their homestead. Peasants live largely in a self-sufficient economy. The amount they buy and sell is small. If their commercial activities are centralized in a fixed locality, say a town, it will take a big area to support it. It is feasible only in those areas where communication is easy and inexpensive, such as in the Lower Yangtze Valley. In most parts of China the periodical market takes the place of the town. It gathers only once in several days. Its size and frequency of gathering can be adjusted to the temporary need from time to time. It seems clear that the permanent town has no place in the traditional rural economy.

The traditional town is the seat of the gentry. The gentry class symbolizes political and financial power. The town in which I was born, and which I know very well, mainly consists of residences of the gentry, rice stores, pawnshops, tea houses, and private gardens. There are also a number of tailors, carpenters, blacksmiths, and goldsmiths and other craftsmen. The rice stores and the pawnshops are financial establishments. The peasants, when pressed by rent or tax or other crises, have to sell their rice to the stores in town at a low price. At the time when their reserves are eaten up, they come to the stores to buy at a high price. The rice stores are therefore similar in nature to the pawnshops. Tea houses, big gardens, and magnificent residences are also the paraphernalia of the gentry. From morning until nightfall, the leisured gentlemen gather in the tea houses to amuse themselves in sipping tea, in listening to the storytellers, in talking nonsense, in gambling, and in smoking opium. It would appear to a New Englander that such a town is no better than a concentration camp of voluntary deserters from life. But, to them, leisure means prestige as well as privilege. By displaying the leisure at their disposal, they stand high in the eyes of the lower classes. The professionals who live in the town are dependent on the gentry for their employment. Few of them keep their own shops. They are called to work in the employers' houses. This reminds us of medieval feudalism in western Europe.

Such towns do not lack their charm. If one is prepared to amuse one's self in an artistic expression of life, there are hundreds of small attractions here that win his admiration. I myself have often missed much of the delicious food of my native town and the specialties of all the towns which I used to visit in my boyhood. I will not hesitate to advise a visitor to Soochow to spend at

least one day in a tea house, where he will be astonished at finding the cultured
eloquence with which the average customer talks and the mellowed and humor-
ous outlook on life he has achieved. But one will be grossly mistaken if one
thinks that this represents the ways and manners of the Chinese mass.

The mass of peasants do not live in the town. They look at the seat of the
gentry with a mixed feeling of repulsion and admiration. They support the living of the minority by paying taxes, rent, and interests. The annual tribute is
their burden. In the Yangtze Valley, with the social conditions of which I am
most familiar, I believe, it will not be exaggerating to say that half of the yield
of the peasants goes to the town. If the economic reason is still not sufficient
to arouse the ill will of the peasant toward the town, he will no longer remain
undisturbed in the village when he finds his unsatisfied wife run away from
home to work as a maid in a gentleman's big house which he dare not enter.
However, the town remains the ideal, the dream, and the incentive of the
peasants. It seems that they are not antagonistic toward the town, nor the
gentry, as such. What they are against is their own inability to become one of
those who exploit them. As long as they believe that paradise is not closed to
them, they have no desire to deny that that is where their own hopes and
wishes lie.

IV

It would be unfair to the gentry if my analysis stops here. So far we have seen
that the gentry is a class which is pre-eminently parasitic. The question then
will be raised as to how such a system of exploitation could persist for a long
period. Is the cultural achievement of the gentry, with which the peasants have
little to do, sufficient to justify their existence? The rich in the town must make
more tangible and concrete contributions before they can win respect and gratitude from the peasants. In the eyes of the peasants the gentry do give them
political protection. But am I contradicting myself when, on the one hand, I
have said that the gentry hold political power for their own interest which
means the protection of their own rights of collecting rent from the peasants,
and, on the other, I now state that the gentry are the protectors of the peasants? It is true that the peasants are the exploited class in the traditional structure and the gentry are their immediate exploiters, but this is true only from
our point of view. For the peasants themselves the situation is not so defined.
As long as the right of private ownership is recognized, rent payment is an approved obligation of the tenants. Usurers are hated, but the rate of interest is
agreed upon when the loans are made. If the gentry are exploiting the peasants,
they do so through institutional means and within institutional limits. Rent and
interest are fixed. Abuse of power is found only when the peasants fail to fulfil
the contract. There is, however, another form of exploitation which is beyond
the control of the peasants, and that is the absolute monarchical power unchecked by popular will and unbounded as the whims of the monarch are
unbounded. Against this power, the peasants have to seek protection from the
gentry. To make this point clear, I have to go further into the power structure
of traditional China.

The center of the power structure is the absolute monarch. From the monarch, power is intrusted to the hierarchy of officials. On the vast continent, with bad communication systems, power is centralized only in name but not in fact. Officials of every rank enjoy such an amount of authority as their immediate superiors will tolerate. "The monarch is as remote as the heaven itself." That which rules the people is the hierarchy of officials. Since the officials are responsible only to their superiors, with the monarch far at the top, there is no legalized mechanism of popular check upon the power. The rights of the people are not protected by law. The welfare of the people is hung by a thread on the good conscience of the power hierarchy. Good conscience rarely appears in those who personify power. Therefore political power becomes sometimes even "more fearful than tigers." Protection from the encroachment of the power upon one's own rights is thus essential. This is achieved not by organized popular action, which results in Western democracy, but by personal approach to the power hierarchy. Since the low official receives power from the one of a higher rank, he has to yield to the will of his superior. If one can influence the superior through personal means, the lower official has to behave amiably toward one, lest he should get into trouble. The direct way of access to the power hierarchy is to enter officialdom one's self. If a man is himself an official, he can protect his and his relatives' private interests not only by the power intrusted in his hands but also by his relation with his fellow-officials. This kind of political maneuver, traditionally known as face-saving, rises from the absence of the rule of law. When a community is ruled by sheer personal will, court politics is inevitable.

It should now be clear why the gentry, being a class of people living on privileges, are anxious to enter into officialdom. If they are not in alliance with the power hierarchy, their position as landowners is threatened. The wrongs done them can never be redressed. Alienation of land by powerful persons is not infrequent. It is a recognized necessity for the rich to hold a position in the hierarchy. Clan organization and affinal confederation are sufficient because they are systems of security through the establishment of a relation to the power hierarchy by kinship.

The gentry mediates between the ruler and the ruled. In the history of China the central power is usually in the hands of alien invaders or social outcasts who seize the political power by unscrupulous means. As soon as the monarch is enthroned, the gentry will join hands with him by filling the rank and file of the officialdom. In their official capacity, they are agents of the ruler, but in their private capacity they are closely related to, and share common interests with, the ruled. Herein lies the popular though not thorough check on the absolute and often alien monarch.

In the traditional system of government the tenacles of the central power stop at the *hsien* (county). Each *hsien* consists of a number of villages which are usually organized locally by villagers. The local organization possesses common property and regulates common enterprises such as religious ceremonies and irrigation. The executives of such an organization are elected not by all the representatives of the families but by the respected elders of the village.

The respected elders are those who possess land and "face," i.e., connection with the officialdom or with the gentry in town. They are the lower rank of the gentry who are not rich enough to leave the village and live in town.

The central power operates on the people in the following way: When the central government orders the magistrate of the *hsien* to collect taxes or conscribe services, the latter will send agents to the village to carry out the order. The agents themselves are conscripts from the villages. They enjoy no prestige in their own community. In practice, they are only messengers of the magistrate. The government order passes unofficially from the hand of the agent to the local headmen who occupy no official position in the government constitution. The order then will be announced and discussed in the village teashops. All those present may participate. No vote will be taken, but the headman will decide according to the public opinion as well to his own sense of appropriateness whether the order should be followed. If the decision is in the negative, the agent will be sent back to the magistrate without achieving anything. The responsibility of the failure in executing the order is his. He will be beaten or otherwise punished for the failure. However, court politics follows on the other hand. The elders of the village will call on the magistrate or ask someone among the town gentry to call on the magistrate for negotiation. Since the gentry have connections with the power hierarchy, the magistrate has to consider their suggestions and modify his order in a way he thinks fit. The actual practice is complicated indeed. The maneuver on both sides may involve the mobilization of a big sphere of the power structure. Sometimes the issue may gradually move up to the monarch himself. Very often the monarch, to grant some personal favor, intervenes in local affairs in a way contrary to his own decrees. For a local government official, the gentry are his opposition, although the opposition is usually not frontal and finally appears in the order from his own superior. Although an official, he is in his private capacity one of the gentry. He will write letters to his fellow-officials asking favor for his own kin, relatives, or local people. The gentry-official is the pivot in the traditional Chinese power structure.

Whatever one may say for or against the traditional pattern, it is clear that, as long as the peasants live in the structure, they have to rely on the gentry for protection against the encroachment of the absolute ruler and his officials.

The gentry differ from the aristocracy in the West in that the former do not form a political party with the responsibility of running a government. Never in the history of China have the Chinese gentry organized their own government. As a class, they never reject any monarch who is able to seize the power and who recognizes the right of landowners. They will enter any government with the purpose of protecting their own kin and local people from the encroachment of the absolute power, but not for the sake of political power itself. They have no sense of political responsibility. They do not even want to remain in their official position for long, and certainly they abhor public duty. I do not think that it is only a matter of pretentiousness that the ideal gentleman is the one who enjoys himself among the people but not in the court. A large bulk of poetry reveals the psychology of retirement of the officials and is popular and typical. The happiest moment of a successful official is when he retires to his own country with high honors. Honor and prestige which the official gentry seek at any price have practical values. They mean security to his own clan and to the people of his locality. In fact, even when he is holding an office in the government, he is at the same time working as a representative of his kin and relatives. The latter function is indeed his main job, but, in order to realize it, he has to take the former. Toward his public position he assumes a negative attitude. He is ready to resign whenever his record and influence are well established and can perform his function as protector of his people without a public office. The gentry as a class are outside the government. They take official positions individually. They are moved by social but not by political responsibility. This is why we should not rank them as aristocracy.

It may also be important to point out here that, owing to their pivotal position in the power structure, the gentry have through long history acquired a set of codes of professional ethics. They preach the doctrine of order: every one should behave according to and be satisfied by the position one occupies in the social structure. The task of Confucius was to set down for each social status its canon of correct behavior. The gentry's interest is not in possessing political power but in maintaining order irrespective of who the monarch is. They will serve him as long as he behaves as a benevolent ruler, but if he becomes despotic and suppresses the peasants too hard, the gentry will exert their pressure against him. On the other hand, if the peasants revolt against the ruler and disturb the social order, they will fight on the side of the monarch. This is their social responsibility. Being a privileged class themselves, they are never revolutionary. Order and security are their sole interests.

V

In discussing the ecological differentiation of the peasants and the gentry, I have shown that those who like to hold their privilege as a leisure class have to stay outside the village. This is because in agriculture there is little hope for the accumulation of wealth. It seems that a peasant who works on the land is bound to the land as a peasant. Therefore, we may ask how the gentry emerges. Of course, we must admit that, since there is no social barrier preventing a peasant from entering into the gentry if he can afford to lead a leisurely life, there will be those hard-working peasants who strive to rise from the bottom. But it will take them several generations to climb up the social ladder, each generation promoting itself a little. Despite thrift and endurance, this is not only a long but also a haphazard way, because in the rural community misfortunes of all kinds are not uncommon. Drought and flood may cause famine. Epidemics may ruin a family. In a period of political disturbance bandits are as bad as locusts in the dry years. It will be most rare for a family to keep up its morale for several generations and to have no misfortune strike them in the meantime.

Another factor which prevents a hard-working and well-to-do peasant family from rising is the high pressure of population. Upon these the pressure of population is particularly strong. For among the leisure class the birth rate is low because of their degenerated physical conditions, and among the poor peasants infantile mortality is high because of the lack of good care. But among hard-working, well-to-do peasants, the birth rate is as high as that of the poor peasants and the death rate is comparatively low owing to their better living standard. Such a family grows fast. If it cannot expand its estate at the same rate, its standard of living will sink in the next generation. It already requires fairly strenuous efforts for a peasant family to maintain its footing, but the hope of rising into the leisure class is slight.

It is quite natural that the common tendency among the peasants is not to rise on the social ladder but rather to sink toward the bottom. A petty owner may become a tenant when he sells his land as misfortune befalls him. He may further sink from a tenant to a landless farm laborer. He may in the end die disgracefully or disappear from the village. These outcasts are desperate. They have nothing to lose but their life of drudgery. They leave the village and plunge themselves into banditry or smuggling, or join the army, or seek employment as servants in big gentry houses. These are economically nonproductive jobs, but it is only by taking up such jobs, in addition to good luck, that the outcasts from the rural society can hope to obtain wealth quickly. Of course, hundreds and thousands of such fortune-seekers die in despair and are forgotten by the world. But, once loosened from the soil, they have freed themselves from the bond of the land. They are the dissatisfied class and thus revolutionary in nature. When the ruling class is strong, they are suppressed. Only a few reach their aim through various kinds of more or less unlawful ways. But if the ruling class is degenerate and weak, they are the uprising group aiming at power. In Chinese history there are several instances where new dynasties were inaugurated by such desperate outcasts.

In peacetime the few successful upstarts when they have obtained wealth will buy land and insinuate themselves into the leisure class. They are looked down upon and looked at with a prejudiced eye by the gentry. Only gradually and especially by means of affinal alliance, are they admitted into the upper layer of the social structure. Not until one of the family members enters into the scholar group and into officialdom is their position in the gentry consolidated.

The gentry are maintained economically by owning land and politically by occupying a position in officialdom. As a landowning class they have the leisure to learn classical literature which is the professional requirement of an official. For nearly a thousand years the monarch has offered regular examinations to recruit officials from the literati. Only a few low classes are excluded from the right to take part in such examinations. Theoretically men from the peasantry are free to enter into competition. And there are notable cases in which a son of a poor peasant learned the classics on the back of his buffalo while he was working in the field and attained high honor in the examination. But, after all, these are exceptions, for otherwise such stories would not be circulated like legends. It is true that in China there is no such social class system as the caste system, but it is another question as to whether the Chinese class system possesses high mobility. I have no statistical information to prove the case, but from studies on existing rural communities it is clear that a child from a peasant family engaged in farm work has little chance of receiving a high-school education. I cannot help being cautious in accepting the popular belief that in the good old days everyone had a chance to become an official through equitable examination. The mobility between the peasantry and gentry has been rather limited. It is needless to add that the existence of the belief among the peasants in the possibility of promotion to the gentry is important because it gives an incentive and eventually stabilizes the structure at large.

Conversely we may ask how frequently the members of the gentry return to peasantry. As far as my own knowledge goes, I cannot find a single case where a good-for-nothing gentleman picks up farming work again. It seems impossible that the gentry should return to the farm. Manual labor is highly deplored in the current ideology in China, even today. The gentry are especially conscious of it. A long gown that signifies leisure is the emblem of honor and prestige and is the last thing a gentleman will cast away. It is worth more than one's life. I had an uncle who became destitute by his fortieth year. He lived in a bare room and was penniless. But he carried on his life as usual in the tearooms and wore his long gowns until his death. The scene of his death was most pathetic. He lingered on at his last moment and was unwilling to close his eyes, as a cousin of my clan put it who visited him on his deathbed. He was worrying that he would not die as a gentleman, dressed in silk and buried in a coffin of good quality. My cousin comforted him by showing him all that he was going to have when he ceased to breathe. He smiled and then passed away in satisfaction. This incident presents in full the inner psychology of the gentry. The question will then arise as to how he could afford to live up to the standard of a gentleman. The answer is that he was helped by his clan members. The clan is a system of mutual security. When I was young, I frequently witnessed the visits of my clan uncles to my home. They were poor, but they talked and laughed without mentioning any financial need. When they left us, my grandmother used to give them a handsome amount of money as a present. My grandmother was not rich then. I knew very well that she had sent a maid to the pawnshop from our back door in order to get enough money to aid our clan members who were in distress. The same spirit leads an official to offer jobs to his clan members regardless of their ability. The sense of responsibility for mutual aid and collective security among the clan members is stronger than the sense of duty as an official of the government.

The system of clan social security which prevails among the gentry encourages dependence especially when the class has kept away from participating in productive work. A child reared in such an environment is detached from the life of the people. He lives in a big house devoid of sunshine; he grows up in the reverence of the past, in the shadow of his ancestors, from whom his privileges are inherited. From the petty court politics among the family members he learns to put on a feigned obedience, is imbued with a sense of futility of all efforts, and is trivial, resigned, conservative, and cowardly. Physically he is weak, slender, and sometimes sterile. Of the six of my clan uncles, three have no children of their own. A similar state of affairs is found among many of my relatives. It seems that the lack of initiative and aggressiveness lead eventually to physical sterility. The gentry in China, like the city dwellers in the West, are the dying population, by which I mean that they cannot replace themselves. They have to rely upon recruits from the countryside.

Posed on the peak of the social pyramid, the gentry possess prestige and privilege. Prestige and privilege attract the daring and the aggressive individuals from the classes below. The new recruits revitalize the gentry, but, when they are assimilated, they become pacified and neutralized. The energy that may cause upheavals is channeled into the petty mobility in the social structure and is finally eliminated in the pattern of leisurely life. The gentry class is in fact a safety valve in social changes. Conservatism becomes the rule of Chinese society, and China as a culture is singular in the history of human kind in its stability and perpetuation.

. . .

In concluding the present paper, I should like to add that a sketch like the present one necessarily oversimplifies the reality. An attempt at making a comprehensive interpretation of the social structure of China is premature because it requires thorough investigation. But to formulate research programs, it is advisable to prepare an outline which will provide hypotheses for investigation. This is the purpose of the present paper. However, it may also be used as reference by those who are interested in a general view of the social structure of China. But this paper should not be taken as conclusive. It serves only as a stimulus for further studies.

The Feudality

HENRI PIRENNE

I. THE DISINTEGRATION OF THE STATE

We are accustomed to give the name of "feudal" to the political system which prevailed in Europe after the disappearance of the Carolingian dynasty. This habit of ours goes back to the French Revolution, which indiscriminately attributed to the feudal system all the rights, privileges, usages and traditions which were inconsistent with the constitution of the modern State and modern society. Yet if we accept the words in their exact sense, we ought to understand, by the terms "feudal" and "feudal system," only the juridical relations arising from the fief or the bond of vassalage,[1] and it is an abuse of language to stretch the sense of these terms to include a whole political order, in which the feudal element was, after all, only of secondary importance, and, if we may say so, formal rather than substantial. We shall follow the common usage, but we shall also call attention to the fact that the most significant feature of the so-called feudal system was the disintegration of the State.

Everything tended to accomplish this disintegration, once it had proved to be materially impossible, after the kingdoms founded by the Germanic invasions were established, to continue the Roman State. Disintegration was already on the way at the close of the Merovingian period, when the monarchy, on which everything depended, recovered its influence for the time being, through its great conquests and its alliance with the Papacy. But these conquests, and this influence, retarded only for a moment the process of disintegration, for the causes of the latter were inherent in the social order itself. The king alone could maintain the political organization of the State. Theoretically the State was monarchical and administrative; but we have seen how weak it was, even under Charlemagne. It was weak because its political constitution did not match its economic nature. Since commerce and the towns had disappeared the State had entered upon a period when the great domains absorbed both the land and the inhabitants, placing the revenue of the former and the arms of the latter at the disposal of a class of magnates. These were rendered the more independent by the fact that their economic life was subject to perturbations; the whole produce of the domain was applied to the maintenance of the domain itself. There was therefore nothing to be feared or expected from the State. This decided the fate of the monarchy. Sooner or later, accordingly as the evolution of society was more or less advanced, it was

From Henri Pirenne, A *History of Europe* (New Hyde Park, N.Y.: University Books, 1956), pp. 146–160. Reprinted by permission of the publisher.

HENRI PIRENNE (1862–1935) was Professor of Medieval and Belgian History at the Universities of Liege and Ghent. The author of many works, including a seven-volume history of Belgium and an economic and social history of medieval Europe, he wrote A *History of Europe*, from which our selection is taken, during World War I while a prisoner of war in Germany.

[1] The old feudal seigneurs, down to the close of the 18th century, were under no illusion in this respect. It was generally admitted by all that "fief and justice have nothing in common." In reality, feudal law was a special kind of law, like commercial law.

doomed to allow its rights and prerogatives to pass to the magnates who were now almost its only subjects, since they had interposed themselves between it and the people, and it was obliged to govern through them. To an ever-increasing extent, its only effective power was that which it derived from its own domains. Where it was reduced to the exercise of a purely political sovereignty its rule soon became purely formal. Deprived of taxes, deprived of the possibility of paying its functionaries, how was it to maintain itself? By throwing itself upon the Church, as it had done in Germany? But this had been possible only because in the time of the Ottos the lay aristocracy was still in an undeveloped condition. And again, the episcopal principalities were themselves destroying the State. Thanks to them the monarch alone was strong from the military point of view. But his governmental efficacy was not enhanced by them, and the State was destroyed notwithstanding his military power. Thus, in the economic circumstances of the age the power of the king was inevitably bound to decline, until it depended entirely on his military activity and his personal prestige. And in fact, since the days of Charlemagne the decadence of the monarchy had progressed very rapidly. The king's position, in respect of the magnates, was growing steadily weaker. Matters had gone so far by the close of the 9th century that the monarchy had become purely elective.

It might have disappeared. It did not disappear, and this was characteristic of the age.[2] It did not occur to the magnates that they could dispense with the king. They still had a lingering sense of the unity of the State. Here, above all, the Church had to intervene, for it did not acknowledge the magnates; for the Church the king was the guardian of the providential order of the world. And he, for his part, protected the Church and guaranteed its property. And the magnates themselves needed a king as judge and arbiter: just as in the law-courts there must be a judge or magistrate who presides over the proceedings and pronounces sentence. The king was indispensable to the social order, to the "public peace." But it was clearly understood that the king reigned and did not govern.

And yet, in law, there was no limit to his power. He took no oath of capitulation. He renounced no prerogative. Theoretically he was absolute. But he was paralysed. The members no longer obeyed the head. As far as appearance went, nothing was changed. The kings continued to employ all the old formulae, to receive, in the official language, all the marks of respect. But they had allowed the reality of power to pass into the hands of the aristocracy. The modern jurists have constructed the prettiest theories of the State of the early Middle Ages, and of the rights of the monarch: but they are only theories. The reality was very different. The State was disintegrating, falling to pieces, and from its ruins it reconstructed itself in another form. After Charles the Bald there were no more capitularies, and not until the 12th century do we find the king acting again in a legislative capacity.

What had happened was simply this: the power had spontaneously declined

[2] The election of the king was a mark of progress in the sense that it assured the unity of the monarchy: there would be no more partitions of kingdoms.

from the hands of the king into those of the aristocracy, which included his officials. We may therefore say, with perfect truth, that the official usurped the functions which he performed. The thing happened quite naturally, without deliberate intention, without any violent disturbances, because the official was the seigneur of many of the persons under his administration, and the proprietor of a good portion of his circumscription.

It should be noted, however, that there was a very clear distinction between his private powers over his estates and his men, and the public power, the crown rights which he exercised in the king's name, but henceforth for his own benefit. He possessed the first in his own name as part of his patrimony. The second he held only by delegation from the crown. If the count, in his country, was supreme judiciary, military commander, collector of what remained of the old Roman *census*, beneficiary of the *droit de gîte* and collector of market tolls, this was because he was a functionary. But all these powers, which he exercised in the king's name, he exercised for his own benefit, and the king could not prevent him from doing so.

Further, the power of the aristocracy broke up and reconstituted for his own benefit the circumscription of the State. The State, since the Merovingian epoch, had been divided into counties. These counties were very small, so small that the count-officials were able easily to cover their counties in the course of a day. But from the 8th century onwards the more powerful of these counts had begun to usurp the power in a number of counties adjacent to their own. Fortunate marriages, friendly arrangements, violence, the king's favour, or the fear which they inspired in him, soon enabled them to amalgamate, in a single territory, a greater or smaller number of the old circumscriptions. The new country established by these encroachments became a principality, just as the count became a prince. The name borrowed from the Roman bureaucracy still adhered to him, but this sometime agent of the central power, having absorbed the power which was delegated to him, and enlarged the circumscription in which he exercised that power, was now, and would remain for centuries, a petty local sovereign.

All this was accomplished in the midst of unspeakable violence and treachery. The 10th century, like the 15th, was an epoch of political assassination. The territorial power of the feudal princes was no more scrupulous in the choice of means than that of the absolutist monarchs or the tyrants of the Renaissance; it was merely more brutal. Each sought to increase his power to the detriment of his neighbour, and any weapon was permissible. The passion for land ruled the actions of all these feudal magnates, and as there was no one to stop them, they struck at each other with all the brutality of their instincts. The king was powerless, and when on occasion he attempted to intervene his functionary made war upon him. It was thus that Charles the Simple died in the prison of the Count of Vermandois.

Nevertheless — and here the feudal element appears — the princes were bound to the king by the oath of fealty. The old subordination of the functionary had been transformed into the oath. The feudal seigneurs were the king's men, his faithful servants. In theory, the king was still the supreme possessor of the powers which had been usurped from him, and this the feudal oath acknowledged. We must not say, therefore, that the feudal system broke down the State, for the truth is the reverse of this. It still maintained a bond — or at least a formal bond — between the king and those parcels of the kingdom of which the great functionaries who had become princes had possessed themselves, and whose feudal oath made them vassals. Here was a principle which the jurists would exploit at a later period, when the king was strong once more. For the time being the king gave way to the seigneurs, and recognized the usurpations which he could not prevent. The hereditary principle was in force among the feudal magnates. The son succeeded to the father, and from the 11th century onwards the hereditary principle was extended to women.

The king, who still regarded himself as the possessor of all the power of the State, was now envisaged by the princes, his great vassals, only from the feudal standpoint. For them he was no more than a magnate to whom they were allied by a contractual bond. They owed him aid and counsel, and the king owed them protection: if he attacked them, taking his king's point of view, they considered themselves justified in marching against him. The princes envisaged the monarchy otherwise than the king himself. But the consequences of this difference of conception were not felt until a later date; and until the 12th century the kings, with rare exceptions, allowed matters to go their way.

Thus, from the end of the 9th and the beginning of the 10th century the State was reduced to an empty form. The provinces had become principalities, and the functionaries princes. The king, except on his own territory, was merely the "enfeoffed sovereign" of his kingdom. A multiplicity of local sovereignties had replaced the old administrative unity derived from the Roman Empire. But it must be recognized that this was the normal and sensible situation, which was in correspondence with the social condition, and therefore with the needs, of the community. The agrarian and domainal constitution of the epoch made it impossible to maintain the administrative unity that even a Charlemagne could not transform into a living reality. How could the political power have remained centralized in the hands of the king at a time when the people were entering *en masse* into the cadres of the great estates, into dependency on the seigneurs? Political power was bound to follow effective power, and to crystallize itself, so to speak, around those who really possessed that power. The protection of human beings is not merely the primordial function of the State: it is also the origin of the State. Now, the king no longer protected his subjects; the magnates protected them. It was therefore necessary and beneficial that they should dismember the State to their own advantage. They certainly had public opinion — or shall we say, the sentiment of the peoples — on their side. Nowhere do we see that the "little man" attempted to save the monarchy. He no longer knew what monarchy was.

It was in the restricted centres of the territorial principalities that a system of government and administration was first organized that actively influenced those who were subject to it. The kingdom was too extensive. It had inevitably to restrict itself to an administration which could not be adequately supervised, and which did not reach the masses. It was otherwise with the new system. The territorial princes were in touch with reality; their private function enabled them to govern effectively a territory of moderate extent: the number of their dependants and vassals was in proportion to its area, and provided them with a staff. Each of these princes set to work in his own way; their methods varied in detail, but were broadly the same. It was this obscure task that was the most important feature of the period, as regards the formation of society, and where it was first undertaken — in the Low Countries and in France — society was more advanced than elsewhere. The kings were in the front of the stage; the emperors occupied themselves with high policy. But it was the princes who created the first original type of political organization that Europe had known since the Roman Empire.

They had, of course, no theory, no conscious conception. Practice automatically fitted itself to the reality.

The foundation of the territorial organization was the landed property of the prince, since it was from this that he derived his power. The principal "counts" of his domain, or the most favourably situated, were provided with defensive works, and became castles (bourgs), the centres of the military, financial, and judicial organization. They were usually great walled enclosures, with dwelling-houses, store-houses, and lodgings for the garrison of knights. A châtelain, whom the prince chose from among his men acted as his substitute in the circumscription, which bore the name of châtellenie. It was the châtelain who commanded the fortress, watched over the countryside, and presided in the local court of justice. In order to support the châtelain and the knights of the castle prestations in kind were levied on the population: and here the principle of the salary made its appearance, a principle unknown to the kings: of payment in the form of fixed dues to be made to the public authority. Moreover, as early as the 11th century we find traces of a county impost (petitio bede), and this was a fresh sign of progress, despite the still primitive form of assessment and collection. Thus, at a time when the king had no financial resources outside his domains, the prince was organizing them. Moreover, the prince minted money, for he usurped the right of coining money with the other crown rights, and he made a handsome profit by debasing the coinage. He had also the market tolls, and, of course, he continued to take his share of the fines.

From every point of view, then, his power was greater than that of the king. For while the king was now elective, the principality was hereditary, and at an early period — as early as the 10th century — the right of sole succession was established, so that the principalities were not divided. It is interesting to note how unchanged they continued until the end of the ancien régime, which preserved them as provinces. The prince, from the 10th century, had a historiography. He had a court, modelled on that of the king: chancellor, marshal, seneschal, cup-bearer. He had his vassals, who were more loyal to him than he was to the king, by reason of their proximity, and the greater disproportion of their powers. He was the advowee of all the monasteries within his territory, and he exacted dues or services from them. The documents call him *princeps, monarcha, advocatus patriae, post Deum princeps*.

He was in actual sense the territorial chieftain, the head of the *patria*, and we should note that in the Latin of the Middle Ages people were beginning to apply this beautiful word to these little local "counties." In them was formed, for the first time, the patriotism which in modern society has replaced the civic sentiment of antiquity. There was something in it of the sense of family, and it was embodied in the man who from father to son was the chief and protector of the group. His armorial bearings became those of the people, and their common loyalty to him was a bond of service. Nothing like this had existed under the Merovingians or Carolingians, and in later periods men had this feeling only for their kings. Modern patriotism, born of the dynastic sentiment, was in the first place nurtured in the principalities.

The prince was really the protector of his men. He discharged his duty in person: his life, and his social function, were active in the extreme. Not only did he lead his men to the wars, and with them fling himself upon the enemy: he also presided in his courts of justice, supervised the work of his tax-collectors, and gave his personal decision in all important questions; and above all, he watched over the "public peace." He assured the safety of the roads, and extended his protection to the poor, and to orphans, widows, and pilgrims; and he fell upon highway robbers and hanged them. He was the supreme justiciary on his own territory, the guardian and guarantor of public order, and in this respect his function was essentially social in character. When one speaks of the "bloodthirsty" feudal magnates one should make reservations. The feudal seigneur was bloodthirsty when abroad, in his enemy's country, but not in his own; and one thing is certain — that society began to receive its political education within the *cadre* of the feudal principalities. The great State of which the principalities were the dismembered parts did not really influence people; its activities were carried on over their heads. The monarchy had designed the framework of political life, introduced Christianity, allied itself with the Church, and created an ideal of royalty which still survived, and would be a force in the future. But it had no actual hold upon men and women. To reach them, to govern them, the immediate, firm, and active power of the local princes was needed. And these princely men-at-arms with the fantastic names, these rough soldiers, despite their pillaging of their neighbours' territories, must be given their place among the civilizers of Europe. In the political and social life of the continent, they were the first instructors.

II. NOBILITY AND CHIVALRY

In the 10th century a new juridical class had sprung up in the European States: the nobility. Its importance is sufficiently shown by the fact that in lay society the nobles alone had political rights. Later on the bourgeoisie would take its place beside the nobility. This place would become more and more considerable, but down to the end of the *ancien régime* it would still be regarded as a secondary place. In the history of Europe the nobles have played — though under very different conditions — almost the same part as the patricians in Roman history, while the bourgeoisie may be compared with the plebeians. It is only in the modern State that they have become merged in the mass of the citizens, much as in the Empire the general bestowal of civic rights effaced the old difference between the patriciate and the plebs.

The noblesse exercised so great and so general an influence over the history of Europe that it is not easy to realize that it constituted an original phenomenon, and one peculiar to the Christian society of Western Europe. Neither the Roman nor the Byzantine Empire, nor the Musulman world, had ever known a similar institution. Doubtless all primitive societies have comprised a nobility of mythological origin. But these nobilities disappeared on the advent of civilization: like the old Germanic nobility, which did not outlive the invasions. The nobility of the Middle Ages, five centuries later, was quite a novel creation, and very different in character.

It was preceded by the powerful aristocracy, partly Roman, and in part consisting of the parvenus and functionaries who had been making their appearance, and playing a more and more important part, since the formation of the new kingdoms. But this aristocracy was not a nobility, in the sense of being a juridical class to which a man belonged by birth. It was merely a social class, which consisted of a group of powerful individuals. Moreover, whatever its actual power, it possessed no privilege in law. The greatest land-owner of Charlemagne's day was in the same position, in a court of justice, as the simple freeman.

Two causes contributed to the formation of the nobility: the constant diminution of the number of freemen, and the feudal form of military service: and of these two causes the second was far more important than the first, and could even have dispensed with its action.

The domainal system, as it expanded, resulted in the juridical degradation of the rural population, reducing it to a more or less complete servitude. Those who had retained their liberty were in a privileged situation, and from the 10th century the word *liber* took on the meaning of *nobilis*. The old juridical usages relating to the family and inheritance now applied only to those privileged persons. The common law of freeman was modified into a special law. The *connubium* was enlarged in Roman law: at the beginning of the Middle Ages it was reduced. Family right was finally the apanage only of the few; and the same was true of free hereditary property (*allodium*).

These freemen, whose numbers it is impossible to estimate, naturally retained the right to bear arms. Their estate enabled them to maintain a war horse. They were above all warriors.

But beside them, and far more numerous — at any rate, in France — was another class of freeman: the vassals. Their means of livelihood was provided not by their personal property, their *allodium*, but by the fief which, in this agricultural age, served as their salary. Like the others, and even more than the others, they were warriors. But unlike the first class, they were not hereditary warriors; for the fief did not pass from father to son unless the son was a good soldier. If the father left only daughters, or sons incapable of bearing arms, the fief lapsed to the seigneur. But such a case was rare. In France, from the time of Charles the Bald, the fiefs were hereditary, and while in Germany their hereditary character was not formally recognized until the reign of Conrad, they were certainly handed down from father to son before that date.

In addition to these free soldiers — some the proprietors of *allodia*, others the holders of fiefs — there were also soldiers who were not free. These were loyal and sturdy serfs whom the seigneurs took with them as bodyguards when they went to the wars, and employed, in times of peace, in confidential posts, as *ministeriales* or *Dienstmannen*; in Germany, more especially, they were numerous, and they constituted the aristocracy of servitude.

All, whether free or not, were united by the sense of professional community, and were regarded with special consideration by the rest of the population; for since all the intellectual functions were allotted to the clergy, only the trade of arms could give the laymen a privileged position in society.

The warrior entered the military class only on coming of age. A special ceremony was necessary before he could be admitted; at this his arms were conferred upon him by the seigneur or by one of his companions. By this ceremony he was consecrated knight, *chevalier*, which meant simply horse-soldier. It gave the recipient of the honour the advantages and the prestige of his position. At first, unless the son of a knight was himself dubbed knight, he was a villein merely, and his daughters, since they could not be knighted, enjoyed no special consideration. But this was evidently a transitory phase; and fact was followed by law. As a general rule, the son of a knight would himself become a knight. He was therefore counted, from birth, as belonging to the military caste; and the daughters of a knight would be regarded as belonging to the same social class. And as soon as this state of affairs was reached — which in France, at all events, was by the close of the 10th century — the nobility was born: that is, a hereditary class, conferring a particular rank in the State, independently of social position. All those who belonged to the *milicia*, or whose ancestors had belonged to it, were *nobiles*. It was not absolutely essential that the "noble" should be free; for in the end the *ministeriales* came to be regarded as nobles.[3]

Thus the class of vassals was practically merged in the nobility. However, nobility did not depend upon the possession of a fief. After all, a man could be knighted who did not possess a fief; and it was not for some time — not until the 13th century — that the plebeian was debarred from the possession of a fief. It was therefore the social function that made the noble; but it was a social function that presupposed economic independence, based upon the noble's personal property (his *allodium*) or his feudal property (his fief). The nobility was really the army. Hence its privileges. They were explained by the nature of the service rendered, and conferred as consideration for that service. The noble did not pay the count an impost on account of his land, because he furnished him with military service. This was the sole privilege, so-called, of the nobility: it had no others. His special juridical situation, his special status in respect of his family, and the special procedure by which he benefited in

[3] But this was not definitely the case until the 14th century.

the law-courts, were merely the survival of the common law of freemen, which had been modified for villeins.

The importance of the nobility resided in its social rôle. Uplifted by its military functions above the rest of the population, in constant touch with the princes, it was the nobility and the nobility alone that furnished the administrative personnel, just as it was the nobility alone that constituted the army. It was from the nobility that the châtelains were chosen, the mayors, and all the other agents of the territorial administration. It was therefore regarded not only as a military but also a political caste. Beside the nobility was the clergy. Below the nobility and the clergy was the mass of plebians, by whose labour they lived; in return for which service the clergy directed their souls while the nobility protected their bodies. This is not a theoretical *a posteriori* view. The writers of the period were perfectly well aware of this mutual relation, and recorded it in plain language.

This nobility was extremely numerous; especially when the domainal system was well developed, so that the number of fiefs could be readily increased. One may say that the evolution of society was in proportion to the numbers, or rather to the density of the chivalry, which decreased as one proceeded from the French frontier in the direction of the Elbe. In France and the Low Countries one could count on finding a number of knights in every country town, and we certainly shall not be far out if we estimate that in these countries they represented at least one tenth of the population.

We must not imagine that their mode of life was especially refined. Their fiefs and their little domains just enabled them to live. Their military equipment consisted of a lance, an iron casque, a buckler, and a suit of buckram. Only the wealthiest knights possessed a coat of mail. They were formidable soldiers, however, and when war left them any leisure they kept themselves in training by means of tourneys that were like veritable battles. They attended them in their hundreds, grouped according to regions, and charged one another heavily until more than one was left on the ground. Further, they were the most turbulent of men, furiously destroying one another in the private wars and family vendettas in which they were continually involved. In vain did the Church, from the close of the 10th century — first of all in France, and later in Germany — restrict the days of battle by the "peace of God"; custom proved to be too strong for it. At the end of the 11th century the chronicler Lambert of Waterloo related that ten of his father's brothers were slain by their enemies on the same day, in an encounter near Tournai; and about the same time the Count of Flanders, Robert the Frisian, drawing up the list of murders committed in the neighbourhood of Bruges, stated that it would take more than 10,000 marks of silver to pay the "compositions" in respect of these murders.

Naturally, in such an environment there was no intellectual culture. Only in the wealthiest families would a clerk teach the daughters to read. As for the sons, who were in the saddle as soon as they could mount a horse, they had no knowledge of anything but fighting. Their literature consisted of soldiers' songs, such as the song that Taillefer sang at the Battle of Hastings. They were violent, gross, and superstitious, but excellent soldiers. Consider the exploits of the Normans in Sicily, the conquest of England, the Flemish knights who so amazed the Emperor Alexis as they passed through Constantinople, and above all the extraordinary enterprise of the Crusades. The qualities that made the knights of France and the Low Countries the finest warriors of their time had nothing to do with race; they were the fruit of training. This training was better in the West because there the chivalry was more numerous, and it was so because of the greater extension of the domainal system.

At the close of the 11th century chivalry was extremely wide-spread. But "chivalrous" manners — by which I mean the code of courtesy and loyalty which distinguished the gentlemen after the age of the Crusades — had as yet no existence. To produce them greater refinement was necessary. Still, the two sentiments on which they were based were already widely diffused among the knights: namely, devotion and honour. Nothing could exceed the piety of these soldiers, despite their superstitions and their brutality. They were scrupulous in their respect for the right of sanctuary: they would halt in their pursuit of an enemy as soon as they saw the towers of a monastery upon the horizon. They followed with exemplary piety the relics which the monks carried in procession through the countryside. They went on distant pilgrimages, to Rome and to Jerusalem; and it would even seem that the songs of the feudal epoch were evolved on the pilgrim routes. As for honour, the sentiment which the modern world has inherited from them, this was wholly a military virtue. It was not precisely the honour of our day, which is more refined. It was, before all, the sentiment of fidelity and loyalty. These knights were ready enough for treachery, but they did not break their given word. Homage (*homagium*) — a word which has gradually lost its full meaning in our language — meant for them the complete offering of their person to their seigneur. Felony was in their eyes the worst of crimes.[4] They regarded everything from the personal point of view, as between man and man. The sentiment of obedience and discipline was entirely foreign to them. The moment that they considered they had been injured they rebelled, and their habit of plain speaking was quite extraordinary. Their economic independence naturally generalized among them certain mental and moral attitudes, which persisted under different conditions, though they assumed more refined forms. It was then that the normal foundation on which the nobility was to build in later times was laid. It was easily comprehensible, and entirely dissimilar to the foundation from which the bourgeoisie rose to a position of influence. To the very last the great majority of the nobility would retain the traces of their descent from a class of men to whom all notions of profit and productive labour were alien. To a certain extent the ancient idea that labour is unworthy of the freeman was revived by the chivalry of Europe. But the freeman of antiquity devoted his leisure, which he owed to the labour of his slaves, to public affairs: the knight of the Middle Ages

4 See Ganelon in the *Chanson de Roland.*

profited by the gift of land which he received to devote himself to the calling of arms and the service of his lord. When centuries had passed, and when the nobility had gradually been ousted from the rank which it held of old, the expression "to live like a nobleman" finally came to mean, "to live without doing anything."

SECTION D

THE WESTERN EXPERIENCE:
POLITICS OF TRANSITION

Introduction

The selections in this section highlight a few aspects of the great transformation of Western Europe and America. The central theme here is the forging of the nation-state from a multiplicity of petty powers and competing jurisdictions. Just as there were variations in the starting point, the feudal structure described in the previous section, so there were variations in the final product: the extent to which authority was centralized and, cutting across this dimension, the varieties of administrative, representative, and legal institutions that emerged as the monarchic regimes, in one way or another, came to terms with the traditional rights and powers of the landed nobility. The comparative study of these institutional varieties has long been a dominant interest of political scientists. Yet much work remains to be done in explaining the sources of these variations in terms of social and economic factors, warfare and military arrangements, and the spread of ideas and technologies among these older "developing nations."

The breakdown of the old order fostered new clashes of interests between the remaining aristocratic privileges and the interests and aspirations of the other social classes. Everywhere such conflicts took on a distinctively modern political form in that they were staged on the larger arena of the nation-state, where interested parties attempted to capture the new center of power, gain access to national decision-making, or otherwise elicit concessions in return for their continued loyalty to the state. How such conflicts were solved, by revolution or by relatively peaceful accommodation, depended in large part on the institutional legacy that the struggle between the crown and the landed nobility had bestowed on succeeding generations. Industrialization fostered still other inequalities and new upheavals in society. Politically, the developments brought the eventual extension of the rights of citizenship to the lower classes and ushered in the politics of the welfare state. Again, this aspect of the great transformation varied greatly, and provides a rich field for comparative analysis. Only with the comparative method can we hope to unravel the significant factors and their pattern of interaction in particular cases.

The first selection, by Otto Hintze, consists of excerpts from a long review essay which criticizes the general approach of constructing comprehensive evolutionary schemes and of explaining political change only by factors internal to societies. Much of this critique has been omitted, because the author's remarks are addressed to a particular, now outdated, theory. Yet this evolutionary approach is still much in vogue today. Hintze, by contrast, demonstrates the significant extent to which the structure of societies is shaped by the external relations between states. Taking account of both sources of change, external and internal, he sketches in bold strokes, but with fine historical scholarship, the forging of the nation-state from its remote antecedents in Greek antiquity and in the Roman empire.

The second selection, by Samuel Huntington, shares this concern with the broader world-historical context in which particular political structures develop. Contrasting the political modernization of Western Europe and North America, he advances the hypothesis that the American political system represents a borrowed version, however elaborated and adapted to colonial conditions, of the constitutional monarchy of Tudor England. Thus in America a very old state became associated with a new society that was free of the deep social cleavages characteristic of Europe. In contrast, the European monarchies first had to break down the privileges and constraints of the feudal structure before a new, modern society could emerge. But in this process there emerged also a new state.

The next two selections deal with two opposing and yet linked tendencies in the Western experience of political change: on the one hand, the new kinds of social antagonism that appeared with the breakdown of the feudal order and the emergence of the national state; on the other, the rise of nationalism, which fostered among the antagonistic groups a shared sense of belonging to the same political community. Combined, these two tendencies lie at the heart of the political integration of the masses through the extension of the rights of citizenship. A continuing process, this aspect will be examined in greater detail in the next section.

The third selection, by Alexis de Tocqueville, consists of a few chapters from the author's work on the French Revolution. Tocqueville compares the institutions of the old order in different European societies and shows how these were breaking down everywhere in the course of political and administrative centralization. Yet this breakdown had proceeded further in France than elsewhere; the French aristocracy had lost to the crown nearly all of their former political functions though they still retained their economic privileges — a circumstance that aroused severe social antagonisms. Though these may have been identified as the proximate cause of the revolution, Tocqueville asks why the French called for a revolutionary solution. Why could the democratization advanced by the state not be completed relatively peacefully as in England, that is, through the gradual extension of the rights of citizenship? Tocqueville argues that the centralization and leveling under the old regime had unintentionally radicalized the people, had isolated and fragmented them, had made them hateful of all inequalities and inequities, and in general had produced a cultural climate of opinion which in times of crisis directed political action to the total reorganization of the state. This provides a striking contrast with the case of England, where the conflicts between the aristocracy and the crown had left a legacy of representative institutions that could be opened to the lower classes; and also with colonial America, where the leveling of social conditions was not the product of state action.

The last selection deals with the rise of national feeling attendant upon the centralization of authority and the decline of parochial loyalties. To be sure, the centralized state was not a product of nationalist fervor. But once nationalism emerged, it went far in enhancing the process of centralization. The article assesses the main factors at work in shaping that integrating sense of national community which helped to focus conflicts of interests on the national political arena, but which at times was also evoked by the state to subordinate partisan interests to some end promoted as the common good.

The State in Historical Perspective

OTTO HINTZE

The relationship between the state and society is one of the most obscure and controversial topics of science. The term "society" has not even a stable and generally recognized referent. Yet our scientific thinking about things social is so suffused with notions of distinct societal and political spheres that any general treatment of the subject calls for a renewed effort at conceptualizing this relationship. And so I shall here attempt an essay of this kind.

The formation of a state seems to rest originally on social groups related by ties of blood and sharing a spatial habitat. Tribes and clans or nations have evidently emerged from such kinship groups by a process of natural growth. This primary nation-building during the prehistoric era included race mixtures probably as often as the secondary nation-building during the historic era; yet a relatively homogeneous type regularly reappears after a few generations. No one has ever observed the primary nation-building. Our earliest knowledge is

Translated by Hans-Eberhard Mueller from "Roschers politische Entwicklungstheorie," Soziologie und Geschichte (Göttingen: Vandenhoeck & Ruprecht, 1964), pp. 3–45 passim, by permission of the publisher. The essay was originally published in Schmollers Jahrbuch, Vol. XXI (1897), pp. 768–881.

OTTO HINTZE (1861–1940) was a specialist in Prussian history who in his later years devoted increasing attention to comparative administrative history. A summary of his work on Prussia is contained in Die Hohenzollern und Ihr Werk (1915). His work on comparative administrative history is contained in three volumes of essays, Staat und Verfassung, Soziologie und Geschichte, and Regierung und Verwaltung. Our selection is from the second of these volumes. A first English translation of a collection of his essays is planned by the University of California Press.

of fragmented nations in which only the parts, usually referred to as tribes or clans, are uniformly organized. This type of social organization has a two-fold nature. One aspect consists in the concrete community-life, which is partially a matter of sharing a portion of the earth's surface and partially a matter of common ancestry. Sometimes also alien groups are attached or taken in, particularly when closed geographic areas become settled while other related groups remain outside the organized areas because the external requirements for an ongoing community-life are missing. The other aspect of this type of social organization consists in a system of institutions for the protection, domination, and governance of the entire human and territorial complex. This side of the organization we call the political, the other the social. Seen from one vantage point, the whole is perceived as the state; seen from the other, it is perceived as society.

While state and society are intimately bound up with one another, the state and the nation may diverge. For society is the (originally narrower) circle of human beings tied together in an ongoing community-life; the nation, however, is that (originally more inclusive) circle in which only those traditions from an earlier period of community are passed down that may survive without a continuous life in common. When we speak of society, we have in mind the mutual needs and the system of communication that tie people together — the sphere of economic life, material culture, and external civilization. When we speak of the nation, we have in mind a common ancestry, a community of language, morals, law, and religion, and, on the higher stages of cultural development, the works of art and literature — in short, the ideal things, the cultural uniqueness, developed in a community of related peoples and passed down from one generation to the next.[1] A national community such as this is much too broad a basis for the formation of a state; it can support a state only insofar as it corresponds to a territorial unit which has attained a level of communication and natural as well as economic resources that renders possible the sort of concrete community we have called a society.

Although it is the natural foundation for the state, society has not been generated by the state, nor is the state merely a natural outcome of the developing social system. No one has observed the origin of either. Whatever we may say is merely inference from the psychological and ethical tendencies inherent in the nature of these organizational forms. One might say that these tendencies mutually condition one another like polar opposites. The cultural forces of the collectivity predominate in the sphere of society. They emphasize above all sentiments of common membership in society at large or in individual groups, and they propagate, so to speak, the life of the whole without the individual being clearly conscious of it. The conscious will and individual inclinations — in short, the personality — predominates in the sphere of the state. It strives to govern, to lead, and to rule. By conceptualizing the state as an organism one thinks primarily about the social base; by conceptualizing it as a personality one conveys the perfectly sound idea that the organization created

---

[1] The concept of a "nation," generally in use during the 19th century, is virtually synonymous with the current concept of "culture." [Tr.]

by the consciously leading will is always a reflection of that will — an extension, so to speak, of its own individuality. All public life, at once social and political, consists of the confluence and opposition of these antagonistic complexes of motives.

In the course of history the institutions of the state and of society become interlaced and suffused to such an extent that they are often difficult to separate. The political relations of power and authority influence the distribution of property and break down the social structure based, if only hypothetically, on social equality; each inequality that arises, in turn, causes a shift in political power. Besides inequality of property, occupational differentiation, if hereditary for a long time, may lead certain groups to acquire a typical style of life. The various processes of social differentiation tend naturally to accompany population growth and improvement of communication; but here, too, the state comes in with legal regulation, sometimes attenuating and sometimes furthering those processes. Status groups and social classes emerging in this way in turn affect the political structure. By and large, one should be able to distinguish the more social from the more political processes according to whether they stem more from the organic life of the community or from conscious intelligence and a will to dominate.

In the social realm there is a tendency to lawful organic development, which the state may follow to an extent while at the same time regulating society. Yet the state is by no means solely determined by society. For the state is not merely a government internally but a sovereign power externally. Throughout history power has been the main goal of the activities of the state; hence its structure depends at least as much on the conditions of its external power position as on the social-structural conditions of its internal governing activity. Since the state must adjust itself not only internally but also externally to the conditions of its existence, the external setting must surely influence the internal social development. . . .

We can agree with Roscher that each individual society, each independently organized group, has a natural tendency to develop in the direction indicated by him.[2] We agree that the stages of social differentiation he has shown may be found almost everywhere and that they are connected with the structure of the state. But this connection is much like the relationship between the development of the human personality and the laws of the species. The latter provide the natural basis for personality development without, however, determining its specific nature. As with human beings, the most interesting things about states only appear once they rise above the organic stratum of the species. Of course, the discovery of the general principles of group life, like the discovery by anthropology of the general principles of the human individual, would be a very important scientific advance. But sociology is still far from this achievement. Moreover, it seems that social structures are affected by historical forces

[2] Wilhelm Roscher, *Politik: Geschichtliche Naturlehre der Monarchie, Aristokratie und Demokratie,* 2nd edition (Stuttgart: J. G. Cotta, 1893). [Roscher's was a neo-Aristotelian theory of stages of political development; like most stage theories, it dealt mainly with internal processes of change and neglected the external relations between states. (Tr.)]

quite differently than biological structures are by consciousness. For the organic life of society determines not only the conscious life of the state, but also vice versa. Hence, natural tendencies of development are frequently deflected in the realm of society and history.

We can also agree that, generally speaking, states develop from more aristocratic to more democratic structures, though even this general statement is subject to several objections that I shall not deal with here. However, it is clear that very little is gained from such general formulae. The most interesting phenomena of political development escape through the wide mesh of this net. Moreover, it should be pointed out that states are subject to a universal as well as a particular development. Seen from this perspective, every formation of a state, indeed cultural development in general, is one great interrelated process among world-historical societies. It is a process in which the particular societies on different courses of development are involved, sometimes in opposition and sometimes in convergence. From this process progressively more advanced, more comprehensive, and more complicated political structures emerge that are not lost in the long run. Viewed in their historical context, particular states are conditioned in many ways by their neighbors and predecessors. From this point of view, a break in, or a deflection of, a particular development is a common phenomenon that explains the many characteristic exceptions to Roscher's scheme. Thus, particular formative processes are independent only to a certain point. Societies move generally along a regular, typical course in the early stages of development. But as soon as they come in closer contact with the great world-historical societies and take part in the universal development of culture, unique, world-historically conditioned types appear. These types are common to a relatively small group of societies and are subject to change depending on temporal and spatial conditions.

Such types are above all the city-state of antiquity and the modern nation-state. Both have emerged in specific world-historical conditions. Thus, city-states, evidently a product of the Mediterranean coastal culture, flourished among the Phoenicians, in Greece, and in Rome. In Greece we find them first and primarily on the eastern coast, in Italy on the western coast. In both places they faced Phoenician cities with which they had communicated since time immemorial. Further inland and on the less traveled coasts the older tribal form of state was preserved longer. In the north, in Macedonia, which was more landlocked and less affected by the Phoenician-Hellenic traffic, this older tribal form developed into a completely different one: a territorial state with a strictly monarchic structure. By developing its military might, this state eventually came to dominate the powerless city-states and to rule the coveted Persian empire. This universal state finally disintegrated. But in the place of the old self-sufficient city-states the larger territorial formations, including also such city alliances as the Achaean, began to dominate in the world of states. However, with the exception of traditionally centralized Egypt, these territorial states, too, tended to dissolve into city districts for reasons of administration, so that actual territorial administrations never developed.

The Roman empire completed this municipal system of administration.

Through a system of unequal alliances the Roman city community extended its power more favorably than Athens had with its system of alliances which gave equal status to all members. A giant conglomeration of dominated city districts was grouped around the ruling capital. Eventually the principle of municipal organization was extended also to the barbaric hinterland, which originally had no city life at all. The administration of this empire was centralized only in the military and fiscal branches. The actual internal administration was left to the city communities in which the decurions were responsible for the collection of taxes. Thus organized, the empire lost its foundation when the economic basis of the city — the exchange of goods with the surrounding country — gave way in the 3rd century owing to the decline of Mediterranean culture, the return to agriculture spreading from the inland outwards, and the development of the colonate and the large economically self-sufficient estates.[3] The cities disintegrated, their economic potential gave way, and with that the whole administrative apparatus of the gigantic empire collapsed.[4]

The municipal form of organization disappeared for a long time and was replaced by the feudal type, which had already been prepared by the economic, administrative, and military transformations of the declining Roman empire. In this context the feudal military system emerged beginning with the Saracen wars of Charles Martel and was followed by the feudal transformation of the administration of the Frankish empire. The division of the latter into counties (*Grafschaftsgaue*) was adapted in Gaul to the old municipal districts and in Germany probably to the ancient political structures from the period of tribal organization. In both cases, the administration became purely provincial and territorial; and in both cases the office was transformed into a fief, which was administered in the king's name but for the holder's benefit. A centralized administration as blocked because of the poor conditions of communication and the prevailing practice of granting lands as a means of compensating the officials.

From this starting point have emerged the forces that have forged over the centuries the modern system of European states. This formative process rests only in part on the unique institutions of the Germanic peoples; it is also closely related to the traditions of the Roman empire. The world-encompassing organization created by Rome did not disappear all at once. The

---

[3] The colonate refers to a system of rights and duties — a kind of serfdom of the soil — which developed during the later Roman empire. The colonus was a hereditary farmer legally attached to the soil. His landlord was not allowed to sell his estate without the coloni, nor the coloni without the estate. Moreover, the landlord had no right to increase the rent or to alter the duties of his tenants. In civil law the colonus was considered a free man, capable of contracting marriage, of making a will, and of initiating legal action pertaining to his tenure. For a fuller description of this system see Ferdinand Lot, *The End of the Ancient World and the Beginnings of the Middle Ages* (New York: Harper Torchbooks, 1961), pp. 107 ff. [Tr.]

[4] Cf. Max Weber, "Die sozialen Gründe des Untergangs der antiken Kultur," *Die Wahrheit*, Vol. VI (1896). [Reprinted in Max Weber, *Gesammelte Aufsätze zur Sozial-und Wirtschaftsgeschichte* (Tübingen: J. C. B. Mohr, 1924), pp. 289–311. There is also an English translation entitled "The Social Causes of the Decay of Ancient Civilization," *Journal of General Education*, Vol. V (1950), pp. 75–88. (Tr.)]

political unity of the West, renewed by Charlemagne, did not actually last very long; but as an idea it stirred the entire Middle Ages and is alive even in the 19th century. Still more important was the mighty organization of the Roman church, the heir to the worldwide dominance of the Roman state. At the height of its power the Roman church, symbolizing the spiritual and religious unity of the West, virtually ruled supreme. Only with the collapse of the church hierarchy did the new states come to life.

East and West Franconia were not yet national states, but parts of the disintegrating Carolingian empire. There was a natural tendency for the empire to disintegrate further and further and for the parts, which were already cohesive in themselves, to become isolated and independent. During the 10th century, a cohesive organization existed in the territories of the great vassals in France and in the tribal areas in Germany, where the landed powers emerged somewhat later owing to the slower advance of the feudal principle. In France one territorial power of feudal origin conquered the others and organized the empire by extending its patrimonial power. In Germany a multiplicity of territorial powers emerged and prevented the centralization of the whole. The different developments of the two lands were due primarily to the different positions of the rulers with regard to the church and the idea of universal politics in the imperialist tradition. Thus, the aftereffects of the Roman influence were significant throughout. Though initially removed from the Roman influence, the Anglo-Saxon state across the channel also came under its spell in indirect but concentrated form during the Norman conquest.

Moreover, the independent and increasingly predominant role of the church in the internal political changes of the Western states has been very significant. The aristocratic and in part also the municipal powers over against the monarchy, the core of the estate (*ständischen*) principle, were developed most strongly among the Romano-Germanic peoples. This development was clearly enhanced by the continuous struggle between the highest spiritual and secular powers, which gave those "intermediate" powers enough play to develop their own strength. In the final analysis, the Magna Carta emerged from a situation fostered by church quarrels. In the conflict between Boniface VIII on the one hand and Edward I and Philip IV on the other, the English parliament gained its power of the purse and the French Estates-General became politically significant for the first time. The conflict between emperor and pope lies also behind the power of the German princes and the imperial estates. Moreover, the unique character and growing significance of the monarchy after the 15th and 16th centuries were determined by the crown's relationship to the spiritual power. Owing to the Reformation in the Protestant countries and the concordates with the Curia in the Catholic lands, authority over the church, important to the governance of the realm, was transferred completely or partially from the pope to the monarch. The kings and princes of more recent times thus became the heirs and assignees of the papacy. Among Catholic kings this was most fully the case in Spain; among Protestant kings the English took the lead. Their authority — one might say the legitimacy of princely sovereignty in general — was not purely secular in origin. During the Middle Ages an educational process had inculcated the masses over the centuries with a sentiment of unconditional subordination and awe in the face of the church and its head. This sentiment was now completely or partially carried over into subordination to the secular head. The latter became the holder of a new religious sovereignty and, in some cases, the actual head of the state church. This political-psychological process played an important role in the emergence of the doctrine of the divine right of kings.

This unique development of both the estate and the monarchic principles distinguishes the states which emerged from the social institution of the Western church from all other states in the world. If we compare the political structures of the Romano-Germanic peoples with those of other culture areas — for example, the areas of the Orthodox church or of Islam — then the difference becomes readily apparent. A politically privileged nobility, one element of the estate principle, developed neither in Russia nor in Turkey, though both had a special kind of feudalism. For in these countries the secular and spiritual power was combined either from the beginning or since very early times. Similar considerations seem to apply to the great East-Asian empires; hence, the theocratic-despotic tendency of the Oriental states.

How the modern representative systems have developed from the estate systems of the Romano-Germanic peoples — partially by way of absolute monarchy — cannot be dealt with here. I merely wish to point out that the unique character of our modern states cannot be explained as a product of isolated individual developments but only as a result of significant influences from the universal world-historical context.

Roscher's complete neglect of this world-historical context of political development is perhaps the most glaring deficiency of his theory. It is also the reason why his theory almost completely misses two important tendencies of political development which have directly and indirectly determined the character and structure of the Western European states. These become apparent especially through a comparison of the classical and the modern eras. One tendency is the progressive abolition of personal servitude and legal inequalities, which affected a part of the population in former times; the other is the emergence of ever larger and more encompassing states in the course of world history.

Political life in antiquity is unthinkable without the fundamental institution of slavery, although its significance may often have been exaggerated. The domestic economy based on slave labor was probably never the decisive economic institution, at least not at the height of the classical culture. . . . Yet it cannot be denied that the unique political life of antiquity rose and declined with the slave economy. The very existence of the Greek city-states depended on the institution of slavery — in fact, the more so as the city communicated with others and participated in the progress of the Mediterranean culture. Like the Greek cities, the Roman municipalities, too, depended for survival on a slave economy: With the decline of the Italian peasantry the character of Roman agriculture was determined by slavery, and interlocal commerce depended more and more on the products of unfree labor. Thus, the regular supply of slaves became an important public concern and the capturing of slaves a chief consideration in warfare.

As the classical world reached its greatest extension, as the Roman empire met the borders of the Germanic forest areas and the Dacian and Syrian steppes, and as the end of foreign wars cut off the supply of slave labor, a curious change occurred, described by Max Weber, which culminated in the collapse of the political order of antiquity. Although the number of slaves in Athens during the Peloponnesian war was only 100,000 against 135,000 freemen, this city of 35,000 citizens was really an aristocracy, even at the height of its democracy. Though the city-states of antiquity and the cities of the Middle Ages are very similar, we cannot subsume both under the same political type; medieval city life made man free, whereas in antiquity, according to Plato and Aristotle, the ideal of citizenship was inseparable from the idea of a slave household.

A world-historical development leads from slavery to serfdom and thence to personal liberty. It is customary to assign the second stage to the Middle Ages and the third stage to the modern era. However, the justification for this practice is controversial. The world-historical conception of the Middle Ages may be confronted with a national-historical conception. There is a Greek Middle Ages as there is a German one; and both share serfdom, among other institutions. There is nothing objectionable in this conception, except that it focuses only on one side of the problem. The question at hand is especially difficult because the national Middle Ages of the Germanic peoples overlaps with a world-historical period of transition, which has also been designated as *medium aevum*, at least in former times. This historical epoch of Latin Christendom is characterized by the predominant position of the church and the culture represented by the church. It is characterized also by the aftereffects of the idea of a universal state and by the institutions of feudalism and serfdom. In the form known to the Middle Ages and the beginning of the modern era, serfdom is not a purely national-historical product but a world-historical phenomenon. It sprang directly from the metamorphoses of a declining Roman slavery. Serfdom is almost more a legacy of antiquity than an inherent product of the Germanic peoples. Serfdom and feudalism go together. They are two sides of one and the same process — of a large-scale division of labor which affected and transformed a population in transition from the primitive conditions of tribal life to the exigencies of an empire. This process originated in the military establishment and eventually governed all public life.

These transformations in the social conditions of Europe were not caused by purely economic factors. In the background we always find the requirements of the nation as a whole, that is, the conditions of a rapidly and radically transformed political existence, thrust from national tranquility onto the stage of world history. Low population density and an exclusively agricultural economy were of course the preconditions for the social cleavage of feudalism. Yet as cities began to develop owing to improved communications, increasing population density, and a returning money economy, this cleavage came to be rooted no longer in the household based on unfree labor but in a new form of enterprise, which uniquely associated free workers with smaller family households. Political entities of greater or lesser independence developed. Freedom, not only for citizens, but for all inhabitants, became an unshakable principle. Thus, these political entities, which for centuries had kept alive a struggle between town and country that was unknown to antiquity, furnished the model for the modern nation-state.

The emergence of serfdom is related to military needs stemming from the general world situation. In the military states on the continent serfdom was preserved longer than in England, which developed early toward the mercantile and industrial type. Owing to the political situation of Europe as a whole, military considerations again rendered necessary the final abolition of serfdom at the very place where, more than anywhere else, it had become the cornerstone of the state. To be sure, the main economic reason for the establishment of serfdom in the north-eastern territories was the rise of large estates since the 16th century. But it is unlikely that this institution could have prevailed through the 18th century without the Prussian king's political interest in maintaining a feudal nobility and an unfree rural population. For the status group of military officers depended on the nobility, while the system of cantons depended on the institution of serfdom. Both of these in turn supported the army and therefore the entire Prussian state. As a result, attempts by the absolute monarchy to emancipate the rural population came to naught for a whole century; emancipation came to pass only once the reform of peasant conditions became a precondition of military reforms which had become inescapable politically. A peculiar reversal of conditions caused the very strata of the population which had become unwarlike during the era of self-equipped armies and which had therefore fallen into servitude to provide the best and most reliable recruits once standing armies, financed and equipped by the state, were established. This change, in turn, eased the people's ascent to liberty. The relationship is not as clear in France as in Prussia; yet it may still be possible to suggest that the military uprising of 1793 finally sealed the decisions of the night of August 4, 1789.

All these changes were not typical, regularly recurring stages of societal development but part of a great universal development, a world-historical process whose influence no nation and no state could escape. Russia emancipated her serfs after the Crimean war. Probably following the European model, she had instituted serfdom at the end of the 16th century, not because her own social development rendered its occurrence necessary, but rather for reasons of state. The experience of the Western European states seemed to promise that serfdom would increase the power of the state. Slavery in the southern states of the United States, moreover, is no proof that this institution may be found in all periods of world history. This was only a local and transitory phenomenon, destined to disappear the moment America entered the community of modern states as an equal member. Finally, the world-historical development in the direction of personal freedom for the masses has occurred even against the grain of economic and natural conditions. It was supported by ethical views and political necessities stemming from the great international context of our cultural life. It is the most significant example of the aforementioned feedback from the conscious historical life to the organic basis of societal existence.

. . . These world-historical processes had an immense influence on the political life of nations, determining the nature of our military organization, our legal and administrative systems, and our party systems. Our political atmosphere today is completely different from that of the Greeks in the period of Hellenism or the Romans under the emperors. The progressive liberation of the masses is a matter of adjustment and extension of the societal base — a change in the human material — upon which the state rests. The other world-historical tendency with which we must deal has to do with the transformation of the spatial base of the state: the progressive enlargement of the governed territories or the extension of the borders within which political development takes place.

The fact of territorial expansion is obvious once we think about the course of ancient history from the Greek city-states to the giant state of the Roman empire and the gradual growth of the modern political structures. It also becomes obvious once we compare the modern type of large nation-states with the more or less confined city districts of antiquity. Between these extremes, however, lie an enormous number of more or less extensive changes which tend to obscure the broader tendency of territorial expansion.

Such large states as Egypt and Babylonia, whose origin we are unable to trace, were carried over into the historical era. They became the points of departure for the unification of the entire Near Eastern culture area by the first great empire in history — the Persian empire. As soon as this empire had conquered the Mediterranean coast, as if following a law of states, war with the smaller states on the Greek coast and the islands became inevitable. But before the victor had been clearly determined, the best forces on both sides were exhausted. A third power, Macedonia, rose up, subjugated both, and founded an even larger empire. Just as the old Persian empire tended to dissolve into satrapies, so this new empire soon dissolved into the Diadochian states under the successors of Alexander. Grown from a city district to a world power, Rome finally incorporated this whole conglomeration of eastern states all the way to the borders of the actual Persian empire. And so the Mediterranean culture, its outposts far inland, forged for centuries a state governing the *orbis terrarum*. But once the forces of the Mediterranean culture weakened, once its foundation — the municipal community — crumbled, this mighty empire, too, fell apart piece by piece in a process of dissolution that lasted centuries. From the ruins, some of which were naturally cohesive, there finally emerged the larger states of the present, growing together more or less slowly in constant friction and mutual displacement.

In this formative process one may distinguish two distinct aspects of a dual tendency: on the one hand, the emergence of universal empires governing an entire culture area; on the other hand, the emergence of more individualized states. In the latter process a state begins to develop in a certain area but does not extend beyond the limits set by the cohesion of the population, the natural unity of the territory, and the possibility for effective administration.

The first type of formative process may be called extensive, the second intensive. The first creates only a loose cohesion and superficial centralization: the state rules more than it administers. The second type, by contrast, is limited to relatively small and homogeneous areas and populations; growing slowly, the state assimilates and organizes, thus forging a strong cohesion through intensive activity. The extensive type rests more on the drive to dominance and exploitation, manifested primarily by some great despots; the intensive type rests more on the social cohesion of a community. Such a community may gradually grow into an empire, but this always presupposes the influence of great rulers. The extensive type of formative process obtained most clearly and purely where a warlike nomadic people, such as the Tartars under Genghis Khan, fell upon a settled agricultural population and erected a system of domination whose administrative purpose was limited to the extraction of tribute. The intensive type, on the other hand, was possible only among a settled agricultural population.

Ratzel has called the peoples of the steppes "spatially extended" in contradistinction to the "spatially confined" peasant peoples.[5] For the nomads' "political concept of space" is infinitely more extended than that of the primitive peasants. Therefore it is not unlikely that the encounter of nomads and peasants at the frontier regions has sparked the intensive type of formative process. However, in the course of history this type became divorced from the nomadic habits of conquerors. It came into its own through increased communication, which produced a homogeneous civilization, uniform habits of life in a cohesive web of nations, and hence the idea of cultural unity. Its actual engine, however, was the political drive to dominate and to master the entire complex of human relationships that seemed capable of centralization. This is achieved by a unified will that orders and guides, by a vision that transcends accustomed patterns of life, that grasps things to come and discovers in them the blueprint of a future edifice of power. Last, but not least, it is achieved by the expansive force of a military organization.

It seems that this ever recurring tendency towards world domination furnished an important lever for the progress of human civilization. However, most of the states which thus emerged, resembled the biblical colossus with feet of clay. They lacked internal cohesion, an ongoing community-life, a permanent social organization at the base. Even the Roman administration cared only about the army and the finances. Everything else was left to the care of the municipal offices. As a result, no unified internal administration with a single perspective developed, nor did a welfare policy to maintain an equilibrium between the demands of the state and the productive capacity of the economy. To centralize this sector of the administration was perhaps impossible in those days; hence, there was always a danger that the administrative system would eventually end up exhausting the population. This is precisely the danger inherent in the lack of intensity in realizing political goals — a characteristic

[5] Friedrich Ratzel, "Der Staat und sein Boden," *Abhandlungen der königlich-sächsischen Gesellschaft der Wissenschaft* (phil.–hist. Klasse), Vol. XVII, No. 4 (1896).

deficiency in the development of these states. The intensive way of forging a state, which we tend to regard as "natural," operates on a smaller scale. Its hallmark is organization and administration, and it is usually at work long before the large states fall apart. Once the work of a state can no longer be accomplished on a universal scale, it devolves naturally on smaller units with the necessary cohesion and organization. And so the process of forging a state begins all over again.

We rarely find a formative process with only one or the other tendency. As a rule the two operate together. The question is merely whether one or the other gains the upper hand or whether both types are in equilibrium. The main criterion is always whether the state has been able to develop an administration that combines the purposes of power and welfare.

The influence of universal state structures upon neighboring or successor states perhaps explains the initially curious fact that at the beginning of history we find several large centralized empires which in the course of further cultural development fragmented or dissolved into loose entities with more or less independent parts. Thus, the empire of Charlemagne and the German-Roman empire ended in territorial fragmentation. There is evidence of this in France as well as in Germany; only the Anglo-Saxon state, untouched by the universal influence, has grown steadily. The west Slavic tribes united in the 10th century under Boleslav Chrobry, only to fragment completely later on. Rachfahl was probably correct in supposing that the Carolingian empire had furnished the model for this development.[6] Similar state structures were the Moravian empire and the empire of Knut the Great. And if Eduard Meyer's reconstruction of the Mycenaean epoch is correct, then we have still another analogous case: fashioned after the model of the Oriental states, the Mycenaean state was a large empire with strong royal powers extending across the Peloponnesus and a part of central Greece. Cultural progress and intensive political development also caused this empire to dissolve into the city-states of the classical period. According to Meyer, the centralized and unified state of the old Egyptian empire similarly gave way to the feudal state of the middle period, in which an effective central power is, of course, no longer discernible.

We know that the tendency to the formation of city-states like those of antiquity has appeared also in more recent times. But these little city republics have as a rule been swallowed up by more encompassing structures. This is partially due to the different geographic conditions of the newer states and above all to the development of overland traffic since the Middle Ages. It is also partially due to the historical experience and customs, to the extension of the political horizon, and to the transformation of the political sense of space in general, which coexistence in one large empire, such as the Roman, was bound to bring about. France, Germany, and Spain were destined, so to speak, to unify more or less completely even before a spontaneous political development of a nationalist character spread from one border to the other. The geographic unity of those areas was discovered in the great states of the Roman

---

[6] Felix Rachfahl, *Die Organization der Gesamtstaatsverwaltung Schlesiens vor dem dreissigjährigen Kriege* (Leipzig: Duncker & Humblot, 1894), pp. 12 ff.

and later the Carolingian empires; and, as Ratzel put it, these natural regions then strove to become political territories. It was a legacy of the past world-historical epoch that these formative processes on the continent were guided by the idea of a larger political unit.

In their really effective and enduring form these states, having developed from several starting points, have grown only gradually and very unevenly into their eventual frame. The development of the Anglo-Saxon state on the British isle, removed from the Roman influence, began with small empires and proceeded to larger ones until the full extent of ethnic unity was achieved. Also in France a really enduring state developed only after the emergence of the feudal territorial powers. Elevated by the Carolingian crown and blessed by the Church, the Capetians through good fortune and determination incorporated one after the other of these territories into their patrimony. Similarly, in Germany an enduring state developed only after the emergence of the petty principalities and the territorial states, which lasted until the foundation of the new empire. In fact, everywhere on the continent the small territorial states preceded the modern nation-states. The development in Germany only represents the clearest, but by no means the only, example. The moving forces of this process are not limited to natural and social factors such as population growth, development of communication, and so on. Rather, they include above all a political drive to power, rivalries and conflicts between neighbors, and the constant pushing and shoving between states by which the European equilibrium reestablished itself in the face of a traditional preponderance of one power with universal tendencies.

It is curious how the various stages of the states' external development corresponded to their internal structure. Thus, the structure of the small territorial states was of the estate-type (*ständisch*); but with the transition from the aggregated territorial state to the unified modern state there usually emerged absolute monarchy. At a later stage of development, once the idea of political unity applied no longer only to the central power, but had become diffused to the entire population, a representative system emerged.

The various causes underlying the enlargement of states seem also to change the internal nature and constitution of the states. Aristotle was already aware of this when he explained the necessity for limiting the size of the polis: its population should be no smaller than necessary for self-sufficiency but also no larger than appropriate for the equally requisite cohesion among the citizenry. If a city grows beyond these limits, then it changes from a political community to a "nation." For Aristotle this meant an unorganized or at least not "politically" organized mass. In more recent times the following development generally took place. The city-state became a nation-state, which entailed a fundamental change in the internal structure and constitution of the state: people today can no longer participate in government through the institutional forms of Greek democracy. When, during the French revolution something like this was attempted, France faced the danger of splitting apart into many small republics, which proved the absurdity of the idea. Rousseau's ideal, to be sure, involved a state of approximately ten thousand citizens; hence, his inability to comprehend the representative system, which until now has been the only way for large modern states to let the people participate in government. . . .

A development toward absolutism often accompanied the emergence of the large unified states in the modern period. In antiquity, the extension of the Roman empire similarly destroyed the foundation of the old republican regime and created the necessity for an absolute monarchy. The agrarian problem, the ruination of the Italian peasantry, the transformation of the militia into a mercenary army and finally into a standing army — all these developments, intimately bound up with the external growth of the state, also forced the destruction of the republican constitution and the rise of an absolute regime. Conversely, everywhere in Greek antiquity the monarchies disappeared where-ever the city-states emerged in their characteristic form. For the municipal character of these little city-states was incompatible with a real monarchy. Finally, the lords spiritual and temporal of the medieval cities declined in the same way once these cities became politically independent.

A real state, not only a municipal but also a political structure, has usually emerged only where a city was the center of a district large enough to guarantee the Aristotelian self-sufficiency. The position of Athens and Sparta in Hellas rested basically on the fact that both had unified a whole territory under their rule — the one through federation and the other through military subjection. At the beginning of the republic, Rome, too, was a city with a large territory; similarly, the thirty-five tribes of the later period, whose topographical reconstruction is to my knowledge no longer possible, must have constituted a rather significant territory. The Italian city-states of the Renaissance might be compared with the German territorial states; however, the German cities did not become as significant, primarily because they did not succeed in acquiring the territorial possessions necessary for political independence.

The territorial state as it emerged in Germany since the 14th and 15th centuries was already a large compound structure. In addition to various private jurisdictions of princes, it was composed in part of city districts and in part of country districts, which, fairly cohesive from time immemorial, were mostly known as "Länder." [7] Switzerland provides a good example of a state which was arrested at the preterritorial stage or rather which developed in a unique federal direction from this starting point. In the provinces of the United Netherlands the territorial mode of development proceeded one step further. But as elsewhere on the North Sea coast this led to an individualization of the territories rather than to an integration of small lands into a larger state. Up till now all studies on the estate structure of the territories have shown that the external and internal formative processes — the development of the territory and the development of the estate structure — went hand in hand. The estate system, an epiphenomenon of the territorial development of states, emerged as soon as an area was consolidated and had grown into a large or

---

[7] A *Land* (pl. *Länder*) is a political territory — a state or part of a state such as a province — with a strong cultural tradition and frequently an ethnic identification. [Tr.]

small "country." Those who had been helpful to the prince in military and financial matters, and continued to be indispensable, took part in the public affairs of the state.

The early development of royal power in France has somewhat obscured the territorial foundation of the political structure. But there, too, it was present, for the ideal unity of France became real only through an unrelenting struggle of the central power with the territorial forces. This battle was fought first against the great vassals and then against the provincial assemblies. It was in the latter, not in the Estates-General, that the life of the estate system pulsated most vigorously and regularly. At the time of Richelieu, France was still at the stage of an aggregated territorial state, unified neither in its constitution nor its administration. The transition occurred only in the 17th and 18th centuries, the period of absolutism and administrative centralization; it was finally completed by Napoleon. As a unified state, moreover, France became the model of development for the entire continent. However, it was no mere imitation or superficial copying that drove the neighbors to forge larger states but a natural reaction and sheer political necessity — in short, an act of self-preservation. Finally, wherever territories combined into a unified state the estate structure gave way to royal absolutism.

England is a special case in this respect. The old English state of the Tudor era was not only the largest but also the healthiest and most powerful territorial state of the period. Its political structure was quite similar to the system of provincial assemblies (landständische Verfassungen) on the continent. Its mercantile significance and its colonial possessions should not deceive us: it was only a small state by European standards. With the ascent of the Stuarts to the throne it became an aggregated territorial state. The problem of integrating England and Scotland immediately raised the question of structural change. Since the Reformation the English crown has derived its greatest strength from its religious sovereignty, which Parliament was unable to limit significantly. By extending the Anglican system to Presbyterian Scotland, the Stuarts evidently strove to unify the two countries under the predominant power of the crown. It was against this measure that Parliament, its position endangered, united with the resisting Scots. What followed was a struggle over centralization and absolutism as on the continent, though with a difference: in England royal power lost the battle. The union between England and Scotland materialized only once the estate system was firmly established (1706). Thus, the union was not a product of the crown, but of Parliament, not an integration of two countries by a monarchic regime subjecting both, but a union of estates or, more precisely, an association of the Scottish with the English parliament.

Ireland's incorporation in 1801 proceeded similarly. Old England became Great Britain, but again the extension of the state had consequences for the internal structure: it destroyed the closed system of the Old-English provincial political structure (landständische Verfassung). Since the Reformation and the Revolution the English state rested on the close relations between church and state. The union with Scotland created problems because the test and corporation acts, legally barring Presbyterian Scotsmen from government offices, had remained in force. Of course, here and there the Protestant dissidents were simply ignored; but when it came to appointing Irish Catholics this practice was no longer tenable, so that the confessions had to be equalized. After a generation of strong resistance the Presbyterians and Catholics were emancipated in 1828 and 1829. As Gneist put it, "This meant a breach in the closed position of the ruling class, in which further reforms could be undertaken." [8] These reforms, not yet completed, have tended to transform the English parliamentary system into a representative system in the continental style and self-government into a central bureaucracy.

The far-reaching changes in our large modern states may to a large extent be conceived as products of political growth. As a growing organism changes its structure, as the addition of mass brings structural refinement and diversity, so it is with states. Improvement of communication, population growth, and increased density were the preconditions for an encompassing political organization of our modern societies. Political centralization, on the other hand, reacted back upon communication and economic life. Schmoller has proved that mercantilism was but the economic-political aspect of that great formative process to which the European states still by and large owe their form and relative power. The enlargement and liberation of markets and the new nationwide division of labor primarily in the realm of production influenced most significantly the information of social classes. The old stratification by estates declined more and more, giving way to new classes based on property and education, on occupation and political position. Finally, this transformation in turn enhanced the development of our representative political systems. . . .

[8] Rudolph von Gneist, "Die Entwicklung der englischen Parlamentsverfassung," in Franz von Holtzendorff, *Encyclopädie der Rechtswissenschaft* (Leipzig: Duncker & Humblot, 1890), Vol. I, p. 1458. Cf. also Rudolf von Gneist, *Englische Verfassungsgeschichte* (Berlin: J. Springer, 1882), p. 717 n.

Political Modernization:
America vs. Europe

SAMUEL P. HUNTINGTON

I. THREE PATTERNS OF MODERNIZATION

Political modernization involves, let us assume, three things. First, it involves the rationalization of authority: the replacement of a large number of traditional, religious, familial, and ethnic political authorities by a single, secular, national political authority. This change implies that government is the product of man, not of nature or of God, and that well-ordered society must have a determinate human source of final authority, obedience to whose positive law takes precedence over other obligations. Rationalization of authority means assertion/ of the external sovereignty of the nation-state against transnational influences and of the internal sovereignty of the national government against local and regional powers. It means national integration and the centralization or accumulation of power in recognized national law-making institutions. Secondly, political modernization involves the differentiation of new political functions and the development of specialized structures to perform those functions. Areas of peculiar competence — legal, military, administrative, scientific — become separated from the political realm, and autonomous, specialized, but subordinate, organs arise to discharge those tasks. Administrative hierarchies become more elaborate, more complex, more disciplined. Office and power are distributed more by achievement and less by ascription. Thirdly, political modernization involves increased participation in politics by social groups throughout society and the development of new political institutions — such as political parties and interest associations — to organize this participation. Broadened participation in politics may increase control of the people by the government, as in totalitarian states, or it may increase control of the government by the people, as in some democratic ones. But in all modern states the citizens become directly involved in and affected by governmental affairs. Rationalized authority, differentiated structure, and mass participation thus distinguish modern polities from antecedent polities.

The political modernization of Western Europe and North America was, of course, spread over many centuries. In general, the broadening of participation in politics came after the rationalization of authority and the differentiation of structure. Significant broadened participation dates from the latter half of the eighteenth century. The rationalization of authority and the differentiation of structure got under way in earnest in the seventeenth century. This article

From World Politics, Vol. XVIII, No. 3 (April 1966), pp. 378–414. Reprinted by permission of the author and publisher.

SAMUEL P. HUNTINGTON is Professor of Government, Harvard University. An authority on military sociology, he is the author of The Soldier and the State (1957), The Theory and Politics of Civil Military Relations (1957), and The Common Defense (1961). He has co-authored Political Power, USA-USSR (1964) with Zbigniew Brzezinski, and has also edited and co-edited numerous other works.

will be primarily concerned with these earlier phases of political modernization in Europe and America.[1]

Three distinct patterns of political modernization can be distinguished: Continental, British, and American. On the Continent the rationalization of authority and the differentiation of structures were dominant trends of the seventeenth century. "It is misleading to summarize in a single phrase any long historical process," Sir George Clark observes, "but the work of monarchy in the seventeenth century may be described as the substitution of a simpler and more unified government for the complexities of feudalism. On one side it was centralization, the bringing of local business under the supervision or control of the government of the capital. This necessarily had as its converse a tendency toward uniformity." [2] It was the age of the great simplifiers, centralizers, and modernizers: Richelieu, Mazarin, Louis XIV, Colbert, and Louvois in France; the Great Elector in Prussia; Gustavus Adolphus and Charles XI in Sweden; Philip IV and Olivares in Spain; and their countless imitators among the lesser realms of the Continent. The modern state replaced the feudal principality; loyalty to the state superseded loyalty to church and to dynasty. "I am more obligated to the state," Louis XIII declared on the famous "Day of Dupes," November 11, 1630, when he rejected the Queen Mother and her claims for family in favor of the Cardinal and his claims for the state. "More than any other single day," Friedrich argues, "it may be called the birthday of the modern state." [3] With the birth of the modern state came the subordination of the church, the suppression of the medieval estates, and the weakening of the aristocracy by the rise of new groups. In addition, the century witnessed the rapid growth and rationalization of state bureaucracies and public services, the origin and expansion of standing armies, and the extension and improvement of taxation. In 1600 the medieval political world was still a reality on the Continent; by 1700 it had been replaced by the modern world of nation-states.

The British pattern of evolution was similar in nature to that on the Continent but rather different in results. In Britain, too, church was subordinated to state, authority was centralized, sovereignty asserted internally as well as externally, legal and political institutions differentiated, bureaucracies expanded, and a standing army created. The efforts of the Stuarts, however, to rationalize authority along the lines of continental absolutism provoked a constitutional struggle, from which Parliament eventually emerged the victor. In Britain, as on the Continent, authority was centralized but it was centralized

[1] For the sake of clarity, let me make clear the geographical scope I give these terms. With appropriate apologies to Latin Americans and Canadians, I feel compelled by the demands of brevity to use the term "America" to refer to the thirteen colonies that subsequently became the United States of America. By "Europe" I mean Great Britain and the Continent. By "the Continent" I refer to France, the Low Countries, Spain, Portugal, Sweden, and the Holy Roman Empire.

[2] George Clark, *The Seventeenth Century* (Oxford: Clarendon Press, 1961), 91.

[3] Carl J. Friedrich, *The Age of the Baroque: 1610–1660* (New York: Harper, 1952), 215–16.

in Parliament rather than in the Crown. This was no less of a revolution than occurred on the Continent and perhaps even more of one.

In America, on the other hand, the political system did not undergo any revolutionary changes at all. Instead, the principal elements of the English sixteenth-century constitution were exported to the New World, took root there, and were given new life at precisely the time they were being abandoned in the home country. These Tudor institutions were still partially medieval in character. The Tudor century saw some steps toward modernization in English politics, particularly the establishment of the supremacy of the state over the church, a heightened sense of national identity and consciousness, and a significant increase in the power of the Crown and the executive establishment. Nonetheless, even in Elizabethan government, the first point of importance is "the fundamental factor of continuity with the Middle Ages." [4] The sixteenth century saw, as Chrimes says, "The Zenith of the Medieval Constitution." The changes introduced by the Tudor monarchs did not have "the effect of breaking down the essential principles of the medieval Constitution, nor even its structure." [5] Among these principles and structures were the idea of the organic union of society and government, the harmony of authorities within government, the subordination of government to fundamental law, the intermingling of the legal and political realms, the balance of power between Crown and Parliament, the complementary representative roles of these two institutions, the vitality of local governmental authorities, and reliance on local forces for the defense of the realm.

The English colonists took these late medieval and Tudor political ideas, practices, and institutions across the Atlantic with them during the great migrations in the first half of the seventeenth century. The patterns of thought and behavior established in the New World developed and grew but did not substantially change during the century and a half of colonihood. The English generation of 1603–1630, Notestein remarks, was "one in which medieval ideas and practices were by no means forgotten and in which new conceptions and new ways of doing things were coming in. The American tradition, or that part derived from England, was at least in some degree established by the early colonists. The English who came over later must have found the English Americans somewhat settled in their ways." [6] The conflict between the colonists and the British government in the middle of the eighteenth century served only to reinforce the colonists' adherence to their traditional patterns. In the words of our greatest constitutional historian, "The colonists retained to a marked

[4] A. L. Rowse, *The England of Elizabeth* (New York: The Macmillan Co., 1951), 262.

[5] S. B. Chrimes, *English Constitutional History*, 2nd ed. (London: Oxford University Press, 1953), 121–23. See also W. S. Holdsworth, *A History of English Law*, 3rd ed. (London 1945), IV, 209 ff.

[6] Wallace Notestein, *The English People on the Eve of Colonization: 1603–1630* (New York: Harper, 1954), xiv. See also Edward S. Corwin, *The "Higher Law" Background of American Constitutional Law* (Ithaca, N.Y.: Great Seal Books, 1955), 74.

and unusual degree the traditions of Tudor England. In all our study of American institutions, colonial and contemporary, institutions of both public law and private law, this fact must be reckoned with. The breach between colonies and mother country was largely a mutual misunderstanding based, in great part, on the fact of this retention of older ideas in the colonies after parliamentary sovereignty had driven them out in the mother country." [7] In the constitutional debates before the American Revolution, the colonists in effect argued the case of the old English constitution against the merits of the new British constitution which had come into existence during the century after they had left the mother country. "Their theory," as Pollard says, "was essentially medieval." [8]

These ancient practices and ideas were embodied in the state constitutions drafted after independence and in the Federal Constitution of 1787. Not only is the American Constitution the oldest written national constitution in the world, but it is also a constitution which in large part simply codified and formalized on the national level practices and institutions that had long existed on the colonial level. The institutional framework established in 1787 has, in turn, changed remarkably little in 175 years. Hence, the American system "can be properly understood, in its origin, development, workings and spirit, only in the light of precedents and traditions which run back to the England of the civil wars and the period before the civil wars." [9] The American political system of the twentieth century still bears a closer approximation to the Tudor polity of the sixteenth century than does the British political system of the twentieth century. "Americanisms in politics, like Americanisms in speech," as Henry Jones Ford put it, "are apt to be Anglicisms which died out in England but survived in the new world." [10] The British broke their traditional political patterns in the seventeenth century. The Americans did not do so then and have only partially done so since then. Political modernization in America thus has been strangely attenuated and incomplete. In institutional terms, the American polity has never been underdeveloped, but it has also never been wholly modern.[11] In an age of rationalized authority, functional specialization, mass democracy, and totalitarian dictatorship, the American political system remains a curious anachronism. In today's world, the American political system is unique, if only because it is so antique.

[7] Charles Howard McIlwain, *The High Court of Parliament and Its Supremacy* (New Haven: Yale University Press, 1910), 386.

[8] A. F. Pollard, *Factors in American History* (New York: The Macmillan Co., 1925), 39. See also McIlwain, *The American Revolution: A Constitutional Interpretation* (Ithaca, N.Y.: Great Seal Books, 1958); and Randolph G. Adams, *Political Ideas of the American Revolution*, 3rd ed. (New York: Barnes & Noble, 1958).

[9] McIlwain, *High Court*, 388.

[10] Henry J. Ford, *The Rise and Growth of American Politics* (New York: The Macmillan Co., 1900), 5. See also James Bryce, *The American Commonwealth* (London: The Macmillan Co., 1891), II, 658.

[11] See the distinction between modernization and political development in Huntington, "Political Development and Political Decay," *World Politics*, XVII (April 1965), 386–430.

II. THE RATIONALIZATION OF AUTHORITY

In seventeenth-century Europe the state replaced fundamental law as the source of political authority, and within each state a single authority replaced the many that had previously existed. America, on the other hand, continued to adhere to fundamental law as both a source of authority for human actions and an authoritative restraint on human behavior. In addition, in America, human authority or sovereignty was never concentrated in a single institution or individual but instead remained dispersed throughout society as a whole and among many organs of the body politic. Traditional patterns of authority were thus decisively broken and replaced in Europe; in America they were reshaped and supplemented but not fundamentally altered. The continued supremacy of law was mated to the decisive rejection of sovereignty.

Undoubtedly the most significant difference between modern man and traditional man is in their outlook on man in relation to his environment. In traditional society man accepts his natural and social environment as given. What is ever will be: it is or must be divinely sanctioned; and to attempt to change the permanent and unchanging order of the universe and of society is both blasphemous and impossible. Change is absent or imperceptible in traditional society because men cannot conceive of its existence. Modernity begins when men develop a sense of their own competence, when they begin to think that they can understand nature and society and can then control and change nature and society for their own purposes. Above all, modernization means the rejection of external restraints on men, the Promethean liberation of man from control by gods, fate, and destiny.

This fundamental shift from acceptance to activism manifests itself in many fields. Among the more important is law. For traditional man, law is an external prescription or restraint over which he has little control. Man discovers law but he does not make law. At most he may make supplementary emendations of an unchanging basic law to apply it to specific circumstances. In late medieval Europe, law was variously defined in terms of divine law, natural law, the law of reason, common law, and custom. In all these manifestations it was viewed as a relatively unchanging external authority for and restraint on human action. Particularly in England, the dominant concept was "the characteristic medieval idea of all authority as deriving from the law." As Bracton put it, "Law makes the King." [12] These ideas remained dominant through the Tudor years and were in one form or another at the basis of the writings of Fortescue, St. Germain, Sir Thomas Smith, Hooker, and Coke. Even after the Act of Supremacy, Parliament was still viewed as a law-declaring body, not a law-making body. Even during the first phases of the constitutional struggles of the seventeenth century, Prynne argued that "the Principal Liberties, Customs, Laws" of the kingdom, particularly those in the "great Charters," were "FUNDAMENTAL, PERPETUAL, & UNALTERABLE." [13]

The obverse of fundamental law is, of course, the rejection of determinate

[12] Corwin, 27.
[13] McIlwain, *High Court*, 51ff., 65.

human sovereignty. For the men of 1600, as Figgis observes, "law is the true sovereign, and they are not under the necessity of considering whether King or Lords or Commons or all three together are the ultimate authority in the state." [14] The sovereignty of law permitted a multiplicity of human authorities, since no single human authority was the sole source of law. Man owed obedience to authority, but authority existed in many institutions: king, Parliament, courts, common law, custom, church, people. Sovereignty, indeed, was an alien concept to the Tudor Constitution. No "lawyer or statesman of the Tudor period," as Holdsworth says, "could have given an answer to the question as to the whereabouts of the sovereign power in the English state." [15] Society and government, Crown and people, existed together in harmony in a "single body politic." The Tudor regime, says Chrimes, "was essentially the culmination of the medieval ideals of monarchical government, in alliance with the assent of parliament for certain purposes, and acknowledging the supremacy of the common law where appropriate. No one was concerned about the location of sovereignty within the State." [16] This indifference to sovereignty made the "whole standpoint" of the most notable expounder of the Elizabethan constitution, Sir Thomas Smith, "nearer that of Bracton than that of Bodin." [17]

Fundamental law and the diffusion of authority were incompatible with political modernization. Modernization requires authority for change. Fundamental changes in society and politics come from the purposeful actions of men. Hence authority must reside in men, not in unchanging law. In addition, men must have the power to effect change, and hence authority must be concentrated in some determinate individual or group of men. Fundamental and unchanging law may serve to diffuse authority throughout society and thus to preserve the existing social order. But it cannot serve as authority for change except for lesser changes which can be passed off as restoration. The modernization that began in the sixteenth century on the Continent and in the seventeenth century in England required new concepts of authority, the most significant of which was the simple idea of sovereignty itself, the idea that there is, in the words of Bodin, a "supreme power over citizens and subjects, unrestrained by law." One formulation of this idea was the new theory, which developed in Europe in the late sixteenth century, of the divine right of kings. Here, in effect, religious and, in that sense, traditional forms were used for modern purposes. "The Divine Right of Kings on its political side was little more than the popular form of expression for the theory of sovereignty." [18]

---

[14] John Neville Figgis, *The Divine Right of Kings* (Cambridge: University Press, 1922), 230. See also Christopher Morris, *Political Thought in England: Tyndale to Hooker* (London: Oxford University Press, 1953), 1.

[15] Holdsworth, 208.

[16] Chrimes, 122–23. See also John Bennett Black, *The Reign of Elizabeth, 1558–1603*, 2nd ed. (Oxford: Clarendon Press, 1959), 206.

[17] Figgis, "Political Thought in the Sixteenth Century," *The Cambridge Modern History* (Cambridge 1904), iii, 748; John William Allen, *A History of Political Thought in the Sixteenth Century* (New York: Methuen, 1960), 262.

[18] Figgis, *Divine Right*, 237.

The doctrine became dominant in France after 1594 and was introduced into England by James I. It admirably served the purposes of the modernizing monarchs of the seventeenth century by giving the sanction of the Almighty to the purposes of the mighty. It was a necessary "transition stage between medieval and modern politics." [19]

In addition, of course, other political theorists responded to the needs of the time by furnishing more "rational" justifications of absolute sovereignty based on the nature of man and the nature of society. On the Continent, Bodin and the Politiques looked into the creation of a supreme royal power which would maintain order and constitute a centralized public authority above parties, sects, and groups, all of which were to exist only on its sufferance. Bodin's *Republic* was published in 1576; Hobbes's *Leviathan*, with its more extreme doctrine of sovereignty, appeared in 1651. Closely linked with the idea of absolute sovereignty was the concept of the state as an entity apart from individual, family, and dynasty. Twentieth-century modernizing Marxists justify their efforts by the needs of the party; seventeenth-century modernizing monarchs justified their actions by "reason of state." The phrase was first popularized by Botero in *Della Ragion di Stato* in 1589. Its essence was briefly defined by another Italian writer in 1614 when he declared, "The reason of state is a necessary violation of the common law for the end of public utility." [20] One by one the European monarchs took to legitimizing themselves and their actions by reference to the state.

In both its religious and its secular versions, in Filmer as well as in Hobbes, the import of the new doctrine of sovereignty was the subject's absolute duty to obey his king. Both versions helped political modernization by legitimizing the concentration of authority and the breakdown of the medieval pluralistic political order. They were the seventeenth-century counterparts of the theories of party supremacy and national sovereignty which are today employed to break down the authority of traditional local, tribal, and religious bodies. In the seventeenth century, mass participation in politics still lay in the future; hence rationalization of authority meant concentration of power in the absolute monarch. In the twentieth century, the broadening of participation and the rationalization of authority occur simultaneously, and hence authority must be concentrated in either a political party or a popular charismatic leader, both of which are capable of arousing the masses as well as challenging traditional sources of authority. In terms of modernization, the seventeenth century's absolute monarch was the functional equivalent of the twentieth century's monolithic party.

On the Continent in the seventeenth century the medieval diffusion of authority among the estates rapidly gave way to the centralization of authority in the monarch. At the beginning of the century, "every country of western Christendom, from Portugal to Finland, and from Ireland to Hungary, had its

[19] *Ibid.*, 258. See Allen, 386; McIlwain (ed.), *The Political Works of James I* (Cambridge, Mass.: Harvard University Press, 1918).
[20] Pietro A. Canonhiero, quoted in Friedrich, 15–16.

assemblies of estates." [21] By the end of the century most of these assemblies had been eliminated or greatly reduced in power. In France the last Estates General until the Revolution met in 1615, and the provincial estates, except in Brittany and Languedoc, did not meet after 1650.[22] By the seventeenth century only six of the original twenty-two Spanish kingdoms retained their *cortes*. The *cortes* in Castile was already suppressed; those in Aragon were put down by Philip II; Olivares subdued Catalonia after a long bloody war. In Portugal the *cortes* met for the last time in 1697. In the kingdom of Naples parliamentary proceedings ended in 1642. The Great Elector put down the estates in Brandenburg and Prussia. The estates of Carniola, Styria, and Carinthia had already lost their powers to the Hapsburgs, who were also able during the early part of the century to curtail the powers of the estates in Bohemia, Moravia, and Silesia. The Danish crown became hereditary in 1665; that of Hungary in 1687. Toward the end of the century, Charles XI reestablished absolute rule in Sweden.[23] By 1700 the traditional diffusion of powers had been virtually eliminated from continental Europe. The modernizers and state-builders had triumphed.

The tendencies toward the substitution of sovereignty for law and the centralization of authority also occurred in England. James I sundered the Crown from Parliament, challenged the traditional authority of the law and of the judges, advocated the divine right of kings. Kings, he said, "were the authors and makers of the laws and not the laws of the kings." [24] James was simply attempting to modernize English government and to move it along the paths already well developed on the Continent. His efforts at political modernization were opposed by Coke and other conservatives who argued in terms of fundamental law and the traditional diffusion of authority. Their claims, however, were out-of-date in the face of the social and political changes taking place. "Coke, like most opponents of the King, had not really grasped the conception of sovereignty; he maintained a position, reasonable enough in the Middle Ages, but impossible in a developed unitary state." [25] Centralization was necessary and at times it seemed that England would follow the continental pattern. But in due course the claims for royal absolutism generated counterclaims for parliamentary supremacy. When James I, Filmer, and Hobbes put the king above law, they inevitably provoked Milton's argument that "the parliament is above all positive law, whether civil or common, makes or unmakes them both." The Long Parliament began the age of parliamentary supremacy. It was then that England saw "practically for the first time a legislative assembly of

---

[21] Clark, 83.

[22] R. R. Palmer, *The Age of the Democratic Revolution* (Princeton: Princeton University Press, 1959), 1, 461: "In 1787 demands were heard for revival of Provincial Estates in various parts of the country. It was a long-delayed reaction against Richelieu and Louis XIV, a demand to make France a constitutional monarchy, not on the English model, but on the model of a France that had long since passed away."

[23] See Clark's summary of constitutional trends, 86–87. See also F. L. Carsten, *Princes and Parliaments in Germany* (Oxford: Clarendon Press, 1959), 436–37; and Holdsworth, 168–72.

[24] "The Trew Law of Free Monarchies," in McIlwain (ed.), *Political Works*, 62.

[25] Figgis, *Divine Right*, 232.

the modern type, — no longer a mere law-declaring, but a *law-making* machine." [26] Fundamental law suffered the same fate in England that it had on the Continent, but it was replaced by an omnipotent legislature rather than by an absolute monarchy.

American development was strikingly different from that in Europe. At the same time that the modernizing monarchs were suppressing the traditional estates, that men were asserting their power to make law, that Richelieu was building an absolute state in France and Hobbes was proclaiming one in England, the old patterns of fundamental law and diffused authority were transported to a new life in the New World. The traditional view of law continued in America in two forms. First, the idea that man could only declare law and not make law remained strong in America long after it had been supplanted by positive conceptions of law in Europe. In some respects, it persisted right into the twentieth century. Secondly, the old idea of a fundamental law beyond human control was given new authority by identifying it with a written constitution. A written constitution can, of course, be viewed as a contract, deriving its authority from conscious, positive human action. But it may also and even concurrently be viewed as a codification of limitations already imposed upon government by custom and reason. It was in this latter sense that men accepted the idea of fundamental law in sixteenth- and seventeenth-century England and embodied it in their colonial charters and declarations of rights. The combination of both theories created a situation in which "higher law as with renewed youth, entered upon one of the great periods of its history. . . ." [27]

The persistence of fundamental-law doctrines went hand in hand with the rejection of sovereignty. The older ideas of the interplay of society and government and the harmonious balance of the elements of the constitution continued to dominate American political thought. In England, the ideas of the great Tudor political writers, Smith, Hooker, Coke, "were on the way to becoming anachronisms even as they were set down." [28] In America, on the other hand, their doctrines prospered, and Hobbes remained irrelevant. Neither the divine right of kings, nor absolute sovereignty, nor parliamentary supremacy had a place on the western shores of the Atlantic. "Americans may be defined," as Pollard has said, "as that part of the English-speaking world which instinctively revolted against the doctrine of the sovereignty of the State and has, not quite successfully, striven to maintain that attitude from the time of the Pilgrim Fathers to the present day." The eighteenth-century argument of the colonists with the home country was essentially an argument against the legislative sovereignty of Parliament.

> It is this denial of all sovereignty [continues Pollard] which gives its profound and permanent interest to the American Revolution. . . . These are American ideas, but they were English before they were American. They were part of that medieval panoply of thought with which, in-

[26] McIlwain, *High Court*, 93–96.
[27] Corwin, 89.
[28] George H. Sabine, *A History of Political Theory*, rev. ed. (New York: Henry Holt & Co., 1950), 455.

cluding the natural equality of man, the view of taxes as grants, the laws of nature and of God, the colonists combatted the sovereignty of Parliament. They had taken these ideas with them when they shook the dust of England off their feet; indeed they left their country in order that they might cleave to these convictions. And now they come back, bringing with them these and other sheaves, to reconvert us to the views which we have held long since but lost awhile.[29]

To the extent that sovereignty was accepted in America it was held to be lodged in "the people." Popular sovereignty, however, is as nebulous a concept as divine sovereignty. The voice of the people is as readily identified as is the voice of God. It is thus a latent, passive, and ultimate authority, not a positive and active one.

The difference between American and European development is also manifest in theories and practices of representation. In Europe, the elimination of the medieval representative bodies, the estates, was paralleled by a decline in the legitimacy accorded local interests. On the Continent the absolute monarch represented or embodied the state. Beginning with the French Revolution, he was supplanted by the national assembly which represented or embodied the nation. In both instances, the collective whole had authority and legitimacy: local interests, parochial interests, group interests, as Rousseau argued, lacked legitimacy and hence had no claim to representation in the central organs of the political system.

The rationalization of authority in Britain also produced changes in representation which stand in marked contrast to the continuing American adherence to the older traditional concepts. In sixteenth-century England both king and Parliament had representative functions. The king was "the representative head of the corporate community of the realm." [30] The members of Parliament still had their traditional medieval functions of representing local communities and special interests. In the late medieval Parliament, "the burgess is his town's attorney. His presence at parliament enables him to present petitions for confirmation of charters, the increase of local liberties, and redress of grievances, and to undertake private business in or near London for constituents." [31] Thus, the king represented the community as a whole, while the members of Parliament represented its component parts. The M.P. was responsible to his constituency. Indeed, an act passed during the reign of Henry V required members of Parliament to reside in their constituencies. In the late sixteenth century this legal requirement began to be avoided in practice, but local residence and local ties still remained qualifications for most M.P.'s.

[29] Pp. 31–33. For a perceptive discussion of the implications that this rejection of sovereignty has for the way in which the political system has adapted to the most modern of problems, see Don K. Price, *The Scientific Estate* (Cambridge, Mass.: Belknap Press of Harvard University Press, 1965), *passim*, but esp. 45–46, 58, 75–78, 165–67.

[30] Samuel H. Beer, "The Representation of Interests in British Government: Historical Background," *American Political Science Review*, li (September 1957), 614.

[31] Faith Thompson, *A Short History of Parliament: 1295–1642* (Minneapolis: University of Minnesota Press, 1953), 59.

"The overwhelming localism of representation in Parliament is its dominant feature," writes Rowse of Elizabethan England, "and gives it vigor and reality. Everywhere the majority of members are local men, either gentry of the country or townsmen. The number of official members, privy councillors and such, is very small, and even they have their roots. . . . An analysis of the representation shows a very small proportion of outsiders, and still smaller of officials." [32] The members not only resided in their constituencies and represented the interests of those constituencies, but they were also paid by their constituencies for their services. Each constituency, moreover, was normally represented by two or three members of Parliament.

The constitutional revolution of the seventeenth century dealt the death blow to this "Old Tory" system of representation. It was replaced by what Beer terms the "Old Whig" system, under which the king lost his active representative functions and the M.P. became "the representative of the whole community, as well as of its component interests." [33] Parliament, as Burke phrased it in the classic statement of the Old Whig theory, is "a *deliberative* assembly of *one* nation, with *one* interest, that of the whole — where not local purposes, not local prejudices, ought to guide, but the general good, resulting from the general reason of the whole." Hence the M.P. should not be bound by authoritative instructions from his constituents and should rather subordinate their interests to the general interest of the entire society. With this new concept came a radical break with the old tradition of local residence and local payment. The last recorded instance of a constituency paying its representatives was in 1678. Increasingly during the seventeenth century, members no longer resided in their constituencies. The statute was "evaded by the admission of strangers to free burghership," and it was finally repealed in 1774.[34] At the same time, the number of multiple-member districts declined, with their complete elimination in 1885. All these developments made Parliament the collective representative of the nation rather than a collection of representatives of individual constituencies. Thus the theory and practice of British representation adjusted to the new face of parliamentary supremacy.

In America, of course, the Old Tory system took on new life. The colonial representative systems reproduced Tudor practices, and subsequently these were established on a national scale in the Constitution of 1787. America, like Tudor England, had a dual system of representation: the President, like the Tudor king, represented the interests of the community as a whole; the individual members of the legislature owed their primary loyalties to their constituencies. The multimember constituencies which the British had in the sixteenth century were exported to the colonial legislatures in America, adapted to the upper house of the national legislature, and extended to the state legislatures

[32] P. 306. Cf. A. F. Pollard, *The Evolution of Parliament*, 2nd ed., rev. (London: Longmans, Green & Co., 1926), 159, who argues that the nationalizing changes began in the late Tudor years.

[33] Beer, 614–15.

[34] Herbert W. Horwill, *The Usages of the American Constitution* (London: Oxford University Press, 1925), 169.

where they remain in substantial number down to the present.[35] Local residence, which had been a legal requirement and a political fact in Tudor England, became a political requirement and a political fact in America. It reflected "the intense localism . . . which persisted in America after it had been abandoned in the mother country." Many key British political figures in the nineteenth and twentieth centuries were able to stay in Parliament because they were able to change their constituencies. "What a difference it would have made to the course of English politics," as one commentator observed, "if Great Britain had not thrown off, centuries ago, the medieval practice which America still retains!" [36] Contrariwise, Americans may view with astonishment and disdain the gap that political modernization has created between the British M.P. and his constituents.[37]

III. DIFFERENTIATION OF STRUCTURE

In comparing European and American development, a distinction must be made between "functions" and "power." In this article, "power" (in the singular) means influence or control over the actions of others, and "function" refers to particular types of activity, which may be defined in various ways. "Powers" (in the plural) will not be used, since most authors use it to mean "functions." It is thus possible to speak with the Founding Fathers of legislative, executive, and judicial functions, and, with Bagehot, of dignified and efficient functions — and also to speak of legal and political functions, military and civil functions, domestic and foreign functions. Governmental institutions may be equal or unequal in power and specialized or overlapping in function.

In Europe the rationalization of authority and the centralization of power were accompanied by functional differentiation and the emergence of more specialized governmental institutions and bodies. These developments were, of course, a response to the growing complexity of society and the increasing demands upon government. Administrative, legal, judicial, and military institutions developed as semi-autonomous but subordinate bodies in one way or another responsible to the political bodies (monarch or parliament) which exercised sovereignty. The dispersion of functions among relatively specialized institutions, in turn, encouraged inequalities in power among the institutions. The legislative or law-making function carried with it more power than did the administrative or law-enforcement function.

---

[35] Maurice Klain, "A New Look at the Constituencies: The Need for a Recount and a Reappraisal," *American Political Science Review*, XLIX (December 1955), *passim*, but esp. 1111–13. In 1619 the London Company aped English practice when it summoned to the first Virginia House of Burgesses "two Burgesses from each Plantation freely . . . elected by the inhabitants thereof."

[36] Horwill, 169–70.

[37] See, e.g., the comments of one American newspaperman covering the 1964 general election: "British members of Parliament aren't oriented toward their constituencies. They don't even have to live in them. . . . Constituencies tend to be regarded as political factories to provide fodder for the national consensus in London. An American Congressman may get 1,500 to 2,000 letters a week from people who elect him. A British MP usually gets no more than 10" (Roderick MacLeish, *New York Herald Tribune*, October 11, 1964).

In medieval government and in Tudor government the differentiation of functions was not very far advanced. A single institution often exercised many functions, and a single function was often dispersed among several institutions. This tended to equalize power among institutions. The government of Tudor England was a "government of *fused* power" (functions) — that is, Parliament, Crown, and other institutions each performed many functions.[38] In the seventeenth and eighteenth centuries British government evolved toward a concentration of power and a differentiation of function. In Great Britain, as Pollard argues, "Executive, legislature, and judicature have been evolved from a common origin, and have adapted themselves to specific purposes, because without that specialization of functions English government would have remained rudimentary and inefficient. But there has been no division of sovereignty and no separation of powers." [39]

In America, in contrast, sovereignty was divided, power was separated, and functions were combined in many different institutions. This result was achieved despite rather than because of the theory of the separation of powers (i.e., functions) which was prevalent in the eighteenth century. In its pure form, the assignment of legislative, executive, and judicial functions to separate institutions would give one institution a monopoly of the dominant law-making function and thus would centralize power. This was in part what Locke wanted and even more what Jefferson wanted. The theory was also, of course, found in Montesquieu, but Montesquieu recognized the inequality of power that would result from the strict separation of functions. The "judiciary," he said, "is in some measure next to nothing." Consequently, to obtain a real division of power, Montesquieu divided the legislative function among three institutions representing the three traditional estates of the realm. In practice in America, as in Tudor England, not only was power divided by dividing the legislative function but other functions were also shared among several institutions, thus creating a system of "checks and balances" which equalized power. "The constitutional convention of 1787," as Neustadt has said, "is supposed to have created a government of 'separated power' [i.e., functions]. It did nothing of the sort. Rather, it created a government of separated institutions *sharing* powers [functions]." [40] Thus America perpetuated a fusion of functions and a division of power, while Europe developed a differentiation of functions and a centralization of power.

In medieval government no distinction existed between legislation and adjudication. On the Continent such institutions as the *Justiza* of Aragon and the French *parlements* exercised important political functions into the sixteenth century. In England, Parliament, an essentially political body, was viewed primarily as a court down to the seventeenth century. The courts of law, as Holdsworth observes, "were, in the days before the functions of government had become specialized, very much more than merely judicial tribunals. In England

[38] McIlwain, *High Court*, xi.
[39] Pollard, *Evolution of Parliament*, 257.
[40] Richard E. Neustadt, *Presidential Power: The Politics of Leadership* (New York: John Wiley & Sons, 1960), 33.

and elsewhere they were regarded as possessing functions which we may call political, to distinguish them from those purely judicial functions which nowadays are their exclusive functions on the continent, and their principal functions everywhere. That the courts continued to exercise these larger functions, even after departments of government had begun to be differentiated, was due to the continuance of that belief in the supremacy of the law which was the dominant characteristic of the political theory of the Middle Ages." [41]

In England, the supremacy of the law disappeared in the civil wars of the seventeenth century and with it disappeared the mixture of judicial and political functions. English judges followed Bacon rather than Coke and became "lions under the throne" who could not "check or oppose any points of sovereignty." In the eighteenth century, Blackstone could flatly state that no court could declare invalid an act of Parliament, however unreasonable it might be. To admit such a power, he said, "were to set the judicial power above that of the legislature, which would be subversive of all government." [42] Parliament had evolved from high court to supreme legislature.

In America, on the other hand, the mixture of judicial and political functions remained. The judicial power to declare what the law is became the mixed judicial-legislative power to tell the legislature what the law cannot be. The American doctrine and practice of judicial review were undoubtedly known only in very attenuated form in late sixteenth-century and early seventeenth-century England. Indeed, the whole concept of judicial review implies a distinction between legislative and judicial functions which was not explicitly recognized at that time. It is, nonetheless, clear that Tudor and early Stuart courts did use the common law to "controul" acts of Parliament at least to the point of redefining rather sweepingly the purposes of Parliament. These actions did not represent a conscious doctrine of judicial review so much as they represented the still "undifferentiated fusion of judicial and legislative functions." [43] This fusion of legislative and judicial functions was retained by American courts and was eventually formulated into the doctrine and practice of judicial review. The legislative functions of courts in America, as McIlwain argues, are far greater than those in England, "because the like tendency was there checked by the growth in the seventeenth century of a new doctrine of parliamentary supremacy." Unlike English courts, "American courts still retain much of their Tudor indefiniteness, notwithstanding our separation of departments. They are guided to an extent unknown now in England by questions of policy and expediency." [44] Foreign observers since De Tocqueville have identified the "immense political influence" of the courts as one of the most astonishing and unique characteristics of American government.

The mixing of legal and political functions in American government can also be seen in the consistently prominent role of lawyers in American politics.

[41] P. 169.
[42] Sir William Blackstone, *Commentaries on the Laws of England*, ed. Thomas M. Cooley (Chicago: Callahan & Co., 1876), i, 90.
[43] See J. W. Gough, *Fundamental Law in English Constitutional History* (Oxford: Clarendon Press, 1955), 27.
[44] McIlwain, *High Court*, ix, 385–86.

In fourteenth- and fifteenth-century England lawyers played an important role in the development of parliamentary proceedings, and the alliance between Parliament and the law, in contrast to the separation between the Estates General and the French *parlement*, helped to sustain parliamentary authority.[45] In Elizabethan England, lawyers played an increasingly important role in Parliament. In 1593, for instance, forty-three percent of the members of the House of Commons possessed a legal education. The Speaker and the other leading figures in the House were usually lawyers. Subsequently, the role of lawyers in the British Parliament declined in significance, reaching a low in the nineteenth century. In the twentieth century only about twenty percent of the M.P.'s have been lawyers. In America, on the other hand, in the colonial governments, in the state governments, and in the national government, the Tudor heritage of lawyer-legislators has continued, with lawyers usually being a majority of the members of American legislative bodies.[46]

Every political system, as Bagehot pointed out, must gain authority and then use authority. In the modern British system these functions are performed by the dignified and efficient parts of the constitution. The assignment of each function to separate institutions is one aspect of the functional differentiation that is part of modernization. It can be seen most clearly, of course, in the case of the so-called constitutional monarchies, but in some degree it is found in almost all modern governments.[47] The American political system, however, like the older European political system, does not assign dignified and efficient functions to different institutions. All major institutions of the American government — President, Supreme Court, House, Senate, and their state counterparts — combine in varying degrees both types of functions. This combination is, of course, most notable in the Presidency. Almost every other modern political system from the so-called constitutional monarchies of Great Britain and Scandinavia to the parliamentary republics of Italy, Germany, and France before De Gaulle, to the Communist dictatorships of Eastern Europe separates the chief of state from the head of government. In the Soviet system, the differentiation is carried still further to distinguish chief of state from head of government from party chief. In the United States, however, the President unites all three functions, this combination being both a major source of his power and

[45] Holdsworth, 174, 184–85, 188–89.

[46] See J. E. Neale, *The Elizabethan House of Commons* (London: Cape, 1949), 290–95; Rowse, 307; Thompson, 169–73; Donald R. Matthews, *The Social Background of Political Decision-Makers* (Garden City, N.Y.: Doubleday & Co., 1954), 28–31; J. F. S. Ross, *Elections and Electors* (London: Eyre and Spottiswoode, 1955), 444; W. L. Guttsman, *The British Political Elite* (New York: MacGibbon & Kee, 1963), 82, 90, 105; D. E. Butler and Richard Rose, *The British General Election of 1959* (London: St. Martin's Press, 1960), 127.

[47] Walter Bagehot, *The English Constitution* (London 1949), 3–4. See also Francis X. Sutton, "Representation and the Nature of Political Systems," *Comparative Studies in Society and History*, ii (October 1959), 7: ". . . the kind of distinction Bagehot made when he talked of the 'dignified' and 'efficient' parts of the English constitution is observed clearly in many states. . . . The discrimination of functions here rests, of course, on an analytical distinction relevant in any political system. It is that between symbolic representation and executive control."

a major limitation on that power, since the requirements of one role often conflict with the demands of another. The combination of roles perpetuates ancient practice. The Presidency was created, as Jefferson declared in 1787, as an "elective monarchy"; the office was designed to embody much of the power of the British king; and the politics that surround it are court politics.[48]

The Presidency is, indeed, the only survival in the contemporary world of the constitutional monarchy once prevalent throughout medieval Europe. In the sixteenth century a constitutional monarch was one who reigned and ruled, but who ruled under law ("non sub homine sed sub Deo et lege") with due regard to the rights and liberties of his subjects, the type of monarch that Fortescue had in mind when he distinguished *dominium politicum et regale* from *dominium regale*. In the seventeenth century this old-style constitutional monarch was supplanted by the new-style absolute monarch who placed himself above the law. Subsequently, the eighteenth and nineteenth centuries saw the emergence of a new so-called "constitutional monarchy" in which a "dignified" monarch reigned but did not rule. Like the absolute monarch he is a modern invention created in response to the need to fix supreme power in a single organ. The American Presidency, on the other hand, continues the original type of constitutional monarchy. In functions and power, American Presidents are Tudor kings. In institutional role, as well as in personality and talents, Lyndon Johnson far more closely resembles Elizabeth I than does Elizabeth II. Britain preserved the form of the old monarchy, but America preserved the substance. Today America still has a king, Britain only a Crown.

In most modern states the legislative function is in theory in the hands of a large representative assembly, parliament, or supreme soviet. In practice, however, it is performed by a relatively small body of men — a cabinet or presidium — which exercises its power in all fields of governmental activity. In America, however, the legislative function remains divided among three distinct institutions and their subdivisions, much as it was once divided among the different estates and other constituted bodies in late medieval Europe. On the national level this arrangement derives not from the ideas of any European theorist but rather from the "institutional history of the colonies between 1606 and 1776." [49] The relations among burgesses, councils, and governors in the colonies, in turn, reflected the relations among Crown, Lords, and Commons in the late sixteenth century.

In modern politics, the division of power between two bodies in a legislative assembly generally varies inversely with the effective power of the assembly as

[48] Thomas Jefferson, Letter to James Madison, December 20, 1787, *Writings* (Washington 1903–05), vi, 389–90; Ford, 293. For an elegant — and eloquent — essay on the President as king, see D. W. Brogan, "The Presidency," *Encounter* (January 1964), 3–7. I am in debt to Richard E. Neustadt for insights into the nature of the American monarchy and into the similarities between White House politics and palace politics. See also Pollard, *Factors in American History*, 72–73: ". . . down to this day the Executive in the United States is far more monarchical and monarchy far more personal than in the United Kingdom. 'He' is a single person there, but 'it' is a composite entity in Great Britain."

[49] Benjamin F. Wright, "The Origins of the Separation of Powers in America," *Economics*, xiii (May 1933), 169 ff.

a whole. The Supreme Soviet has little power but is truly bicameral; the British Parliament has more power but is effectively unicameral. America, however, is unique in preserving a working bicameralism directly inherited from the sixteenth century. Only in Tudor times did the two houses of Parliament become formally and effectively distinguished, one from the other, on an institutional basis. "The century started with Parliament a unitary institution, truly bicameral only in prospect." When it ended, the growth in "the power, position, and prestige of the House of Commons" had made Parliament "a political force with which the Crown and government had to reckon." [50] The sixteenth century represented a peak of bicameralism in English parliamentary history. Each house often quashed bills that had passed the other house, and to resolve their differences the houses resorted to conference committees. Originally used as an "occasional procedure," in 1571 the conference committee was transformed into "a normal habit." In Elizabethan Parliaments, conferences were requested by one or the other house on most bills; the conference delegations were at times instructed not to yield on particular items; and when there were substantial differences between the versions approved by the two houses, the conference committee might substantially re-write the entire bill, at times at the urging and with the advice of the Queen and her councillors. Although all this sounds very contemporary, it is, in fact, very Tudor, and it is this conference committee procedure that was carried over into the colonial legislatures and then extended to the national level. In Great Britain, however, the practice died out with the rise of cabinet responsibility to the Commons. The last real use of "Free Conferences," where discussion and hence politics were permitted, occurred about 1740.[51]

The participation of two assemblies and the chief executive in the legislative process caused the continuation in America of many other legislative methods familiar to Tudor government. An assembly that legislates must delegate some of its work to subordinate bodies or committees. Committees made their appearance in the Tudor Parliament in the 1560's and 1570's. The practice of referring bills to committees soon became almost universal, and the committees, as they assumed more and more of the functions of the House, became larger and more often permanent. The committees were also frequently dominated by those with a special interest in the legislation that they considered. Bills concerned with local and regional problems went to committees composed of members from those regions and localities.[52] By the turn of the century the larger committees had evolved into standing committees which considered all matters coming up within a general sphere of business. This procedure reflected the active role of the Commons in the legislative process. The procedure was, in turn, exported to the colonies in the early seventeenth century — particularly to

[50] Neale, *Elizabeth I and Her Parliaments* (New York: St. Martin's Press, 1958), I, 16–17.

[51] *Ibid.*, 235, 287, 387–88, 412–13; G. F. M. Campion, *An Introduction to the Procedure of the House of Commons* (London: P. Allen & Co., Ltd., 1929), 199; Ada C. McCown, *The Congressional Conference Committee* (New York: Columbia University Press, 1927), 23–37.

[52] Rowse, 307.

the Virginia House of Burgesses — where it also met a real need, and 150 years later was duplicated in the early sessions of the national Congress. At the same time in England, however, the rise of the cabinet undermined the committee system that had earlier existed in Parliament; the old standing committees of the House of Commons became empty formalities, indistinguishable from Committees of the Whole House, long before they were officially discontinued in 1832.

The division of the legislative function imposed similar duties upon the Speaker in the Tudor House of Commons and in subsequent American legislatures. The Tudor Speaker was a political leader, with a dual allegiance to the Crown and to the House. His success in large measure depended upon how well he could balance and integrate these often conflicting responsibilities. He was the "manager of the King's business" in the House, but he was also the spokesman for the House to the Crown and the defender of its rights and privileges. He could exercise much influence in the House by his control, subject to veto by the House, over the order in which bills were called up for debate and by his influence on the "timing and framing of questions." The struggle between Crown and Parliament in the seventeenth century, however, made it impossible for the Speaker to continue his loyalties to both. His overriding duty was now to the House, ánd, in due course, the impartiality of Onslow in the eighteenth century (1727–1761) became the norm for Speakers in the nineteenth and twentieth centuries. Thus in Britain an office that had once been weighted with politics, efficient as well as dignified, radically changed its character and became that of a depoliticized, impartial presiding officer. In America, on the other hand, the political character of Tudor Speakership was perpetuated in the colonial assemblies and eventually in the national House of Representatives.[53]

The sharing of the legislative function among two assemblies and the chief executive gives a strikingly Tudor character to the contemporary American law-making process. In Elizabethan England, Rowse observes, the "relations between Crown and Parliament were more like those between President and Congress than those that subsist in England today." [54] The Tudor monarchs had to badger, wheedle, cajole, and persuade the Commons to give them the legislation they wanted. At times they were confronted by unruly Parliaments which pushed measures the monarch did not want, or debated issues the monarch wished to silence. Generally, of course, the monarch's "legislative program," consisting primarily of requests for funds, was approved. At other times, however, the Commons would rear up and the monarch would have to withdraw or reshape his demands. Burghley, who was in charge of Parliamentary relations for Elizabeth, "kept a close eye on proceedings and received from the Clerks during the session lists showing the stages of all bills in both Houses." [55] Elizabeth regularly attempted to win support in the Commons for her proposals by sending messages and "rumours" to the House, by exhorting and instructing

[53] Neale, *House of Commons*, 381 and *passim*; Holdsworth, 177; Campion, ii, 52–54.
[54] P. 294.
[55] Neale, *House of Commons*, 411.

the Speaker on how to handle the business of the House, by "receiving or summoning deputations from the Houses to Whitehall and there rating them in person," and by "descending magnificently upon Parliament in her coach or open chariot and addressing them" personally or through the Lord Keeper.[56]

Although the sovereign did not "lack means of blocking obnoxious bills during their progress through the two Houses," almost every session of Parliament passed some bills that the Crown did not want, and the royal veto was exercised. Although the veto was used more frequently against private bills than against public ones, important public measures might also be stopped by the Crown. During her reign Elizabeth I apparently approved 429 bills and vetoed approximately 71. The veto, however, was not a weapon that the Crown could use without weighing costs and gains: ". . . politics — the art of the possible — were not entirely divorced from Tudor monarchy. Too drastic or ill-considered a use of the royal veto might have stirred up trouble." [57] The tactics of Henry VIII or Elizabeth I in relation to their Parliaments thus differed little from those of Kennedy or Johnson in relation to their Congresses. A similar distribution of power imposed similar patterns of executive-legislative behavior.

The differentiation of specialized administrative structures also took place much more rapidly in Europe than it did in America. The contrast can be strikingly seen in the case of military institutions. A modern military establishment consists of a standing army recruited voluntarily or through conscription and commanded by a professional officer corps. In Europe a professional officer corps emerged during the first half of the nineteenth century. By 1870 the major continental states had developed most of the principal institutions of professional officership. England, however, lagged behind the Continent in developing military professionalism, and the United States lagged behind Great Britain. Not until the turn of the century did the United States have many of the institutions of professional officership which the European states had acquired many decades earlier. The division of power among governmental institutions perpetuated the mixing of politics and military affairs, and enormously complicated the emergence of a modern system of objective civilian control. Even after World War II, many Americans still adhered to a "fusionist" approach to civil-military relations and believed that military leadership and military institutions should mirror the attitudes and characteristics of civil society.[58]

[56] Rowse, 294–95.

[57] Neale, *House of Commons*, 410–12, and *Elizabeth I and Her Parliaments, passim.* Until the eighteenth century, Privy Councillors, of course, functioned as advisers to the King much as cabinet members now do to the President. Perhaps reflecting both this similarity and the later drastic change that took place in the British cabinet is the fact that in the United States the executive leadership is still called "the Administration," as it was in eighteenth-century Britain, while in Britain itself, it is now termed "the Government."

[58] See, in general, Huntington, *The Soldier and the State* (Cambridge, Mass.: Harvard University Press, 1957), *passim.*

American reluctance to accept a standing army also contrasts with the much more rapid modernization in Europe. In the sixteenth century European military forces consisted of feudal levies, mercenaries, and local militia. In England the militia was an ancient institution, and the Tudors formally organized it on a county basis under the Lord Lieutenants to take the place of the private retinues of the feudal lords. This development was a step toward "domestic tranquility and military incompetence," and in 1600, "not a single western country had a standing army: the only one in Europe was that of the Turks." [59] By the end of the century, however, all the major European powers had standing armies. Discipline was greatly improved, uniforms introduced, regulations formalized, weapons standardized, and effective state control extended over the military forces. The French standing army dates from Richelieu; the Prussian from the actions of the Great Elector in 1655; the English from the Restoration of 1660. In England the county militia continued in existence after 1660, but steadily declined in importance.

In America, on the other hand, the militia became the crucial military force at the same time that it was decaying in Europe. It was the natural military system for societies whose needs were defensive rather than offensive and intermittent rather than constant. The seventeenth-century colonists continued, adapted, and improved upon the militia system that had existed in Tudor England. In the next century, they identified militia with popular government and standing armies with monarchical tyranny. "On the military side," as Vagts says, "the war of the American Revolution was in part a revolt against the British standing army. . . ." [60] But in terms of military institutions, it was a reactionary revolt. The standing armies of George III represented modernity; the colonial militias embodied traditionalism. The American commitment to this military traditionalism, however, became all the more complete as a result of the War of Independence. Hostility to standing armies and reliance on the militia as the first line of defense of a free people became popular dogma and constitutional doctrine, even though these were often departed from in practice. Fortunately, however, the threats to security in the nineteenth century were few, and hence the American people were able to go through that century with a happy confidence in an ineffective force protecting them from a nonexistent danger. The militia legacy, however, remained a continuing element in American military affairs far into the much more tumultuous twentieth century. It is concretely manifest today in the political influence and military strength of the National Guard. The idea that an expert military force is better than a citizen-soldier force has yet to win wholehearted acceptance on this side of the Atlantic.

[59] J. H. Hexter, *Reappraisals in History* (Evanston, Ill.: Northwestern University Press, 1962), 147; and Clark, 84. On the fundamental changes in European military practice, see Michael Roberts, *The Military Revolution: 1560–1660* (Belfast n.d.).

[60] Alfred Vagts, A *History of Militarism*, rev. ed. (New York: Meridian Books, 1959), 92. See generally Louis Morton, "The Origins of American Military Policy," *Military Affairs*, xxii (Summer 1958), 75–82.

IV. TUDOR POLITY AND MODERN SOCIETY

The rationalization of authority and the differentiation of structure were thus slower and less complete in America than they were in Europe. Such was not the case with the third aspect of political modernization: the broadening of political participation. Here, if anything, America led Europe, although the differences in timing in the expansion of participation were less significant than the differences in the way in which that expansion took place. These contrasts in political evolution were directly related to the prevalence of foreign war and social conflict in Europe as contrasted with America.

On the Continent, the late sixteenth and the seventeenth centuries were periods of intense struggle and conflict. For only three years during the entire seventeenth century was there a complete absence of fighting on the European Continent. Several of the larger states were more often at war during the century than they were at peace. The wars were usually complex affairs involving many states tied together in dynastic and political alliances. War reached an intensity in the seventeenth century which it had never reached previously and which was exceeded later only in the twentieth century.[61] The prevalence of war directly promoted political modernization. Competition forced the monarchs to build their military strength. The creation of military strength required national unity, the suppression of regional and religious dissidents, the expansion of armies and bureaucracies, and a major increase in state revenues. "The most striking fact" in the history of seventeenth-century conflict, Clark observes, "is the great increase in the size of armies, in the scale of warfare. . . . Just as the modern state was needed to create the standing army, so the army created the modern state, for the influence of the two causes was reciprocal. . . . The growth of the administrative machine and of the arts of government was directed and conditioned by the desire to turn the national and human resources of the country into military power. The general development of European institutions was governed by the fact that the continent was becoming more military, or, we may say, more militaristic." [62] War was the great stimulus to state-building.

In recent years much has been written about "defensive modernization" by the ruling groups in non-Western societies, such as Egypt under Mohammed Ali, the eighteenth- and nineteenth-century Ottoman Empire, and Meiji Japan. In all these cases, intense early efforts at modernization occurred in the military field, and the attempts to adopt European weapons, tactics, and organization led to the modernization of other institutions in society. What was true of these

[61] Clark, 98; Quincy Wright, A *Study of War* (Chicago: University of Chicago Press, 1942), I, 235–40. See also Clark, *War and Society in the Seventeenth Century* (Cambridge: University Press, 1958), *passim*.

[62] *Seventeenth Century*, 99, 101–2. See also Wright, 256: ". . . it would appear that the political order of Europe changed most radically and rapidly in the seventeenth and twentieth centuries when war reached greatest intensity. The seventeenth century witnessed the supersession of feudalism and the Holy Roman Empire by the secular sovereign states of Europe. The twentieth century appears to be witnessing the supersession of the secular sovereign states by something else. Exactly what cannot yet be said."

societies was also true of seventeenth-century Europe. The need for security and the desire for expansion prompted the monarchs to develop their military establishments, and the achievement of this goal required them to centralize and to rationalize their political machinery.

Largely because of its insular position, Great Britain was a partial exception to this pattern of war and insecurity. Even so, one major impetus to the centralization of authority in English government came from the efforts of the Stuart kings to collect more taxes to build and man more ships to compete with the French and other continental powers. If it were not for the English Channel, the Stuart centralization probably would have succeeded. In America in the seventeenth century, however, continuing threats came only from the Indians. The nature of this threat, plus the dispersion of the settlements, meant that the principal defense force had to be the settlers themselves organized into militia units. There was little incentive to develop European-type military forces and a European-type state to support and control them.

Civil harmony also contributed significantly to the preservation of Tudor political institutions in America. Those institutions reflected the relative unity and harmony of English society during the sixteenth century. English society, which had been racked by the Wars of the Roses in the fifteenth century, welcomed the opportunity for civil peace that the Tudors afforded. Social conflict was minor during the sixteenth century. The aristocracy had been almost eliminated during the civil wars of the previous century. England was not perhaps a middle-class society but the differences between social classes were less then than they had been earlier and much less than they were to become later. Individual mobility rather than class struggle was the keynote of the Tudor years. "The England of the Tudors was an 'organic state' to a degree unknown before Tudor times, and forgotten almost immediately afterward." [63] Harmony and unity made it unnecessary to fix sovereignty in any particular institution; it could remain dispersed so long as social conflict was minimal.

The only major issue that disrupted the Tudor consensus was, of course, religion. Significantly, in sixteenth-century English history the Act of Supremacy meant the supremacy of the state over the church, not the supremacy of one governmental institution over another or one class over another. After the brief interlude of the Marian struggles, however, the shrewd politicking and popular appeal of Elizabeth restored a peace among religious groups which was virtually unique in Europe at that time. The balance between Crown and Parliament and the combination of an active monarchy and common law depended upon this social harmony. Meanwhile on the Continent, civil strife had already reached a new intensity before the end of the sixteenth century. France alone had eight civil wars during the thirty-six years between 1562 and 1598, a period roughly comprising the peaceful reign of Elizabeth in England. The following fifty years saw Richelieu's struggles with the Huguenots and the wars of the Fronde. Spain was racked by civil strife, particularly between 1640 and 1652 when Philip IV and Olivares attempted to subdue Catalonia. In Germany, princes and parliaments fought each other. Where, as frequently hap-

---

[63] McIlwain, High Court, 336; Rowse, 223 ff.

pened, estates and princes espoused different religions, the controversy over religion inevitably broke the medieval balance of powers between princes and parliaments.[64]

English harmony ended with the sixteenth century. Whether the gentry were rising, falling, or doing both in seventeenth-century England, forces were at work in society disrupting Tudor social peace. The efforts to reestablish something like the Tudor balance broke down before the intensity of social and religious conflict. The brief period of Crown power between 1630 and 1640, for instance, gave way "to a short-lived restoration of something like the Tudor balance of powers during the first year of the Long Parliament (1641). This balance might perhaps have been sustained indefinitely, but for the rise of acute religious differences between the Crown and the militant Puritan party in the Commons." [65] In England, as in France, civil strife led to the demand for strong centralized power to reestablish public order. The breakdown of unity in society gave rise to irresistible forces to reestablish that unity through government.

Both Puritan and Cavalier emigrants to America escaped from English civil strife. The process of fragmentation, in turn, encouraged homogeneity, and homogeneity encouraged "a kind of immobility." [66] In America, environment reinforced heredity, as the common challenges of the frontier combined with the abundance of land to help perpetuate the egalitarian characteristics of Tudor society and the complexity of Tudor political institutions. And paradoxically, as Hartz has pointed out, the framers of the Constitution of 1787 reproduced these institutions on the federal level in the belief that the social divisions and conflict within American society made necessary a complex system of checks and balances. In reality, however, their Constitution was successful only because their view of American society was erroneous. So also, only the absence of significant social divisions permitted the continued transformation of political issues into legal ones through the peculiar institution of judicial review.[67] Divided societies cannot exist without centralized power; consensual societies cannot exist with it.

In continental Europe, as in most contemporary modernizing countries, rationalized authority and centralized power were necessary not only for unity but also for progress. The opposition to modernization came from traditional interests: religious, aristocratic, regional, and local. The centralization of power was necessary to smash the old order, break down the privileges and restraints of feudalism, and free the way for the rise of new social groups and the develop-

---

[64] Friedrich, 20–21; Sabine, 372–73.

[65] Chrimes, 138.

[66] Louis Hartz, *The Founding of New Societies* (New York: Harcourt, Brace & World, 1964), 3, 4, 6, 23. Hartz's theory of fragmentation furnishes an excellent general framework for the analysis of the atrophy of settlement colonies, while his concept of the American liberal consensus in large part explains the preservation of Tudor political institutions.

[67] Hartz, *The Liberal Tradition in America* (New York: Harcourt, Brace, 1955), 9–10, 45–46, 85–86, 133–34, 281–82.

ment of new economic activities. In some degree a coincidence of interest did exist between the absolute monarchs and the rising middle classes. Hence European liberals often viewed favorably the concentration of authority in an absolute monarch, just as modernizers today frequently view favorably the concentration of authority in a single "mass" party.

In America, on the other hand, the absence of feudal social institutions made the centralization of power unnecessary. Since there was no aristocracy to dislodge, there was no need to call into existence a governmental power capable of dislodging it.[68] This great European impetus to political modernization was missing. Society could develop and change without having to overcome the opposition of social classes with a vested interest in the social and economic status quo. The combination of an egalitarian social inheritance plus the plenitude of land and other resources enabled social and economic development to take place more or less spontaneously. Government often helped to promote economic development, but (apart from the abolition of slavery) it played only a minor role in changing social customs and social structure. In modernizing societies, the centralization of power varies directly with the resistance to social change. In the United States, where the resistance was little, so also was the centralization.

The differences in social consensus between Europe and America also account for the differences in the manner in which political participation expanded. In Europe this expansion was marked by discontinuities on two levels. On the institutional level, democratization meant the shift of power from monarchical ruler to popular assembly. This shift began in England in the seventeenth century, in France in the eighteenth century, and in Germany in the nineteenth century. On the electoral level, democratization meant the extension of the suffrage for this assembly from aristocracy to upper bourgeoisie, lower bourgeoisie, peasants, and urban workers. The process is clearly seen in the English reform acts of 1832, 1867, 1884, and 1918. In America, on the other hand, no such class differences existed as in England. Suffrage was already widespread in most colonies by independence, and universal white manhood suffrage was a fact in most states by 1830. The unity of society and the division of government meant that the latter was the principal focus of democratization: The American equivalent of the Reform Act of 1832 was the change in the nature of the Electoral College produced by the rise of political parties, and the resulting transformation of the P esidency from an indirectly elected, semi-oligarchical office to a popular one. The other major steps in the expansion of popular participation in the United States involved the extension of the electoral principal to all the state governors, to both houses of the state legislatures, to many state administrative offices and boards, to the judiciary in many states, and to the United States Senate. Thus, in Europe the broadening of participation meant the extension of the suffrage for one institution to all classes of society, while in America it meant the extension of the suffrage by the one class in society to all (or almost all) institutions of government.

[68] *Ibid.*, 43.

In Europe the opposition to modernization within society forced the modernization of the political system. In America, the ease of modernization within society precluded the modernization of the political system. The United States thus combines the world's most modern society with one of the world's most antique polities. The American political experience is distinguished by frequent acts of creation but few, if any, of innovation. Since the Revolution, constitutions have been drafted for thirty-eight new political systems, but the same pattern of government has been repeated over and over again. The new constitutions of Alaska and Hawaii differ only in detail from the constitution of Massachusetts, originally drafted by John Adams in 1780. When else in history has such a unique series of opportunities for political experiment and innovation been so almost totally wasted?

This static quality of the political system contrasts with the prevalence of change elsewhere in American society. A distinguishing feature of American culture, Robin Williams has argued, is its positive orientation toward change. In a similar vein, two observers have noted, "In the United States change itself is valued. The new is good; the old is unsatisfactory. Americans gain prestige by being among the first to own next year's automobile; in England, much effort is devoted to keeping twenty-five-year-old cars in operating condition." [69] In three centuries, a few pitifully small and poor rural settlements strung along the Atlantic seaboard and populated in large part by religious exiles were transformed into a huge, urbanized, continental republic, the world's leading economic and military power. America has given the world its most modern and efficient economic organizations. It has pioneered social benefits for the masses: mass production, mass education, mass culture. Economically and socially, everything has been movement and change. Politically, however, the only significant institutional innovation has been federalism, and this, in itself, of course, was made possible only by the traditional hostility to the centralization of authority. Fundamental social and economic change has been combined with political stability and continuity. In a society dedicated to what is shiny new, the polity remains quaintly old.

Modernity is thus not all of a piece. The American experience demonstrates conclusively that some institutions and some aspects of a society may become highly modern while other institutions and other aspects retain much of their traditional form and substance. Indeed, this may be a natural state of affairs. In any system some sort of equilibrium or balance must be maintained between change and continuity. Change in some spheres renders unnecessary or impossible change in others. In America the continuity and stability of government has permitted the rapid change of society, and the rapid change in society has encouraged continuity and stability in government. The relation between polity and society may well be dialectical rather than complementary. In other societies, such as Latin America, a rigid social structure and the absence of social and economic change have been combined with political instability and the

[69] Robin Williams, *American Society*, 2nd ed., rev. (New York: Alfred A. Knopf, 1961), 571; Eli Ginzberg and Ewing W. Reilley, *Effecting Change in Large Organizations* (New York: Columbia University Press, 1957), 18–19.

weakness of political institutions. A good case can be made, moreover, that the latter is the result of the former.[70]

This combination of modern society and Tudor polity explains much that is otherwise perplexing about political ideas in America. In Europe the conservative is the defender of traditional institutions and values, particularly those in society rather than in government. Conservatism is associated with the church, the aristocracy, social customs, the established social order. The attitude of conservatives toward government is ambivalent: Government is viewed as the guarantor of social order, but it also is viewed as the generator of social change. Society rather than government has been the principal conservative concern. European liberals, on the other hand, have had a much more positive attitude toward government. Like Turgot, Price, and Godwin, they have viewed the centralization of power as the precondition of social reform. They have supported the gathering of power into a single place — first the absolute monarch, then the sovereign assembly — where it can then be used to change society.

In America, on the other hand, these liberal and conservative attitudes have been thoroughly confused and partly reversed. Conservatism has seldom flourished because it has lacked social institutions to conserve. Society is changing and modern, while government, which the conservative views with suspicion, has been relatively unchanging and antique. With a few exceptions, such as a handful of colleges and churches, the oldest institutions in American society are governmental institutions. The absence of established social institutions, in turn, has made it unnecessary for American liberals to espouse the centralization of power as did European liberals. John Adams could combine Montesquieu's polity with Turgot's society much to the bafflement of Turgot. Nineteenth-century Europeans had every reason to be fascinated by America: It united a liberal society which they were yet to experience with a conservative politics which they had in large part forgotten.

V. TUDOR POLITY AND MODERNIZING SOCIETIES

Recently much has been made of the relevance to the currently modernizing countries of Asia, Africa, and Latin America of the earlier phases of modernization in the United States. It has been argued that the United States was and still should be a revolutionary power. The American Revolution, it has been said, "started a chain reaction" beginning with the French Revolution and leading on to the Russian Revolution which was "the American Revolution's child, though an unwanted and unacknowledged one." [71] But the effort to see connections and/or parallels between what happened in America in the eighteenth century and what is happening in Asia, Africa, and elsewhere in the twentieth century can only contribute to monstrous misunderstandings of both historical experiences. The American Revolution was not a social revolution like

[70] Merle Kling, "Toward a Theory of Power and Political Instability in Latin America," *Western Political Quarterly*, IX (March 1956), 21–31. [See also this volume, pp. 489–502. (Ed.)]

[71] Arnold J. Toynbee, "If We Are To Be the Wave of the Future," *New York Times Magazine*, November 13, 1960, 123.

the French, Russian, Chinese, Mexican, or Cuban revolutions; it was a war of independence. Moreover, it was not a war of independence of natives against alien conquerors, like the struggles of the Indonesians against the Dutch, or of the Vietnamese or the Algerians against the French, but was instead a war of settlers against the home country. Any recent parallels are in the relation of the Algerian *colons* to the French Republic or of the Southern Rhodesians to the United Kingdom. It is in these cases, in the last of the European "fragments" to break their European ties, that the eighteenth-century experience of America may be duplicated. These, however, are not parallels of which American liberal intellectuals and statesmen like to be reminded.

The case for the relevance of the American experience to the contemporary modernizing countries has also been couched in terms of the United States as "The First New Nation." The United States, it has been argued, was the first nation "of any consequence to emerge from the colonial dominance of Western Europe as a sovereign state in its own right, and to that extent it shares something in common with the 'emerging nations' of today, no matter how different they may be in other respects." [72] The phrase "new nation," however, fails to distinguish between state and society, and hence misses crucial differences between the American experience and those of the contemporary modernizing countries. The latter are, for the most part, more accurately described by the title of another book: "Old Societies and New States." [73] America, on the other hand, was historically a new society but an old state. Hence the problems of government and political modernization that the contemporary modernizing states face differ fundamentally from those that confronted the United States.

In most countries of Asia, Africa, and Latin America, modernization faces tremendous social obstacles. The gaps between rich and poor, between modern elite and traditional mass, between the powerful and the weak — gaps that are the common lot of "old societies" trying to modernize today — contrast markedly with the "pleasing uniformity" of the "one estate" that existed in eighteenth-century America. As in seventeenth-century Europe these gaps can be overcome only by the creation of powerful, centralized authority in government. The United States never had to construct such authority in order to modernize its society, and hence its experience has little to offer modernizing countries today. America, De Tocqueville said, "arrived at a state of democracy without having to endure a democratic revolution" and "was born equal without having to become so." So also American society was born modern; and it hence was never necessary to construct a government powerful enough to make it so. An antique polity is compatible with a modern society but it is not compatible with the modernization of a traditional society.

The Latin American experience, for instance, is almost exactly the reverse of that of the United States. After independence the United States continued es-

---

[72] See Seymour Martin Lipset, *The First New Nation* (New York: Basic Books, 1963), Part I; J. Leiper Freeman, "The Colonial Stage of Development: The American Case," unpubl. paper, Comparative Administration Group, 1963, 4.

[73] See Clifford Geertz (ed.), *Old Societies and New States: The Quest for Modernity in Asia and Africa* (New York: The Free Press of Glencoe, 1963).

sentially the same political institutions it had had before independence, which were perfectly suited to its society. At independence the Latin American countries inherited and maintained an essentially feudal social structure. They attempted to superimpose on this social structure republican political institutions copied from the United States and revolutionary France. Such institutions had no meaning in a feudal society. These early efforts at republicanism left Latin America with weak governments which until the twentieth century lacked the authority and power to modernize the society. Liberal, pluralistic, democratic governments serve to perpetuate antiquated social structure. Thus in Latin America an inherent conflict exists between the political goals of the United States — elections, democracy, representative government, pluralism, constitutionalism — and its social goals — modernization, reform, social welfare, more equitable distribution of wealth, development of a middle class. In the North American experience these goals did not conflict. In Latin America, they often clash head on. The variations of the North American political system which North Americans would like to reproduce in Latin America are simply too weak, too diffuse, too dispersed to mobilize the political power necessary to bring about fundamental change. Such power can be mobilized by revolution, as it was in Mexico and Cuba, and a historical function of revolutions is to replace weak governments by strong governments capable of achieving social change. The question for Latin America and similarly situated countries is whether other ways short of violent revolution exist for generating the political power necessary to modernize traditional societies.

However it occurs, the accumulation of power necessary for modernization makes the future of democracy rather bleak. Countries, such as France and Prussia, which took the lead in political modernization in the seventeenth century have had difficulty in maintaining stable democracy in the twentieth century. Countries in which the seventeenth-century tendencies toward absolute monarchy were either defeated (England), stalemated (Sweden), or absent (America) later tended to develop more viable democratic institutions. The continued vitality of medieval estates and pluralistic assemblies is associated with subsequent democratic tendencies. "It is no accident, surely," Carsten observes, "that the liberal movement of the nineteenth century was strongest in those areas of Germany where the Estates survived the period of absolute government." [74] Similarly, in seventeenth-century Spain, Catalonia was the principal locus of feudal opposition to the centralizing and rationalizing efforts of Olivares, but in the twentieth century it has been the principal locus of Spanish liberalism and constitutionalism. In eighteenth-century Europe also, the conflict between traditional liberties and modernizing reforms was a pervasive one, and the conservative and even reactionary efforts of the "constituted bodies" to maintain and to restore their privileges laid the basis for later, more popular, resistance against despotism. [75]

[74] P. 434; Friedrich, 20–25.
[75] Palmer, *passim*, but esp. 323–407. Of the Belgian revolution of 1787 against Joseph II, Palmer writes (p. 347), "The issue was clear. It was between social change and constitutional liberty. Reform would come at the cost of arbitrary government over-

If a parallel exists between seventeenth-century modernization and twentieth-century modernization, the implications of the former for the latter are clear. Despite arguments to the contrary, the countries where modernization requires the concentration of power in a single, monolithic, hierarchical, but "mass," party are not likely to be breeding grounds for democracy.[76] Mass participation goes hand-in-hand with authoritarian control. As in Guinea and Ghana, it is the twentieth-century weapon of modernizing centralizers against traditional pluralism. Democracy, on the other hand, is more likely in those countries that preserve elements of traditional social and political pluralism. Its prospects are brightest where traditional pluralism is adapted to modern politics, as appears to be the case with the caste associations of India and as may be the case with tribal associations in some parts of Africa. So also, Lebanon, the most democratic Arab country — indeed, perhaps the only democratic Arab country — has a highly traditional politics of confessional pluralism.[77] Like the states of seventeenth-century Europe, the non-Western countries of today can have political modernization or they can have democratic pluralism, but they cannot normally have both.

In each historical period one type of political system usually seems to its contemporaries to be particularly relevant to the needs and demands of the age. In the era of European state-building in the seventeenth century, the "pattern-state," to use Sir George Clark's phrase, was the Bourbon monarchy of France. Indeed, the new state that emerged in that century, as Clark argues, "may be called the French type of monarchy not only because it reached its strongest and most logical expression in France, but also because it was consciously and deliberately copied elsewhere from the Bourbon model." [78] This type of cen-

---

riding the articulate will and historic institutions of the country. Or liberty would be preserved at the cost of perpetuating archaic systems of privilege, property, special rights, class structure, ecclesiastical participation in the state. It was a revolution against the innovations of a modernizing government — in a sense, a revolution *against* the Enlightenment. It was not in this respect untypical of the time."

Compare this with David Apter's conclusion that in contemporary Africa "the degree of autocracy which emerges after independence is in virtual proportion to the degree of antagonism the government shows to tradition" (*The Political Kingdom in Uganda* [Princeton: Princeton University Press, 1961], 476).

[76] See Immanuel Wallerstein, *Africa: The Politics of Independence* (New York: Vintage Books, 1961), 159–63; and Ruth Schachter (Morgenthau), "Single-Party Systems in West Africa," *American Political Science Review*, LV (June 1961), 294–307, for the case for the liberal and democratic potential of single-party states. For more realistic evaluations, see Martin L. Kilson, "Authoritarian and Single-Party Tendencies in African Politics," *World Politics*, xv (January 1963), 262–94; and Aristide Zolberg, "The African Mass-Party State in Perspective," unpubl. paper prepared for Annual Meeting, APSA, September 1964.

[77] See Lloyd I. and Susanne Hoeber Rudolph, "The Political Role of India's Caste Associations," *Pacific Affairs*, xxxiii (March 1960), 5–22; Lloyd I. Rudolph, "The Modernity of Tradition: The Democratic Incarnation of Caste in India," *American Political Science Review*, LIX (December 1965), 975–89; and Michael C. Hudson, "Pluralism, Power, and Democracy in Lebanon," unpubl. paper prepared for Annual Meeting, APSA, September 1964.

[78] *Seventeenth Century*, 83, 90–91.

tralized, absolute monarchy met the paramount needs of the time. In the late eighteenth and nineteenth centuries, the pattern-state was the British parliamentary system. The countries of Europe then faced the problems of democratization and the incorporation into the polity of the lower social orders. The British system furnished the model for this phase of modernization. Today, in much of Asia, Africa, and Latin America, political systems face simultaneously the needs to centralize authority, to differentiate structure, and to broaden participation. The system that seems most relevant to the simultaneous achievement of these goals is a one-party system. If Versailles set the standard for one century and Westminster for another, the Kremlin may well be the most relevant model for the modernizing countries of this century. The heads of minor German principalities aped Louis XIV; the heads of equally small and backward states today may ape Lenin and Mao. The primary need their countries face is the accumulation and concentration of power, not its dispersion, and it is in Moscow and Peking and not in Washington that this lesson is to be learned.

Nor should this irrelevance of the American polity come as a great surprise. Historically foreigners have always found American society more attractive than the American polity. Even in the seventeenth and eighteenth centuries, as Beloff observes, "the political appeal of the new country was less potent than the social one." [79] De Tocqueville was far more impressed by the democracy of American society and customs than he was by its democratic institutions of government. In the last century Europeans have found much to emulate in American business organization and in American culture, but they have found little reason to copy American political institutions. Parliamentary democracies and one-party dictatorships abound throughout the world. But surely one of the striking features of world politics is the rarity of other political systems based on the American presidential model.

The irrelevance of the American polity to the rest of the world, however, must not be overdone. It is of little use to societies that must modernize a traditional order. But, as the American experience itself demonstrates, a Tudor polity is quite compatible with a modern society. Consequently it is possible, although far from necessary, that as other societies become more fully modern, as the need to disestablish old, traditional, feudal, and local elements declines, the need to maintain a political system capable of modernization may also disappear. Such a system will, of course, have the advantage of tradition and of association with successful social change, so the probabilities are that it will not change greatly. But at least the possibility exists that there may be some evolution toward an American-type system. The "end of ideology" in Western Europe, the mitigation of class conflict, the tendencies toward an "organic society," all suggest that the European countries could now tolerate more dispersed and relaxed political institutions. Some elements of the American system seem to be creeping back into Europe from which they were exported

[79] Max Beloff, *The Age of Absolutism: 1660–1815* (London: Hutchinson's University Library, 1954), 168–69.

three centuries ago.[80] Judicial review has made a partial and timorous reappearance on the Continent. After De Gaulle, the constitution of the Fifth Republic might well shake down to something not too far removed from the constitution of the American Republic. Mr. Harold Wilson was accused, before and after coming to power, of acting like Mr. President. These are small straws in the wind. They may not mean anything. But if they do mean anything, they mean that the New Europe may eventually come to share some of the old institutions that the New World has preserved from an older Europe.

[80] See, e.g., Stephen Graubard (ed.), *A New Europe?* (Boston: Houghton Mifflin, 1964); Stanley Hoffmann, "Europe's Identity Crisis: Between the Past and America," *Daedalus,* xciii (Fall 1964), 1249, 1252–53. On the role of the courts see Taylor Cole, "Three Constitutional Courts: A Comparison," *American Political Science Review,* liii (December 1959), 963–84; and Gottfried Dietze, "America and Europe — Decline and Emergence of Judicial Review," *Virginia Law Review,* xliv (December 1958), 1233–72.

Selections from
*The Old Regime and the
French Revolution*

ALEXIS DE TOCQUEVILLE

HOW ALMOST ALL EUROPEAN NATIONS HAD HAD THE SAME INSTITUTIONS AND HOW THESE WERE BREAKING DOWN EVERYWHERE

The various races which, after overthrowing the Roman Empire, ended up by forming the nations of modern Europe had different ethnic origins, came from different regions, and spoke different languages — indeed, the only thing they had in common was their barbarism. Once these races were firmly entrenched within the boundaries of the Empire, there followed a long period of intertribal warfare, and when at last this period ended and their respective territorial limits had been stabilized, they found themselves isolated from each other by the ruins they themselves had caused. Civilization was practically extinct,

From *The Old Regime and the French Revolution* (pp. 14–19, 22–32, 57–60, 77–81) by Alexis de Tocqueville. Copyright © 1955 by Doubleday & Company, Inc. Reprinted by permission of the publisher.

ALEXIS DE TOCQUEVILLE (1805–1859) was a French lawyer, statesman, and writer. He has written a brilliant summary of English history and, in collaboration with Gustav de Beaumont, a study of the penitentiary system in the U.S.A. Although his book *The Old Regime and the Revolution,* from which our selection is taken, is not as well known as his classical *Democracy in America,* it is also an outstanding work in historical sociology. He wrote the former after his retirement from active politics, occasioned by the coup d'état of December 1851. J. P. Mayer has recently published a complete French edition of his works.

public order nonexistent; communications had become difficult and precarious, and the great European family was split up into a number of hostile communities, each an independent unit. Yet within this incoherent mass there developed with remarkable suddenness a uniform system of law.

These institutions were not an imitation of Roman law; indeed, they were so unlike it that those who at a later date set out to transform them lock, stock, and barrel took Roman law as the starting-off point for their reforms. The system we are now discussing was an original creation, vastly different from any other code of laws devised for the maintenance of the social structure. Its various elements dovetail neatly into each other, forming a symmetrical whole quite as coherent as our modern legal and constitutional codes, and were skillfully adapted to the needs of semi-barbarian peoples.

An inquiry into the circumstances under which this system of law took form, developed, and spread throughout Europe would take me too far afield, and I merely draw attention to the undoubted fact that it prevailed to a greater or lesser extent in every part of Europe during the Middle Ages and to the exclusion of all other forms of law in many countries.

I have had occasion to study the political institutions of medieval France, England, and Germany, and the more deeply I went into the subject, the more I was struck by the remarkable similarity between the laws and institutions in all three countries; indeed, it seemed extraordinary that nations so unlike and having so little intercourse with each other should have built up systems of law so close akin. True, they vary greatly, almost infinitely on points of detail (as was only to be expected), but their basis is everywhere the same. Whenever in my study of the constitution of ancient Germany I came on a political institution, a law, a local authority, I felt sure that If I searched long enough I would find its exact parallel, or something substantially the same, in France and England — and thus it always was. With the result that each of the three nations helped me to a better understanding of the other two.

The administration of all three countries derived from the same general principles; the political assemblies were composed of the same elements and invested with the same powers. The community was divided up on the same lines and there was the same hierarchy of classes. The nobles held identical positions, had the same privileges, the same appearance; there was, in fact, a family likeness between them, and one might almost say they were not different men but essentially the same men everywhere.

Urban administrations were alike and the rural districts governed in the same manner. The condition of the peasant varied little from one country to another; the soil was owned, occupied, and cultivated in the same way and the cultivator subject to the same taxes. From the Polish frontier to the Irish Sea we find the same institutions: the manor (*seigneurie*), the seigneurial court presided over by the lord; the fief, the quitrent, feudal services, trade, and craft guilds. Sometimes the names were identical in all countries and, more surprising still, behind all these institutions, and sponsoring them, was the same ideology. It is not, I think, going too far to say that in the fourteenth century the political, social, administrative, judicial, and financial institutions — and even the literary productions — of the various European countries had more resemblance to each other than they have even in our time, when the march of progress seems to have broken down all barriers and communications between nations have so vastly improved.

It is no part of my present plan to trace the gradual decline of this ancient constitution of Europe, and I confine myself to pointing out that by the eighteenth century its disintegration had progressed so far that it was half in ruins. Generally speaking, this disintegration was less pronounced in the east of the continent than in the west, but its effects were visible in every part of Europe.

This progressive decay of the institutions stemming from the Middle Ages can be followed in records of the period. It is well known that each *seigneurie* maintained the registers of landed property known as *terriers*, in which were recorded the boundaries of the various fiefs and *censives* (dependent holdings paying rent), the dues payable, the services to be rendered, the local customs. In the thirteenth- and fourteenth-century registers I examined I was much impressed by the skill with which they were drafted, their clarity, and the intelligence of the men compiling them. In later periods, however, there is a very definite falling off; the *terriers* become more and more obscure, ill ordered, incomplete, and slovenly despite a rise in the general level of intelligence in France. In fact, it would seem that while the French people were advancing toward a high standard of civilization, their political structure was relapsing into barbarism.

Even in Germany, where the old European constitution had retained its primitive features to a greater extent than in France, many of its institutions had already passed out of existence. But it is not so much by noting what had disappeared as by studying the condition of such institutions as survived that we best can measure the ravages of time. True, the forms of municipal government, thanks to which the chief German towns had developed during the fourteenth and fifteenth centuries into small, enlightened republics, thriving and self-sufficient, still existed; but they were now a mere empty show. To all appearances their mandates were still in force, the officers appointed to see to their observance bore the same titles and seemed to carry on as in the past. But the spirit of local patriotism and strenuous endeavor, and the virile, pioneering virtues it promoted, had passed away. In short, these ancient institutions, while keeping their original forms, had been drained of their substance.

All such public powers, creations of the Middle Ages, as still survived were affected by the same disease; it sapped their vitality and they fell into a decline. What was still worse, a number of institutions which, though not actually deriving from that period, linked up with it and bore traces of this association to any marked extent followed suit. Even that political freedom which had given rise to so many fine achievements in the Middle Ages now seemed doomed to sterility whenever it still bore the slightest imprint of its medieval origin; even the aristocracy seemed to be falling into a senile decay. Wherever the provincial assemblies had kept unchanged their ancient structure they hindered rather than helped the march of progress; indeed, they seemed impervious to the spirit of the age. Moreover, they were ceasing to hold the allegiance of the populace at large, who were growing more and more inclined to put their faith in the royal house. The antiquity of these institutions did not ensure respect for them. On the contrary, the older they grew, the more they were discredited and, paradoxically enough, the weaker they became and the more they seemed to have lost their power to harm, the more they were disliked. "The present state of affairs," wrote a contemporary German whose sympathies were with the old régime, "seems to be in bad odor with nearly everybody and heartily despised. This sudden aversion for everything that is old is indeed a strange phenomenon. The 'new ideas' are bandied about within the family circle, creating an atmosphere of restlessness, and we find our modern German housewives clamoring to get rid of furniture that has been in the family for generations." Nevertheless, it was a period of steadily increasing prosperity in Germany no less than in France. But — and this is a point on which I would lay stress — all that was vital, most active in the life of the day, was of a new order; indeed, not merely new but frankly hostile to the past.

It must be remembered that the royalty of this time had no longer anything in common with the royalty of the Middle Ages. It had different prerogatives, was animated by a different spirit, played a different part, and inspired sentiments of quite another order. It must be remembered, too, that local governments had broken down and made way for a central administration staffed by a bureaucracy that was steadily undermining the power of the nobility. These new authorities employed methods and were guided by ideas which the men of the Middle Ages had never dreamed of and would certainly have discountenanced, since the social system to which they applied was, to the medieval mind, inconceivable.

The same thing was happening in England, though at first sight one might think that the ancient European constitution still functioned there. True, the old names and the old offices were retained; but in the seventeenth century feudalism was to all intents and purposes a dead letter, classes intermingled, the nobility no longer had the upper hand, the aristocracy had ceased to be exclusive, wealth was a steppingstone to power, all men were equal before the law and public offices open to all, freedom of speech and of the press was the order of the day. All this lay quite outside the purview of the medieval mind, and it was precisely these innovations, gradually and adroitly introduced into the old order, that, without impairing its stability or demolishing ancient forms, gave it a new lease of life and a new energy. Seventeenth-century England was already a quite modern nation, which, however, venerated and enshrined within its heart some relics of the Middle Ages.

. . .

WHY FEUDALISM HAD COME TO BE MORE DETESTED IN FRANCE THAN IN ANY OTHER COUNTRY

At first sight it may appear surprising that the Revolution, whose primary aim . . . was to destroy every vestige of the institutions of the Middle Ages, should not have broken out in countries where those institutions had the greatest hold and bore most heavily on the people instead of those in which their yoke was relatively light.

At the close of the eighteenth century serfdom had not yet been completely abolished anywhere in Germany; indeed, in most parts of that country the peasants were still literally bound to the land, as they had been in the Middle Ages. The armies of Frederick II and Maria Theresa were composed almost entirely of men who were serfs on the medieval pattern.

In most German states in 1788 the peasant was not allowed to quit his lord's estate; if he did so, he was liable to be tracked down wherever he was and brought back in custody. He was subject to the jurisdiction of his lord, who kept a close eye on his private life and could punish him for intemperance or idleness. He could neither better his social position, change his occupation, nor even marry without his master's consent, and a great number of his working hours had to be spent in his master's service. The system of compulsory labor, known in France as the *corvée,* was in full force in Germany, and in some districts entailed no less than three days' work a week. The peasant was expected to keep the buildings on his lord's estate in good repair and to carry the produce of the estate to market; he drove his lord's carriage and carried his messages. Also he had to spend some years of his youth in his lord's household as a member of the domestic staff. However, it was possible for the serf to become a landowner, though his tenure was always hedged round with restrictions. He had to cultivate his land in a prescribed manner, under his lord's supervision, and could neither alienate nor mortgage it without permission. In some cases he was compelled to sell its produce, in others forbidden to sell it; in any case he was bound to keep the land under cultivation. Moreover, his children did not inherit his entire estate, some part of it being usually withheld by his lord.

It must be thought that I am describing ancient or obsolete laws; these provisions can be found even in the code drawn up by Frederick the Great and put in force by his successor at the very time when the French Revolution was getting under way.

In France such conditions had long since passed away; the peasants could move about, buy and sell, work, and enter into contracts as they liked. Only in one or two eastern provinces, recent annexations, some last vestiges of serfdom lingered on; everywhere else it had wholly disappeared. Indeed, the abolition of serfdom had taken place in times so remote that its very date had been forgotten. However, as a result of recent research work it is now known that as early as the thirteenth century serfdom had ceased to exist in Normandy.

Meanwhile another revolution, of a different order, had done so much to improve the status of the French peasant; he had not merely ceased to be a serf, he had also become a landowner. Though this change had far-reaching consequences, it is apt to be overlooked, and I propose to devote some pages to this all-important subject.

Until quite recently it was taken for granted that the splitting up of the landed estates in France was the work of the Revolution, and the Revolution alone; actually there is much evidence in support of the contrary view. Twenty years or more before the Revolution we find complaints being made that land was being subdivided to an unconscionable extent. "The practice of partitioning inheritances," said Turgot, writing at about this time, "has gone so far that a piece of land which just sufficed for a single family is now parceled out between five or six sons. The result is that the heirs and their families soon find they cannot depend on the land for their livelihood and have to look elsewhere." And some years later Necker declared that there was "an inordinate number" of small country estates in France.

In a confidential report made to an Intendant shortly before the Revolution I find the following observations: "Inheritances are being subdivided nowadays to an alarming extent. Everybody insists on having his share of the land, with the result that estates are broken up into innumerable fragments, and this process of fragmentation is going on all the time." One might well imagine these words to have been written by one of our contemporaries.

I have been at great pains to make, as it were, a cadastral survey (i.e., of the distribution of land) of the old régime and have to some extent, I think, succeeded. Under the provisions of the law of 1790, which imposed a tax on land, each parish was required to draw up a return of all the privately owned land within its boundaries. Most of these documents are lost, but I have discovered some in certain villages and on comparing them with their modern equivalents have found that in these villages the number of landowners was as high as half, often two thirds, of the present number. These figures are impressive, and all the more so when we remember that the population of France has risen by over twenty-five per cent since that time.

Then, as in our own day, the peasant's desire for owning land was nothing short of an obsession and already all the passions to which possession of the soil gives rise in present-day France were active. "Land is always sold above its true value," a shrewd contemporary observer remarked, "and this is due to the Frenchman's inveterate craving to become a landowner. All the savings of the poorer classes, which in other countries are invested in private companies or the public funds, are used for buying land."

When Arthur Young visited France for the first time, among a multitude of new experiences, none impressed him more than the extent to which ownership of the soil was vested in innumerable peasant proprietors; half the cultivable land was owned by them. "I had no idea," he often says, "that such a state of affairs existed anywhere" — and in fact none such existed outside France.

There had once been many peasant proprietors in England, but by now their number had greatly dwindled. Everywhere in Germany and in all periods a limited number of free peasants had enjoyed full ownership of the land they worked. The special, often highly peculiar laws regulating the cultivator's ownership of land are set forth in the oldest German *Books of Customs,* but this type of ownership was always exceptional, there never were many of these small landed proprietors.

It was chiefly along the Rhine that at the close of the eighteenth century

German farmers owned the land they worked and enjoyed almost as much freedom as the French small proprietor; and it was there, too, that the revolutionary zeal of the French found its earliest adepts and took most permanent effect. On the other hand, the parts of Germany which held out longest against the current of new ideas were those where the peasants did not as yet enjoy such privileges — and this is, to my mind, a highly suggestive fact.

Thus the prevalent idea that the breakup of the big estates in France began with the Revolution is erroneous; it had started long before. True, the revolutionary governments sold the estates owned by the clergy and many of those owned by the nobility; however, if we study the records of these sales (a rather tedious task, but one which I have on occasion found rewarding) we discover that most of the parcels of land were bought by people who already had land of their own. Thus, though estates changed hands, the number of landowners was increased much less than might have been expected. For, to employ the seemingly extravagant, but in this case correct, expression used by Necker, there were already "myriads" of such persons.

What the Revolution did was not to parcel out the soil of France, but to "liberate" it — for a while. Actually these small proprietors had much difficulty in making a living out of the land since it was subject to many imposts from which there was no escaping.

That these charges were heavy is undeniable, but, oddly enough, what made them seem so unbearable was something that, on the face of it, should have had the opposite effect: the fact that, as in no other part of Europe, our agriculturists had been emancipated from the control of their lords — a revolution no less momentous than that which had made them peasant proprietors.

Although the old régime is still so near to us in time — every day we meet persons born under its auspices — it already seems buried in the night of ages. So vast was the revolution that has intervened that its shadow falls on all that it did not destroy, and it is as if centuries lay between the times we live in and the revolutionary epoch. This explains why so few people know the answer to the quite simple question: How was rural France administered previous to 1789? And indeed it is impossible to give a full and accurate answer without having studied not the literature but the administrative records of the period.

I have often heard it said that though they had long ceased to play a part in the government of the country as a whole, the nobility kept in their hands, right up to the end, the administration of the rural districts; that, in fact, the landed proprietor "ruled" his peasants. This idea, too, seems based on a misconception of the true state of affairs.

In the eighteenth century all that touched the parish, the rural equivalent of the township, was under the control of a board of officials who were no longer agents of the seigneur or chosen by him. Some were nominated by the Intendant of the province, others elected by the local peasantry. Amongst the many functions of these officials were those of assessing the tax to be paid by each member of the community, of keeping churches in repair, of building schools, of summoning and presiding over the parish assemblies. They supervised the municipal funds, decided how these were to be expended, and in litigation to which the parish was a party acted as its representatives. Far from controlling the administration of parish affairs the lord had no say at all in them. All members of the parish councils were ex officio public servants or under the control of the central power (as will be explained in the following chapter). As for the lord, he rarely figured as the King's representative in the parish or as an intermediary between him and its inhabitants. He was no longer expected to see to the maintenance of law and order, to call out the militia, to levy taxes, to publish royal edicts, or to distribute the King's bounty in times of shortage. All these rights and duties had passed into the hands of others and the lord was in reality merely one of the inhabitants of the parish, differentiated from the others by certain exemptions and privileges. His social rank was higher, but he had no more power than they. In letters to their sub-delegates the Intendants were careful to point out that the lord was only "the first resident."

When we turn from the parish to the larger territorial unit, the canton, we find the same arrangement; the nobles play no part, collectively or individually, in the administration of public affairs. This was peculiar to France; in all other countries what was the chief characteristic of ancient feudalism persisted to some extent and possession of the land carried with it the right to govern the people living on it.

England was administered as well as governed by the great landed proprietors. Even in those parts of Germany, for example Prussia and Austria, where the ruling Princes had been most successful in shaking off the control of the nobility in the conduct of affairs of State, they had allowed the nobles to retain to some extent the administration of the rural areas. Though in some places they kept a firm hand on the local lord, they had not, as yet, supplanted him.

The French nobility, however, had long ceased to play any part in public administration, with one exception: the administration of justice. The leading nobles retained the right of delegating to judges appointed by them the trial of certain kinds of suits and still issued police regulations, from time to time, that held good within the limits of their domains. But the central authority had gradually curtailed and subordinated to itself the judicial powers of the landed proprietor; to such an extent that the lords who still exercised them regarded them as little more than a source of revenue.

The same thing had happened to all the special powers of the nobility; on the political side these powers were now defunct and only the pecuniary advantages attaching to them remained (and in some cases had been much increased). At this point something must be said about those lucrative privileges which our forefathers usually had in mind when they spoke of "feudal rights," since it was these that most affected the life of the general public.

It is hard to say today which of these rights were still in force in 1789 and in what they consisted. There had been a vast number of them and by then many had died out or been modified almost out of recognition; indeed, the exact meaning of the terms in which they are described (about which even contemporaries were not very clear) is extremely hard to ascertain today. Nevertheless, my study of works by eighteenth-century experts on feudal law and my researches into local usages have made it clear to me that the rights still functioning in 1789 fell into a relatively small number of categories; others survived, no doubt, but they were operative only in exceptional cases.

Of the old seigneurial *corvée*, or statutory labor obligation, traces remained everywhere, but half obliterated. Most of the toll charges on the roads had been reduced or done away with, though there were few provinces in which some had not survived. Everywhere the resident seigneur levied dues on fairs and markets, and everywhere enjoyed exclusive rights of hunting. Usually he alone possessed dovecotes and pigeons, and it was the general rule that farmers must bring their wheat to their lord's mill and their grapes to his wine press. A universal and very onerous right was that named *lods et ventes*; that is to say an impost levied by the lord on transfers of land within his domain. And throughout the whole of France the land was subject to quitrents, ground rents, dues in money, or in kind payable by the peasant proprietor to his lord and irredeemable by the former. Varied as they were, all these obligations had one common feature: they were associated with the soil or its produce, and all alike bore heavily on the cultivator.

The lords spiritual enjoyed similar privileges. For though the Church derived its authority from a different source and had aims and functions quite different from those of the temporal power, it had gradually become tied up with the feudal system and, though never fully integrated into it, was so deeply involved as to seem part and parcel of it.

Bishops, canons, and abbots owned fiefs or quitrents in virtue of their ecclesiastical status, and usually monasteries had seigneurial rights over the villages on whose land they stood. The monastery had serfs in the only part of France where serfdom had survived, employed forced labor, levied dues on fairs and markets, had the monopoly of the communal wine press, bakehouse, mill, and the stud bull. Moreover, the clergy enjoyed in France — as indeed in all Christian Europe — the right of levying tithes.

The point, however, on which I would lay stress is that exactly the same feudal rights were in force in every European land and that in most other countries of the continent they pressed far more heavily on the population than in France. Take, for example, the lord's right to forced labor, the *corvée*. It was rarely exercised and little oppressive in France, whereas in Germany it was stringent and everywhere enforced.

Moreover, when we turn to the feudal rights which so much outraged our fathers and which they regarded as opposed not merely to all ideas of justice but to the spirit of civilization itself (I am thinking of the tithe, irredeemable ground rents, perpetual charges, *lods et ventes*, and so forth, all that in the somewhat grandiloquent language of the eighteenth century was styled "the servitude of the land"), we find that all these practices obtained to some extent in England and, indeed, are still found there today. Yet they do not prevent English husbandry from being the best organized and most productive in the modern world; and, what is perhaps still more remarkable, the English nation seems hardly aware of their existence.

Why then did these selfsame feudal rights arouse such bitter hatred in the heart of the French people that it has persisted even after its object has long since ceased to exist? One of the reasons is that the French peasant had become a landowner, and another that he had been completely emancipated from the control of his lord. (No doubt there were other reasons, but these, I think, were the chief ones.)

If the peasant had not owned his land he would hardly have noticed many of the charges which the feudal system imposed on all real estate. What could the tithe matter to a man who had no land of his own? He could simply deduct it from the rent. And even restrictions hampering agriculture mean nothing to an agriculturist who is simply cultivating land for the benefit of someone else.

Moreover, if the French peasant had still been under his lord's control, the feudal rights would have seemed much less obnoxious, because he would have regarded them as basic to the constitution of his country.

When the nobles had real power as well as privileges, when they governed and administrated, their rights could be at once greater and less open to attack. In fact, the nobility was regarded in the age of feudalism much as the government is regarded by everyone today; its exactions were tolerated in view of the protection and security it provided. True, the nobles enjoyed invidious privileges and rights that weighed heavily on the commoner, but in return for this they kept order, administered justice, saw to the execution of the laws, came to the rescue of the oppressed, and watched over the interests of all. The more these functions passed out of the hands of the nobility, the more uncalled-for did their privileges appear — until at last their mere existence seemed a meaningless anachronism.

I would ask you to picture to yourself the French peasant as he was in the eighteenth century — or, rather, the peasant you know today, for he has not changed at all. His status is different, but not his personality. See how he appears in the records from which I have been quoting: a man so passionately devoted to the soil that he spends all his earnings on buying land, no matter what it costs. To acquire it he must begin by paying certain dues, not to the government but to other landowners of the neighborhood, who are as far removed as he from the central administration and almost as powerless as he. When at long last he has gained possession of this land which means so much to him, it is hardly an exaggeration to say that he sinks his heart in it along with the grain he sows. The possession of this little plot of earth, a tiny part, his very own, of the wide world, fills him with pride and a sense of independence. But now the neighbors aforesaid put in an appearance, drag him away from his cherished fields, and bid him work elsewhere without payment. When he tries to protect his seedlings from the animals they hunt, they tell him to take down his fences, and they lie in wait for him at river crossings to exact a toll. At the market there they are again, to make him pay for the right of selling the produce of his land, and when on his return home he wants to use the wheat he has put aside for his daily needs, he has to take it to their mill to have it ground, and then to have his bread baked in the lord's oven. Thus part of the income from his small domain goes to supporting these men in the form of charges which are imprescriptible and irredeemable. Whatever he sets out to do, he finds these tiresome neighbors barring his path, interfering in his simple pleasures and his work, and consuming the produce of his toil. And when he has done with them, other fine gentlemen dressed in black step in and take the greater part of his harvest. When we remember the special temperament of the French peasant proprietor in the eighteenth century, his ruling interests and passions, and the treatment accorded him, we can well understand the rankling grievances that burst into a flame in the French Revolution.

For even after it had ceased to be a political institution, the feudal system remained basic to the economic organization of France. In this restricted form it was far more hated than in the heyday of feudalism, and we are fully justified in saying that the very destruction of some of the institutions of the Middle Ages made those which survived seem all the more detestable.

· · ·

HOW THE IDEA OF CENTRALIZED ADMINISTRATION WAS ESTABLISHED AMONG THE ANCIENT POWERS, WHICH IT SUPPLANTED, WITHOUT, HOWEVER, DESTROYING THEM

At this stage it may be well to sum up briefly the state of affairs. . . . We find a single central power located at the heart of the kingdom and controlling public administration throughout the country; a single Minister of State in charge of almost all the internal affairs of the country; in each province a single representative of government supervising every detail of the administration; no secondary administrative bodies authorized to take action on their own initiative; and, finally, "exceptional" courts for the trial of cases involving the administration or any of its officers. Is not this exactly the highly centralized administration with which we are familiar in present-day France? True, its forms were less clearly defined, its procedures less co-ordinated, and the government machinery ran less smoothly than it does today; nonetheless, it was the same in all essentials. Nothing vital has been added to or taken from it. The only change is that the centralization of power in France has become far more conspicuous now that all the relics of the past have been pruned away.

Most of the institutions described above were subsequently adopted by other countries — indeed, replicas of them can now be seen in many parts of the world — but at the time of which I am writing they were peculiar to France and they had, as I shall now set forth, a very great influence not only on the Revolution itself but on its aftermath.

That it was possible to build up modern institutions of this kind in France within the shattered framework of the feudal system may seem surprising at first sight. It was a task calling for much patience and adroitness rather than for the exercise of force and authoritarian methods. When the Revolution broke out, very little of the old administrative structure had actually been destroyed; but a new substructure, so to speak, had gradually been pieced together.

There is nothing to show that in carrying out this difficult task the government of the old régime was following any premeditated scheme. It merely yielded to the instinctive desire of every government to gather all the reins of power into its own hands and, despite the multiplication of secondary powers, this instinct never failed to take effect. Representatives of the former ruling class retained their rank and titles, but all effective authority was gradually withdrawn from them. They were not so much expelled from their former spheres of influence as edged out of them. Taking advantage of the apathy of some and the unenlightened egotism of others, the central administration stepped into their place; far from seeking to amend their shortcomings it made these serve its turn, and ended up, almost everywhere, by replacing them with a single representative of government named the Intendant, whose very title was a new creation.

The only obstacle the central power encountered in carrying out its vast program was the judiciary; but even in this domain it succeeded in grasping the substance of power, leaving only the shadow of it to its rivals. It did not exclude the parlements from the administration but little by little extended its authority so as to usurp practically the whole field assigned to them. In certain states of emergency, during periods of famine for example, when feelings ran high amongst the people and the local authorities saw a chance of asserting themselves, the central government allowed the parlements to take charge for the duration of the crisis and to make a great show of beneficent activity (historians have tended to give prominence to these episodes). But once the crisis was over, the government stepped in again, and discreetly but firmly resumed its control of everything and everyone within the affected areas.

When we closely study the conflicts between the parlements and the royal power we find that it was almost always in the field of politics, not in that of administration, that these clashes took place. Usually the bone of contention was a new tax; that is to say the matter at issue was not of an administrative order but concerned exclusively the power of legislation — a power which, constitutionally, neither of the parties involved had any better right than the other to arrogate to itself.

These disputes are found to intensify in violence the nearer we come to the revolutionary period. And with the rising tide of popular feeling, the parlements tended more and more to take a hand in politics while, as a result of the increasing efficiency (due to long, cumulative experience) of the central power and its officers, the parlements concerned themselves less and less with matters of an administrative order in the strict sense. Thus the French parlement became less and less an administrative and more and more a demagogic body.

Moreover, with the passing years the central power constantly opened up new fields of action into which the courts of law, owing to their inadaptability and conservatism, were incapable of following it. For they had no precedents to go on and were inhibited by routine. The social order was in the throes of a rapid evolution, giving rise to new needs, and each of these was an added source of power to the central government, since it alone was in a position to satisfy them. Whereas the activities of the courts were limited to a well-defined field, those of the central government were being steadily extended, along with civilization itself.

With the approach of the Revolution the minds of all the French were in a ferment; a host of new ideas were in the air, projects which the central government alone could implement. Thus, before overthrowing it, the Revolution increased its powers. That, like so much else, the State machine had been brought to a high state of perfection is evidenced by all the records of the period. The Controller-General and the Intendants of 1790 were quite other than the Controller-General and the Intendants of 1740. The administration had been thoroughly overhauled, and though it employed the same officials, they were actuated by a very different spirit. In proportion as the central power at once widened its sphere of action and paid more heed to details, it had become more systematic in its methods and more efficient. Moreover, now that it had the entire nation under its control, it could afford to be more lenient, to give more suggestions, fewer peremptory orders.

That ancient institution, the French monarchy, after being swept away by the tidal wave of the Revolution, was restored in 1800. It was not, as is often supposed, the principles of 1789 that triumphed at that time (and are still incorporated in the French administrative system); on the contrary, it was the principles of the old order that were revived and have been endorsed by all successive governments.

If I am asked how it was possible for this part of the old régime to be taken over en bloc and integrated into the constitution of modern France, my answer is that the reason why the principle of the centralization of power did not perish in the Revolution is that this very centralization was at once the Revolution's starting-off point and one of its guiding principles. Indeed, I would go so far as to say that whenever a nation destroys its aristocracy, it almost automatically tends toward a centralization of power; a greater effort is then needed to hold it back than to encourage it to move in this direction. All the authorities existing within it are affected by this instinctive urge to coalesce, and much skill is needed to keep them separate. Thus the democratic revolution, though it did away with so many institutions of the past, was led inevitably to consolidate this one; centralization fitted in so well with the program of the new social order that the common error of believing it to have been a creation of the Revolution is easily accounted for.

.   .   .

HOW FRANCE HAD BECOME THE COUNTRY IN WHICH MEN WERE MOST LIKE EACH OTHER

One of the things which cannot fail to strike an attentive student of the social system under the old order is that it had two quite contradictory aspects. On the one hand, we get an impression that the people composing it, at least those belonging to the upper and the middle classes — the only ones that is to say who catch the eye — were all exactly like each other. Nevertheless, we also find that this seemingly homogeneous mass was still divided within itself into a great number of watertight compartments, small, self-contained units, each of which watched vigilantly over its own interests and took no part in the life of the community at large.

If we bear in mind the number of these minute gradings and the fact that nowhere else in the world were citizens less inclined to join forces and stand by each other in emergencies, we can see how it was that a successful revolution could tear down the whole social structure almost in the twinkling of an eye. All the flimsy barriers between the various compartments were instantaneously laid low, and out of the ruins there arose a social order closer knit and less differentiated, perhaps, than any that the Western World had ever known.

I have pointed out how local differences between the various provinces had long since been obliterated throughout practically the entire kingdom; this had greatly contributed to making Frenchmen everywhere so much like each other. Behind such diversities as still existed the unity of the nation was making itself felt, sponsored by that new conception: "the same laws for all." For as the eighteenth century advances, we find an ever increasing number of edicts, Orders in Council, and royal mandates imposing the same regulations and the same procedures on all parts of the kingdom. Not only the governing class but also the governed endorsed this concept of a standardized legislative system valid everywhere. Indeed, it underlies all the successive projects of reform put forward during the three decades preceding the Revolution. Two centuries earlier any such projects would have been quite literally unthinkable.

Not only did the provinces come to resemble each other more and more, but within each province members of the various classes (anyhow those above the lowest social stratum) became ever more alike, differences of rank notwithstanding. This is borne out conspicuously by the *cahiers* (written instructions given to the deputies) presented by the different Orders at the meeting of the Estates-General in 1789. Allowing for the fact that the parties who drew up these memoranda had strongly conflicting interests, they seem remarkably alike in tenor.

When we turn to the proceedings of the earliest Estates-General we find a very different picture: the middle class and the nobility then had more common interests, more points of contact, and displayed much less antipathy towards each other — even if they still gave the impression of belonging to different races. Though with the passing years the privileges which made a cleavage between these two important sections of the community had not merely been maintained but in some respects intensified, the lapse of time had worked towards a certain leveling out of their differences in all else.

For during several centuries the French nobility had been getting steadily poorer. "Despite its privileges," a man of gentle birth, writing in 1755, laments, "the nobility is being starved out, and all its wealth passing into the hands of the Third Estate." Yet the laws protecting property owned by the nobility had not been modified and to all appearances its economic position was unchanged. Nonetheless, the more its power declined, the poorer it became.

It would seem that in all human institutions, as in the human body, there is a hidden source of energy, the life principle itself, independent of the organs which perform the various functions needed for survival; once this vital flame burns low, the whole organism languishes and wastes away, and though the organs seem to function as before, they serve no useful purpose. The French nobility still had entails (Burke, indeed, observed that in his day entails were commoner and more binding in France than in England), the law of primogeniture, the right to perpetual dues on the land, and, in fact, all their vested interests had been left intact. They had been released from the costly obligation of defraying their own expenses on active service in the army and, nevertheless, had retained their immunity from taxation; that is to say they still profited by the exemption after being relieved of the obligation. Moreover, they now enjoyed several financial advantages unknown to their ancestors. And yet, in proportion as both the instinct and the practice of leadership declined among them, their wealth passed out of their hands. This gradual impoverishment of the French nobility was largely due to the breaking up of the great landed estates, to which we have already drawn attention. The nobleman had sold his land, plot by plot, to the peasants, keeping only the seigneurial dues which safeguarded the semblance, but not the reality, of his overlordship. In several French provinces — for example the Limousin, of which Turgot gives us so good a description — the erstwhile seigneurs eked out a hand-to-mouth existence; they had hardly any land of their own, and dues and quitrents were almost their only source of income.

"In this *généralité*," wrote an Intendant at the beginning of the century, "there are still several thousand noble families, but not fifteen of them have an income of twenty thousand *livres* a year." The position is lucidly summed up in a note handed by the Intendant of Franche-Comté to his successor (in 1750). "The nobles in these parts are worthy folk but very poor, and as proud as they are poor. Their prestige has sadly declined. It is not bad policy to keep them in this state, for thus they are obliged to have recourse to us and to carry out our wishes. They have formed a closed society, to belong to which a man must prove his right to four quarterings on his escutcheon. It meets only once a year, and it is not officially recognized; merely tolerated. The Intendant is always present at this society. On such occasions, after dining and attending Mass in a body, these worthy gentlemen go home, some on foot, and some on old, worn-out hacks. It's quite a comical sight — as you will see for yourself."

This gradual impoverishment of the nobility was not peculiar to France. It was taking place in all parts of the continent where the feudal system was in process of dying out without being replaced by a new form of aristocracy. In German territory, along the Rhine, the decadence of the indigenous nobility was particularly marked and attracted much attention. England was the one exception. There the old nobility had not only retained but greatly increased its wealth; its members were still the richest and most influential of the King's subjects. True, new families were coming to the fore, but their wealth was no greater than that of the ancient houses.

In France the commoners alone seemed to be taking over the wealth that was being lost by the nobility, to be growing fat at their expense. Yet there was no law preventing the middle-class man from ruining himself or helping him to amass a fortune. All the same he steadily grew wealthier and frequently became as rich as, sometimes richer than, the nobleman. Moreover, his wealth often took the same form; though usually residing in a town, he owned land in the country and sometimes even bought up entire seigneurial estates.

Education and a similar style of living had already obliterated many of the distinctions between the two classes. The bourgeois was as cultivated as the nobleman and his enlightenment came from the same source. Both had been educated on literary and philosophic lines, for Paris, now almost the sole fountainhead of knowledge for the whole of France, had cast the minds of all in the same mold and given them the same equipment. No doubt it was still possible at the close of the eighteenth century to detect shades of difference in the behavior of the aristocracy and that of the bourgeoisie; for nothing takes longer to acquire than the surface polish which is called good manners. But basically all who ranked above the common herd were of a muchness; they had the same ideas, the same habits, the same tastes, the same kinds of amusements; read the same books and spoke in the same way. They differed only in their rights.

I doubt if this leveling-up process was carried so far in any other country, even in England, where the different classes, though solidly allied by common interests, still differed in mentality and manners. For political freedom, though it has the admirable effect of creating reciprocal ties and a feeling of solidarity between all the members of a nation, does not necessarily make them resemble each other. It is only government by a single man that in the long run irons out diversities and makes each member of a nation indifferent to his neighbor's lot.

The Rise of
National Feeling in
Western Europe

ROYAL INSTITUTE OF INTERNATIONAL AFFAIRS

In theory, the old universalism of the Roman Empire remained intact throughout the Middle Ages. The Emperor was the head of a complicated but symmetrical hierarchy at whose base stood the actual cultivator of the soil. Every

From Royal Institute of International Affairs, *Nationalism* (London: Oxford University Press, 1939), pp. 8–21. Reprinted by permission of Oxford University Press, publisher of *Nationalism*, under the auspices of the Royal Institute of International Affairs.

unit formed part of a single system; the civilized world was still a single whole.

Moreover, the theory was to some extent realized in practice. However ramshackle the political structure of the Holy Roman Empire may have been, the one and indivisible Church was a constant and powerful unifying force. The onrush of the barbarian invasions had driven most knowledge inside the Church, which accordingly imposed not only a uniform religion but (possessing as it did a virtual monopoly of education) a uniform language and culture. The Latin of the medieval clerk was admittedly not a very pure Latin, but the very fact of its impurity proves that it was a live language, constantly adapted to the needs of the different days, and thus widely understood.

> It was not only the language of literature, of the Church, of the Law-courts, of all educated men, but of ordinary correspondence; the language in which a student will write home for a pair of boots, or suggest that it is the part of a discreet sister to inflame the affection of the relations, nay even the brother-in-law, of a deserving scholar who at the moment has neither sheets to his bed nor shirts to his back, and in which she will reply that he is sending him two pairs of sheets and a hundred solidi, but "not a word to my husband, or I shall be dead and destroyed!" [1]

Besides the men of learning, another order shared to a certain, if steadily decreasing, extent in this uniform medieval culture: the men of war. They, too, belonged to a universal order which was coterminous with Christendom. The "international" wars of the Middle Ages were wars waged by the whole of Christendom against the infidel beyond the pale; any other war was, strictly speaking, civil war, although the distinction tended quickly to be lost to sight. The medieval knight had at any rate his smattering of Latin, and stood far nearer to the "clerk" than to the tiller of the soil who could speak only in his local tongue. During the earlier Middle Ages (as compared with later periods) a French knight, like a French priest, had more in common with a knight or a priest from Italy or Germany than with a French peasant.

The political structure of medieval, by comparison with modern, Europe was also surprisingly uniform. Local variations of course existed, but the principles which governed the relations between an overlord and his vassals were everywhere much alike, while it long remained the practice for powerful men to hold lands in more than one country.[2] The various European States were developing so slowly that there was relatively little difference in the amount of progress which each had made. The influence of the Roman Empire caused the legal systems of most lands to be based upon somewhat the same foundations, which were in addition shared by the law of the Church. Medieval political theory, partly as a result of the uniformity of organization, did not display any great

---

[1] Helen Waddell, *The Wandering Scholars* (London: Constable & Co., Ltd., 1927), p. x.

[2] Professor F. M. Powicke, in his *Loss of Normandy* (Manchester: Manchester University Press, 1961), suggests that the nation came into existence when Philip Augustus in 1204 gave the Norman nobles the choice of staying in Normandy and giving up their English lands, or of going to England and giving up their Norman lands.

dissimilarities, and it is some time before we can say with confidence that the form of any treatise on the subject has been affected by the country in which it was written.

In other respects, the uniformities of medieval life were perhaps less important than the differences which existed between the inhabitants of one locality and those of another.[3] The striking feature of the social system of the world at all periods prior to the Renaissance was not so much its cosmopolitanism as its parochialism. The whole structure was based on the "subsistence economy" of an immense number of small units, each of which was virtually self-contained. There were few contacts between the units; travelling was difficult and trade was for some time confined to luxuries. The vagueness of the allegiance which a feudal baron owed to his overlord was in a large degree due to the difficulties which the overlord had to encounter in making his presence felt. Indeed the relative amount of influence which the Empire retained, by comparison with the various kingdoms, was due to the inability of any unit above the smallest to take concerted action on a wide scale. When men reckoned in terms of villages, Europe was as much — or as little — a reality as England and France.

Partisan loyalty, love of the familiar and hatred of the stranger were at work throughout the Middle Ages to produce sentiments towards the various units which were remarkably like those now felt towards a nation. In the France of the tenth and eleventh centuries, *patria* was used of each individual province, and not of the whole country.[4] Wherever men of different origins came into contact strife was likely to result. Medieval universities were torn by brawls between the different "nations," although the members of both "nations" might belong to one and the same State. In 1284 a chronicler records that

> as there is a natural loathing between men and serpents, dogs and wolves, horses and gryphons, so is there between the Pisans and the Genoese, Pisans and men of Lucca, Pisans and Florentines.[5]

In 1279 a commissary of a French abbey who was sent to visit daughter foundations in England reported of one that

> the prior is a good, wise, humble and discreet man, albeit an Englishman.

The crusades may have been in theory the only true "international" wars of the Middle Ages, but there was almost as much strife between the Christians who went on them as there was fighting between Christians and infidels. The sacking of Constantinople and Zara during the Fourth Crusade is notorious, while one participant in that expedition wrote to the Pope that

---

[3] It must be remembered that the records from which we draw our knowledge of the Middle Ages were largely written by clerks, who were probably the most cosmopolitan class.

[4] See Handelsmann, in *Bulletin of the International Committee of Historical Sciences*, vol. ii, no. 2, Oct. 1929.

[5] Salimbene, quoted in G. G. Coulton, "Nationalism in the Middle Ages," *Cambridge Historical Journal*, vol. v, no. 1, 1935, where a number of interesting examples are collected, from which all those reproduced here are taken.

it is very important for this business that the Germans should not march with the French; for we cannot find in history that they ever were at accord in any momentous common enterprise.[6]

Hatred of foreign traders was evident from an early date; the Black Prince got into trouble with Parliament for favouring them in the matter of a monopoly of Cornish tin, while the presence of Hansa merchants in London led to considerable unrest during the reign of Richard II.

It is going too far to say that these examples prove the existence of national feeling in the modern sense of the term. There is little to show that any particular significance was yet attached to lines of "national" division in deciding whether a man should be welcomed or shunned. That Frenchmen should be unpopular in England was natural and not very important, so long as the inhabitants of Nether Wallop were coldly received in Over Wallop. National feeling can only be said to appear when men from one part of England are regarded throughout the whole of the rest of the country as being kith and kin, in contrast to "foreigners" who dwell in other lands beyond the sea. The contrast was becoming felt more and more vividly as the Middle Ages progressed, and the chief factor which contributed to its development was undoubtedly the increasing authority of the central government. For that reason, it became most pronounced in those States of Western Europe where the kings were able to consolidate their power over a fairly large area.

There were many reasons why strong governments should have first appeared on the European seaboard of the Atlantic. In the first place, this area was shielded by the rest of Europe from the barbarian invaders who pressed forward from Asia, so that after the inroads of the Norsemen had come to an end, the rulers were not much distracted by external upheavals in their work of internal consolidation. The English were specially fortunate in this respect, being isolated by the sea from the Continent of Europe, and by hill-country from the weaker and more primitive groups who shared their island with them. The French were also favoured by geography since they possessed in the Île de France a solid central core from which they could ultimately expand to Burgundy, Lorraine, and Brittany. But geographical features were not in themselves the determining factor, since Italy, which possesses the most perfect natural frontiers of any European country except Britain, was much later in achieving unity. Spain, which has better natural frontiers than France, was at the same time more exposed to Saracen invasion from North Africa.

A more decisive factor would appear to have been the relative effectiveness of the authority and attraction exercised by the Holy Roman Empire. In England and France the imperial power had always seemed remote and rather nominal, and was never really strong enough to interfere with the activities of the royal government. In the German lands, on the other hand, the Empire remained a living force. The Emperor was usually the most powerful German monarch, and the strength which might in other circumstances have gone to weld together a unitary German State was squandered outside Germany in a

[6] Coulton, *op. cit.*

prolonged struggle against the Pope. At a later date the association of the Habsburg Emperors with the Spanish throne, and Spanish ambitions in Italy, similarly thwarted the consolidation of Spain. In Italy the power of the Papacy continued right down to 1870 to place a barrier in the way of Italian unity.

The part played by the organization of the Church in Western Europe deserves to be noticed in this connexion. Long before France and Britain had acquired single governments, the Papal chancery was referring to Gallia and Anglia as distinct units.[7] The medieval Church adapted itself to the kingdoms which were growing up, making their divisions those of its organization, and within each of them it exercised a strong centralizing influence.[8] The technique of civil administration was partly borrowed from the Church, while the nascent bureaucracy, which was the chief moving force behind the royal power, was at first largely composed of Churchmen, and continued to contain a certain number of them throughout the Middle Ages. The support which the Church gave to the various monarchies was, of course, limited, and as the power of the latter grew, they became less tolerant of the privileges which the Church demanded as a reward.

Lastly, a certain part must be attributed to accident. It was luck that a man of the ability and strength of Henry II should have come to the throne in England after the anarchy of Stephen. It was luck, again, that in France the houses of Capet and afterwards of Valois should have continued so long without being exposed to the dangers of a disputed succession.[9]

The establishment of a strong central power had economic effects of the first importance. It guaranteed the permanence of settled conditions, and the protection of individuals against any arbitrary force except its own. The State began to provide security and certainty, although, of course, both had their limits. The merchants were protected by the rules of contracts. The privileges granted to towns were a safeguard of their freedom. Whereas towns had previously been the economic unit because these conditions could only be found inside their walls, their place began to be taken by the wider area of the State as soon as law and order were effectively organized over that area. Travel became simpler and safer. The monarchs, assisted by jurists, maintained the continuity of a body of rules which were considered as an external expression of justice. The stimulus to the development of the economic system, in which so much depends upon the anticipation of future conditions and therefore on some degree of stability, was tremendous. Specialization for a non-local market could now replace production for subsistence. The range of commodities ex-

---

[7] Coulton, *op. cit.*

[8] See Friedrich Hertz in *Fahrbuch für Soziologie. I. Ergänzungsband: Nation and Nationalität*, 1927.

[9] Freeman, in his *History of Federal Government*, attributed the early consolidation of France and England to the fact that in each of these countries, although in a different way, the king became directly related to every one of his subjects. Ousting the great feudal intermediaries in France, the king was, by various means, continually adding the feudal domains of his vassals to his own; in England, he was strong enough to make the power of his vassals over his subjects less compelling than the power of his own officers. In Germany, on the other hand, the Diet became in effect a congress of governments, and unity was lost.

changed, and the distance over which exchange took place, began to grow. Money came into general use,[10] the doctrine of the just price lost some of its influence, and a primitive banking system was gradually created.

These developments brought into existence a new kind of wealth, and a new wealthy and therefore influential class. Whereas the earlier Middle Ages had known virtually no form of property except land, which was almost entirely in the hands of the feudal lords or of the Church, the wealth of the new merchants consisted of goods and (at a slightly later date) of capital. They lived in towns since towns were the principal markets with the result that towns rapidly grew in size and influence.[11]

A struggle for power was bound to ensue between the old order and the new, between the barons and the Church on the one side, and the new merchant class on the other. But the king, who had his own reasons for fearing the turbulent feudal lord and the equally insubordinate abbot or bishop, had already taken up the struggle against them on his own account. It was natural that the merchant class should give its support to the only power that was likely to establish the settled conditions on which its livelihood depended, and it was natural that the king should readily accept an alliance which gave him the money and mercenaries essential to the assertion of his authority. The king and the merchant had a common interest in the growth of a centralized State and an organized bureaucracy subordinate to the royal authority. Thus in Western Europe that transformation of the economic and social order which is marked by the emergence of a middle class was first the result and then in part the cause of the establishment in each State of a supreme and sovereign government.[12] As Acton observes, "the development of absolute monarchy by the help of democracy is the one constant characteristic of French history." [13]

In its origin the centralized State was in no sense the product of national feeling. But once the process of consolidation had begun, a group feeling began to be generated, and no doubt became before long a contributory factor to the continuation of the process. The length to which centralization was carried, largely owing to the fresh opportunities which were offered by the hitherto unparalleled development of the economic system, meant that this group feel-

[10] The guarantee of value which was given by coinage in a royal mint was an important factor in promoting the use of a common money.

[11] If, as some writers have maintained, the growth of the middle class was the exclusive cause of the development of national feeling, it might have been expected that the town, rather than any larger area, would have formed the political unit of the rising society, since the merchants in each town composed a unified body. National feeling does appear to have become marked earlier in towns than in the country-side, and in some areas, such as north Italy, the town did become the unit. That this was not the case in England and France can only be explained by the fact that the monarchical government had already gone some way towards establishing its authority on a national basis.

[12] The enforcement of royal authority was considerably helped by the invention of gunpowder, which made useless the customary weapons of the medieval knight; and this invention was not unconnected with economic progress.

[13] Lord Acton, *History of Freedom and Other Essays* (London: Macmillan & Co., 1906), p. 279. By "democracy" Acton meant the middle class.

ing became generalized and attained an intensity such as had never before been developed over a correspondingly wide area. Not only was the unit larger, but the proportion of people sensitive to the feeling of community was greater. For that reason the term "nation" seems for the first time in history fully appropriate.

It is, however, interesting to trace the process by which national feeling and the consciousness of national distinctiveness developed, and to show how the existence of a single sovereign government, run first and foremost in the interest of a single man, made an indispensable contribution to the process. The following appear to have been the principal factors which were at work:

(1) The need to express orders and inquiries in a form which would be intelligible to all broke down the monopoly of Latin as the language of every one who mattered, and brought about the gradual acceptance of the native tongue as the regular medium of intercourse. In England, the process was complicated by the presence of a third language, namely French, and it may have contributed to the development of English national feeling that the English language had to establish itself in opposition, not only to a universal language, but also to the tongue particular to another and frequently hostile State. The process had been virtually carried to completion by 1362, when Froissart records that Parliament began to hold its sessions in English "parce que la langue française est mal comprise du peuple."

English and French had not only to break down the opposition of rival tongues but to establish themselves as uniform languages over the area in which they were spoken. The mode of speech of educated Englishmen and educated Frenchmen had to become in some degree standardized; and this was achieved when the East Midland variety of the Midland dialect and the *Langue d'Oil* were respectively recognized as standard English and standard French. These dialects were in fact those of the central administration and of its law courts; the East Midland dialect, besides being the language of the government, was in addition that of the vice-comites in the shires and of the capital city with its business. The extent to which a language becomes standardized in a given area ultimately depends on the amount of travel and intercourse within that area. The security provided by the royal governments did much to increase intercourse throughout the respective kingdoms.

It would be false to assume that the creation of a distinctive State-wide language was in itself tantamount to the creation of the nation. Dante, though he contributed immensely to the development of Italian, was an advocate of the universal sovereignty of a German Emperor, while Chaucer, although he was a pioneer of the English language and keenly alive to individual character, never suggests that his pilgrims are types peculiar to England. But the adoption of uniform languages over considerable areas must obviously have exercised a potent influence both in binding the inhabitants of any single area to one another and in differentiating them from the rest of the world. The full importance of this influence lies in the fact that culture follows language, and that the literature written in that language will form one of the proudest parts of the national heritage.

(2) Just as the State spoke in a single language throughout the entire country, so it everywhere enforced a single set of laws. At the end of the Dark Ages, each district had had its own customs, and the history of government during the Middle Ages is largely a history of the process by which the law of the centre not only spread through the country, but increased in bulk at the expense of local practices. Along with the law, and partially incorporated in it, went a vast body of conventions of social behaviour. The extension of the law created another common link between members of the State, which also served to distinguish them from members of other States. England provides an outstanding example. Common Law, being based upon precedent and thus upon a particular set of customs, served to differentiate the developing English society from the feudal type. When an attempt was made to bring in Saint Louis of France as an arbitrator, his authority was denied because, being a foreigner, he could not know the English law.[14] In this connexion, it is significant that throughout the Middle Ages English Common lawyers should have displayed the greatest dislike both of the Civil Law and of Canon Law, which were based upon Roman foundations. One of the most serious charges brought against John Tiptoft was that he had, when Constable, introduced into England the "Law of Padua."

(3) The rise of the new merchant class, as well as of the bureaucracy who were the king's agents, meant a vast increase in the number of those who owned property and who had what is commonly called "a stake in the country." The new class, having interests to defend as well as the resources with which to defend them, became politically conscious and acquired a political outlook which was necessarily very different from that of the barons. The evolution in industrial and commercial technique, of which the growth of the commercial classes was a sign and a result, involved increasing division of labour and exchange, which was not only more intensive but occurred over a wider area. In particular, the freeing of trade in land facilitated migration and made possible greater social diversification. A growth in the amount of specialized knowledge, with a consequent growth in diversification of function, adds to mutual interdependence, so that one result of the development was to give greater cohesion to life within each of the various units. Such cohesion as had previously existed had been due to the common government imposed from above. The effect of common government was not supplemented and intensified, more common interests were created, and an awareness of those already existing became easier.

(4) The rapid expansion of a class which had new ideas to express, and the development of national languages and literature, were bound up with the rise of a secular education and culture. The breakdown of the monopoly of Latin meant the breakdown of the ecclesiastical monopoly of education. The new well-to-do and leisured class wanted to learn to think, and to train their children to think, on lines adapted to their new requirements. Even where the Church retained control of education, it was compelled to make concessions to the needs of the new rich, who were often its most munificent patrons. Thus cul-

---

[14] James I subsequently met with opposition on similar grounds from Coke and his colleagues.

ture took on, for the first time since the fall of the Roman Empire, a secular flavour. Moreover, in detaching itself from the universal tradition of the Church, it attached itself to the new tradition of each particular state; that is to say, to something which would soon justify a claim to the title of "national tradition." The invention of printing, itself part of the process which was creating the new merchant class, helped greatly towards this secular education.

(5) The contributions which political, economic, linguistic, and cultural factors were making to the creation of national feeling were powerfully reinforced by the effects of hostile contact between the incipient national groupings. This was brought about when the rulers of the centralized State called their subjects to fight against members of other similar units. The Hundred Years' War (supplemented, in the case of England, by the wars against the Scots) was the factor which ultimately did more than anything else to develop a feeling of conscious nationalism in England and France. War, as has already been suggested,[15] not only compelled co-operation between the members of one State, but also intensified the differences which distinguished them from the members of the other. It is true that the English monarchs fought on the pretext that they were kings of France as well as of England, and that the Burgundians (who might well be considered as Frenchmen) were fighting on the English rather than on the French side. But these were merely symptoms of the rudimentary stage which national feeling had as yet reached. It is, on the whole, a sound tradition which associates the birth of the French nation with the name of Joan of Arc. Joan heard voices, hailed Charles VII as the vassal of the King of Heaven, and was burnt as a witch. But the medieval setting of her career need not blind us to the essential nature of her achievement. By her emphasis on the coronation at Rheims and her call to drive out the English she became, consciously or unconsciously, the first champion of French unity and independence; and the Burgundians were merely fighting in rearguard action in defence of a doomed order of society.

On the English side, the *Libelle of English Policy* reflects the undeniable national feeling which prevailed among the merchant adventurers at the beginning of the fifteenth century.

> Shall any prynce, what so be hys name . . .
> Be lorde of sea and Flemmynges to our blame
> Stoppe us, take us and so make fade the floures
> Of Englysshe state and disteyne oure honnoures.

The author is not interested in the conquest of France, but he would like to see England mistress of the seas.

> Now then, for love of Cryste and of his joye,
> Brynge yet Englande out of troble and noye;
> Take herte and wite and set a governaunce,
> Set many wites wythouten variaunce
> To one accorde and unanimite
> Put to gode wylle for to kepe the see,

[15] Cf. Chap. I, p. 2.

Furste for worshyp and for profite also,
And to rebuke of eche evyl-wylled foo.
Thus shall richesse and worship to us longe . . .
The ende of bataile is pease sikerlye,
And power causeth pease final verily . . .
Kepe then the see, that is the wall of Englond,
And then is Englond kept by Goddes sonde.[16]

His attitude suggests that it was perhaps a sound instinct which led Shake-speare to depict Agincourt as a demonstration of English patriotism and Henry V as the first of England's patriot kings.

In the next century, when the great discoveries, through their effect upon the trade routes, had given an additional impetus to English commerce, privateers and merchant adventurers carried national rivalries on to the high seas. The spirit which had been roused by war with France was inflamed still further by war with Spain. And by this time, religion had provided the States of Europe with a further source of opposition and differentiation.

(6) The modern conception of the nation remained seriously incomplete so long as the Church was organized on a universal rather than on a national basis. In the revolt against Rome, economic and moral as well as religious motives were at work, for the wealth of the Church made it a tempting prey and its indolence an easy target. The political implications of the Reformation were as important as the religious ones, and it is no accident that Luther should be regarded as a pioneer of German national feeling. England provides an outstanding example of the process by which the power of the Church was broken, and made subordinate to that of the State. The struggle began as early as the twelfth century, and ended under the Tudors in a complete victory for the State and for the new national tradition. Here again the influence of the king was all important. The initial steps in the rejection of Papal authority were due to the personal wishes of Henry VIII, and the monarchy was sufficiently strong to impose the form of worship which it preferred upon the whole country, though it left an aftermath of religious discord which deeply affected English history for the next century and a half.[17]

In France, which lay nearer to Rome, the religious struggle was keener and the Crown (held at this period, as luck would have it, by a succession of weaklings) proved less dominant; there was a period when it seemed likely that the country, like Germany, would be permanently split on religious lines. This disaster was narrowly averted by the policy of Henri IV, which was rendered possible by the fact that a sufficient proportion of the population, under the leadership of the *Politiques*, thought of themselves first as Frenchmen, and only second as Catholics or Protestants. A solution was ultimately reached by the compromise of Gallicanism, which involved the establishment of a national Church politically independent and owing allegiance to Rome on doctrinal

---

[16] *Libelle*, lines 43–7, 1064–72, 1090–1, 1096–7. "Noye" = harm; "sonde" = grace. The poem was written about 1437.

[17] The keenness of the struggle is reflected in the anti-Catholic legislation which remained in force till the nineteenth century, and which still survives in the exclusion of Catholics from the throne and from the Woolsack.

matters alone. The compromise worked well enough, though it did not prevent the religious issue from remaining a potentially disruptive force in French politics even in quite recent times.

Some writers have seen a close connexion between the rise of nationalism and the decline of religion. Bryce described the "sentiment of nationality" as

> a sentiment comparatively weak in the ancient world and in the Middle Ages, and which did not really become a factor of the first moment in politics till the religious passion of the 16th and 17th centuries had almost wholly subsided, and the gospel of political freedom preached by the American and French Revolutionaries had begun to fire men's minds.[18]

There can be little doubt that, as the power of the State and its impact upon the individual increased, it acted with increasing effect as a magnet attracting the loyalty which human beings desire to concentrate on some object more permanent and extensive than is provided by their personal lives. One consequence of this development was that the collective passions which formerly found expression in disputes about religious doctrine or practice tended increasingly to find expression in nationalism.

(7) The present analysis would be deficient if it failed to touch upon the familiar fact that representative government was born in the States of Western Europe, and in particular in England. The establishment of this form of government, to which the kings largely contributed, not only enabled those citizens who had become politically conscious to feel that they had a share and personal responsibility in the State, but also stimulated the growth of political consciousness. Thus were laid the foundations of that association between nationalism and democracy which reached its culminating expression during the nineteenth century.

By these means, among which those dependent on government action played a considerable part, the people of England and France were slowly and without deliberate purpose being given common distinguishing marks. They were gradually becoming aware that they formed a community, the members of which were like one another and unlike anybody else. That is to say, a sense of community was being generated over a sufficiently wide area for the group to merit the name of "nation." The cohesion which resulted increased enormously the efficiency of the State in relation to its neighbours, both as regards war and trade. The acquisition of a common stock of knowledge and feeling enabled men to handle problems of government in more effective and more closely integrated groups than had even been possible before.

Thus by about the end of the sixteenth century in England, and soon afterwards in France, the making of the modern nation within the framework of the unified State was complete. France, through the absorption of Burgundy, attained its modern national limits. The union between England and Scotland made Great Britain to all intents and purposes a single State; and in place of

18 James Bryce, *Studies in History and Jurisprudence* (Oxford: Oxford University Press, 1901), i, 268.

the English nation, the new conception of a British nation slowly emerged. The centuries succeeding the Reformation saw a steady continuation of the economic development which the new security of life and the growth of strong centralized government had set in motion in Western Europe. In this development the purely economic forces, the strong centralized governments, and the growing awareness of national unity all combined to reinforce one another. In particular, the deliberate exploitation of the resources of the State as a unit under the direction of the government and in competition with other similar units, which is described by the name of "Mercantilism," not only caused the economic system to make progress which might otherwise have remained unachieved, but also heightened national feeling.

In the meanwhile, the balance of forces within the nation had shifted. The foundations of the nation-State had been laid by an alliance between the monarchy and the new middle class which had combined with the king to break the power of feudalism. Now that the common enemy had been destroyed, the alliance had lost its meaning; and the attempt of the monarchy to govern in its own interest became a hindrance to further development both of material prosperity and of national feeling. Once again these developments occurred first and most conspicuously in England. In the English civil wars of the seventeenth century those interests which had formerly aided the monarchy to build up a strong central government now combined to wrest that government out of the hands of the king. Moreover, this step lay on the direct path of economic progress. In the Middle Ages the establishment of royal courts of justice had been an inestimable boon to merchants. Now, further progress required the security of the Act of Settlement of 1701, which laid down that judges should in future continue to hold office unless removed by Parliament, and so ended all danger of a public-spirited judge being dismissed at a royal whim. In another aspect, the Revolution of 1688 was a proof of the strength which national feeling had attained, since the coercive power of the head of the State could be curbed and shared out among the whole body of well-to-do citizens, and even religious diversity could be tolerated without breaking down national unity. In France the Revolution of 1789 performed the same function as the English civil wars and Revolution of the seventeenth century; and Napoleon came to complete the task of national unification.

The essential feature of these movements, which reflected the economic development made possible by increased stability and other favourable conditions created by the growth of strong governments, and which were carried to completion in the nineteenth century, was the broadening of the basis of the nation-State. This was now built up, not on a strong central autocracy, but on an ever-widening foundation of popular support. And this placing of the State on a popular basis involved a change, which was only gradually achieved, in the general conception of the nation. In earlier times the State had been regarded as the personal property and concern of the monarch, in which private individuals had little or no part. As a larger proportion of the population came to participate in politics, the conception was widened to allow them a place beside the proprietor. But to regard the citizens as being joint and equal proprietors was a more difficult change, since it involved turning the State from something personal into something abstract. Yet the contemporary idea of the nation can only be said to be complete when the group linked by common national feeling has been organized politically as a modern popular State. The next subject therefore calling for consideration is the development of the theory of the nation, which is indissolubly linked with the development of the theory of the State.

SECTION E

THE WESTERN EXPERIENCE: POLITICS OF THE MODERN STATE

E 1 / Social Groups Considered Politically

Introduction

While the "society" and "state" of our title refer to concrete social phenomena, we can also speak in analytical terms of "social" and "political" dimensions of action; and as long as these analytical dimensions are not reified carelessly, they can aid us in discussing politics in the nation-state.[1] In the Weberian tradition which we follow here, the "social" includes both natural groups formed by actions based upon a sense of communal solidarity or cultural identification and associations formed by actions based upon considerations of ideal and material interest. The "political," on the other hand, includes two aspects: formal authority structures, that is, the organization of those who rule; and the beliefs in legitimacy which serve to unite, at least to a degree, the rulers and the ruled, and which provide the framework for the conflicting interactions of social groups. These dimensions, then, provide the tripartite division for our analysis of politics in modern and modernizing states in Sections E and G.

The first of our subsections, entitled "Social Groups Considered Politically," focuses on the natural groups and associations of the "social" order. Under this heading a wide variety of topics may be studied by political sociologists. The selections we have chosen concentrate on the lower classes of society (Bendix), interest groups in their relations to public bureaucracies (Ehrmann), and groups based on political, ethnic, or religious affiliations (Lipset). All such groups can, but need not, have political influence, though the more complex and powerful interest-based organizations almost inevitably tend to impinge on

[1] For discussions of this distinction, see Reinhard Bendix and Seymour M. Lipset, "Political Sociology, an Essay and Bibliography," *Current Sociology*, Vol. VI (1957), especially pp. 87–88. In anthropological writings, a closely corresponding distinction is that made by Claude Levi-Strauss between "structures of communication" and "structures of subordination"; see *Anthropologie Structurale* (Paris: Plon, 1958), pp. 303–351. The dialectical relationship between society and political power, and their mutual relationship through the process of legitimation, as well as the specificity of the political structures of authority are also stressed in the contributions of Michel Crozier, Gaston Fessard, Georges Davau, and Leo Hamon in *Pouvoir et Société, Recherches et Débats* (C.C.I.F. Desclée de Brouwer, Paris, 1966).

the political order to achieve their goals. Within the national society they constitute the basic cleavages, which the political sociologist views as influences upon the decision-making and decision-implementing institutions of the political order, whether or not such decisions are actually arrived at or carried out. They affect the electoral process (the most formal way in which modern states institutionalize conflict), but they also function independently of voting, which is only an intermittent part of a more or less continuous political process. Most notable here, perhaps, is their influence upon the bureaucracies which administer political decisions. In recent years some theories of politics have emphasized this group-aspect, sometimes to the exclusion of the institutional framework of authority. However, recognition of the political effects of social cleavages should not be carried that far, since the very notion of "politics" presupposes some institutional framework with reference to which such groups may be "considered politically."

Social classes are groups arising from the economic aspects of the division of labor; unlike interest groups, they need not possess a formal organization. In our first selection, Bendix describes the extension of citizenship to the lower classes in a dozen Western European countries. These classes entered the arena of national politics by gaining gradual access to what T. H. Marshall has categorized as civil, political, and social rights. Such an extension of rights was one way in which social protest was accommodated and groups were brought into the national community rather than become a revolutionary threat to it; thus, Bendix's article provides also a final chapter to the process of transition to the modern nation-state described in Section D. Bendix compares the different Western European experiences, couching his analysis in terms of a dialectical interplay between the plebiscitarian and the representative principles, the first involving a direct, the second a mediated, relation between the individual and the nation-state. The right of incorporation for business organizations and the right to form workingmen's associations and trade unions are seen as changes in the representative principle from its medieval version of estate representation to modern "functional" representation; the rights of education and voting, on the other hand, are entailed in a direct relation between individual and state.

While Bendix's discussion deals with one of the great problems and achievements of the past, Ehrmann's article brings us to a central dilemma of the contemporary nation-state. In an era of increasingly complex and powerful organizations, the legislative and executive branches of government in Western industrial societies are losing power to administrative officials, while the latter are influenced increasingly by the interest groups with which they interact. These interest groups may include professional, religious, and many other types of associations, but of major and almost overwhelming importance are large industrial corporations and, secondarily, labor unions. In Ehrmann's view, this confluence of special-interest organizations threatens the formal political structure and the public interest it is supposed to ensure.

Bendix concludes that the endurance of the Western European political system depends on maintaining the tension and balance between the plebiscitarian and representative principles. One kind of breakdown is represented when, in his words, totalitarian states destroy pluralistic associations "in the interest of implementing the plebiscitarian principle alone under the aegis of a one-party state." Another dissolution of the balance is that projected by Ehrmann, when the relatively more plebiscitarian formal institutions of electoral systems and parliaments lose significance vis-à-vis "functional" economic organizations in interaction with bureaucracies (see also the discussion of this problem by Weber in Section F2). Both articles thus deal not only with past and present problems of the nation-state but also with admittedly speculative considerations of its future in the societies which gave birth to it.

Lipset's article is, in contrast, ahistorical as well as more inclusive in dealing with non-Western, European, and North American states. Further, while Ehrmann discusses a threat to the formal political structure, Lipset focuses on it, in examining various relationships between political parties, their social bases, and systems of representation. With the stability of the democratic political system taken as the goal, attention is directed to the significance of electoral laws and the legal structure of the polity for the attainment of this goal. However, more important in the present context than this prescriptive orientation is his attempt as a sociologist to demonstrate the significance of formal institutional structures. This is a needed corrective, since the bulk of sociological writing in this field tends to analyze social groups to the exclusion of the institutional structure within which these groups are politically active.

The Extension of
Citizenship to the
Lower Classes [1]

REINHARD BENDIX

ELEMENTS OF CITIZENSHIP

In the nation-state each citizen stands in a direct relation to the sovereign
authority of the country in contrast with the medieval polity in which that
direct relation is enjoyed only by the great men of the realm. Therefore, a core
element of nation-building is the codification of the rights and duties of all
adults who are classified as citizens. The question is how exclusively or inclu-
sively citizenship is defined. Some notable exceptions aside, citizenship at first
excludes all socially and economically dependent persons. In the course of the
nineteenth century this massive restriction is gradually reduced until eventually
all adults are classified as citizens. In Western Europe this extension of national
citizenship is set apart from the rest of the world by the common traditions of
the *Ständestaat*.[2] The gradual integration of the national community since the
French Revolution reflects these traditions wherever the extension of citizenship
is discussed in terms of the "fourth estate," that is, in terms of extending the
principle of *functional representation* to those previously excluded from citizenship. On the other hand, the French Revolution also advanced the *plebiscitarian principle*. According to this principle all powers intervening between the
individual and the state must be destroyed (such as estates, corporations, etc.),

From Reinhard Bendix, *Nation-Building and Citizenship* (New York: John Wiley &
Sons, 1964), pp. 74–104. Reprinted by permission of the publisher.

REINHARD BENDIX is Professor of Sociology, University of California, Berkeley. His
publications include *Higher Civil Servants in American Society* (1949), *Work and
Authority in Industry* (1956; MacIver Award, 1958), *Max Weber* (1960), and *Nation-
Building and Citizenship* (1964). With Seymour M. Lipset, he has co-authored *Social
Mobility in Industrial Society* (1959) and co-edited *Class, Status and Power* (1953,
1966).

[1] The following section was written jointly with Dr. Stein Rokkan, Christian Michel-
sen Institute, Bergen, Norway. I have adapted the original essay. . . . Subsequent
formulations will emphasize the classificatory sense in which the term "lower classes" is
used. The question is left open which sections of the "lower classes" develop a capacity
for concerted action and under what circumstances. Although in some measure a
response to protest or the result of anticipating protest, the extension of citizenship
occurred with reference to broadly and abstractly defined groups such as all adults
over 21, or women or adults having specified property holdings, fulfilling certain
residence requirements, etc. Such groups encompass many people other than those who
have few possessions, low income, little prestige, and who because of these disabilities
are conventionally understood to "belong" to the lower classes. The reference here is
to the larger, classificatory group of all those (including the "lower classes") who were
excluded from any direct or indirect participation in the political decision-making
processes of the community.

[2] So much so that the historian Otto Hintze denies the *indigenous* development
of constitutionalism anywhere else. See his "Weltgeschichtliche Vorbedingungen der
Repräsentativverfassung," in *Staat und Verfassung* (Göttingen: Vandenhoeck & Ruprecht, 1962), pp. 140–185.

so that all citizens as individuals possess equal rights before the sovereign, national authority.[3]

A word should be added concerning the two adjectives "functional" and "plebiscitarian." The phrase "functional representation" derives from the medieval political structure in which it is deemed proper, for example, that the elders or grand master of a guild represent it in a municipal assembly. Here function refers generically to any kind of activity considered appropriate for an estate. Used more broadly, the term "function" designates *group-specific activities or rights and duties*. As such it encompasses both, observations of behavior and ethical mandates of what is thought proper. The latter imply very different theories of society, however. In medieval society the rank and proper functions of the constituent groups are fixed in a hierarchical order. In modern Western societies this older view has been superseded by concepts of group function which presuppose the ideal of equality, except where medieval connotations linger on. The term "plebiscite" refers to the *direct vote on an important public issue by all qualified electors* of a community. The broader the community, the more minimal the qualifications stipulated for the electors, and hence the larger the number of persons standing in a direct relationship to public authority, the more will the plebiscitarian principle conflict with the functional. The specific meaning of both principles varies naturally with the definitions of group-specific activities and the extent and qualifications of community membership.

Various accommodations between the functional and plebiscitarian principle have characterized the sequence of enactments and codifications through which citizenship became national in many countries of Western Europe. To examine this development comparatively the several rights of citizenship must be distinguished and analyzed. In his study of *Citizenship and Social Class*, T. H. Marshall formulates a threefold typology of rights:

— *civil* rights such as "liberty of person, freedom of speech, thought and faith, the right to own property and to conclude valid contracts, and the right to justice";
— *political* rights such as the franchise and the right of access to public office;
— *social* rights ranging from "the right to a modicum of economic welfare and security to the right to share to the full in the social heritage and to live the life of a civilized being according to the standards prevailing in the society." [4]

---

[3] These two models have been analyzed in terms of the distinction between the representative and the plebiscitarian principle by Ernst Fraenkel, *Die Repräsentative und die Plebiszitäre Komponente im Demokratischen Verfassungsstaat* (Heft 219–220 of Recht und Staat; Tübingen: J. C. B. Mohr, 1958). The ideology of plebiscitarianism is documented in J. L. Talmon, *The Origins of Totalitarian Democracy* (New York: Frederick A. Praeger, 1960).

[4] The essay referred to has been reprinted in T. H. Marshall, *Class, Citizenship and Social Development* (Garden City, New York: Doubleday & Co., Inc., 1964), pp. 71–72. The following discussion is greatly indebted to Professor Marshall's analysis.

Four sets of public institutions correspond to these three types of rights:

the *courts*, for the safeguarding of civil rights and, specifically, for the protection of all rights extended to the less articulate members of the national community;

the local and national *representative bodies* as avenues of access to participation in public decision-making and legislation;

the *social services*, to ensure some minimum of protection against poverty, sickness, and other misfortunes, and the *schools*, to make it possible for all members of the community to receive at least the basic elements of an education.

Initially, these rights of citizenship emerge with the establishment of equal rights under the law. The individual is free to conclude valid contracts, to acquire, and dispose of, property. Legal equality advances at the expense of legal protection of inherited privileges. Each man now possesses the right to act as an independent unit; however, the law only defines his legal capacity, but is silent on his ability to use it. In addition, civil rights are extended to illegitimate children, foreigners, and Jews; the principle of legal equality helps to eliminate hereditary servitude, equalize the status of husband and wife, circumscribe the extent of parental power, facilitate divorce, and legalize civil marriage.[5] Accordingly, the extension of civil rights benefits the inarticulate sections of the population, giving a positive libertarian meaning to the legal recognition of individuality.

Still, this gain of legal equality stands side by side with the fact of social and economic inequality. Tocqueville and others point out that in medieval society many dependent persons were protected in some measure against the harshness of life by custom and paternal benevolence, albeit at the price of personal subservience. The new freedom of the wage contract quickly destroyed whatever protection of that kind had existed.[6] For a time at least, no new protections are instituted in place of the old; hence class prejudice and economic inequalities readily exclude the vast majority of the lower class from the enjoyment of their legal rights. The right of the individual to assert and defend his basic civil freedoms on terms of equality with others and by due process of law is *formal* in the sense that legal powers are guaranteed in the absence of any attempt to assist the individual in his use of these powers. As Anton Menger observed in 1899: "Our codes of private law do not contain a single clause which assigns to the individual even such goods and services as are indispensable

---

[5] See R. H. Graveson, *Status in the Common Law* (London: The Athlone Press, 1953), pp. 14–32. For details of these legal developments in Germany, Austria, Switzerland, and France, see J. W. Hedemann, *Die Fortschritte des Zivilrechts im 19. Jahrbundert* (Berlin: Carl Heymanns Verlag, 1910 and 1935), two volumes. A brief survey of the background and extent of these developments in Europe is contained in Hans Thieme, *Das Naturrecht und die europäische Privatrechtsgeschichte* (Basel: Halbing and Lichtenhahn, 1954). A more extended treatment is contained in Franz Wieacker, *Privatrechtsgeschichte der Neuzeit* (Göttingen: Vandenhoeck & Ruprecht, 1952), esp. pp. 197–216 and *passim*.

[6] Alexis de Tocqueville, *Democracy in America* (New York: Vintage Books, 1954), II, pp. 187–190.

to the maintenance of his existence." [7] In this sense the equality of citizenship and the inequalities of social class develop together.

The juxtaposition of legal equality and social and economic inequalities inspired the great political debates which accompany the nation-building of nineteenth-century Europe. These debates turn on the types and degrees of inequality or insecurity that should be considered intolerable and the methods that should be used to alleviate them. The spokesmen of a consistent *laissez-faire* position seek to answer this question within the framework of formal civil rights. Having won legal recognition for the exercise of individual rights, they insist that to remain legitimate the government must abide by the rule of law. It is consistent with this position that in most European countries the first Factory Acts seek to protect women and children, who at the time are not considered citizens in the sense of legal equality.[8] By the same criterion all adult males are citizens because they have the power to engage in the economic struggle and take care of themselves. Accordingly, they are excluded from any legitimate claim to protection. In this way formally guaranteed rights benefit the fortunate and more fitfully those who are legally defined as unequal, while the whole burden of rapid economic change falls upon the "laboring poor" and thus provides a basis for agitation at an early time.

This agitation is political from the beginning. One of the earliest results of the legislative protection of freedom of contract is the legislative prohibition of trade unions. But where legislative means are used both to protect the individual's freedom of contract and deny the lower classes the rights needed to avail themselves of the same freedom (i.e., the right of association), the attacks upon inequality necessarily broaden. Equality is no longer sought through freedom of contract alone, but through the establishment of social and political rights as well. The nation-states of Western Europe can look back on longer or shorter histories of legislative actions and administrative decisions which have increased the equality of subjects from the different strata of the population in terms of their legal capacity and their legal status.[9] For each nation-state and for each

[7] Anton Menger, *The Right to the Whole Product of Labor* (London: Macmillan and Co., 1899), pp. 3–4.

[8] Ideological equalitarianism as well as an interest in breaking down familial restrictions upon the freedom of economic action were presumably the reason why protection was first extended to these most inarticulate sections of the "lower class." For a critical analysis of the German Civil Code of 1888 exclusively in terms of the economic interests its provisions would serve, see Anton Menger, *Das bürgerliche Recht und die besitzlosen Volksklassen* (Tübingen: H. Laupp'sche Buchhandlung, 1908). The book was originally published in 1890. This perspective omits the self-sustaining interest in formal legality which is the work of legal professionals and leads to the prolonged conflict between legal positivism and the doctrine of natural law. See in this respect the analysis of Max Weber, *Law in Economy and Society* (Cambridge, Mass.: Harvard University Press, 1954), pp. 284–321. See also the illuminating discussion of this point in Fr. Darmstaedter, *Die Grenzen der Wirksamkeit des Rechtsstaates* (Heidelberg: Carl Winters Universitätsbuchhandlung, 1930), pp. 52–84.

[9] When all adult citizens are equal before the law and free to cast their vote, the exercise of these rights depends upon a person's ability and willingness to use the legal powers to which he is entitled. On the other hand, the legal status of the citizens involves rights and duties which cannot be voluntarily changed without intervention by the State. A discussion of the conceptual distinction between capacity as "the legal

set of institutions we can pinpoint chronologies of the public measures taken and trace the sequences of pressures and counterpressures, bargains and maneuvers, behind each extension of rights beyond the strata of the traditionally privileged. The extension of various rights to the lower classes constitutes a development characteristic of each country. A detailed consideration of each such development would note the considerable degree to which legal enactments are denied or violated in practice. It would thus emphasize how the issue of the civic position of the lower classes was faced or evaded in each country, what policy alternatives were under consideration, and by what successive steps the rights of citizenship were extended eventually. A full analysis could illuminate each step along the way, but it would also obscure the over-all process of nation-building.

For taken together, the developments of the several European countries also constitute the transformation from the estate societies of the eighteenth to the welfare state of the twentieth centuries. A comparative study of this transformation from the standpoint of national citizenship will inevitably appear abstract if juxtaposed with the specific chronology and detailed analysis of successive legislative enactments in each country. However, such a study will have the advantage of emphasizing the truth that, considered cumulatively and in the long run, legislative enactments have extended the rights of citizenship to the lower classes and thus represent a genuinely comparable process in nineteenth- and twentieth-century Europe.

The following discussion is limited to one aspect of Western European nation-building: *the entry of the lower classes into the arena of national politics.* Only those policies are considered which have immediate relevance for lower-class movements seeking to enter national politics.[10] The decisions on the *right to form associations* and on the *right to receive a minimum of formal education* are basic, for these rights set the stage for the entry of the lower classes and condition the strategies and activities of lower-class movements once they are formally allowed to take part in politics. Next, the actual *rights of participation* are analyzed in terms of the extension of the *franchise* and the provisions for the *secrecy of the vote.* Considered together, the extension of these rights is indicative of what may be called the civic incorporation of the lower classes.

A BASIC CIVIL RIGHT:
THE RIGHT OF ASSOCIATION AND COMBINATION

Civil rights are essential to a competitive market economy in that "they give to each man, as part of his *individual* status, the power to engage as an *inde-*

---

power of doing" and status as "the legal state of being" is contained in Graveson, *op. cit.,* pp. 55–57.

10 Accordingly, only incidental consideration is given to the initial and the terminal phases in this process of change: the breakup of estate-societies through the extension of civil rights and the final codification and implementation of welfare rights in our modern, "mass-consumption" societies.

pendent unit in the economic struggle." [11] By taking cognizance only of persons who possess the means to protect themselves, the law in effect accords civil rights to those who own property or have assured sources of income. All others stand condemned by their failure in the economic struggle according to the prevailing views of the early nineteenth century. The abstract principle of equality underlying the legal and ideological recognition of the *independent* individual is often the direct cause of greatly accentuated inequalities. In the present context the most relevant illustration of this consequence is the law's insistence that the wage contract is a contract between equals, that employer and worker are equally capable of safeguarding their interests. On the basis of this formal legal equality, workers in many European countries were denied the *right to combine* for the sake of bargaining with their employers.

However, this denial of the right to combine raised conceptual and political difficulties from the beginning. Civil rights refer not only to the rights of property and contract but also to freedom of speech, thought, and faith which include the freedom to join with others in the pursuit of legitimate private ends. Such freedoms are based on the *right of association* — an accepted legal principle in several European countries (France, England, Belgium, Netherlands) which nevertheless decided to prohibit the workers' *right to combine*. It was held that conditions of work must be fixed by agreements freely arrived at between individual and individual.[12] Such legal prohibitions were distinguished, however, from the right to form religious or political associations in so far as associations not specifically prohibited by law were legal. Accordingly, enactments singled out workmen of various descriptions by special regulations in order to "uphold" the principle of formal equality before the law.

The distinction between association and combination was not made in all countries, however. To understand this contrast we must recall the traditional approach to the master-servant relationship which was similar in many European countries. Statutory enactments had been used to regulate the relations between masters and servants and to control the tendency of masters and journeymen to combine in the interest of raising prices or wages. Such regulation increased in importance as guild organizations declined, though governmental regulations were often made ineffective by the new problems arising from a quickening economic development. Efforts to cope with these new problems could take several forms.

The government could attempt to use an extension of the traditional devices. This approach worked temporarily in England but gave way to the distinction between associations which were allowed and workers' combinations which were prohibited. In the Scandinavian countries and Switzerland the traditional policies proved more successful. These countries remained predominantly agricultural until well into the nineteenth century. They experienced a re-

---

[11] Marshall, *op. cit.*, p. 87. Italics added.

[12] See statement by Le Chapelier, author of the French act prohibiting trade unions of July 1791, as quoted in International Labour Office, *Freedom of Associations* (ILO Studies and Reports, Series A, No. 28; London: P. S. King & Son, 1928), p. 11. Further references to this five-volume work will be given in the form *ILO Report*, with the number and pages cited.

markable proliferation of religious, cultural, economic, and political associations which followed the breakdown of the estate society. Except for a few cases of violent conflicts, their governments did little or nothing either to restrict or to legalize these activities. There were differences here also in the various efforts to cope with the mounting unruliness of journeymen and agricultural workers. But none of these countries went as far as England in enacting special prohibitory legislation designed to stamp out rather than curb combinations of workingmen. In this traditional setting with its estate ideology such a prohibition would have violated the widely accepted right of association.

Such reservations did not prevail in Prussia and Austria, where by the end of the eighteenth century conventional absolutist controls over journeymen's associations were extended to a general prohibition of all "secret assemblies" as in the Prussian Civil Code of 1794. This prohibition was directed principally against Free Masons and other early forms of quasi-political organizations, which were springing up in response to the ideas and events of the French Revolution (such legislation was used against workingmen's combinations as well). A specific prohibition of the latter occurred in Prussia only in the 1840's, although in Austria it had occurred already in 1803. This absolutist approach may be considered together with analogous policies elsewhere which had much the same general effect on workingmen's combinations. In Italy and Spain restrictions of associational activity were traditional and local and hardly required specific legislative enactments to ensure their implementation. In France, on the other hand, the plebiscitarian tradition of direct state-citizen relations led to the promulgation of the famous *Loi Le Chapelier* in 1791, and this tendency to restrain all associations was further strengthened under Napoleon. Here was ample evidence that absolutism and plebiscitarian rule are mutually compatible.

Finally, in England, the early invidious distinction between associations and combinations proved difficult to maintain in the long run. The right of association permitted political agitation through which the prohibition of trade unions could be opposed. Although the Act of 1824 repealing the anticombination laws was not effective, its early passage is evidence of opposition to the harsh prosecution of workingmen's combinations. We have seen that these repressive measures need to be balanced against others in which violations went unpunished, because employers would not lodge complaints and magistrates would not act in the absence of a complaint.

When the decline of the guild system together with the increasing pace of economic development suggested the need for new regulations of master-servant relations and of journeymen's associations, the several Western European countries responded with three broadly distinguishable types of policies. The Scandinavian and Swiss type continued the traditional organization of crafts into the modern period, preserving the right of association at the same time that they extended the statutory regulation of master-servant relations and journeymen's associations to cope with the new problems. In modified form this variant represents the medieval concept of liberty as a privilege, a concept which certainly allows for a statutory reinforcement of existing arrangements. The sec-

ond, absolutist type is exemplified by the Prussian prohibition first of journeymen's associations, then of all secret assemblies, and finally of the newly formed
workingmen's combinations — in keeping with the policy of enlightened
absolutism which seeks to regulate all phases of social and economic life. This
type represents a major break with the tradition of liberty as a corporate privilege in so far as the king destroys all powers intervening between himself and
his subjects, though this destruction could be just as thoroughgoing under
plebiscitarian auspices. Finally, the liberal policy exemplified by England went
from the earlier regulation of guilds and the master-servant relationship to a
policy which combined the specific prohibition of workingmen's combinations
with the preservation of the right of association in other respects. Thus, liberalism with its invidious distinction between association and combination
represents a halfway mark between the preservation of the right of association
(as this was understood in the premodern social structure of Europe) and the
complete denial of the right of association which was an outgrowth of absolutist
and plebiscitarian opposition to the independent powers of estates and corporations.

Countries of the first type are characterized by relatively insignificant histories of repression, while countries of the other two types suppressed workingmen's combinations by outright prohibition or severe statutory regulations for
periods ranging from 75 to 120 years. We can compare countries in terms
of this interval between the first decisive measures taken to repress tendencies
toward workingmen's combinations and the final decision to accept trade
unions. In Denmark, for example, that interval comprised 49 years, in England
76 years, and in Prussia/Germany either 105 or 124 years, depending on
whether we consider 1899 or 1918 as the date most appropriate for the legal
recognition of trade unions. But the dating of such intervals is problematic.
The early acts of repression inevitably blurred the distinction between a mere
extension of traditional regulations and a novel and harsher prohibition which
singled out the newly developing working class. It is also difficult to date the
final legalization of trade unions precisely, since in most cases such legalization
occurred gradually. However, these difficulties of dating do not invalidate the
rough, threefold typology of the policies which have guided the extension of
the right of association to the lower classes in Western Europe.

The legal right to form associations combines the plebiscitarian with the
functional principle. Whenever *all* citizens possess this right, we have an instance of plebiscitarianism in the formal sense that everyone enjoys the same
legal capacity to act. However, in practice only some groups of citizens take
advantage of the opportunity, while a large majority remain "unorganized."
Thus, in the developing nation-states of Western Europe private associations
exemplify the functional principle of representation on the basis of common
interests, in contrast with the medieval estates that collectively enjoyed the
privilege of exercising certain public rights in return for a common legal
liability. It was recognized early that organizations based on common economic
interests would perpetuate or re-establish corporate principles analogous to

those of the medieval period.[13] In his argument against mutual benefit societies, Le Chapelier expresses this view in his 1791 speech before the Constituent Assembly to which reference was made earlier:

> The bodies in question have the avowed object of procuring relief for workers in the same occupation who fall sick or become unemployed. But let there be no mistake about this. It is for the nation and for public officials on its behalf to supply work to those who need it for their livelihood and to succour the sick. . . . It should not be permissible for citizens in certain occupations to meet together in defence of their pretended common interests. There must be no more guilds in the State, but only the individual interest of each citizen and the general interest. No one shall be allowed to arouse in any citizen any kind of intermediate interest and to separate him from the public weal through the medium of corporate interests.[14]

This radically plebiscitarian position which does not tolerate the organization of any "intermediate interest" is difficult to maintain consistently. For the individualistic tendencies of the economic sphere, which are partly responsible for this position, are likewise responsible for legal developments which undermine it. A growing exchange economy with its rapid diversification of transactions gives rise to the question how the legal significance of each transaction can be determined unambiguously. In part, this question is answered by attributing "legal personality" to organizations such as business firms and hence by separating the legal spheres of the stockholders and officials from the legal sphere of the organization itself.[15] Incorporation establishes the separate legal liability of the organization and thus limits the liability of its individual members or agents. Although "limited liability" was denounced for a time as an infringement of individual responsibility, massive interests were

---

[13] We do not go into the question of the continuity or discontinuity between medieval and modern corporations, a problem treated at length in the writings of Figgis, Gierke, Maitland, and others.

[14] Quoted in *ILO Report*, No. 29, p. 89. Le Chapelier's statement reflects the principle enunciated by Rousseau: "If, when the people, sufficiently informed, deliberated, there was to be no communication among them, from the grand total of trifling differences the general will would always result, and their resolutions be always good. But when cabals and partial associations are formed at the expense of the great association, the will of each such association, though *general* with regard to its members, is *private* with regard to the State: it can then be said no longer that there are as many voters as men, but only as many as there are associations. By this means the differences being less numerous, they produce a result less general. Finally, when one of these associations becomes so large that it prevails over all the rest, you have no longer the sum of many opinions dissenting in a small degree from each other, but one great dictating dissentient; from the moment there is no longer a general will, and the predominating opinion is only an individual one. It is therefore of the utmost importance for obtaining the expression of the general will, that no partial society should be formed in the State, and that every citizen should speak his opinion entirely from himself. . . ." See Jean Jacques Rousseau, *The Social Contract* (New York: Hafner Publishing Company, 1957), pp. 26–27.

[15] Weber, *Law in Economy and Society*, pp. 156–157 ff. The editors have added references to the extensive literature in this field.

served by this new device and objections based on the concept of obligation
were quickly overcome. Incorporation is a most important breach in the strictly
plebiscitarian position. It represents a first limitation of that radical individualism which stands for strictly formal equality before the law and against the
formation of "intermediate interests."

Marshall states that in the field of civil rights "the movement has been . . .
not from the representation of communities to that of individuals [as in the
history of parliament], but from the representation of individuals to that of
communities." [16] The device of incorporation and the related principle of
limited liability make it possible for an economic enterprise to take risks and
maximize economic assets on behalf and for the benefit of individual shareholders. Through its officials the enterprise performs a representative function in the sense that it makes decisions and assumes responsibilities for
the collectivity of its investors, which is frequently composed of other corporate
groups as well as of individuals. Through much of the nineteenth century this
representative function of the corporation was confined to economic goals.
However, such concepts as "corporate trusteeship," the development of public
relations, and direct political participation by many large corporations suggest
that in recent decades this earlier restriction has been abandoned — a development whose significance for citizenship still needs to be explored.

These considerations provide useful background for an understanding of the
special position of trade unions. As Marshall points out, trade unions:

> . . . did not seek or obtain incorporation. They can, therefore, exercise
> vital civil rights collectively on behalf of their members without formal
> collective responsibility, while the individual responsibility of workers in
> relation to contract is largely unenforceable. . . .[17]

If we take the prohibition or severe restriction of combinations as our starting
point, then the development of trade unions also exemplifies the movement
of civil rights from the representation of individuals to that of communities.
This collective representation of the economic interests of the members arises
from the inability of workers to safeguard their interest individually. Trade
unions seek to raise the economic status of their members. The workers organize in order to attain that level of economic reward to which they feel entitled — a level which in practice depends on the capacity to organize and
to bargain for "what the traffic will bear." These practical achievements of
trade unions have a far-reaching effect upon the status of workers as citizens.
For through trade unions and collective bargaining the right to combine is
used to assert "basic claims to the elements of social justice." [18] In this way
the extension of citizenship to the lower classes is given the very special meaning that as citizens the members of these classes are "entitled" to a certain
standard of well-being, in return for which they are only obliged to discharge
the ordinary duties of citizenship.

[16] Marshall, op. cit., p. 94.
[17] Ibid., p. 93. The following discussion is based on Marshall's analysis on pp. 93–
94, but our emphasis differs somewhat.
[18] Ibid., p. 94.

The legalization of trade unions is an instance of enabling legislation. It *permits* members of the lower classes to organize and thus obtain an equality of bargaining power which a previously imposed, formal legal equality has denied them. But to achieve this end it becomes necessary, as we saw, to discriminate in favor of "combinations" by allowing them legal exemptions without which the disadvantaged groups are unable to organize effectively. In other words, civil rights are used here to enable the lower classes to participate more effectively than would otherwise be the case in the economic and political struggle over the distribution of the national income.

However, many members of the lower classes either do not avail themselves of the opportunities afforded them by the law or are prevented from doing so by the exclusivist or neo-corporatist devices of established trade unions. Hence, *in effect* legal opportunities have turned into privileges available to workers who are willing and able to organize in order to advance their economic interests. Such privileges are buttressed, in turn, by legal, extralegal, and illegal devices to make union membership obligatory or nonmembership very costly. Thus, the right to combine turns out to be a "privilege of those organized in trade unions." In a sense this is a measure of the weakness of corporatist tendencies in modern Western societies, since the same right more generally applied would mean that every adult belongs to an organization representing his occupation. Instead, the right to combine has given rise to a "corporatist enclave." The very effectiveness of exclusive practices by trade unions makes membership quasi-obligatory, however beneficial, and unwittingly it is often related to the failure of drives for new members. In this way the right to combine can be used to enforce claims to a share of income and benefits at the expense of the unorganized and the consumers. This exceptional position of *some* trade unions has not altered the *principle* that civil rights are permissive rather than obligatory, though it may be said to have infringed upon it. This permissiveness of civil rights needs special emphasis in the present context because of the contrast with the second element of citizenship, *social* rights, to which we now turn.

A BASIC SOCIAL RIGHT:
THE RIGHT TO AN ELEMENTARY EDUCATION

The right to an elementary education is similar to the "right to combine." As long as masses of the population are deprived of elementary education, access to educational facilities appears as a precondition without which all other rights under the law remain of no avail to the uneducated. To provide the rudiments of education to the illiterate appears as an act of liberation. Nonetheless, social rights are distinctive in that they do not usually permit the individual to decide whether or not to avail himself of their advantages. Like the legislative regulation of working conditions for women and children, compulsory insurance against industrial accidents, and similar welfare measures, the right to an elementary education is indistinguishable from the duty to attend school. In all Western societies elementary education has become a duty of citizenship, perhaps the earliest example of a prescribed minimum enforced by all the powers of the modern state. Two attributes of elementary education make it into an element of citizenship: the government has authority over it, and the parents of all children in a certain age group (usually from 6 to 10 or 12) are required by law to see to it that their children attend school.

Social rights as an attribute of citizenship may be considered benefits which compensate the individual for his consent to be governed under the rules and by the agents of his national political community.[19] It is important to note the element of agreement or consensus which is at the root of the *direct relationship between the central organs of the nation-state and each member of the community*. But in now turning to a consideration of social rights, we find that this plebiscitarian principle of equality before the sovereign nation-state involves duties as well as rights. Each eligible individual is *obliged* to participate in the services provided by the state. It is somewhat awkward to use the term "plebiscitarian" for this obligatory aspect of citizenship as well. Yet there is a family resemblance between the right of all citizens to participate (through the franchise) in the decision-making processes of government and the duty of all parents to see to it that their children in the designated age groups attend school. In the fully developed welfare state citizens as voters decide to provide the services in which citizens as parents of school children are then obliged to participate. The right to vote is permissive, whereas the benefits of school attendance are obligatory. But both are principles of equality which establish a direct relationship between the central organs of the nation-state and each member of the community, and this direct relationship is the specific meaning of *national* citizenship.

It may be useful to reiterate the major distinctions at this point. There is first the distinction between an indirect and direct relation between the nation-state and the citizen. We have discussed the *indirect* relationship in the preceding section in connection with the *rights to association* and the *right to combine*. Although these civil rights are in principle available to all, in practice they are claimed by classes of persons who share certain social and economic attributes. Thus, group (or functional) representation is of continued importance even after the earlier, medieval principle of privileged jurisdictions has been replaced by equality before the law. In now turning to the *direct* relationship between the nation-state and the citizen, we consider *social* rights before we turn to the discussion of *political* rights. The extension of social rights with its emphasis upon obligation may leave privilege intact and broadens the duties and benefits of the people without necessarily encouraging their social mobilization, whereas the extension of the franchise unequivocally destroys privilege and enlarges the active participation of the people in public affairs.

There is clear indication that on the Continent the *principle* of an elementary education for the lower classes emerged as a by-product of enlightened absolutism. In Denmark, for example, Frederick IV established elementary schools on his own domains as early as 1721 and provided them with sufficient

---

[19] This formulation is indebted to the perceptive analysis by Joseph Tussman, *Obligation and the Body Politic* (New York: Oxford University Press, 1960), Chap. II.

resources and a permanently employed teaching staff. Attempts to follow through with this policy failed, because the landed proprietors evaded their responsibility for the employment and remuneration of teachers by imposing charges for teacher salaries on the peasants who could ill afford them. Following the principal measures alleviating the obligations imposed on the peasants (1787–88), Frederick VI proceeded to establish a new organization of elementary schools which has remained the basis of national education in Denmark since 1814.

This Danish development may be compared with the corresponding development in Prussia, where the program of a system of national education also developed early. The profoundly conservative purpose of this program is not in doubt. In 1737, a basic Prussian school law was issued with the commentary that it had grieved the king to see youth living and growing up in darkness and thereby suffering damage both temporally and to their eternal souls. On this occasion the king donated a sum to facilitate the employment of capable teachers, and for several decades thereafter the Prussian kings and their officials promoted the scheme on the basis of such incidental appropriations. By 1763 an ordinance was issued regulating school affairs for the entire monarchy and including provisions for disciplinary measures against teachers who neglect their duties, thus at least envisaging a regular administration of the schools. At the same time efforts were made to alleviate the teacher shortage by earmarking special funds for this purpose. These measures encountered difficulties, because parents were reluctant to send their children to school and local bodies would not assume their share of the financial responsibility. In 1794, the schools (together with the universities) were declared institutions of the state, and in the ensuing years the whole system of national education became part of the national liberation movement against Napoleon. Although some officials publicly expressed doubts concerning the usefulness of literacy for the ordinary man, military defeat and patriotic enthusiasm generally removed such doubts. Official declarations demanded that all subjects without exception should be provided with useful knowledge; national education would raise the moral, religious, and patriotic spirit of the people.[20] In all probability national education became acceptable to the conservative rulers of Prussia on the ground that it would help to instill loyalty for king and country in the masses of the population. It is well to remember, however, that in the field of military recruitment the same effort to mobilize the people in the wars of liberation led to great controversies and provoked a very strong reaction among ultra-conservatives, once the immediate danger was passed.[21] Thus, enlightened absolutism may be considered the reluctant or equivocal pioneer of extending social rights to the people. Absolutist rule endorses the principal that nothing should intervene between the king and his people, and hence that the king out of his own free will distributes benefits among them. But absolutism naturally insists that the

[20] The preceding two paragraphs are based on A. Petersilie, *Das Öffentliche Unterrichtswesen* (Vol. III of Hand- und Lehrbuch der Staatswissenschaften; Leipzig: C. L. Hirschfeld, 1897), I, pp. 203–204, 158–166, and *passim*.

[21] For details see the excellent study by Gerhard Ritter, *Staatskunst und Kriegshandwerk* (Munich: R. Oldenbourg, 1959), I, Chaps. 4 and 5.

people are the king's subjects; it rejects the idea of rights and duties derived from and owed to the sovereign authority of the nation-state.[22]

The ideas of national citizenship and a sovereign national authority are basic concepts of liberalism. They have special relevance for education, because in Europe teaching had been in the hands of the clergy for centuries. Accordingly, the schools were under clerical rather than political authority so that pupils to receive an education are subject to this special jurisdiction. This clerical control is destroyed, where absolutist rulers or the nation-state assume authority over the schools. In Lutheran Prussia such secular control over education could be imposed without difficulty. When ministers of the church as well as teachers are subject to the sovereign authority of the king, it is easy to recruit the ministers into the teaching profession. But when, as in France, the Catholic clergy is under an authority separate from that of the state, the establishment of a national system of education and hence of a direct relationship between each citizen and the government becomes incompatible with the existing system. In his *Essai d'education nationale*, published in 1763, La Chalotais opposes the clergy's control of education by demanding that the teaching of letters and science should be in the hands of a secular profession. After observing that distinguished men of letters are laymen rather than clerics, and that "idle priests" overrun the cities while the country is deprived of clergy, La Chalotais continues:

> To teach letters and sciences, we must have persons who make of them a profession. The clergy cannot take it in bad part that we should not, generally speaking, include ecclesiastics in this class. I am not so unjust as to exclude them from it. I acknowledge with pleasure that there are several . . . who are very learned and capable of teaching. . . . But I protest against the exclusion of laymen. I claim the right to demand for the Nation an education that will depend upon the State alone; because it belongs essentially to it, because every nation has an inalienable and imprescriptible right to instruct its members, and finally because the children of the State should be educated by members of the State.[23]

The statement parallels the plebiscitarian principle enunciated by Le Chapelier which was quoted earlier.[24] Where Le Chapelier had argued against mutual

[22] The significance of absolutist regimes for elementary education varied with the prevailing religious beliefs of the country. In Austria, elementary education was organized by the government as early as 1805, with the clergy acting as the supervisory agent of the state. In Catholic countries with less religious unity than Austria such an approach did not prove possible; in France, for example, the traditional Catholic claim to superintend education was challenged in the 1760's with the suppression of the Jesuits and the endorsement of a nationally organized system of lay education. Again, in countries with Protestant state churches (Prussia, Denmark, Norway, and Sweden) little or no conflict developed as the unity of church and state in the person of the monarch allowed for the ultimate authority of government over elementary education, with ministers of the church acting in this field as agents of the monarch or (later) of a ministry for education and ecclesiastical affairs.

[23] See La Chalotais, "Essay on National Education," in F. de la Fontainerie (ed.), *French Liberalism and Education in the Eighteenth Century* (New York: McGraw-Hill Book Company, 1932), pp. 52–53.

[24] See page 241.

benefit societies on the ground that no "intermediate interest" should be allowed to separate any citizen from the "public weal through the medium of corporate interests," La Chalotais here echoes the same idea in his argument against the clergy. There must be a profession of teachers which is entirely at the disposal of the state, in order to implement a program of instruction in which nothing intervenes between the "children of the State" and the teachers who are members and servants of the state.

At a later time the principle of a national system of elementary education also became acceptable to the emerging industrial work force. Among laborers the desire to become educated was strong, partly to better their chances in life, partly to see to it that the children had a better chance than their parents, and partly in order to give additional weight to the political claims made on behalf of the working class. If this desire led to voluntary efforts to provide educational facilities for workers, as it did notably in England and Germany, such action was largely a response to the fact that no other facilities were available to them. Once these facilities became available, voluntary efforts in the field of workers' education declined (though they did not cease), another indication of the relative weakness of corporatist tendencies.

It is probable, therefore, that systems of national education develop as widely as they do, because the demand for elementary education cuts across the spectrum of political beliefs. It is sustained by conservatives who fear the people's inherent unruliness which must be curbed by instruction in the fundamentals of religion and thus instill loyalty to king and country. Liberals argue that the nation-state demands a citizenry educated by organs of the state. And populist spokesmen claim that the masses of the people who help to create the wealth of the country should share in the amenities of civilization.

Compulsory elementary education becomes a major controversial issue, however, when governmental authority in this field comes into conflict with organized religion. Traditionally, the Catholic Church regards teaching as one of its inherent powers, with the work of instruction being conducted by the religious orders. In this view the *corporate* principle is paramount in so far as the Church administers man's "spiritual estate" and in this realm possesses the exclusive right and duty of *representation*. This principle was challenged during the eighteenth century in France, and conflict over clerical or lay control of education has lasted to this day. Similar conflicts have also persisted in Protestant countries in which the population is sharply divided over religious issues. That is, a national system of elementary education has been opposed wherever the Church or various religious denominations have insisted upon interposing their own educational facilities between their adherents and the state. Thus, such countries as England, Belgium, and the Netherlands have been the scene of protracted struggles over the question whether or under what conditions the national government should be permitted to give assistance or exercise authority in the field of elementary education. In England, for example, voluntary contributions in aid of education amounted, in 1858, to double the amount of support provided by the government. Since 1870 a new system of state schools has been developed, not as a substitute for the schools based on voluntary contributions, but in addition to them. Thus, until well into the modern period local and voluntary efforts preserve elements of "functional representation," despite the steady growth of a national (plebiscitarian) system of education.[25] Perhaps the most outstanding example of the corporate or representative principle in education is provided by the Netherlands with its three separate school systems: one Catholic, one Calvinist, and one secular-humanist. The significant fact here is that all three systems are financed by the government and all three are based on the principle of obligatory attendance, thus neatly combining the plebiscitarian principle in finance with the representative principle in the organizational and substantive control over the educational process.

POLITICAL RIGHTS:
THE FRANCHISE AND THE SECRET VOTE

This strain between estate orientation and nation orientation in the determination of policy is even more apparent in the debates and enactments concerning *rights of political participation*: the right to serve as a representative, the right to vote for representatives, and the right of independent choice among alternatives.

The basic condition for the development toward universal rights of participation was the *unification of the national system of representation*. In the late Middle Ages the principle of territorial representation had on the Continent increasingly given way to a system of representation by *estates*: each estate sent its separate representatives to deliberate at the center of territorial authority and each had its separate assembly.[26] Only in England was the original system of territorial representation retained: the House of Commons was not an assembly of the burgher estates but a body of legislators representing the constituent localities of the realm, the counties and the boroughs. The greater openness of English society made it possible to keep up the territorial channels of representation, and this, in turn, set the stage for a much smoother transition to a unified regime of equalitarian democracy.[27]

Regardless of the principle of representation in these *anciens régimes*, only the economically independent heads of households could take part in public life. This participation was a right they derived not from their membership in

[25] See the historical sketch of the English educational development in Ernest Barker, *The Development of the Public Services in Western Europe* (New York: Oxford University Press, 1944), pp. 85–93 and the comparative account by Robert Ulich, *The Education of Nations* (Cambridge, Mass.: Harvard University Press, 1961), *passim*.

[26] The primary authority on the history of corporate estates and their representation is still Otto von Gierrke, *Das deutsche Genossenschaftsrecht* (Berlin: Weidmann, 1868), I, pp. 534–581.

[27] This question of territorial vs. functional representation is at the heart of the debate over the reasons for the survival of Parliament during the age of absolutism. Otto Hintze has stressed the historical continuities between medieval and modern forms of representation and has argued that the two-chamber polities beyond the reach of the Carolingian Empire offered the best basis for the development of pluralist, parliamentary rule. See his "Typologie der ständischen Verfassungen des Abendlandes," *Staat und Verfassung*, pp. 120–139.

any national community but from their ownership of territory and capital or from their status within legally defined functional corporations such as the nobility, the church, or the guilds of merchants or artisans. There was no representation of individuals: the members of the assemblies represented recognized stakes in the system, whether in the form of property holdings or in the form of professional privileges.

The French Revolution brought about a fundamental change in the conception of representation: the basic unit was no longer the household, the property, or the corporation, but the *individual citizen*; and representation was no longer channeled through separate functional bodies but through a *unified national assembly* of legislators. The law of August 11, 1792, went so far as to give the franchise to all French males over 21 who were not servants, paupers, or *vagabonds*, and the Constitution of 1793 did not even exclude paupers if they had resided more than six months in the *canton*. The Restoration did not bring back representation by estates: instead the *régime censitaire* introduced an abstract monetary criterion which cut decisively across the earlier criteria of ascribed status.

A new phase in this development opened with the Revolution of 1848 and the rapid spread of movements for representative democracy through most of Europe. Napoleon III demonstrated the possibilities of plebiscitarian rule, and leaders of the established elites became increasingly torn between their fears of the consequences of rapid extensions of the suffrage to the lower classes and their fascination with the possibilities of strengthening the powers of the nation-state through the mobilization of the working class in its service.[28] These conflicts of strategy produced a great variety of transitional compromises in the different countries. The starting points for these developments were the provisions of the *Ständestaat* and the postrevolutionary *régime censitaire*, and the end points were the promulgations of universal adult suffrage. But the steps taken and the paths chosen from the one point to the other varied markedly from country to country and reflected basic differences in the dominant values and character of each social structure.[29]

We may conveniently distinguish five major sets of criteria used in limiting the franchise during this transitional period: (1) traditional *estate* criteria: restriction of franchise to heads of households within each of the established status groups as defined by law; (2) *régime censitaire*: restrictions based on the value of land or capital or on the amounts of yearly taxes on property and/or

[28] See H. Gollwitzer, "Der Cäsarismus Napoleons III im Widerhall der öffentlichen Meinung Deutschlands," *Historische Zeitschrift*, Vol. 152 (1952), 23–76. In a number of countries the demands for universal manhood suffrage became intimately tied in with the need for universal *conscription*. In Sweden the principal argument for the breakup of the four-estate *Riksdag* was the need for a strengthening of national defense. In the Swedish suffrage debates, the slogan "one man, one vote, one gun" reflects this tie up between franchise and military recruitment.

[29] The details of these developments have been set out in such compendia as Georg Meyer, *Das parlamentarische Wahlrecht* (Berlin: Haering, 1901), and Karl Braunias, *Das parlamentarische Wahlrecht* (Berlin: de Gruyter, 1932), Vol. 2.

income; (3) *régime capacitaire:* restrictions by literacy, formal education, or appointment to public office; (4) *household responsibility* criteria: restrictions to heads of households occupying own dwellings of a minimum given volume or lodged in premises for a given minimum rent; (5) *residence* criteria: restrictions to citizens registered as residents either in the local community, the constituency, or the national territory for a given minimum of months or years.

The Norwegian Constitution of 1814 provides a good example of an early compromise between estate criteria, the *régime censitaire* and the *principe capacitaire.* The franchise was given to four categories of citizens: two of these, the *burghers* of incorporated cities and the *peasants* (freeholders and lease-holders), corresponded to the old estates; a third, applicable only in cities and towns, was defined by ownership of real estate of a given minimum value; and the fourth was simply made up of all officials of the national government. This system gave a clear numerical majority to the farmers, but as a political precaution the interests of the burghers and officials were protected through inequalities in the distribution of mandates between urban and rural constituencies.[30] The simplicity of the social structure made the Norwegian compromise a straightforward one: the age-old division between peasant and burgher estates corresponded to an established administrative division into rural districts and chartered towns, and the only class of voters explicitly placed above this territorial-functional division was the king's officials, the effective rulers of the nation for several decades to come.

Much more complex compromises had to be devised in multinational polities such as Austria. In the old Habsburg territories the typical *Landtag* had consisted of four *curiae:* the nobles, the knights, the prelates, and the representatives of cities and markets. The *Februar-patent* of 1861 kept the division into four *curiae,* but transformed the estate criteria into criteria of *interest representation.* The nobles and the knights were succeeded by a *curia* of the largest landowners. The ecclesiastical estate was broadened into a *curia* of *Virilstimmen* representing universities as well as dioceses. The burgher estate was no longer exclusively represented by spokesmen for cities and markets, but also through the *chambers of commerce and the professions:* this was the first recognition of a corporatist principle which was to become of central importance in the ideological debates in Austria in the twentieth century. To these three was added a *peasant* division: this was new in the national system; direct peasant representation of the type so well known in the Nordic countries had only existed in Tyrol and Vorarlberg. The most interesting feature of the Austrian sequence of compromises was the handling of the lower classes so far excluded from participation in the politics of the nation. True to their tradition of functional representation, the Austrian statesmen did not admit these new citizens *on a par* with the already enfranchised, but placed them in a new, a fifth *curia, die allgemeine Wählerklasse.* This, however, was only a transitional measure: eleven years later even the Austrian *Abgeordnetenhaus*

---

[30] See Stein Rokkan, "Geography, Region and Social Class: Cross-Cutting Cleavages in Norwegian Politics," in S. M. Lipset and Stein Rokkan (eds.), *Party Systems and Voter Alignments* (New York: The Free Press of Glencoe, forthcoming).

fell in with the trend toward equalitarian mass democracy and was transformed
into a unified national assembly based on universal manhood suffrage.[31]

The rise of commercial and industrial capitalism favored the spread of the
régime censitaire. The ideological basis was Benjamin Constant's argument
that the affairs of the national community must be left to those with "real
stakes" in it through the possession of land or through investments in business.
The *principe capacitaire* was essentially an extension of this criterion: the
franchise was accorded not only to those who own land or have invested in
business but also to those who have acquired a direct interest in the maintenance of the polity through their investments in professional skills and their
appointment to positions of public trust. The implicit notion is that only such
citizens can form rational judgments of the policies to be pursued by the
government. A Norwegian authority on constitutional law links the two elements together in his statement: "Suffrage . . . should be reserved to the
citizens who have *judgment* enough to understand who would prove the best
representatives, and *independence* enough to stick to their conviction in this
matter." [32]

This question of criteria of intellectual independence was at the heart of the
struggles between liberals and conservatives over the organization of the suffrage. Liberals favored the *régime censitaire* and feared the possibilities of
electoral manipulation inherent in the extension of the suffrage to the economically dependent. Conservatives, once they recognized the importance of
the vote as a basis of local power, tended to favor the enfranchisement of the
"lower orders": they had good reason to expect that, at least on the patriarchal
estates in the countryside, those in positions of dependence would naturally
vote for the local notables. This conflict reached a climax in the discussions
at the German National Assembly in Frankfurt in 1848–49. The Constitutional
Commission had recommended that the franchise should be restricted to all
independent citizens, and this term was at first interpreted to exclude all
servants and all wage earners. This interpretation met with violent protests in
the Assembly. There was general agreement that subjects who received public
assistance or were in bankruptcy were not independent a id should be excluded
from the franchise, but there was extensive disagreement on the rights of
servants and workers. The left claimed full rights for the lower classes and was
only moderately opposed by the conservatives. The result was the promulgation
of universal manhood suffrage. As it happened, this law could not be enforced
at the time: it took another 17 years until Bismarck was able to make it the
basis for the organization of the *Reichstag* of the North German Federation.
The Prussian Chancellor had already had the experience of a system of uni-

---

[31] A useful account of these developments in Austria is found in Ludwig Boyer,
Wahlrecht in Österreich (Vienna, 1961), pp. 80–85. It is interesting to compare the
Austrian mixture of medieval estate-orientation and modern corporatism with the Rus-
sian provisions for the *Duma* in 1906; see Max Weber's detailed analysis in "Russlands
Übergang zum Scheinkonstitutionalismus" *Gesammelte Politische Schriften* (Tübingen:
J. C. B. Mohr, 1958), pp. 66–126.

[32] T. H. Aschehoug, *Norges nuverende Statsforfatning* (Christiania: Aschehoug,
1875), Vol. I, p. 280.

versal suffrage, but a markedly unequal one — the Prussian system of three-class
suffrage introduced by royal decree in 1849. Under that system the "lower
orders" had been given the right to vote, but the weight of their votes was
infinitesimal in comparison with those of the middle classes and the landowners. This system had obviously served to bolster the power of the *Guts-
besitzer*, particularly east of the Elbe: the law had simply multiplied by *n* the
number of votes at their disposal, since they counted on being able to control
without much difficulty the behavior of their dependents and their workers at
the polls.[33] Bismarck detested the three-class system for its emphasis on
abstract monetary criteria and its many injustices, but he was convinced that a
change to equal suffrage for all men would not affect the power structure in the
countryside: on the contrary it would strengthen even further the landed
interests against the financial. Generally, in the countryside the extensions of
the suffrage tended to strengthen the conservative forces.[34]

There was much more uncertainty about the consequences of an extended
suffrage for the politics of the urban areas. The emergence and growth of a
class of *wage earners outside the immediate household* of the employer raised
new problems for the definition of political citizenship. In the established socio-
economic terminology their status was one of dependence, but it was not evident that they would inevitably follow their employers politically. The crucial
battles in the development toward universal suffrage concerned the status of
these emerging strata within the political community. A great variety of transitional compromises were debated and several were actually tried out. The
basic strategy was to underscore the structural differentiations within the wage-
earning strata. Some varieties of *régime censitaire* in fact admitted the better
paid wage workers, particularly if they had houses of their own.[35] The
householder and lodger franchise in Britain similarly served to integrate the
better-off working class within the system and to keep out only the "real
proletariat," migrants and marginal workers without established local ties. The
retention of residence requirements has served similar functions even after the
disappearance of all economic qualifications for suffrage: these restrictions are
adhered to most stubbornly in the provisions for local elections.

Another set of strategies in this battle to control the onrush of mass democracy comprises the institutions of *weighted* suffrage and *plural votes*.

[33] For a recent detailed account see Th. Nipperdey, *Die Organisation der deutschen
Parteien vor 1918* (Düsseldorf: Droste, 1961), Chap. V. For a parallel with conditions
in the similarly structured rural areas of Brazil, see the chapter by Emilio Willems in
Arnold Rose (ed.), *The Institutions of Advanced Societies* (Minneapolis: University of
Minnesota Press, 1958), p. 552: "The main functions of *suffrage was that of preserving*
the existing power structure. Within the traditional pattern, suffrage added opportunities
for displaying and reinforcing feudal loyalty. At the same time, it reinforced and legalized the political status of the landowner."

[34] See D. C. Moore, "The Other Face of Reform," *Victorian Studies*, V (September
1961), pp. 7–34 and G. Kitson Clark, *The Making of Victorian England* (London:
Methuen, 1962), especially Chap. VII.

[35] A special tax census taken in Norway in 1876 indicates that more than one-quarter
of the urban workers who were on the tax roles were enfranchised under the system
adopted in 1814: by contrast only 3 per cent of the workers in the rural areas had
been given the vote. See Statistisk Centralbureau ser. C. No. 14, 1877, pp. 340–341.

The crudest examples are no doubt the Austrian *Kurien* and the Prussian three-class system: universal suffrage is granted, but the weights of the votes given to the lower classes are infinitesimal in comparison with those of the established landed or financial elite. The most innocuous system of plural voting is perhaps the British provision for extra votes for university graduates and for owners of business premises in different constituencies. Sociologically the most interesting is the Belgian system of plural voting devised in 1893: universal manhood suffrage is introduced, but extra votes are given not only on *capacitaire* criteria but also to *pères de famille* upon reaching the respectable age of 35. The basic motive is clearly to underscore structural differentiations within the lower strata and to exclude from the system the elements least committed to the established social order.

Closely related to these strategies is the stubborn resistance to changes in the delimitation of constituencies. Rapid urbanization produces glaring inequalities even under conditions of formally equal universal suffrage. The injustices of the Prussian districting provisions were the object of acrimonious debate for decades. The extreme solution adopted in the Weimar Republic — the establishment of a unitary system of proportional representation for the entire Reich — no doubt gives every voter the same abstract chance to influence the distribution of seats, but at the same time brings to the fore the inherent difficulties of such standardization across localities of very different structure. The continued overrepresentation of rural areas in the United States is another example.

The entry of the lower classes into the political arena also raises a series of problems for the *administration of elections*. Sociologically the most interesting issue is the safeguarding of the *independence of the individual electoral decision*. The defenders of estate traditions and the *régime censitaire* argue that economically dependent subjects cannot be expected to form independent political judgments and would, if enfranchised, corrupt the system through the sale of votes and through violent intimidation. Corrupt practices were, of course, widespread in many countries long before the extension of the suffrage, but the enfranchisement of large sections of the lower classes generally provides added incentive to reforms in the administration and control of elections. The secrecy of the ballot is a central problem in this debate.[36]

The traditional notion was that the vote was a public act and only to be entrusted to men who could openly stand by their opinions. The Prussian system of oral voting was defended in these terms, but was maintained for so long largely because it proved an easy way of controlling the votes of farm laborers.

The secret ballot essentially appeals to the liberal urban mentality: it fits as another element into the anonymous, privatized culture of the city, described by Georg Simmel. The decisive factor, however, is the emergence of the lower-class vote as a factor in national politics and the need to neutralize the threatening

---

[36] A recent one-nation account of the development of standards for the control of elections is Cornelius O'Leary, *The Elimination of Corrupt Practices in British Elections, 1868–1911* (Oxford: Clarendon Press, 1962).

working-class organizations: the provisions for secrecy isolate the dependent worker not only from his superiors but also from his peers. Given the state of electoral statistics, it is very difficult to determine with any exactitude the effects of secrecy on the actual behavior of workers at the polls. But it seems inherently likely, given a minimum amount of cross-class communications, that secrecy helps to reduce the likelihood of a polarization of political life on the basis of social class.

In this respect the secret ballot represents the national and plebiscitarian principle of civic integration, in contrast to working-class organizations which exemplify the principle of functional representation. That is, the claims of trade unions and labor parties which seek recognition for the rights of the *fourth estate* are counterbalanced by the claims of the *national* community and its spokesmen. The provision for secret voting puts the individual before a personal choice and makes him at least temporarily independent of his immediate environment: in the voting booth he can be a national citizen. The provisions for secret voting make it possible for the inarticulate rank and file to escape the pressure for political partisanship and at the same time put the onus of political visibility on the activists within the working-class movement. In sociological terms we can say, therefore, that the national electoral system opens up channels for the expression of secret loyalties while the political struggle makes it necessary for the party activist to publicize his views and expose himself to censure where he deviates from the "establishment." [37]

CONCLUDING CONSIDERATIONS

The extension of citizenship to the lower classes of Western Europe can be viewed from several complementary points of view. In terms of the comparison between the medieval and the modern political structure the discussion exemplifies the simultaneous trends toward equality and a nationwide, governmental authority. The constitution of a modern nation-state is typically the fountainhead of the rights of citizenship, and these rights are a token of nationwide equality. Politics itself has become nationwide, and the "lower classes" now have the opportunity of active participation.

The preceding discussion has stressed the over-all similarity of the Western European experience, arising from the common legacies of European feudalism. The estate assemblies and parliaments of the eighteenth century provide the immediate background for the development of modern parliaments and for the

[37] Some socialist parties try to counteract these effects of secret voting by establishing intimate ties with trade unions. Note in this respect the controversy over the political levy paid by members of British trade unions as discussed in Martin Harrison, *Trade Unions and the Labour Party since 1945* (London: Allen & Unwin, 1960), Chap. 1. Trade union members who wish to be excused from payment hand a "contracting-out" form to their branch secretary, but although the payment is nominal and the procedure simple, controversy has been intense, in part because "contracting-out" is a public act which indirectly jeopardizes the secrecy of the ballot.

conception of a right to representation which was gradually extended to previously unrepresented sections of the population. This extension has two, more or less disparate, elements. According to the plebiscitarian idea, all adult individuals must have equal rights under a national government; according to the functional idea, the differential affiliation of individuals with others is taken as given and some form of group representation is accepted. The two ideas reflect the hiatus between state and society in an age of equality. When the extension of legal, political, and social rights becomes a principle of state policy, abstract criteria must be used to implement these rights. Hence, there are recurrent attempts to define in what respects all persons must henceforth be considered equal. However, the society continues to be marked by great inequalities. Hence, all adults who would take advantage of their legal, political, and social rights naturally associate with one another in order to advance their claims as effectively as possible, and such associations reflect (or even intensify) the inequalities of the social structure. The preceding discussion has shown that the relations between the plebiscitarian and functional ideas are frequently paradoxical.

Formal equality before the law at first benefits only those whose social and economic independence enables them to take advantage of their legal rights. Efforts to correct *this* inequality take many forms, among them regulations which enable members of the lower classes to avail themselves of the right of association for the representation of their economic interests. However, these regulations in turn do not reach those individuals or groups who will not or cannot take advantage of the right of association. Accordingly, equality before the law unwittingly divides a population in a new way. Further legal provisions attempt to deal with remaining inequalities or cope with newly emerging ones, for example, the institution of the public defender where the defendant is unable to take advantage of his right to counsel, or efforts to protect the rights of shareholders who are unable to do so under existing legislation. As yet there are only debates concerning the best ways of protecting members of trade unions against possible violations of their individual rights by the organization which represents their economic interests. The principle of formal legal equality may be called "plebiscitarian" in the sense that the state directly establishes each individual's "legal capacity." In addition, special provisions seek to reduce in various ways the unequal chances of individuals to use their rights under the law. In the latter case the rule-making authorities "represent" the interests of those who do not or cannot use their legal powers.

The right and duty to receive an *elementary education* may be considered another way of equalizing the capacity of all citizens to avail themselves of the rights to which they are entitled. Although elementary education provides only a minimal facility in this respect, it is perhaps the most universally approximated implementation of national citizenship, all other rights being either more permissive or selective in character. As such, public elementary education exemplifies the plebiscitarian component of the nation-state, since school attendance is not only incumbent upon all children of a certain age group but also depends on the financial contribution of all taxpayers.[38] But here again, formally instituted equalities give rise to or are the occasion for new types of inequalities. Those concerned with teaching and the organization of schools join together because of common professional and economic interests. These specialists in education often develop organizations with entrenched opinions concerning education. As such, teachers as a group confront parents as individuals, just as they confront the state with the influence of their organization in all matters affecting their interests. More indirectly, public elementary education helps to articulate, however inadvertently, the existing residential divisions within the community, since children will be assigned to schools closest to their area of residence and the school population will reflect the social characteristics of residential areas. Efforts to counteract these consequences of the functional principle such as the Parent-Teacher Associations. and the reassignment of children among different school districts as in the United States are examples of plebiscitarianism within the system of public education. In addition, there is the prolonged resistance of denominational groups against public education as such, to which reference was made earlier. The plebiscitarian principle is resisted since the agencies of the church or the denominations, by controlling the curriculum, seek to represent the special religious and cultural interests of parents as members of their respective congregations. Religious groups thus use the right of association to implement their special concerns in the field of education, though they differ widely in terms of whether and to what extent they rely financially on tax support or on assessments of their congregations.

With regard to the *franchise* the conflicts between the plebiscitarian and the representative principles may be divided into the two phases of a variously restricted and a universal right to vote. The restrictions we have reviewed are typically administrative criteria to which functional significance is imputed. When the right to vote is made dependent upon a certain level of income, tax payment, property ownership, or education, it is assumed that those who meet minimum standards in these respects also share social and political views compatible with the established social order. It is also assumed that the representatives elected from these strata of the population will be notables capable of thinking and acting in terms of the whole community. This legal recognition of the representative principle is in large part abandoned once the right to vote has become universal. Yet the plebiscitarian principle of the right to direct participation by all adults as eligible voters is quite compatible with an acceptance of group differences and various indirect forms of functional representation. The electoral process itself is greatly influenced by the social differentiation of the voting public, and it is supplemented at many points by other influences on policy formation, many of them depending on special interest groups. Social differentiation and interest groups result in modifications of the plebiscitarian

[38] Children attending elementary school are more numerous than taxpayers since school attendance allows for no exemptions as does the tax system. Indeed, even the children of resident aliens are subject to this requirement, but this may be considered an administrative convenience, a welfare measure, a preparation of potential citizens, and so on rather than a matter concerning the principle of national citizenship.

principle and in new inequalities which may in turn provoke countermeasures in order to protect the plebiscitarian principle of equality of all adults as eligible voters.

Accordingly, the extension of citizenship to the lower classes involves at many levels an institutionalization of abstract criteria of equality which give rise both to new inequalities and new measures to deal with these ancillary consequences. The system of representative institutions characteristic of the Western European tradition remains intact as long as this tension between the plebiscitarian idea and the idea of group-representation endures, as long as the contradiction between abstract criteria of equality and the old as well as new inequalities of the social condition is mitigated by ever new and ever partial compromises. The system is destroyed when, as in the totalitarian systems of recent history, these partial resolutions are abandoned in the interest of implementing the plebiscitarian principle alone under the aegis of a one-party state.

Interest Groups
and the Bureaucracy
in Western Democracies

HENRY W. EHRMANN

. . . Herrschaft ist im Alltag primaer: Verwaltung.*
Max Weber, *Wirtschaft und Gesellschaft.*

The preoccupation of political scientists with the activities and the influence of interest groups can lead to a realistic understanding of the political process only if we also acquire an understanding of the institutions through which the groups are compelled to function and of the milieu in which they move.[1] This comparative essay is concerned with the interaction of public administration and interest groups since policies originated by them mirror rather distinctly both the plural patterns of power and the functional specialization which exist

From *Revue Française de Science Politique* (Presses Universitaires de France éditeurs), Vol. XI (September 1961), pp. 541–568. Reprinted by permission of the author and publisher.

Henry W. Ehrmann is Professor of Law and Political Science, Dartmouth College. A specialist in business, labor, and politics in France, he has been visiting professor at Bordeaux, Grenoble, and Nice. He is the author of *French Labor from Popular Front to Liberation* (1947) and *Organized Business in France* (1957), and the editor of *Interest Groups on Four Continents* (1958) and *Democracy in a Changing Society* (1964).

* In everyday affairs domination is primarily administration. [Ed.]
[1] Cf. M. Fainsod, "Some Reflections on the Nature of the Regulatory Process," *Public Policy*, I (1940), p. 298.

in countries of a highly develped economy. In such societies the resolution of even the most important issues is transferred from the general level of policy-making downwards to a combination of institutions among which the administrative bureaus are most prominent. The "separate whirlpools of policy formation" which have been described as typical of the United States exist elsewhere as well.[2] Moreover the subsystem in which public servants and group representatives meet offers frequently a glimpse of a counter-system to representative democracy.

In the modern welfare state political power is increasingly substituted for economic power and problems whose solution was previously left to private initiative have become public issues. Pressed for manifold decisions for which they are ill-equipped parliament and frequently also the political executive entrust discretion to the bureaucrats (1) as holders of the technical knowledge that is needed to bring about the intended political results; (2) as the wielders of the instrumentalities of economic and social planning where neither the legislator nor the executive know exactly which ultimate results are desirable (3) as conflict resolvers who are, at least implicitly, asked to break a deadlock between contradictory claims and values especially when the legislature has embodied its own doubts and hesitations into the law.[3]

The diminished role of parliament has been paralleled usually, if somewhat unexpectedly, by a decrease in the weight of the political executive. Where Ministers used to tell the civil servants what the public would not stand for, the bureaus are now in direct contact with an organized public, viz., the interest groups. If a high degree of governmental controls has increased the power of Ministers and of their departments, such power is counterbalanced by their dependence on outside organizations. From the perspective of the bureaucracy interest groups are audience, advisors, and clients, foremost participants in the process of bargaining over governmental policy. From the perspective of pressure politics the administrative bureaus are a decisive center of power although this does not mean that for the interest groups their contacts with the bureaucracy have everywhere replaced other forms of influence.

In all Western democracies the consequences of such a configuration are discussed in fairly similar terms. Is there a danger, it is asked, that the groups, acting through a subsystem over which external controls have weakened, exercise an inordinate amount of influence, or can the civil service because of its disinterestedness, knowledge and permanency be relied upon to act as a check on group influence? [4]

[2] Cf. E. S. Griffith, *Congress. Its Contemporary Role* (New York: New York University Press, 1951), p. 112; and H. J. Spiro, *Government by Constitution* (New York: Random House, 1959), p. 340.

[3] Cf. W. A. R. Leys, "Ethics and Administrative Discretion," *Public Administration Review*, III (1943), p. 23.

[4] In France pioneering studies on the subject have been undertaken by J. J. Meynaud. Cf. especially "Les groupes d'intérêt et l'administration en France," *Revue Française de Science Politique*, VII (1957), pp. 573–593; and his *Les Groupes de Pression en France* (Paris: A. Colin, 1958), pp. 203–216. Since it can be assumed that to readers of this journal the situation in France is known better than that in other countries, this paper pays somewhat scant attention to France. My article, "French Bureaucracy and

OBJECTIVES OF GROUP-BUREAUCRACY CONTACTS

Today extensive consultation between group leaders and civil servants is generally considered as a "fundamental democratization" of the administrative process.[5] If in Europe official collaboration with the groups is praised openly only since the war, European administrators have practiced it for as long a time as Americans. The British may describe what they are doing as a mere form of courtesy of good manners, the Germans may praise it as a necessary departure from the methods of the *Obrigkeitsstaat*. What matters is that there exists by now in all countries widespread agreement on the propriety and convenience of continuous consultation both when the bureaus are drafting legislation and when they administer enacted laws. "We should be very loath to make any recommendations which might have the incidental effect of impeding or restricting liaison between Government Departments and the public": [6] this conclusion reached by a British Committee set up *inter alias* to investigate the role of interest groups as intermediaries, would today be echoed almost everywhere.

The administrator turns to the group leader in order to obtain an understanding for the practices and customs of that part of the society that is affected by his ruling. Without the benefit of a sounding board the official feels that he is unable to correctly forecast the results of his actions. What at first has been merely useful, becomes soon necessary.[7] Where the sources of official information, statistical and otherwise, are as notoriously insufficient as in France and Italy, many bureaus must rely constantly on the data provided by trade associations, trade-unions or other groups. But also in other countries the administration is compelled to utilize the groups as technicians and experts rather than as partisan advocates even though their advice may be that of an expert *engage*.[8] Information flows in either direction. The groups frequently serve as channels for those explanations of its policy which the administration wishes to communicate to the public but feels it cannot convey directly. Where, as in France, important interest groups pay little attention to the cultivation of outside contacts, the bureaucracy complains that it has altogether inadequate means of conveying and interpreting its programs.[9]

Organized Interests," *Administrative Science Quarterly*, V (1961), pp. 534–555 may be considered as complementary to the present one.

[5] Cf. K. Mannheim, *Man and Society in an Age of Reconstruction* (London: Paul, Trench and Trubner, 1940), p. 44.

[6] *Report of the Committee on Intermediaries* (London: H. M. Stationery Office, 1950), p. 69.

[7] Cf. Political and Economic Planning, *Advisory Committee in British Government* (London: Allen and Unwin, 1960), pp. 99–105; and A. Leiserson, *Administrative Regulation: A Study in Representation of Interests* (Chicago: University of Chicago Press, 1942), p. 53.

[8] Cf. J. Meynaud, *Technocratie et Politique* (Lausanne: Etudes de Science Politique, 1960), p. 38, and J. Palombara, "The Utility and Limitations of Interest Group Theory in Non-American Field Situation," *The Journal of Politics*, XXII (1960), p. 47.

[9] For details, cf. H. W. Ehrmann, *La Politique du Patronat Français* (1936–1955) (Paris: A. Colin, 1959), pp. 182 ff. For the situation in Great Britain, cf. *Report on Intermediaries, op. cit.*, p. 69.

Even more important than the channeling of information is the general decentralization of governmental functions which the group-bureaucracy relationship affords. Where the administration lacks technical knowledge or considers its apparatus inadequate for the performance of incumbent tasks, yet hesitates to add more bulk to the governmental machinery, the burden of executive responsibility may be shifted to well organized interest groups. In the United States such an abdication of administrative functions to a wide variety of licensing boards gives to the groups powers that are often not better controlled than that of medieval guilds. In the field of labor relations and social insurance most European democracies practice the "self-government" of unions and management.

Where organs of consultation and cooperation are lacking, the administration will frequently create them. In all countries, especially in the wake of war-time or emergency controls, the need of the bureaucracy for contacts with groups has been stimulus for the organization of interests. Some of the large confederations or *Spitzenverbaende* owe their existence to the initiative of the government.[10]

If such are the main objectives of the cooperation between group and bureaucracy, it is natural that in the eyes of the administration not all groups are equal. It will prefer those that have given proof of representing the wishes of their membership, those whose information has been found reliable and whose staff is not only competent but also attuned to style and working methods of the civil service. Were it only because of their search for rationality civil servants will most of the time prefer to deal with large-scale organizations: "their representatives can usually appreciate the larger view even when they disagree with it, and they have a surer and more intellectual approach to what is politically and economically feasible." [11] With some exceptions only groups which represent sectional interests as industry, agriculture or labor will be admitted to regular consultation or be used for the decentralization of administrative departments more difficult and will therefore frequently seek other channels of influence.

POINTS OF GROUP ACCESS

Either on their own initiative or prodded by the Ministry with which they have dealings, the groups will shape their organizational structure so as to resemble the institutions they wish to influence. The resulting parallelism between the structure of public administration and of interest groups does much to facilitate informal and continuous group access. Wherever the government regulates multiple aspects of the national economy, an increasing functional specialization leads to the consolidation of clientele administrations animated by a clientele orientation. The groups find greatest satisfaction in their contacts with what the French call the "vertical" administrations and which correspond

---

[10] For examples, cf. W. J. M. Mackenzie, "Pressure Groups in British Government," *British Journal of Sociology*, VI (1955), p. 144.

[11] B. Chapman, *The Profession of Government. The Public Service in Europe* (London: Allen and Unwin, 1959), p. 318.

to the Sponsoring Departments in Great Britain, to the regulatory commissions or clientele administrations in the United States. As technical advisors to these agencies they shape much of the actual regulatory process; as public they make the administrator fully aware of the point of view taken by the interests they represent. Natural alliances between bureau head and group leader are formed; if necessary they are directed against such "outsiders" as other administrations and the rival interests they may sponsor, against the political executive or against parliament. In the United States the mutual support of groups and clientele administrations has often complicated if not obstructed the efforts of the President and of Congress to make the government serve broader public interests.[12] Usually both agencies and groups have a common interest in the continuation of vigorous regulation; the prestige if not the survival of both may depend on it.

If other civil servants grow sometimes extremely critical of the mentality and the rulings of their colleagues in the clientele agencies, it can be answered that the conditions they criticize appear endemic in any agency performing such tasks. They are the natural outgrowth of the process of regulation, of its organizational structure and of the underlying philosophy of functional representation. Yet it cannot be denied that in many countries the point has been reached where the trend towards specialized organizations runs afoul of the need for a macro-economic policy.[13] The narrower the clientele, the less capable becomes the administrative agency of resisting pressures. When the government tries occasionally, as has been the case in Western Germany, France and Great Britain, to remedy the prevailing situation by combining administrations, the violent protests that have come from the interest groups, are an indication of what they stand to lose.

More amply discussed than other phases of group influence is the cooperation in which organized interests and administrations engage in order to prepare legislation. Especially in such small countries as Sweden and Switzerland, Belgium and the Netherlands, all known for their frank acknowledgement of a pronounced pluralism, the bureaucracy, when drafting bills, leans heavily on a constituency composed of interest groups. The *Vernehmlassung* in Switzerland and the *remissyttranden* in Sweden do not only enable the groups to comment extensively and at every stage on the legislative proposals of the government; their opinions, if they have not already modified the bills, are also transmitted to parliament. Often the collaboration between bureaucracy and groups will result in unanimous agreement on bills which parliament is then asked to endorse.

[12] Cf. C. Hyneman, *Bureaucracy in a Democracy* (New York: Harpers, 1950), p. 64. For the interesting, somewhat abnormal situation that arose in the United States while Mr. Benson was Secretary of Agriculture, see J. L. Freeman, "The Bureaucracy in Pressure Politics," *The Annals of the American Academy of Political and Social Sciences*, CCCIXX (1958), p. 17.

[13] Cf. L. L. Jaffé, "The Effective Limits of the Administrative Process: A Revaluation," *Harvard Law Review*, LXVII (1954), p. 1113. The same point is made for England, after much praise for interest group consultation, by L. Tivey and E. Wohlegemuth, "Trade Associations as Interest Groups," *The Political Quarterly*, XXIX (1958), p. 71.

To be sure, complaints that parliament is most of the time confronted with a *fait accompli* are quite common. "Le Parlement passe de plus en plus pour un décor dans lequel on apparait quand les jeux sont faits," remarks a Belgian author, and a British author, and a British observer concludes that "if White-hall (i.e. the Bureaucracy) can claim the monopoly of knowledge and the agreement of the interested parties . . . (it is strengthened) at the expense of Westminster (i.e. parliament)." [14] Although the practices that have become widespread in all of Western Europe can hardly be reconciled with classical theories of democratic representation, parliament knows full well that it will never be able to match the bureaucracy group effort in its attention to detail. The more thoroughly group opinion has been explored beforehand the less need will there be for amendments, costly in time and effort, by members of parliament. Besides being indicative of the general decline of parliamentary opposition,[15] this situation had to be accepted by the elected representatives when it became apparent that to an increasing extent the citizen prefers the concrete involvement in interest group activities to the identification with political parties.

The fact that in the Third and Fourth Republics the legislative process has remained, and in the United States still remains more traditional has compelled the interest groups to divide their efforts between the bureaucracy and the parliamentary committees. The American Congress, it is true, is better equipped than European parliaments, to collect expert and group advice. Since the French constitution of 1958 has all but squashed the amending power of the National Assembly as extravagant, groups have, except in extraordinary situations, deserted the couloirs of the Palais Bourbon and are cultivating now almost exclusively the administrative bureaus.[16]

FORMS OF GROUP ACCESS

One can easily exaggerate the difference between situations in which the bureaucracy negotiates with pressure groups and where it merely consults them. It is generally impossible to measure the relative influence that groups exert over administrative decisions. But how much influence is exercised will depend less on the label describing the exchange than on the eagerness with which the decision-maker seeks advice and negotiation and on the persuasiveness with which both are offered.[17]

[14] Cf. W. J. Ganshof Can Der Meersch, *Aspects du Régime Parlementaire Belge* (Bruxelles: Librairie Encyclopédique, 1956), p. 129; and K. C. Wheare, *Government by Committee* (Oxford, Oxford University Press, 1955), p. 67; see also E. Gruner, *Die Wirtschaftsverbände in der Demokratie* (Erlenbach-Zurich: Rentsch Verlag, 1956), pp. 97 ff.

[15] Cf. O. Kirchheimer, "The Waning of Opposition in Parliamentary Regimes," *Social Research*, XXIV (1957), pp. 127–156.

[16] Why the circumstances surrounding the parliamentary deliberations of the law on the new status of the private schools proved an exception to this generalization, cannot be discussed here.

[17] Cf. H. Simon, "Decision-Making and Administrative Organization," *Public Administration Review*, IV (1944), pp. 24–25; and Palombara, *op. cit.*, p. 39.

More important is a distinction between formal, institutionalized consultation and informal contacts. Both exist in all countries, but their legal significance and actual effect may be very different. The so-called advisory committees, usually attached to a specific administration are everywhere, whatever other functions they may fulfill, an instrumentality of interest group influence. In Great Britain a recent census of such committees counted 484 on the level of the central government alone, more than one-fourth of them attached to the Ministry of Agriculture, that of supply and the Board of Trade.[18] The very proliferation of such committees forces many governmental departments to constantly "keep in touch"; at almost every step it is necessary to take into account a large number of reasons and arguments.

In most cases interest groups propose committee members for nomination or nominate them outright. For these groups there is therefore no need for hammering at the doors of the Ministries; they are constantly being invited in and have acquired the status that stems from being immensely useful. They also may acquire the inside information that enhances their position in regard to their own membership. This however does not change the fact that the advice which the groups tender, may not present to the bureaucracy sufficient alternatives for action.[19] Where the acceptance of the committee's advice has become habitual, because the bureaucracy hesitates to formalize any decision for which the groups concerned do not want to take the responsibility, the groups are in fact, vested with administrative authority. In most countries it seems to take particular courage to by-pass agricultural organizations which contributes to an inflation of the group-ego. Yet it is still true that frequently the outcome will depend on the forcefulness of the administrator to whom the committee reports.

For being less useful the larger and less technical committees have also less weight. This explains in part why the various Economic Councils have never fulfilled the expectations of pluralists and administrators who hoped that the councils would, by combining the advantages of expertness and publicity, relieve the pressures of the lobbies. In countries such as Germany and Great Britain where they once existed they have been abandoned. The French experience remains inconclusive, and the same must as yet be said about the Dutch Economic Council although as an institutionalized representation of the "Estates" the latter seems to have become an effective "shadow parliament." [20]

Besides the official committees which are used by the administration as seals of democratic legitimacy, informal face-to-face contacts remain important for the groups since they are more interested in the substance than in the form

[18] Cf. P.E.P., *op. cit.* listing pp. 193–217 all existing committees as well as the major nominating bodies, mostly interest groups.

[19] For parallel criticism of the situation in the United States and in France, see C. Wirtz, "Government by Private Groups," *Louisiana Law Review*, XIII (1953), p. 440, and G. Lavau, "Political Pressures by Interest Groups in France," H. Ehrmann (ed.), *Interest Groups on Four Continents* (Pittsburgh: University of Pittsburgh Press, 1958), pp. 82–84.

[20] Cf. H. Daalder, "Parties and Politics in the Netherlands," *Political Studies*, III (1955), pp. 1–16; but see for France, H. Seligson, "An Evaluation of the Economic Council of France," *Western Political Quarterly*, VII (1954), pp. 35–50.

of power. In countries like France and Finland where the fragmentation of interests is pronounced, the flight into informal and confidential contacts follows often the breakdown of communications in the more or less publicly conducted committees.[21] But informal daily contacts are usual also in the United States and Germany. In Great Britain they have been described as forming the very basis of a "quasi-corporatism." In Sweden a "Thursday Club" brings together high civil servants, representatives of industry and finance to engage in serious planning business over the dinner table.[22]

Formal as well as informal consultation will have some of the consequences which resulted when in the United States the Tennessee Valley Administration found it necessary to bargain with local centers of power for their support.

Such cooperation led unavoidably to an acceptance by the T.V.A. of the entire pattern of Southern economic, race and class relations.[23] Almost any bureaucracy which in order to ensure its own stability makes outside organizations part of the policy-making administrative structure, will find that in the process the groups may succeed in modifying character and even the role of governmental instrumentalities. The regular consultation of groups, indispensable as it might be, is likely to lead to commitments which have restrictive consequences for official policy and the behavior of authority.

A farther reaching "colonization" of the bureaucracy occurs where groups determine the personnel policy of the administration and where therefore personal relations have become institutionalized in a somewhat drastic fashion. Here differences between various countries continue to exist. In Great Britain one considers "sinister" what has become common practice in Western Germany. In France there are at most social sanctions against the civil servant who has incurred the displeasure of an interest group, and if a group wishes to see a particular *fonctionnaire* put in charge of a certain assignment, it must act surreptitiously. In Belgium, on the other hand, outside pressure on promotions, though no longer on appointments, remains strong and gives the groups an effective lever on decision-making. In Italy the influence of groups affiliated with the dominant Christian Democracy seems to loom large in the thinking of civil servants about their career.[24] Whether or not the non-existence of life-tenure makes the Swiss civil servant amenable to pressures coming from a particularly well developed network of interest groups, has not been investigated

[21] For a report on Finland revealing and striking similarities to the French situation, see L. Krusius-Ahrenberg, "The Political Power of Economic and Labor-Market Organizations: A Dilemma of Finnish Democracy," Ehrmann (ed.), *op. cit.*, pp. 33–59.

[22] For England cf. S. H. Beer, "Pressure Groups and Parties in Britain," *The American Political Science Review*, L (1956), p. 9; for Sweden, cf. H. Thorelli, "Formation of Economic and Financial Policy: Sweden," *International Social Science Bulletin*, VIII (1956), p. 270.

[23] Cf. P. Selznick, *TVA and the Grass Roots* (Berkeley: University of California Press, 1949), pp. 12, 265 and *passim*.

[24] These and other data on Italy and Belgium are gleaned, with the permission of the authors, from unpublished reports by Professors V. Lorwin and J. Palombara submitted to the Conference held in September 1960 under the auspices of the Social Science Research Council.

so far. Cases of group leaders entering the administration are known in the United States as well as Sweden, though presumably in Sweden interest group personnel will sever all of their former connections.

It is not easy to find a common denominator for the factors which in different countries have made it possible to operate, as it were, from within the administrative hierarchy. The degree of and the belief in the political neutrality of the civil service is obviously an important factor. In Germany, the politization of the bureaucracy, though it had started earlier, reached its apogee in the Third Reich. Denazification, the distrust of the occupying powers of the civil service, and the rapid re-emergence of the interest groups after the war while political parties were still discredited, combine to explain a situation in which certain groups consider certain administrative jobs their fief. Some bureaus have been described as "feudal dukedoms," and administrative autonomy is threatened wherever the civil servant knows that he occupies his post because of the *satisfecit* of an interest group.[25] In the United States some of the regulatory commissions have come under the sway of the economic forces they were set up to control partly because presidential appointments of commissioners have drawn freely on interest representatives who were presumably considered to possess expert knowledge. The result has been in many cases a perversion of the law which the regular courts can seldom correct.[26] In Belgium the politization of promotions is a legacy of ideological, religious and cultural-linguistic conflicts. There, as well as in Italy, the colonization of parts of the administration is effected through the political parties which may act as agents for the groups. It would be an unwarranted generalization to expect this to be true in all political systems where interest groups are massively involved in party affairs or at least in party finances, since the case of Great Britain clearly refutes such an assumption.

Whether or not the groups succeed in "boring from within" tactics or whether their access to decision-making is confined to other channels is quite obviously determined by the framework of the institutions and by the traditions within which the groups operate.

CONTROLS OF THE BUREAUCRACY-GROUP RELATIONSHIP

In all democratic systems administrative decisions are subject to a variety of administrative, political and judicial controls.[27] The decisive question seems to

[25] Cf. T. Eschenburg, *Herrschaft der Verbände?* (Stuttgart: Deutsche Verlagsanstalt, 1956), pp. 16 ff.; and W. Weber, in *Der Staat und die Verbände* (Heidelberg: Verlag Recht und Wirtschaft, 1957), p. 22. For the influence of German veterans' organizations on the recruitment of the officers' corps in the new army cf. K. W. Deutsch and L. J. Edinger, *Germany Rejoins the Powers* (Stanford: Stanford University Press, 1959), p. 96.

[26] Cf. James M. Landis, *Report on Regulatory Agencies to the President-Elect* (Washington: Government Printing Office, 1960), esp. pp. 11–17.

[27] For reasons of space the effectiveness of judicial controls in various countries cannot be examined here. Moreover this is as yet a largely unexplored question.

be how deeply the available controls can penetrate into the subsystem in which groups and bureaucracy interact.

The fact that different Ministries vary in their outlook on the desirability or the danger of group influence determines the nature of certain intra-administrative controls. The competence of an administration and its position in the hierarchy may generate enough independent power to change decisions that have been made elsewhere, e.g., by clientele agencies or in another administrative environment where groups have weighed heavily. The Treasury (in the United States together with the Bureau of Budget) seems to fulfill this role in many countries; in such different systems as Great Britain and France it exercises its prerogatives in very similar fashion. For all their differences in style (persuasion here, haughtiness there) Treasury and *Rue de Rivoli* are always waiting to turn something down, to be the guardians of the general interest in a universe seething with special interests and to use budget compliance as a means of administrative-political control. Even in Sweden where a curious 18th century tradition of keeping executive policy separate from routine administration compels the groups to work on both levels, the budget is the main device of curbing the autonomy of the Central Administrative Boards in charge of administration proper.[28] But everywhere treasury controls are somewhat blunted by the fact that if they are carried too far, an over-centralization of final decision-making is bound to occur.

The way in which intra-bureaucratic arbitration is organized has a bearing on pressure group activities. Muddled responsibilities may transform the dialogue between group and regulatory agency into a colloquium between private and public bureaucracies. In such a situation the best informed, i.e., usually the best organized groups can play on intra-bureaucratic feuds and peddle information from one agency to another. Should the lack of effective arbitration leave the situation so unsettled that administrative immobilism sets in, the groups will either be happy with a *status quo* that serves them well or they will have to appeal to forces outside the bureaucracy. In any country difficulties of reaching decisions on the ministerial level are likely to impede long-range programming by officials which in turn might make the bureaus listen with more benevolence to short-term causes pleaded by the groups. Such a situation arose in England during the last period of the war-time coalition; it has been chronic in Finland and during much of the Fourth Republic. On numerous occasions the French bureaucracy took major political decisions under the cloak of an administrative ruling and more than once under pressure from organized interests — the "solution" of the Moroccan crisis in 1953 is a well-known case in point.[29]

The point has been made that where a strong and disciplined legislature exercises political controls the civil service is in a better position than elsewhere to hold the dam against special interests, for otherwise the interests penetrate the bureaucracy and undermine its neutral, instrumental character.[30] A com-

---

[28] Cf. Thorelli, *op. cit.*, pp. 262–264.
[29] Cf. Meynaud, "Les groupes d'intérêt etc.," *op. cit.*, p. 584.
[30] G. Almond, Rapporteur, "A Comparative Study of Interest Groups and the Politi-

parative inquiry seems to suggest that while such a penetration occurs everywhere, its effects depend on many factors besides the ability of parliament to articulate and aggregate group demands. Where parliament is organized so as to function, usually through committees, as a body for intensive legislative initiative and even current administration, this will have its repercussions for the structure and the workings of the subsystem. In the United States and the now defunct French Republics the interaction between committee chairmen, bureau heads and clientele groups provide a different field for group activities from that existing in Great Britain or other countries where parliament is concerned with the discussion of broad policy issues rather than with influencing legislation.

If it is true that the British official has to sustain relatively few pressures coming directly from Westminster, this does not mean that existing controls will always shield him from direct group intervention. Only in rare situations can he protect himself against group demands by obtaining appropriate directives from his Minister. On the other hand many French civil servants maintain that during the years of the Fourth Republic they were perfectly capable of insulating themselves from parliamentary pressures transmitting demands emanating from interest groups. They considered themselves safe from such intervention just because the National Assembly did not muster efficient parties which might have aggregated interests behind the closed doors of a caucus or an executive committee meeting. Since it was well-known which deputies were the appointed spokesmen of particular special interests, it was easy to discredit their demarches in the governmental bureaus. Undoubtedly the contempt which many French civil servants harbor for the politician is much greater than that of his British or American colleague and results in bureaucratic unwillingness to grant a sympathetic hearing to most deputies.[31] Developments in the Fifth Republic are contradictory. Certain groups, especially those representing small and marginal interests, which in the past had an easy access to parliament and its committees, were compelled to seek other channels, some of them leading through the ministerial *cabinets*. But at least so far one cannot conclude that the drastic transformation of parliamentary functions has had any clear incidence on the relationship between groups and bureaucracy.

There is evidence that in all Western democracies political and technological developments led to a weakening of controls over the administration. Though the civil servant is steadily gaining ascendancy over the politician, his own autonomy does not always increase correspondingly. In the absence of a clear political impulse the bureaucracy finds it often necessary to lean heavily on the interest groups for advice and cooperation and subsequently identifies itself more easily with their demands.

---

cal Process," *American Political Science Review*, LII (1958), p. 280. For the situation in the United States, see J. L. Freeman, *The Political Process. Executive Bureau-Legislative Committee Relations* (Garden City, N.Y.: Doubleday & Co., 1955).

[31] Cf. R. Grégoire, *Réflexions sur le Problème des Réformes Administratives* (Paris: Cours ENA, 1951), p. 23.

BUREAUCRATIC MENTALITY
AND ENVIRONMENT AS FACTORS
IN GROUP ACCESS

Which are the factors making civil servants personally amenable or resilient to group influence? From the angle of the old controversy as to whether the high civil service should be turned over to the expert-technician or to the amateur-generalist there is evidence that the latter knows better how to defend himself against special interests. For Max Weber the absence of emotional involvement distinguishes the administrator from the politician.[32] But the technically trained bureaucrat in charge of highly specialized regulation becomes frequently as committed to causes as his clients and seems incapable of the stoical realism and open-mindedness which his generalist colleagues are proud to push to the point of professional agnosticism. In France the state engineers, distributed over many agencies and excellently trained though they are, are regarded by their colleagues to be least capable of thinking in terms of long-range generalized interests and therefore easily swayed by the pleadings of articulate groups. The strong identification of the administrator with his agency and its clientele will be lessened by the mobility which a unified civil service generates more easily than a highly stratified bureaucracy whose *grands corps* are fairly strictly separated.

In many countries civil servants, rather than being men of ideas pride themselves on enjoying a freedom from ideas.[33] But then interests may be more convincing than political doctrines and the civil servant might judge the vagaries of party politics more severely than the concrete and closely reasoned arguments of interest groups. Does the character training to which monarchical and aristocratic traditions in Great Britain and Sweden are still submitting the civil service elite have an immunizing effect? [34] The French scoff at it. But they admit that their pre-war training which provided solitary preparation for mastery, left the official without sufficient initiation in the skills of negotiation, so important in dealings with interest groups. The almost exclusively legalistic training of the German and Italian civil servant, while satisfactory to the generalists' orientation, tends to provide the administrator with a perspective which leaves the concrete content of administrative issues in a zone of indecision and confusion. A focus on the abstract might create a void into which interest group leaders can move to press their demands.[35]

Because of the controls they exercise over other sectors of the bureaucracy, the differences in attitude of the officials of the British Treasury and the French Ministry of Finance are noteworthy. The British staff is lacking specialized training but is now imbued with a practical philosophy: Keynesian thinking. The French Inspectorate of Finance (and there are close parallels

[32] Cf. the significant quotations from various writings by M. Weber in R. Bendix, *Max Weber, an Intellectual Portrait* (Garden City, N.Y.: Doubleday & Co., 1960), p. 421.

[33] Cf. C. H. Sisson, *The Spirit of British Administration and Some European Comparisons* (Oxford: Blackwell's, 1959), p. 23.

[34] Cf. Chapman, *op. cit.*, p. 93.

[35] A point developed by Palombara in his unpublished paper, *op. cit.*

to its outlook in Belgium) is highly trained in the techniques of public finance but so preoccupied with monetary considerations that, at least until recently, a philosophy of economic development was alien to its members.[36] It appears that the Treasury control is more effective when it is called upon to arbitrate between conflicting claims. The *Rue de Rivoli* has, especially in an inflationary situation, the tendency to turn down everybody until its defenses are breached from without.

It is sometimes argued that the degree to which an administrative agency is permeable to organized interests is a function of its age: the more recent administrations, especially those established in the wake of war-time and post-war controls are said to lack the traditions of autonomy and to be as yet too unsure of themselves to develop the standards that are needed in their relationship with interest groups. This seems to be an unwarranted generalization.[37] In most countries an enumeration of Ministries, noted for granting easy access to interest groups, include old-time administrations as well as newer ones. It is still the specialized clientele agency, whether new or old, which is most given to quasi-corporatist practices. Hence function and not age seems to be the decisive factor.

For the time being it rather appears that the younger generation of civil servants is more fully aware of the problems inherent in their contacts with organized interests. Whether they are correct when they boast of having developed a mentality and techniques that insure a greater autonomy to the bureaucracy remains to be seen. In Saskatchewań [38] and in France the conjuncture of political circumstances and of thorough reforms in the training of top administrators could be a reason for change. But one notes also in Holland a more frankly technocratic orientation of the younger civil servants: if they believe to have acquired the political skill which is necessary in their contacts with interest groups, they have even less sympathy than their elders for the professional politician.

Social cohesion and a strongly developed corporate life make undoubtedly for bureaucratic autonomy. Frequently however, the social origin of the top-bureaucrats facilitates feelings of kinship with groups outside the administration and notably with a milieu that dominates the private sector of the economy. These attitudes, noted equally in France and in Great Britain, have their impact on the relationship between officials and those who come to represent in their bureaus the major interests of the nation. In Western Germany the business elite and their professional spokesmen are much closer to the foreign service and the military than both are to the political elites presently ruling the country.[39] Similar affinities based not only on social origin and edu-

---

[36] For England, cf. S. H. Beer, *Treasury Control* (New York: Oxford University Press, 1956), pp. 58, 95. For France, P. Lalumière, *L'Inspection Générale des Finances* (Paris, 1959).

[37] For France this hypothesis is advanced by Meynaud, "Les groupes d'intérêt etc.," *op. cit.*, p. 580. For Italy it is rejected by Palombara, "The Utility etc.," *op. cit.*, p. 44.

[38] For observations on Saskatchewan, see S. Lipset, *Agrarian Socialism*, quoted here from R. Merton *et al.* (eds.), *Reader in Bureaucracy* (Glencoe, Ill.: The Free Press, 1952), p. 228.

[39] Cf. Deutsch and Edinger, *op. cit.*, pp. 99–100.

cation but also on manners, style and outlook exist now elsewhere when most of the influential interest groups are employing a personnel that is particularly attractive for the civil service and that has been described in the United States as the "counter-elite of the private governments." [40] There is nothing involved here that could be characterized as collusion. But administrators are likely to be receptive to proposals which stem from sources comparable to those from which their own attitudes and values have been derived.[41]

The professional aspirations of the civil servant may include plans for a switch to private employment. In both France and the United States this phenomenon is particularly frequent and provokes strikingly similar attitudes both before and after the transfer has taken place.[42] The official who looks forward to a business career is generally able to develop during his term of office a concept of independent public service without thereby spoiling his chances for a change in employment. Nevertheless the fact that he who regulates today expects to spend his later days representing the other side, is apt to be reflected in the general outlook of the civil servant. In general the *pantouflard* will be employed in an activity with which he was familiar while in government service, if he is not simply now doing what he was previously called upon to control. He is almost always hired because of his expert knowledge of public administration, its personnel, its methods and policies. When he calls on his former colleague to transact business with him the cordiality of their contacts will greatly further the symbiosis of officialdom and private interests.

STANDARDS FOR THE DEFENSE
OF THE PUBLIC INTEREST

It has become evident from the foregoing that the political efforts of interest groups directed at influencing administrative decisions show a great deal of uniformity in all Western democracies. Held against existing similarities the effect of diverse political institutions of sharply different political cultures pales in comparison. It remains quite true that the degree of political homogeneity of a society, and the consensus achieved by its citizens will have an important impact on the way in which private conflicts are taken into the public domain and group claims are transformed into public policy. The general effect which the interest group system has on the political process in countries like France and Italy may still be very different from that produced in Great Britain or the Scandinavian countries. But where they interact with the bureaucracy (and at least as long as they interact) group leaders will even in countries with a

---

[40] H. Morgenthau, "Our Thwarted Republic," *Commentary*, XXX (1960), p. 484. The entire article is a sharp attack on the place of interest groups in the American political system of today.

[41] Cf. R. W. Gable, "Interest Groups as Policy Shapers," *The Annals of the American Academy of Political and Social Sciences*, CCCIXX (1958), p. 91.

[42] The description of the American situation by Jaffe, *op. cit.*, pp. 1132 ff., could be taken as an exact portrayal of the mentality of the *pantouflard* in France.

fragmented, isolative political culture [43] show a somewhat unexpected degree of consensus and of loyalty to the rules of the game.

To seek a hearing in governmental bureaus, to act as advisor and consultant implies on the part of the groups at least a momentary, but probably a lasting commitment to the political system, the acceptance of common values include the acknowledgement of the fact that every social service state controls a large share of the national income through administrative decisions and that it is the proper role of the bureaucracy to adjust conflicting group claims. The more regularly such an arbitration occurs, the more will even the temporarily dissatisfied groups have confidence in the stability of the state, however much they may decry, as they did for instance in the Fourth Republic, the instability of governments. In the perhaps extreme case of Sweden the general standard of values is so commonly accepted and the function of the state has become so technical that politics appear to administrators as well as to groups as a kind of applied statistics.[44] But also in societies where distrust frequently destroys the basis of pragmatic behavior, mutual fears of group leader and officials of being manipulated by the other side will subside. A high degree of agreement on basic issues coupled with a high degree of concern with narrowly delimited policies impinging mostly upon technical fields creates an atmosphere in which there is a premium on moderation.[45]

It is true that in order to participate in the bargaining process of the subsystem a group must be confident that its demands can be handled there. Any group that has major demands upon society and state will go elsewhere than to the bureaucracy: it may turn to the party system, transform itself into a party if the parties fail, or take to violence. The British and German tradeunions early in the century, Dorgeres in the Thirties, Poujade in the Fifties are examples of such attempts of translating political power into economic power. Just as the "time for law has not yet come while opposite convictions still keep a battle front against each other," [46] the administration cannot fulfill its function as a mediating authority in regard to groups which give expression to fundamental discontents. Where the disruption of the consensus divides the community into armed camps, the bureaucracy risks to be transformed into a battalion of one of the armies.[47] But the situation is fundamentally different when permanently organized groups seek, through their own bureaucracies, the assistance of officialdom to translate their economic power into favorable regulation.

In that process the administrator is faced with the task of utilizing, if at all possible, the currents of special interests with which he is surrounded, for the discovery of the public interest.[48] It is significant that in all Western de-

[43] For an interesting typology of different countries of Western Europe cf. Almond, *op. cit.*, p. 274.

[44] Cf. Thorelli, *op. cit.*, p. 272.

[45] Cf. H. Eckstein, *Pressure Group Politics. The Case of the British Medical Association* (Stanford: Stanford University Press, 1960), p. 156.

[46] O. W. Holmes, *Collected Legal Papers* (London: Constable, 1920), p. 295.

[47] Fainsod, *op. cit.*, p. 322.

[48] Cf. P. Herring, *Public Administration and the Public Interest* (New York: McGraw-Hill Book Co., 1936), p. 134 and *passim*.

mocracies practitioners and theorists of public administration discuss the concept of the public interest in very similar terms, though in Anglo-Saxon countries their terminology might be colored by Bentham, while elsewhere it is influenced by Rousseau.[49] The way in which the bureaucrat will assess his role in discovering the "x-factor in the political equation," namely the public or general interest, is highly significant for his self-image and thereby for his dealings with organized interests. One finds in most countries a variety of schools reviewing the search for the general interest in a different light. There are those who believe in the ability of the expert-technician to distill the Public Will from a rationalization of the decisional process with apparently little room left for discretion. There are also the "philosopher-administrators" whose creed, whether they admit it or not, comes close to an organic theory of the state since they trust their intuition for a recognition of the common good even though the public which allegedly wills it, is unaware of its concrete content. Apostles of apolitical Darwinism may hold that the invisible hand will find a counter-lobby for each lobby, and that from the group struggle the public interest will spontaneously emerge.[50]

But of late, and especially since the war, the sociological reality of the administrative process has been grasped more clearly and insights have spread that attribute to the bureaucracy less sweeping though not less exacting functions. In reality the official will have to select among the interests pressing on him some that are more readily identified with his concept of the public welfare than others. Here demands must be fused, their dormant interests must be awakened so that they can be opposed to others that have long been vocal. All this might, though it must not necessarily, increase for the bureaucracy its freedom of maneuver. The choices which it will communicate to the groups as well as to other parts of the political system, become an expression of the policy to which the administration is committed.[51]

Understood in this way the concept of public interest, rather than being, as it was considered earlier a standard for administrative behavior, becomes the post-hoc label for the resolution of group conflict. Just as the interplay of interests is regarded as legitimate in a pluralist society, the form in which their claims affect administrative decision-making is legitimized by a reference to the public or common interest. Since the well-organized pressure groups which find recognition and frequently, satisfaction in the subsystem, are similarly structured in many countries, and since they also act similarly at least as long as they are addressing the bureaucracy, it can only be expected that the process of and the procedures for legitimization have many similarities from one country to the other.

[49] Cf. the discussion on Bentham and Rousseau by a British and a French observer in Ehrmann (ed.), op. cit., pp. 278–280.

[50] On the concept of the public interest and the various schools which have formed in regard to it cf. G. A. Schubert, "The Public Interest in Administrative Decision-making; Theorem, Theosophy or Theory?" *American Political Science Review*, LI (1957), pp. 346–368; and F. Sorauf, "The Public Interest Reconsidered," *Journal of Politics*, XIX (1957), especially pp. 617, 628.

[51] Cf. Fainsod, op. cit., p. 320.

This does not mean that in all Western democracies decisions reached in the bureaucracy-group system will produce identical results. It is true that everywhere and only with some exceptions, sectional interest groups are better at conservation than at development, more prone to protect vested rights than to face new problems. The power of the bureaucracy on the other hand may be utilized either to maintain an existing equilibrium or to tilt the balances so as to create a new equilibrium. Which way the decision goes may, but must not be decided in the subsystem. Whether special interests will in the end further or obstruct the achievement of a viable policy will depend not only on the degree of autonomy which the bureaucracy has preserved, but on impulses that come from other parts of the political system. Economic policies followed after the war in different European countries provide contrasting examples. In Sweden powerful and self-conscious interest groups were not less responsible for assuring economic stability than the government. In England governmental initiative, backed by a disciplined parliamentary majority was needed to produce similar results. But in France organized business and labor, preying upon a weak political executive and upon parliament, inaugurated policies which for long years veered between the alternatives of inflation and recession.

SUBSYSTEM INTO NEO-FEUDALISM?

The generally smooth functioning of the group-bureaucracy subsystem contributes greatly to the efficiency of modern government; but also has its dangers, acute or latent, for the democratic process. In the eyes of those who doubt that there exists a metaphysical "general interest" and who admit that administrators can "find" the common good only by reference to the interests and demands which surround them, it is neither avoidable nor inherently bad that pressure groups have an impact on decision-making. According to this view the democratic process is not disturbed by the mere fact that the administration seeks legitimacy for its decision by group consultation and that the groups wish to see legitimacy bestowed on them by being admitted to the consultation-decision circuit. The decisive question is rather whether in concrete situations the sharing of power between groups and bureaucracy perverts the democratic method of formulating policies.[52]

A number of anguishing questions can nowhere be answered satisfactorily. On which basis are some groups admitted and others excluded? It is a truism that society is not vocal and that the expressed demands of society are usually the demands of vocally organized groups.[53] In some countries there might be agreement as to which groups are representative of the publics in whose name they are speaking. Elsewhere this might be impossible were it only for the fact that many sectional groups will try to identify their demands with the interests of the general public and will have successfully manipulated public opinion to lend verisimilitude to their claim. A decision by the administration to invite certain interest groups rather than others to take part in the regulatory process

[52] Cf. Gable, *op. cit.*, pp. 92–93.
[53] Cf. L. Lancaster, "Private Administration and Public Administration," *Journal of Social Forces* (1934), p. 291.

might reflect a state of tension between formal authority and social or economic power; it might deflect a possible threat coming from such powers. It might, however, also lead to policies quite different from those which a wider, but inarticulate public would have approved.

In most countries the articulation of demands by the consumer "group" encounters particular difficulties. What these demands are is most of the time an unexplored mystery. To expect the administrator to be constantly mindful of the existence of unorganized consumer interests is probably unrealistic. Consumer demands or revolts used to assert themselves rather through political parties, and obviously most likely through opposition parties. Hence, the Present-day decline of the role of political opposition in most democracies tends to consolidate from yet another side the relative weight of organized interests interacting with the bureaucracy.

Although serious conflicts are infrequent between groups and the administration, it should not be assumed that intra-group conflict is always solved benevolently nor that the interests of all group members are represented fairly.[54] The more efficient its own organization, the easier it becomes for the group to determine which interests will be expressed and which will be silenced. In fact when they sift and arbitrate between conflicting claims of their membership interest groups fulfill an important political function. How satisfactorily they perform this role might depend upon procedures for accountability and in general on the social and political climate. But it is certain that the effects of such group activities can very seldom be controlled by the bureaucracy. (In France some efforts in this direction have been made by the newer administrations when they sought to break the grip of group leaders who were all too devoted to the practices of economic malthusianism.)

The possible misrepresentation of member interests is all the more serious since even in countries where the functioning of parliamentary institutions is unimpaired, a creeping pluralism has rendered the right to an isolated existence very precarious. In many cases, of which the cartel situation is only one of the better known, an individual or a subgroup wishing to balk the decisions made in their name by the leadership of an interest organization can do so only at the risk of ostracism and economic ruin. Where citizens owe their livelihood and security to the groups, their primary loyalties will easily belong to the interest groups rather than to the state.[55] Thereby a situation remindful of feudal arrangements is created and these arrangements are solidly underpinned in the relationship between groups and bureaucracy.

What a Swiss writer has called the *Unio Mystica*, the merging of state and group power [56] is strengthened by the fact that at present in most countries group leaders and bureaucrats are frequently united by bonds of similar origin, education and outlook. The subsystem turns into a subsociety. Its members are drawn to each other by mutual respect which enhances the understanding

[54] Cf. Jaffe, *op. cit.*, p. 251.
[55] Cf. Morgenthau, *op. cit.*, p. 481.
[56] Cf. F. Marbach, here quoted from E. Gruner, *op. cit.*, p. 109.

for each other's position but also induces both sides to consider personalities, institutions and ideas outside the subsystem as a possible disturbance. The outside however is the wider public. By a frequently diffident attitude towards the public at-large the amalgam formed by groups and bureaucracy derives its characteristics of a counter-system to political democracy.

At least in countries of continental Europe administrators and group leaders are also likely to share feelings of hostility against politics and of disdain for the politician. Since their foremost standards are efficiency and effectiveness they may believe that by de-politicizing and presumably neutralizing decisions one can arrive at technically perfect solutions which are all but insensitive to the variations of the political conjuncture. Partly such a belief may simply reflect a middle-class distaste for political struggle; in the United States the preference of millions of citizens to participate in public life through civic groups rather than through party channels is another expression of this distaste. In their self-image the partners of the subsystem are cleansed of political motivations and are engaged in what has been correctly called a "non-traditional kind of engineered neo-corporatism." [57] It is indeed preferable to stress the non-traditional character of the phenomenon rather than to trace it in Great Britain to the old whig theory of representation, in the United States to a grass-root concept of democracy, in continental Europe to a revival of the *Ständestaat* or to catholic notions. The striking similarity in present-day attitudes is far more significant than their possibly differing historical derivation.

In their common resistance to politics the technicians who collaborate in the subsystem hope to bring about, among other desirable results, that close union of public and private decision-making which in France has recently been christened *économie concertée*.[58] Objectively they may multiply states within the state and thereby reconstitute the technicalities of a feudal system.[59] Should under such circumstances administrative creativity collapse, political decisions would amount to little more than an endorsement of the lowest common denominator of what the affected groups are willing to concede. It may be unavoidable that in any modern state the administrative stream is frequently threatened by "the embolism of off-setting groups." But a mentality which disdains politics and strives for technical perfection "rejects the very solvents that would reduce the obstruction." [60]

Then the creative impulse needed to serve the ends of a broader public policy must come from outside the subsystem, most likely from the political executive or from parliament and its parties. In the end this amounts everywhere to the problem which has been stated by an American author: "How much de-centralization can the political system stand before some redress in the form

57 Cf. Spiro, *op. cit.*, p. 340.

58 F. Bloch-Lainé, *A la Recherche d'une "Economie Concertée"* (Paris, 1959). The author is however fully aware of the technocratic dangers inherent in such a constellation.

59 Cf. M. Waline, "Les résistances techniques de l'administration au pouvoir politique," *Politique et technique* (Paris: Presses Universitaires, 1958), p. 173.

60 Cf. E. Latham, *The Politics of Railroad Coordination, 1933–1936* (Cambridge, Mass.: Harvard University Press, 1959), p. 277.

of centralized power becomes necessary to maintain or re-establish the equilibrium of the system as an integrating unit?" [61]

Two opposite, though not necessarily mutually exclusive dangers arise. One might ask whether such redress will always be possible after bureaucracy and groups have been given near-unlimited opportunities for autonomous action. And after the equilibrium is re-established a government strong enough to check the deeply rooted neo-feudalism may at least in certain societies also be strong enough to destroy the freedom of all.

The ghost of Jean-Jacques has not been laid.

[61] A. Leiserson, *Parties and Politics* (New York: Alfred A. Knopf, 1959), p. 304.

Party Systems and
the Representation
of Social Groups

SEYMOUR M. LIPSET

. . . [One form of "sociological determinism" stresses] the influence of national value systems on specific institutions. This . . . determinism is properly subject to the criticism that it ignores ways in which men may change their society and its values by changing its structure. We know that men may modify their conditions of existence by changing the laws which govern them, a process which may be the first step on the road to changing values. . . .

In order to generalize about the significance of a nation's constitutional system in stabilizing its polity, we need concepts which permit us to distinguish the role played by the legal structure from the effect of various social forces within the polity. A step in this direction has been taken by Talcott Parsons.[1] He has argued that the polity can be seen as providing generalized leadership for the larger social system in setting and attaining collective goals, and that this is acknowledged by interested social groups who supply general-

"Party Systems and the Representation of Social Groups," Chapter 9 of *The First New Nation*, by Seymour M. Lipset, © 1963 by Seymour M. Lipset, Basic Books, Inc., Publishers, New York. Reprinted by permission of the author and publisher.

SEYMOUR M. LIPSET is Professor of Government and Social Relations, Harvard University. Prior to teaching at Harvard, he was at the University of California, Berkeley. Among his numerous publications are *Agrarian Socialism* (1950), *Union Democracy* (1956, with Martin Trow and James Coleman), *Social Mobility in Industrial Society* (1956, with Reinhard Bendix), *Political Man* (1960; MacIver Award, 1962), and *The First New Nation* (1963).

[1] Talcott Parsons, "Voting and the Equilibrium of the American Political System," in Eugene Burdick and Arthur Brodbeck (eds.), *American Voting Behavior* (Glencoe, Ill.: The Free Press, 1959), pp. 80–120; see also William Mitchell, *The American Polity* (New York: The Free Press, 1963).

ized support in the expectation of "a good life," as they understand it. Within this polity, a variety of social groups form and advocate the particular policies that eventually result in the specific decisions of public officers, which then become binding on all citizens. The competitive struggle within the elite, sometimes for generalized but usually for specific support, gives those outside the authority structure *access* to political power.

This process works through the representation system.[2] It is given shape by those institutional practices which have been developed in democratic societies — notably party systems and interest organizations — to facilitate interchange between authority and the spontaneous groupings of society. This internal differentiation produces its own power structure and its own problems of integration which within limits may also affect the stability of the polity.

Within the representative system, some of the aspirations of the subgroups in the society are transformed into demands; these demands are then killed, compromised, or magnified into issues that are fed into the authority system as party policies or as the detailed recommendations of interest groups. Inchoate loyalties are turned into organized support. Thus the system provides grist for the political mill and also some of the power that drives it, depending upon how far the polity derives its effectiveness and legitimacy from organized support.

On the other hand, the representative system also receives information and public policy commitments from the authority structure wherein decisions are reached and implemented. These in turn shape the demands within the system, and legitimate the leadership and domination. This "input" from the side of authority may be general (political leadership at various levels, party discipline) or specific (electoral laws, regulation of the lobby), suppressing some demands, raising others into issues, and enforcing compromise. Into the social base the political system puts the political education of citizens and the political consciousness of groups. Whether or not these have consequences that are functional for the polity as a whole depends largely upon the form and working of the representative structure.

Viewed in this way, representation is neither simply a means of political adjustment to social pressures nor an instrument of manipulation. It may contribute to the maintenance or dissolution of primary ties, to the perception of common or diverse interests, to the socialization or alienation of elites, to the effectiveness or feebleness of the polity in attaining societal goals, and to the political unity or incoherence of society as a whole. This chapter will consider some aspects of the behavior of social groups in politics, taking into account the political alternatives which face the electorates of different countries, with special reference to the ways in which various party systems organize and affect their social bases. It is not primarily concerned with the *differentials* between power wielded by various social groups, nor will economic variables be given

[2] For a comprehensive summary of definitions, see John A. Fairlie, "The Nature of Political Representation," *The American Political Science Review*, 34 (1940), pp. 236–248, 456–466; for articles dealing with various aspects of the system, see Harry Eckstein and David E. Apter (eds.), *Comparative Politics* (New York: The Free Press, 1963), pp. 97–132.

much prominence. Its aim is to show how certain combinations of relationships between parties and social bases contribute to the possibility of stable and efficient government.

Parties are by far the most important part of the representative structure in complex democratic societies. Such societies show some variation in the salience of particular solidary groupings as the source of demands and support; but generally, under contemporary industrial conditions, the stratification system has been the prime source of sustained internal cleavage — classes have been the most important bases of political diversity.[3]

The character and number of the political parties in a country are perhaps the chief determinants of the extent to which the government acts through a stable system of interchanges between the key solidary groups and the political elite. Discussions of the causes and consequences of diverse party systems often turn upon the question of whether it is social structure or electoral arrangements that mainly determine the different types. Some argue that the character and number of parties flow almost directly from the social cleavages in a country; others have claimed that the electoral system in use — proportional representation or the single-member district plurality method — has been the main source of stability or instability in democracies. On the whole, there is a sham dispute. There is no reason to believe either that social cleavage creates political cleavage, or that political cleavage will give rise to social controversies. As Maurice Duverger has said: "The party system and the electoral system are two realities that are indissolubly linked, and even difficult sometimes to separate by analysis." [4]

SOCIAL STRUCTURE AND THE CHARACTER OF THE PARTY SYSTEM

The representative system may be said to have a singular influence on the stability of the polity only when the economic and social conditions for stable democracy . . . have been taken into account. Yet, paradoxically, these conditions affect the workings of the democracy precisely through their influence on the representative system. The ability of a democratic political system to

---

[3] They, of course, are far from being the only important such bases. Others, such as religious, ethnic, or linguistic groups, regions, and rural-urban groupings, have formed the basis for separate parties or differential backings for particular parties. For a detailed discussion of the way in which different groups have varied in support for parties in different democratic countries, see S. M. Lipset, *Political Man: The Social Bases of Politics* (Garden City, N.Y.: Doubleday & Co., 1960), pp. 228–282.

[4] Maurice Duverger, *Political Parties* (London: Methuen, 1954), p. 204. Duverger's book, however, is the best recent effort to demonstrate the causal effect of electoral systems. A sophisticated critique of Duverger and the general emphasis on electoral systems may be found in G. E. Lavau, *Partis politiques et réalités sociales* (Paris: Armand Colin, 1953); see also Aaron Wildavsky, "A Methodological Critique of Duverger's *Political Parties*," in Eckstein and Apter, *Comparative Politics*, pp. 368–375. There is a comprehensive statement of all the arguments for and against proportional representation in Alfred De Grazia, *Public and Republic* (New York: Alfred A. Knopf, 1951). A good general discussion of the theory of electoral systems is D. Hogan, *Election and Representation* (Cork: Cork University Press, 1945). Differing analyses and points of view are reprinted in Eckstein and Apter (eds.), *Comparative Politics*, pp. 247–324.

win or retain the support of different solidary groupings depends largely on whether all the major parties already accept democratic principles. If some parties reject the system, it may break down even if democracy is favored by a substantial majority.

The evidence seems quite clear that stable democracies are largely to be found in more well-to-do nations, where greater wealth is associated with patterns which reduce internal tension — for example, more equal distribution of income and of education, less emphasis on barriers between classes, and the existence of a relatively large middle class. In addition, the stability of democratic systems depends upon the extent to which they have retained or developed legitimacy, a "believed-in title to rule," for the political elite. Such legitimacy, as we have seen, has been most secure where the society could admit the lower strata to full citizenship and to the rights of participation in the economic and political systems, and could at the same time allow the traditionally privileged strata to keep their high status while yielding their power.

But if legitimacy and economic development define the boundaries within which political conflict occurs, there nevertheless remains great variation in the nature of party systems. Why do they take so many different forms? I have suggested that to some extent this depends upon the ways in which varying combinations of value orientations have permeated the attitudes toward stratification in a nation. The basic (and obvious) fact is that the more clear-cut the status demarcation lines in a country, the more likely there exist explicitly strata-oriented parties. The failure of Canada and the United States to develop a major working-class party, and the relative stability of their democratic systems, may be partially explained by the difficulty of developing a working-class political consciousness where no rigid status groups already existed to create a perception of common interests. On the European continent, workers were placed in a common class by the value system of the society, and they absorbed a political "consciousness of kind" from the social structure. Marxists did not have to teach European workers that they formed a class; the ascriptive values of the society did it for them.

In the English-speaking parts of the Commonwealth, Labour parties have been class oriented and class based, yet much less imbued with class feeling than those of continental Europe, as is shown by their early willingness to cooperate with bourgeois parties, and their consistent opposition to Marxist and revolutionary ideology. The absence of a base for intense class conflict is also affirmed by the bent toward a two-party system which has characterized their politics, since inherent in a two-party system is the need for cooperation among diverse strata. In Australia and New Zealand, this pattern may be explained, as it can in Canada and the United States, by the absence of feudal tradition. In Britain, the weakness of working-class extremism is often attributed to the country having borne the early tensions of industrialization before the rise of modern socialism, and, after the working-class movement had appeared, to its prosperity. On the other hand . . . the uniquely "open" and "responsible" character of the British aristocracy enabled it to retain power and influence late into the capitalist period, thus helping to soften the antagonism of the working classes to the state and to society.[5]

The great emphasis on status differentiation in Germany may also have been responsible for the large number of middle- and upper-class parties, each representing a distinct status group on a national or regional basis and each possessing its own ideology, which existed in pre-Nazi Germany.[6] Similarly, it has been suggested that the relative failure of the German Socialists to gain rural backing, and their weakness among the poorer urban working class, reflected the hostility of the better paid and more skilled workers, who dominated the movement, toward other depressed segments of the population such as the so-called *Lumpenproletariat* — a hostility which has not existed in other countries.[7] The split within the working class between Socialists and Communists in Weimar Germany was also partly due to this status consciousness of the skilled workers in the Social-Democratic Party, who left the more depressed sector to be recruited by the Communists. Robert Michels has pointed out how their sense of superiority was reflected in party literature, which attacked the Communists by arguing that their supporters were largely the shiftless *Lumpenproletariat*.[8] . . .

The discussion so far has sketched some of the conditions under which support will be available for *different* kinds of political leadership. But the number and nature of political parties, the claims they stake out, and the policies they advocate, do not result automatically from underlying social cleavages. Political systems possess a certain (varying) autonomy within the larger social system, and it is appropriate to ask how the restraints imposed by the political order itself affect the capacity of parties to provide generalized leadership in different countries.

SOCIAL STRUCTURE AND ELECTORAL SYSTEMS

Concern with formal constitutional provisions has generally been outside the province of political sociology. Sociologists tend to see party cleavages as reflections of an underlying structure, and hence, wittingly or not, frown on efforts to present the enacted rules of the game as key *causal* elements of a social structure. The sociologist's image of a social system, all of whose parts are interdependent, is at odds with the view of many political scientists, who believe that such seemingly minor differences in systems as variations in the

[5] Joseph Schumpeter, *Capitalism, Socialism and Democracy* (New York: Harper & Bros., 1947), pp. 134–139.

[6] Sigmund Neumann, *Die deutschen Parteien: Wesen und Wandel nach dem Kriege* (Berlin: Junder und Dunnhaupt, 1932); Theodor Geiger, *Die soziale Schichtung des deutschen Volkes* (Stuttgart: Ferdinand Enke, 1932), p. 79.

[7] See Robert Michels, "Die deutschen Sozialdemokratie, I: Parteimitgliedschaft und soziale Zusammensetzung," *Archiv für Sozialwissenschaft und Sozialpolitik*, 26 (1906), pp. 512–513; Robert Lowie, *Toward Understanding Germany* (Chicago: University of Chicago Press, 1954), p. 138. For detailed evidence that the contemporary German Social-Democratic Party remains weak among the less skilled, a pattern which remains almost unique among left parties, see Lipset, *Political Man*, pp. 240–241.

[8] Robert Michels, *Sozialismus und Fascismus I* (Karlsruhe: G. Braun, 1925), pp. 78–79.

way in which officials are elected can lead to stability or instability. An examination of comparative politics suggests that the political scientists are right, in that electoral laws determine the nature of the party system as much as any other structural variable.

The available evidence gathered together by political scientists such as E. E. Schattschneider, F. A. Hermens, Maurice Duverger, and many others indicates that proportional representation encourages the appearance or continuance of more relatively large parties than does the plurality system, in which the candidate receiving the most votes in an electoral unit is elected. Wherever we find a two-party system working (wherever the usual situation is the alternating control of government by one of two parties, with an over-all majority of representatives) we find also an electoral system which debars from representation in government those parties which cannot win a plurality of votes in a geographical election district. On the other hand, every country which uses proportional representation has four or more parties represented in the legislature and, except in Norway, Sweden, and Ireland in recent decades, absolute parliamentary majorities of one party have been extremely rare.

If enough cases existed for analysis, the following rank-order correlation might be found between electoral systems and the number of political parties: presidential system with single-member districts and one plurality election — two parties; parliamentary system with single-member districts and one plurality election — tendency to two parties; parliamentary system with single-member districts and alternative ballot or run-off (second) election — tendency to many parties; proportional representation — many parties. . . .

The motives underlying the electorate's refusal to sustain third parties, in systems where the candidate with the most votes is elected and where third parties are effectively barred from representation, have been analyzed in detail in the numerous studies of electoral systems, and I will not discuss them here. Essentially, polarization between two parties is maintained by those factors which lead people to see a third party vote as a "wasted vote." [9]

PARTY SYSTEMS AND THE BASES
OF SOCIAL CLEAVAGE

The interrelated effects of electoral systems and social cleavages may be seen in a comparison of the party systems in different parts of the British Commonwealth, in the United States, and in France.

There is general recognition that stable two-party government works best in Great Britain. Members of Parliament are elected in single-member constituencies in which one factor — class position — is the basic source of political difference.[10] Differences based on regions, religious or ethnic allegiances,

[9] See Duverger, *Political Parties*, pp. 224–228, 246–250; and E. E. Schattschneider, *Party Government* (New York: Rinehart and Co., 1942), pp. 80–84.

[10] "British politics are almost wholly innocent of those issues which cross the social lines in other lands, for example, race, nationality, religion, town and country interests, regional interest, or the conflict between authoritarian and parliamentary methods." See John Bonham, *The Middle Class Vote* (London: Faber and Faber, 1954), pp. 194–195; and Leslie Lipson, "The Two-Party System in British Politics," *American Political Science Review*, 47 (1953), pp. 337–358.

urban-rural conflicts, or past historical feuds are unimportant or affect groups too small to organize on their own behalf. But if two-party government presents its best and simplest face in Britain, multi-party government has created the most difficult and complicated conditions in France. Until the Gaullist presidential system began to press the French parties together, France had at least six important political groupings, in addition to some minor ones. For many decades it has been divided between clericals and anti-clericals, supporters and opponents of a planned economy, and supporters and opponents of parliamentary government, with a few rural-urban and regional cleavages as well. Table [I] shows the ways these differences have been reflected in French party life during the period from 1955 to 1963.[11]

Table [I]

Overlapping of Cleavages in France *

CLERICAL			
PLANNED ECONOMY		FREE ECONOMY	
Parliamentary	*Anti-Parliamentary*	*Parliamentary*	*Anti-Parliamentary*
M.R.P.		Independents	U.N.R.
(Catholics)	(left Gaullists)	(conservatives)	(Gaullists)
ANTI-CLERICAL			
PLANNED ECONOMY		FREE ECONOMY	
Parliamentary	*Anti-Parliamentary*	*Parliamentary*	*Anti-Parliamentary*
Socialists	Communists	Radicals	Poujadists †

* Adapted from a somewhat similar diagram in Duverger, *Political Parties* (London: Methuen, 1954), p. 232.
† Now practically dead.

Before De Gaulle created a presidency directly elected by the people, France appeared to be a country whose social fragmentation dictated the need for a multi-party system, whatever electoral laws were in force. The fact remains, however, that the various parliamentary electoral systems in use throughout most of the history of the Third, Fourth, and Fifth republics encouraged the creation or perpetuation of small parties. The experiences of Britain and France, standing near the extremes of stable and unstable government, might suggest that the nature of group differences is the key to the number of parties in a system; yet even for these nations this conclusion may be questioned. Since

[11] The table, of course, oversimplifies present divisions. Almost no political group in France is actually for a "free economy." The Gaullist government has continued and even extended the comprehensive system of planning begun under the Fourth Republic. This system, however, is a voluntary one; private industry need not conform, though the state has extensive powers through its ownership of banks, insurance companies, and many industries. Communist and Gaullist "anti-parliamentary" positions are quite different. The first favors a dictator; the second, an "American-type" president.

the development of adult suffrage, Britain has never had a *pure* two-party system. In the late nineteenth century there was a strong Irish third party; before World War I, four parties were represented in the Commons: the Liberals, the Conservatives, the Irish, and Labour; between 1918 and 1931 three major parties were represented; and since then the Liberal Party has remained a serious electoral force even though the plurality system minimizes its strength in Parliament.[12]

French political history offers striking examples of the ways in which formal political institutions may decisively affect political cleavage, and therefore the stability of the democratic system. Despite deep-rooted social tensions and lack of consensus on fundamental political, religious, and economic issues, the Third Republic's electoral system diverted considerable support from the anti-democratic extremists. Its double ballot effectively stopped the French Communist Party from becoming a major force during this period. For after an auspicious start in 1921, supported by a majority of the former Socialist Party and controlling its principal newspaper, *L'Humanité*, it lost ground seemingly because it was unable to elect members to the Chamber. As a revolutionary party opposed to constitutional government, it would not combine with other parties for the decisive second ballot, so that many of its potential voters obviously returned to the Socialist fold. Thus in 1928, the Communists secured 11 per cent of the vote in the first ballot, but only 14 out of 600 seats. In the following election of 1932, held in the depths of the depression, the Communist first-ballot vote dropped to 8 per cent, and it elected less than 2 per cent of the representatives. Almost half the Communist first-ballot supporters backed candidates of other parties on the second ballot, though the Communists did not withdraw any candidates. Even Communist party discipline and the worst depression in history could not induce many voters to "waste" their ballots. Similarly, Maurice Duverger notes "the complete impossibility"

---

[12] For a detailed report on the issues and facts involved, see D. E. Butler, *The Electoral System in Britain, 1918–1951* (New York: Oxford University Press, 1953). Though many argue from historical evidence that the British two-party system derives from particular national characteristics, since two parties or tendencies preceded the introduction of the present single-member constituency in the mid-nineteenth century, this argument also may be questioned. G. E. Lavau, *Partis politiques et réalités sociales,* has pointed out that the House of Commons had unstable majorities, with members shifting their support from government to opposition throughout much of the nineteenth century. Duverger contends that in France itself the contemporary complex political substructure was built "upon the fundamental conflict which dominated the nineteenth century, that between conservatives and liberals. . . . The principal actors were a landowning aristocracy, bound to monarchical principles . . . and, opposed to this aristocracy, an industrial, commercial and intellectual bourgeoisie, attracted to the principles of political liberty. . . . The first phase in the moulding of the prevailing spirit in modern Europe ended with the appearance and development of the socialist parties. . . . Between 1900 and 1914, the bipartisan tendency which had dominated the preceding century was replaced everywhere by a swing towards tripartisanship; the 'conservative-liberal' duo now changed to a 'conservative-liberal-socialist' trio." Maurice Duverger, "Public Opinion and Political Parties in France," *American Political Science Review,* 46 (1952), p. 1070. See also Club Jean Moulin, *L'État et le citoyen* (Paris: Éditions du Seuil, 1961), pp. 249–253, 325–343.

for fascist and right-wing extremist movements "to obtain any representation in parliament," although there were many strong fascist groups during the 1930's.[13]

The Communists became a major force in French politics only after they pretended to give up their opposition to parliamentary government, and formed the Popular Front coalition with the Radicals and Socialists in 1936. This enabled them to increase their first-ballot percentage to 15.6, and their representation in the Chamber from 11 to 72.[14]

But if the Third Republic demonstrated how electoral rules may punish and inhibit parties which oppose the system, the Fourth Republic showed how different rules may facilitate the ruin of democracy by nourishing such parties.[15] Throughout its history, the Fourth Republic employed different versions of proportional representation. Its last Parliament, elected in 1956, was hampered by the presence of 150 Communists and 50 Poujadists. The latter, who secured about 10 per cent of the vote, could probably have elected no candidates under the double ballot with single-member constituencies. The Fifth Republic, having returned to that system, elected only ten Communists and one Poujadist to its first Chamber and 40 Communists to its second. The Communist gains between 1958 and 1962 were largely a result of an informal electoral alliance with the Socialists. And for the first time in French history, the combination of a strong presidential system and the absence of proportional representation has given one tendency, the Gaullists, a parliamentary majority.

The United States and Canada offer a still more complex picture of the way in which party systems can be affected by the interrelationship between social cleavages and methods of election. For though two-party politics have predominated at the national level in both countries, it is clear that their solidarity structure is in some ways more like that of France than that of Britain. Both are divided among class, ethnic, religious, and regional lines, and while the chief issues for groups like the southern whites or the French Canadians tend to separate them from the rest of the nation, internally they remain sharply divided over non-ethnic questions.

It seems likely that if the United States had ever adopted proportional rep-

---

[13] *Political Parties*, pp. 319–320; see also F. A. Hermens, *Europe between Democracy and Anarchy* (Notre Dame, Ind.: University of Notre Dame Press, 1951), pp. 41–44, and Club Jean Moulin, *L'État et le citoyen*, pp. 349–350.

[14] For a detailed account of the events leading up to this election as well as an analysis of the vote, see Georges Dupeux, *Le Front populaire et les élections de 1936* (Paris: Armand Colin, 1959).

[15] "It is especially important, in order to understand what the fundamental political problems of France actually are, to investigate why the state for too many years has seemed so completely powerless to hold the antagonisms and the divisions between the parties within reasonable bounds and to make the divergent forces act in concert for the general welfare. This raises the question of political institutions, the most important problem facing France. *The present difficulties in this sphere stem from the fact that the political institutions that were adopted in 1946 in no way satisfy the requirements of the economic, social, and political situation. . . .*" François Goguel, *France under the Fourth Republic* (Ithaca, N.Y.: Cornell University Press, 1952), p. 146. (Emphasis mine.)

resentation or even the second ballot run-off, it would have developed several main parties, such as the following: 1) a labor party, based on urban workers and perhaps on ethnic minorities outside the South; 2) a northern conservative party, based on the urban middle class and the higher-status ethnic and religious groups; 3) a southern conservative party, comparable in support to the *ante-bellum* southern Whigs and Constitutional Unionists, i.e., the urban middle classes, and the more well-to-do rural whites; 4) a southern populist party, based on the lower white strata comparable to those who backed the Jacksonian Democrats in the 1830's and 1840's, Breckenridge and the secessionist Democrats in the election of 1860, and various "populist" parties and agrarian factions of the Democrats in the late nineteenth century; and 5) a farmer's party, based on rural elements outside the South. There would probably also have been a number of smaller parties from time to time.

Such differentiation has been prevented, not only by the disadvantages which the American presidential system lays on small parties, as discussed above, but also by the peculiar device of the party primary. This arrangement, by which different factions within the party may compete in state-conducted, intra-party contests to determine party candidates and officials, permits the interests and values of different groups, which elsewhere would give rise to separate parties, to be expressed within the major parties. First, the various groups have been forced by the electoral system to identify with one or the other of the two major blocs on whatever basis of division matters most to them; [16] then their differences are fought out within each party in the primaries, although they may often still lead to cross-party alliances in Congress afterward.

Few observers have been willing to recognize how comparable are the social bases for multiple parties in France and the United States, and how far the difference between them in political stability has been due to varying constitutional structures. The French two-ballot system may be regarded as a functional equivalent to the American primary elections. In both cases, different tendencies may compete in various ways up to the decisive final election. Thus, in most elections of the Third Republic, "at the first ballot few candidates could obtain an absolute majority, so that at this stage there was no fear of splitting the vote and no deterrent to 'splinter parties'; but at the second this fear became as effective as in Britain. *Most constituencies then had a straight fight between a candidate of the Right and one of the Left.*" [17]

[16] The one other country which I know of that has a system akin to the American primaries is Uruguay, the most stable democracy in Latin America. In Uruguay, the various factions within the two major parties may each nominate a presidential candidate. On election day, the voters choose the man they prefer. When votes are counted, the party which has a majority, counting the votes of *all* its presidential candidates, wins the election, and the candidate of that party who received more votes than any other one of the party is elected president. In other words, Uruguay combines the primary and the final election on the same ballot.

[17] Philip Williams, *Politics in Post-War France* (New York: Longmans, Green and Co., 1954), p. 310. (Emphasis mine.) This book contains an excellent discussion of the nature and effects of the French electoral systems. For a detailed description of the way in which the double ballot worked in the first elections of the Fifth Republic in 1958, see Philip Williams and Martin Harrison, "France 1958," in D. E. Butler (ed.), *Elections Abroad* (New York: St. Martins, 1960), pp. 13–90.

Under the Third Republic, the electoral alliances which gave decisive majorities to the Left or Right would always break down in parliament, hence the constant reshuffling of cabinets. The common assumption that these coalitions were so fragile because they tried to harmonize incompatible views and interests — such as those of the Radicals, as the party of small business, with those of the Socialists, as the workers' party — overlooks the fact that these differences have been no sharper than some *within* the American parties. The divergencies on domestic issues between conservative southern Democrats and left-liberal northern Democrats, or on foreign affairs between Republicans from the provincial Midwest and Republicans from the metropolitan centers of the East, with their close ties to international big business, are fully as great. The American party factions have been held together largely by the presidential system. Thus, the changing congressional majorities on questions which cut across party lines are comparable to the shifts in the Chamber as new issues were taken up. Since in America this cannot change the party in control of the executive, however, there has been continuity of executive action and also a substantial amount of party loyalty in important congressional votes, as David Truman has demonstrated.[18] And the "American" elements introduced into the French constitution by General De Gaulle seem to be having comparable effects on the party system there.

Canada is perhaps an even more interesting case of interaction of the various elements which have been discussed. Its social structure and bases for political division are complex and comparable to the American and French. It retains, however, the British electoral and parliamentary system, which requires disciplined parliamentary action and does not permit the American practices of cross-party alignments in the House, of ideological divergencies between local party machines, or the resolution by public primary elections of differences within the parties. Whenever a Canadian region, class, ethnic group, or province comes into serious conflict with its party of traditional allegiance, it must either change over to the other party, with which it may be in even greater disagreement on other issues, or form a new "third" party. The result of combining this social diversity with a rigid constitutional structure has been the regular rise and fall of relatively powerful "third" parties. Every single Canadian province, except Prince Edward Island and New Brunswick, has been governed for some time since World War I by a "third" party. At least three such parties, the Progressives in the 1920's and, since 1933, Social Credit (monetary reformers supported by farmers and small businessmen) and the socialist Cooperative Commonwealth Federation (CCF), renamed in 1961 the New Democratic Party, have had significant strength in a number of provinces. Nationalist parties, often at odds with one another, have arisen in Quebec; one of them, the *Union Nationale*, governed the province almost unbrokenly from 1936 to 1957. Most recently, in 1962, Social Credit, which was almost non-

[18] David Truman, *The Congressional Party: A Case Study* (New York: John Wiley & Sons, 1959); see also Duncan MacRae, Jr., *Dimensions of Congressional Voting* (Berkeley: University of California Press, 1958); and V. O. Key, Jr., *Politics, Parties and Pressure Groups* (New York: Thos. Y. Crowell, 1958), p. 729.

existent in Quebec in the 1958 election, won twenty-six constituencies in the national election in that province, and it retained most of this strength in the 1963 election. The rise and fall of these parties, mainly at the provincial level, are not the result of any general discontent in Canada, but largely of the inter-action between constitutional arrangements and social and economic divisions.[19]

Although the Canadian two-party system has repeatedly broken down, it has been able, especially on the national level, to reabsorb most of the rebellious elements, since the single-member plurality method of election necessarily represses minorities. At the provincial level, however, it has been much easier for them to survive by becoming one of the two major *local* parties. Unlike the situation in the United States, in which state and presidential elections are often on the same ballot, in Canada this never occurs. Hence, voters are not pressed to bring their national and provincial party preferences into line.

South Africa, which also combines British constitutional procedure with complex internal bases of cleavage, has exhibited the same rapid rise and fall of minor parties as Canada. Within the limits of the dominant ethnic divisions, other sources of conflict still exist. Thus for long periods the Afrikaners were divided into two parties; today they are united in the National Party, but the English are split. In addition to the old but sharply declining Labour party, a number of parties, mainly English, have come into being in the last decade as splinters from the United Party. All these minor parties have met, in an ag-gravated form, the same difficulties as the Canadian.[20]

In New Zealand, the two non-socialist parties merged after Labour had risen to a position in which it seemed able to win a three-cornered fight. Social Credit has shown on at least two occasions that it could get the support of about 10 per cent of the New Zealand electorate, but, being unable to win seats, it has failed to sustain any permanent strength.[21] In Australia, the two major non-socialist parties — the Country and Liberal parties — have not merged, but generally follow a policy of exchanging seats and refraining from competition.[22]

[19] See S. M. Lipset, "Democracy in Alberta," *Canadian Forum*, 34 (1954), pp. 175–177 and 196–198. For British Columbia, where Social Credit rose from no seats to the provincial government in one election, see H. F. Angus, "The British Columbia Election, 1952," *Canadian Journal of Economics and Political Science*, 18 (1952), pp. 518–525; and Margaret Ormsby, *British Columbia: A History* (Vancouver: Macmillan, 1958), pp. 477–489.

[20] See Gwendolen M. Carter, *The Politics of Inequality, South Africa Since 1948* (New York: Frederick A. Praeger, 1958); for a further report see R. R. Farquharson, "South Africa 1958," in D. E. Butler (ed.), *Elections Abroad* (New York: St. Martins, 1960), pp. 229–275.

[21] Peter Campbell, "Politicians, Public Servants, and the People in New Zealand, I," *Political Studies*, 3 (1955), pp. 196–197.

[22] Although the Country and Liberal parties usually do not run against each other and act, in effect, electorally as the rural and urban wing of the non-socialist party, the continued existence of two such parties is facilitated by the fact that Australia has adopted the preferential ballot system with the single-member constituency. Under this system voters list the order of preference for all candidates on the ballot. Thus when there are Liberal and Country candidates in the same constituency, a Liberal voter will mark the Country candidate as his number two choice, and Country party supporters will do the same for the Liberals. This system has also encouraged occa-sional splits from the Labour Party, since minority party candidates can pick up first

Similar electoral alliances took place in some of the Scandinavian countries before the introduction of proportional representation.

Conversely, in one former dominion of the British Crown, Eire, which has a relatively simple basis for political cleavage, the perpetuation of proportional representation ever since the birth of the Irish Republic in 1922 has meant the continued existence of at least five parties. Only one party, Fianna Fáil, has been able to govern without a coalition under these conditions. The second largest party, Fine Gael, which is somewhat more conservative, can hope to form a government only with the help of minor and often more leftist parties, such as Labour and the Republicans.[23]

Had Eire adopted the British election system, it would now no doubt have a stable two-party system and cabinets as responsible as the United Kingdom. This failure, like some other Irish difficulties, must be attributed to the English, because when yielding power in southern Ireland, they insisted on a system of proportional representation to ensure representation of Protestant and other more pro-Commonwealth minorities. Fianna Fáil, as the dominant party, has tried hard to change the electoral system, but as in other countries the smaller parties oppose such changes for fear that the single-member plurality district system would weaken their electoral position. The result is that the need for "inter-party" governments has led to periodic breakdowns in the traditional pattern of responsible cabinet government.[24]

Similarly, in Israel, another state once governed by Great Britain, independence was followed by the continuance of the system of proportional representation previously used in elections to the council of the Jewish Agency, the dominant pre-independence organ of the Zionist community. Hence, in this immigrant society formed by men from many states and cultures, over thirty different parties have taken part in the elections. There have been at least five different socialist parties, excluding the Communists, represented in the Knesset, and some half dozen religious parties. Basically, however, the Israeli political structure consists of three groups: the socialist parties, the largest of which, the Mapai, has about 40 per cent of the vote, while the others have between 10 and 15 per cent; the non-socialist secular parties, which range from liberal to conservative (in the American sense of the terms), and which poll about 30 to 35 per cent of the vote; and the religious parties, which poll from 10 to 15 per cent and are divided fairly equally between pro- and anti-socialist groups. A single-member district plurality system would probably create a two-party system, socialist versus conservative, with each party bidding for the support of

---

votes without these votes being permanently lost to the major party backed by such protest voters. The Democratic Labor Party, a right-wing split from Labour, has urged its followers to vote Liberal as their second preference as a means of pressing the Labour Party to accept their terms. See J. D. B. Miller, *Australian Government and Politics* (London: Duckworth, 1954), pp. 85–86.

[23] See Enid Lakeman and James D. Lambert, *Voting in Democracies* (London: Faber and Faber, 1955), pp. 223–230.

[24] Basil Chubb, "Cabinet Government in Ireland," *Political Studies*, 3 (1955), p. 272.

the religious. This solution is favored by Mapai, the largest party in the country; but, as in Ireland, it is opposed by the others, since none of them feels certain of survival without proportional representation. An Israeli social research institute, in a study of the effects of electoral systems on national life, has strongly urged a change in the Israeli system.

> In sum: while the present system of proportional representation aggravates existing social evils in the Israeli society, i.e., absolute rule of central party machines, deepening social divisions and the perpetuation of factional fanaticism, the system of constituency election is designed to counteract and finally to eliminate them, by weakening party power at the centre, placing emphasis on common, integrative, cohesive elements in our society and encouraging the growth of tolerance, fellow-feeling and social compromise. . . .
>
> The condition for constructive democratic life in the country becomes largely a function of the development of social forces which can combat and counteract these negative features [toward intense destructive conflict]. And the web of social institutions is the most potent powerful instrument at our disposal to accomplish this end.[25]

Maurice Duverger has described the conscious and successful effort made in Belgium to prevent a two-party system reasserting itself when the Socialists rose to second place, displacing the anti-clerical Liberal opposition, after the adoption of universal manhood suffrage in 1893. By the next election in 1898, the Liberals had declined to parliamentary insignificance with only thirteen seats. Rather than see the Liberals disappear, which would have meant, eventually, a Socialist government, the Catholics, who were then in power, introduced proportional representation and thus preserved the Liberals as a major third party.[26] The anti-clerical vote has almost always been above 50 per cent, but the Socialists have never reached 40 per cent, while the Liberals have constantly secured between 10 and 15 per cent.[27]

The strain between the institutionalization of specific social cleavages in a multi-party structure and a plurality electoral system is aggravated by the distorted representation which usually results. The major party whose support is most evenly distributed throughout the country tends to be over-represented, and sometimes the largest single party does not win the most seats. In Canada between 1935 and 1957 the Liberal party dominated Parliament with overbearing majorities, though it had a majority of the electorate on only one occasion.[28] Similarly, in India the Congress Party has over 75 per cent of the seats in the House with less than 50 per cent of the vote, while the Communist Party ruled the Indian state of Kerala for one term with a legislative

25 Beth Hillel (Society for Social Research in Israel), *Electoral Reform in Israel* (Tel Aviv: Beth Hillel Publications, 1953), pp. 24, 26.

26 Duverger, *Political Parties*, pp. 246–247.

27 Felix E. Oppenheim, "Belgium: Party Cleavage and Compromise," in Sigmund Neumann (ed.), *Modern Political Parties* (Chicago: University of Chicago Press, 1958), p. 167.

28 Gwendolen M. Carter, "The Commonwealth Overseas: Variations on a British Theme," *ibid.*, p. 104.

majority based on 35 per cent of the electorate.[29] In 1945, the British Labour Party took over with an overwhelming majority of 146 seats in the House of Commons, and nationalized a number of industries, despite the fact that over half of the electorate had voted for non-socialist candidates. Conversely, the three British Conservative governments since 1951 have governed with parliamentary majorities although the country had given a majority of its votes to Labour and the Liberals.[30]

Essentially, the evidence suggests that whatever potential cleavages exist in the social structure, there is a fundamental incompatibility between a multi-party system and a plurality method of election; where the two co-exist, the instability is ultimately resolved by a change to one of the following situations: 1) a change in the electoral system to proportional representation, which preserves declining parties and facilitates the growth of new ones; 2) an arrangement by which different parties continue to exist, but support each other in more or less permanent alliances; 3) mergers between parties which re-create a two-party situation, as has occurred a number of times with American third parties; or 4) the elimination over time of the weaker parties and a return to a two-party system, as has occurred in various countries of the Commonwealth and in the United States.

CONSEQUENCES OF THE DIFFERENT SYSTEMS

A number of consequences for the nature of representation and the stability of democracy have been attributed to the two-party and the multi-party systems.

In a two-party system, both parties aim at securing a majority. Hence, they must seek support among groups which may be preponderantly loyal to their opponents and must avoid accentuating too heavily the interests of their customary supporters. Elections become occasions for seeking the broadest possible base of support by convincing divergent groups of their common interests. The system thus encourages compromise and the incorporation into party values of those general elements of consensus upon which the polity rests. For similar reasons the system encourages emphasis by both parties upon material interests (concessions and patronage) as against a stress upon ideal interests, thus reducing ideological conflict.[31] The "out" party can always realistically aspire to gain office within a few years, and this has the effect of stifling exaggerated commitments on its part to ideal or ideological goals which may gain votes but embarrass office holders, and it also reinforces the adherence of the opposition to the "rules of the game." The weakness of ideology that is inherent in two-

[29] Avery Leiserson, *Parties and Politics* (New York: Alfred A. Knopf, 1958), p. 286.

[30] Detailed discussion of the relation between votes and seats in the British system can be found in R. B. McCallum, *The British General Election of 1945* (New York: Oxford University Press, 1947), pp. 277–292; for a table giving votes and seats in British elections since 1900, see Samuel Beer, "Great Britain: From Governing Elite to Organized Mass Parties," in Sigmund Neumann (ed.), *Modern Political Parties* (Chicago: University of Chicago Press, 1958), p. 57.

[31] See Carl Friedrich, *Constitutional Government and Democracy* (Boston: Ginn and Co., 1950), pp. 416–417; Parsons, "Voting and the Equilibrium of the American Political System," *op. cit.*

party systems has the further consequences of reducing intense concern with particular issues dividing the parties, and sharpening the focus on party leaders. The plebiscitary nature of electoral struggles in two-party systems is largely an effect of the system itself.

In a multi-party system, where parties do not hope to gain a majority, they usually seek to win the greatest possible electoral support from a limited base. They therefore stress the interests of that base and the cleavages which set it apart from other groups in society. The party's function as a representative of a group is separated from the function of integrating the group in the body politic, which requires a stress on similarities with others and commitments to them.[32] The multi-party system with proportional representation in fact substitutes the interest group (or group of common believers) for the territorial unit as the basis of representation.[33] The small size of many parties and the absence of a need in most multi-party systems for compromise at the electoral level enhances the ideological content of the conflict. This divisiveness encouraged by a multi-party system is perpetuated by the tendency of most parties to attack most virulently those with whom they have most in common and with whom they thus compete for a similar vote; this magnifies the differences between them.

The two-party system helps to maintain the commitment of the entire electorate to the system itself, rather than to the regime, and encourages the elector to devote his efforts to the quite clear-cut task of replacing the incumbents with their traditional opponents. The necessity for coalition government in most multi-party systems — where the lesser parties wield so disproportionate an influence that election results may scarcely affect the composition of the government — deprives the elector of the feeling that he is able to turn out leaders who have forfeited his confidence, and weakens his commitment to the system as a whole.

There are, however, conditions under which a two-party system is *less* conducive to the preservation of democratic order than is a multi-party system. The two-party system works best where it is based on an elaborate, cross-cutting solidarity structure, in which men and groups are pulled in different directions only by their diverse roles and interests. Wherever the solidarity structure is polarized by class, race, or religion, and the political lines follow those of social cleavage, a two-party system may intensify internal conflict rather than help to integrate the society. For example, the first Austrian republic (1919–1934) was largely a two-party system, but one which was divided along the interrelated lines of religion, class, and region. The parties represented two almost completely separate cultural units, and the civil war which followed was a nearly

[32] See F. A. Hermens, *The Representative Republic* (Notre Dame, Ind.: University of Notre Dame Press, 1958), p. 201.

[33] "Electoral procedures based on territorial . . . [as distinct from 'representation through interest-groups'] is [sic] precisely the technique for the organic integration of the whole. As a matter of principle the individual delegate represents the entire area. The ensuing separation into parties according to *political* tendencies implies then only differences of belief concerning the means by which the welfare of the nation is to be achieved." Georg Simmel, *The Web of Group Affiliations* (Glencoe, Ill.: The Free Press, 1955), p. 194.

inevitable consequence of the system.[34] Similarly, in Italy today the lines of division between the Christian Democrats and the Communist opposition are such as to reduce consensus rather than increase it. In South Africa, a division into two parties largely based on two ethnic groups, the Afrikaner Nationalists and English United Party, is destructive of national unity and democratic norms.[35]

In general, where the class struggle is superimposed upon a conflict between religion and irreligion, or between different ethnic groups — wherever opposing groups see elections as a fight between good and evil, so that conversion from one political faith to another is almost impossible — a two-party system is more destructive of political stability than is one which center parties can mediate between extreme opponents. Consequently, though it may be validly argued that a two-party system makes for a more stable and effective democratic polity than a multi-party one, this is true only if both actors in the system accord a certain degree of legitimacy to each other; each party must be willing to view the other as an acceptable alternative government. . . .

The differences between the two types of party system must be tested also for their capacity to provide generalized leadership in return for generalized support, to serve as the interchange mechanism between the solidary groups of society and the wielders of political power. The experiences of Western industrial society suggest that, in general, a two-party system is much the better adapted to these needs.

The ability of the two-party system to provide for generalized leadership is closely linked to the fact that one party always represents the government and actually rules the country, so that the party in power *temporarily* becomes identical with the State. Both parties are organized to be able to take full responsibility, at home and abroad, for the conduct of the nation's affairs; the opposition is always conscious of its role as the government of tomorrow, and in order to be able to *govern* it must look beyond electoral victory to its chance of inspiring at least some confidence among the supporters of the other party. Insofar as the party itself overtly represents interests, these are represented *within* the party and disciplined by the necessity of being able to govern in the na-

[34] For a detailed description of the system and an analysis of the events leading to the downfall of the first Austrian republic, see Charles Gulick, *Austria: From Hapsburg to Hitler* (Berkeley, Calif.: University of California Press, 1948). A recent study of elections in the first and second republics demonstrates that the second one is genuinely different from the first in that the two major parties, though based on the same groups as before 1934, have much more support today within "opposition strata" than their predecessors did. Thus the conservative People's party is much stronger today among workers, residents of Vienna, Protestants, and irreligious people, than was the pre-1934 Christian Social party. Conversely, the Socialists, though weaker in Vienna, are much stronger in the outlying provinces than earlier, and they have considerably increased their vote among peasants. Paralleling the growth of the two parties within segments once overwhelmingly opposed to them has been a sharp decline in ideological cleavage. The conservative party is no longer a Christian or Catholic party, and the Socialists have dropped their adherence to Marxist doctrine. See Walter B. Simon, "Politische Ethik und Politische Struktur," *Kölner Zeitschrift für Soziologie und Sozialpsychologie*, 11 (1959), pp. 445–459.

[35] Carter, *op. cit.*

tional interest; the same applies to the party's relationship with pressure groups. A party, in these circumstances, is above all a way of organizing citizens to take part in *public* affairs. It is clearly damaging to a party, especially to the party in power, if it appears in a light where its opponents can accuse it of obvious favoritism to a group of party supporters. Further, since the legitimacy of a party rests ultimately upon its actual or potential effectiveness as a *national* government, there is strong pressure on both parties in a two-party system to reduce or eliminate ideology as a basis for political decision. The access of a given party to the full power of the state is quite straightforward so long as almost everyone is convinced that it will use that power to solve problems from a national standpoint.

In contrast to the two-party system, where each party tries to appear as a plausible representative of the whole society, multi-party systems have been mainly based upon the premise that a party should consciously represent the private interests of a section of the population. Only the State, and no one party, can claim to represent the interests of the whole. Thus individuals are citizens, and enjoy public roles, in relation only to the State, not to the party; and patriotism tends to be found only in action which "transcends" party, rather than as a value which can infuse party action as such. As a result, bourgeois and peasant parties have tended to reflect rather than sublimate the *incivisme* of their constituents. Minority working-class parties have often regarded constitutionalism — the basis of any notion of public interest — as a matter of socially irrelevant technicalities, and parties of the right have been tempted to aspire to a position "above parties."

But while almost all minority parties in a multi-party system could ideologically reject responsibility for the political community at large, many have in fact found themselves wielding State power in coalition governments. The consequent divorce between party symbols and party actions for all who participate in coalitions, and the bargaining necessary to fill public offices and obtain parliamentary support, may lead to cynicism or to attitudes resembling that unmediated attachment to abstractions which, as Philip Selznick argues, is a source of irresponsibility, extremism, and manipulability in mass society.[36] These extreme manifestations have, of course, appeared in some multi-party systems only under conditions of stress. It seems likely, however, that multi-party systems accentuate the development of such dangerous traits, while two-party systems are better able to resist political and civic irresponsibility on the part of different solidary groups and their representatives.

While the two-party system has these great advantages, under certain conditions a multi-party system may produce a relatively permanent coalition cabinet which adequately reflects the main groupings of society and can effectively interchange leadership and support. In such systems all parties become, in a sense, "State parties." This development seems to have occurred in Switzerland and, to a lesser degree, in Austria, Uruguay, Benelux, and the Scandinavian countries. There is some reason to anticipate that the Swiss "solution" to the

[36] Philip Selznick, *The Organizational Weapon* (New York: McGraw-Hill Book Co., 1952), pp. 276–291

problem of multi-party government — the inclusion of all democratic parties in the cabinet, so that issues are fought out there as well as in the parliament — may spread to other countries as well.

CONCLUSION

Political sociologists tend to regard formal political devices as peripheral items, having little effect upon the main features of societies. One purpose of this chapter has been to distinguish between the more "natural" elements in the social structure, derivative from the value system . . . , which influence the political process and the enacted rules which help determine the nature of parties and of representation. As we have seen in the American example, constitutions and electoral systems are the outcome of particular decisions which may permanently affect the type of social system which a country develops. It is especially important to emphasize this at a time when men in various new nations are trying to set up democratic procedures and to foster an open society. For sociologists to treat formal political structures as epiphenomena is not only wrong from a theoretical point of view, but may also reinforce the appeal of a vulgar Marxism which would have democracy wait solely upon economic development. . . .

Wherever democracy has not been institutionalized, whether in the old states of Europe or the new states of Asia and Africa, it is important to recognize that particular political forms will not emerge automatically in response to developments in other parts of the social system.[37] Whether these states develop a stable interchange of leadership and support in a democratic framework also depends in part on the rules they adopt for their polities. The study of the social effects of diverse constitutional arrangements should remain a major concern for the student of politics and comparative institutions.

[37] For a detailed analysis of the factors which influence political forms in these societies, see Edward Shils, *Political Development in the New States* (The Hague: Mouton, 1962); see also S. N. Eisenstadt, "Sociological Aspects of Political Development in New States," in his *Essays on Sociological Aspects of Political and Economic Development* (The Hague: Mouton, 1961), pp. 9–53.

Introduction

In its traditional approach political science analyzes the structure of authority in terms of "established" institutions like government, the courts, the legislature, and others. The German sociologist Georg Simmel contrasted such "large social formations" with the vast number of less conspicuous interactions, without which formal institutions could not exist. The phrase "political sociology" embodies this contrast in that the adjective still reminds us of political *institutions*, while the noun refers to innumerable, unnamed *interactions* among men in society.[1] When sociologists focus attention on the interactions among officials, or between officials and some segment of the public, we should be aware (as the previous section suggests) that they take the institutional "structure of authority" as given. The selections we have chosen illustrate how these two emphases can be combined by examining interaction patterns with due regard for the institutional contexts in which they occur.

The essay by Max Weber is taken from a longer political pamphlet originally published as a series of newspaper articles during World War I (in 1917). The author gives a passionately political analysis of governmental practices in Imperial Germany by using an ideal contrast between bureaucrat and politician. The official must exercise his judgment and skill, but his duty is to place these at the service of higher authority; ultimately he is responsible for the implementation of assigned tasks. The politician, on the other hand, must demonstrate — despite the compromises he is obliged to make — that he adheres to a political line on which he stakes his case and for which he assumes personal responsibility. The ideal of the official is impartiality and expertise in the service of decisions made by others; the ideal of the politician is partisanship and a powerful drive to make decisions for the community as a whole. This ideal distinction serves Weber as a framework for the analysis of political *practices* in Imperial Germany. Though the comparison between two types of govern-

---

[1] See Kurt H. Wolff (ed.), *The Sociology of Georg Simmel* (Glencoe, Ill.: The Free Press, 1950), pp. 9–10.

mental functions is internal to the country studied, Weber implicitly challenges us to make comparable analyses of the political process in other countries.

The next two selections are more explicitly comparative. Neustadt shows that in England and the United States the same crucial functions of governmental leadership are performed by different institutional arrangements, while institutional structures that look alike actually perform different functions. Another, more general comparison between the two countries is contained in the analysis by Shils, who relates the difference between the American and the British approach to publicity and secrecy to the contrast between a populist and an aristocratic political tradition. Here emphasis is placed on the high degree to which a populist government is subjected at every point to direct influence upon its decision-making and decision-implementing process in contrast to an "aristocratic" government which can operate on the assumption that the autonomy of decision-making and implementation is accepted by the public at large.

The final selection by Bendix presents a contrast. Certain cultural preconditions of Western European authority structures are used as a framework for an analysis of the distinguishing characteristics of Soviet political institutions, as these stand revealed in the structure of factory management. Emphasis is placed on the double hierarchy of authority through the Communist party and the planning agencies of government. The two hierarchies and their various subordinate units are coordinated in a manner that seeks to monopolize decision-making at the top and push responsibility downwards — a pattern that contrasts sharply with the more diffuse distribution of decision-making and of responsibility in authority structures marked by a largely uncoordinated multiplicity of parties and interest groups.

Bureaucracy and Political Leadership

MAX WEBER

I. BUREAUCRACY AND POLITICS

In a modern state the actual ruler is necessarily and unavoidably the bureaucracy, since power is exercised neither through parliamentary speeches nor monarchical enunciations but through the routines of administration. This is

Translated by Guenther Roth from Max Weber, *Economy and Society*, edited by Guenther Roth and Claus Wittich (New York: Bedminster Press, 1968). Copyright © 1968 Bedminster Press International AB. Reprinted by permission.

MAX WEBER (1864–1920) was a German lawyer, economic historian, and sociologist. Many of his works are available in English translation (see note under Guenther Roth). A comprehensive bibliography of his writings is contained in Marianne Weber's biography. The available translations are listed in R. Bendix, *Max Weber: An Intellectual Portrait* (1962).

true of both the military and civilian officialdom. Even the modern higher-ranking officer fights battles from the "office." Just as the so-called progress toward capitalism has been the unequivocal criterion for the modernization of the economy since medieval times, so the progress toward bureaucratic official-dom — characterized by formal employment, salary, pension, promotion, specialized training and functional division of labor, definite jurisdiction, documentary procedures, hierarchical sub- and super-ordination — has been the equally unambiguous yardstick for the modernization of the state. . . . The democratic state no less than the absolute state eliminates administration by feudal, patrimonial, patrician or other notables holding office in honorary or hereditary fashion, in favor of employed officials, who decide on all our every-day needs and problems. . . .

In the Church the most important outcome [of the Vatican Council] of 1870 was not the much-discussed dogma of infallibility but the universal episcopate, which reinforced the ecclesiastic bureaucracy (Kaplanokratie) and, in contrast to the Middle Ages, turned the bishop and the parish priest into mere officials of the central power, the Roman Curia. The same bureaucratic trend prevails in the big private enterprises of our time, the more so, the larger they are. Private salaried employees grow statistically faster than the workers.

It is simply ridiculous if our literati believe that non-manual work in the private office is in the least different from that in a government office. Both are basically identical. Sociologically speaking, the modern state is an enterprise just like a factory: this exactly is its historical peculiarity. Here as there the authority relations have the same roots. The relative independence of the artisan, the putting-out manufacturer, the free peasant, the travelling associate (*Kommendatar*), the knight and vassal rested on their ownership of the tools, supplies, finances and weapons, with which they fulfilled their economic, political and military functions and maintained themselves. In contrast, the hierarchical dependence of the worker, the administrative and technical employee, the assistant in the academic institute *as well as* the dependence of the civil servant and soldier is due to the fact that their respective means, which are indispensable for the enterprise and for making a living, are concentrated in the hands of the entrepreneur or the political ruler. . . . This all-important economic fact: the "separation" of the worker from the material means of production, destruction, administration, academic research, and finance in general is the common basis of the modern state, in its political, cultural and military sphere, and of the private capitalist economy. In both cases the disposition over these means is in the hands of that power whom the bureaucratic apparatus (of judges, officials, officers, supervisors, clerks and non-commissioned officers) directly obeys or for whom it is available in case of need. This apparatus is nowadays equally typical of all those organizations. Its existence and function are inseparably cause and effect of this concentration of the means of operation — in fact, the apparatus is its very form. Increasing "nationalization" means today unavoidably increasing bureaucratization.

The "progress" toward the bureaucratic state, adjudicating and administering according to rationally established law and regulation, is nowadays very closely related to the modern capitalist development. The modern capitalist enterprise rests primarily on *calculation* and presupposes a legal and administrative system, whose functioning can be rationally predicted, at least in principle, by virtue of its fixed general norms, just like the expected performance of a machine. The modern capitalist enterprise cannot accept what is popularly called "khadi-justice": adjudication according to the judge's sense of equity in a given case or according to the other irrational means of law-finding that existed everywhere in the past and still exist in the Orient. The modern enterprise also finds incompatible the theocratic or patrimonial governments of Asia and of our own past, whose administrations operated in a patriarchal manner according to their own discretion and, for the rest, according to inviolably sacred but irrational tradition. . . .

II. THE REALITIES OF PARTY POLITICS

Within the political parties bureaucratization progresses in the same fashion as in the economy and public administration.

The existence of the parties is not recognized by any constitution or, at least in Germany, by any law, although they are today the most important political vehicles for those ruled by bureaucracy — the citizens. Parties are inherently voluntary organizations based on ever renewed recruitment, no matter how many means they may employ to attach their clientele permanently. This distinguished them from all organizations with a definite membership established by law or contract. Today the goal of the parties is always vote-getting in an election for political positions or a voting body. A hard core of interested members is directed by a leader or a group of notables; this core differs greatly in the degree of its hierarchical organization, yet is nowadays often bureaucratized; it finances the party with the support of rich sponsors, economic interests, office seekers, or dues-paying members. Most of the time several of these sources are utilized. The hard core also defines program and tactics and selects the candidates. Even in mass parties with very democratic constitutions, the voters and most of the rank and file members do not (or do only formally) participate in the drafting of the program and the selection of the candidates, for by their very nature such parties develop a salaried officialdom. The voters exert influence only to the extent that programs and candidates are adapted and selected according to their chances of receiving electoral support.

No moralizing complaint about the nature of campaigning and the inevitable control of minorities over programs and candidates can abolish the parties, or change their structure and methods more than superficially. The conditions for establishing an active party core (like those for establishing trade unions, for example) and the "rules of war" on the electoral battlefield can be regulated by law, as was done several times in the United States. But it is impossible to eliminate the struggle of the parties, if an active parliamentary representation is to exist. . . .

In modern states political parties may be based primarily on two different principles. They may be essentially organizations for job patronage, as they have been in the United States since the end of the great differences about the interpretation of the Constitution. In this case they are merely interested in putting their leader into the top position so that he can turn over state offices to his following, the regular and the campaign staffs of the party. Since the parties do not have substantive principles, they compete against one another by writing those demands into their programs from which they expect the greatest impact. This type of party is so distinct in the United States because of the absence of a parliamentary system; the popularly elected president of the Union controls — together with the Senators — the patronage of the vast number of federal jobs. Despite the resulting corruption this system was popular since it prevented the rise of a bureaucratic caste. It was technically feasible, as long as even the worst management by dilettanti could be tolerated in view of the limitless abundance of economic opportunities. The increasing necessity of replacing the untrained party protégé and sometime-official with the technically trained career official diminishes progressively the parties benefices and results inescapably in a bureaucracy of the European kind.

The second type of party is primarily ideological (*Weltanschauungspartei*) and intended to accomplish the realization of substantive political ideals. In relatively pure form this type was represented by the Catholic Center party in the eighteen seventies and the Social Democrats before they became bureaucratized. In general, parties combine both types: they have substantive goals which are set by tradition, hence modifiable only by degrees, but they also want to control job patronage. First of all, they want to put their leaders into the major *political* offices. If they are successful in the electoral struggle, the leaders and functionaries can provide their following with secure state jobs during the party's dominance. This is the rule in parliamentary states; therefore, the ideological parties, too, followed this path. In non-parliamentary states [such as Imperial Germany] the parties do not control the patronage of the top offices, but the most influential parties can usually pressure the dominant bureaucracy into conceding non-political jobs to their protégés, next to the regular candidates recommended through their own connections with officials; hence, these parties can exercise subaltern patronage.

In the course of the rationalization of campaign techniques during the last decades, all parties have moved towards bureaucratic organization. The individual parties have reached different stages of this development, but at least in mass states the general direction is clear. Joseph Chamberlain's "caucus" in England, the rise of the "machine," as it is significantly called, in the United States, and the growing importance of party officialdom everywhere, including Germany, are all stages of this process; in Germany it proceeds fastest in the Social Democratic party — quite naturally, since it is the most democratic party. . . . The power of the parties rests primarily on the organizational effectiveness of these bureaucracies. The mutual hostility of the party machines much more than programmatic differences accounts for the difficulties of merging parties. . . .

III. BUREAUCRATIZATION AND THE NAIVETÉ
OF THE LITERATI

Of course, there are many differences between the various kinds of bureaucracy: between the civilian and the military administration, between state and
party, between community, church, bank, cartel, producers' co-operative, factory, and interest group (such as employers' associations or the *Bund der
Landwirte*). The degree to which unpaid notables and interest groups participate also varies greatly. Neither the party boss nor the board members of a
stockholding company are bureaucrats. Under the various forms of so-called self-
government notables or elected representatives of the government or the taxpayers may constitute a corporate group or individual organs vis-a-vis the
bureaucracy and have co-determining, supervisory, advisory and sometimes executive functions. The last phenomenon occurs particularly in the municipal
administrations. However, we are here not interested in them. . . . In our context it is decisive that in the administration of *mass associations* the trained
career officials always form the core of the apparatus; their discipline is the
absolute precondition of success. This is increasingly so, the larger the association is, the more complicated its tasks are, and above all, the more its existence
depends on power — whether it involves a power struggle on the market, in
the electoral arena or on the battlefield. This is especially true of the political
parties. Doomed is the system of local organization by notables, which still
exists in France — whose parliamentary misère is due to the absence of bureaucratized parties — and partly in Germany. In the Middle Ages this system
dominated all kinds of associations, and it still prevails in small and medium-
sized communities, but nowadays "respected citizens," "leading man of
science," or whatever their label, are used merely as advertisement, not as carriers of the decisive everyday routines. . . .

Just as the Italians and after them the English [masterly] developed the modern capitalist economy, so the Byzantines, again the Italians, the territorial
states of the absolutist age, the French revolutionary centralization and, sur-
passing all of them, the Germans perfected the rational, functional and specialized bureaucratic organization of all forms of domination from factory to army
and public administration. For the time being the Germans have been outdone
only in the techniques of party organization especially by the Americans. The
present world war means the world-wide triumph of this form of life, which was
advancing at any rate. . . . It is true that bureaucracy is by far not the only
modern form of organization, just as the factory is by far not the only type of
commercial enterprise, but both determine the character of the present age
and of the foreseeable future. The future belongs to bureaucratization, and it is
evident that in this regard the literati pursue their calling — to provide a salvo
of applause to the up-and-coming powers — just as they did in the age of
laissez-faire, both times with the same naiveté.

Bureaucracy is distinguished from other historical agencies of the modern
rational order of life by its far greater *inescapability*. History shows that wher-

ever bureaucracy gained the upper hand, as in China, Egypt and, to a lesser extent, in the later Roman empire and Byzantium, it did not disappear without the total collapse of the supporting culture. However, these were still, relatively speaking, highly irrational forms of bureaucracy: "patrimonial bureaucracies." In contrast to these older forms, modern bureaucracy has one characteristic which makes its inescapability much more definite: rational specialization and training. The Chinese mandarin was not a specialist but a gentleman with a literary and humanistic education. The Egyptian, Late Roman or Byzantine official was much more of a bureaucrat in our sense of the word. But compared to the modern tasks, his were infinitely simple and limited; his attitude was in part tradition-bound, in part patriarchally, that means, irrationally oriented. Like the businessman of the past, he was a pure empiricist. The modern official receives a professional training, which unavoidably increases, corresponding to the rational technology of modern life. . . . Whenever the modern specialized official comes to predominate, his power proves practically indestructible since the whole organization of elementary want satisfaction has been tailored to his mode of operation. A progressive elimination of private capitalism is theoretically conceivable. . . . What would be the practical result? The destruction of the steel frame of modern industrial work? No! The abolition of private capitalism would simply mean that the management of the nationalized or socialized enterprises would become bureaucratic. Are the daily working conditions of the salaried employees and the workers in the state-owned Prussian mines and railroads perceptibly different from those in big business enterprises? In truth, there is even less freedom since every struggle against a state bureaucracy is hopeless and since, in principle, nobody can appeal to an agency which would be interested in limiting it, contrary to what is possible in relation to a private enterprise. *That* would be the whole difference.

State bureaucracy would rule *alone*. The private and public bureaucracies which now work next to, and potentially against, each other and hence check one another to a degree would be merged into a single hierarchy. This would be similar to the situation in ancient Egypt, but it would occur in a much more rational and inescapable form.

An inanimate machine is mind objectified. Only this provides it with the power to force men into its service and to dominate their everyday working life as completely as is actually the case in the factory. Objectified intelligence is also that animated machine, the bureaucratic organization, with its specialization of trained skills, its division of jurisdiction, its rules and hierarchical relations of authority. Together with the inanimate machine it is busy fabricating that frame of bondage which men will perhaps be forced to accept some day, powerlessly, just like the fellahs in ancient Egypt. This might happen, *if* their ultimate and sole yardstick for the direction of their affairs is a merely technically superior administration, that means, a rational bureaucratic administration with the corresponding welfare benefits. Bureaucracy can accomplish this much better than any other structure of domination. This structure, which our unsuspecting literati praises so much, might easily be reinforced by fettering every individual to his job — notice the beginnings in the system of fringe benefits — , to his class — through the increasing immobility of the property distribution — , and perhaps to his occupation — through liturgic requisition-ing for the state, that means, through imposing state functions on occupational associations. This structure would be all the more indestructible, if "corporate" organizations of the ruled would be affiliated with the bureaucracy, and in truth subordinated to it, as in the forced-labor states of the past. An "organic," Oriental-Egyptian stratification would arise, but in contrast it would be as strictly rational as a machine. Who would want to deny that such a potentiality lies in the womb of the future? . . . Who would not smile about the fear of our literati that political and social development might bring us too much "individualism" or "democracy" or similar things, and about their anticipation that "true freedom" will light up only when the present "anarchy" of economic production and the "party machinery" of our parliaments will be abolished in favor of "social order" and "organic stratification" — that means, in favor of the pacifism of social impotence under the tutelage of the only really inescap-able power: the bureaucracy in state and economy.

IV. THE POLITICAL LIMITATIONS OF BUREAUCRACY

Given the basic fact of the irresistible advance of bureaucratization, the question about the future forms of political organization can only be asked in the following way:

1. How can one possibly save *any remnants* of "individualist" freedom in any sense? After all, it is a gross self-deception to believe that without the achievements of the Age of the Rights of Man any one of us, including the most conservative person, can go on living his life. . . .

2. In view of the growing indispensability of the state bureaucracy and its corresponding increase in power, how can there be any guarantee that powers will remain which can check and effectively control the tremendous influence of this stratum? . . .

3. A third question, and the most important of all, is raised by a consider-ation of the inherent limitation of bureaucracy proper. It can easily be seen that its effectiveness has definite limitations in the public and governmental realm as well as in the private economy. The "moving spirit," the entrepreneur here and the politician there, differs in substance from the official. . . . The prime minister is formally a salaried official with pension rights. He differs from most officials in that, according to most constitutions, he can be dismissed or resign at any time. Much more striking is the fact that only he does not need to prove formal specialized training. This indicates that the meaning of his position dis-tinguishes him, after all, from other officials, as it does the entrepreneur and the director general in the private economy. Actually, it is more accurate to say that he is supposed to be something different. And so it is indeed. If a man in a leading position is an "official," no matter how qualified, in the spirit of his performance — a man, that is, who works dutifully and honorably according to rules and instruction, then he is as useless at the helm of a private enterprise as

of a government. Unfortunately, our own government has proven this point.

The difference is rooted only in part in the kind of performance expected. Independent decision-making and imaginative organizational capabilities in matters of detail are usually demanded of the "officials," and very often also expected in larger matters. . . . The difference lies in the type of *responsibility*, and this in fact determines the different demands addressed to both kinds of positions. An official who receives a directive which he considers wrong can and is supposed to object to it. If his superior insists on its execution, it is his duty and honor to carry it out as if it corresponded to his innermost conviction, and to demonstrate in this fashion that his sense of duty stands above his personal preference. It does not matter whether the imperative mandate originates from an "agency," a "corporate body" or an "assembly." This is the ethos of the office. A political leader acting in this way would deserve contempt. He will often be compelled to make compromises, that means, to sacrifice the less important to the more important. If he does not succeed in demanding of his master — be it a monarch or the people — , "You either give me now the authorization I want from you, or I will resign," he is a *Kleber* (one who sticks to his post), as Bismarck called this type — not a leader. "To be above parties," in truth, to remain outside the realm of the struggle for power, is the official's role, but this struggle and the resulting personal responsibility is the lifeblood of the politician and the entrepreneur.

Since the resignation of Prince Bismarck, as a result of his elimination of all political talent, Germany has been governed by "bureaucrats." Germany continued to maintain a military and civilian bureaucracy that was superior to all others in the world in terms of integrity, education, conscientiousness and intelligence. The military and, by and large, also the domestic performance during the war has proven what can be achieved with these means. But what about the handling of German foreign policy during recent decades? The most benign thing said about it was that "the victories of the German armies made up for its defeats." . . . What was lacking was the direction of the state by a *politician* — not by a political genius, to be expected every few centuries, not even by a great political talent, but simply by a politician.

V. THE LIMITED ROLE OF THE MONARCH

This brings us straight to the discussion of those two powers which alone can be controlling and directing forces in the modern constitutional state, next to all-encompassing officialdom: the *monarch* and *parliament*.

The position of the German dynasties will emerge unscathed from the war, unless there is a great deal of imprudence and nothing is learnt from the mistakes of the past. . . .

However, in the modern state the monarch can never and nowhere be a counterforce against the pervasive power of the professional bureaucrats. He cannot supervise the administration, for it is a professionally trained apparatus and the modern monarch is never an expert, with the possible exception of military matters. Above all, the monarch is never a politician who received his training within the machinery of the parties or of diplomacy. . . . He does not gain his crown through a party contest, and the struggle for power is not his natural milieu. He does not experience the harsh realities of party life by descending into the political arena, rather he is removed from them through his privilege. There are born politicians, but they are rare. The monarch who is not one of them becomes a threat to his own and to the state's interests if he attempts to govern by himself, like the Tsar, or to exert influence with political means — "demagogy" in the broadest sense of the word — , in speech and writing, for the sake of propagating his ideas or of projecting his personality. . . . However, this temptation, nay, necessity arises inevitably for a modern monarch if he is confronted only by bureaucrats, that means, if parliament is powerless, as it has been the case in Germany for decades. Even from a purely instrumental viewpoint this has severe drawbacks. If there is no powerful parliament, the monarch is today dependent upon the reports of officials for the supervision of the work of other officials. This is a vicious circle. A natural consequence of such allegedly "monarchic" government, which is without a responsible political leader, is the continuous war of the various ministries against one another, as was typical of Russia and as has also occurred in Germany up to the present. This conflict of "satraps" involves most of the time not only differences of opinion, but also personal rivalries; the clashes between the ministries serve their chiefs as vehicles in the competition for the ministerial positions, if these are treated merely as bureaucratic benefices. Then court intrigues, not material reasons or qualities of political leadership, determine incumbency. . . .

Let us now turn to parliament.

VI. WEAK AND STRONG PARLIAMENTS, NEGATIVE AND POSITIVE POLITICS

Modern parliaments are primarily representative bodies of those ruled with bureaucratic means. After all, a certain minimum of consent on the part of the ruled, at least of the socially important strata, is a precondition of the durability of every, even the best organized, domination. Parliaments are today the means of manifesting this minimum consent. . . . However, as long as a parliament can support the complaints of the citizens against the administration only by rejecting appropriations and other legislation or by introducing unimportant motions, it is excluded from positive participation in government. Then it can only engage in "negative politics," that means, it will confront the administrative chiefs as if it were a hostile power; as such it will be given only the indispensable minimum of information and will be considered a mere drag-chain, an assembly of impotent fault-finders and know-it-alls. . . .

Things are different when parliament has accomplished the following:

Either the administrative heads must be recruited from its midst — the *parliamentary system* proper — , or they require the express confidence of its majority for holding office, or they must at least resign upon losing its confidence — the *parliamentary selection* of the leaders; in this case, they must account for their actions exhaustively, with parliament or its committees investigating them — *parliamentary accountability* of the leaders; moreover, they must run the administration according to the guidelines approved by parliament — *parliamentary control* of the administration. Then the leaders of the dominant parties have necessarily a positive share in government. . . .

Whether you hate or love parliamentary politics — you cannot eliminate it. Parliament can only be made politically powerless, as Bismarck did with the Reichstag. In addition to the general consequences of "negative politics," the weakness of parliament has other results (which can be better understood if we first recall the role of a strong parliament): Every conflict in parliament involves not only substantive issues but also personal power struggles. Wherever parliament is so strong that, as a rule, the monarch entrusts the government to the spokesmen for a clear-cut majority, the parties contest the highest executive position. The fight is then carried by men who have great political power instincts and highly developed qualities of political leadership, and hence the chance to take over the top positions; for the survival of the party outside parliament, and the countless ideal, and partly very material, interests bound up with it require that capable leaders get to the top. Only under such conditions can men with political temperament and talent be motivated to subject themselves to this kind of selection.

Matters are completely different, if under the label of "monarchic government" the appointment to the top positions is subject to bureaucratic advancement or accidental court acquaintance, and if a powerless parliament must submit to such a government. In this case, too, personal ambitions, apart from substantive issues, naturally play a role, but in very different, subaltern forms, and in directions which they have pursued in Germany since 1890. Besides representing the local economic interests of influential voters, petty subaltern patronage becomes the major concern of the parties. . . .

On the other hand, this system permits qualified bureaucrats who yet have no trace of statesman-like talent to assert themselves in a leading political position until some intrigue forces them out in favor of a similar personage. Thus, we have no less party patronage than any other country, but we have it in dishonestly veiled form and in a manner which always favors certain partisan views acceptable at court. However, this partiality is by far not the worst aspect of the matter. It would be politically tolerable if it afforded at least an opportunity for recruiting leaders from these court parties. However, this is not the case. The recruitment of leaders capable of guiding the nation is possible only in a parliamentary system, or at least under conditions which make the top positions available to parliamentary patronage. Here we encounter a purely formal obstacle embedded in the constitution.

VII. THE CONSTITUTIONAL WEAKNESSES OF THE REICHSTAG AND THE PROBLEM OF LEADERSHIP

. . . Stripped of all phraseology, our so-called monarchic government amounts to nothing but this process of *negative selection*, which diverts all major talents to the service of capitalist interests. For only in the realm of private capitalism is there today anything approaching the selection of men with leadership talents. Why? Because *Gemütlichkeit* in this case, the rhetoric of the literati, comes to an end as soon as economic interests involving millions and billions of Marks and tens and hundreds of thousands of workers are affected. And why is there no such selection in government? Because one of the worst legacies of Bismarck's rule has been the fact that he considered it necessary to. cover his caesarist regime with the *monarch's legitimacy*. His successors, who were no Caesars but sober bureaucrats, imitated him faithfully. The politically uneducated nation took Bismarck's rhetoric at its face value, and the literati provided the usual applause. This stands to reason because they examine the future officials and consider themselves officials and fathers of officials. Their resentment is directed against everybody who seeks and gains power without legitimizing himself through a diploma. Since Bismarck had taken over all the worrying about public affairs, and foreign policy in particular, the nation permitted itself to be talked into accepting something as "monarchic government" which in truth amounted to the unchecked rule of the bureaucracy. Under such a system qualities of political leadership have never been born and brought to fruition anywhere in the world. Our civil service has indeed men with leadership qualities: we certainly would not want to deny this here. However, the conventions and typical features of the bureaucratic hierarch severely impede the career opportunities of such talents, and the whole nature of modern officialdom is most unfavorable to the development of *political* independence (which must be distinguished from the inner freedom of the private individual). The essence of politics — as we will have to emphasize time and again — is struggle, the recruitment of allies and of a voluntary following; to get training in this difficult art is impossible under the career system of the *Obrigkeitsstaat*. It is well-known that Bismarck's school was the Frankfurt Federal Council. In the army, training is directed toward combat, and this can produce military leaders. However, for the modern politician the proper palaestra are the parliament and the public; neither competition for bureaucratic advancement nor anything else will do as an adequate substitute. Of course, this is only true of a parliament and a party whose leader takes over the government.

Why in the world should men with leadership qualities be attracted by a party which at best can change a few budget items in accordance with the voters' interests and provide a few minor benefices to the protégés of its bigshots? What opportunities can it offer to potential leaders? The merely negative politics of parliament is reflected today in the most minute details of the agenda of the Reichstag and the conventions of the parties. I know of quite a few cases in which young political talents were simply suppressed by the old guard of deserved local notable and party bigwheels. This happens in every guild, and it is quite natural in a powerless parliament, since there guild instincts prevail. A party oriented toward sharing governmental power and responsibility could never afford this; every member would know that the survival of the party and of all the interests which bind him to it depends upon its subordination to qualified leaders. Nowhere in the world, not even in

England, can the parliamentary body as such govern and determine policies. The broad mass of deputies functions only as a following for the leader or the few leaders who form government, and it blindly follows them *as long as* they are successful. *This is the way it should be.* Political action is always determined by the "principle of small numbers," that means, the superior political maneuverability of small groups. In mass states, this caesarist element is ineradicable.

However, this element alone guarantees that *responsibility* toward the public rests upon clearly identifiable persons; responsibility would evaporate within an assembly governing at large. This is especially true of a democracy proper. . . .

Just like every other human organization, the selection of political leaders through the parties has its weaknesses, but these have been exposed ad nauseam by German literati during the last decades. Of course, the parliamentary system too expects of the individual that he subordinate himself to a man whom he can often accept only as the "smaller evil." But the *Obrigkeitsstaat* gives him no choice at all and imposes upon him bureaucrats instead of leaders, which certainly makes for a bit of a difference. Moreover, plutocracy flourishes in Germany as much as in other countries, only in a different form. The literati depict the great capitalist powers in the darkest colors and without any competence, yet there must be solid reasons behind the fact that these very powers, which know their interests better than those armchair theorists, range themselves unanimously on the side of the bureaucratic *Obrigkeitsstaat* and against democracy and parliamentarism. In particular is this true of heavy industry, the most reckless of these capitalist powers, but the reasons remain beyond the ken of the literary philistines. In their moralizing fashion, they score the fact that the party leaders are moved by the will to power and their following by selfish interest in office-holding — as if the bureaucratic aspirants were not as career- and salary-minded and inspired by the most selfish motives. The role of demagogy in the power struggle is demonstrated to everybody by the current newspaper campaign about who should be foreign minister, a campaign encouraged from certain official quarters. This proves that an allegedly monarchic government facilitates the most pernicious misuse of the press in the pursuit of office and of inter-departmental rivalries. This state of affairs would not be aggravated in any parliamentary system with effective parties.

The motives of party members are no more merely idealist than are the usual philistine interests of bureaucratic competitors in promotion and benefices. Here as there, personal interests are usually at stake (and this will not change in the vaunted state of corporate solidarity, which the literati envision). It is of crucial importance that, at the least, these universal human frailties do not prevent the selection of capable leaders. But this is possible only in a party whose leaders know that in case of victory they will have the powers and the responsibilities of government. Only then is this selection possible, but it is not assured by it. For only a working, not just a speech-making parliament can provide the ground for the growth and selective ascent of genuine leaders, not merely demagogic talents. A working parliament, however, is one which supervises the administration by continuously sharing its work. Before the war, this was not possible in Germany, but afterward it must be possible, or we will have the old *misère*.

White House
and Whitehall

RICHARD E. NEUSTADT

Cabinet government, so-called, as practiced currently in the United Kingdom, differs in innumerable ways — some obvious, some subtle — from "presidential government" in the United States. To ask what one can learn about our own system by viewing theirs, may seem far-fetched, considering those differences. But actually the question is a good one. For comparison should help us to discriminate between shadow and substance in both regimes. A look down Whitehall's corridors of power might suggest a lot of things worth noticing in Washington.

For a President-watcher, who tries to understand the inner workings of our bureaucratic system by climbing inside now and then, and learning on the job, it is no easy matter to attempt comparison with the eternal life of Whitehall. How is one to get a comparable look? Those who govern Britain mostly keep their secrets to themselves. They rarely have incentive to do otherwise, which is among the differences between us. Least of all they are inclined to satisfy the curiosities of academics. Even we colonials, persistent though we are and mattering as little as we do, find ourselves all too frequently treated like Englishmen and kept at bay by those three magic words: "Official Secrets Act." Why not? Nothing in the British Constitution says that anyone outside of Whitehall needs an inside view. Quite the reverse. If academics know, then journalists might learn, and even the back-benchers might find out. God forbid!

In Britain governing is *meant* to be a mystery. And so it is. Only in the memoirs of participants does one get glimpses, now and then, of operational reality. And even the most "indiscreet" of recent memoirs veil the essence of the modern system: the relations between ministers and civil servants in the making of a government decision.

From *The Public Interest*, No. 2 (Winter 1966), pp. 55–69. Reprinted by permission of the author and publisher.

RICHARD E. NEUSTADT is Professor of Government, Associate Dean of the School of Public Administration, and Director of the Institute of Politics, Harvard University. He is the author of *Presidential Power, The Politics of Leadership* (1960). He was presidential advisor to President John F. Kennedy.

For four years I have made a hobby of attempting to poke holes in Whitehall's defenses, and to take a closer look than either interviews or books afford. Partly this has been a "busman's holiday": having roamed one set of corridors, I find the temptation irresistible to look around another. Partly, though, I have been tempted by the thought that a comparison of set likenesses and differences would add a new dimension to President-watching.

To test that proposition, let me raise two simple points of difference between their system and ours.

First, we have counterparts for their top civil servants — but not in our own civil service.

Second, we have counterparts for their cabinet ministers — but not exclusively, or even mainly, in our cabinet.

If I state these two correctly, and I think I do, it follows that in our conventional comparisons we all too often have been victims of semantics. Accordingly, in our proposals for reform-by-analogy we all too often have confused function with form. I find no functions in the British system for which ours lacks at least nascent counterparts. But it is rare when institutions with the same names in both systems do the same work for precisely the same purpose. Thus, the most important things that I bring back from my excursioning in Whitehall are a question and caution. The question: what is our functional equivalent? The caution: never base analysis on nomenclature. These seem to be embarrassingly obvious. But it is astonishing how frequently they are ignored.

I

"Why are your officials so passionate?" I once was asked in England by a bright, young Treasury official just back from Washington. I inquired with whom he had been working with there. His answer: "Your chaps at the Budget Bureau."

To an American, those "chaps" appear to be among the most *dis*passionate of Washingtonians. Indeed, the Budget staff traditionally prides itself on being cool, collected, and above the struggle, distant from emotions churning in the breasts of importunate agency officials. Yet to my English friend, "They took themselves so seriously . . . seemed to be crusaders for the policy positions they thought made sense . . . seemed to feel that it was up to them to save the day. . . ." If this is how the Budget Bureau struck him, imagine how he would have felt about some circles in our Air Force, or the European Bureau of the State Department, or the Office of Economic Opportunity, or the Forest Service for that matter, or the Bureau of Reclamation, or the National Institutes of Health!

His inquiry suggests two further queries. First, out of what frame of reference was he asking? And second, is it sensible of him (and most of us) to talk of our own budgeteers as though they were his counterparts? These questions are pertinent because I think we are very far from candid with ourselves about the way we get *his* work done in *our* system.

This young man was a Principle-with-prospects at the Treasury. By definition, then, he was a man of the Administrative class, the elite corps of the British civil service. More important, he was also an apprentice-member of the favored few, the elite-of-the-elite, who climb the ladder *in* the Treasury. With skill and luck and approbation from his seniors he might someday rise to be a Mandarin. And meanwhile he would probably serve soon as personal assistant to a Cabinet minister. In short, he had the frame of reference which benefits a man whose career ladder rises up the central pillar of the whole Whitehall establishment toward the heights where dwell the seniors of all seniors, moulders of ministers, heads of the civil service, knights in office, lords thereafter: the Permanent Secretaries of the Cabinet and the Treasury.

English civil servants of this sort, together with their foreign office counterparts, make up the inner core of "officials," civilian career men, whose senior members govern the United Kingdom in collaboration with their ministerial superiors, the front-bench politicians, leaders of the parliamentary party which commands a House majority for the time being. Theirs is an intimate collaboration, grounded in the interests and traditions of both sides. Indeed it binds them into a Society for Mutual Benefit: what they succeed in sharing with each other they need share with almost no one else, and governing in England is a virtual duopoly.

This is the product of a tacit treaty, an implicit bargain, expressed in self-restraints which are observed on either side. The senior civil servants neither stall nor buck decisions of the Government, once these have been taken in due form. "Due Form" means consultation with these senior civil servants, among other things; but having been consulted, these officials act without public complaint or private evasion, even though they may have fought what they are doing up to the last moment of decision. They also try to assure comparable discipline in lower official ranks, and to squeeze out the juniors who do not take kindly to it.

The senior politicians, for their part — with rare and transient exceptions — return this loyalty in full measure. The politicians rarely meddle with official recruitment or promotion: by and large, officialdom administers itself. The politicians preserve the anonymity of civil servants both in Parliament and in the press. Officials never testify on anything except "accounts" (an audit of expenditures), and nobody reveals their roles in shaping public policy. Ministers take all kudos for themselves — likewise the heat. They also take upon themselves protection for the status of officialdom in the society: honors fall like gentle rain at stated intervals. They even let career civil servants run their private offices, and treat their personal assistants of the moment (detailed from civil-service ranks) as confidentially as our department heads treat trusted aides imported from outside. More important, the politicians *lean* on their officials. They *expect* to be advised. Most important, they very often follow the advice that they receive.

This is an advantageous bargain for both sides. It relieves the politicians of a difficult and chancy search for "loyal" advisers and administrators. These are in place, ready to hand. And it relieves civil servants of concern for their security in terms both of profession and of person. No wonder our career men appear "passionate" to one of theirs; theirs have nothing at stake except policy!

So a Treasury-type has everything to gain by a dispassionate stance, and nothing to lose except arguments. To be sure, since he feels himself with reason to be one of an elite, ranking intellectually and morally with the best in Britain, this is no trifling loss. If parliamentary parties were less disciplined than they now are, or if he had back-benchers who identified him, he could afford to carry arguments outside official channels, as his predecessors sometimes did a century ago — and as *military* officers still do, on occasion. But party discipline calls forth its counterpart in his own ranks. And party politicians on back-benches have no natural affinities with civil servants — quite the contrary. The civil servant really has no recourse but to lose his arguments with grace and wait in patience for another day, another set of ministers. After all, he stays, they go. And while he stays, he shares the fascinating game of power, stretching his own mind and talents in the service of a reasonably grateful country.

The Treasury-type is a disciplined man; but a man fulfilled, not frustrated. His discipline is the price he pays for power. Not every temperament can take it; if he rises in the Treasury, he probably can. But there is more to this than a cold compromise for power's sake. Those who rise and find fulfillment in their work do so in part because they are deliberately exposed at mid-career to the constraints, the miseries, the hazards which afflict the human beings who wield power on the political side. They know the lot of ministers from observation at first hand. Exposure makes for empathy and for perspective. It also makes for comfort with the civil servant's lot. Whitehall's elites gain all three while relatively young. It leaves them a bit weary with the weight of human folly, but it rids them of self-righteousness, the bane of *our* career men — particularly endemic, of course, among budgeteers.

A Treasury-type gains this exposure through that interesting device, the tour of duty in a minister's private office as his personal "dogsbody." The private secretary, so called, serves his master-of-the-moment as a confidential aide, minding his business, doing his chores, sharing his woes, offering a crying towel, bracing him for bad days in the House, briefing him for bad days in the office. Etcetera. Remarkably by our standards, the civil service has preempted such assignments for its own. (Do not confuse a minister's private secretary with mere *parliamentary* private secretaries who are drawn from the back benches of the House.) Still more remarkably, the politicians feel themselves well served and rarely dream of looking elsewhere for the service. I know an instance where a minister confided in his private secretary a secret he told no one else save the Prime Minister, not even his Permanent Secretary, the career head-of-department, "lest it embarrass him to know." The Permanent Secretary was the private secretary's boss; yet the secret was kept as a matter of course. This, I am assured, is not untypical: "ministerial secrets" are all in the day's work for dogsbodies.

Accordingly, the one-time private secretary who has risen in due course to be permanent secretary of a department knows far more of what it feels like to perform as a politician than his opposite number, the department's minister, can ever hope to fathom in reverse. A William Armstrong, for example, now joint-head of Treasury, whose opposite number is the Chancellor of the Exchequer, spent years as private secretary to a previous Chancellor who was among the ablest men in the cabinets of his time. Draw the contrast with our own career civil servants.

Our budgeteers imagine that they are the nearest thing to Treasury civil servants. For this, no one can blame them. Much of our literature suggests that if they are not quite the same as yet, a little gimmickery could make them so. Many American political scientists have bemused themselves for years with plans to borrow nomenclature and procedures from the British side, on the un-stated premise that function follows form. But it does not.

Functionally, our counterparts for British Treasury-types are *non*-career men holding jobs infused with presidential interest or concern. They are "in-and-outers" from the law firms, banking, business, academia, foundations, or occasionally journalism, or the entourages of successful Governors and Sen-ators — along with up-and-outers (sometimes up-and-downers) who relinquish, or at least risk, civil service status in the process. Here is the elite-of-the-elite, the upper-crust of our "Administrative class." These are the men who serve alongside our equivalents for ministers, and who share in governing. One finds them in the White House and in the *appointive* jobs across the street at the Executive Office Building. One finds them also on the seventh floor of State, and on the third and fourth floors of the Pentagon; these places among others.

Let me take some names at random to suggest the types. First, the proto-type of all: Averill Harriman. Second, a handful of the currently employed: David Bell, William Bundy, Wilbur Cohen, Harry McPherson, Paul Nitze. Third, a few recent "outers" almost certain to be back, somehow, sometime: McGeorge Bundy, Kermit Gordon, Theodore Sorensen. Fourth, a long-time "outer" who is never back but always in: Clark Clifford. Three of these men got their start as government career men, two as academics, two in banking, two in law, and one on Capitol Hill. The numbers are but accidents of random choice; the spread is meaningful.

The jobs done by such men as these have no precise equivalents in England; our machinery is too different. For example, McGeorge Bundy as the Presi-dent's Assistant for National Security Affairs was something more than Prin-cipal Private Secretary to the Prime Minister (reserved for rising Treasury-types), a dogsbody-writ-large, and also something different from the Secretary of the Cabinet (top of the tree for them), a post "tradition" turns into an almost Constitutional position, certainly what we would call an "institutional" one. Yet the men in those positions see a Bundy as their sort of public servant. They are higher on the ladder than my young friend with the question; they do not take budgeteers to be their counterparts; they know a Senior Civil Servant when they see one.

Every detail of our practice is un-English, but the general outline fits. One of our men appears on television; another testifies against a bill; a third and fourth engage in semi-public argument; a fifth man feeds a press campaign to change the President's mind; a sixth disputes a cabinet member's views in open meeting; a seventh overturns an inter-agency agreement. So it goes, to the perpetual surprise (and sometimes envy?) of the disciplined duopolists in Britain. Yet by *our* lights, according to *our* standards, under our conditions, such activities may be as "disciplined" as theirs, and as responsive to political leadership. The ablest of our in-and-outers frequently display equivalent restraint and equal comprehension in the face of the dilemmas which confront our presidential counterparts of their Cabinet politicians.

The elite of our officialdom is not careerist men in the British sense (although, of course, our in-and-outers have careers); why should it be? Neither is it the President with his department heads. They, too, are in-and-outers. We forget that the duopoly which governs Britain is composed of *two* career systems, official and political. Most ministers who will take office through the next decade are on the scene and well identified in Westminster. The permanent secretaries who will serve with them are on the Whitehall ladders now; a mere outsider can spot some of them. Contrast our situation — even the directorships of old-line bureaus remain problematical. Who is to succeed J. Edgar Hoover?

We have only two sets of true career men in our system. One consists of Senators and Congressmen in relatively safe seats, waiting their turn for chairmanships. The other consists of military officers and civil employees who are essentially technicians manning every sort of specialty (including "management") in the Executive establishment. Between these two we leave a lot of room for in-and-outers. We are fortunate to do so. Nothing else could serve as well to keep the two apart. And *their* duopoly would be productive, not of governance, but of its feudal substitute, piecemeal administration. We can only hope to govern in our system by, and through, the Presidency. In-and-outers are a saving grace for Presidents.

II

Since 1959, English commentators frequently have wondered to each other if their government was being "presidentialized." In part, this stemmed from electoral considerations following the "personality contest" between Harold Macmillan and Hugh Gaitskell in that year's general election. In part, too, it stemmed from the impression left by Macmillan's active premiership — re-enforced this past year by the sight of still another activist in office, Harold Wilson.

Despite their differences in style, personality, and party, both Macmillan and Wilson patently conceived the Cabinet Room in Downing Street to be the PM's office, not a mere board-room. Both evidently acted on the premise that the PM's personal judgment ought, if possible, to be decisive. Both reached out for the power of personal decision on the issues of the day. Macmillan did so through offstage maneuver, while avowing his fidelity to cabinet consensus. With perhaps a bit more candor, Wilson does the same. Hence discussion about trends toward "presidential" government.

Yet between these two Prime Ministers there was another for a year, Sir

Alec Douglas-Home. And by no stretch of the imagination could his conduct in office have been characterized as presidential. On the contrary, by all accounts he was a classic "chairman of the board," who resolutely pushed impending issues *out* of Number 10, for initiative elsewhere, by others. He managed, it is said, to get a lot of gardening done while he resided there. I once asked a close observer what became of the initiatives, the steering, the maneuvering, which Home refused to take upon himself. He replied:

> When ministers discovered that he really wouldn't do it, they began to huddle with each other, little groups of major figures. You would get from them enough agreement or accommodation to produce the main lines of a government position, something they could try to steer through Cabinet. Or if you didn't get it, there was nothing to be done. That's how it began to work, outside of Number 10, around it.

That is how it would be working now, had there been but a slight shift in the popular vote of 1964.

The British system, then, has *not* been presidentialized, or not at least in operational terms. For, as we learned with Eisenhower, the initiatives a President must take to form "the main lines of a government position" cannot survive outside the White House precincts. Toss them out and either they bounce back or they wither away. A president may delegate to White House aides ("ok, S.A."), or to a Foster Dulles, but only as he demonstrates consistently, day-in-and-out, that they command his ear and hold his confidence. Let him take to his bed behind an oxygen tent and they can only go through motions. Eisenhower's White House was a far cry from 10 Downing Street in the regime of Douglas-Home. That remains the distance Britain's system has to travel toward a presidential status for prime ministers.

But even though the system did not make an activist of Douglas-Home, his predecessor and successor obviously relished the part. The system may not have required them to play it, but they did so, and the system bore the weight of their activity. In externals, Number 10 looks no more like the White House under Wilson than it did a year ago. But, in essence, Wilson comes as close to being "President" as the conventions of *his* system allow. He evidently knows it and likes it. So, I take it, did Macmillan.

How close can such men come? How nearly can they assert "presidential" leadership inside a cabinet system? Without endeavoring to answer in the abstract, let me record some impressions of concrete performances.

First, consider Britain's bid for Common Market membership four years ago, which presaged an enormous (if abortive) shift in public policy, to say nothing of Tory Party policy. By all accounts, this "turn to Europe" was Macmillan's own. The timing and the impetus were his, and I am told that his intention was to go whole-hog, both economically and politically. As such, this was among the great strategic choices in the peacetime politics of Britain. But it never was a "Government decision." For those, by British definition, come in Cabinet. Macmillan never put the issue there in candid terms. Instead he tried to sneak past opposition there — and on back-benches and in constituencies — by disguising his strategic choice as a commercial deal. The

Cabinet dealt with issues of negotiation, *en principe* and later in detail, for making Britain part of Europe's economic union without giving up its Commonwealth connections (or farm subsidies). One minister explained to me:

> Timing is everything. First we have to get into the Common Market as a matter of business, good for our economy. Then we can begin to look at the political side. . . . Appetites grow with eating. We couldn't hold the Cabinet, much less our back-benchers, if we put this forward now in broader terms. . . .

Accordingly, the move toward Europe had to be played out in its ostensible terms, as a detailed negotiation of a commercial character. This took two years; and while the tactic served its purpose within Tory ranks, these were the years when France escaped from the Algerian war. By the time negotiations neared their end, Charles de Gaulle was riding high at home. Macmillan tiptoed past his own internal obstacles, but took so long about it that his path was blocked by an external one, the veto of de Gaulle.

Second, take the Nassau Pact of 1962, which calmed the Skybolt crisis between Washington and London even as it gave de Gaulle excuses for that veto. Macmillan was his own negotiator at the Nassau Conference. He decided on the spot to drop his claim for Skybolt missiles and to press the substitution of Polaris weaponry. He wrung what seemed to him an advantageous compromise along those lines from President Kennedy. Then and only then did he "submit" its terms to the full Cabinet for decision (by return cable), noting the concurrence of three potent ministers who had accompanied him: the Foreign, Commonwealth, and Defense Secretaries. With the President waiting, the Cabinet "decided" (unenthusiastically, by all accounts) to bless this *fait accompli*. What else was there to do? The answer, nothing — and no doubt Macmillan knew it.

Third, consider how the present Labour Government reversed its pre-election stand on Nassau's terms. Within six weeks of taking office, Wilson and his colleagues became champions of the Polaris program they had scorned in opposition. Their back-benchers wheeled around behind them almost to a man. It is no secret that the Prime Minister was the source of this reversal, also its tactician. So far as I can find, it was his own choice, his initiative, his management, from first to last. He got it done in quick-time, yet he did it by maneuvering on tiptoe like Macmillan in the case of the Common Market (with just a touch of the shot-gun, like Macmillan in the Nassau case). When Wilson let Polaris reach the Cabinet for "decision," leading ministers, both "right" and "left," already were committed individually. By that time also, Wilson had pre-tested back-bench sentiment; he had "prematurely" voiced to an acquiescent House what would become the rationale for Cabinet action: keeping on with weapons whose production had already passed a "point of no return."

Superficially, such instances as these seem strikingly unpresidential. In our accustomed vision, Presidents do not tiptoe around their Cabinets, they instruct, inform, or ignore them. They do not engineer *faits accomplis* to force decisions from them, for the Cabinet does not make decisions; Presidents decide. A Kennedy after Birmingham, a Johnson after Selma, deciding on their civil rights bills, or a Johnson after Pleiku, ordering the bombers north, or Johnson last December, taking off our pressure for the multilateral force, or Kennedy confronting Moscow over Cuba with advisers all around him but decisions in his hands — what contrasts these suggest with the maneuvers of a Wilson or Macmillan!

The contrasts are but heightened by a glance at their work-forces: Presidents with twenty-odd high-powered personal assistants, and a thousand civil servants in their Executive Office — Prime Ministers with but four such assistants in their private Office (three of them on detail from departments) and a handful more in Cabinet Office, which by definition is not "theirs" alone. Differences of work-place heighten the effect still more: 10 Downing Street is literally a house, comparing rather poorly with the White House before T.R.'s time. The modern White House is a palace, as Denis Brogan keeps reminding us, a physically-cramped version of the Hofburg, or the Tuileries.

Yet beneath these contrasts, despite them, belying them, Americans are bound to glimpse a long-familiar pattern in the conduct of an activist Prime Minister. It is the pattern of a President maneuvering around or through the power-men in his Administration *and* in Congress. Once this is seen, all contrasts become superficial. Underneath our images of Presidents-in-boots, astride decisions, are the half-observed realities of Presidents-in-sneakers, stirrups in hand, trying to induce particular department heads, or Congressmen or Senators, to climb aboard.

Anyone who has an independent power-base is likelier than not to get "ministerial" treatment from a President. Even his own appointees are to be wooed, not spurned, in the degree that they have their own attributes of power: expertise, or prestige, or a statute under foot. As Theodore Sorensen reported while he was still at the White House:

> In choosing between conflicting advice, the President is also choosing between conflicting advisers. . . . He will be slow to overrule a cabinet officer whose pride or prestige has been committed, not only to save the officer's personal prestige but to maintain his utility. . . . Whenever any President overrules any Secretary he runs the risk of that Secretary grumbling, privately if not publicly, to the Congress, or to the press (or to his diary), or dragging his feet on implementation, or, at the very worst, resigning with a blast at the President.

But it is men of Congress more than departmental men who regularly get from Pennsylvania Avenue the treatment given Cabinet ministers from Downing Street. Power in the Senate is particularly courted. A Lyndon Johnson (when he served there), or a Vandenberg in Truman's time, or nowadays an Anderson, a Russell, even a Mansfield — to say nothing of a Dirksen — are accorded many of the same attentions which a Wilson has to offer a George Brown.

The conventions of "bipartisanship" in foreign relations, established under Truman and sustained by Eisenhower, have been extended under Kennedy and Johnson to broad sectors of the home-front, civil rights especially. These never were so much a matter of engaging oppositionists in White House undertakings as of linking to the White House men from either party who had influence to spare. Mutuality of deference between Presidents and leaders of congressional opinion, rather than between the formal party leaderships, always has been the essence of "bipartisanship" in practice. And men who really lead opinion on the Hill gain privileged access to executive decisions as their customary share of "mutual deference." "Congress" may not participate in such decisions, but these men often do: witness Dirksen in the framing of our recent Civil Rights Acts, or a spectrum of Senators from Russell to Mansfield in the framing of particular approaches on Viet Nam. Eleven years ago; Eisenhower seems to have kept our armed forces out of Indo-China when a projected intervention at the time of Dien Bien Phu won no support from Senate influentials. Johnson now maneuvers to maintain support from "right" to "left" within their ranks.

If one seeks our counterparts for Wilson or Macmillan as Cabinet tacticians, one need look no further than Kennedy or Johnson maneuvering among the influentials both downtown *and* on the Hill (and in state capitals, or among steel companies and trade unions, for that matter). Macmillan's caution on the Common Market will suggest the torturous, slow course of JFK toward fundamental changes in our fiscal policy, which brought him to the point of trying for a tax cut only by the end of his third year. Macmillan's *fait accompli* on Polaris brings to mind the Southeast Asia Resolution Johnson got from Congress after there had been some shooting in the Tonkin Gulf — and all its predecessors back to 1955, when Eisenhower pioneered this technique for extracting a "blank check." Wilson's quiet, quick arrangement for the Labour Party to adopt Polaris has a lot in common with the Johnson *coup* a year ago on Federal aid to education, where a shift in rationale took all sorts of opponents off the hook.

British government may not be presidential, but our government is more prime-ministerial than we are inclined to think. Unhappily for clarity of thought, we too have something called a Cabinet. But that pallid institution is in no sense the equivalent of theirs. Our equivalent is rather an informal, shifting aggregation of key individuals — the influentials at both ends of Pennsylvania Avenue. Some of them may sit in what we call the Cabinet as department heads; others sit in back rows there, as senior White House aides; still others have no place there. Collectively these men share no responsibility nor any meeting ground. Individually, however, each is linked to all the others through the person of the President (supported by his telephone). And all to some degree are serviced — also monitored — by one group or another on the White House staff. The former "Bundy Office," or the "Sorensen Shop" which one might best describe now as the Moyers "sphere of influence," together with the staff of legislative liaisoners captained until lately by Lawrence O'Brien — these groups, although not tightly interlocked, provide a common reference-point for influentials everywhere: "This is the White House calling. . . ." While we lack an institutionalized Cabinet along British lines, we are evolving an equivalent of Cabinet Office. The O'Brien operation was its newest element, with no precursors worthy of the name in any regime earlier than Eisenhower's. Whether it survives, and how and why, without O'Brien become questions of the day for Presidency-watchers.

The functional equivalence between a British Cabinet and our set of influentials — whether Secretaries, Senators, White House staffers, Congressmen, or others — is rendered plain by noting that, for most intents and purposes, their Cabinet members do the work of our congressional committees, our floor-leaderships, and our front-offices downtown, all combined. The combination makes for superficial smoothness; Whitehall seems a quiet place. But once again, appearances deceive. Beneath the surface, this combine called "Cabinet" wrestles with divergencies of interest, of perspective, of procedure, of personality, much like those we are used to witnessing above ground in the dealings of our separated institutions. Not only is the hidden struggle reminiscent of our open one, but also the results are often similar: "bold, new ventures" actually undertaken are often few and far between. Whitehall dispenses with the grunts and groans of Washington, but both can labor mightily to bring forth mice.

It is unfashionable just now to speak of "stalemate" or of "deadlock" in our government, although these terms were all the rage two years ago and will be so again, no doubt, whenever Johnson's coattails shrink. But British government is no less prone to deadlock than our own. Indeed I am inclined to think their tendencies in that direction more pronounced than ours. A keen observer of their system, veteran of some seven years at Cabinet meetings, put it to me in these terms:

> The obverse of our show of monolithic unity behind a Government position, when we have one, is slowness, ponderousness, deviousness, in approaching a position, getting it taken, getting a "sense of the meeting." Nothing in our system is harder to do, especially if press leaks are at risk. You Americans don't seem to understand that. . . .

In the Common Market case, to cite but one example, the three months from October to December, 1962 were taken up at Brussels, where negotiations centered, by a virtual filibuster from the British delegation. This drove some of the Europeans wild and had them muttering about "perfidious Albion." But London's delegates were not engaged in tactical maneuvering at Brussels. All they were doing there was to buy time for tactical maneuvering back home, around the cabinet table. The three months were required to induce two senior ministers to swallow agricultural concessions every student of the subject knew their government would have to make. But Britain could not move until those influential "Members of the Government" had choked them down. The time-lag seemed enormous from the vantage point of Brussels. Significantly, it seemed short indeed to Londoners. By Whitehall standards this was rapid motion.

One of the checks-and-balances in Britain's system lies between the PM and his colleagues as a group. This is the check that operated here. A sensible

Prime Minister is scrupulous about the forms of collective action: overreaching risks rejection; a show of arbitrariness risks collegial reaction; if they should band together his associates could pull him down. Accordingly, the man who lives at Number 10 does well to avoid policy departures like the plague, unless, until, and if, he sees a reasonable prospect for obtaining that "sense of the meeting." He is not without resources to induce the prospect, and he is at liberty to ride events which suit his causes. But these things take time — and timing. A power-wise Prime Minister adjusts his pace accordingly. So Macmillan did in 1962.

Ministerial prerogatives are not the only source of stalemate or slow motion in this system. If members of a Cabinet were not also heads of great departments, then the leader of their party in the Commons and the country might be less inclined to honor their pretensions in the Government. A second, reenforcing check-and-balance of the system lies between him and the senior civil servants. To quote again, from the same source:

> The PM has it easier with ministers than with the civil servants. The ranks of civil servants do not work for *him*. They have to be brought along. They are loyal to a "Government Decision" but that takes the form of action in Cabinet, where the great machines are represented by their ministers.

The civil servants can be his allies, of course, if their perceptions of the public interest square with his; then all he needs to do is to bring ministers along. Something of this sort seems to have been a factor in the Labour Government's acceptance of Polaris: Foreign Office and Defense officials urged their masters on; Treasury officials remained neutral. The PM who first manages to tie civil servants tighter to his office than to their own ministries will presidentialize the British system beyond anything our system knows. But that day is not yet. It may never come.

So a British Premier facing Cabinet is in somewhat the position of our President confronting the Executive Departments and Congress combined. Our man, compared to theirs, is freer to take initiatives and to announce them *in advance* of acquiescence from all sides. With us, indeed, initiatives in public are a step toward obtaining acquiescence, or at least toward wearing down the opposition. It is different in Downing Street. With us, also, the diplomatic and defense spheres yield our man authority for binding judgments on behalf of the whole government. Although he rarely gets unquestioning obedience and often pays a price, his personal choices are authoritative, for he himself is heir to royal prerogatives. In Britain these adhere to Cabinet members as a group, not to the Prime Minister alone. True, he can take over diplomacy, as Neville Chamberlain did so disastrously, and others since, or he can even run a war like Winston Churchill. But Chamberlain had to change Foreign Secretaries in the process, and Churchill took precautions, making himself Minister of Defense.

Still, despite all differences, a President, like a Prime Minister, lives daily under the constraint that he must bring along *his* "colleagues" and get action from *their* liege-men at both ends of the Avenue. A sensible Prime Minister is always counting noses in Cabinet. A sensible President is always checking off his list of "influentials." The PM is not yet a President. The President, however, is a sort of super-Prime Minister. This is what comes of comparative inquiry.

III

For over half a century, a great number of studious Americans have sought to fasten on our system, frankly imitating Britain, both a senior civil service drawn from career ranks and a Cabinet drawn from Congress. Meanwhile, without paying much attention to such formulations, our governmental practice has been building *ad hoc* counterparts. I have given two examples and could offer many more, but I hope these suffice to make the point.

The in-and-outers of whom we depend to do at presidential level what the Treasury-types of Whitehall do at Cabinet level deserve much more notice than they have so far received. They are a political phenomenon to study. They also are a political resource to nurture. Their care-and-feeding should concern our schools of public service not less but rather more than that of civil servants who remain in career ranks. (At least this is a proposition we shall test at Harvard with the new resources we are to obtain in memory of that notable recruiter, John F. Kennedy.)

As for our Cabinet-substitute, the shifting set of influentials, few things are more interesting in our system than the still inconclusive signs that we *may* now be on the verge of a new institutional breakthrough, a pragmatic innovation in our Constitution which might match those of the Roosevelt-Truman years. For White House staffing in the years of Kennedy and Johnson, combined with Johnson's tendency to use some senior Senators as though they were Executive advisers — these together, if sustained, could lay the basis for new patterns of relationship we someday would discover had become an institution. It is, of course, too soon to tell. Truman, in his early years, also leaned a lot on certain Senators. Eisenhower's staffing innovations mostly were a flash-in-the-pan. Influentials on the Hill are not yet tied to the presidential circle with anything like the firmness or the mutual satisfaction (relatively speaking) of the ties which bind their counterparts downtown. Perhaps they never will be. But if they ever are to be, the Johnson years appear a likely time.

These among others are the thoughts a look at Whitehall can suggest to a watcher of Washington — provided one is careful to distinguish form from function.

Two Patterns of Publicity, Privacy, and Secrecy: The United States and Great Britain

EDWARD A. SHILS

I. INTRODUCTORY REMARKS

The past decade has been the decade of the secret. Never before has the existence of life-controlling secrets been given so much publicity and never before have such exertions been made for the safeguarding of secrets. Of the three great powers, the Soviet Union represents the extreme of secretiveness. There, publicity is governmentally controlled and, although used far more widely than in any previously known oligarchy (for the Soviet Union is, after all, a populistic regime despite the impotence of the populace), it is used only by the government. It is never used against the government, and the secrets of the government are immune from publicity as long as the government wishes to keep them so. Publicity is directed against malefactors in the government on lower levels and against leaders who have failed. Privacy in the Soviet Union is not a legitimate area; insofar as it exists, it exists only on sufferance or out of negligence. The requirements of secrecy predominate.

The equilibrium of privacy, secrecy, and publicity which has been characteristic of the Western liberal democracies does not exist in the Soviet Union. Except as a feeble aspiration which never came to life, it never existed in Tsarist Russia. There too governmental secrecy predominated, although in a far more slipshod manner, and publicity was the timorous hope of the undeveloped liberal professions. Privacy was the area of life left over by the negligence and incompetence of the government. But, preoccupied with the fear of revolutionary conspiracies, the government infiltrated much of the society and what would otherwise have been the private zone of many of its members. Tsarist Russia was the only great state of the nineteenth and early twentieth centuries in which the ruling groups were perpetually occupied with the danger of conspiracy. The concern with secrets was an obsessive concern. In Great Britain and the United States the traditions of publicity and privacy were sufficiently strong to hold in check the occasionally surging anxiety about conspiracy. In Great Britain the equilibrium has continued largely intact and, despite minor fluctuations in crises and a long-run trend in favor of increased publicity, it does not seem likely to change greatly in the near future. In the

Reprinted by permission of The Macmillan Company and the author from *The Torment of Secrecy* (pp. 36–57) by Edward A. Shils. © The Free Press, a Corporation, 1956.

EDWARD A. SHILS is Professor of Social Thought and of Sociology, University of Chicago, and Fellow at King's College, Cambridge. He has co-translated some of Mannheim's and Weber's works, and has co-edited (with Talcott Parsons and others) *Toward a General Theory of Action* (1951) and *Theories of Society* (1961). He has written *The Atomic Bomb in World Politics* (1948), *The Present State of American Sociology* (1948), *The Torment of Secrecy* (1956), *Political Development in the New States* (1962), *The Intellectual Between Tradition and Modernity* (1961), and numerous articles published in various professional journals.

United States it has often verged towards disequilibrium. The disequilibrium is threatened by a continually mounting pressure of publicity and a fluctuatingly powerful preoccupation with secrecy, bound together in the peculiar affinity characteristic of populism under strain.

II. THE AMERICAN PATTERN:
LUXURIATING PUBLICITY

The United States has been committed to the principle of publicity since its origin. The atmosphere of distrust of aristocracy and of pretensions to aristocracy in which the American Republic spent its formative years has persisted in many forms. Repugnance for governmental secretiveness was an offspring of the distrust of aristocracy.

In the United States, the political elite could never claim the immunities and privileges of the rulers of an aristocratic society. Moreover, the suspicion of governmental intentions and the low esteem in which politicians and administrators were held after the Jacksonian revolution lowered the barriers to publicity on the governmental side and increased the insistence on publicity from the side of the governed.

All this occurred before the appearance of the press of the metropolitan masses. The development of sensational popular journalism coincided with the efflorescence of political and intellectual populism and followed on the flowering of governmental corruption in the tremendous economic expansion of the post-Civil War period. The result was the formation of a tradition of muckraking and exposure of the dark deeds of local, state, and federal governments, and of private business corporations. If was then that the ethos of the American journalistic profession was formed. It viewed the world as its oyster which had only to be pried open to be enjoyed. The ideal of the "scoop" meant that the journalist had always to be on the prowl for undisclosed secrets which would be of interest to his audience — and governmental secrets in an anti-governmental society were always so. American governments in that period offered much that was intriguing in this respect. There was always some corruption or shady dealing at one point or other in the vast, shambling structure of American government, and there was enough disgruntlement and talkativeness among those who had shared in it to reward the inquisitiveness of the journalistic investigator.

Government too marched in tune with the times, for politicians also lived in the tradition of publicity. Congressional investigations fitted perfectly into the populistic pattern of saving the people from the schemes of the powerful. It also met the journalists' need to uncover dark secrets and to assure the populace that their interests were being protected from their enemies in high and remote places.

The First World War, indirectly through the impetus it gave to the study of psychology and directly through the promotion of a belief in the efficacy of propaganda, sent America further into the direction of publicity. In the 1920's, mass production, national prosperity and advertising intensified the pressure for publicity. The growth of mass communications, films, radio and later television, only strengthened and gave new opportunities to a powerful impulse already very well developed.

By the end of the first quarter of the present century, the principle of aggressive publicity which had become deeply entrenched over the preceding hundred years thus found a special professional custodian. The supreme value and self-constituted task of the journalistic, advertising, and mass communication professions, reinforced by tradition, the Constitution, and their own professional interests and the pleasures of professional virtuosity, became the maintenance and furtherance of publicity. No society has ever been so extensively exposed to public scrutiny as the United States in the twentieth century.

The widely ranging freedom of the press has been repeatedly reaffirmed in the United States. The freedom to comment on court proceedings while a trial is still going on and the freedom of the press to publish anything it can obtain and to protect its sources are only a few among many instances of the dominance of publicity in American life. Few institutions refuse to acknowledge that dominance. Organizations which would appear to gain little from publicity feel the obligation to have a public relations department; universities, churches, learned societies accept unquestioningly the importance of "public relations."

The government admits without a qualm the rightfulness of publicity. The President's press conference, the press conferences of Cabinet officers, fireside chats, even television broadcasts of cabinet meetings attest the thoroughgoing permeation of the executive branch by the principle of publicity. Cabinet members and undersecretaries send out with the aid of ghost writers a continuous flow of articles to the popular periodicals. Generals, active and retired, find it almost impossible to be silent when so many opportunities in press, radio and television are offered. And the unending sequence of dinners of political, professional, religious, and business organizations gives the executive branch ample opportunity to spread its views, ill- or well-thought-out, before the nation.

The legislative branch too avails itself of the newest facilities for diffusing its news while the floors of Congress, not designed for the most modern forms of publicity, sink into the background. Congressional debate as a means of instructing the public yields to television, press conferences, and radio.

Few voices are raised in criticism of this ocean of publicity, and those which are raised are discredited as soon as they are heard.

The influence of the Genteel Tradition with its aversion for publicity suffered a gradual decline concurrently with the growth of the cultural independence of the Middle and Far West. The rise into the intelligentsia of the offspring of the ethnic groups which fell outside the sphere of hegemony of culture of the Eastern seaboard bred a generation in which restraint was not a virtue, in which distance, deference, and reserve were not esteemed. Self-restraint was equated with snobbery. The desire for privacy was described as "stand-offishness." Traditional American friendliness, which had always been critical of "side," moved with the times and the decline of etiquette. Traditional American talkativeness by its nature has been inherently antipathetic to privacy. Talk must have an object — either oneself or the other person. The need to be in contact and in communication with the other person is itself a breach in the wall of privacy.

No society could ever eliminate privacy completely. There are too many inhibitions on the one side and too much lack of curiosity on the other to permit the private zone around an individual, a friendship, or a corporate body to be entirely eroded. American society in the last two decades has, however, gone very far, certainly further than most great societies living in the western liberal tradition have gone. This is by no means without its positive aspect. No other large-scale society possesses the internal self-perceptiveness of American society. The various social classes and groups are more aware of each other, empathize with each other more readily and respond more readily to each other's expectations than in any European society. The whole process of the erosion of privacy and formation of a broad public sensitivity is to be seen in microcosm in the development of the social sciences, and especially sociology and social psychology, in the United States.

In the second quarter of the present century, the phenomenal growth of the social sciences, first in University studies and then in lay culture, has accustomed the new educated class to penetration into the privacy of others. Psychoanalysis and even more, its popularization, have had a similar effect. The ethos of an educated class more preoccupied with the observation of their own and other's private selves than any since the flowering of European romanticism has weakened the barriers against the flood of publicity.

American culture has become "wide open," and any efforts to close it are rearguard actions. There were and are occasional acts of censorship, precipitated by fundamentalists in reaction against modern secular culture, or by the extremists of sexual purity or by one of the great urban churches opposed to the temptations which the modern film or literature places before its parishioners. Even the moral rigorists who espouse suppression and try to enforce it are strong proponents of publicity. Picketing of theaters exhibiting "immoral" films, press conferences and congressional investigations are characteristic of latter-day efforts to restrict the free movement of the organs of publicity. Even suppression is achieved or sought through publicity.

American culture is a populistic culture. As such, it seeks publicity as a good in itself. Extremely suspicious of anything which smacks of "holding back," it appreciates publicity, not merely as a curb on the arrogance of rulers but as a condition in which the members of society are brought into a maximum of contact with each other. Favoring the exposure of practically every aspect of life, it is uneasy in the presence of those who appear to be withholding something. It is not always tolerant, and its occasional intolerance derives in large part from alarm over folds and convolutions in the fabric of society in which might lie hidden unknown dangers, temptations and disruptions.

This intolerance is by no means incompatible with publicity. On the contrary, publicity is one of the instruments by which populistic intolerance operates.

With its devotion to publicity on such a scale, it could scarcely be expected that in its normal state Americans would have much sympathy with secrecy, particularly governmental secrecy. Within the government, secrecy was at a minimum until the Second World War. Even the military, which in liberal societies is the chief locus of secrecy, was not granted many prerogatives in this respect in the United States nor did it aspire to them. When General Groves, who has played a monumental role in bringing secrecy to the forefront of American consciousness, was asked during the hearings on Dr. Oppenheimer whether he had much experience of security during his army career, he said he had never done so until the Manhattan Project. "The Army as a whole didn't deal with matters of security until after the atomic bomb burst on the world because it was the first time that the Army really knew there was such a thing, if you want to be perfectly frank about it!"

The U.S. Army had very little security training. Soldiers who might be captured in battle were cursorily instructed not to give anything away to their interrogators; there was ample classification and overclassification. There was, however, very little security-consciousness in the Army before the Second World War, and even during the war it was lax. A United States general shortly before D-Day disclosed the date of the attack at a cocktail party in London and his irresponsibility, although not matched, was approached in the general belief that security precautions were a bureaucratic ritual. They were a ritual which had to be observed because security officers could make things unpleasant, but there was little cognizance that the precautions were really necessary.

Within the civilian branches of the government, where secrecy had even feebler roots, "security-consciousness" was very faint.

Without seeking to make a brief for either Mr. John Service, who allegedly passed documents to the staff of *Amerasia*, or for any other American official who has turned confidential documents over to his friends of the press, or who has taken them home or shown them to unqualified persons, it must be remembered that security-consciousness is something new in America. How incomplete it is even now is evident from the continuous flow of inside information in the columns of certain journalists and the premature publication of the Yalta documents because they had obviously been, through some official's own unauthorized decision, placed in the hands of the *New York Times*.

In an individualistic society where the sense of institutional identity is often weak and where the principle of publicity is so central to the national culture, the only relationship between publicity and secrecy would, if men were reasonable, be one of conflict.

The situation is not, however, quite so simple. There are points at which publicity, overreaching itself, also doubles back on itself. At the extremes there is an affinity of opposites. Whereas most Americans take publicity in their stride and are affronted by secrecy, there are some, a small but vigorous minority, who are equally and extremely attracted by both.

There are persons for whom publicity is not just part of the accepted rules of the game of American social life, but to whom it is a means to salvation itself. Like secrecy, which might be functional or magical, so publicity can be practiced and accepted as the normal pattern of relationships among individuals and institutions or it can be endowed with sacred properties and surrounded with excited sentiments.

The American love of publicity is of both types. The former predominates, but there is always a tinge of the latter in it, particularly among the professionals of publicity. In a small sector of the population the balance is reversed and the magical protectiveness of publicity has the upper hand. It is in these circles that the preoccupation with secrecy is greatest — secrecy not in any rational sense, but rather secrecy as a source of danger and as a saving refuge. There is an irrational adhesion of the three elements: fear of secrets, dependence on secrets, and dependence on publicity.

This adhesion has, of course, been sharply catalyzed by the crisis attending the atomic bomb, but it was always a tendency of American populist radicalism of "right" and "left." Populist radicalism of the right has sought its salvation in an all-embracing patriotic homogeneity, within which place has been found for the secrecy of protective organs ranging from the Ku Klux Klan to the Federal Bureau of Investigation and the Atomic Energy Commission.

III. HYPERPATRIOTISM AND THE FEAR OF CONSPIRACY

The weaker sense of privacy in America makes for a flimsier attachment to corporate bodies and a fainter assimilation of their traditions. During the Second World War Professor Denis Brogan once said that whenever he was asked by a British civil servant going to Washington for the first time what useful counsel he could offer, he replied that the first thing to bear in mind in confronting an American official was that one was dealing not with the representative of an institution but with an individual. There is, of course, an element of hyperbole in this insight, but it is sound. Institutional loyalties are rather weaker in America than in England. The result is twofold: greater individual expressiveness on the one hand and occasionally a greater responsiveness and intensity of attachment to the more remote national or class or ethnic symbols.

In the United States these broader and yet diverse symbols rise frequently and excitingly to men's minds. Less firmly entrenched in private concerns, attention and sentiment shift easily towards distant public objects. Threats to public objects are envisaged with an almost eager rapidity and "crisis," "crossroads," and "last chances" are too often conjured up when the symbols of the nation come to the fore. There is a close affinity between the idea of the nation and the thought of crisis.

Within professions and professional societies, within occupational groups, within business enterprises, within churches and schools and school systems, and universities, all having their own traditions and their own criteria of recruitment and achievement, their own heroes and ideals, the emergence of an alleged national crisis attenuates autonomy and enfeebles the will to autonomy. At institutional ceremonies and in the internal regulation of institutional life in which the traditions of the institution might be celebrated and honored, there is a tendency in America for the symbols of the nation to come forward and for menaces to its safety to be discussed. At numerous ceremonial dinners, in sermons, at commencement addresses and alumni meetings, at meetings of bar and medical associations, at dedications of buildings and the inauguration of officers of associations, the celebration of the traditions and the past achievements of the club or association or sect are passed over in order to speak at length on the menace presented by America's ceaselessly conniving enemies. Like the Pole who, in the well-known anecdote about the competition for the best essay on the elephant, wrote on "The Elephant and the Polish Question," in the United States there is a perhaps too-ready tendency to invoke the national symbols and give them supremacy over the symbols of private bodies and separate institutions when it is really unnecessary for the well-being and military security of the nation.

Attachment to the most public of symbols, extreme "politicization" to the point of ideological possession, the anchoring of one's soul in the sphere of ultimate politics is the product of a state of mind which sees only white and black. Since all that is not white is not obviously black, it must be "really" black in the sense that it hides its blackness under a disguise. The wicked hide their wickedness under the conspirator's mask of innocence.

Worry about conspiracy has been a constant feature of American life for half a century at least. It has fluctuated in its significance, most of the time remaining the obsession of obscure and uninfluential ranters, but at other times, and especially in the past ten years, rising in intensity and extending its range of influence.

Anxiety about conspiracy brings with it a distortion of the conception of individual responsibility. The peculiar idea of moral infection in consequence of association with individuals of indelible wickedness leads to the notion of "guilt by association." Conspiracy is conceived, not necessarily as oriented towards the performance of specific acts, but as the harboring of certain general states of mind in seclusion or secrecy. The tendency to prosecute for conspiracy has been growing in American practice over the past twenty-five years, a period which coincides with an upward swing of populism. Mr. John Lord O'Brian has observed that "Congress for the past twenty-five years has been consistently endeavoring to establish in our jurisprudence the doctrine of guilt by imputation or belief or 'guilt by association.'" (*Harvard Law Review*, Vol. 61, p. 603.)

The pseudo-crises generated by fears of subversion by secretly working forces are the creations of populist demagogy and they in turn stir up the most stormy passions of populistic demagogy. The demand for complete disclosure, for a complete ironing out of the creases and unevenness in loyalty to the nation, imposes a great strain on the pluralistic institutional system.

Populistic radicalism almost always harbors, alongside of its fear of secrets, a belief in their salvationary character. In the traditional forms of revolutionary and counterrevolutionary radical populism, the need to keep secrets was concentrated on the inner circle of the conspiratorial band. American populism of the 1940's and 1950's has a new type of secret to engage its feverish worriment and love, namely, scientific secrets.

Science, which for so long had lived apart and to itself, has increasingly in the present century shown how much it could contribute to technology, welfare and defense. In the time of war when all autonomous institutions were being pressed to renounce some of their autonomy, the discovery was made that what science produced could make all the difference to national strength. Under pressure to divulge and not to divulge, science and scientists have fallen into a tormenting cross fire. Offering the quintessence of the most salvationary secrets, scientists have, at the same time and for the same reason, been drawn into the arena of publicity. Never has the tension of secrecy and publicity been so great as it has been in the United States in the past decade, and never has privacy been under such bombardment as since 1945. For almost a decade in the United States the equilibrium of privacy, publicity and secrecy was slipping out of order. It reached a maximum of disequilibrium in the winter and spring of 1954.

A society with as strong a tradition of pluralism as the United States does not lose its equilibrium indefinitely. It has great powers of righting itself. The populistic tendencies of American political sentiment have to contend with the resistance of other tendencies which are just as integral to it. The country has repeatedly shown its capacity to put its wildness behind it — as it did after the flurries of the First World War. And since the summer of 1954 it has once more demonstrated its balancing capacity. The technical problems of secrecy still remain and they are not easy to solve even in the calm light of reason. For the time being, however, the mad passions which endow publicity and secrecy with sacred properties have been repressed. They have been forced back into the lairs where they have always found a home in America, and the normal equilibrium of American life with publicity uppermost has been largely re-established.

IV. THE BRITISH PATTERN: THE BULWARK OF PRIVACY

The equilibrium of publicity, privacy, and secrecy in Great Britain is more stable and its deviations from the normal state are smaller than they are in the United States. Like America, Great Britain is a modern, large-scale society with a politicized population, a tradition of institutional pluralism, a system of representative institutions and great freedom of enquiry, discussion, and reporting. Like America, it also has a sensational popular press which goes to the limits in the infringement of privacy — limits which are narrower in Great Britain than in the United States. It also produces demagogues of great oratorical gifts, capable of arousing political passions and, as in the United States, they seldom attain the highest positions of authority. Yet this tells us very little about Great Britain because the differences are considerable. Despite occasional outbursts of acrimony and gross abuse, British political life is strikingly quiet and confined. Modern publicity is hemmed about by a generally well-respected privacy. Secrecy is acknowledged and kept in its place.

Although democratic and pluralistic, British society is not populist. Great Britain is a hierarchical country. Even when it is distrusted, the Government, instead of being looked down upon, as it often is in the United States, is, as such, the object of deference because the Government is still suffused with the symbolism of a monarchical and aristocratic society. The British Government, of course, is no longer aristocratic. Only the House of Lords remains, although in a greatly diminished form, as an instrument and symbol of aristocratic prerogative. The members of the Government come from all classes, primarily from the middle and upper-middle classes, but they participate in a set of institutions which has about it the aura of aristocracy and it enjoys therefore the deference which was given to that aristocracy. It enjoys the deference which is aroused in the breast of Englishmen by the symbols of hierarchy which find their highest expression in the Monarchy. Although the British Government is as democratic as any in the world, the institutions through which the Government operates still enjoy the respect which their aristocratic incumbents once aroused and which connection with the Crown still confers.

British participation in political life is somewhat greater than participation in the United States, but it does not express populist sentiments. The mass of the politically interested citizenry does not regard itself as better than its rulers. In contrast with the United States, the mandatory conception of the legislator does not find much support in Britain outside a small and radical section of the Labour Party. The ordinary citizen does not regard his own judgment as better than, or even as good as, his leaders'.

Walter Bagehot said many years ago that the English Constitution worked because the English were a deferential people. England has undergone many changes since Bagehot wrote; the peerage has been brought down, the Court is no longer so prominent and the great London houses have descended from their glory. The distribution of opportunity is far more equalitarian now than it was in 1867, and organizations supported by the working classes share in the power to an extent which seemed impossible at that time. But in the distribution of deference, Britain remains a hierarchical society.

The acceptance of hierarchy in British society permits the Government to retain its secrets, with little challenge or resentment. The citizenry and all but the most aggressively alienated members of the elite do not regard it as within their prerogative to unmask the secrets of the Government, except under very stringent and urgent conditions. For the same reason, the populace is ordinarily confident that their rulers can be counted upon to keep secret that which has to be kept secret.

The deferential attitude of the working and middle classes is matched by the uncommunicativeness of the upper-middle classes and of those who govern. The secrets of the governing classes of Britain are kept within the class and even within more restricted circles. The British ruling class is unequalled in secretiveness and taciturnity. Perhaps no ruling class in the Western world, certainly no ruling class in any democratic society, is as close-mouthed as the British ruling class. No ruling class discloses as little of its confidential proceedings as does the British. The televising of a cabinet meeting, such as happened recently in the United States, was profoundly shocking to British political circles.[1] The broadcast of the proceedings of a Parliamentary Committee or a Royal Commission would not be tolerated in Great Britain. Even the wireless discussion of issues about to come before Parliament is regarded as an intrusion into the autonomous sphere of the House of Commons. Even the most central public bodies are regarded as having an appropriate privacy which must be respected.

In contrast with the United States, where government documents are made available to historians without long delay, in Britain governmental papers which are not published at the time as part of government policy, are opened to scholarly inspection only after a very long lapse of time and even then with restrictions. Government officials, Cabinet ministers and their biographers always tread with discretion in personal and political matters. Again the contrast with America is very great. The memoirs of American political figures, although not always entirely written by themselves, disclose far more of the inner workings of party, government, and department than is the case in Britain. Only on very rare occasions does a British public figure, in his autobiography, make personal remarks disclosing his opinion of his fellow politicians or officials. There is practically no book in the modern literature of British political autobiography comparable to the late Harold Ickes' recent autobiographical works in which rivals are excoriated and enemies denounced in a language of extraordinary harshness. It is not that British politicians do not have animosities and mean thoughts of their colleagues and opponents. They have them in ample measure, but the rules of privacy forbid their public expression, beyond a narrow circle of equals.

What is spoken in privacy is expected to be retained in privacy and to be withheld from the populace.[2] When journalists are confided in, it is with the expectation that the confidence will be respected. "Government by leaks" in Great Britain is extremely infrequent. It is not a technique of warfare of one department against another or of one official against another.

The traditional sense of privacy of executive deliberations characteristic of the ruling classes of Great Britain has imposed itself on the rest of the society and has established a barrier beyond which publicity may not justifiably penetrate. Nowhere is this more evident than in the conduct of the British press, through which the impulse towards publicity is expressed.

The press in Great Britain, with all its vulgarity and all its curiosity about the great, keeps its place. For all the criticism of the Government of the day, the press maintains its distance and seldom pries into the affairs of the bureaucracy. Certainly it never comes anywhere near the practice of the American press in such matters. Sensational though much of the press is, it seeks sensations of unveiled privacy in the main elsewhere than in the disclosure of the

[1] The dominance of public events in British political life by television engineers and camera men as has happened on various occasions in the United States, is quite inconceivable.

[2] The journalist who discloses what is said behind the wall of privacy breaks the rules. He arouses the resentment of those on the "inside" and the curiosity of those on the "outside," but in both circles he is known to be doing the unusual thing.

vices of government. Muckraking in the American style is not one of the features of the British press, even the most sensational type. The exposures of governmental misdeeds featured in the British press are largely those uncovered by the Opposition or by some meticulously conscientious member of the Government. It is only then that political scandal-mongering is rendered legitimate.

The awe of the press before the majesty of Government is expressed also in the silence of the press about cases under trial in the courts. Whereas in the United States, the newspaper treatment of trials may involve editorial comments on the issues and parties, interviews with some of the principals and even analysis of the jurors and their deliberations, in Great Britain the newspapers must acquiesce in the exclusion of these areas from the scope of their professional virtuosity.

The British journalist, in his dealings with the government, handles himself as if he were an inferior of the person clothed with the majesty of office. His esteem for his own profession does not permit him to look on judges, members of Parliament and civil servants as if they were dependent upon him for publicity which he had in his power to give or withhold. Politicians in Great Britain like publicity, but their conception of what is possible and permissible usually falls within fairly narrow limits. The press conference plays a far smaller part in Whitehall and Westminster than it does in Washington. The balance of power between Government and the press favors the Government in Great Britain and the press in the United States.

In this manner, publicity in Great Britain is held in check. The Governments of Great Britain are not secretive in the way of an absolutist regime. Parliamentary debates are more fully reported than are Congressional debates in the United States and they are more widely discussed. A continuous flow of White Papers, Royal Commission Reports, Select Committee Reports, etc., throw light on the action and intentions of the Government. In the main, journalists are content to leave it at that. The secrets of the Government are not only protected by an Official Secrets Act and the strong silencing sense of corporate obligation on the part of ministers and civil servants; they are sustained too by the journalists' restraint in the presence of Governmental secrecy.

The professionals of publicity, political and journalistic, not being quite so fascinated by the secrets of the Government, do not feel their integrity and status dependent on the unravelling of secrets. Accordingly, they do not, like some American populist publicists and politicians, act as if salvation depended on secrecy as well as publicity. Very few strong complaints were made in Britain in 1948 that the Government's newly stated policy for keeping "security risks" out of sensitive positions was not sufficiently stringent. The defection of Maclean and Burgess, scarcely more than the misdeeds of Fuchs, Nunn May and Pontecorvo did not rouse a great outcry in Britain for far more stringent restraints on those entrusted with secrets.[3] There was practically

---

[3] It is possible that the slackness of British security which allowed Burgess and Maclean to escape notice so long arose from the mutual confidence of the different sectors of the ruling classes.

no demand for stricter measures against civil servants; the recent decision of the Government to increase the number of sensitive positions from which Communists would be excluded was not the product of popular pressure, in the House of Commons or in the press or in any organizations. Miss Rebecca West's suggestion that scientists have a special disposition towards treason found a louder echo in the United States than in Great Britain.

Secrecy is less fascinating in Great Britain because privacy is better maintained and publicity less rampant. The balance produced by the moderation of the demand for publicity, respect for the integrity of secrets and insensitivity to the magic of secrecy rests then on hierarchy, deference and self-containment. Self-containment is a part of the pluralism of British society.

By pluralism we mean the firm attachment and simultaneous and intermittent loyalty to a plurality of corporate and primordial bodies; to family, profession, professional association, regiment, church, chapel, club, and football team, political party, friends, and nation. Pluralism entails the more or less simultaneous exercise of attachments to these diverse objects and the maintenance of a balance among them so that none is continuously predominant. It is not rootlessness. On the contrary, it depends on solid bonds, on the enjoyment of traditions and the belief in the supra-individual character of the institution and of the members' obligations to them. But it does not permit such a degree of absorption into any one of the groups that members would be blind to the claims and values of others.

It is the reverse of specialization of interest and concentration of loyalty. In Great Britain, politics, ideally and in practice, is not permitted to claim all of an individual's attention. Naturally, the politician will usually prize political activity above most others, but he will feel compelled to show an interest in other fields of activity as well and to show himself to be a well-rounded human being. The scientist is expected not to allow science to rule out every other interest or concern. The situation is the same in other professions. The multiplicity of interest which this standard maintains in each individual means that passions are less frequently absorbed by single objects. In consequence, fanaticism appears less frequently in British ruling circles in the twentieth century than it does in many other modern countries. The reality of the propertied and leisured classes, devoting themselves in an amateur way to politics, sports and philanthropy, scarcely exists any longer in Great Britain, but the tradition which it set going, however, is still a force among men whose condition in life is very different.

The tradition of the amateur, with its aversion to specialization, is a major constituent in the internal solidarity of the British ruling classes, regardless of their class of origin. It promotes amicable relations within the elite and amicable dispositions and a ready empathy with one another. Mutual trust reduces the fear of secretiveness and the need for publicity. In such a situation there is less fear on the part of sensitive persons that secrets are being kept from them. The feeling of affinity which members of the elite in Great Britain have towards one another, the feeling of proximity and of understanding which they have for one another despite all disagreements and antagonisms, restrains the tendency to fear hidden secrets. It increases the acceptability of secrecy within the elite since it symbolizes an acknowledgment of equality. By increasing the solidarity of the elite it increases the capacity to keep secrets within the group and reduces the disposition to "leak" secrets in order to show "outsiders" that one is "on the inside." The internal solidarity and mutual confidence of the elite is accompanied by a greater insensitivity to the sentiments of those outside.

The respect for one's "betters" and the mutual trust within the ruling classes are infused with a general disposition towards a lack of interest in the private affairs of the next man. In all classes of the population in England, men can live close to one another, work with one another and even be friends for a long time while remaining quite ignorant of each other's affairs and past. This ignorance is partly a function of indifference, partly of tact and the belief that the other's affairs are his own business.

There is less active curiosity in England on the part of one individual about another. There is less probing, there is less quick empathy, and less readiness to imagine oneself into the state of mind of another person. The general lack of social understanding, the ignorance of the social structure of Great Britain which one finds in so many sections of the British population — the blindness about British society which one finds in the educated classes — means that alongside of the broad sense of unity, which reduces anxiety, there is also a lower level of mutual, imaginative penetration and less of an impulse to penetrate into the interior life of other persons.

This does not mean that there is not gossip, often of a very malicious sort, or that there is not pathological curiosity, a considerable market for literature about the private life of the royal family, or a considerable audience for scandal from the divorce courts. England has all of these. But they all exist within the matrix of a quite striking acceptance of the legitimacy of the privacy of one's fellow man. The person who keeps to himself in Britain will be less criticized than he would be in America. The difference in the sense of privacy contributes to the maintenance of the equilibrium by offering resistance to pressures for publicity and for the search for salvation in the opposite of publicity, namely, the concentration of secrecy.

Through the spirit of privacy, the deferential attitude towards government is reinforced. If anybody in Britain would have grounds to feel that the ruling group was secretive, it would be the lower and middle classes who are so excluded from "inside" knowledge. Much more is withheld in Britain than in America from the scrutiny of the public. Yet the ruling classes in Great Britain are respected, and they are entitled, in the eyes of the mass of the population (lower-middle class and working class, rural and urban) to possess their secrets as long as they are not obviously harming anyone. Thus the circle is turned, and an equilibrium of secrecy, privacy, and publicity kept stable.

Although the British and the official spokesmen of their corporate institutions are much afflicted with national conceit, on the whole they are less preoccupied with the symbols of nation and of national unity than some of the more vociferous Americans. Those who are so preoccupied get less of a hearing and are less influential. On ceremonial occasions, the national symbols are less frequently invoked and less intensely invoked in Great Britain than in America. In the United States a trade or professional association, being addressed at a conference, is more likely to learn about the threat of Communism and the needs of national defense. In Great Britain this is less likely to be so. The fact of nationality lies less continuously and less restlessly on the minds of the British upper and upper-middle classes. It is not that there are not in all political positions in Great Britain, hyperpatriots who refer everything they discuss to a British standard and find it wanting. There are many Englishmen, especially since the war, who have Britain on their minds over all else. But they do not, on the surface at least, seem to be defending themselves from external attack. British jingoism does not seem to be in such need of the internal homogeneity of society as its American counterpart. American hyperpatriotism seems always to call for loyalty, maximal loyalty, while British national conceit is capable of being unworried by the internal heterogeneity of British society. The British phenomenon is directed towards foreigners; the American towards other Americans as well as foreigners.

Feeling less exposed to attack from hidden enemies allied to external enemies, there is less need for publicity to root them out and to uncover their secrets. Less preoccupied with secrets and indeed accepting a mild type of secrecy as a normal mode of life, there is more confidence that such secrets as are deemed necessary will not be stolen or disclosed with harmful intentions. Just as the British are less perceptive of crisis than the Americans and more apt to deny their existence, while the Americans tend to overemphasize them, so British security measures tend towards an over confident and gentlemanly laxity and inefficiency, while American security measures tend towards excessive and unnecessary rigidity and comprehensiveness.

The two patterns which we have just described have much in common. It would be impossible for two large-scale, highly industrialized, highly democratic liberal countries to exist at opposite poles. In each of the countries there is normally an equilibrium of publicity, privacy, and secrecy. Each of the countries has, however, a somewhat different weighting of the elements. In America it is publicity, in Britain privacy, and even a matter-of-fact, unemotional, unmagical secrecy which weigh a lot more heavily than the other elements in the culture. In America, for the balance to be maintained, there must be a perpetual struggle to keep publicity and a nervous worry about secrets, good and bad, from inundating individual and corporate privacy. In Britain the equilibrium requires a constant alertness lest the privacy of the upper stratum in government and culture proves too great a bulwark against publicity.

The specifically British disequilibrium, which is restricted in range, is the preponderance of privacy and traditional governmental secretiveness over publicity. The specifically American disequilibrium is the preponderance of publicity and its attendant stress on salvationary secrecy over privacy.

The Cultural and Political
Setting of Economic
Rationality in Western
and Eastern Europe

REINHARD BENDIX

The Soviet system of domination is a new historical phenomenon. On the basis of modern technology, through the organizational structure of a ruling totalitarian party, and by the whole gamut of material incentives and modern as well as ancient devices of tyranny this system has achieved rapid economic growth. In this respect as well as in its atomization of civil society it differs fundamentally from the patrimonial despotism of the ancient and oriental world. The present paper seeks to characterize this type of domination by contrasting the cultural and political setting of "economic rationality" in Western and Eastern Europe.[1]

The term "economic rationality" may mean many things, but I shall use it here in a deliberately restricted sense, referring to work habits and to the expectations regarding governmental action respectively. Work habits are rational in this sense when they possess method and a steady as well as intense expenditure of effort. Administration is rational in this sense when it is characterized by an orientation toward norms and thus permits relatively stable expectations with regard to the conduct of official business. Both forms of rationality are ordinarily thought to presuppose that the norms governing work and the conduct of public business stay put for reasonable lengths of time. I am here concerned with the social origin of a set of preferences which the economist takes as given in his approach to the problem.

In Western Europe rational *work habits* were strongly influenced by the Protestant Ethic. Though the direction of this influence is amply documented, Max Weber's original essay on this theme left unspecified how religious ideas might have become influential in the conduct of individuals. And his later sociology of religion made this influence of ideas on conduct still more problematic since he emphasized the great emotional, social, and intellectual distance between religious leaders and the mass of the people. Nevertheless, Weber did not neglect this question, even though he did not explore it fully. In his essay on the Protestant sects he pointed out that sectarian religions

From *Russian and East European Studies: Value and Plan, Economic Calculation and Organization in Eastern Europe*, ed. Gregory Grossman (Berkeley and Los Angeles: University of California Press, 1960), pp. 245–261. Reprinted by permission of the University of California Press.
[1] In keeping with the intentions of this comparative analysis my formulations will be ideal-typical. They are designed to characterize the problematics of a totalitarian regime in one respect at least, rather than to analyze specific solutions. I should make clear that on the empirical side my own work in this field consists so far of a case study of industrial relations and specifically of managerial ideologies in East Germany. Since my purpose here is typological, I have sought to abstract from the specific conditions of this satellite country on the basis of a reading knowledge of Soviet conditions. My hope is that experts on Soviet Russia will find my analysis to be compatible with the Soviet experience.

provided incentives as well as sanctions which were designed to inculcate methodical work habits and which forced the individual through social pressure to conform to the standards of the community.

> The member of the sect had to have qualities of a certain kind in order to enter the community circle. . . . In order to hold his own in this circle, the member had to *prove* repeatedly that he was endowed with these qualities. . . . For, like his bliss in the beyond, his whole social existence in the here and now depended upon his "proving" himself. . . .
>
> According to all experience there is no stronger means of breeding traits than through the necessity of holding one's own in the circle of one's associates.[2]

Weber did not investigate the diffusion of the ideas which were inculcated in this manner, but he made it clear that they had retained their influence long after the conditions of their origin had disappeared. Today, "the idea of duty in one's calling prowls about in our lives like the ghost of dead religious beliefs." [3] One can summarize Weber's contention by stating that he attributed to the ideas expressed in Puritan preaching the spirit of sober zeal and rationality which he also found characteristic of capitalist economic activities. He looked to the social pressure of the sectarian community for the "mechanism" of internalization; and he believed that once launched these ideas attained a momentum of their own owing to their affinity with economic activities and to their secularized diffusion in all phases of modern culture.[4]

With this Western European background in mind it may be instructive to examine the Russian experience with the idea of finding "functional equivalents" for the change of orientation which Puritanism helped to bring about in traditional economic activities.[5] To be sure, the emergence of economic rationality in Russia was in part associated with the diffusion of ideas which may be traced back to Puritanism. When Lenin spoke of adopting the Taylor system without its capitalist abuses or when Alexander Blok wrote a poem in praise of "Communist Americanism," they were clearly borrowing techniques and images of advanced industrialization.[6] But diffusion is only a small part of the story. During the 1920's Russia experienced an "outbreak" of technocratic zeal which is comparable in some ways to the enthusiasm for in-

[2] Max Weber, *Essays in Sociology*, tr. and ed. by H. H. Gerth and C. W. Mills (New York: Oxford University Press, 1946), p. 320.

[3] Max Weber, *The Protestant Ethic and the Spirit of Capitalism* (New York: Scribner, 1930), p. 182.

[4] For other aspects of Weber's study of economic rationality in Western Europe see pp. 249 ff.

[5] The following discussion elaborates comparisons and contrasts which are analyzed in a preliminary way in my *Work and Authority in Industry* (New York: John Wiley & Sons, 1956), pp. 204–211.

[6] They were not the first, of course. For a useful survey of the developing concern with industrialization, see Alexander Gerschenkron, "The Problem of Economic Development in Russian Intellectual History of the 19th Century," in Ernest J. Simmons (ed.), *Continuity and Change in Russian and Soviet Thought* (Cambridge, Mass.; Harvard University Press, 1955), pp. 11–39.

ventions in mid-eighteenth-century England. As an example of the type of evidence I have in mind I refer to Fülöp-Miller's *The Mind and Face of Bolshevism,* in which the author surveys the technocratic zeal of the 1920's as it found expression in poetry, drama, novels, and films, in demonstrations, billboards, and other public displays, in the slogans of pamphleteers and in theoretical discussions. The revolutionary grandiloquence of all this was well expressed in a declaration of the Central Labor Institute, which was founded in 1920 by A. K. Gastev, who was characteristically both a poet and an industrial engineer.

> The cultural level of the masses is low, yet they believe themselves close to a turning-point in history. Their spirit is growth, they await great determining gestures, they dream of great men, who are leaders, they anticipate the advent of gigantic technical powers. Europe and America are guarding established traditions, while Eastern Europe witnesses a spring-flood of an incomparable love of life, an unlimited belief in progress. The land of tremendous rivers, unruly hurricanes, steppes without limit, which is peopled by pilgrims and pioneers, will give birth to an unusual patriotism and will call into life courageous men of daring deeds and accomplishments. . . .[7]

This passage not only expresses the revolutionary fervor of the period, but makes clear also that this fervor linked technocratic ideals with nationalism and that by itself it had nothing to do with rationality. The spirit expressed in Gastev's proclamation was zealous, but hardly sober.

This second element came to the fore as the product of organization. Gastev's institute was discontinued, probably because his "bourgeois" methods of analyzing bodily movements after the manner of Taylor and Gilbreth could only be made the basis of individual instruction and efficiency ratings as in the West. It is symptomatic that at about the same time a mass campaign to inculcate methodical work habits was launched by the Red Army and then in offices and enterprises. Small groups were organized in order to fight "for the proper use and economy of time." Under the impetus of activists these groups were organized in the Time League, whose members were obliged to keep a card on which they recorded their daily activities. The ideas espoused by this organization were as identical with the Puritan principles of daily conduct as two such divergent sets of ideas can get; even the device of a daily record is similar to the diaries which Puritan Divines commended to their parishioners as a means of making sure that their time was not spent in activities harmful to the soul.[8] It may be suggested that — at least in this initial

---

[7] Quoted in Franziska Baumgarten, *Arbeitswissenschaft und Psychotechnik in Russland* (München: R. Oldenbourg, 1924), p. 13. My translation.

[8] Whether the work habits which resulted from these campaigns actually became more rational is another question. The Stakhanovite campaigns, beginning in the 1930's, would indicate that they did not. The fact that Stakhanovism is still an important incentive method does not necessarily mean, on the other hand, that no improvement in the direction of more rational work habits has occurred, although Stakhanovism by itself is the opposite of steady and intense work effort. The fact that this type of special purpose campaign is endemic in the Soviet system does not rule out the

period — the methods which Communist and trade-union activists used to in-culcate work habits of steady intensity were closely similar to the examinations of conscience, the daily scrutiny of conduct, and the public disclosure and discussion of individual failings characteristic of the sectarian community. Perhaps, the pedagogical techniques of A. S. Makarenko reflected as well as influenced these early methods of agitation. Makarenko's emphasis on the precedence of collective goals over individual values together with his skillful manipulation of shame and guilt within the adolescent peer group as a means of inculcating discipline and work habits are reminiscent of the collectivism and techniques of social control in the sect, both at their best and their worst.[9]

Several striking differences between the Western European and the Russian "case" must now be noted. First, there is an important difference in back-ground. The Puritan revolution occurred in line with many correlated de-velopments favoring economic rationality; it was a manifestation of ethical rationalism that had its roots in the Old Testament prophets and in the mes-sage of Jesus. As far as I know, the Russian revolution had no comparably favorable background for the development of economic rationality, though a recent study suggests that the zeal of the 1920's had deep roots indeed in an anti-Western Messianic tradition.[10] Second, there is a difference in timing. In Western Europe the Puritan ethic of work developed and became diffused (in secularized form) for two centuries, before the advance of industrialization brought about the utilization of this ethic in rationalizing the methods of work performance and the organizational structure of the modern enterprise. In Russia an ethic of work and industrialization developed simultaneously, whether we take as the beginning date the rapid development of railroads in the 1880's or the revolution of 1917. Presumably, this difference in timing meant that at the level of work performance economic rationality was firmly established in Western Europe long before the modern requirements of industrial organization emerged; and even then more than a century inter-

---

possibility of a cumulative change in the direction of rationality. The tactics of evasion which have been studied intensively at the managerial level, may be used at the level of the workers as a means of making a steady intensity of work possible despite the Stakhanovite campaigns. My guess is that this would depend on an ac-ceptance of the industrialization drive as a national cause, and if so that acceptance might well be a partial result of the Stakhanovite movement. For evidence of a rejection of both and hence of a barely disguised hostility between workers and "activists" of any kind see my *Work and Authority in Industry*, pp. 400 ff.

[9] See A. S. Makarenko, *Ausgewaehlte Paedagogische Schriften* (Berlin: Volk and Wissen, 1953), pp. 25–45, 77–89, and the interesting study of Makarenko's work as a whole in Frederic Lilge, A. S. *Makarenko, An Analysis of His Educational Ideas in the Context of Soviet Society* (University of California Publications in Education, Vol. 15, No. 1; Berkeley and Los Angeles: University of California Press, 1958). It may be added that Makarenko explicitly used the mutual dependence and the solidarity of the military unit as his model.

[10] Emanuel Sarkisyanz, *Russland und der Messianismus des Orients* (Tübingen: J. C. B. Mohr, 1955). As a layman in this field I can only record my impression that the author's very interesting emphasis may have led him to underestimate the influence of Russian revolutionary thought of the European enlightenment, especially the idea of progress through science. This is my reason for referring to the "technocratic ideals" of the 1920's.

vened between Adam Smith and Frederick Taylor. In Russia, on the other hand, the development of industry coincided with the felt need for a rational organization of work. Third, there is a major difference of ideas between a secular utopia linked to invidious contrasts between Mother Russia and a universal enemy, on the one hand, and a transcendental conception of God's relationship to a community of believers, on the other. The many ramifications of this point need not be considered in the present context. Fourth, there is a major difference between inculcation of work habits which occurs through interaction among members of a religious community and diffuses from there, and a comparable inculcation which occurs throughout the nation (rather than within the community) and through the organized drive of a totalitarian party.

All of these differences have a bearing on another aspect of economic rationality which I would like to call "the stability of expectations." In the Western European experience men increased the zeal (intensity) and rationality (method) of their work effort because in their economic transactions and in relation to government they came to know what to expect — at least in certain respects. But the study of totalitarian government is teaching us today that men may also increase the zeal and rationality of their work effort when they are systematically led to distrust one another and when in certain respects they are deliberately prevented from knowing what to expect. I now turn to a closer examination of this contrast.

In his study of economic rationality Max Weber buttressed his assertions concerning Puritanism with a series of related studies. These dealt with the ethical rationalism of the Old Testament prophets, with the decline of kinship ties in urban communities due to the equality of citizens as Christian believers and as armed defenders of their city, and with the emergence of legal and administrative rationality in the Catholic church, the absolute monarchies, and the legal profession of Western Europe. All these developments had in common that they tended to promote *stable expectations* in economic transactions. Following Weber I shall relate this important aspect of economic rationality first to the Protestant Ethic and then to the system of legal domination which emerged with the development of absolute monarchy.

Puritanism placed major emphasis upon a double aspect of man's unremitting service to God. To prove worthy of the gifts and opportunities which God had placed at man's disposal, he must not permit anything to interfere with the productive use of his time; thus, all emotional ties are a danger to man's immortal soul for they easily divert him from the service to which God has called him. This innerworldly asceticism as Weber called it, resulted in a profound depersonalization of family and neighborhood, for it demanded that man treat his next of kin and his associates with sober detachment, lest his love for them or their love for him jeopardize the work to which God had called him. And this emotional detachment within the community also reduced the emotional distance between its members and the strangers beyond the "gate." For hatred is as dangerous to the soul as love, and where the relation to one's associates is detached, it becomes difficult to distinguish it from one's relations with strangers which are similarly detached. Subsequently this detachment often gave rise to a calculating approach in all human relationships, but originally this attitude had a profoundly ethical basis. Implicit in the Puritan ethic was the demand that man should order *all* his personal relationships with the same detachment so that he may be single-minded in attending to the purpose in life which transcends all mundane concerns. The significance of this orientation for economic rationality may be summarized in Weber's words:

> Originally, two opposite attitudes toward the pursuit of gain exist in combination. Internally, there is attachment to tradition and to the pietistic relations of fellow members of tribe, clan, and house-community, with the exclusion of the unrestricted quest of gain within the circle of those bound together by religious ties; externally, there is absolutely unrestricted play of the gain spirit in economic relations, every foreigner being originally an enemy in relation to whom no ethical restrictions apply; that is, the ethics of internal and external relations are categorically distinct. The course of development involves on the one hand the bringing in of calculation into the traditional brotherhood, displacing the old religious relationship. As soon as accountability is established within the family community, and economic relations are no longer strictly communistic, there is an end of the naive piety and its repression of the economic impulse. This side of the development is especially characteristic of the West. At the same time there is a tempering of the unrestricted quest of gain with the adoption of the economic principle into the internal economy. The result is a regulated economic life with the economic impulse functioning within bounds.[11]

Thus, interpersonal reliability was buttressed by diminishing both the emotional involvement among the true believers within the community and the emotional distance between them and persons on the outside. This proved to be an essential element in economic transactions in that it furthered the development of mutual trust among men who sought and recognized in each other the same criteria of trustworthiness. The built-in secularization of the Puritan ethic (which John Wesley noted when he said that piety produced riches, and riches a decline of religion), therefore, led on the positive side to established norms of economic conduct albeit at the price of personal detachment and of a tendency toward calculation in human relations.[12]

[11] Max Weber, *General Economic History* (London: Allen and Unwin, n.d.), p. 356.

[12] In Weber's eyes this tendency to obliterate the distinction between the in-group and out-group in economic affairs was associated with the decline of kinship ties and the religious equality of Christian believers in the cities of Western Europe. He contrasted this development especially with the persistent communalism of the Oriental cities with their taboo against commercialism among insiders and their "no-holds-barred" attitude toward the exploitation of outsiders. See Max Weber, *Wirtschaft und Gesellschaft* (Tübingen: J. C. B. Mohr, 1925), II, 528–544. More recently, Benjamin Nelson has shown that this transition from a double to a single standard of economic ethic was intimately related to the whole history of Christian universalism. See his *The Idea of Usury, From Tribal Brotherhood to Universal Otherhood* (Princeton: Princeton University Press, 1949).

These unanticipated and secularized consequences of Puritanism were not, however, the only and perhaps not the most important foundation for the development of stable expectations in economic transactions. In his sociology of law and in his study of domination Weber demonstrated that certain legal and administrative developments had favored this aspect of rationalism in Western culture. Under a traditional system of domination stable expectations in economic affairs could not develop readily. The belief in sacred norms which sustained this system was typically combined with the endorsement of paternal authority which was essentially arbitrary. And the irrationality of such personal arbitrariness in the organization of government was matched by the irrationality of a legal system which consisted of many autonomous jurisdictions whose conflicts had to be resolved by compromise or forced settlement in the absence of a nationally valid and codified body of laws. Weber showed that stable expectations became possible when the development of legal procedure and administrative organization gradually brought about an orientation toward abstract norms which were regarded as valid. For the discussion to follow it will stand us in good stead if I summarize here the essential elements of his definition of legal domination in the modern state. Such a system of domination exists when the political community possesses the following characteristics:

A legal order which is subject to change by legislation and which has binding authority over all citizens and most actions within its area of jurisdiction.
Binding authority under law means that all use of force within the body politic is regarded as legitimate only if it is either permitted or prescribed by the legally constituted government, i.e., if it is in accordance with enacted statute.
An administrative apparatus conducts official business in accordance with legislative regulation. This means that
The persons who occupy positions of authority are not personal rulers, but superiors who temporarily occupy an office by virtue of which they possess limited authority.
The work of these officials is done
on a continuous basis
under supervision
on the basis of documents.
As a result the officials are characterized by the following attributes:
They are personally free and appointed to their position on the basis of contracts;
Their loyalty is enlisted on the basis of the faithful execution of their official duties;
Their appointment and job placement depends on their technical qualifications;
Their administrative work is a full-time occupation;
Their work is rewarded by a regular salary and by prospects of regular advancement in a lifetime career.[13]

[13] This list of attributes is a paraphrased synopsis of several enumerations in which Weber variously discusses the characteristics of the modern state, of the legal order, of administration under the rule of law, and of the social position of officials. See Max Weber, *The Theory of Social and Economic Organization* (New York: Oxford Uni-

The most important characteristics of this type of bureaucratic government under the rule of law consist in the conscious orientation toward abstract norms and consequently in the depersonalization of the exercise of authority. By elaborating the contrast between this type of domination and the system of traditional authority Weber showed that under a legal order and a bureaucratic organization of government the stability of expectations was substantially increased.

If we now turn to the Russian development it is easy to see that the contrast with the Western European development is very great. There is, I take it, no analogue for the gradual emergence of mutual trust within autonomous groups which Weber examined in the context of the urban community and the Protestant sects. The destruction of urban and sectarian group autonomy by the tsarist rulers has often been traced. And I merely add here that the same consideration applies to the Russian aristocracy, which was divided for centuries into rival kinship groups. Their competition for the social rank bestowed at court and through governmental office prevented the emergence of a cohesive status group of landed notables.[14] This absence of group autonomy is related to the fact that in Russia a modern state in Weber's sense did not develop. During the nineteenth century the foundation of a legal order through codification was laid in Western Europe, whereas in Russia attempts in this direction failed. And this absence of a rule of law was reflected in the autocratic rule of the tsar which helped to perpetuate a government of rival administrative cliques and hence prevented the development of a bureaucracy in Weber's sense of that term.[15] These allusions may suffice as a reminder of the historical background which accounts for the absence of stable expectations and of legal and administrative rationality in Russia. My purpose is to analyze the possibility of rationality under a totalitarian regime despite the absence of these elements. Since Weber's work contains the most extensive analysis of the cultural conditions which favored such rationality in Western Europe, it seems worthwhile to test the utility of his approach by using it as a frame of reference for this typological analysis of totalitarian government. In order to do this, it is necessary to spell out his analysis of bureaucracy with regard to the problem of power.[16]

---

versity Press, 1947), pp. 154, 156, 329–336; and Max Weber, *Essays in Sociology*, pp. 198–204.

[14] See the illuminating contrast of city and bourgeoisie in Western Europe and Russia by Otto Brunner, *Neue Wege der Sozialgeschichte* (Göttingen: Vandenhoeck and Ruprecht, 1956), pp. 80–115, and the brief survey in my *Work and Authority*, pp. 117–128. The classic work by Leroy-Beaulieu is perhaps still the best analysis of the relation between the Russian aristocracy and the tsarist court and government.

[15] A telling analysis of the administrative consequences of autocratic rule will be found in Max Weber, *Gesammelte Politische Schriften* (München: Drei Masken-Verlag, 1920), pp. 156–158, and *passim*.

[16] For reasons of space I confine myself to a discussion of bureaucracy. Weber also examined the beliefs in natural law which legitimized legal enactments in terms of ideas that transcend the positive law. Totalitarianism obviously depends in part upon

An ideally functioning bureaucracy represents the most efficient method of solving large-scale organizational tasks. But the conditions of efficiency can also be conditions which lead to a subversion of the rule of law, and hence to the transformation of bureaucracy from an instrument of power into a decision-making body. Most important in this respect is the knowledge of the official. This knowledge is technical, so far as appointments depend on educational qualifications, and it is specifically administrative so far as organizational know-how is acquired through day-to-day experience with the minutiae of administration. Under modern conditions the only alternative to administration by officials who possess such knowledge is administration by dilettantes. And this alternative is ruled out wherever the expert performance of administrative functions is indispensable for the promotion of that order and welfare which is regarded as mandatory by the decision-making powers. Thus, the technical and organizational knowledge of the official is a sign of his indispensability and hence of his power, unless he is controlled by persons who possess not only the authority to supervise him but also the knowledge to do so effectively. The latter condition was especially important in Weber's view, because officials tend to buttress their superiority as technical and organizational experts by treating official business as confidential and by thus securing their work against outside inspection and control. This tendency toward secrecy becomes imperative wherever the power interests of an organization are at stake in its contest with hostile organizations, for concealment may improve the chances of success. But the tendency prevails even where this justification does not apply: every bureaucracy will conceal its knowledge and operation unless it is forced to disclose its conduct of affairs, and it will, if need be, simulate the existence of hostile interests in order to justify such concealment. Such practices will subvert the rule of law, because an administration which cannot be inspected and controlled, will tend to become a law unto itself.[17]

Weber's discussion of this issue was concerned with the task of establishing effective parliamentary control over the bureaucracy, because in imperial Russia and Germany the problem was that autocratic monarchs who sought to exercise supreme authority, were in fact in the hands of uncontrolled bureaucratic cliques or powerful chancellors. He asserted that a parliamentary regime would create or restore the system of legal domination, because its enactments would reflect the constellations of interest in the population as well as the minimum consensus needed for every system of domination. Because of this dependence of parliament on public opinion he could assume that the norms enacted into law would remain for reasonable lengths of time. For Weber it was, therefore, principally a question of establishing political control over a functioning bu-

ideas of legitimacy which underlie its legal system and which differ strikingly from the traditions of natural law and legal positivism which have been basic to the system of legal domination in Western Europe. See the discussion in Max Weber, *Law in Economy and Society,* ed. and tr. by Max Rheinstein and E. A. Shils (Cambridge, Mass.: Harvard University Press, 1954), pp. 284–321.

[17] These points are discussed in Max Weber, *Theory,* p. 339; *Essays in Sociology,* pp. 232–235; and *Gesammelte Politische Schriften,* p. 171.

reaucracy, because the latter "is easily made to work for anybody who knows how to gain control over it." [18] In a totalitarian regime the problem of political control is essentially different, because the issues which Weber analyzed must be resolved there on the basis of ever-changing norms in keeping with the revolutionary rationale of the Party. Like all bureaucracies the officials of such a regime will practice the arts of concealment, but the Party cannot be satisfied with establishing control over the apparatus at the top only, because it wishes to do more than supervise the routine functioning of that apparatus. The following pages will describe what I conceive to be the principle of totalitarian rule in an effort to show its rationality, given the forced pace and the frequent changes in policy which have characterized the process of industrialization in the Soviet Union.

Under totalitarian rule every organized activity is thought to be politically significant and is subjected in principle to two interlocking hierarchies of authority. One of these hierarchies is always the Party, the other varies with the field of activity. The operation of these hierarchies may be analyzed here in terms of a hypothetical factory. One hierarchy of authority extends from the Presidium (or Politbureau) of the Party through the successive levels of the planning authorities of government down to the director of the individual enterprise. The director has to follow the detailed plans issued to him by the superordinated planning agencies, though as Professor Berliner has shown, he will where possible take a hand in the formulation of these plans so as to facilitate the successful operation of the enterprise.[19] Within the limits stipulated by the economic plan the director has absolute authority over the enterprise. An official textbook on industrial organization states that "the Director of the factory . . . is the agent of the Soviet State. He determines the ways and means by which the enterprise can fulfill the tasks set for it by the economic plan." [20]

The other hierarchy of authority also descends from the Presidium of the Party, but then goes through the Party-secretariats at the several geographic levels down to the Party secretary in the factory. The basic organizational unit of the Party consists of rank and file members recruited among the employees of the factory, but here we need only be concerned with the leaders of the party-cell, that is, its activists and the Party secretary who (in East Germany at least) is a full-time appointee of the higher Party authorities. Although these local Party leaders must follow the specific directives issued by the Party, their general functions are described as a regular aspect of industrial organization. That is to say, the Party cell must support the absolute authority of the factory director by mobilizing the workers "for the fulfillment of production plans, for the strengthening of labor discipline, and for the development of socialist competition." At the same time, the Party cell is also called upon to "fight against mismanagement, control the administrative activity, and strengthen the masses

[18] Weber, *Essays in Sociology*, p. 229.

[19] See Joseph S. Berliner, *Factory and Manager in the USSR* (Cambridge, Mass.: Harvard University Press, 1957), chap. 14.

[20] S. E. Kamenizer, *Organisation und Planung des sozialistischen Industriebetriebes* (Berlin: Verlag Die Wirtschaft, 1953), p. 110. My translation.

in the struggle against bureaucratism and against conduct inimical to the state." [21]

The official interpretation denies the existence of any conflict between the absolute authority of the director and the apparently overlapping functions of the party cell. The latter is said to support the director's authority and to aid in the implementation of managerial directives. The Party's struggle against bureaucratism and other deviations and failings is but another phase of its responsibility for aiding in the fulfillment of production goals and safeguarding the interests of the state. None of this, it is said, limits in any way the principle of "one-man management," for the director has ultimate responsibility for maximum production, he is enjoined to fight against "bureaucratism," and he is frequently instructed to rely on the support of the Party organization in meeting his responsibilities. The director and the Party cell are ultimately subject to the authority of the Party, whether the director is a member of the Party or not, and of course most of them are. Hence, the goals of both are the same, and they are enjoined to collaborate in "fulfilling and overfulfilling" the plan. But despite this prescribed identity of goals and despite the common subordination to the same ultimate authority the division between management and "labor" is nominally retained. The director represents management, while the Party cell represents the Party which in turn is said to represent and lead the workers. However, the conflicts between management and "labor" which might result from common interests and patterns of thought within each group, are officially eliminated.

This is clearly revealed in the so-called collective agreements between management, the trade union, the Party cell, and individual "activists." With regard to the usual stipulations concerning wages and the conditions of employment, these "agreements" can only repeat what is already contained in the authoritative directives of the planning agencies. However, the agreements also have a substantive content which consists of pledges by all signatories concerning the detailed duties each obliges himself to fulfill during the coming year. A textbook on Soviet labor law defines this institution as an agreement between management and the trade-union representatives of the workers, "in which the *reciprocal obligations* of the participants are set down with regard to the fulfillment and overfulfillment of the production plan, the improvement of the organization of work and of labor safety, as well as the improvement of the material and cultural living conditions of workers and employees." [22] Thus, the collective agreements are in fact declarations of loyalty to the dictatorial Party, which pledge each group and individual to the utmost exertions and to eternal vigilance against the "enemies" of the regime. The complete centralization of control at the top of the two hierarchies is paralleled at the bottom by a joint pledge of "comradely coöperation and mutual help" on the part of all participants. Management and labor are not antagonistic classes and conflicts

[21] *Ibid.*, p. 134–135.
[22] N. G. Alexandrov (ed.), *Lehrbuch des Sowjetischen Arbeitsrechts* (18. Beiheft zur Sowjetwissenschaft; Berlin: Verlag Kultur und Fortschritt, 1952), p. 161. My italics and translation.

cannot exist, because "all have the common goal of increasing labor productivity, of improving the material well-being and the cultural level of the workers." [23]

In this formal description of the two interlocking hierarchies of authority I have limited my illustrations to a hypothetical factory for the sake of simplicity. I must now add for the sake of accuracy that this principle of a double government applies throughout the society. That is to say, every factory, every government office, every unit of the army and the secret police, as well as every cultural or social organization is subject to two authorities rather than one. For the work of each unit is programed, coördinated, and supervised by some government agency. And it is also propagandized, expedited, criticized, organized, spied upon, and incorporated in special-purpose campaigns by the Party cell within the organization, and that Party cell is of course subject to the higher Party authorities. Thus, the actual work done in any specific organizational unit *and* in its supervising agency (or agencies) is expedited, criticized, and spied upon by Party cells which are responsible neither to the director of the unit nor to the head of its supervising agency, but which are separately accountable to the independent hierarchy of the Party.[24]

At first glance, this whole arrangement bears out the common view that dictatorships inevitably develop a superbureaucracy with its inefficiency and confusion. But as Weber pointed out a generation ago in his study of rationalism in Western culture, what appears irrational from one point of view may well be rational from another.[25] And in view of the manifest success of Soviet industrialization an analysis of totalitarian rule has the task of seeing the organizational rationale which has achieved that success. This rationale can be stated in the framework of Weber's analysis. An ideally functioning bureaucracy

[23] *Ibid.*, p. 157. It may be added that these agreements are the product of a 30-year development, which is traced briefly in *ibid.*, pp. 156–161.

[24] For an attempt to depict this structure in the form of an organizational chart for East Germany I refer to my *Work and Authority in Industry*, pp. 356, 359. I should add that my interpretation differs from that contained in C. J. Friedrich and Z. K. Brzezinski, *Totalitarian Dictatorship and Autocracy* (Cambridge, Mass.: Harvard University Press, 1956). Though I agree with the authors' emphasis on the difference between autocracy and totalitarianism, I wonder whether it is useful to state that difference entirely in terms of Friedrich's descriptive syndrome of official ideology, a single mass party, a technologically based monopoly of arms and mass communications, and a system of police control. Apparently this doubt is shared by the coauthor who has pointed out that this syndrome leaves out the "institutionalized revolutionary zeal" of the Party. See Z. Brzezinski, "Totalitarianism and Rationality," *American Political Science Review*, L:3 (Sept., 1956), 754. I have attempted to include this essential element and to point out its institutionalization in the double hierarchy of government.

[25] See Weber, *Protestant Ethic*, p. 26. For this reason it does not appear useful to me to conceptualize the inefficiency of totalitarian government by showing that in many respects it is the reverse of Weber's concept of bureaucracy. See Friedrich and Brzezinski, *op. cit.*, pp. 185–186, where the authors refer to the process of "debureaucratization," in which such characteristics of bureaucracy as centralization, separation of functions, recruitment on the basis of qualifications, objectivity and secrecy of official business have been abandoned under the influence of one-party rule. There is no doubt, of course, concerning these effects of totalitarianism, but one would have to know about the degree of bureaucratization (in Weber's sense) under tsarist rule, before one may properly speak of "debureaucratization."

in his sense is the most efficient method of solving large-scale organizational tasks, but only if these require the orderly administration of public affairs under the rule of law. However, a continuous and dependable operation which combines efficiency with a more or less stable norm orientation, is usually obtained at the price of some inflexibility for the sake of maintaining the rule of law and achieving an equitable administration of affairs. Such a bureaucracy may not function properly where the task is the rapid industrialization of a nation. Under the simulated combat conditions of a totalitarian regime the norms which govern conduct do not remain for any length of time. In the face of an unremitting drive for prodigies of achievement officials will tend to use their devices of concealment for a systematic, if tacit "withdrawal of efficiency" (Veblen). They will do so not only for reasons of convenience, but also because the demands made upon them by the regime are "irrational" from the viewpoint of expert knowledge and systematic procedure.[26] The party, on the other hand, must prevent the types of concealment which make such collective inaction possible while putting all executive officials under maximum pressure to utilize their expertise to the fullest extent. This, I take it, is the rationale of a double hierarchy of government, which places a party functionary at the side of every major official in order to prevent concealment and apply pressure. In a totalitarian regime these two hierarchies would be required, even if all key positions in government and industry were filled with party functionaries. For a functionary turned executive official would still be responsible for "fulfilling and overfulfilling" the plan, while the new party functionary would still be charged with keeping that official under pressure and surveillance.[27]

This "double government" of a totalitarian regime has certain consequences, which have been variously noted and which are related to the tendency of the regime to centralize authority at the top while shoving responsibility for results downwards.[28] At the level of policy this tendency has corollaries which possess a rationale of their own, at least from the viewpoint of the regime. The industrial situation may again be used for illustration. I noted earlier that in the textbook version of the Soviet regime the Party cell is given a regular function in the operation of a factory, but that this function is double-headed, so to speak. The Party must support the director in mobilizing the workers for the

[26] We have it on the authority of a thoroughly compliant Communist functionary in East Germany that "the word 'impossible' is banned once and for all from the vocabulary of the German language" and that "the functionaries must learn that what was correct yesterday is already outdated and incorrect today." See Walter Ulbricht, *Der Fünfjahrplan und die Perspektiven der Volkswirtschaft* (Berlin: Dietz-Verlag, 1951), p. 91, and in *Lehren des XIX. Parteitages der KPdSU für den Aufbau des Sozialismus in der DDR* (Berlin: Dietz-Verlag, 1952), p. 56.

[27] It should be added that the effort to prevent concealment and exert pressure to procure greater performance is not confined to executive officials. The techniques of mass agitation are surveyed in Alex Inkeles, *Public Opinion in Soviet Russia* (Cambridge, Mass.: Harvard University Press, 1950), esp. pp. 67–131. For a case study of agitation in East German industry see my *Work and Authority in Industry*, pp. 400–433.

[28] I assume that this is the tendency Barrington Moore has in mind in his slightly different formulation in *Terror and Progress* (Cambridge, Mass.: Harvard University Press, 1954), p. 17.

overfulfillment of the plan, but it must also control the administrative activity and fight against mismanagement. This type of directive gives rise to a familiar refrain of industrial relations under the Soviet system. The Party organization in a factory will be admonished not to interfere with the work of management, because this violates the principle of "one-man management" and constitutes a usurpation of economic functions by the Party. However, the Party will also be reminded that it is duty-bound to help management in overcoming the difficulties facing the enterprise and that it must be vigilant in the detection of evasive and bureaucratic practices on the part of management. There are many examples of this kind, all of which indicate that the regime demands of its functionaries the simultaneous maximization of conflicting goals. Officially, it is denied that these goals conflict: the Party secretary and the director are leading members of the same Party organization and are admonished to discuss and resolve all decisive questions. But although this desired collaboration is endorsed as the principle of "collective leadership," that principle stands opposed not only to the principle of "one-man management" but it is also hedged in by the determined campaigns of the Party against collusive practices between executive officials and Party functionaries.[29]

This institutionalization of conflicting standards in the textbook version of the regime reflects the centralization of authority at the top and the allowance of controlled flexibility under pressure at the level of operations.[30] It may be stated as a principle of totalitarian rule that it implements its unremitting drive for achieving the possible by continually demanding the impossible. Conflicting demands are "on the books" and thus legitimate every demand the highest Party authorities decide to make. Under these conditions the hierarchy of Party functionaries may be said to serve the purpose of demanding the impossible,

[29] From a Chinese source we have a formulation of the principle of "collective leadership" which reveals clearly that the collaboration envisaged is based on mutual distrust, or Bolshevik partisanship in the official terminology. "By collective leadership we understand a system, in which all principal questions must be decided by all leading personalities on the basis of careful examination and collective discussion. . . . No one should presume to decide principal questions by himself. . . . Collective leadership is the most important means to secure unity, improve criticism and self-criticism, and *facilitate the control of each functionary* regardless of his position." Quoted from a Chinese Communist newspaper in *Ostprobleme* VI (May, 1954), 731. My italics and translation. The party's opposition to collusive practices which underlies this formulation is spelled out in the comments on "cadre policy" by N. Khrushchev, *Report to the Nineteenth Party Congress on Amendments to the Rules of the CPSU (b)* (Moscow: Foreign Languages Publishing House, 1952), pp. 23–25.

[30] In his comments on this paper Professor Eckstein remarked that among the conflicting goals there exists a scale of priorities, but that these priorities are frequently implicit, rather than explicit. My point is that this implicit character of the priorities together with abrupt changes in policy is aided by the institutionalization of conflicting goals in the textbook version of the regime, because this institutionalization increases the freedom of abrupt decision making at the center and intensifies the planned uncertainty below. Where officials are told to maximize both productivity and safety, failure to do either *can* be punished, while the authorities through their administration of incentives, controls, and penalties may in effect opt for productivity at the expense of safety. If this leads to production breakdowns, the officials will be called to account for their neglect of safety measures. In this way, an implicit scale of priorities is combined with the formal institutionalization of conflicting goals.

that is, the simultaneous maximization of conflicting goals, at any rate if they perform their tasks adequately from the viewpoint of the regime. Where some success has been achieved, more success may be possible, and it is the responsibility of the Party in this system to test continually whether this "more" can be achieved. The top agencies of the Party, therefore, treat every one of their own directives as a minimum, because officially the "impossible" cannot be allowed to exist if the pressure is to be maintained below. Moreover, the Party authorities are well aware of evasions and collusive practices at the operational level. And although the pressure is presumably tempered and allocated in order to allow for the necessary maneuvering and to obtain the maximum of the possible, the official viewpoint of the regime is to consider all evasions or collusions as evidence of slack which may be taken up by additional pressure. The Party jargon reflects this orientation by speaking of "still further successes" which proper political agitation will make possible, thus asserting at the same time that the Party is eminently successful but that its functionaries can still do much more in tapping the underutilized resources of the country and the hallowed initiative of the masses. Thus, there is a constant demand for "overfulfillment" and it is standard practice to treat every successful performance as a *prima facie* indication that more could have been accomplished. At the agitational level there is in principle no reliable sign of success.

At the level of operations this drive of the Party meets with considerable, tacit resistance. In his striking analysis of the "web of 'mutual involvement'" Berliner has shown that Party officials and industrial managers support each other in their illegal practices, because their performance is judged by the same criteria.[31] A casual reading of this study might make it appear as if the relations between political functionaries and managers were free of tensions and conflicts of interest as long as the enterprise is successful, and that the drive of the Party for greater achievements was so much empty commotion. But this conclusion does not follow from the available evidence. Berliner himself has emphasized that illegal practices are condoned only where they lead to successful performance in terms of the official criteria, and that the collusion which makes such practices possible disintegrates quickly with the first signs of impending failure.[32] In addition, we have considerable evidence for the assertion that "the drive for industrial expansion comes almost wholly from the top."[33] My hunch is that both lines of analysis are right in their respective emphases on collusive alliances at the bottom *and* on organizational drive from the top through the agencies of the Party. Perhaps the experts would have to "give" a little on each

---

[31] *Berliner, op. cit.*, chaps. 13–16.

[32] *Ibid.*, pp. 295–300. One may wonder whether the portents of failure are easily discerned in this bureaucratic environment, and hence whether the collaboration between operating and control officials is as free of tension even in the successful enterprise, as the former Soviet managers make it appear.

[33] See Moore, *op. cit.*, pp. 71 and *passim*. See also Merle Fainsod, *How Russia Is Ruled* (Cambridge, Mass.: Harvard University Press, 1955); David Granick, *Management of the Industrial Firm in the USSR* (New York: Columbia University Press, 1954); Leopold Haimson, "Decision Making and Communications in Russian Industry," *Studies in Soviet Communication* (Cambridge, Mass.: Center for International Studies, Massachusetts Institute of Technology, 1952), vol. 2; and other studies.

side to become compatible with each other. This is already implicit in the fact that illegal practices thrive most where they lead to successful economic performance. Presumably this fact indicates a degree of that economic rationality which is feasible under totalitarian conditions. For to the extent that collusion leads to economic growth rather than to the "withdrawal of efficiency," it would seem to be evidence for the fact that during the last generation the regime has in part produced a built-in ethic of work performance which does not possess a steady intensity, but which is nevertheless "rational" in the sense of being adapted to the bureaucratic fits and starts of forced industrialization.[34]

This speculation is related to the fact that the conflicting goals which are "on the books" cannot be enforced simultaneously. The result is a characteristic jerkiness of Party policy which tends to engage in campaigns for the achievement now of the one and now of the other goal, although officially the Party demands the simultaneous maximization of both.[35] There is a kind of organizational logic in this phenomenon. The executive officials and Party functionaries of the regime develop a "sixth sense" for changes of the Party line, which may be detected in a daily press known to be an authoritative organ of the Party. Under the systematic pressure of the regime which pushes responsibility downward, implementation of the new Party line will eventually lead to exaggerations which make a "reversal" of that line mandatory, although officially this takes the form of emphasizing the "other" goal which is also "on the books." This history of industrial relations with its alternating emphasis on "one-man management" and "contact with the masses" is a case in point. A recent discussion of industrial reorganization makes the same point by examining the policy of decentralization in terms of the new problems created by that policy which may eventually lead to renewed centralization.[36] If this characterization is correct, it may not be too fanciful to suggest that at the apex of a totalitarian regime the authorities find themselves forced to "reënact" a kind of organizational simulation of the business cycle with its cumulation of indices of performance in alternate directions.

A suggestion concerning future developments is implicit in the comparative analysis I have presented. Those observers who envisage more rationality in economic behavior and organizational methods as a consequence of techno-

[34] The energy and willingness with which such adaptations are made is perhaps evidence of a belief that the successful drive for industrialization legitimates the regime. But while this rationale for the drive is accepted, its bureaucratic manifestations and police-state methods are not. See R. A. Bauer, A. Inkeles, and C. Kluckhohn, *How the Soviet System Works* (Cambridge, Mass.: Harvard University Press, 1956).

[35] This fact has been used as the basis for an organizational model by A. G. Frank, "The Organization of Economic Activity in the Soviet Union," *Weltwirtschaftliches Archiv*, LXXVIII (1957), 104–156. The author speaks of the selective enforcement of conflicting standards in order to maximize both authority at the center and flexibility in operation. As discussed in the text I am inclined to emphasize the more or less "cyclical" character of policy enforcement. But this emphasis is compatible with Frank's interpretation, and my analysis of the underlying organizational structure may be regarded as a supplement to his economic analysis which relies in good part on the work of Berliner, Granick, Holzman, and others.

[36] See Alec Nove, "The Soviet Industrial Reorganization," *Problems of Communism*, VI (Nov.–Dec., 1957), 19–25.

logical imperatives, seem to neglect the type of rationality in the Soviet system of domination which exists already. The interest in rationality which we rightly attribute to managers and technicians, can be satisfied in many ways, and it is in fact a very ambivalent interest. A generation ago Max Weber pointed out that the demand of businessmen for formal legal rationality was always combined with their concern for substantive justice wherever this affected their interests, that businessmen had been ready to come to terms with arbitrary types of government, and that the increasing rationality of legal and administrative procedure had in large part been the result of professional status groups like lawyers or government officials.[37] Rationality in any line of activity was in his view the precarious end product of struggles among competing groups, and the collusive practices of Soviet managers and technicians are certainly not evidence of impending struggles of that kind.[38] We are left, therefore, with the alternative that the drive for industrialization might diminish and that the ability of the party to manipulate the double hierarchy of government would decline.[39] If it occurred, such a change would be difficult to assess in the short run, because no single development such as the changes in police controls and the administrative reorganization which accompanied the recent succession crisis, can be taken as a dependable indication. But since the drive for industrial expansion has been legitimated from the beginning either by the threat of war or by the simulated condition of combat which we call the cold war, its relaxation would occur only when this legitimation disappears. And the leaders of the Party will seek to avoid this eventuality by perpetuating the cold war and by thus buttressing their continued drive for industrial expansion through the manipulation of the double hierarchy of government.

[37] See Weber, *Law in Economy and Society,* pp. 266–268, 277–278, 317–321.

[38] Nor is it too useful to suggest that more rational organizational methods would come into being, "if only the party could be satisfied with the status quo." This suggestion of Brzezinski contradicts his own definition of totalitarianism and hence amounts to the proposition that rationality increases when totalitarianism declines. Given the complexity of preconditions which makes any type of rationality possible, this is too simple a perspective. See Brzezinski, *op. cit.,* p. 762. See the more circumspect analysis of "creeping rationality" in Moore, *op. cit.,* pp. 189–191.

[39] Some consequences of this possibility are projected in Moore, *op. cit.,* pp. 191–192.

E 3 / Aspects of Legitimacy

Introduction

To exercise authority every government relies on a combination of coercion and reward. But even coercion must be based on *principles of legitimacy:* rules which state who has the *right* to be obeyed; only then can coercion help to provide a stable basis for authority. (See Collins, Section B.) Typically, a government endeavors to have its authority accepted by the populace, and hence it must strive to live up to the principles it has enunciated. But a government's dilemma is that by living up to its principles of legitimacy, it limits its own power and submits to a standard by which it can be criticized. Moreover, such principles or standards are not immutable; contingencies always arise which prompt decisions that are not easily squared with abstract guidelines. Accordingly, it is difficult for governments to adhere to their own principles of legitimacy consistently, but it is also hazardous to change them. For when governments violate their own justificatory principles or attempt to alter them, they provide a focus around which opponents can organize support.

In modern industrial or industrializing societies, legitimating principles become particularly important in the political struggle. To run a modern economy, every government to some degree regulates economic activities, controls industrial conflicts, and provides services such as education and social security. At the same time, industrialization mobilizes the populace, drawing it out of isolated localities and making it possible for the masses to become politically organized. (See Royal Institute of International Affairs, Section D.) For the first time, a major part of the populace is brought into extensive contact with politics; simultaneously, the government becomes more relevant to the life of the people by providing services and regulating economic affairs. Under these circumstances, social groups acquire particular interests in influencing the government and at the same time acquire the means of making their interests known.

To be sure, pre-industrial oligarchies, surviving into the industrial era, generally continue their traditional attempts to keep the people out of politics and confine political struggle to the battles and intrigues of nobles and court cliques. But the economic mobilization of the masses provides a political resource that cannot be long ignored by political elites old or new. A new form of politics emerges: one in which appeals to the masses for support are a crucial means in the struggle for power.

Mass politics has been institutionalized under two major forms of legitimacy: democratic and totalitarian. Democracy develops where competing elites achieve a balance of power, such that none can effectively monopolize control of the government. Under these circumstances, the legitimacy of the incumbent group depends primarily on its selection in a "fair contest" and by its support for the rules of the democratic game; the rulers' selection itself depends on the bargains they make with supporting social groups by promising certain services or policies. Totalitarian rule, on the other hand, is the result of the victory of a single elite and the elimination of all competing elites. The ruling elite, in these circumstances, justifies itself on the ground that it has mass support from *everyone* while suppressing opposing elites on the ground that they represent only narrow, selfish interests. In order to make this claim, such competing elites and interests must generally be defined as illegitimate, as not belonging to the citizenry. Hence, totalitarian governments stress purges of "alien" groups, whether these are defined as classes, races, or agents of foreign powers. In an era of mass politics, the elite that wants to monopolize power and eliminate the political contest must "externalize" the opposition that inevitably exists in *any* political system. It can maintain the principle that it alone represents the people only by finding periodic scapegoats [1] and by sponsoring mass participation in ceremonial affirmations of support for the government.[2]

All modern governments, whether democratic or totalitarian, must regulate disputes and provide social services. These are the areas in which inevitable conflicts of interest arise among individuals and social groups, and the way governments handle these matters determines not only their short-run support but also the popular belief in their legitimacy (see Bendix, Section E1).

The way in which disputes are regulated is particularly crucial in a democracy, because democracy is itself a form of dispute-settlement. Dahrendorf compares Germany and Britain, to show that law courts and labor dispute procedures may be based either on the principle that these institutions should uphold the rules of a "fair contest" between competing groups or individuals, or

[1] Thus, scapegoating is not solely, or even necessarily, a psychological phenomenon; totalitarian leaders, as *individuals*, may not personally engage in stereotyping or projecting of aggressions but may merely use a very important political tactic, dictated by the dynamics of their principles of legitimacy.

[2] These are not descriptions of two mutually exclusive systems of government; rather, "democracy" and "totalitarianism" have been presented here as *analytical types* of the legitimating principles that elites may use in modern mass politics: the former principle is used by elites that operate (or hope to operate) in a situation of political competition, the latter principle by elites that have attained or hope to attain sole control of power. Thus, it is possible to have totalitarian parties or totalitarian tactics in a competitive system. Also, the two types of justification may be used by the same elite, in varying combinations; thus, an elite may stress its adherence to the rules of the democratic game and also engage in scapegoating and claims of universal support.

on the principle that a monolithic consensus should be made to prevail. If conflict is recognized as legitimate in these subsidiary areas of social life, then the parliamentary competition of political democracy is similarly upheld. However, a parliamentary regime, such as the Weimar Republic, in a society in which courts and labor relations procedures express the principle of consensus rather than competition is inherently unstable.

Pekelis' comparison of Continental civil law and Anglo-American common law shows that the courts are crucial in maintaining democracy, because they may function as regulators of political competition as well as of private conflicts. Pekelis echoes Tocqueville's theme (Section D) that individualism and the centralization of authority may go together; there are more extensive legal protections for the individual in the civil law countries, where courts are merely an administrative arm of the government, than in the more independent common law courts, where the community may tyrannize the individual. However, the crucial point is not the autonomy of the individual; it is rather that the participation of the local community in court procedures — through the jury and through community influence on the judge — makes the court relatively independent of the central government. Thus, the courts can rule on the legitimacy of government actions and thereby limit the power of ruling elites to a degree that the purely parliamentary competition of political parties cannot achieve in more centralized governments.[3]

The final two pieces examine the political implications of social services: social security and higher education. Rimlinger shows how social security is handled as a contractual, insurance-type relationship between the individual and the government in the U.S., whereas the U.S.S.R. the totalitarian government invokes the principle of benevolent care to justify using social security as arbitrary reward and punishment in matters of political loyalty and economic performance. Ben-David and Collins, finally, deal with the political dilemmas of educational policy in Europe, Russia, and Latin America.[4] Governments commit themselves to providing opportunities for social advancement through education and academic freedom to scholars who carry the nation's culture and develop its knowledge; but governments are often unable or unwilling to live up to these principles. In the classical instance of 19th-century Russian educational policy, the pendulum-swings between violations by the government of some of its avowed principles and attempts to rectify these violations resulted in growing political estrangement of the educated classes. In the end, this autocratic regime fell, partly because it was unable to fulfill the promises implicit in its own principles of legitimacy.[5]

---

[3] It is worth noting that there is far less difference between the centrally administered legal systems of the politically unstable European democracies and the Soviet legal system than between these European legal systems and the decentralized Anglo-American legal systems. See Doris Joras, "The Soviet Judge and the American Judge," *Baylor Law Review*, Vol. 5 (1952–1953), pp. 18–37.

[4] The universities in these countries are all state supported, unlike in the United States.

[5] See Reinhard Bendix, *Work and Authority in Industry* (New York: John Wiley & Sons, 1956), for further comparative studies on this theme.

Legal Techniques
and Political Ideologies:
A Comparative Study

ALEXANDER H. PEKELIS

The problem with which we are going to deal is one of comparative law, a discipline probably even more illusory than legal science itself. A body of laws represents in itself neither a social reality nor a social ideal. One of the difficulties that every historian faces in trying to reconstruct a period of the past with the help of legal monuments is due to the great variety of relations existing between legal rules and social reality.[1] So, e.g., legal monuments generally contain in an inextricable confusion at least two contradictory types of rules: rules which are a simple restatement of an existing custom, and rules which are enacted with the very purpose of reversing existing customs and which, in terms of social reality, should be read as we read the negative of a snapshot: white for black and black for white.

The science of comparative law suffers from the same difficulties, and can acquire a meaning only if it faces them in full and becomes a part of the history of civilization. But in this endeavor, comparative law runs the risk of losing its character of legal science. Once engaged on the sociological path, the temptation to drop the technique of strictly legal approach altogether is great. The difficult task before the comparative lawyer is that of reading the technical results against the light of a more general political, social, and historical experience.[2]

We shall attempt the comparison between some typical principles of the common law at large with those which prevailed — prior to the advent of totalitarian regimes — in what we may call Latin countries. We are conscious of all the methodological qualifications involved in the idea of comparison between *types*, based necessarily on a somewhat arbitrary classification. On the other hand, only *typical* characteristics are the proper subject matter of comparative research. The first condition for the solution of this methodological difficulty is to be found, as is usually the case with many "preliminary problems," in the completion of one or more concrete pieces of work.

From *Michigan Law Review*, Vol. 41, No. 4 (February 1943), pp. 665–692. Reprinted by permission.

ALEXANDER H. PEKELIS (1902–1946) was born in Russia. He was educated in Germany, Austria, Italy, and England, and taught in Italy, France, and the U.S.A. He was Professor at the New School for Social Research in New York when he died in 1946. He is the author of *Il Diritto Come Voluntà Costante* (1930). Our selection was previously published in a collection of his essays edited by Milton R. Konvitz under the title *Law and Social Action* (1950).

[1] See, particularly with regard to studies of foreign law, Justice Holmes in Diaz v. Gonzales, 261 U.S. 102, 43 S. Ct. 286 (1923). See also Rudolf von Jhering, *Geist des roemischen Rechts*, 2nd ed. (Leipzig: Breitkopf und Hertel, 1866), Vol. 2, p. 133.

[2] See H. E. Yntema, "Roman Law as the Basis of Comparative Law," in *Law, A Century of Progress* (New York: New York University Press, 1937), Vol. 2, p. 373; Lepaulle, "The Function of Comparative Law," *Harvard Law Review*, Vol. 35 (1922), p. 853; Max Rheinstein, "Teaching Comparative Law," *University of Chicago Law Review*, Vol. 5 (1938), p. 615.

In justifying, however, the classification adopted for the present investigation, we might say why we centered it upon some aspects of the law of the Latin type instead of engaging in the more familiar comparison between common law and civil law at large. Such comparative studies have often treated, on the civilian side, institutions of German law to an extent unwarranted by the importance, however great, of the systems of that type on the Continent. Europe is by no means coextensive with Germany, and it might add to the completeness of the picture to put the emphasis on a different group of countries, for a change. We thought, furthermore, that such an approach was bound to yield results somewhat different from those of studies of the dominant type, since the countries of the German type, although strongly influenced both by the political ideologies and the legal techniques which originated from the so-called Latin countries of Europe, still retain too many old Teutonic institutions and attitudes to present a sufficiently striking contrast with the common-law system. Finally, the expression "civil law" is generally associated with the countries of the European Continent, while we are trying to emphasize the fact that the contrast between the two systems we are studying means, today, practically a contrast between North and South America, between English and Latin America.

Among the most frequent general statements concerning the typical features of the common law we find the assertion of its individualistic character, for which it is sometimes praised and sometimes condemned; and, of course, even more often we find the general statement asserting the individualistic character of the American way of life.[3] It may therefore be interesting to see whether and to what extent a strictly technical legal test would lead to the substantiation or the refutation of that general assertion.

We do not attempt to give an exact definition of individualism. It is safe, however, if not trite, to say that under individualism we all understand a particular type of relationship between individuals and society, and precisely a type of relation in which the interests of the individual and those of society are balanced at a point relatively favorable to the individual. It is, of course, a relative or comparative statement and therefore the existence of individualistic features in a given society can best be ascertained only by comparing it with other existing societies rather than with ideal standards. And in this study the aggregate of the means and devices used by a given society in order to enforce upon the individual the laws of that society, the amount of social pressure used for this purpose, may be fairly indicative of the degree of individualism

---

[3] See Roscoe Pound, "Puritanism and the Common Law," *Kansas Bar Association Proceedings*, Vol. 27 (1910), p. 48; F. H. Bohlen, "The Moral Duty to Aid Others As a Basis of Tort Liability," *University of Pennsylvania Law Review*, Vol. 56 (1908), p. 220, reprinted in Bohlen, *Studies in the Law of Torts* (Indianapolis: The Bobbs-Merrill Co., 1926), p. 294; Bryce, "The Influence of National Character and Historical Environment on the Development of the Common Law," *Can. Law Times*, Vol. 28 (1908), p. 89; Marc Ancel, *La "Common Law" d'Angleterre* (Paris: Rousseau, 1927), p. 206; Charles W. Eliot, *The Conflict Between Individualism and Collectivism in a Democracy* (New York: C. Scribner's Sons, 1910), p. 5; Frederick Jackson Turner, *The Frontier in American History* (New York: H. Holt and Co., 1920), pp. 30 ff.

existing in that society. It seems to us, in other words, that a comparison between the different techniques of enforcement used in the common-law countries and in other types of legal systems may be significant in our investigation.

We shall start our investigation at the very point at which the literature of comparative law generally stops: we shall ask ourselves what happens *after* the judicial decision has been rendered. A good romantic novel ends with a marriage. But sometimes the tragedy starts just afterward. One of our finest scholars of comparative law concludes a recent article of his by stating that "The problems which courts have to decide are essentially the same on both sides of the Atlantic and, I venture to say, eighty per cent or even more of the solutions are the same." [4] We think that a far greater degree of dissimilarity between the two systems would have been discovered had the problem of enforcement been given more thorough consideration.

We are going to start with a very simple, even naïve remark: the common law knows an institution, called *contempt of court*, which to our mind is most important for the working of the whole legal system. Legal writers do not indulge too often in rationalizing on this institution, probably because it belongs to the self-evident presuppositions of the legal method. It is, in a certain sense, not surprising that a striking contrast between the two legal systems we are considering may be found just in connection with this institution. The existence of such a contrast becomes certain when we give full weight to the fact that the self-evident common-law principle of responsibility for contempt is, as principle, simply unknown in the civil-law countries, at least to the extent to which it represents a sanction for nonperformance of substantive duties.

It may be said that in the Latin countries the relation between the courts and the parties is in general far less close, I should say less intimate, than here. The Anglo-American idea of responsibility for contempt means, indeed, that the party who does not abide by certain specific decrees emanating from a judicial body is a contumacious person and may, as a rule, be held in contempt of court, in the king's mercy, so to say, and consequently fined and jailed. And although the institution is not utilized to the same extent in all areas of enforcement, it is still a highly characteristic illustration of the philosophy underlying the whole mechanism of the Anglo-American legal machinery.

Now, this very concept of contempt simply does not belong to the world of ideas of a Latin lawyer. It just does not occur to him that the refusal of the defendant to deliver to the plaintiff a painting sold to the latter, a purely *private* matter between plaintiff and defendant, may, as soon as a judicial order is issued, become a matter to a certain extent *personal to the court*, and that the court may feel hurt, insulted, "contemned," because its order has been neglected or willfully disobeyed.

The Latin conception of the means of enforcement is of a far more mechanical or formalistic character: it is a play with certain rules, traps, catches, and loopholes; and the court itself is one of the cogs of the mechanism, a party to the play. It does not occur to the actors that you have to bow to the judge's

[4] Rheinstein, "Common Law and Civil Law — A Comparison," *Pennsylvania Bar Association Quarterly*, Vol. 12 (1940), p. 19.

will, or that you may be punished by him, or, even more absurd, *blamed* for
not having complied with his orders. The court says that the painting belongs
to the plaintiff? Very well, let him try to get it! He may send the sheriff, and
the defendant certainly will not prevent him from coming into his house and
looking for the painting; if he is lucky enough to find it *there*, not elsewhere,
well, he has won. Neither the sheriff nor the court can ask where the
defendant put the painting. Once, in Italy, a simple-minded creditor who, by
special leave, assisted at the futile attempt to attach a painting in the debtor's
house, requested the sheriff to inquire of the defendant where the painting
had been put. A general chorus of laughs and chuckles, in which even the
plaintiff's attorney joined, was the answer. The Anglo-American solution of
this situation, namely, to send the debtor to jail until he chooses to deliver the
painting — theoretically for life — simply does not occur to the Latin lawyer.
His first reaction to this common-law practice is generally: "Don't you think
that this kind of punishment is a little too severe for a simple refusal to deliver?" The answer of the common lawyer — which only adds to the astonishment of the civil lawyer — is that of course we are faced here with so-called
civil contempt; there is no punishment involved; the proceeding is not a criminal one. He just disobeyed — a term that for a Latin lawyer's ear is likely to
suggest a parent-child relation, rather than a court-party relation — he has
disobeyed the court, he has been a bad boy, and he has to stand in the corner
until he changes his mind. Nothing mysterious about it!

The enforcement device known to the civil law of the Latin countries, which
is compared frequently to the contempt sanction,[5] is the French "astreinte."
This is a pecuniary sanction imposed by the court for every single future act
or single period of violation of a judicial decision. This sanction can either
consist in the simple means of liquidation of damages *in futuro* or have a
comminatory or coercive character. The line between the two forms is not
always easily drawn, but it is obvious that only to the extent to which the
astreinte has the latter character is it an enforcement device at all, and only
to that extent does it fall within the scope of our investigations.

It is true that some apparently impressive instances of strong pressure
exerted by astreintes assessed in amounts obviously beyond any possible liquidation of damages can be found on are often quoted in support of the analogy.
We believe, however, that a closer analysis of the astreinte not only shows that
its role is altogether incomparable, in terms of legal reality, with that of the
sanction for contempt but also illuminates the deep contrast in the political
approach to the problems of enforcement.

First of all, the decision of a tribunal granting an astreinte never operates in
personam. That is to say, the debtor can never be imprisoned for nonperformance of the order. This evidently takes away the usefulness of astreinte in cases
where the inadequacy of damages is due to the difficulty of collecting them.
Second, and this is their most surprising feature, astreintes do not operate in

---

[5] See Amos, "Specific Performance in French Law," *Law Quarterly Review*, Vol. 17
(1901), p. 373; Brodeur, "The Injunction in French Jurisprudence," *Tulane Law Review*, Vol. 14 (1940), p. 211.

rem either. Strange as it seems, *creditors cannot collect the astreinte* that has been assessed by the court. No process by execution or otherwise assists them. The decision remains on a merely platonic plane. If, despite the judicial threat, the debtor persists in his refusal to comply, the only thing the creditor can do is to go back to the tribunal in order to make the provisional decision final.[6] But this making the decision final is a somewhat euphemistic description of what really happens to the first decision through the process of "finalization." In it, the astreinte judgment is, and has to be, *deprived* of every comminatory element and reduced to a simple liquidation of damages. Planiol and Ripert describe in the following way the dilemma confronting the French judges:

> Now the amount actually collected by the creditor must be measured by the damage suffered by him and serves only to repair it. Indeed, either the judges intended from the beginning to render a final decision, and they had to confine themselves to the allowance of damages calculated in the usual way; or they intended to render a comminatory judgment whose amount they could fix arbitrarily but which cannot be enforced as it is and is subject to revision in order to be reduced to an assessment of damages. This is to say, the penal element which it may be appeared at the beginning, will vanish at this moment and will not materialize.[7]

As the French Supreme Court puts it, an astreinte is *either* comminatory *or* final.[8]

In other words, the French judge finds himself in the somewhat peculiar position of one who may threaten but who may not carry out his threat. Strictly speaking, astreinte becomes nothing more than strong language intended to impress the recalcitrant loser of a law suit. If, however, the latter is not impressed to the point of performance, so much the worse for the winner. The court has done for him all it possibly could do: it used strong language against his opponent. It is an open secret that before giving the winner title for execution the court *must* reduce the amount of the astreinte to the size of the damage suffered. True enough, there is every reason to expect that in assessing such damages the court will solve many if not all doubts about the actual amount of the damage in favor of the winner. But this judicial discretion is strictly limited by the court's duty to explain in its opinion the way in which the damage has been appraised (duty to motivate). It is safe to say, therefore, that there is nothing in the powers of a French tribunal in this respect that might exceed the powers inherent in the Anglo-American system of assessment of damages by unmotivated jury verdict.

One cannot help wondering why the French tribunals use astreinte at all if it is just an unrealizable threat. The answer is probably twofold. First of all

---

[6] E.g., Coquelin v. Société des Comédiens Français (Ct. App. Paris, April 21, 1896) Dalloz 1897.2.177, 182; Consorts Lantzenberg v. Veuve Dreyfus, (Ct. App. Dijon, April 28, 1910) Dalloz 1912.2.36; Fouché v. Consorts Chancerelle, (S. Ct., Jan. 20, 1913) Sirey 1913.1.388; Société hôtelière de Marseille et de la Riviera v. Comte de Beauregard, (Ct. App. Aix, Feb. 15, 1937) Dalloz Hebdo. 1937.211.

[7] Marcel F. Planiol and G. Ripert, *Traité pratique de droit civil français* (Paris: Librairie générale de droit et de jurisprudence, 1931), Vol. 7, p. 95.

[8] Galbrum v. Durand, (S. Ct., March 14, 1927) Sirey 1927.1.232.

it must be remembered — and astreinte is a revealing institution from this viewpoint — that shadows and ghosts and words and powerless threats have a reality of their own. They might and in fact do impress people, laymen and lawyers, to an extent far greater than that justified by rational expectation. In the second place, the somewhat futile comminatory astreinte is still the first step toward the "final astreinte" which consists in the anticipatory liquidation of damages generously measured and payable from period to period. The efficacy of the periodical form given to the compensatory sanction increases, of course, its secondary deterring effect. But this is, by and large, all that can be said to explain the existence of astreinte. In investigating the psychology of a game one may discover that bluffing is an important weapon and maintain, if in the mood for paradoxes, that to have or not have cards in one's hands does not make much difference. But we should not be misled by elegant contemplations on the marginal effects of an institution lest we lose sight of its main lines. Astreinte is an institution substantially different from contempt of court. It is a bluffing threat by naked words and does not really add to the dignity of the courts, at least as understood in the common-law countries. The truth of the matter is that the French — judges, lawyers, and laymen — do not believe in what constitutes the essence of the Anglo-American legal system, i.e., the existence of an inherent contempt power of judges as a fundamental attribute of their being judges. Characteristically enough, a scholar of the standing of Professor Esmein felt the necessity of writing a learned article in which, with the help of historical and political arguments, he attempted to prove that French judges do have contempt powers, and tried to give a foundation to astreinte in its comminatory character.[9] But his has been and is a *vox clamans in deserto*. His main contention, that judges have imperium — a self-evident truth to every common lawyer — presents itself to the French public as a heterodox doctrine militating against the general consensus of jurists and politicians. The work of Esmein has been largely admired, widely quoted, unanimously rejected. In the field of astreinte the French judges could never get rid of a certain timidity, an unequivocal symptom of their "bad conscience." Esmein tried in vain to tranquilize them (and in so doing he was abandoning his basis of inherent-imperium doctrine) by pointing to some secondary provisions of the French Code. But the provisions were actually saying the contrary of what Esmein attempted to read into them, and every lawyer knew it. One of the highest courts of France, the Conseil d'Etat, speaking of the astreinte, considered it a useful and necessary contrivance but without any juridical foundation and a *"procédé antijuridique."* [10] Instead of a self-evident, primary, and fundamental attribute the judges possess as a matter of principle, we find in France an arrangement confined to the back yard of legal principles, created timidly on the margin of, and perhaps against, the Code, this sacred and dominating body of law, an enforcement device surprisingly enough not enforceable itself.

[9] Esmein, "L'Origine et la logique en matière d'astreintes," 2 *Revue trimestrielle de droit civil* 5 (1903).
[10] Le Noir, (Council of State, Jan. 27, 1933) Dalloz 1934.3.68.

It must be added that in Latin countries other than France even this timid "astreinte," this shadow of contempt proceedings, has been considered a tyrannical device opening the door to the worst evils of judicial arbitrariness.[11] Indeed, despite the wide influence exercised by the French civil code in almost all countries of the romance language group of Europe and America, in none of them, with the exception of one Swiss canton, Geneva, has astreinte been received. A few unsuccessful attempts to introduce it have been made in Europe and in America. The lack of such attempts in the majority of the countries, and their failure where they were made, seem equally revealing of a certain historical tradition, if not of a deep-rooted conception of legal relations at large.

This conception is clearly distinguishable, to say the least, from that prevailing in the common-law countries. While Anglo-American equity bluntly confesses to act in personam, the idea which dominates the civil law of the Latin type is still *nemo ad praecise factum cogi potest*.[12] What is meant by this formula is not simply that a man *cannot* be coerced into acting in a certain way. That statement would be of a doubtful philosophical value. Indeed, if no line between coercion and inducement were drawn, the statement would be incorrect: *coactus voluit tamen voluit*, says another handy Latin maxim. If, on the other hand, the line between inducement and coercion were drawn somewhere, the statement would mean simply that an event is not an *act* if it is coerced, and thus shrink to mere tautology. But under a philosophical cloak, the formula offers political content, and mirrors the conviction that courts cannot, that is to say, *should not*, use personal coercion upon a man in order to obtain his acting in a certain way.

The most common form of personal coercion is represented, probably throughout the world, by the sanctions of the penal law, and these obtain, of course, on the European Continent to the same extent as elsewhere. But the uniqueness of the common-law sanction consisting in imprisonment for civil contempt lies in the fact that, unlike the criminal sanctions, it is imposed not so much *quia peccatum est*, not as a *consequence* of a certain act, but *ut agitur*, in order to provoke an act. The legal significance of punishment is in its etiological character, whereas that of the contempt sanction is in its teleological aspect; punishment is mainly a willed *consequence* of human behavior; jail for contempt is mainly a *means* of bringing about certain behavior. Even when the criminal sanctions are explained not on the theory of retribution but on that of deterrence (*ne peccetur* as opposed to the *quia peccatum est*), the intended effect is that of an indirect action upon men generally, not that of directly coercing the punished person into a certain behavior. It is true, of course, that whatever be the theory upon which punishment is predicated, the

[11] Belgium: Commune d'Engis v. Compagnie d'Electricité de Seraing, (S. Ct., Jan. 24, 1924) Pasicrisie Belge 1924.1.151; Italy: Giorgio Giorgi, *Teoria delle obligazioni nel diritto moderno italiono*, 7th rev. ed. (Torino: Unione tip.-editrice torinese, 1930), p. 238; Argentina: Machado, *Esposición y comentario del codigo civil argentina* (1932), Vol. 3, p. 349; Colombia: Fernando Velez, *Estudio sobre el derecho civil colombiano* (Medellín: C. A. Molina, 1926), Vol. 6, p. 229.

[12] See Planiol and Ripert, *Traité pratique de droit civil français*, Vol. 7, p. 76.

threat of punishment induces the threatened to behave in a certain way, and that this effect looms large in the intentions of the lawmakers. But the contempt sanction still differs from the punitive one in the exclusiveness of its coercive purpose, in its functional structure well adapted to its aim. The magnitude of the pressure is measured not by what has been done (be it the heinousness of the crime or other elements) but by the resistance to be overcome. Once the will of the person subject to treatment is bent, coercion ceases. The judge jailing the reluctant party engages in an active struggle with the will of the latter, and as soon as he changes his attitude he is freed, even though the injury which caused the proceedings has meanwhile become incapable of reparation. The future behavior of the defendant or of other individuals is incomparably less in the foreground in a criminal case. What happened — the crime — is now beyond the powers of judges and parties. The law imposes certain consequences, and repentance, reparation, good behavior, reformation, and future deterrence are only secondary characters in the play. In every type of society you can jail a man or put him to death *because* he did something. But in many societies the doubt is raised whether it is proper to jail him for a single day *in order* to do violence to his incoercible freedom to do or not to do something. Has society an enforceable claim to his specific behavior? Everywhere that contempt sanction obtains the answer is "yes"; where it is missing, the answer is "no."

The same criterion makes it possible to distinguish the contempt sanction (particularly in its pecuniary form) from the sanction of damages and other noncriminal sanctions. Here again it must be conceded and pointed out, from the outset, that an element of coercion or inducement is obviously present in every sanction. What makes for the uniqueness of the contempt sanction is that it is the only one which, in order to achieve the restoration of the legal order, counts upon and aims to provoke the co-operation of the debtor. All other sanctions rely upon a certain behavior of agents of the government directly aiming at the achievement of certain objective results consisting generally in the transmission to the injured party of certain things and/or values from the possession or ownership of the debtor. The structure and mechanism of the sanctions is shaped in a way to dispense completely with co-operation. As matter of fact, the debtor is not expected to *act*, and not even to *forbear* to act, but only to *suffer* other people's action, to *pati*.

Execution, e.g., is not directed against the debtor, whose person remains free from every compulsion, but only against his goods. He might care to stop the march of execution through voluntary compliance. And in this sense every sanction functions as inducement or coercion of the debtor. But this is a collateral and accidental aspect of sanctions other than those for contempt: they may be brought to ultimate and satisfactory conclusion without having exercised the slightest effect upon the debtor's behavior. Only the contempt sanction is directed against the debtor's person, has its magnitude measured not by that of the wrong committed or the injury inflicted but by the expected resistance and the need of bending the reluctant will. Inducement or coercion is not a secondary, accidental, or implicit aspect of this sanction, but represents its essential and exclusive functions conditioning and shaping its structure. The sanction for civil contempt stands alone as a *pure enforcement device*; its sole and avowed purpose is that, declared impossible by Continental law, of *cogi ad praecise factum*, i.e., to coerce a man into a certain behavior.[13]

It is probable that at this point the question spontaneously arises: what are the remedies upon which the creditor in Latin countries may count? These remedies consist primarily in the award of damages. This is of course a common-law remedy as well, being the typical, if not the only, remedy at law as distinguished from equitable relief.

Let us see, therefore, how this common remedy of damages works in the two legal systems. For if, by any chance, the remedy of damages were stronger in the civil-law countries than in the common-law countries, this could offset the weakness derived from the lack of specific relief. But on examination of the two systems, it appears that the opposite is true.

Take, for instance, the case of libel or slander: in many cases the issue fought by the lawyer in this country is to find out whether or not special damages have to be shown in order to make the defendant liable. The ruling of the court that the plaintiff must show special damages because the oral defamation did not fall into any of the classes of slander per se is often considered a substantial defeat for the plaintiff. But this is all a plaintiff in a typical Latin country can reasonably hope for in any event; the idea of getting what is called here general damages does not even occur to him. The only recovery he can secure in any case is these meager special damages, and he knows that he has to prove specifically and concretely each and every penny thereof. It is true that you speak sometimes about moral or nonpecuniary damages. But how modest and cautious they are! According to the doctrine prevailing in Italy, they may be awarded only in the case of a criminal offense, and even there some writers contend that the monetary reparation is justified only to the extent to which these moral damages have produced financial loss.[14] The same result obtains substantially in Latin American countries.[15] The rule is even more strict in Germany.[16] In France and in Belgium, things are apparently different, but a student who makes the effort to go beyond the words of the decisions and look into the actual awards of damages will find rather instructive results. Thus, in defamation cases the awards average between 5,000 fr. ($200) and 100 fr. ($4). And these latter cases are by no means six-cent

[13] For an attempt at a general classification of enforcement devices somewhat along the above lines, see Alexander H. Pekelis, *Diritto come volontà constante* (Padova: A. Milani, 1931), pp. 94–104, 121–131.

[14] E.g., Ronsini v. Lettieri, (S. Ct., May 21, 1932) Il Foro Italiano (1932) 57.1.1322, and Unione Italiana Tramways Electrici v. Marugo, (S. Ct., May 7, 1934) *Rivista di diritto privato* 1935.2.17. See also Montel, "La Réparation des dommages moraux en droit italien," 64 *Bulletin de la Société de Législation Comparée* 361 (1934).

[15] E.g., for Argentina: Scaramussi v. Parma, (Ct. App. Rio de Janeiro, June 18, 1907) Juris. Civil V 187.394. For Brazil, see Clovis Bevilaqua, *Codigo civil dos estados unidos do Brazil, commentado*, 4th ed. (Rio de Janeiro: F. Alves, 1939), Vol. 5, p. 321.

[16] Bürgerliches Gesetzbuch, (1938) art. 253. See also zu Dohna, "Die Stellung der Busse im reichsrcchtlichen System des Immaterialgueterrechts," 1 *Abhandlungen des kriminalistischen Seminars an der Universität Berlin*, N.F., No. 4, esp. 443–444 (1902).

verdicts; they are considered to be genuine compensation for the injury suffered. Malicious and intentional libel by big newspapers results as a rule in
verdicts for about 500 fr. ($20), hardly enough to compensate the unfortunate
plaintiff for the inconvenience of prosecution, and certainly by no means a
deterrent penalty.[17] In a single case there was a substantial deviation from the
average range of recovery. A French nobleman, M. de Brissac, succeeded in
collecting 75,000 fr. ($3,000) from an American motion picture company,[18]
but even that sum does not appear substantial when compared with the
£25,000 ($125,000) awarded in 1934 by an English jury in the analogous
case of *Princess Youssoupoff* v. *Metro-Goldwyn-Mayer*.[19] That is why a European newspaper would classify under the heading "Things American" —
"Americana" — the news that a girl in New York has been awarded $5,000
because the defendant kissed her in the street.

These instances are but an illustration of the general contrast, based, on the
one hand, upon the existence of such institutions as exemplary or multiple
damages and, on the other, upon the idea — fundamental for the modern
civil lawyer — that damages are strictly a compensation for injury suffered.
This explains why he does not understand institutions such as nominal, punitive, and multiple damages. The concept that, while judicially ascertaining
your damages to amount to $100, the judge may award you $200 or $300
simply does not fit into the structure of a contemporary civil-law system. And
the comparative investigation of the law of damages only stresses further the
greater energy of the common-law enforcement technique.

Thus, considering, among other instances, the "civil" contempt of court
involving fine and imprisonment, thinking of punitive and multiple damages,
we cannot help feeling that the line separating public law and private law in
Europe is far less clear-cut in Anglo-American countries, and that a certain
penalistic flavor is a characteristic of the whole common-law system. But it
is probably impossible fully to understand the true spirit of common law without recognizing and frankly admitting its religious and moralistic character.
The philosophy of the civil-law countries is that law has to do with the *external*
behavior of man in society, and questions of conscience are reserved to the
moral forum. The law has to translate its aims in a series of *objective* rules
which will be the guide of the individual, who is bound only by what is said,
and who is free where loopholes are to be found in the network of the laws.
Franz von Liszt, the great German criminologist, used to contend that the
criminal code is the Magna Charta of the criminal.[20] No law, and particularly
no court, shall meddle with the conscience of the litigants. While this is the

---

[17] E.g., Callman-Lévy and Psichari (Anatole France) v. X., (Ct. App. Paris, April
24, 1936) Dalloz-Hebdo. 1936.319; and Me. Roche v. Bozon Viallé, (Ct. App.
Chambéry, Oct. 22, 1936) Gaz. Pal. 1936.2.780. See also Givord, *La Réparation du
préjudice moral* (Grenoble: Imprimerie Boissy et Colombi, 1938), p. 258.

[18] De Brissac v. Société Paramount des Films, (Civ. Trib., Dec. 1, 1926) Dalloz-
Hebdo. 1927.127.

[19] (Ct. App. 1934) 50 T.L.R. 581, 99 A.L.R. 864.

[20] Von Liszt, "Die deterministischen Gegner der Zweckstrafe," 13 *Zeitschrift fuer
die gesamte Strafrechtswissenschaft* 325 at 357 (1893).

secular civil-law approach, we have on the other side, in England, a Court of Chancery, which had its very origin in the aim, to use its own words, to meddle with the "Conscience of the Party." [21] The Court of Chancery was of course not an ecclesiastical court: but it is just its secular structure and its secular functions that make certain aspects of its tradition significant. The fact that until 1529 the Lord Chancellor had always been a high ecclesiastic dignitary, that he exercised civil jurisdiction in his capacity of the Keeper of the King's Conscience, and that his devices were those used widely in ecclesiastic tribunals contribute to the obliteration of a clear-cut line between the techniques of ecclesiastic and secular courts. And we are not surprised to find lay chancellors using a typically ecclesiastical language. For instance, the opinion in the famous case of the Duke of Norfolk, decided as late as 1682, was based in part on the reasoning that certain long-lasting arrangements of property holdings could not be protected by the law because they disclosed a mentality inconsistent with that of a true Christian: "Such do fight," said Lord Nottingham, "against God, for they pretend to such a stability in human affairs as the nature of them admits not of." [22]

The influence of religious beliefs upon the economic development and the very origin of English capitalism has been the subject of many valuable and famous studies.[23] The influence of religious philosophy and ecclesiastical technique upon the substantive and adjective law was not less important. As a matter of fact, this influence is probably the only factor in the development of Anglo-American legal institutions that can show a continuity of more than a thousand years. Almost two centuries before the Norman invasion, Alfred the Great thought it advisable to begin his Dooms with the re-enactment of a somewhat revised edition of the Ten Commandments. Thus, in section 3 he made legislatively certain that "in six days Christ wrought the Heavens and the Earth, the Seas and All Creatures that are in them and rested on the seventh day and therefore the Lord hallowed it." [24] And the Commandments are still a part of the law of the land. Thus, a few months ago, a judge in Pittsburgh held a witness in contempt of court who, in a divorce suit, said, "My mother is not a lady." "Honor thy father and thy mother, as the Lord thy God hath commanded thee," says the Bible. American tradition backs the Pittsburgh judge. We find, for instance, a paragraph in the Blue Laws of New Haven reciting: "If any child above sixteen years old and of sufficient understanding shall curse or smite his natural father or mother he shall be put to death . . . Exodus Ch. 21, verse 17; Leviticus 20; Exodus 20:15." The same provision is to be found in section 13 of the 1671 version of the Liberties of

[21] Arguments Proving from Antiquity the Dignity, Power, and Jurisdiction of the Court of Chancery, 1 Chan. Rep. (Appendix) 1 at 47, 21 Eng. Rep. 576 at 587 (1616).

[22] Duke of Norfolk's Case, 3 Cas. Ch. 1 at 31, 22 Eng. Rep. 931 (1682).

[23] See, e.g., Max Weber, *The Protestant Ethic and the Spirit of Capitalism*, trans. T. Parsons (New York: C. Scribner's Sons, 1930); R. H. Tawney, *Religion and the Rise of Capitalism* (London: J. Murray, 1926).

[24] B. Thorpe, *Ancient Law and Institutes of England* (London: Eyre and Spottiswoode, 1840), pp. 44–45.

the Massachusetts Bay Colony. We all know that biblicism was extremely strong in American colonial life; a great number of the laws enacted in New England contained as a usual feature a reference to the biblical passage deemed to be their truest source of authority. To "deny God or His creation or government of the world" was one of the capital offenses in the Massachusetts Colony, and probably not there alone.

One of the most impressive consequences of the influence exercised by the ecclesiastic procedural technique through the medium of the equity courts upon the administration of justice at large is to be found in the creation of a closer, almost confessional, atmosphere in the relation between the court and the party. This somewhat vague atmosphere has materialized in at least two very precise legal relationships, which can be described as the duty of disclosure and its far-reaching complement, the right of investigation. The decisive importance of this duty and this right for our investigation becomes clear when we consider that, under the rules of civil procedure in Latin countries, no person may testify under oath in his own cause, not even if willing to do so. You cannot be a witness in your own case any more than you can be a judge in your own case. In the Anglo-American system, on the contrary, every party has the right today to testify under oath in his own case, and has, as a rule, a strong interest in doing so. It is true that we sometimes see a party take an oath in, say, an Italian or a French court, but never as a *witness*. The party may swear upon a given formula. He cannot be examined, much less cross-examined. The party's oath is not a means of finding the truth; it is rather a means of closing a litigation haphazardly, or a chance taken by a party who feels he is going to lose and tries to put his opponent under pressure by making him swear to his allegations. This, of course, makes the party oath an institution of very limited practical importance, and it is in no way comparable to the cross-examination of the parties under oath which takes place in the common-law countries. Prior to 1933 there were a few exceptions to this rule; the most prominent of these was the Austrian *Parteivernehmung*, shaped expressly on the British pattern,[25] and an outstanding and rare instance of successful reception of a common-law institution on the European Continent.

The situation of the defendant in a criminal proceeding is not less significant. I do not know of a single civil-law country in Europe or America in which the defendant in a criminal suit is allowed to take the stand in order to make declarations under oath. This is, however, the defendant's privilege today in England and in all but one of the American jurisdictions, a situation perfectly in line with one of the most basic chancery traditions. This right of the defendant to testify is, of course, at the same time quite a burden, and the defendant who fails to avail himself of the privilege is liable as a matter of fact to discredit himself in the eyes of his judges. At the International Congress of Criminal Law held in Palmero in 1933, the question of the defendant's oath appeared to be almost the only point of unbridgeable conflict between

[25] See 2 Pollak, System des Oesterreichischen Zivilprozessrechts mit Einschluss des Exekutionsrechtes, 2nd ed., 687–688 (1932).

the common and the civil lawyers.[26] The attitude of the latter was that the defendant has to be given a chance in his struggle against the accusation. After the criminal code, the code of criminal procedure becomes the Magna Charta of the criminal. The argument of the civil lawyers — and it is noteworthy that one of the most violent indictments of the United States's system of criminal proceedings was read by the delegate from Cuba — was that in order to make the common-law guarantees against self-incrimination effective, not only the duty but also the right to testify in their own case must be taken from the parties; otherwise the *prejudice de facto* is an incentive to perjury.

This sweeping duty of disclosure in Anglo-American countries is beyond doubt of ancient origin. The Court of Chancery subpoenaed the defendant to present himself before the court and to file under oath an answer containing the full disclosure of all facts pertaining to the cause. This duty of disclosure reached its climax in the proceedings before the High Commission and its ex officio oath, which invited the thunders of Sir Edward Coke, who argued that judges "ought not examine *partem ream*, upon their oath." To prove the point, he explicitly had recourse to a civil-law principle, and went on to say "for as a civilian said, that this was *inventio diaboli ad destruendas miserorum animas ad infernum*." [27] The High Commission disappeared, King Charles I was beheaded, but it is still the spirit of the chancery, and not that of Lord Coke, which rules common-law procedure.

The importance of *the right to investigate* and of *the duty to disclose* goes, in Anglo-American society, far beyond the scope of judicial activity. Even where there is no question of violation of existing laws, an individual may be subpoenaed to appear before an administrative agency or a legislative investigating committee and disclose every detail of his business and his life, and a subpoena *duces tecum* may order him to produce every possible kind of record or document pertinent to the inquiry. We tried to explain elsewhere the reasons for our belief that the power of the American administrative agencies and the scope of their activity are much greater than those of administration in civil-law countries. Here it is enough to stress the fact that the subpoena is the main weapon of administrative and legislative investigating bodies. Without the duty to disclose, their activities are unthinkable, and indeed an investigation as sweeping, for instance, as that described by Judge Pecora in his *Wall Street under Oath* [28] is a phenomenon practically unknown in the civil-law countries. In France, for instance, the powers of the parliamentary committees are uncertain at best, and the success of their investigations practically depends upon the willingness of witnesses to testify.[29] The timid legislative reform of 1914 failed to change the situation substantially, but did not escape the vigilant attention

[26] Troisième Congrès international de droit pénal, Actes du Congrès 491–533 (1935).

[27] 12 Coke 26, 77 Eng. Rep. 1308 (1607).

[28] Ferdinand Pecora, *Wall Street under Oath; the Story of Our Modern Money Changers* (New York: Simon and Schuster, 1939).

[29] See Joseph Barthélemy, *Essai sur le travail parlementaire et le système des commissions* (International Institute of Public Law, 1934), Vol. 5, p. 245.

of leading constitutional lawyers and statesmen, who, like Duguit, Barthélemy, and Reynaud, were ready to see in it an obvious violation of the doctrine of separation of powers and a curtailment of the fundamental rights of man and citizen.[30] The ideological strength of this individualistic principle was such that even the indignation provoked by events like the Panama scandal or the Stavisky affair was not sufficient to swing the balance of public opinion. Not even in Germany, where the Weimar constitution followed the English precedent by introducing the principle of parliamentary investigation, was the situation different. An early episode is probably sufficient to show the difficulties with which the reception of the common law on European soil usually meets. The German right-wing leader Helfferich, while testifying before a parliamentary committee, declared that he would not answer any question put to him by Oscar Cohn, one of the members of the committee. The outraged committee, in the climax of its fury, assessed a fine of no less than 300 semi-inflated marks. The order was sent for collection to a local court, which apparently upheld certain procedural exceptions of the contumacious witness and canceled the fine.[31] It is highly probable that an English or American committee would, in a similar case, have kept Mr. Helfferich in jail "as long as we please." [32]

It is important for the purpose of our investigation to note that this far-reaching duty of disclosure in common-law countries has its roots not only in the clerical and moralistic manners of approach we have spoken about but also in another characteristic of the common-law tradition. The feature is represented by the importance of the control that the community at large exercises over the individual. To a certain extent the law represents always and everywhere social custom and public opinion about what is wrong and what is right. But the common-law countries possess a series of institutions which succeed in maintaining a constant relationship between the state of law and the state of public opinion, and particularly the state of opinion of the immediate community to which a given individual belongs.

The main device through which this constant check is effectuated is probably the institution of the jury, and, possibly even more, of the grand jury. Trial by jury is the birthright of every Englishman, accepted and guaranteed in the Constitution of the United States. It may be worth while to recall some of the ancient English institutions, which may place in relief the true significance of the jury.

One of these institutions is the tithing, or the frankpledge. It is an old Saxon institution that existed in England long before the Norman conquest, and the Norman invaders were only too glad to develop and strengthen it. It is said that each boy, on reaching the age of fourteen, was obliged to find some such

[30] See Leon Duguit, *Traité de droit constitutionnel*, 2nd ed. (Paris: E. de Boccard, 1924), Vol. 4, pp. 398 ff.; Barthélemy, "Les Limites du pouvoir législatif," *Revue politique et parlementaire*, Vol. 125 (1925), pp. 455 ff.; *Le Temps*, Nov. 14, 1925.

[31] See W. Jellinek, "Revolution und Reichsverfassung," *Jahrbuch des oeffentlichen Rechts der Gegenwart*, Vol. 9 (1920), p. 91.

[32] See, e.g., *Cong. Globe*, 42nd Cong., 3rd sess. (1873), p. 982.

pledge or be *committed to prison*,[33] and it is an interesting circumstance that the frankpledge was not unknown to Colonial America, and seems to have been in effect in Pennsylvania.[34]

We do not think there is any need to comment on the significance of such an institution. Its underlying philosophy is obviously that it is the quality of being a good neighbor that makes a man a good citizen, or better, a citizen at all, that gives him his political status and his personal liberty. Other institutions were inspired by the same philosophy. Take, for instance, the compurgation, or wager of law. A defendant in a criminal or civil proceeding could purge himself by his simple oath, provided, of course, he presented himself to the court with a sufficient number of oath-helpers, or compurgators. This means, of course, that good neighborliness not only imposed certain duties but could pay very well indeed in certain contingencies through this institution of the wager of law. The latter was common to all Teutonic tribes, but England is the only country in which, as late as 1833, it required statutory abolition.[35]

Against this background, the origin of the jury takes on a particular meaning. It is to be remembered that this reform was not imposed, as some seem still inclined to think, by humanitarian reformers against a cruel royal tyranny. The jury, a device invented by the royal courts, was sometimes rather cruelly imposed upon litigants or at least upon certain types of litigants. A descendant of Norman conquerors, in his "rugged individualism," probably would consider as his inalienable birthright the right to trial by battle, and not a trial by jury, which would expose him to the mercy of his peers. He wanted to fight his opponent sword in hand, and kill him or hear the groveling word "craven" issue from his throat — even at the risk of being killed himself. And even the humble Saxon would sometimes prefer the terrible trial by ordeal, the judgment of God, who in His infinite mercy and justice had so many times miraculously saved innocents from accusation and persecution. Rather a deal with God than with the neighbors, who had been bad neighbors to him or to whom he had been a bad neighbor. Of course, the more peaceful part of the population was only too happy to pronounce the sacramental words that represented the waiver of their birthright to the ancient forms of trial, and say, "I put myself upon the country, for better or for worse." But a few of them would refuse to pronounce these words, and rather than submit to the ersatz of the voice of God — the voice of the people — they would submit to the *peine forte et dure*, being pressed to death.

We think that the jury, not only in its historical origins but also in its practical functioning, particularly in the small and medium-sized communities, represents a principle manifestly contrasting with the more formalistic or legalistic functioning of a Latin court appointed by a central authority. This

[33] Thomas Blount, A *Law-Dictionary* (London: H. Heringman, 1670), "Frank Pledge" and "View of Frankpledge."

[34] For an urgent recommendation to introduce the frankpledge, see Granville Sharp, *A General Plan for Laying Out Towns and Townships on the New-acquired Land in the East Indies, America or Elsewhere* (London, 1794), pp. 13–15.

[35] 3 & 4 Will. IV, c. 42, § 13 (1833).

method of selecting the judiciary, especially since it is coupled with the fact that — at least in civil proceedings — the personal appearance of the parties is a rare occurrence, tends to dehumanize the trial. Not only does the judge not know John or Jack personally, as in some small communities the jurors do, but the considerations of being liked or disliked by his neighbors cannot generally affect the judge's appraisal. He has before him certain facts, or, better still, certain legal facts, and to these facts, *as they appear in the files*, he has to apply the law.

One of the fundamental principles of civil-law procedure is that a fact-finding tribunal cannot use in the trial its private knowledge of the facts in issue.[36] In theory, analogous rules exist in common-law countries. But it is of course an open question to what extent the personal knowledge of the jurors gathered from newspapers and even from back-fence gossip may influence their decision. The old rule that the jurors *had* to know the facts of their own knowledge has of course long been reversed. Nevertheless, more than one defendant could, even today, make the old objection: "These men have their hearts big against me and hate me because of this ill report which is surmised against me," and therefore refuse to put himself upon "the good folk of this Vill." [37] It is often said that the institution of the jury is declining in America and England.[38] However, the reliance upon the judgment of the community and particularly the small community is still extremely strong. The mobilization of millions of soldiers in a nation at war through the selection system operated by local draft boards is certainly a new triumph for the law of the neighbors, and a feature unthinkable on the European Continent.[39]

Let us see how the institution of the jury works in those civil-law countries in which this institution is known. Once again the picture is easily drawn, the differences being of macroscopic dimensions. To begin with, there the jury *never* intervenes in private litigations, nor does it deal with misdemeanors, except possibly those committed by the press. Thus, in effect trial by jury is limited to felonies — or better — certain exceptional classes of felonies, numerically an insignificant fraction of the total judicial life. Of particular interest is the fate of the jury in Latin America. Many of the South American constitutions, following the example of the United States, explicitly declared the jury to be the birthright of every citizen, a guarantee of democracy. Actually, however, the jury system has never assumed great importance in the South American countries.[40] In some nations, in spite of the constitutional

[36] See F. Stein, *Das private Wissen des Richters, Untersuchungen zum Beweisrecht beider Prozesse* (1893) pp. 138 ff.; René Savatier, *Nouveau Dictionnaire pratique de droit* (Paris: Jurisprudence Générale Dalloz, 1933), Vol. 2, p. 224.

[37] *The Court Baron*, Maitland and Baildon, ed., 4 *Publications of the Selden Society* 63 (1891).

[38] See, e.g., Howard, *Criminal Justice in England* 308–310 (1931); Emery, "Government by Jury," 24 *Yale L. J.* 265 (1915).

[39] Compare also the functioning of local rationing boards described by R. Oppenheimer in a forthcoming article in 43 *Col. L. Rev.* (1943).

[40] See 3 Garcia, *Juicio oral*, esp. pp. 520–566 (1938); M. Costa, *O Jury* (1938), *passim*, and Bergé, "Etude sur le jury en droit comparé," 6 *Revue de l'Institut de Droit Comparé* 1 at 7–14, 86 *et seq.* (1913).

reception of the jury, no statutes were ever passed providing for trial by jury. Other countries, while passing such statutes, limited them commonly to criminal cases, and even there the jury was not favorably received and was applied to a very limited number of cases. In several recent revisions of codes of criminal procedure, trial by jury has been almost completely eliminated because, to use a characteristic expression of a Mexican writer, the jury is "contrary to the rhythm of judicial life in Mexico." [41]

The German experience is strikingly similar. The jury, which had been introduced in the German legal world under the influence of the French Revolution, was abolished by simple governmental decree in 1924. With the exception of a few experts, this act was met with almost complete indifference in the country.[42] One can imagine how different would have been the reaction of the people of the United States had a president tried to abolish trial by jury by executive order — even in the midst of an emergency as grave as the one Germany was facing in 1924.

In civil-law countries the jury plays almost no political role whatsoever, and does not have that social significance which it has in England and the United States. A study by Dr. Alvin Johnson has shown the educational importance of the jury in a small New England community.[43] Alexis de Tocqueville remarked, more than a century ago, that if trial by jury is not always the best possible way to accomplish justice for the parties, it is of the greatest moral benefit to the jurors. But the jury is not only the object of education — it is also an educator.[44] In amplifying this, we have to consider that in civil-law countries the jury — if it intervenes at all — can render only a decision analogous to the common-law "special verdict," that is, the jury has to answer specific interrogatories limited as far as possible strictly to questions of fact. In this country, on the contrary, it is the duty of the trial court to expound the law to the jury. The jurors are not only going to ascertain the facts; it is equally their function to apply to those facts the law which the trial court has had to explain or translate to them. This job of translating law into plain, popular language, or of reviewing the translation made by the court below, to which the most influential class of common lawyers — I mean the judges — are daily compelled, is a kind of job that a European jurist faces perhaps once in his life, when, rather reluctantly, he has to deliver a paper on legal problems at what is called over there a people's university. The everyday link between judge and jury, between law and plain English, makes again for the popular, neighborly character of the common-law institutions. This may also be one of the many reasons why the common-law writers indulge less in efforts at generalization and systematization than do the civil-law writers. The need to expound the

---

[41] Gonzales Bustamante, *Principios de derecho procesal penal mexicano* 189 (1941).

[42] See Mannheim, "Trial by Jury in Modern Continental Criminal Law," 53 *L. Q. Rev.* 388 at 404 (1937).

[43] Johnson, "The Substance of American Democracy," in Max Ascoli and Fritz Lehmann (eds.), *Political and Economic Democracy* (New York: W. W. Norton and Co., 1937), pp. 320–321.

[44] De Tocqueville, *Democracy in America*, trans. by Reeve, 2nd ed., 195–200 (1836).

law to a lay jury would break down every ambitious excursion into the higher spheres of jurisprudence.

If we try now to give an answer to the question we formulated at the beginning, we must say that the aspects of legal life in England and America which we have just examined do not substantiate the contention of the individualistic character of the common-law technique. On the contrary, the strength of the enforcement devices, the clerical and moralistic character of legal approach at large, the duty of disclosure, the close control exercised by the community upon the individual and upon the law, if compared with the analogous legal institutions of the Latin countries, seem to disclose rather a more collectivistic than a more individualistic character of the common-law system. Does this mean, however, that the contention of the individualistic character of the common law and of the American social structure is only and simply a commonplace? And were it but a commonplace, would not we still have to account for its rise and appeal?

We ask leave to submit an explanation and to a certain extent a reconciliation of our preceding remarks with the prevailing individualistic thesis. It seems to us that what is generally considered as and taken for the individualistic aspect of American life is simply the existence and coexistence of a plurality of communities and — let's not be afraid of this quantitative element — of an extremely great number of communities of various types. Through a kind of optical error this phenomenon of decentralization of collectivistic pressure, which by its very decentralization only *increases* in power, has sometimes been taken for individualism. "Things are so well arranged in America that the strict allegiance to collective behaviour is called individualism," remarked Max Ascoli many years ago, and added, "The highways are filled with cars running towards the solitude of the country." [45] When, for instance, such students of the structure of American society as F. J. Turner or C. W. Eliot emphasize the individualistic and antisocial character of the early American colonists, stressing at the same time the importance of the family, the group, the town, and the section, in American life,[46] they identify individualism with intolerance of a *central* authority. As a matter of fact, what they called individualism seems to be in reality collectivism within a smaller group, and what they called the antisocial tendency may be simply an antigovernmental one.

Now is this only a question of words? Is what we would call collectivism or pluricollectivism just what is usually classified as individualism? We think that, to say the least, the use of the term individualism greatly beclouds the true issue. Should it be admitted that what is typical for the English and American way of life is not the lack of social control but its decentralized character, then, e.g., the popular issue individualism and free enterprise versus collectivism and social control appears as a phantom issue that neglects the third and decisive

[45] Max Ascoli, *Intelligence in Politics* (New York: W. W. Norton and Co., 1936), p. 199.

[46] See Turner, *The Frontier in American History*, esp. pp. 125, 258–268; Eliot, *The Conflict Between Individualism and Collectivism in a Democracy*, esp. pp. 7, 8, 31, 91.

element, the factual prevalence of a strong social control in its decentralized pluralistic form.

We could speak of an essential federalism of America and we would not, of course, have in mind just forty-eight or forty-nine American jurisdictions. We think of a wider and deeper network composed of a plurality of legal systems enjoying an extremely great amount of autonomy. Not only the forty-eight states but the smaller territorial communities, the unions, the churches, the trade associations, the exclusive groups, the fraternities, the various klans, the vigilantes, the pressure groups — all these cellular organisms have their own written and unwritten laws, their own enforcement devices, their own forms of social control, their own framework of pressure. When we see the individual challenging the power of the central authority he does not, as a rule, act as an individual. He acts as a member of one of these communities. He is one of the tithing. He presents himself with his neighbors or with others with whom he has common interests. He leans upon the power that even the smallest community has.

Before the rise of the modern state, the existence of a plurality of legal orders was probably too obvious to be remarked on. But even after the claim of the state for the monopoly of lawmaking had made itself felt, the existence of nonofficial systems of law was recognized. As early as 1878, the German jurist August Thon affirmed the existence of a plurality of legal orders, some of which were even illegal, as the Roman Church under the Roman Emperors.[47] Benedetto Croce published in Italy in 1906 a clear exposition of the pluralistic theory.[48] The names of the modern English pluralists are well known.[49] But an investigation into the real structure of these legal systems, representing, so to speak, as many states within the state, is almost completely neglected. To give only a single instance, in spite of the enormous development of commercial arbitration in this country, not a single systematic report on the content of the arbitration awards has been published here. The fact would be amazing if one did not suspect that at certain stages of development lack of publicity and systematization is probably the condition of growth, and if one did not recall the reluctance of early equity to keep records, publish reports, and become aware of its compliance with precedents.

At least to a certain extent this lack of legal data on the various minor and less formal legal organisms existing in society at large, such as the constitutions of trade unions and trade associations, etc., is probably responsible for certain formalistic limitations to the investigations of the school of institutional

[47] See F. W. Thon, *Rechtsnorm und subjectives Recht; Untersuchungen zur allgemeinen Rechtslehre* (Weimar: H. Bohlau, 1878), esp. XI–XII, pp. 7–8.
[48] See Benedetto Croce, *Riduzione della filosofia del diritto alla filosofia dell' economia* (Napoli, 1907, reprinted 1926).
[49] See, among many, John Figgis, *Churches in the Modern State* (London and New York: Longmans, Green and Co., 1913); George D. H. Cole, *Guild Socialism Re-stated* (London: Fabian Society, 1920); Harold J. Laski, *The State in Theory and Practice* (New York: Viking Press, 1935) and *Studies in the Problem of Sovereignty* (New Haven: Yale University Press, 1937); and Ernest Barker, *Political Thought in England from Herbert Spencer to the Present Day* (New York: H. Holt and Co., 1915), esp. pp. 175–83.

economics. It appears to us that studies of the forms of social or collectivistic controls of economic activity have the tendency to confine the research to the regulation exercised by legislature and court, by the legal agencies in their most narrow sense. Even when outstanding scholars go to work on topics such as monopolistic competition or the economics of imperfect competition, questions in which the consideration of the extent and ways of functioning of group behavior and group control would seem inevitable, they either maintain themselves "in an atmosphere rarefied by the adoption of very severe simplifying assumptions" [50] or limit their study mainly to the problems of state controls.[51]

We find, to be sure, that some economists discuss controlling social factors other than state control.[52] But their statements are usually either overgeneralized statements of principles or investigations on too specific topics. There appears to be as well a lack of any developed techniques or methodology for dealing with the factors of nonofficial controls, and we are probably still far from a systematic treatment of the problem of pluralism in the economic field.

It is certain that much more must be done in the field of law and in the field of economics before public opinion is to realize that the historical development of the American economy cannot be interpreted as a phenomenon of the growth of individual enterprise, and that the real choice is not, and never has been, between freedom of enterprise and state control. This historical development can be viewed only in terms of the relationship between various types of social controls and their relative checks and balances in the total economy. The complete insight into these social controls, which could be outlawed but not destroyed by these anti-trust laws, is probably the prerequisite for every type of efficient economic legislation.

We cannot fully understand the political significance of the pluralistic structure unless we are aware of the fact that centralization of power and individualism are far from being contradictory and inconsistent. They may sometimes appear as concurrent and complementary concepts. A historical concurrence of this kind probably explains the tyranny of Renaissance Italy, and why France has been at the same time a typically centralized and a typically individualistic country. The distant boss, the stranger-judge, and other features of centralized government may be more favorable to the development of individualism than the pressure of government by neighbors in a decentralized state. The formalistic and legalistic approach which the very fact of centralization develops by necessity brings about a form of individualism which sees its Magna Charta even in the most severe code. It can be said, further-

[50] Joan Robinson, *Economics of Imperfect Competition* (London: Macmillan and Co., Ltd., 1933), p. 327. See also Edward H. Chamberlin, *The Theory of Monopolistic Competition* (Cambridge, Mass.: Harvard University Press, 1936).

[51] See, e.g., Arthur R. Burns, *The Decline of Competition* (New York and London: McGraw-Hill Book Co., 1936), p. 522.

[52] See, e.g., John M. Clark, *Social Control of Business* (Chicago: University of Chicago Press, 1939); John R. Commons, *Legal Foundations of Capitalism* (New York: Macmillan Co., 1932); Thorstein Veblen, *The Theory of Business Enterprise* (New York: C. Scribner's Sons, 1940) and *Absentee Ownership and Business Enterprise in Recent Times: The Case of America* (New York: B. W. Huebsch, Inc., 1923).

more, that the connection between centralized despotism and individualistic tendencies of a country is probably a two-way proposition, and that the strong individualistic attitude of the population may be the source of a decline of political interests and communal solidarities, and become the ideal ground for the rise of antidemocratic institutions.

The strong collectivistic pressure typical for the common-law countries is, on the other hand, outweighed by the fact that the closely controlling communities are here so numerous that, as a practical matter, the great majority of individuals can find a community that suits them more or less perfectly, and to which they may adjust themselves more or less painlessly. Only the "rugged individualists," the eternal dissenters, the true outsiders will have a much harder time in the common-law countries than in what used to be in the past a typical European democracy.

The historical tradition of the pluralistic approach in England and America is very strong. We shall mention here only an example which, although on a different plane, is nonetheless an extremely significant manifestation of this way of thinking. We refer to the known episodes of the struggle among the English courts that constitute in our opinion an absolutely unique feature. The history of the European Continent knows of struggles and conflicts between barons and states, towns and empires, state and church, feudalism and central power. But it does not present us with a struggle between two courts both emanating from the same authority, fighting each other in a period in which that very authority exercised a very strong *central* power. And that is what happened during the Tudor and Stuart periods in England. The King's Bench would, for instance, render a judgment in favor of a plaintiff, but the Court of Chancery, on the prayer of the defendant, would enjoin the winning party from exercising his rights recognized by the King's Bench, and would jail him for contempt if he tried to enforce the mandate of the King's Bench. The latter would then issue a writ of habeas corpus and free him. Sir Edward Coke, Chief Justice of the King's Bench, tried even to indict the Master in Chancery under the Statute of Praemunire for having interfered with the judgment of the King's Bench, and, as Bacon said, "make the Chancellor sit under a hatchet, instead of the King's arms." [53] James I intervened in this conflict between his two courts and decided it, upon the advice of Bacon, in favor of the Chancellor, thus maintaining the plurality of independent courts in his kingdom. He fully appreciated the advantages of a legal polytheism and would not deprive the Olympus of the common law of one of its most industrious gods, the court of equity.

In a way, this royal decision, restated in England by statute in 1872,[54] is also a methodological justification of this paper. It must be conceded, indeed, that most of its conclusions rely on rules and practices of equity rather than on those of common law proper. If we thought this to be a proper approach, it is because equity appeared to be the ultima ratio of the Anglo-American law, prevailing wherever it came in conflict with the common law proper. We

[53] Bacon, *Letters and Life*, Spedding, ed., 91 (1872).
[54] The Supreme Court of Judicature Act, 1873, 36 & 37 Vic., c. 66.

must also be conceded that the latter, considered in itself, appears rather similar to the civil law at large. But the very idea of considering common law proper *in itself* implies a disregard for the functional unity of the institutions studied. We are inclined to explain the conclusions reached by the prevailing doctrine of comparative law by a certain neglect of equitable institutions. To us the main distinguishing feature of the common-law countries is in the fact that not common law but equity prevails there. If someone were compelled to explain the essence of civil law to a common lawyer in one sentence, he could perhaps say that civil law is what common law would have been if it had never known a court of chancery. It is true that the answer would hardly be helpful, the picture suggested being probably beyond the imagination of a common lawyer.

The picture of conflicting and coexisting jurisdictions is equally inconceivable to a Latin or even a German lawyer, who believes in the *Einheit der Rechtsordnung*, the uncompromising and sometimes cruel unity of the legal order. Our late colleague, Nino Levi, had long ago noted in his special field this contrast of approach between the English and the Italian type of regulation.[55] The former left the findings of the civil and criminal courts completely independent of one another; the latter declared that the civil judge is strictly bound by the findings of the criminal court, and thus reaffirmed the irretractability of the judicial decision upon the same set of facts, and the fundamental unity of the legal order.

This need for unity probably reached one of its climaxes during the French Revolution. In 1790 two significant events took place in Paris. In that year the first steps leading to the establishment of the metric system were taken in France in order to supersede the medieval complexity of weights and measures. It is true that the French influence strongly felt in the United States in that period manifested itself also in this field through Jefferson's proposals to introduce a decimal division of the various units. But this project, adopted in France, was, except in the matter of currency, rejected in this country; symmetry, legal or arithmetical, has evidently never been a decisive argument in the common-law countries.

The second event that took place in France in that very year of 1790 was the enactment of the famous *Décret sur l'Organisation Judiciaire*, directing judges to *refrain from the interpretation of laws* and to consult the central legislative authority whenever need for such interpretation should arise.[56] And we certainly do not have to point out that the adoption of a principle depriving judges of their power to interpret statutes would be inconceivable in a common-law country, even during the excitement of a revolution. Not even the *dissenting* opinions of the judges are here considered seditious or subversive. In Europe, with the significant exception of Switzerland, a judge who would dare to reveal publicly or in private conversation that he disagreed with his brethren on the bench would be guilty of grave misconduct, liable to

[55] Nino Levi, *La Parte civile nel processo penale italiano*, 2nd ed. (Padova: A. Milani, 1936), p. 3.

[56] Décret sur l'Organisation Judiciaire, August 16–24, 1790, Tit. II, art. 1, no. 12.

impeachment and removal. The court is considered a unity, its voice is the *viva vox juris*, and it must be assumed that the judges can speak but in a unisonal chorus. The contrapuntal conception of law in common-law countries is shown by the importance that dissenting opinions have in the process of legal change.

We do not forget, on the other hand, that the exigency of unity and of geometric perfection of the legal world has deep roots in human nature. Ptolemy was the first man to give scientific foundation to the hypothesis that the world is a sphere. It is said that the origin of his conception was not a strictly mathematical reasoning, but rather an aesthetic intuition. Since the world could not have been created, he felt, but beautiful and perfect, and since the sphere is the most beautiful and perfect form human mind can conceive, our earth must necessarily be a sphere. I personally have always admired the pathos of abstractness which inspired such a thought. Here was a man who did not have sufficient affection and love for what makes for mortal beings the beauty of the world in which they live — the unevenness of the landscape, the shape of mountains, the fanciful ribbon of rivers. To him beauty was something else: an abstract and cool geometric perfection. The Egyptian certainly had in his soul the spirit of the race of Semitic shepherds who, in sleepless dreams under the nocturnal sky at the borders of the desert, conceived the dogma of monotheism.

I must add, on the other hand, that my admiration for Ptolemy is equaled only by my admiration for the man who first had the extraordinary daring to conceive the idea that while singing or playing two or more themes simultaneously you could bring about, not a terrible musical cacophony or political anarchy, but a newer, better, more perfect union and beauty. The strong fabric of the common law, the social structure of the common-law countries, building a unity of their very variety, represent one of the most astonishing achievements of legal and political contrapuntal harmony.

Civil law and common law represent, therefore, not only the two main legal systems of western civilization but also two fundamental trends of human nature. It would be childish to try to find out which one is better. It is only unfortunate that their mutual contact has so far been rather limited. A greater reciprocal influence of the ideas inspiring the two systems is probably one of the prerequisites for a real understanding between English America and Latin America and, through it, of the unity and survival of the western civilization at large. Their deeper interpenetration could eventually become an important factor in the development of less imperfect forms of human coexistence.

Conflict and Liberty:
Some Remarks on the Social
Structure of German Politics

RALF DAHRENDORF

If anyone trained in the English tradition of legal thought came to follow the preparation and conduct of a German criminal case, he would notice a number of telling differences. In fact, each of the three principal characters involved in the great drama of the trial — judge, counsel for the defence, and counsel for the prosecution — differs in important details, both in the theory and practice of criminal law, from its English counterpart. The judge, far from being the referee in a contest of parties or, in Erving Goffman's delightful description of this role, a chairman who, as "go-between," provides his audience (in this case: the jury) with cues as to their appropriate reactions to the evidence and arguments presented, is in fact more like a "player-manager" — and one, of course, who is always on the winning side. A German judge not only guards the rules of the game, but takes an active hand in the examination of witnesses and, above all, withdraws with the jury and guides its deliberations throughout. The judge is a civil servant (*Beamter*), so is counsel for the prosecution, but counsel for the defence is usually a private citizen. In both the general social and the specific legal context this status tends to become a disadvantage which is aggravated by the fact that often counsel for the defence does not have access to all the evidence before the trial. He is thus hardly an equal opponent of the prosecutor, but rather a beggar for clemency (and indeed the most frequent plea of the defence is that of extenuating circumstances). It is symptomatic that until quite recently counsel for the defence was physically placed, in many German courtrooms, somewhat below counsel for the prosecution whose official title of state attorney (*Staatsanwalt*) connotes an air of authority. The state attorney's is clearly the crucial role in a German criminal case; it is indeed two roles which may be regarded as barely compatible. Before the trial opens, the state attorney represents what a widely used legal commentary describes without irony and indeed with some justification as "the most objective authority in the world." He has every available means — files and witnesses, laboratory tests and police information, etc. etc. — at his disposal in order to work out "the truth." Evidently, this usually takes a long time — which is one of the reasons why many months, and sometimes years elapse between the original arrest and the opening of the trial in Germany. Evidently also, the trial itself loses in importance, if "the truth" has been worked out beforehand — which explains in part why it is often felt by critics of German criminal-law procedure that the accused is assumed guilty once the trial has been opened at all.

From *British Journal of Sociology*, Vol. XIV (1963), pp. 197–211. Reprinted by permission of the author.

RALPH DAHRENDORF is now Professor of Sociology at the University of Konstanz, West Germany. Previously he was Professor of Sociology, Tübingen University. He has written extensively on politics, stratification, industrialism, and conflict theory. He has written *Class and Class Conflict in Industrial Society* (1959), *Society and Democracy in Germany* (1967), and recently *Essays in the Theory of Society* (1968).

Above all, the state attorney undergoes a curious change of character when, on the day the trial begins, he slips from the role of an impartial "objective" investigator of "the truth" into that of a naturally partisan counsel for the prosecution.

It is evident that brief descriptions of this kind cannot do justice to complex legal traditions; they ignore, moreover, the actual similarities of seemingly widely divergent institutions: a clever defence counsel may transform a German criminal trial into a contest of the English type, just as a clever English judge may influence the course of the trial far beyond his role of referee. Rather than as a starting point for the analysis of legal systems as such, this brief sketch of criminal-law procedure can however serve as a useful metaphor for a feature of German social structure which seems worth exploring a little more fully: Wherever opposing interests meet in German society, there is a tendency to seek authoritative and substantive rather than tentative and formal solutions. Many institutions of German society have been and still are set up in such a way as to imply that somebody or some group of people is "the most objective authority in the world," and is therefore capable of finding ultimate solutions for all issues and conflicts. In this manner, conflict is not regulated, but "solved"; and it appears worth examining some of the social patterns, political implications, historical causes, and philosophical bases of this procedure.

The problem underlying these remarks seems no less important for its obviousness. For the German social scientist, the failure of liberal democracy in Germany continues to be a challenge of far more than antiquarian interest. While we all hope that history will not repeat itself, we can clearly not be certain that another 1933 is going to be impossible in Germany — and we know that representative government has proved precarious in many other countries as well. Thus it may be suspected that the pathology of liberty in Germany involves features which can, at other times and in other combinations, be found elsewhere as well, and that therefore — if for no other reason — an analysis of the conditions of illiberty in Germany is of more than local importance.

The failure of German democracy in 1933 has been attributed to numerous causes, ranging from the Treaty of Versailles to the national character of the Germans as described by Tacitus, from the unique personality of Hitler to the prevalence of authoritarian personalities throughout the country, from the depression of 1929 to the extremist desires of the German middle class. While some of these causes are likely to have something to do with the breakdown of the Weimar Republic, they constitute a curiously unsystematic medley of history and metaphysics which fails to amount to a convincing and controllable analysis of the situation. Perhaps the sociologist is capable here to go a step or two beyond previous attempts at explanation. Political institutions are anchored in social structure — or if they are not, they are likely to remain paper constitutions, of which admittedly we have come to see many since that "most perfect democratic constitution ever" (as some historians still describe the Weimar Constitution of 1919). But what is it in societies that guarantees, or, more modestly, helps the success of a given set of political institutions? What are, more particularly, the social bases of the liberal (as against the totalitarian) version of political democracy? Evidently, it would be presumptuous to try and provide more than a very partial and tentative answer to this large question. In the following consideration I am guided by what may be called a theory, or, more modestly, a hope that liberal democracy presupposes four sets of social conditions: first, the effective realization of an equal status of citizenship for all participants in the political process; secondly, the presence of competing élites and interest groups none of which is capable of monopolizing the roads to power; thirdly, the prevalence of a set of values which, by contrast to the private virtues of withdrawal and non-participation, may be described as public virtues; and, finally, the acceptance of differences of opinion and conflicts of interest as an inevitable and indeed creative element of social life. These reflections will be confined to the fourth factor, i.e. to conflict and its treatment in Germany. Our main question is therefore: What is it in the ways in which conflict is dealt with in the institutions of German society that can help to explain the apparent impossibility to establish successful and lasting democratic political institutions?

Let us return for a moment to the example of criminal-law procedure. A criminal case, and in particular the drama of the trial, may be thought of in terms of a conflict of interests. In its crudest interpretation, it involves a clash between the interest of the prosecution to prove and that of the defence to disprove the guilt of the accused. In German criminal law, the task of finding out who was guilty is accomplished by setting up an elaborate machinery of research and investigation — the position and office of the state attorney. In this manner, what might be regarded as a situation of conflict is in fact conceived as one of a concerted search for truth. As a consequence, the function of the trial is less that of a contest for the judgment of common sense as embodied in the jury than one of making "the truth" public, considering extenuating circumstances and drawing the conclusions stipulated by the legal code. In the place of debate and argument, an agency is set up to find the ultimate solution: "the most objective authority in the world."

In an important sense, however, the example of criminal law is merely a metaphor for social modes of dealing with conflicts. There is a fundamental difference between the clash of interests in a criminal case — for civil-law suits this would not be equally true — and, say, the clash of interests in a wage dispute or an election campaign. In the legal situation, there is no unavoidable uncertainty about the issue at hand: "The truth" is in principle available in the sense that the crime has been committed, and that somebody has committed it. In industrial or political conflicts, on the other hand, "the truth," i.e. the good or right solution of particular issues is fundamentally uncertain, because its proof lies in the future. For this reason, it could be said that English legal procedure has borrowed the ethics of uncertainty from other areas — from the methodology of science or the constitution of politics — in which it is more clearly appropriate. For this reason also, we have to turn now from the legal system to other social institutions.

Conflict begins at home. The family, like any other institution, may be regarded as a system of conflict regulation. Now, the authoritarian character of the German family has become a favourite with most political and literary critics of German society ever since Heinrich Mann's novels and Max Horkheimer's collection of studies on *Autorität und Familie*. Occasionally, one encounters the notion that the German father is, or at least used to be, a combination of judge and state attorney: presiding over his family, prosecuting every sign of deviance and settling all disputes by his supreme authority. It is debatable, however, whether one can draw as sweeping conclusions from this alleged observation as has been done by some, including the authors of the *Authoritarian Personality*. Today, German legislation goes further than that of almost all other countries in guaranteeing equal rights to women; and so far as earlier periods are concerned, it would appear at least open to question whether the father in Wilhelminian Germany was really so much more authoritarian than his counterpart in Victorian England or in any other society of the *fin de siècle*.

A rather more pertinent illustration of the ways in which discussion and debate are dealt with in German society may be found in the educational system. When Max Weber advanced his thesis of the desirability of a value-free approach to social science, and in particular his demand for a complete abstention from value judgments in academic teaching, one of his main points was that "in the lecture-room where one sits in front of one's listeners, they have to be silent and the lecturer has to speak." For this reason (so Weber argued) it would be irresponsible to exploit the situation by mixing values with facts. But may it not be that the educational situation envisaged by Weber is as dated (and placed) as, say, Freud's notion of the super-ego as the internalized father? Is it not conceivable that academic teaching could be conducted in such a way that the students do not "have to be silent," and that the lecturer is exposed to questions, objections, debate, and discussion? It would be rewarding to explore the implications of these — rhetorical — questions for the demand of a value-free social science. As far as attitudes to debate and conflict are concerned, they point to a conception of the educational situation which is characteristic of German society. The institution of the *Vorlesung* in the universities, which effectively protects the lecturer from all uncomfortable questions and objections, is clearly — and, by the way, in contrast to Humboldt's idea of the *universitas magistrorum et scholarium* — based on a definition of the situation according to which teaching is not a process of exchange and dialogue, but one in which "the truth" is passed on by its professed possessors to ignorant children. Once again, we find a situation of debate and contest reinterpreted in hierarchical terms.

With all due caution and without trying to overstate the case it might also be pointed out in this context that in the past liberal democracy seems to have flourished in countries in which there was also a fairly widespread interest in so-called non-conformist churches and sects. It is evidently more than daring to offer generalizations about the large number of such religious groups which exist in the present world. With this grain of salt, however, it may be argued that while some non-conformist groups are more dogmatic in their theology, many of them tend to be more democratic in their organization than established churches. By "democratic" in this rather loose sense is meant the influence of the lay element in church affairs, the ways in which dignitaries are elected and controlled, the amount of discussion permitted, and the like. Before this background it may therefore be relevant to remark that German Protestantism has always, and especially in the Eastern provinces, tended to the established type, and that nonconformist groups have never played a significant part at all. Even today — at a time, that is, when they are under no public pressure and when interest in some of them is growing — only about 3 per cent of the population of Western Germany are not members of the two great churches, Protestant and Roman Catholic (and of this minority many do not belong to any church at all).

The general pattern of conflict regulation — or, more appropriately, of conflict evasion — which is characteristic of the legal and educational systems, the family and the church, reappears in the German system of industrial relations. Here too the search for ultimate and authoritative solutions prevails over the establishment of rules of the game which would regulate the disputes between management and labour. Since 1918, if not before, the history of industrial relations in Germany has been marked by two related features: first, by a tendency for industrial affairs to be settled by state intervention — whether legislative, executive, or judicial — rather than the autonomous operation of the private organizations of management and labour; and secondly, by a tendency on the part of both management and labour to devise new types of industrial organization (a new "constitution of the enterprise," as it is generally called) rather than find a *modus vivendi* with respect to their contradictory interests. By many representatives of labour and management, the state is considered an authority that provides ultimate solutions for industrial disputes; the unbroken chain of ideologies of structural change — of workers' councils and a "community of the enterprise" (*Betriebsgemeinschaft*), of co-determination and partnership — documents the hope that such ultimate solutions can be found.

But the case of industrial relations is of particular interest in our context, because here, more clearly than in other institutional orders, it becomes apparent that the attempt to evade or eliminate conflict by finding ultimate solutions, does not succeed. Despite the expectations attached by many to legislative measures of industrial re-organization both after the First and the Second World Wars, there was no noticeable decrease in industrial conflict in Weimar Germany, and today, after the admittedly comparatively peaceful years of reconstruction, there are signs that disputes between labour and management are growing rather than decreasing in intensity. What is more, it appears that the very measures devised to take the sting out of industrial disputes and create a state of lasting industrial peace in fact have the opposite consequence. Why this should be so, can be demonstrated by a brief analysis of the two great institutional changes effected in German industry since 1918 — both legislative acts, and both affecting the constitution of the enterprise: the establishment of works councils in 1920, and the introduction of co-determination in 1951.

Consider first the German works councillor, whose functions differ so significantly from those of his English equivalent, the shop steward. He is the only living heritage of the brief triumph of the Council, or Soviet Movement after 1918, and his construction bears the traces of this ideology. Works councillors in Germany have no formal relations to the trade unions (who are represented in the enterprise by their own officials); they occupy their place with reference to the individual enterprise alone. Here, the law of 1920 ascribes to them the task of "representing the common economic interests of the employees (manual and clerical workers) vis-à-vis the employer *and of supporting the employer in realizing the purposes of the enterprise.*" The new and extended law of 1952 (*Betriebsverfassungsgesetz*) documents by a long list of control and decision-making functions of the works council (most of them in that most sensitive sphere of the exercise of authority which concerns the hiring and firing, promotion and supervision of personnel) that "realizing the purposes of the enterprise" is a managerial job, and that therefore the works council is at least in part an extension of management. Under these conditions the explicit stipulation is not surprising that "employer and works council have to abstain from every measure that might endanger the work and peace of the enterprise. In particular, employer and works council must not carry out any measures of industrial conflict against each other."

Now more than forty years old, the works council has of course long found its place in the German industrial scene. Many useful and necessary tasks are performed by works councils in many firms. But occasionally, especially in the last years, the general public was shocked by the news that in a large and well-known enterprise the majority of works councillors elected were known Communists. It is at such points that the apparent incompatibilities in the role of the works councillor become evident. More than the foreman, he must be a master and is the victim of double talk; indeed his is an "institution on the borderline" (as Fürstenberg has described it) of at least three not altogether friendly countries: management, labour, and the unions. Whatever the works councillor does, he must do injustice to one of his groups of reference. Since his existence neither eliminates the causes nor settles the issues of industrial conflict, it complicates the fronts of dispute and therefore leads to uncontrolled outbursts of resentment and protest.

All this is *a fortiori* the case with the creature of the co-determination law of 1951, the labour manager (*Arbeitsdirektor*). As a consequence of this law, workers are accorded the right to participate, by their representatives, in the management of enterprises in the coal, iron, and steel industries. This right takes two institutional forms. On the one hand, the supervisory boards (*Aufsichtsräte*) in these industries are composed of equal numbers of owners' and workers' representatives (with a "neutral" chairman, the famous "thirteenth man"); on the other hand a labour manager appointed in agreement with the labour representatives on the supervisory boards joins the managing directors (*Vorstand*). As with the works councils, industrial practice has on the whole led to workable solutions for these constructions. For the supervisory boards, this often means that, in clear deviation from their original legal functions, they have become bargaining bodies of a kind; as far as the labour managers are concerned, they have (as Pirker predicted soon after the enactment of the law) more or less taken over the functions of personnel managers — a position previously unknown in German industry. But since these workable solutions have evidently little relation to the great expectations attached to the law by its Christian Democratic and Social Democratic promoters, they too complicate and thereby aggravate the conflicts between labour and management. As if the problem of oligarchic rule in trade unions were not enough, resentment of the elected representatives in the enterprise is added, for many workers, to resentment of union bosses and, of course, management. It is always difficult to interpret wildcat strikes (of which Germany has seen quite a few in recent years); but it may be suspected that at least some of them are spontaneous and undirected expressions of the sense of frustration with their own representatives that emerges from all recent studies of workers' evaluation of co-determination.

The preceding sketch obviously presents a highly simplified picture of German industrial relations. There are many points at which the German scene differs little from that of Britain or other industrial countries. In so far as the institutional treatment of industrial conflict in Germany does differ from that elsewhere, it seems however to bear out my thesis. In its most distinct aspect, the history of industrial relations in Germany is a history of ultimate solutions. The fact that as such it is also a history of failures has not deterred management, or labour, or the great political parties from continuing their search for the perfect constitution of the enterprise. But whoever tries to evade or eliminate open conflict, risks guerilla warfare, and that means, the impossibility of rational conflict regulation. The study of German industrial relations shows that industrial conflict cannot be either wished or legislated away — and that therefore, by implication, the interests of those concerned as well as of the community at large are probably better served by an effective machinery of industrial conciliation and arbitration than by a perfect constitution of the enterprise.

The attitude to conflict inherent in various institutions of German society has of course a long and in part distinguished history in political and legal history. Probably the most significant and certainly, in our context, the most relevant representative of this tradition was Hegel. In his dialectics of substantive morality (Sittlichkeit), the third and final part of his Philosophy of Law, he introduces the three categories which form the terminological arsenal of every defender of the attitude in question here: family, civil society, and the State. Hegel of course does not simply "introduce" these categories; he presents them as that necessary sequence of both qualitative preference and historical development which is meant by his version of the term "dialectics." The family — the thesis of this dialectical structure — is for Hegel the primary, original community of men, a kind of Gemeinschaft in which the individual disappears as such, and exists (as Hegel says) "not as a person for itself, but as a member." But the family is neither systematically nor historically the final form of social and political organization. Rather, Gemeinschaft has to give way to Gesellschaft, the family to civil society — the antithesis of substantive morality. Hegel's analysis of civil society is justly famous; it is one of the brilliant accounts of the new society emerging from the French revolution as well as one of the intellectual roots of the work of at least the young Marx. But those who praise this analysis often overlook the fact that for Hegel the world of interests and needs, conflicts and antagonisms that is civil society is merely a step in a dialectical process, and that, as antithesis or opposition, it is the negative step, i.e. the one which throughout his constructions he always liked least. Thus, family and civil society are *aufgehoben* in the triple sense of this German word — abolished, conserved, and lifted to a higher level — in the State. Above the interests and conflicts of civil society, the State acts as ultimate, tranquil, impartial authority. Hegel's statements to this effect have often been quoted: "The State is the reality of the moral ideal. . . . The State, as the reality of the substantial will . . . is the reasonable in and for itself. This substantial unity is absolutely unmoved purpose for itself within which freedom achieves its highest right, just as this ultimate purpose has the highest right against the individuals, whose highest duty it is to be members of the State."

Quoting Hegel as extensively as this is more than a lapse from sociological analysis to intellectual history. Through legal and political theory, Hegel has influenced German politics more than any other thinker. But even where no such direct influence can be demonstrated, his dialectics of substantive morality is a perfect description of many features of political organization in Germany (and perhaps, in other continental countries, past and present, as well).

If one was looking for a formula to describe the constitution of Bismarck's German Empire, none could be more appropriate than the dialectics of State and civil society. There was a parliament within which the various and often divergent interests of civil society, organized in political parties, were represented. But the debates of the *Reichstag* were not regarded as either legal or factual sources of legislation or of the control of the executive. Decisions were made elsewhere by authorities which looked upon themselves and were looked upon by others as impartial adjudicators of right and wrong ("the reality of the moral ideal") above the petty disputes and conflicts of the parties. — In the structure of the executive, this notion of the State as the ultimate authority and source of law and morality was and is clearly expressed by the preferential position accorded to civil servants (and within the civil service to lawyers as the institutional interpreters of substantive morality). The Prussian "civil service ethos" of duty, incorruptibility, loyalty, and disinterestedness is a direct consequence of the moral ideal as embodied in the State. — One of the most striking features of recent German history is the extent to which the labour movement, and above all the Social Democratic Party has taken over this suspicion of interests and the belief in the impartial authority of the State. Lassalle, of course, was a Hegelian, and in his *Workers' Programm* he tried to convince his audience that the State was so clearly the embodiment of the moral ideal that not even Bismarck's Empire could be really bad. But Lassalle did not remain alone. All great Social Democratic leaders — Bebel, Ebert, Schumacher above all — believed in the privileged position of the State versus the comparative pettiness of civil society, i.e. of interests, parties, parliaments, conflicts, and the like. — That the invidious distinction between the State and civil society, or authority and conflicts of interest, went far beyond political philosophers and party leaders, has only recently been demonstrated again by Kurt Sontheimer in his study of anti-parliamentary currents in the Weimar Republic. In so far as parliamentary government was ever accepted in Weimar Germany, it was accepted as a second best solution, often indeed as a mere mechanism for finding the right man or men, i.e. him or those who know all the right answers. Thus, for many elections and parliamentary debates seemed acceptable as a procedure of personnel selection, but not as a method of government. Throughout the years from 1918 to 1933 there was widespread antipathy against "party strife," "the rule of interests," "the politics of bargaining," and the whole "system" which did not manage to rise from the grime of civil society to the splendour of the State.

To English ears, the usage of the word "state" imported here from everyday German must sound decidedly odd. Statements like "The State is the ultimate source of authority" or indeed "The State is the reality of the moral ideal" seem to provoke, if phrased in English, a question which to many Germans would seem almost sacrilegious: Who is it who represents this State and hides behind the personified abstraction? Which groups do in fact dominate government and determine, directly or indirectly, the course of the country? These questions lead directly to an historical explanation of the prevalence of the attitude to conflict under discussion. But before I follow this lead, it seems appropriate to try and state the thesis of this analysis as it is implied by the title of *Conflict and Liberty*.

In political debate, if not in political theory, the claim is often heard today that political democracy presupposes the "total democratization of society." The word offends the ear; but, more than that, it involves a very imprecise notion of both democracy and society. Following Schumpeter's well-known definition, parliamentary democracy may be described as "that institutional arrangement for arriving at political decisions in which individuals acquire the power to decide by means of a competitive struggle for the people's vote." But it can be shown that this distinctive arrangement is strictly appropriate for the political community only. It is hard to see how an army could serve its purpose if its officers had to campaign for office among their soldiers. However liberal a school system may be, the election of teachers and professors by pupils and students would probably not help the quality of teaching. While some children may dream of electing their parents, the resulting kinship system would be a novelty even for the most widely travelled anthropologist. Even in enterprises, industrial or otherwise, it would seem that the fact of ownership — whether private or public — and the requirement of continuity forbid the introduction of strictly democratic institutions. As a matter of fact, many attempts to "democratize" these and other institutions have been undertaken in this century of large-scale social experiments, but so far as can be judged they have all failed and been abandoned, thereby providing empirical confirmation of the apparent impossibility to extend the procedures of political democracy to other institutions of society.

There is, however, implicit in the institutions of parliamentary democracy, an attitude to conflicts of interest as they emerge from the differential placement of people in society, which can be applied in other institutional areas as well. In its abstract core, this attitude involves (1) the acceptance of differences of opinion and interest as inevitable; (2) concentration on the modes rather than the causes of conflict; (3) the setting-up of institutions which provide conflicting groups with binding channels of expression; (4) the development of rules of the game by which the conflicting parties abide. What these rules of the game, and the context within which they operate, are like in detail, depends largely on the specific requirements of the institutions concerned. Thus, a system of conciliation and arbitration in industry, teaching procedures based on discussion and dialogue in universities, a machinery for lodging and hearing complaints in the army, and many other detailed modes of channelling differences of interest, may be fully appropriate equivalents of parliamentary government in the polity. While there may thus be a wide variety of institutional arrangements in the various spheres of social organization, it is the thesis of this paper that parliamentary democracy cannot work except in the context of a society the institutions of which are everywhere based on the acceptance and rational canalization of conflict.

Wherever their is social life, there is conflict. But while this sociological law — if such it is — would suggest that the liberal attitude to conflict sketched before is also the only realistic one, human history has seen more violation than acceptance of this law. Techniques of suppressing conflict are older than the word "totalitarian" with which we describe them today. Not infrequently, such techniques are embellished by ideologies of conflict resolution, according to which there can be disinterested authorities and organizational solutions eliminating the causes of conflict. I suggest that neither the totalitarian nor the authoritarian approach to social conflict can work, but that both tend to their own supersession by revolutionary upheavals or, more frequently, by the unplanned emergence of patterns which in fact if not in theory amount to the rational regulation of conflict. But this is a statement about that "long run" which renders so many sociological generalizations faintly irrelevant. Looking back into history and looking round in the present, it is hard to deny that there was and is rather less rationality than we might hope for.

What is the relevance of these different approaches to conflict for the cause of liberty? It may be said that in the sense in which the rational attitude to conflict regulation is a pragmatic implication of parliamentary government, it is also a precondition of that liberty of the individual which is guaranteed by representative democracy. But this is only part of what is meant here. Different attitudes to conflict involve different views of the human condition. If one is prepared to accept the existence of opposing views and use their conflict as a stimulus to social development, this implies the notion that man is living in a world of constitutional uncertainty. In the terms of the economist, we are always, and not just accidentally, lacking some of the information that would be required to decide what is true and what is good. Since no human being knows all the answers, the only way to avoid the dictatorship of wrong answers is to see to it that at all times and in all areas it remains possible to give more than one answer. Conflict is liberty, because it is the only adequate expression of the multiplicity and incompatibility of human interests and desires in a world of uncertainty.

At least in the past, however, this has not been — to quote the title of Leonard Krieger's important study — *The German Idea of Freedom*. The suspicious ties of freedom and necessity or freedom and authority in German political thought have often been noticed; Krieger adds to these the historical connection of the ideas of freedom and the sovereignty of the numerous provinces and principalities before the establishment of the Empire. In a sense, what some would describe as a Baconian view of man was and is prevalent in Germany: Perhaps, not all of us are living in a world of certainty, but it is possible for some, by hard work or by calling, to acquire certain knowledge about truth and justice. What is needed in politics as in all other social institutions is therefore not the freedom of accepted conflict, but the search for those who are in the possession of certain knowledge. Authority is for them, and they are made for the possession of authority.

At this point, the abstract discussion of attitudes to conflict and their implications meets the analysis of German social institutions. Once again we may ask: who are the select few whose claim to certain knowledge is accepted by the many, and who are evidently the secret of that abstract personality, the State? And since in this form the question still contains a strong element of ideological distortion of reality: How is it that in Germany, in a modern, industrial society, this notion of the State and of the chosen few — or indeed, the chosen one — continued to be accepted for so long?

Thorstein Veblen was one of the first authors to point out, in his spirited if sloppy study of *Imperial Germany and the Industrial Revolution*, that industrialization is by no means as great a unifying force of societies as many seem to think even today. While the rapid expansion of industrial production in Imperial Germany has certainly resulted in profound changes in German society, its more striking feature is how this process was incorporated in the earlier traditions of German society. Today, we tend to describe these traditions as "pre-industrial." But in fact, the German case was the first to prove that the social relations characteristic of feudal conditions everywhere need not disappear either immediately or entirely as industrialization sets in. The authoritarian welfare state and the industrial feudal society may appear contradictions in terms, but in Germany they were not contradictions in reality (unless one wants to regard the very explosiveness of these combinations as one of the sources of the instability of German politics after 1871).

Due to her peculiar version of the process of industrialization and modernization, Germany failed to develop for a long time any one of the four conditions of democracy mentioned earlier. The hidden truth of the State as the reality of the moral ideal was an established ruling class of Prussian, Protestant civil servants, soldiers, diplomats, and landed aristocrats. The process of dissolution and dislodgement of this group took more than half a century, and was finally accomplished only by the intense, and often overlooked, struggle of the Nazis against Prussia and her tradition. Equality of participation was long restricted not only by formal privileges such as the three-class electoral law of Imperial

Prussia, but above all by equally effective informal restrictions of political participation including the influence of local economic and religious powers. In this manner, the attitude of non-participation, of withdrawing to the family as the appropriate unit of social membership, of private rather than public virtues, remained the predominant value of German society, praised in German literature and practiced in German politics alike. For this is the other side of the assumption that some are in possession of certain knowledge: that the many are resigned to their impotence and renounce any claim to participation or even protest.

Evidently, in this context social conflict appears as a rather ugly concomitant of civil society which has to be superseded. In the ideology of feudal society there is no conflict between lords and subjects. For the lords, the subjects are but children who need a mixture of paternal severity and paternal care. The seemingly contradictory combination of the most advanced system of social welfare of the time, and the outlawing of the socialist parties and union in Bismarck's Germany is symbolic of an attitude to conflict according to which formal antagonisms are unnecessary since there is an authority capable of settling their issues once and for all.

It would be presumptuous to claim that this analysis provides an explanation of the specific events of 1933, much less of those of 1938 and after. Indeed, one of the melancholy failings of sociological analysis seems to be that specific events escape its crude generalities altogether. But it may be suggested that one of the underlying reasons why liberal democracy failed to gain a sure foothold in German society can be found in an attitude to social conflict which is informed by an authoritarian belief in the capacity of some to gain certain knowledge about truth and justice. It is before this background that the vanity of the political venture of the Weimar Republic becomes apparent and its failure understandable.

No task seems more difficult than to conclude these observations with a few remarks about the present. But since the question of the future of liberty is asked no less anxiously inside as outside Germany, the attempt to venture, however briefly and tentatively, into this uncertain territory may be excused.

In the first place, there are of course many indications that the social substratum of German politics has changed rather less than the more visible political institutions themselves. It is true, one of the leading opinion research institutes which has asked a national sample annually since 1951, "Do you believe that it is better for a country to have several parties, so that different opinions can be expressed freely, or but one party, so that there is as much unity as possible?" has found a consistent decrease in the proportion of those who favoured a one-party system from over 20 per cent to about 10 per cent. But perhaps the question is phrased in too rational a manner. In fact there are many Germans who favour several parties, so that there can be as much unity as possible between them; or, in other words, the multi-party system seems to be popular to the extent to which it does not function as such, but leads to all-party coalitions and unanimous decisions. Such tendencies to a new exclusion of parliament and establishment of a kind of presidential regime — sometimes called "chancellor democracy" — as there are, have perhaps been exaggerated; but undoubtedly the State is still a very prominent institution in the Federal Republic (to say nothing of the German Democratic Republic of East Germany). In other social institutions, analogous conclusions might be drawn. My exemplary analyses of the legal and educational systems, the family and the church, apply to the present no less than to the past; and in industrial relations both unions and management are still busy devising new constitutions of the enterprise.

On the other hand, this is clearly a very one-sided picture. There is always more continuity in social than in political history; the inertia of social institutions is greater than that of political constitutions. It is not surprising therefore that he who looks for the past in contemporary Germany in fact finds many traces of it. But there are indications of new departures as well: in the legal system where substantive and procedural reforms of considerable consequence have been worked out and in part introduced ("*Grosse Strafrechtsreform*"); in the field of family relations by legislation as well as unplanned developments to a condition of partnership; in the schools and universities where the older authoritative type of teaching is today clearly on the defensive; in industrial relations where American criticisms and experience are beginning to bear fruit; in the organization of the political executive where the old "civil service ethos" is increasingly being replaced by an economic ethos deplored by many, but possibly indicative of a less privileged place of the State in a society which is more nearly capitalist in character than the industrial feudalism of Imperial Germany.

It is too early to say with any degree of confidence which direction German social and political development is going to take. For one matter, there is the fundamental instability of the political and social systems of both Germanies of the present caused by the fact of the division of the country which remains a latent source of nationalist revival. But even apart from the re-unification issue, developments in the Western part of Germany are in the balance. While I feel that the social condition of the Federal Republic holds out more hope for the maintenance of liberty than there has ever been in German history, all that can safely be concluded from these remarks is that one of the developments to watch is that of the attitude to conflict implied by Germany's social and political institutions.

Social Security,
Incentives, and Controls
in the U.S. and U.S.S.R.

GASTON V. RIMLINGER

One of the most important developments in the relationship between the state and the individual citizen during the present century has been the growth in the rights of the citizen to claim economic services and cash benefits from the state. Social security programs, which have appeared in nearly every country of the world, are a central feature of this development.[1] Their main purpose has been the prevention of poverty through protection of the individual and his family against loss of income and against certain financial burdens. The growth of these rights, while greatly enriching the status of citizenship, has always been confronted with certain fundamental economic and social questions.[2] What is likely to be the long-run effect on the work habits and productivity of the mass of the people once a nation has eliminated the fear of destitution? Will a growing sense of security increase productivity? Or is it likely that the more surely individuals can count on essential services and minimal incomes, the greater will be the danger of drifting into indifferent work habits? Such a drift would probably take the form of a subtle change in values rather than a dramatic shift in attitude. Whatever the effect may be, it must certainly depend on the nature of the rights granted, social values and attitudes, and a country's economic and socio-political order.

The historic stress on individualistic self-reliance and political freedom and restrictions on state intervention under American capitalism are often considered polar opposites of the collectivist mentality and institutions of Soviet socialism. The Soviet system is based on highly centralized economic and political control and inevitably fosters the individual's economic dependence on the

From *Comparative Studies in Society and History*, Vol. IV, No. 1 (November 1961), pp. 104–115, 123–124. Copyright by The Society for the Comparative Study of Society and History. Reprinted by permission of the author and publisher.

GASTON V. RIMLINGER is Professor of Economics, Rice University, Houston, Texas. He is an expert on labor problems and social security. His Ph.D. thesis was a study of labor protest in British, American, and German coal mining prior to 1914 (1956). He has published numerous articles in professional journals and is currently at work on a comprehensive comparative study of social security systems.

[1] A note on terminology. "Social security" in this paper is used as a generic term for governmental measures designed to protect individual or family income and to provide certain services. It includes social insurance, public assistance, and social service. "Social insurance" is used to refer specifically to programs with work-related benefits which are financed at least in part by specific taxes. "Public assistance" is used for programs financed out of general revenue with benefits given on the basis of need. Most of the discussion will have reference to social insurance programs.

[2] Those opposing social security programs have always stressed presumed harmful effects. Those who favor them are more interested in finding out at what point and under what conditions public income guarantees may have adverse economic effects. T. H. Marshall throws interesting light on this question in tracing the growth of citizenship rights from the acquisition of civil rights in the 18th century, to political rights in the 19th, to social rights in the 20th century. See *Citizenship and Social Class* (Cambridge, Eng.: Cambridge University Press, 1950).

state. These divergent environments offer an opportunity for a comparative approach to the complex questions raised above. This article uses the comparative method to explore the relationship between social security rights and production implications in the two countries.

Aside from the inherent interest of this question, its discussion is made timely by the remarkable recent increases and anticipated growth in social security expenditures in many countries, including the U.S. and U.S.S.R.[3] How these large sums and the administrative agencies controlling them will affect economic behavior and processes is becoming increasingly important.[4] For purposes of dealing with this question, we may look upon social security as a system of secondary income distribution, a system which is different in its distributive principles and primary objectives from the economy's functional income distribution. Functional income payments go to employed factors of production. They perform their productive function when they attract and allocate these factors in accordance with economic efficiency. Income from social security, on the other hand, is oriented, at least in the first instance, to the needs of its beneficiaries rather than the requirements of the production process. Social security payments go chiefly to totally or partially unemployed and unemployable persons, in other words, persons who are in the main separated from productive activity. As all income payments, they tend to have an impact on both the supply and the demand side of the economy's output. Social security income affects the economy's level of effective demand; its timing and amount can be designed to contribute to economic stability. To have an effective impact on the supply side, the distributive pattern and eligibility conditions of social security must be coordinated with functional income distribution and with other factors affecting production costs.

Many problems are inherent in the attempt to make social security serve adequately the needs of its beneficiaries and at the same time use it as an instrument of economic incentive and control. To see how the U.S. and the U.S.S.R. differ in their approaches to these problems, we shall begin with an examination of social security rights, since these determine the principles of benefit distribution in the two countries.

[3] In the U.S. public income-maintenance program expenditures rose from $9.149 billions in 1949–50 to $26.146 billions (projected) in 1959–60. The U.S.S.R. state social insurance budget rose from 17.2 billion rubles in 1950 to 70.2 billion rubles (planned) in 1960. Figures for the U.S. are from Ida C. Merrian, "Social Security Status of the American People," *Social Security Bulletin*, XXIII, No. 8 (August 1960), p. 8. U.S.S.R. data are from "Tsentral'noe Statisticheskoe Upravlenie pri Sovete Ministrov SSSR," *Narodnoe Khoziaistvo SSSR v. 1958 Godu* (Moscow, 1959), p. 906, and from A. Larin, "Leniskie Printsipy Sotsial'nogo Strakhovanii, Vottloshchaiutsia v Zhizni," *Okhrana Truda i Sotsialnoe Strakovanie*, No. 3 (March 1960), p. 9.

[4] The broader implications of social security are stressed particularly in recent German literature. See, for instance, H. Achinger, *Sozialpolitik als Gesellschaftspolitik* (Hamburg, 1958), and H. Hensen, *Die Finanzen der sozialen Sicherung im Kreislauf der Wirtschaft* (= *Kieler Studien*, No. 36) (Kiel, 1955). Myrdal also stresses the need to integrate the social security edifice in Sweden with "the whole system of public policies." G. Myrdal, *Beyond the Welfare State* (New Haven: Yale University Press, 1960), p. 66.

SOCIAL SECURITY RIGHTS AND
BENEFIT DISTRIBUTION

The American System. Social security income, unlike functional income, cannot be distributed "blindly" through the working of an impersonal market mechanism. The state has to decide under what circumstances and in what degree individuals and their families will be supported. Such decisions are necessarily interrelated with prevailing views on the powers and duties of the state, the rights and responsibilities of individuals, and on an evaluation of the economic justification of support and its consequences.

The interaction of these factors in the shaping of a country's social security system is a complex historical process. Only a broad outline of major shifts in ideas and attitudes leading to the present American system can be sketched here. The absence of serious social security planning in America until the 1930's was not due to any stifling of widespread demands for such benefits. This absence, a historian points out, "reflected a positive philosophy . . . that it was up to the individual to work, save, and succeed." [5] It was an affirmation of a faith in a certain uniqueness of the country's economic and social system. According to the dominant views, the country was so full of opportunities for economic self-help that support by the state could be largely ignored or rejected as both harmful and unnecessary.

To be sure, insecurity and personal misfortune were not denied, nor could cases of chronic poverty be entirely overlooked. But insecurity was considered an essential stimulus to economic drive, and relief of personal misfortune was a task for voluntary private charity.[6] Chronic poverty, on the other hand, was accounted for largely in terms of character deficiency. The poorest groups were made up mainly of Negroes and recent immigrants. In the explanation of their lot, sociological theories about racial characteristics, which were most in vogue during the decades of heavy immigration, reinforced the arguments about individual shortcomings as a cause of economic distress. So long as shiftlessness, laziness, lack of prudence and forethought, or ungrateful children, which may be evidence of faulty rearing and care by the parent, were regarded as the source of indigence, the poor could have no strong claim against society. On the contrary, to give them assistance might only encourage their "evil" habits and help them escape the "natural" punishment for their weaknesses.

The provision of restricted public assistance to recognized paupers was, of course, part of Anglo-American tradition, and its legitimacy, in the sense of acceptability to the community, was not in doubt while America industrialized. The legitimacy of social insurance, however, was an entirely different matter, for it meant superimposing upon the private enterprise system state planned

[5] F. L. Allen, "Economic Security: A Look Back and A Look Ahead," in The American Assembly, *Economic Security for Americans* (New York: Graduate School of Business, Columbia University, 1959), p. 14.

[6] The most forceful presentation of this view is probably in William G. Sumner, *What Social Classes Owe to Each Other* (New York: Harper and Brothers, 1883).

support of individuals and families, regardless of their need and without deterrent.

The implied dependence on the state was felt to pose serious threats to individual freedom, thrift, and self-help, which have always been considered the backbone of American economic vitality. The presence of these deep feelings about a fundamental incompatibility of such compulsory measures with the American free enterprise system helps to account for the fact that by the early 1930's the United States, the most important industrial power in the world, was at the same time the greatest laggard among industrial countries in the development of social security. For a quarter of a century protection against industrial accidents alone was thought to be an acceptable field for social insurance. And this was made acceptable by an extension of the concept of employer liability and reliance on state policy power, rather than on any welfare state concept. Other forms of social insurance were associated with socialism and state paternalism. They were sensed to be the product of class-conscious governments, governments which admit that not all citizens have equal opportunities, that some social groups cannot fully provide for themselves and are therefore entitled to special protection.

Rather interesting shifts in ideas and attitudes occurred when the spectacular distress of the 1930's made massive state relief measures unavoidable. Now it was officially recognized not only that large numbers of people were becoming economically dependent through no fault of their own, but also that this was a permanent rather than merely a temporary problem.[7] While this recognition removed some of the obstacles to the introduction of social security, it did not eliminate the deeply-rooted American dislike for any arrangement which ties the welfare of large numbers of individuals to benefits provided by the state. In defense against latent and overt arguments that such an arrangement threatens individual freedom and economic self-reliance, the framers of the American social security system put great emphasis on the idea that social security, unlike ordinary relief measures, was not at all a government handout but mainly a social mechanism for the realization of the traditional ideas of economic self-help. Professor J. Douglas Brown, a staff member of the Committee on Economic Security appointed by President Roosevelt, has stated recently: "We wanted our government to provide a mechanism whereby the individual could prevent dependency through his own efforts . . . To us social security was a social mechanism for the preservation of individual dignity. . . ."[8] According to this view, the American approach to social security is a conservative force which strengthens rather than weakens economic self-help and other individualistic values.

[7] See the President's message to Congress, June 8, 1934, *Congressional Record*, LXXVIII, Part 10, pp. 10769–10771; and the report of the Committee on Economic Security in U.S. House of Representatives, 74th Congress, 1st Session, *Hearings Before the Committee on Ways and Means on H. R. 4120* (Washington, D.C., 1935), pp. 19–20.

[8] "The American Philosophy of Social Insurance," *Social Service Review*, XXX, No. 1 (March 1956), p. 3.

Although social security inevitably involves governmental intervention in the distributive process, the basic concern of the American approach was to keep this intervention as passive as possible. This concern, due to individualistic and equalitarian legacies, accounts for certain fundamental features of American social insurance programs which significantly affect their distributive aspects. First, the extent and levels of benefit have always been geared to an acceptable minimum, rather than to universality of coverage and comprehensiveness of benefit at maximum feasible levels. Second, the programs treat all individuals alike, without relating eligibility to socio-economic status, which until recently was typical of European programs. Third, and most fundamental, benefits under these programs are said to be on a "contributory-contractual" basis.

The stress on the concept of contract has ideological rather than legal significance. Official educational literature at the inception of the system emphasized the idea that benefits were not to be a matter of state benevolence, which presumably could subject them to governmental whims, but a "matter of right." Of course, in any country where social security is established by law, individuals who qualify under the law obtain benefits as a matter of statutory right. The American concern with benefits as a "matter of right" has to do with the basis of this right. Many countries, including the Soviet Union, treat social security as a "constitutional" or "social" right, something to which the individual is conditionally entitled simply because he is a member of the given social collectivity.[9] But the philosophy of social solidarity which underlies this conception of social security clashes hard with traditional American individualism. The guiding idea in American social insurance is that the *individual earns* the right to benefit through payment of contributions by himself and on his behalf. Although workers in many countries pay contributions, these do not usually carry the significance they do in the United States, where they imply a quasi-contractual relationship between the citizen and the state. Nevertheless, the act of contributing, while it has important political advantages, can only bind the government morally, rather than legally, to render specified benefits.

The emphasis on relating benefits to a contributory contractual basis, which precludes financing from general revenue, is an outstanding manifestation of the traditional ideals of self-help and independence carried over into a governmental "mutual help" program. It reflects the desire for a system under which the individual would merely use the governmental mechanism to help himself, without otherwise relying on state aid. It reflects also a desire to safeguard individual independence by establishing a "contractual" relationship which limits governmental discretion in the collection of contributions and distribution of benefits. Thus, the contributory-contractual principle, which is the basic distributive principle of American social insurance, is intimately related to American social values and attitudes. It puts the right to social security on a modified self-help basis, which is in the main a restrictive approach. It restricts

---

[9] For a discussion of this idea see C. Marti Bufill, *Tratado comparado de Seguridad Social* (Madrid: Ministerio de Trabajo, Instituto Nacional de Previsión, 1951), pp. 106 ff.

benefits to those by or for whom contributions have been paid, while many needy persons may be overlooked.[10]

One implication of a strict interpretation of the principle is that total accumulated contributions should determine the level of the disability or old age pension to which an individual is entitled, but in practice this emphasis on the equitable interest presents many problems and has been progressively diluted in the evolution of Old Age, Survivors and Disability Insurance. Our main concern here, however, is with the restrictions the contributory contractual approach puts on the use of social insurance funds and institutions for purposes of promoting incentive and effecting control. Although individual benefits are only indirectly related to contributions by or for the individual, the U.S. Congress insists that total disbursements of benefits stay within the limits of contributed funds and interest. This approach tends to impose rather inflexible income and expenditure patterns and calls for maintaining definite relationships between contributions and benefits over time. To safeguard the financial integrity of the system, and hence the individual's unhindered right to benefits, it is felt that contributions and disbursements must be governed solely by the internal requirements of the programs. What this implies for economic policy will be discussed after an examination of the exactly opposite Soviet approach.

The Soviet System. If the atomistic concepts of society and the economy underlying nineteenth century capitalism were a hindrance to the introduction of social security, the sense of solidarity and the relationship of state and society in socialist ideology were highly congenial to it. The Soviet citizen's right to social security rests on a historical basis which goes back to the early years of Russian socialism. Although Marx made only an incidental reference in his writings to "funds for those unable to work," [11] Lenin showed repeated interest in this question and has earned, if not all, at least some of the honor done him by Soviet writers in this field. The first record of Lenin's interest in this matter dates to 1895, when he included social security proposals in the reform program he was then preparing.[12] He also is given major credit for the social security demands embodied in the "Labor Program" adopted in 1903 by the Second Congress of the Russian Social Democratic Workers' Party. The measures envisaged at that time called for "State insurance for old people and people completely or partially incapacitated, out of a special fund created by a special levy on the capitalists." [13] Most important, however, was the plan he advanced at the Prague Conference of the Bolshevik Party in 1912, a plan

[10] In a strict legal sense this is not quite correct since an employer's failure to pay social security taxes does not thereby deprive his employees of their right to benefits if their employment is covered by the law. For persons not eligible the American system relies on public assistance, which pays benefits on the basis of demonstrated need.

[11] K. Marx, *Critique of the Gotha Programme* (London: Lawrence and Wishart, 1943), p. 10.

[12] "Leninskaia Strakhovaia Programma," *Okhrana Truda i Sotsial'noe Strakhovanie,* No. 5 (November, 1958), pp. 68–72.

[13] The program is contained in M. Dewar, *Labour Policy in the U.S.S.R., 1917–1928* (London: Royal Institute of International Affairs, 1956), pp. 158–159.

which called for comprehensive insurance of all wage and salary earners against unemployment and all losses of capacity to work. Benefits were to equal the worker's wage and be paid for entirely by the employer and the state, but control of the system was to be completely in the hands of the insured.[14] Although Lenin's program was part of an attempt to belittle the rather limited social insurance scheme then under consideration by the Tsarist government, it nevertheless supplied the foundation for the prominence of social security among the means by which the Soviet state would carry out its welfare policy.

For the Bolsheviks, social security, as the preamble to the 1903 Program indicates, was a means to strengthen the workers' "capacity to fight for their emancipation." [15] Lenin was convinced, and his successors still are, that capitalism is incompatible with genuine social security. He urged his followers to agitate against the "illusory" Tsarist proposals and assured them that "the necessary condition for the realization of insurance reforms that answer the real needs of the proletariat is the definitive overthrow of Tsarism. . . ." [16] After the Tsarist government had established its modest insurance scheme, the Bolsheviks urged their followers to participate in its administration and use it for revolutionary purposes.[17] The struggle for the overthrow of Tsarism and capitalism became in part a struggle for the establishment of comprehensive social security, which has been considered one of the main fruits of the "victory of the working class over capitalism." In the very first days of its existence, on November 14, 1917, the Bolshevik government felt compelled to issue a declaration acknowledging that the "Russian proletariat has placed on its banners comprehensive social insurance for all hired workers and for all urban and rural poor," and that the government "shall without delay proceed with the promulgation of decrees for total social insurance." [18] The Declaration also enunciated five principles, of clear Leninist inspiration, on which to base the planned system: (1) inclusion of all wage and salary earners and all urban and rural indigents, (2) coverage of all income hazards, (3) financing entirely by employers, (4) compensation to equal at least full wages in case of loss of work capacity and unemployment, (5) complete self-administration by the insured.

Taken literally, these principles are not a little heroic. They are just as naive as the once prevalent American attitude that any socially guaranteed income scheme is bound to have adverse incentive effects. An almost unrestricted promise to wage and salary earners of full wage compensation, combined with "complete self-administration" by those who draw benefits but do not bear the cost, would in time inevitably have adverse effects on work habits. It is not

[14] V. I. Lenin, *Sochineniia*, 4th ed. (Moscow, 1948), XVII, p. 427.

[15] Dewar, *op. cit.*, p. 158.

[16] Lenin, *op. cit.*, p. 428.

[17] See the resolutions of the Central Committee of the Russian Social Democratic Workers' Party in 1913–1914, in Nauchno-Issledovatel'skii Institut Professional'nogo Dvizheniia, VKP(*b*) *i Profsoiuzy o Sotsial'nom Strakhovanii* (Moscow, 1934), pp. 44–48.

[18] A. S. Krasnopol'skii, *Osnovnye Printsipy Sovetskogo Gosudartsvennogo Sotsial'nogo Strakhovaniia* (Moscow, 1951), pp. 13–14.

surprising that when these promises were put into the form of concrete programs they were pragmatically trimmed to the dimensions of reality.

It is not possible to consider here the multitude of decrees and directives
which began to be issued in 1917. They reflect experimentation in method
as well as important shifts in policy in response to changes in the economic
situation and in over-all economic policy. Many of the early, generous measures
existed mainly on paper and had very limited practical significance in an era
of monetary instability. However, the evolution of Soviet social security
policy since then is of great interest from the point of view of the questions
raised at the beginning of this paper. Having committed itself not only to a
comprehensive social security program but also to a government controlled
economy, the Soviet rulers soon realized the labor discipline and productivity
implications of social security. Somehow they had to decide in what manner the
distribution of social security benefits should be guided by the needs of the
beneficiaries or by the requirements of the production process.

The evolution of Soviet policy toward extensive use of social security payments and institutions for purposes of economic incentive and control will be
considered below. To understand this evolution one must bear in mind not only
the character of the Soviet economic and political order but have some
acquaintance with basic Soviet social insurance ideas. The government's conception of the citizen's right to benefits enters into many decisions where the
interests of beneficiaries and those of the economy in general are not necessarily
identical. It influences the determination of eligibility, the fixing of the structure and level of benefits, and administrative practices. In all these areas the
government can discriminate between individuals and groups according to its
view of their rights and needs and the broader interest of state and country.
It was for the express purpose of restricting this kind of discrimination, and the
exercise of power over individual welfare it implies, that the founders of the
American system stressed the "contributory-contractual" principle and the idea
that the individual *earns* his benefits.

The character of Soviet thought in this respect is quite the opposite from
the American, although no less ambiguous. It stresses, on the one hand, that
benefits are a free gift from the state, an act of governmental benevolence, a
manifestation of social humanism. Soviet workers have been told by their
leaders that every "figure in the state social insurance budget . . . breathes
the warmth and paternal care which our leader and teacher Comrade Stalin
manifests daily and hourly toward all people, great and small." [19] On the other
hand, as noted earlier, social security is treated also as an historic right of the
working population, a right which has been incorporated into the Constitution.
Article 120 of the Constitution (1936, as amended) states in part that
"Citizens of the U.S.S.R. have the right to maintenance in old age and also
in case of sickness and disability." Conditions governing the receipt of benefits

[19] Statement by N. M. Shvernik at a meeting of trade union activists, May 25, 1938,
quoted in A. S. Krasnopol'skii, "On the Nature of Soviet State Social Insurance,"
Current Digest of the Soviet Press, III, No. 46 (Dec. 29, 1951), 4, translated from his
article in *Sovetskoe Gosudarstvo i Pravo*, No. 6 (June 1951), pp. 62–69.

and the benefit structure can be quite different depending on the extent to which they are based on the theory that benefits are a free gift or on the theory that they are a basic right of the worker. As a gift benefits can legitimately serve primarily the purpose of the giver, but as a right they definitely limit the freedom of the giver. The possibility of the theoretical conflict suggested here disappears, however, for all practical purposes, when attention is paid to Article 12 of the Constitution, which is an important corollary to Article 120. Article 12 states in part that "Work in the U.S.S.R. is a duty and a matter of honor for every able-bodied citizen, in accordance with the principle: 'He who does not work, neither shall he eat.' "

In the context of the questions raised earlier it is highly significant, and certainly not accidental, that a constitution which guarantees the individual's maintenance also imposes upon him the duty to work. And conversely, the duty to work implies a right to maintenance that goes beyond any individual merit of support, since maintenance of the worker is then more nearly like the maintenance of capital. In fact, the concept of the maintenance of the efficiency of the "human capital" is a basic and highly interesting ingredient of Soviet social insurance thought. "In the society which is founded on labor, where the exploitation of man by man has been eliminated . . . , where people are treated as the *most valuable capital* . . . comprehensive care of aged and disabled members is natural and inevitable." [20] Actual practice, as will be seen below, has become more consistent with this revealing statement in recent years than was the case earlier.

Nevertheless, income maintenance rights in the Soviet Union, as in the United States, are conditional rather than absolute. Being a citizen, or a piece of "human capital," is not sufficient for benefit eligibility. Moreover, in neither country do eligible citizens have an equal right to support; both relate benefits to previous wages, in contrast to the more egalitarian British and Swedish systems, which pay mainly flat benefit amounts.[21] But even if in the two countries studied differential benefits serve similar incentive purposes, the concepts behind these differentials reveal interesting differences. In America the higher paid worker pays a larger contribution, and, on the basis of the "contributory contractual" principle, is entitled to higher benefits. But the Russian worker cannot "earn" differential benefits in the sense that the American worker does, unless his earnings are somehow related to payment for benefits. But that would undermine the idea that benefits are a gift of the state and would weaken the propaganda value of the system as well as its flexibility in the pursuit of broader economic and political goals. Furthermore, contractual social insurance concepts run counter to Soviet ideas about the nature of the relationships between individuals and the state.

In Soviet thinking, benefits are in the nature of a *reward* for loyal performance of duties, which is not quite compatible with the contractual idea of

[20] Krasnopol'skii, *Osnovnye Printsipy* . . . , p. 54. Italics are mine.

[21] It is noteworthy, however, that in 1959 both Great Britain and Sweden introduced graduated benefits on top of a flat base rate, which is a move away from the traditional income equality aim in favor of incentive considerations.

an *exchange* of benefits for premium payments. Krasnopol'skii, in one of the few theoretical examinations of the Soviet system, puts particular stress on this point:

> . . . mutuality and reciprocity . . . are not to be found in the mutual relations or the parties in state social insurance. The obligation here lies not on both parties, but only on one — the agency of state social insurance is under obligation to issue funds and to set and pay pensions or other forms of subsistence . . . , whereas the worker or employee has no reciprocal obligations to the agencies of state social insurance.[22]

This deliberate avoidance of the contract fiction has the virtue of being consistent with the other fiction, that benefits are a gift, but it implies a rejection of the Soviet wage principle "to each according to his work," which would be one way of justifying differential benefits. Krasnopol'skii clearly states the inapplicability of the wage principle to social insurance, for benefits are not a payment for work done. But, he argues, "The level of consumption that the given person has reached is taken into consideration when he is granted disability aid out of the special funds set aside for purposes of socialist mutual aid." [23] Soviet benefits are, in fact, always related to recent earnings, even in the case of old age benefits. The contractual approach would suggest, of course, that they be based on the total amount of contributions paid, that is, on the total period in covered work.

Nevertheless, just as the American system has never awarded benefits in direct proportion to total contributions, so is it impossible to provide a simple principle of Soviet benefit distribution. The Soviet government has always used the social security system in a highly pragmatic manner, to suit its economic and social planning purposes. It feels free to discriminate between union and non-union members and between individuals with identical earnings engaged in different occupations, industries, or locations. The government also feels free to introduce non-economic eligibility criteria. For instance, an individual may count as part of his work record required for old-age pension eligibility the time he spent in "bourgeois" jails for revolutionary activity and periods he was unemployed for political reasons in "bourgeois" countries. On the other hand, those who committed a crime against the state in enemy occupied territory during the war or as displaced persons may not count their war-time work record toward meeting the required work stage for old-age pension eligibility.[24]

It is apparent from the foregoing analysis that the distributive philosophy of a social security system is a product of historically interacting forces and is

---

[22] "On the Nature of Soviet State Social Insurance," p. 6. It may be worth pointing out also that while in America a worker may institute a civil suit in a U.S. court to enforce his benefit claim, Soviet courts have no such jurisdiction. This does not mean that a Soviet worker can be arbitrarily deprived of his benefits, but the fact that the trade unions and administrative agencies make final decisions reflects an important difference in the conception of the worker's right. See N. G. Aleksandrov, *Sovetskoe Trudovoe Pravo*, 2nd ed. (Moscow, 1959), pp. 359-363.

[23] Krasnopol'skii, "On the Nature of Soviet State Social Insurance," p. 5.

[24] V. I. Merkulova and I. M. Sakharova, *Pensii po Strarosti* (Moscow, 1957), p. 31.

necessarily intimately related to a country's economic and political system. American social insurance concepts have developed in an environment with strong individualistic and laissez faire traditions. Consequently, the American system tries to minimize the role of the state and restrict it as much as possible to the passive provision of a legal framework and administrative machinery. The American social insurance system, in effect, is somewhat of a public trustee of the properties of many individuals, which gives it a semi-autonomous existence. It operates mainly in the interests of "insured" individuals, and its overriding purpose is to meet its obligations to them. In the Soviet Union, on the other hand, social security has always been the mainstay of social welfare policy. Attempts, in the early years of the regime, to make it a quasi-independent undertaking were definitely suppressed.[25] By emphasizing the role of the state as a dispenser of "free" benefits and shunning the concept of individual equitable interest, the Soviet system has facilitated the development of social security as an integral part of the command economy.

· · ·

CONCLUSION

The aspiration for economic security is a powerful force in the evolution of an economic system, whether it is centrally planned or organized by markets. How this force is channeled will depend on historically conditioned economic, social, and political factors. A basic lesson of American experience has been to show the weakness of the old argument, closely associated with the puritanical work ethic of early industrial capitalism, that a lessening of insecurity by social means impairs individual incentive and initiative. Many observers, indeed, argue the opposite case. The danger in following this line of argument beyond the context of limited programs is that it leads to the controversial proposition that the structure and levels of social security programs should be designed to promote incentive, labor discipline, and other economic objectives. By comparison with a Soviet-type economy, a democratic capitalistic system does not present a favorable setting for exploiting the economic incentive and control potentials of social security schemes. Although it is often argued that social security serves as a bulwark of the private enterprise system, there is nevertheless a latent conflict between the stress on individual economic responsibility, individual freedom, and reliance on automatic market processes, and the centralized planning against economic insecurity represented by social security. To minimize this conflict and restrict centralized planning and control, the American approach has been to keep social security measures at a minimum acceptable level and think of benefit distribution in quasi-contractual terms. Consequently, American social security gives precedence to the specific rights of insured individuals over general economic objectives.

The pattern of adaptation of social security to the planned Soviet economy

[25] On administrative developments see G. V. Rimlinger, "The Trade Union in Soviet Social Insurance: Its Historical Development and Present Function," *Industrial and Labor Relations Review* (April 1961).

is substantially different. Instead of being hampered by individualistic pre-conceptions, Soviet social security payments and institutions are based on concepts which facilitate the system's integration with central planning and aid in the control and management of the work force. Theoretically, Soviet spokesmen do not recognize any conflict between individual interests and social goals. On the contrary, they see in social welfare measures an unmistakable manifestation of the basic harmony underlying a socialist society and economy. But Soviet experience has revealed two opposite dangers of an unqualified acceptance of this view. It may lead, as it did initially in the Soviet case, to naively generous but economically impractical and hence self-defeating social security programs. Or it may lead, as it did during the industrialization period, to painful sacrifices of individual welfare for the sake of promoting broader economic aims.

A Comparative Study
of Academic Freedom
and Student Politics

JOSEPH BEN-DAVID AND RANDALL COLLINS

. . . The usual aim [of a university] is an administration without any coercion and with a great measure of active participation of those administered. An essential requirement for this is mutual trust. This is presumably established on the basis of the same considerations we generally use in making individual decisions. Where the risks are unknown or great, general trustworthiness becomes decisive; where the risks are small — either because of the triviality of the affair, or because the odds are known to be low, personal acquaintance will be less important.

Translated to the problem of academic freedom, these considerations manifested themselves partly in attempts at the restriction of the academic privileges to a very small number of people, amounting to the definition of the academics as an elite rather than a profession; and partly in attempts at the restriction of the functions of academic institutions to fields in which patterns and outcomes of training and research are known well enough to regard the risks as negligible.

From *Student Politics*, edited by Seymour M. Lipset, © 1967 by Basic Books, Inc., New York. Reprinted by permission of the authors and publisher.

JOSEPH BEN-DAVID is Associate Professor of Sociology at the Eliezer Kaplan School of Economics and Social Science, Hebrew University, Jerusalem. He is the author of "Professions in the Class Structure of Present-Day Societies" (*Current Sociology*, 1963–1964) and editor of *Agricultural Planning and Village Community in Israel* (1964). He has written many articles on the sociology of professions, of education, and of science, and is currently writing *Science and Society* for the Modern Foundation of Sociology Series.

Different academic systems have chosen different ways to minimize their risks. Some have preferred to create a restricted elite, failing to take advantage of extending the uses of the university. Others, starting out somewhat later, tried to exploit fully the potentials of the university. Since this made the establishment of personal trust such as can exist among small circles of people rather difficult, they have tried to reduce their risks by specifying as far as possible procedures and results. Whether the one or the other course is taken, trust is more easily established in situations which are reasonably well known to both parties. Such is the case where people and roles of the same kind as the universities are expected to produce have existed for a long time, and where the intellectual activities engaged in by the university are continuous with activities engaged in outside the university. On the other hand, misunderstanding is likely to arise in the absence of concrete models so that agreement has to be based on abstract principles. Besides, the absence of role-models in society makes it difficult to adjust the supply of graduates to the demand for their services. As the exact size and nature of this latter are unknown, the expectations concerning the rewards for university studies will be unrealistic, and frustration will be inevitable. The tensions resulting therefrom may seriously jeopardize academic freedom.[1]

We shall therefore expect different kinds of conflicts about academic freedom, and different kinds of outcomes in four types of university systems (cf. Table [1]).

TABLE [1]
Types of University Systems by
Aim and the Availability of Models

| | | MODEL | |
AIM		Available	Unavailable
to employ and train {	elite	Type I	Type II
	expert	Type III	Type IV

Theoretically an eightfold classification would be required, since there may be systems where professors are considered as an elite, but not necessarily the students, and vice versa. Since, however, in practice the two tend to go together, it is preferable not to complicate the scheme. It must be made clear that the dichotomization of the components is arbitrary. All university systems, as well as the majority of the individual universities, try to turn out an elite and at the same time train experts who are not necessarily destined to become an elite. These are only differences of emphasis which form a continuum. A scale of reasonable validity can be established by simply taking the ratio of students to population. These ranged in 1958 from 185 per 10,000 of general population in the United States to 19 per 10,000 in Britain and less than that in most

---

[1] J. Ben-David, "Professions in the Class System of Present-Day Societies," *Current Sociology*, Vol. XII, No. 3 (1963–64), pp. 273–275.

of the Latin American and Middle Eastern countries. Continental Europe
is much nearer this respect to the lower than to the upper end. These differences have been, with few exceptions, stable since the beginning of this century.[2] These variations reflect differences of purpose: the European systems had
started out and were meant to be first and foremost elite intellectual institutions, providing positions for the leaders in scholarly and scientific fields. At
the same time they were responsible for the training of an intellectual and
political elite, as well as some of the higher professions which, to some extent,
share in the elite status. Leading lawyers, physicians and clergymen have been
traditionally part of the central elite of European countries, while the rank and
file, alongside of teachers in the European *gymnasia* and *lycées,* have had a respected place among local notables. To perform this function, it was not
necessary to have large numbers of teachers or students. These people were
not expected to make very important direct contributions to the economy; they
were only supposed to contribute to it indirectly by creating new knowledge and
providing excellent leadership for the country. Restriction of admission, as long
as it was done according to impeccable standards, was considered an advantage,
it safeguarded quality.

In those countries, on the other hand, in which the ratios are high — the
prototype of which has been the U.S. — the system as a whole has been designed to train experts and to extend research into fields which, partly perhaps
because they had not been considered worth specialized attention, promised
to yield useful results quickly. This is not to say that the elite function of
education was lost sight of. The universities do train the elite in these systems
too. Besides, expertise and research which produces new knowledge are a kind
of leadership. The difference between these and the previously discussed elite
systems is that the expert systems do not regard it as a debasement of the
university to also train people for positions which are not elite roles.

The difference is not limited to the range of fields taught at universities, but
extends also to the way they are taught. The elite type of university, even when
it requires high technical standards from its staff, does not care much about
the technical training of the students. This, it assumes, will be acquired by
trial and error, or through in-practice training and not necessarily in the university. It suspects professional schools — the ideal solution is that of English
medical schools, in which the university medical schools concentrate on the
basic fields, whereas clinical training is provided in teaching hospitals possessing
considerable autonomy and only loosely tied to the university.[3] Ideally this

---

[2] *Ibid.,* p. 263.

[3] "Elite" as opposed to "expert" is a distinction between diffuseness and specificity.
The academic in the elite systems has to be an expert too, but that is not a sufficient
condition. His expertise itself is judged according to criteria of diffuseness. Such questions typically asked as, "Is his specialization broad enough, or important enough?"; "Is
he not merely a good technician?" imply (a) that the academic person has to cover a
broader segment of fields than those who are merely "experts"; and (b) that he must
possess qualities of leadership which are not easily defined, only intuitively distinguishable when compared with those who do not possess those qualities.

type of university is an academy, the staff of which also does a limited amount of teaching, but has practically no responsibility for training.

The prototype of the expert university, on the other hand, is the professional school. Even if it teaches pure science or humanities, it endeavors to impart to the student the actual tools for his research. Thus, the most original innovation of the American universities has been the graduate school which is an extension of the techniques of training in professional schools to all the arts and sciences.

The distinction between countries in which models are available and those in which they are not, is also a matter of a continuum. In most countries there are fairly clear-cut models of physicians or engineers, and in few is it clear what the model is for a young man studying for an arts degree. The situation also changes through time: where there is no model today there may be one tomorrow. At the same time, a distinction can be made between systems in which the university trains and educates for roles which are well known and accepted in the society, and systems which are created by a traditional, or at any rate uneducated, elite for the purpose of eventually reforming themselves or increasing their efficiency through training new and better qualified people of a kind that do not exist yet in the country.

In England, France, the U.S., and probably some other countries, modern higher education developed in the nineteenth century, shortly after the changes in occupational system and the rise of an educated class. The universities of Oxford, Cambridge, or Paris, at least since the sixteenth century, have not had the privilege of intellectual leadership. For a long time, in fact, they were followers rather than leaders. In both countries during the eighteenth century, and in England in the nineteenth as well, many of the most outstanding scholars, intellectuals, and scientists did not hold academic positions. The change was instigated partly by this non-academic intelligentsia, who were civil servants, politicians, professionals, or — especially in England — simply wealthy people often of noble descent.[4] The kind of people who should form the academic elite, as well as the nature of the products, were not in question. There was consensus between those who taught at the universities and those who decided about the fate of university budgets as civil servants, donors, or politicians. They all belonged to the same class and spoke the same language. Similarly there had been a long non-university tradition in higher education, scholarship, science, and technology in the U.S. before the country seriously embarked on the reform of its higher education. Although this has been true for the Northeastern part of the country, elsewhere the situation has often been one of the "non-model": governments and/or philanthropists of pioneering and educationally backward states setting up institutions to bring their own areas up to the standards of the East.[5]

The best known examples of non-model systems are Austria, Prussia, and

---

[4] D. S. L. Cardwell, *The Organization of Science in England* (London: Heinemann, 1957), pp. 46–51.

[5] Hofstadter and Metzger, *op. cit.*, pp. 413–414.

Russia in the eighteenth century, and the latter also in the nineteenth century (or the reformed system of the USSR in the twentieth). In all of these cases the universities were established by a minority of educated rulers and officials with the purpose of creating a new educated elite of the Western type, not to replace landed aristocracy as the mainstay of the respective regimes, but to educate the latter and selectively introduce into it able people of non-aristocratic origin. Apparently, similar conditions prevailed in Japan and China at the end of the nineteenth and early twentieth centuries, when their modern systems of higher education were established, as well as in the Eastern and Southern European, Latin American, Asian, and African countries at various times in the nineteenth and twentieth centuries. Obviously, there is a great deal of variation here concerning the efficiency and determination of those in power to carry through their attempts at modernization, and thus change a situation of "non-model" into one in which the model becomes available. Still the two categories are clearly enough distinguishable.[6]

Clearly, these types present separate and distinct problems for the maintenance of academic freedom. We shall try to explore these by taking each type in turn. We shall not give a detailed account and classification of the existing academic systems, but seek to present models of the working of those which seem to be most representative of each type.

Type 1: Elite Systems with Accepted Models. There is a nearly perfect example of this type in the English academic system. Germany, the Scandinavian countries, and France presumably also belong to this type, but the workings of these, especially that of France, are much more complex. We shall, therefore, describe the model mainly with reference to England.

The governing of this type of system is effectively shared between the academics who have complete autonomy in running their own affairs, and the government which has effective means of letting its views be known and seriously considered without openly interfering with the universities. This is so because there are no basic differences between the two sides involved. The exchange of opinion between the higher civil servants and the leadership of the universities takes place either through a formally constituted body (like the University Grants Commission in Britain, or the Chancellor of the Universities in Sweden), as well as informally since the people know each other quite well. The civil servants are of similar education and background as the university professors, so that there are no barriers to communication between them.

One of the important effects of this situation is that the civil servants form an effective buffer between politics and the universities.[7] Certain parties may have opinions about the necessity of making the universities more representative, or they may want to look into the finances of the universities. In these

---

[6] It should be possible to define them in quantitative terms by relating the numbers and kinds of students at the early stages of modern university growth to the numbers of trained and qualified people in the ruling elites, or in the country in general.

[7] Don K. Price, *Government and Science* (New York: New York University Press, 1954), p. 122; Lord Chorley, "Academic Freedom in the United Kingdom," *Law and Contemporary Problems*, 28 (Summer, 1963), pp. 647–671.

cases some solution is worked out informally which then makes the execution of the policies acceptable to the academics as well as to the politicians.

Thus, even though there may be a good deal of public discussion and criticism of the universities, there is no attempt to interfere with their autonomy. It is taken for granted that, whatever changes may prove to be desirable or necessary, they will be carried out autonomously by the universities. The consensus necessary for such a degree of trust is the result of keeping the academic system exclusive, small, and so highly selected as to command universal or near-universal respect. Conservatism is the price paid for this: academic innovations, whether in education or research, have to be relegated to peripheral parts of the system, since the elite cannot take chances without endangering its status. An example of this in England has been the great hesitancy of Oxford and Cambridge (particularly the former) in making provision for the social sciences: economics was introduced only in the 1920's, and then without adequate library facilities or sufficient staff; psychology achieved its first chairs in 1931 and 1947 at Cambridge and Oxford, respectively; sociology was introduced only in 1961, and still does not have a chair at either institution. There have been similar lacks in medical science, particularly in the integration of basic and clinical research.[8]

At first sight this delay does not seem too inefficient. It is logical to develop new things by trying them out on a small scale in a peripheral setting, and then decide on the basis of experience whether to pursue or drop the matter. The trouble is that this kind of wisdom only occurs retrospectively in the pages of official histories. For a new field to succeed, those who believe in it have to be given a chance to fight for it with as good resources as they can possibly muster, and to vie for as good students as they are capable of attracting. By being shunted to a third-rate university, or to some kind of more gilded academic ghetto where there is no chance of getting disciples or support for research, the novelty is doomed to failure.

This, however, is beside the point here. The purpose of this paper is not to investigate the innovative capability of different systems, but to study academic freedom. From this point of view, the important thing is that the situation is not perceived as an unjust limitation of the opportunities by a privileged clique, but as a fair, if not perfect, system. The possibilities for this lie in the efficiency of selection and allocation. Limitations and restrictions are perceived as just, if their rationale is reasonable and their administration equitable. As long as the elite does reasonably well what it is supposed to do, people have a good grasp of what the criteria of admission into the elite are and the elite does not make life too difficult for the rest, there will be a feeling of justice. This is assured by the existence of what we have called a "model." That is, when academic systems have been shaped by successful people in their own image. The image is well reflected throughout the educational system, and children from a very

[8] A. Flexner, *Universities: American, English, German* (New York: Oxford University Press, 1930), pp. 289–296; E. G. Boring, *A History of Experimental Psychology*, 2nd ed. (New York: Appleton-Century-Crofts, 1950), p. 494; Howard Becker, *Social Thought from Lore to Science*, 3rd ed. (New York: Dover Books, 1961), Vol. 3, p. XCVIII.

early age are made aware of it, and learn what their chances are. Expectations are geared to reality, and there are no (or insignificantly few) aspirants for academic careers, especially for top positions, who will have to be frustrated. Since, therefore, much of the envy is taken out of competition — or disposed with at an early age before the personality is formed in its final shape — there is no vindictiveness on the part of the elite, and no aggression on the part of those professionals and intellectuals who are not academics.[9] To the extent that some of the latter feel that the definition of the academic fields and roles should be broadened, they will be listened to and often given a chance "to prove" themselves. They will rarely succeed, although they will be treated fairly enough to end up blaming only themselves.[10]

Another way of bringing the educational system in accord with available social models has been the conscious attempt to make the composition of the academic elite representative of all the important political and social groups. Universities may make (and have made) efforts to find a person of working class origin for a position, or to have a communist or two on their staff. Such steps, if taken before the emergence of a frustrated group of alienated anti-establishment intellectuals, lend to this type of system an air of generosity and limitless tolerance and freedom. In fact, however, when combined with the selective, elite-oriented, process of education, this policy has the effect of giving the system maximum stability and of enhancing to the limit its conservative tendencies. Since selection is thorough and efficient, and consensus about important things great, the likelihood of individual dissent having any disrupting effect on the system is negligible. The effectiveness of scientific policy-making by a small group which knows itself to be the best in a certain field in the country, and is recognized by the relevant others as such, will not be affected by one of its members publicly advocating communism or free love. The same member, when it comes to professional policy-making, may be the "soundest" or even the most conservative of all. And, if members of the group, possibly including even the dissenter, have been known for a great many years to the civil servants who advise the minister (or, perhaps, to the minister himself, too), then no one will come to suspect them of being politically or morally unsound, and therefore not to be supported by public money. Paradoxically, the tolerance probably also reduces the dissenter's effectiveness as a propagator for his subversive non-academic interests. Having been admitted to the establishment and not being victimized by it for his views and activities, his activities only confirm the fairness of the system. The rebel himself will

---

[9] Glen H. Elder Jr., "Life Opportunity and Personality: Some Consequences of Stratified Secondary Education in Britain," *Sociology of Education*, 38 (Spring, 1965), pp. 173–202. In addition we are indebted to Professors Max Gluckman and Hilde Himmelweit for information about different enquiries showing the decisive effect of the ranking system within and between schools on the self-perception and level of aspiration of students in England.

[10] Cf. Michael Young, *The Rise of Meritocracy: 1870–2033* (London: Thames and Hudson, 1958), for a semi-literary presentation of this atmosphere and its imagined consequences.

usually feel so and his revolutionary fervor will be blunted.[11] But even if he does not feel this, his public will. A brilliant scientist and scholar victimized for his views in his academic career makes a very good agitator. As a martyr he is a living indictment of the system. But the same person, treated fairly, is living propaganda for the *status quo*.

Such a system is in near perfect balance, with a minimum of conflict and a maximum feeling of freedom. Compared with more enterprising systems, it may seem too restrictive both in its expansion of scope and its selection of personnel. But for those within it, it provides a stable, fair, and predictable system. Lack of innovativeness is counterbalanced by flexibility and openness for suggestions of reform and innovation coming from outside the society, or — in principle — even from within.

The French system, operating in a much more impersonal way, achieves similar results. There is an elaborate system of selection and allocation which produces a somewhat similar elite as in England, but instead of reducing conflict and effective dissent through group consensus, the same end is achieved there, though probably accompanied by qualitatively different emotions, through careful isolation and delimitation of spheres of influence.[12]

Type II: Elite Systems without Models in Society. While Type I tends toward a more or less stable balance, this second type is the most likely to be out of balance. This is implied in its very purpose, since it is founded in order to foster social change. Simply because these systems were all instigated by more advanced examples, they were initially built so as to create conflict. Historically, the line of educational reform leading to social conflict (and often culminating in revolution) can be traced back as far as the seventeenth century. The enlightened circles of France propagandizing for the establishment of the Academy of Sciences and Baconian educational ideas and supported by "modernizing" civil servants like Richelieu or Colbert, had English models before their eyes. The movement which arose as a result eventually played an important role in the overthrow of the old regime. The reforms of Austrian and German higher education in the end of the eighteenth and early nineteenth centuries were first an imitation and then a reaction to French models; Russian higher education, established mainly in the nineteenth century, took its model mainly from Germany; the even newer systems of higher education in Latin America, Asia, and Africa have usually followed one of those three models.

The common characteristic of all these imitations has been that they are not mere adoptions of innovations in education and research made elsewhere, but deliberate attempts at facilitating a change in the character and/or composition of the ruling elite, and/or the creation of entirely new secondary elites, by

[11] On the general point of the cooptation of dissenters by controlling elites, cf. Philip Selznick, "Foundations of the Theory of Organizations," *American Sociological Review*, 13 (February, 1948), pp. 25–35.
[12] Michel Crozier, *The Bureaucratic Phenomenon* (Chicago: The University of Chicago Press, 1964), pp. 238–244.

means of the educational reform. This distinguishes the present type from such cases as the adoption of certain features of the German academic system in the nineteenth century by English, French, and American universities. In these earlier cases the "models" for educated administrators, politicians, professionals, or even scientists and scholars had existed prior to the adoption of the foreign pattern. The innovation was a means of producing more and better of the same kinds of people as already existed in society. This, of course, might have led eventually to unexpected political problems. But the replacement of existing elites with a new one, or the introduction of a new stratum in society, is bound to lead to direct conflict. No existing elite will put up gracefully with an open attempt to transform and replace it, and even less will young men reared as future elite according to models of more advanced societies admit to the authority of a traditional ruling class. One can postulate, therefore, that at some point attempts will be made by the authorities to regulate the university and tell professors what to teach and what not to teach, and what in general should be the model they present to their students. It is nearly inevitable that under such circumstances students, and at least some of the teachers, will become politically rebellious.

Since, therefore, this is a system which by definition starts from imbalance, no single case can be regarded as representative of it. Some systems never attain balance, so that the universities become permanent centers of intellectual and political conflict over a long period of time; others manage to establish some kind of a balance which may be more or less precarious depending on conditions to be specified. We shall, therefore, attempt first to describe a model of chronic disequilibrium, based mainly on the nineteenth century Russian and twentieth century Latin American cases, and then referring to the well-known case of Germany in the nineteenth and early twentieth century, we shall treat an example of a temporarily successful establishment of balance.

One of the distinguishing features of these systems, compared with the previous type, is the high degree of formalization of the rights and privileges of the academic person, and the academic corporation. In principle these may appear as not too different from the arrangements of the first type — both are designed to ensure the autonomy of the profession — but in the first type of system there are few or no laws to define these rights, so that in principle it would probably be quite easy for any government which so desired to impair them without any change in the legal situation. The necessity of spelling out the rights in the non-model systems is the result of lack of communication and mutual trust between the academics and the rulers. Almost immediately after the establishment of the new University of Berlin in 1809, which was to serve as a model of academic freedom, there arose conflicts in Berlin and elsewhere about a variety of issues concerning the freedom of teachers to participate in opposition politics, present religiously heterodox views, and a variety of major and minor issues concerning freedom of publication, academic self-government, and honors. Such difficulties were, however, prevented wherever the minister of education was a cultivated person with good connections to the academic world. Since, however, the majority of the politicians and higher civil servants at that time were not people who valued intellectual achievements nearly as much as they valued noble birth or political and military excellence, the autonomy of the profession was constantly in danger and, therefore, required formal safeguards.[13] In countries like nineteenth century Russia, or Latin America today, where military dictatorship is always an imminent possibility, these needs have been even greater.[14]

How effective are such formal safeguards in preserving, or — since there are often countries where civil freedom is very limited — creating academic freedom? Of course, no safeguards help against a government which wants and has the power to disregard them. But, as has been noted, most governments most of the time do not want to tamper with the universities and the academic profession. Formal safeguards, therefore, have some value since violating them will be regarded as a breach of legitimacy which governments can ill afford. The problem, however, is to what extent the formal safeguards, even if more or less honored by the government, will ensure that the autonomous academic community will use its power to promote an ever-growing freedom of enquiry. The assumption that by granting to the academic community visibly high status and responsibility, the norms of scholarship and science will prevail is based on some kind of concept of *noblesse oblige*. Unfortunately what is true of other cases of privileged nobility is true of the academic case as well, namely that the rule has been abuse of privilege. Only under circumstances where the privilege was rather limited, have such groups lived up to their obligations out of their own free will. The conditions of "non-model" societies, however, are usually such that the privileged academic community will be corrupted sooner or later.

Even minor matters of chicanery and honor will have their effect. Where lack of personal power means subjection to arbitrary authority, and lack of special honors means dishonor, university professors will fight for these, and, since they fulfill an important function and are able people, will sooner or later succeed. They will become part of, or at least friendly with a corrupt ruling group, which inevitably involves a measure of corruption. Such corruption which replaces academic standards with nepotism and subordinates scholarship to politics had been widespread in nineteenth century Russia, and is said to be even worse in many Latin American countries today. The tragic thing is that many who do not want to be corrupted by the rulers,' and oppose the falsification of the purpose of the university through turning it into one of the fortresses of personal privilege, often end up by similarly falsifying these objectives by using their privileged position as a lever for opposition politics. Morally their stand may be impeccable. There is an excellent argu-

---

[13] Franz Schnabel, *Deutsche Geschichte im Neunzehnten Jahrhundert* (Freiberg: Herder, 1934), Vol. 3, pp. 140–141; Frederic Lilge, *The Abuse of Learning* (New York: Macmillan, 1948), pp. 20–23, 30–34; Richard Graf du Moulin Eckart, *Geschichte der deutschen Universitäten* (Stuttgart: Enke, 1929), p. 350.

[14] This is not to say that they actually obtained such safeguards. In Russia they never have. In Latin America, on the other hand, they did. Cf. Luigi Einaudi, "University Autonomy and Academic Freedom in Latin America," *Law and Contemporary Problems, Special Issue: Academic Freedom*, 28 (Summer, 1963), pp. 636–646.

ment for giving priority to the larger interests of defending freedom and justice over academic duties. But the line between a temporary situation of emergency in which the professor and the student, as well as the doctor, the lawyer, the merchant, and the worker, must leave their places of work and study to man the barricades and fight for justice, and a situation in which one has to go on working and to use one's spare time for discharging one's political and civic duties, has to be clearly drawn. If everyone else works, but professors (and/or students) supported by public funds and special facilities and immunities conferred upon them to pursue their studies, use those facilities and immunities for political activity, they may come dangerously near to abusing their privileges. There are situations in which this is justified. But one should not include those under academic freedom; these rather involve a deliberate abandonment of the professional concerns of the academic in order to engage in something much more important than any professional obligation. This seems to have been the case in many individual instances in a great many places. But where — as it seems to be the case in some of the Latin American (and Southern European) countries — professors have come to regard their positions, conferring on them high status, public visibility, immunities, and income (or access to income), as sinecures provided by the State to engage in politics, then whatever the worth of those politics, they are abusing academic freedom.[15] Not only because freedom and facilities meant to be used for the advancement of knowledge are thus diverted to other ends, but because almost inevitably such actions will be justified by an ideology which identifies intellectual activity with activist politics, and thus opposes or even suppresses free and unbiased enquiry in all ideologically sensitive fields. What starts out (and in individual cases may continue to be) as a justified subordination of intellectual freedom to the cause of freedom in general, may then turn into a threat to the principle of freedom of inquiry.

Even more serious problems arise because of the difficulty in controlling the students. Since models are non-existent, criteria of student selection cannot be too efficient. Besides, since the society is backward relative to the educational model it adopts, it will tend to lack a similar range of alternatives as the model for useful and respectable non-elite professional jobs for those who cannot make the elite. Finally, even those who are suitable in every respect to enter the elite, will usually find that they are admitted by the ruling class only with very specialized qualifications and on sufferance, and then only to positions of secondary importance. It is almost inevitable, therefore, that many are admitted to universities and their aspirations raised without any hope of realizing them. Even those who due to exceptional ability and/or the fact that they come from upper class families, should expect elite status, will also encounter difficulties for a number of reasons. Almost inevitably, the system will be fairly inefficient, since the country will usually lack enough people of sufficient qualification to teach at a university, and even those qualified will

[15] Frank Bowles, *Access to Higher Education*, Vol. I, Paris: UNESCO and the International Association of Universities, 1963, pp. 147–152; Rudolph P. Atcon, "The Latin American University," *Die Deutsche Universitätszeitung*, 17 (February, 1962), pp. 9–48.

lack experience and know-how to run such an institution. Worse yet, where the faculty has been corrupted, the able students will become very cynical; where the faculty is honest, students will learn to despise even more that kind of authority to which they are expected to subordinate themselves when leaving the university; and when the faculty is partly corrupted and partly honest they may conclude that the whole existing adult society makes no sense. In any case they are likely to be in a situation of the type Durkheim called *anomie*, where norms of conduct are unreliable and do not lead to their expected ends. Thus the students become alienated from the very ruling class which had created the university. The honeymoon period with enlightened absolutist rulers is followed by absolute disillusionment on both sides.

This general pattern, which has a great many variations, is most clearly discernible in Russia in the nineteenth century and in present day Latin America. The sequence of events in Russia was somewhat like this. The modern university started out as an institution to which Messianic hopes for social betterment were attached. After a very short time, however, the hopes went sour. Instead of preparing themselves for entering slots in society which they were intended to enter, the students grew impatient with both society and the slots, and organized themselves for (or at least threatened) subversion. This was followed by government attempts to restrict entrance into universities, and to control what happened in them. This action caused even more dissatisfaction. The restrictions were perceived as injustices by those who were now prevented from entry, and their sense of injustice was incensed by the corrupt and erratic way admission was administered. Those who were admitted became alienated nonetheless, since they were made to suffer from the usually stupid attempts at controlling the instruction, speech, writing, and thought. Eventually the futility and injustice of the restrictive measures were recognized, and a new liberal era began, starting a new cycle of the vicious circle. This is in a schematic way what happened in Russian higher education starting from early in the nineteenth century with the reforms of 1804 and lasting until the first World War. The cycles were: first, a liberalization under Alexander I with the reforms of 1804, followed by a reaction after the Napoleonic War of 1812, and culminating in the Decembrist Revolt of 1825. The restriction of admissions to an ever-smaller elite and the tightening controls over the teachings and the curriculum, followed in the reign of Nicholas I, 1825–1855. Alexander II brought a new period of liberal reform, approximately during the years 1856–1866, but conflicts led to spasmodic repressions throughout the remainder of the reign, ending with the assassination of the tsar in 1881; Alexander III instituted a severe reaction until 1894, but student strikes and other forms of defiance continued; reforms were attempted in 1901, but without quelling the tide of disturbances. Revolution broke out in 1905, and liberal and reactionary policies fluctuated rapidly thereafter until the Revolution of 1917 ended forever the tsarist educational experiments.[16]

[16] Nicholas Hans, *History of Russian Educational Policy* (London: P. S. King, 1931); Hans-Eberhard Müller, *State, Society and Education: The Russian Case in the Nineteenth Century* (unpublished M.A. thesis, Department of Sociology, University of California, Berkeley, Calif., 1966).

As a result student culture became overwhelmingly politicized, and students came to regard academic freedom as equivalent to freedom of speech and agitation. The intellectual atmosphere which resulted from this was one of doctrinaire adherence to ideologies and the spread of ideological intolerance.[17] If all this did not completely exhaust Russian intellectual creativity, it was probably due to proximity to Western Europe. The best Russian intellectuals, irrespective of their field of activity, had studied in France and Germany, or Switzerland, published in German and French, and/or were exposed to publications coming from those countries. This counteracted the tendencies for intellectual corruption and complete politicization inherent in the internal conditions.

The parallel between nineteenth century Russia and present-day Latin America is particularly interesting, since this latter area has had some revolutions. As a result individuals and groups from the alienated intelligentsia have found their way to supreme power. Due to the existence of many independent states in the area, there has been no period of time since the second half of the nineteenth century, without the existence in some of the countries of relatively liberal regimes respecting the independence and autonomy of the universities.

What, however, these countries have in common with pre-World War I Russia has been their social structures. These latter have been left virtually unaffected by political change: there is everywhere a very narrow and conservative stratum of extremely rich and conservative landowners; an overwhelmingly large and abjectly poor and backward peasantry and urban lumpen-proletariat and in between a small, economically insecure mobile and relatively educated middle class.

Since the universities have been modeled on elitist European examples — Spanish traditions going back to the middle ages and the universities of Continental Europe — they imbue the students with aspirations for leadership. But in these economically backward and unstable countries the only way to obtain positions of economic security and honor (for those who were not born into such position) is through political power or patronage. Therefore, even though the proportion of university trained people in positions of responsibility is among the highest in the world, this remains an extreme non-model situation nevertheless. The professionals in high positions are there not as a result of their training, but of political success or connections. There are no models in society of the kind of elite roles for which the universities are supposedly training their students — creative scientists and scholars, high grade professionals, or broadly educated intellectuals with a keen sense for practical affairs whose services are rewarded because of their superior intellectual training and abilities.

The very high degree of legally safeguarded freedom (which is actually observed in some of the countries) is used deliberately and consciously to secure for those connected with the university far-going privileges to engage in politics. Furthermore, this freedom is often used to prevent improvements of

[17] Richard Pipes (ed.), *The Russian Intelligentsia* (New York: Columbia University Press, 1961), p. 10.

academic standards, or to suppress the expression of views unpalatable to an important political faction, or simply to victimize certain individuals.

This case is particularly important since unlike the Russian failure which could be attributed to the insufficiency of the safeguards of academic freedom and to constant interference by bumbling autocratic governments, the failure of the Latin American university must be blamed on the actions of relatively autonomous scholars and students. If nevertheless the results have been similar or worse than those in Russia, they have to be attributed to the dynamics of elite non-model systems.[18]

In contrast to these failures of elite non-model systems Germany, or rather the system of German language universities, in the nineteenth century is considered a great success. Here autonomy was used wisely and responsibly. The universities had not been deflected from the pursuit of the highest standards of science and scholarship for a period of more than one hundred years. The people appointed were generally of a high caliber, the quality of the lectures, seminars, and research was among the best in the world, the graduates were well trained and the German universities attracted many of the best students from all over the world. Much of this success has been attributed to the specific arrangement of academic freedom prevailing in the German universities.[19]

We should like to suggest, however, that those formal arrangements were not a sufficient condition for the scientific success of the universities. An abuse of these freedoms in a manner similar to Latin America (or their suppression similar to Russia or under Peron, in Argentina) was only prevented by a set of circumstances which had nothing to do with these formalities.

We shall trace now the way the system had worked. The first effect of the new freedom of the Prussian universities was indeed an attempt to politicize them on the one hand, as in present-day Latin America, and to regulate them authoritatively as in Russia, on the other. One of the first and most famous manifestations of the newly won freedom of the academic profession and of the students was the Wartburgfest in 1817 — a festival arranged by the student organizations to commemorate the Jubilee of the Reformation. One of its

[18] Gabriel del Mazo, *La reforma universitaria* (1918–1940) (La Plata: Edicion del Centro Estudiantes de Ingeniera, 1941), 3 vols.; and his *Estudiantes y gobierno universitario*, 2nd ed. (Buenos Aires: Elateneo, 1956); Roberto MacLean y Estenos, *La Crisis Universitaria en Hispano-America* (Mexico, D. F.: Universidad Nacional, 1956), pp. 51–56, 73–75; Focion Febres Cordero, *Reforma universitaria* (Caracas: Universidad Central de Venezuela, 1960), pp. 65–68; Arthur P. Whitaker, *The United States and Argentina* (Cambridge, Mass.: Harvard University Press, 1954), pp. 67–74, 152–53; Frank Bonilla, "The Student Federation of Chile: 50 years of Political Activity," *Journal of Inter-American Studies*, 2 (July, 1960), pp. 311–334; Kalman H. Silvert, *The Conflict Society: Reaction and Revolution in Latin America* (New Orleans, Hauser, 1961), pp. 162–182; and his "The University Student" in John J. Johnson (ed.), *Continuity and Change in Latin America* (Stanford: Stanford University Press, 1964), pp. 206–226. On the general setting of the problem cf. S. M. Lipset, "Values, Education and Entrepreneurship in Latin America," in S. M. Lipset and Aldo Solari (eds.), *Elites and Development in Latin America* (New York: Oxford University Press, forthcoming).

[19] Friedrich Paulsen, *The German University: Its Character and Historical Development* (New York: Macmillan, 1895), pp. 85–86; Flexner, *op. cit.*, 1930, pp. 317–320.

features was the burning of books which were not in accordance with the taste of one of the principal ideologists of the "youth" movement, Professor Massmann. Several other professors were active in fomenting extremist nationalist movements among the students, and their agitation led amongst other things to the murder of the Austrian playwright Kotzebue and to several anti-semitic outbursts.[20]

The authorities started reacting to this by restricting entrance to the universities so as to prevent the admission of students from popular backgrounds who might be insecure and potentially subversive. There were also attempts to discipline academic teachers with an ineptness similar to the Tsarist government.[21] But the worst, nevertheless, did not follow. In addition to the fact that the German ruling class contained a much greater minority of enlightened and educated people than its Russian counterpart, German universities had the advantage of decentralization. Whenever one of the governments decided to interfere high-handedly with a university, the academic elite of that university usually had the choice of resigning and finding a haven in another state which happened to have a more enlightened ruler at that time, or just taking an opportunity of the occasion, so as to benefit its own university. As a last resort there was also democratic Switzerland with its German-language universities. Moreover, reactionary measures against the universities were never general, so that the system developed by the initiative taken first in one place, and then in another. This decentralization could have such a favorable effect, of course, only because of the unevenness of the situation; the lack of "models," of sympathetic, educated men in society, was not completely general throughout German society; thus, it was less in a position of "non-model" than Russia or Latin America.[22]

The outcome was a strengthening of genuine research and learning, since this was in the long run the most useful strategy from the point of view of the profession. Playing autonomous politics, as in Latin America, was not tolerated anywhere in the area, and would not have been easible anyway due to the greater differentiation of society. Becoming martyrs for freedom in general, as in Russia, was not necessary. There was a third and respectable possibility of practicing professional freedom efficiently. Although in the beginning the inefficiencies of a "non-model" situation caused considerable damage, competitive

---

[20] Du Moulin Eckart, *op. cit.*, p. 222; Carl Brinkmann, *Der Nationalismus und die deutschen Universitäten im Zeitalter der deutschen Erhebung, Sitzungsverichte d. Heidelberger Akademic d. Wissenschaften*, Philosophisch-historische Klasse (1931/32) 3, Abhandlung (Heidelberg: Carl Winters, 1932). Cf. especially pp. 72–78 for parallels with late 19th century Russia and p. 72 for social background — insecure, downwardly mobile parents — of alienated students.

[21] After the number of students in Prussia had increased from 3311 (or 29.3/100.000 of population) to 15,751 (52.5/100.000) between 1820–1830, measures were taken to restrict entrance. The figures for the following decades were 1841: 11,593; 1851: 12,314; 1861: 13,248 (34.0/100.000, 34.2/100.000; 33.8/100.000). These figures and the description of the measures are based on Volker Eisele, "Democratization in German Higher Education" (unpublished seminar paper, Dept. of Sociology, University of California, Berkeley, 1965).

[22] Schnabel, *loc. cit.*

pluralism prevented complete bankruptcy and brought about rapid improvement.

The balance which emerged and the conditions under which it eventually broke down between the two World Wars precisely reflect these various forces. The political freedom of the academic profession as well as of the students was limited. It was assumed that the academic teacher as a civil servant had to have political and ideological convictions acceptable to the rulers. Even though the majority of the academic profession opposed the *Lex Arons,* passed by the Prussian legislature in 1898, requesting positive identification with the government, they would have preferred Arons to resign his position as a *Privatdozent* in physics, believing that activity in the Social-Democratic party was inconsistent with the "civil service" position of the member of a university.[23] Political prejudice and extremism of the kind acceptable to the ruling class (extreme chauvinism, incitement to war, anti-semitism) were on the other hand quite frequent among university professors. It went without saying that Jews were discriminated against in appointments, and that the appointment of Catholics and Protestants was often influenced by considerations of religious politics. Liberal academics did not accept these things. But apart from being active in liberal politics outside the university, as some of them were, the only thing they could do about it within the university was to try to keep the institution on as high a level, and as far above and away from topics which might open it to contact with the outside world, as possible. They opposed everything that might have implied value judgments or technological application, arguing that those were matters to be discussed and taught elsewhere. In principle, of course, this attitude is impeccable, and everyone would accept Paulsen's statement that "Ein gebundener Unterricht ist kein wissenschaftlicher" (a restricted education is not a complete one), and it probably was the best way to reduce attempts at controlling the university, or corrupting the integrity of the staff. But it should be clear that it was a compromise, and not a clear and simple criterion of what is academic and therefore what should be free. This is evident from the actual decisions made. Theology was an acceptable discipline, but sociology was usually not; medicine and law were traditional subjects, but engineering or business administration was kept outside the universities. The principle, therefore, cannot be taken too seriously. It was an adjustment to a precarious situation. Academic freedom could be maintained only in limited subjects which were old and venerable so that they became part of the unquestioning routine and in those which either because of their highly abstract nature, or, at times, because of their complete remoteness from any practical application or social implications were absolutely certain not to produce any friction.[24]

Thus academic freedom, as it actually existed, was a Janus-faced institution and none of its faces represented that ideal of beauty which had been so often

---

[23] Friedrich Paulsen, *The German Universities and University Study* (New York: Longmans, Green, 1906), pp. 228–231.
[24] Ben-David and Zloczower, *op. cit.*

attributed to it. On the one hand, academics shared the honors, emoluments, and privileges of the ruling classes in an authoritarian society, and only a negligible minority felt any pangs of conscience. To the extent that violations were "localized," the majority tolerated abuse and corruption, such as enumerated (right wing bias, etc.), and often actively participated in them. On the other hand, they were good enough professionals not to want the system to be totally corrupted into one of the domains of ascribed privilege reflecting the exercise of bureaucratic power. In this concern they agreed with the liberal minority. Building up the university into a kind of holy shrine, and establishing impressive rituals to symbolize the elevated status of the place and the profession, were acceptable to all. They added even more status to those who were corruptible, and they could be used by the honest academics as weapons against corruption.

Thus the successful institutionalization of academic freedom in this elite non-model setting has to be attributed to the effective decentralization of the system. The academic profession was able to maintain a decent measure of autonomy and freedom in a relatively authoritarian society, because it had been able to opt out easily from oppression. The establishment of German unity did not change this situation, because (a) it did not include the Austrian lands and Switzerland, and (b) because by that time the German system, which had started out as "international" in the German language area, had already become the center of a new cosmopolitan world of universities. German universities had trained most of the academic elite of Eastern and the rest of Central Europe, much of that of England and the U.S., and practically all the new academic elite of Japan. Thus the German university professor had a role of international significance and influence which no German government could attack without hurting its own international standing.

This outcome was a more or less satisfactory solution only for those who had been admitted into the academic profession. The majority of the students, however, had to find their way within German society, and face its general authoritarianism. From their point of view the privileges of the established academics, strictly restricted to a few lucky incumbents of positions and a limited number of recognized academic fields, appeared as arbitrary intellectual authoritarianism. They reacted to this situation by the creation of a variety of what might be described as intellectual sects. Marxism with its tendency to build up a whole intellectual establishment parallel to the universities, psychoanalysis with only slightly more modest aims at intellectual self-sufficiency, and a variety of less well developed instances, such as that of Nietzsche and his followers, were all, at least in part, expressions of discontent and alienation by scholars and intellectuals who felt that they had been driven out into the wilderness by the academic establishment.[25] There are obviously limits to who can and cannot

[25] For the invidious atmosphere concerning university honors cf. Samuel and Thomas, *op. cit.*, pp. 116–117. The ideologies of the period are described in Karl Löwith, *Von Hegel bis Nietzsche* (Zürich-New York: Europa Verlag, 1941); for some of the sociological aspects of the psychoanalytic movement cf. J. Ben-David, *op. cit., American Journal of Sociology*.

be absorbed in an academic (or any other) establishment which exist every-where. But it makes all the difference whether these limits are perceived as legitimate means to the purpose of the university, or whether they are seen as illegitimate monopolization of scarce opportunities and honors for in-tellectual work. In Germany there was a widespread feeling of this latter kind, resulting from the defensive conservativeness of the academic profession, wary of moving out of time-tested precedents into intellectual fields which might have involved them in conflict with the ruling elite, or undermine the justi-fication of their high privileges and immunity from control.

The intellectual movements which arose in this situation were often con-nected with extremist politics of the left, or the right. The question is how these onsets of student-intellectual unrest resembling those in Russia and Latin America were prevented from politicizing the university to the extent of seriously interfering with the quality of studies, as it happened in those coun-tries. This was achieved by (a) emphasizing reasonably high and honest academic standards; in this respect there was much less room for feelings of cynicism and normlessness than in Russia, or in Latin America; (b) the "non-model" situation was mitigated by numerous exceptions: for the intellectual elite of the students there existed at different times reasonably good prospects for suitable careers at the universities, secondary schools, and professions; and for those coming from the upper and upper-middle class — who formed a considerable part of the student body — there were good and intellectually quite acceptable careers in the civil service or the military. The potential al-liance of these student elites with the insecure and subversive part of the student body was further prevented by the existence of exclusive student organizations which kept these higher class students apart from the others and placed them in a separate environment within the university which closely resembled in its social structure, if not necessarily in human values, the English and French elite institutions.[26] Thus finding themselves in a framework of interlocking elites, including part of the faculty and important sectors of the ruling class, the elite student culture was politically innocuous. This pattern explains why the crises of the system occurred in the beginning, before these new elite frameworks were consolidated. After World War I when, as the com-bined result of attempts at democratization and inflation, these frameworks broke down, the way was opened to extremists skillfully using the dubious symbols of valor and virility of the old upper classes to unite their descendants with many of the hopeless mass of students from the lower middle classes in a movement promising to make them all into an elite, not at the expense of the lower classes, but of so-called lower races.[27]

The success of the German universities cannot, therefore, be attributed to the institutions of academic freedom and the freedom of students. Similar institutions elsewhere did not prevent deterioration; there was a considerable measure of political and ideological corruption in German universities too. As

---

[26] Paulsen, *op. cit.*, 1895, pp. 189–194; Samuel and Thomas, *op. cit.*, pp. 120–121.
[27] W. Kornhauser, *The Politics of Mass Society* (New York: Free Press, 1959), pp. 187–192.

in Latin America the decentralization of the system enhanced the formal autonomy of the universities. Unlike Latin America, however, the decentralized system was much more pluralistic, with some parts of it very near, and all parts of it closer to the model end of the continuum than either Latin America or Russia. Because of the much greater mobility of staff and students, the German system was also much more competitive than the other two systems dealt with here. Thus academics had not only rights and privileges, but also an opportunity to prove the value of real excellence.

In this context a word should be said about the formal freedoms of the students, which have not been dealt with yet. These consisted in an agreement to transfer enrollment credits from one university to another, and to reduce the formal requirements for attending classes and passing intermediate examinations to a minimum.[28] Interestingly, these freedoms have not been imitated elsewhere, and have rarely been mentioned as a desirable model. Indeed they are of a quite different kind than those of the academic body. They are not privileges of a traditional, corporate kind, but freedoms in the liberal-democratic sense. They have probably contributed a very great deal to the competitive nature of the system, serving as a check on the professors — if students did not like the way a part of their subject was taught at one institution they could go elsewhere; and they must have increased satisfaction by allowing the students to find the most congenial place for themselves by trial and error. Finally, they served to correct some of the shortcomings of the elite system. As said, such a system makes no point of training the student. The university staff is small. The most important thing is that they should be excellent. No particular care is taken that every aspect of the field should be covered, and even less that the actual techniques of research should be taught. This, of course, greatly enhances the insecurity of the student in a "non-model" system, since he cannot safely look forward to a place of work or professional practice with traditions of technical excellence and socialization of the novice. By allowing the students to move from one place to another they could make up for some of these deficiencies. Thus while the structure of the individual university definitely places this system in the elite category, the working of the system as a whole pushes it along some way towards the "expert" end of the continuum.

The validity of this explanation can be tested by reference to more recent parallels. The most interesting of these is Japan. Its academic system had been in many ways the best and most successful imitation of the German system. The possibility and value of granting complete academic freedom to a highly selected intellectual elite of international standing was clearly recognized by the leaders of educational reform, though they were aware of the problems which might result from this for the maintenance of the stability of an otherwise authoritarian system. Great care was taken, therefore, to isolate the university system, to justify and legitimate the isolation by true adherence to high standards, and to ensure the loyalty of the graduates to the system by linking them through informal cliques to the elite (reminiscent of the function

28 Paulsen, *op. cit.*, 1895, pp. 187–88, 201.

of German student corporations). Having linked its universities from the outset into the most advanced international network and possessing a considerable educated and honest administrative class, as well as a potential middle class — like Germany — Japan had avoided in the beginning the instabilities attending the Russian and the Latin American systems. Yet after World War I a class of unemployable and increasingly radicalized intellectuals emerged as in Germany, which was open to ideologies of national superiority like their German counterparts.[29]

A parallel to Latin American developments may emerge soon in Africa. Prior to independence there had arisen in most places a conflict between the colonial ruling class and the embryonic native educated class possessing English or French education, spearheading more or less broadly based nationalist movements. With the attainment of independence these educated groups found themselves in a situation where they had easy access to power, and great potential influence on educational policies. Individuals, or as in the case of the Mobutu administration in Congo, groups, attained actual power. But despite their progressive intentions, they have not been able to change the class structure. Apart from those having very great wealth, politics remains the main avenue to comfort and security. Those who are in the educational system have retained a completely and usually unrealistically elitist view of education. The expectations of the students concerning their futures as educated members of their societies are so unrealistic, in view of the actual opportunities which those societies can offer, that they are bound to become hopelessly frustrated. The relative success of some of the local universities in actually living up to the British or French ideal of a university and maintaining ivory towers of almost European academic standards, and more than European standards of living in splendid isolation from their environments, is apt to lead within a generation or two to a situation resembling Latin America.[30] The existence of culturally coherent, but politically decentralized, areas (particularly in English-speaking Africa), and extreme economic backwardness coupled with unstable, revolutionary politics, is closely parallel to the situation prevailing in Latin America. On the other hand, both the English- and the French-language African universities are closely attached to effective, high-standard European academic systems, which has not been the case in Latin America. This is a circumstance favoring the maintenance of international academic standards and preventing such far-reaching politicization of the university as occurs in Latin America. If other things remain unchanged, the situation may then develop somewhat in the same direction as in India, where a few institutions and individuals oriented towards the outside world struggle for high standards amidst a flood of academic pettiness, decadence, and politicization.

[29] Michio Nagai, "The University and the Intellectual," *Japan Quarterly* (Autumn, 1964), pp. 46–52; Herbert Passin, "Japan" in James S. Coleman (ed.), *Education and Political Development* (Princeton: Princeton University Press, 1965), pp. 272–312.

[30] Cf. James S. Coleman (ed.), *op. cit.*, articles by Coleman, pp. 35–50; Francis X. Sutton, pp. 51–74; Michel Debeauvais, pp. 75–91; Ayo Ogunsheye, pp. 123–143; Coleman, pp. 353–371; Anthony H. M. Kirk-Greene, pp. 372–407; Dwaine Marwick, pp. 463–497.

There is finally the possibility that these elite systems will turn into expert systems. This had actually occurred in the more or less recent past in the USSR and in Japan. In both cases the transition took place under extraordinary conditions; revolution in Russia, and defeat followed by foreign occupation in Japan. Otherwise the transition from an elite to an expert system of universities is very difficult, since it is inevitably opposed by the only experts available. These are necessarily the products of an elite system and they will perceive the transition to an expert system as a threat to their status as well as to their values.

This resistance notwithstanding, it is possible that the Russian and Japanese examples will eventually be followed. This may occur not because of the immanent instability of the elitist system in developing societies — this could just as well become chronic as in Latin America — but because the internationally most influential system — the American one — is an expert system, as are the two others next in size and potential influence, those of the USSR and Japan. Since the African systems are linked to international networks they may re-orient themselves — especially the English-language ones — to the U.S. pattern.

SECTION F

POLITICS OF MODERNIZATION:
WESTERN IMPACT AND NATIVE RESPONSE

Introduction

In the social sciences fashionable phrases may be a needed shortcut to communication, but they are also a fertile source of misleading connotations. "Politics of modernization" is a case in point. In current usage "modernization" tends to be seen as a process that *has* occurred in the geographic West and is *now* occurring in the non-Western world under different and more difficult conditions. Some of the difficulties are ascribed to particular forms of non-Western traditions, others to the colonial past. But the writings on "modernization" — except for some works on imperialism — tend to deal with Western and non-Western societies in isolation, as separate political systems which differ only in the degree and speed of their advance. This approach is erroneous, because it suggests that "modernization" is a process of the present or recent past, and because it treats all societies as independent systems. Yet "modernization" began with European expansion in the late 15th century, and societies around the world have experienced relationships of dominance and dependence ever since.

The introduction to this volume refers to the growth of the modern nation-state and the impact of this Western development abroad. These two world-historical transformations occurred concurrently: as nation-states developed in Western Europe, world empires were created overseas through commercial expansion and eventually through colonial regimes.[1] To put it another way, as Europeans created the modern political order, the arena of their economic and political actions was extended beyond the geographical limits of Western civilization. And as the range of their actions expanded, the structures of non-Western societies were changed irrevocably. Whenever it occurs, political change results from the confluence of internal developments and external influences. But in the non-Western world, the impact of the West has been

[1] For a useful discussion of the factors influencing imperialism, including conditions in non-Western societies as well as in the expanding Western nations, see John Gallagher and Ronald Robinson, "The Imperialism of Free Trade," *Economic History Review*, Vol. VI (1953), pp. 1–15.

an external factor of decisive significance. This continues to be the case even in the era of anti-colonial movements, because political independence cannot at one stroke undo the legacy or the continuing fact of Western economic and political supremacy. Thus in an interrelated process "modernization" in the West has occurred, and continues to occur, under conditions of dominance; "modernization" in the non-West, under conditions of dependence.

This section deals with the Western impact and its consequences for the political order of non-Western societies. Three types of impact, varying along a continuum of exercise of direct colonizing force, may be distinguished. First, the material superiority of Western societies has served as a threat underlining the urgency of social change and as an example broadening the choices of action for various groups in the affected countries. As Von Laue argues in the case of Russia, the resulting emulation and cultural borrowing have undermined traditional forms of authority, leading to a "revolution from without" and creating the conditions of a later internal revolution.

Second, in various areas of the world Western expansion has interfered economically and/or politically with the existing structure of societies but without establishing direct colonial rule. Such interference has weakened native elites and social structures, though the estimate of this effect must depend on an assessment of those elites and structures prior to that interference. Results have varied from merely a continuing political instability to developments culminating in an indigenous revolution. In his work on Communist China, Schurmann describes the preconditions of the latter, with brief comparative references to the English, French, and Russian revolutions. In China the political and economic impact of the West greatly enhanced the growing weakness of the traditional Confucian elite. Eventually a Western-influenced movement, which was originally focused on the coastal cities, was able to organize peasant unrest and take advantage of a long tradition of peasant rebellion when the Japanese invasion facilitated a merging of nationalist sentiment with these long-standing discontents. The uniqueness of the Chinese revolutionary experience lies in this ability of a military and political organization to mobilize populist energies, and Schurmann suggests that China sees herself as the significant model for emulation, not so much for the industrial goal itself, as for the revolutionary and organizational means of reaching it. This possibility, as well as the role of the Japanese in China and elsewhere in Asia, illustrates the fact that it is not only the West whose impact must be taken into account.

Direct Colonial rule makes a third type of impact: [2] the replacement of a traditional political structure by European rule, with European bureaucratic and economic institutions established in native territories, run for the purposes of colonial rule and staffed by European colonial officials, natives educated for the purpose, and often by "foreigners" from other non-Western societies whose

---

[2] This can itself be treated as a variable: under various forms of legal colonial rule, Western governments adopted varying policies of "direct" and "indirect" rule. Furnivall himself devotes much of his work to distinguishing the results of direct British rule in Burma from the more indirect policies of the Dutch in Indonesia.

immigration was stimulated by European rule. Thus J. S. Furnivall argues that under colonial domination, resulting from the imposition of this complex Western economic and administrative machinery, a society lacks a "social will," i.e., common values integrating and unifying the population. What results is a *plural society*, of implanted and unintegrated institutions, populated by various racial-cultural groups performing their different roles in the division of labor. Unity is precarious because an imposed political rule has little or no legitimacy in the eyes of the people, and there are few accepted "rules of the game" that could mitigate the clashing interests of various cultural sections of the population. Thus, the West has provided the model for the nation-state to much of the world, has laid the economic foundations of increased communication and interaction, and in some cases has created the political arena in which conflicts of social groups are focused and can potentially be accommodated. At the same time, for many areas of the world, colonial encouragement of a plural society has made the creation of a nation-state more difficult.

Our final article by Balandier deals with Africa. In contrast to the emphasis of most writers on non-European nationalism, Balandier describes the continuing and developing reaction of the African masses to alien rule as revealed in myths which may be considered the equivalent of political ideologies. In this schema messianic movements, early professional associations, and later explicitly political movements all find their place. Further, in colonized societies, emulation is forced upon the members of these societies. Natives are made acutely aware that they are stigmatized as inferior by the colonial rulers and that their culture is considered primitive.[3] Hence, cultural nationalism — negritude, the search for an "African personality" — is an important part of their reaction.

The selections assembled in this section and in the following sections also raise a major theoretical issue. As our title suggests, the separation of "state" from "society" is an ideal-typical attribute of the nation-state. Participation in public affairs is no longer monopolized on the basis of hereditary privilege by specific social groups. The inhabitants of a national territory are now common citizens of a political community, struggling to obtain a greater share in the distribution of the national product as well as greater participation in the exercise of authority.[4] If this is taken to be the "modern" political order, then Russia and China represent a "post-modern" order. In these countries the most important political institution is no longer a patrimonial structure bound up with hereditary privilege nor a state as the focus of political struggle of "organized interests" within the society. Rather, it is the modernizing one-party state, which is "totalitarian" in the sense that central authority is used to politicize and organize society on all levels in a conscious attempt to transform that society. The designation of such a regime as "post-modern" is in keeping with our emphasis on the limited geographic and temporal applicability

[3] See the description of this stigmatizing process in Erving Goffman, *Stigma* (Englewood Cliffs, N.J.: Prentice-Hall, 1965). Cf. also Albert Memmi, *The Colonizer and the Colonized* (New York: The Orion Press, 1965).

[4] See Reinhard Bendix, *Nation-Building and Citizenship* (New York: John Wiley & Sons, 1964), p. 106.

of concepts like the nation-state, political party, social class, and others. This historicity of concepts cannot be avoided by defining universal functions that political structures perform, for there is not only change *of* the concrete political institutions in societies but these institutions themselves take on varying functions under the changing conditions of history. It remains to be seen what concepts may be most appropriate when the institutional framework of the non-Western countries has become more clearly delineated than it is today.

Imperial Russia
at the Turn of the Century:
The Cultural Slope and the
Revolution from Without

THEODORE H. VON LAUE

The expansion of Europe has been a much-discussed process. Unfortunately the publicists' and historians' interest has commonly been limited to surface aspects of power, to political, economic, and intellectual penetration. Yet a closer acquaintance reveals the existence of a yet deeper layer of hostile infiltration, a subtler and more subversive onslaught on native values and traditions. The "underground" portions of western expansion have hitherto rather escaped notice, let alone analysis, although among their victims their force was felt deeply if confusedly. Thus an anonymous journalist writing in Russia late in 1896 pointed to that melting away of native guideposts under the western impact when he lamented that "*under the influence of historical conditions and progress many phenomena which distinguished Russian nationality are now changing and therefore prove no longer to be genuine and unchangeable. . . .*"[1] No hallowed custom, no authority remained unimpaired, even though the surface structure of society and government was preserved and the sovereignty of the state untouched. The termites of western influence were eating away the substance and left only facades. And the invisible portion of

From *Comparative Studies in Society and History*, Vol. III, No. 4 (July 1961), pp. 353–367. Copyright by the Society for the Comparative Study of Society and History. Reprinted by permission of the author and publisher.

THEODORE H. VON LAUE was for many years Professor of History, University of California, Riverside. He is now at the Washington University, St. Louis. An authority on modern European and Russian history, he has written *Leopold Ranke, the Formative Years* (1950), *Sergei Witte and the Industrialization of Russia* (1963), and *Why Lenin? Why Stalin? A Reappraisal of the Russian Revolution 1900–1930* (1964).

[1] *Moskovskiia vedomosti*, No. 3 (1897), 3rd January, in the column "dnevnik pechati" (italics my own).

western power, its ability to serve as a universal model, proved in the long run even more devastating than armies, battleships, or stocks and bonds.

This paper will deal with the deeper substratum of the western outreach as it affected imperial Russia in an age when the spontaneous western penetration reached an all-time peak, on the latter 1890's, and when the forces and conditions that led to the revolutions of 1917 were first shaped in final form. (Much of the subsequent analysis, however, applies equally to all the years before 1914.) The theme is an observation made by Clifton R. Breckinridge, the American minister to Russia, who attended the coronation of Nicholas II in May 1896. The ceremonies, so he reported to Washington,[2] surpassed anything previously seen. But the most noteworthy feature of the pageant was "the strange blending of the old things and the new." "It is not simply," so he explained, "that the old ceremonials were preserved out of affection for the past and kept in company with the historic structures of the Kremlin and Moscow, but they are still used as a positive force, of great effect as governing the majority of the peoples of the Empire, and along with them come abundantly the ideas and appliances of modern civilization and government." Was this happy union of things old and new a historic fact or a figment of Mr. Breckinridge's imagination?

A modern observer investigating the truthfulness of this comment by looking over a sample of census data, import statistics, and contemporary newspapers and periodicals, and progressing from simple to complex phenomena may well come to a very different conclusion and find that old and new, native and western elements were bitterly at odds with each other. He would not unnaturally first turn to the great census of the Russian Empire carried out, after years of preparation, on 28 January 1897, the first of its kind ever undertaken in Russia. Here was an example of the blending of the old and the new, a western technique tried out by the government to measure the quantity and quality of the human raw material with which it must work. Yet the intruder from the present is soon made aware of the familiar flaw: the modern design did not fit the Russian realities.[3] The government had made no effort to solicit the cooperation of the professional statisticians. The experts had heard of the forthcoming census only through an announcement of the International Statistical Institute at Bern in August 1895. They had then asked for permission to convene a congress to discuss the problems raised by a Russian census: many professional groups in these years were making plans for all-Russian conventions. But the government had refused it. As a result, the census turned out to be a purely bureaucratic affair. And worse: the *chinovniks* entrusted with the task were not masters of statistical method, nor did they have time amidst their numerous other duties to acquaint themselves with the technical details. The critics proved right. The Central Statistical Commission attached to the

[2] Clifton R. Breckinridge to Secretary of State Olney, 22 June 1896. National Archives, Washington, D.C.

[3] For the following see A. Kotelnikov, *Istoriia proizvodstva i razrabotki vseobshchei perepisi naseleniia 28-go ianvaria* (St. Petersburg, 1901), and V. P. Kadomtsev, *Professionalnyi i sotsialnyi sostav naseleniia evropeiskoi Rossii* (St. Petersburg, 1909), p. 11 ff.

Ministry of the Interior, which administered the census, ran into difficulties while evaluating its data; it was soon attacked by the Ministry of Finance, which had a much superior staff of statisticians. Each Ministry then accused the other of incompetence; in the end it took the Russian government far longer to publish the results than the Germans with their census of 1895. Furthermore, the results presented by the census, it was pointed out, were unreliable, because the government had taken no steps to acquaint the public at large with the meaning of its project. The prevalent suspicion toward all officials had made the answers given to the census takers highly untrustworthy. The peasants and businessmen were afraid of higher taxes and therefore had minimized their earnings or concealed their religion, knowing the dire consequences of religious dissent. And how could one determine literacy, when the only question asked under this heading was: "Can you read?" Even the timing of the census was attacked. In January many peasants were working in the cities or in the factories. The results thus unduly augmented the figures for urban and industrial employment; they made Russia look more modern than she really was.

Taking the imperfect data with which the Imperial government had to work one finds then that on 28 January 1897 the Russian Empire counted 125.7 million inhabitants, 93.4 million of whom lived in European Russia.[4] Most of them were young, the average age being a mere 26 years (and the life expectancy 32 years!).[5] Of these multitudes only 13.4% were classified as urban. But this figure had little meaning since the government arbitrarily decided which settlement was to be counted town or village. It was perhaps more accurate to estimate the proportion of the urban population in the total to be around one-fifth.[6] But then, Russian statisticians asked, how could anyone tell where the peasants who shifted seasonally between town and country really belonged? The neat classifications of the census originating in the West could hardly be adapted to the fluid conditions of employment in Russia.

One aspect of the census proves particularly revealing in this context, the literacy rates for the various *sosloviia* (categories of subjects) into which the population was divided. Taking the hereditary nobility first, not even three-quarters of all men in that estate were counted as literate, and even slightly fewer of the women.[7] The proportion of the sexes was reversed, however, when it came to high school education for the nobility: 23% of the noble women had graduated from the *gimnasium* but only 20% of the men. Yet it was clearly the nobility which furnished the bulk of the university students (71%) and monopolized the enrollment in the equivalent military schools (95%). The most literate *soslovie*, not unexpectedly, were the priests, who boasted a rate of 77%; yet their wives hung back with only 66%. As for the population at large the relatively high figures given thus far were radically levelled down. Only

[4] *Obshchii svod po imperii rezultatov razrabotki dannykh po vseobshchei perepisi naseleniia proizvedennoi 28 ianvaria 1897 goda*, I (St. Petersburg, 1905), p. iii.

[5] These from Warren W. Eason's paper "Population Changes" in Cyril Black (ed.), *The Transformation of Russian Society since 1861* (Cambridge, Mass.: Harvard University Press, 1960).

[6] *Ibid.*

[7] See pp. xvi-xix in *Obshchii svod po imperii rezultatov* cited above.

33% of the men in European Russia and a mere 14% of the women were registered as literate. Yet there was hope. If one took the age group from 10–19, nearly three-quarters of the boys were literate and over half of the girls. In the next generation, in short, the literacy rate would rise conspicuously. On the other hand it was clear that it would still remain far below that of the Great Powers of western Europe, who counted among their population only five percent illiteracy or less. Even the United States, despite its influx of unschooled immigrants, boasted a 90% literacy rate.

Scrutinizing the regional distribution of literacy in European Russia,[8] one can observe a curious effect: a general decrease in literacy sloping down toward the east and southeast. The highest literacy was recorded in the Baltic provinces; thence the rate fell off steadily, though unevenly, toward the Urals and Caspian Sea. The cities stood out as minor peaks on this slope, or a province like Iaroslav as a high plateau; and there were ravines of illiteracy reaching, as around Pskov, almost up to the crest. Yet the general nature of the slope was undeniable. The same phenomenon emerges again when one probes into the rates for mortality and births, which like the illiteracy rate can serve as an excellent index of Russian backwardness. All of these indices stood low in western Europe, a proof of its high cultural standards, the death rate around 20/1000, and the birth rate around 30/1000. In Russia, on the other hand, the average death rate was 31/1000, the birth rate over 49/1000. And within Russia the same gradient that had been so obvious in the comparison between western Europe and Russia continued. Scanning the regional distribution of births and deaths, one discovers the same sloping decline, not exactly coinciding with the relief of the literacy map but in the over-all effect conforming to it. The highest standards and, by the same token, the lowest general mortality and birth rates prevailed along the Baltic coast. Thence conditions deteriorated as one advanced to the east and southeast. If there was one special surface on this slope, it was a trough falling below the average in the central black soil provinces racked by famine and agricultural depression. The same sloping gradient also prevailed in the infancy death rate or, in what Russian statisticians called "financial productivity," the accumulation of local capital.

The cultural slope inside Russia, however, was only a continuation of the gradient issuing from western Europe. A contemporary statistician employed by the Ministry of Finance who was compiling comparative statistics in a number of fields, provided many illustrations of the cultural descent from Europe into Russia.[9] He was contrasting the position of Russia with that of the other Great Powers in the reign of Alexander III, but his conclusions applied equally to the present reign. As for the number of steam engines per 1,000 inhabitants, Russia with 22 stood far behind Italy (44), Austro-Hungary (55), Germany (155), the United States (248), and Great Britain (332); in her building of

[8] See the excellent charts for the following in *Kartogrammy i diagrammy k iubileinomu sborniku tsentralnago statisticheskago komiteta ministerstva vnutrykh del* (St. Petersburg, 1913).

[9] S. O. Gulishambarov, *Sravnitelnaia statistika Rossii v mirovom khoziaistve i v riadu velikikh derzhav v tsarstvovanii imperatora Aleksandra III, 1881–1894* (St. Petersburg, 1905), *passim.*

ships she was outdone by all of these except Austro-Hungary. In the number of letters sent by mail Russia (with 620 million) was far eclipsed by Great Britain (3.2 billion), Germany (4 billion), France (2.2 billion), or Austro-Hungary (1.4 billion); only the Italians, who numbered merely one-quarter of the population of Russia, posted fewer letters than the Russians. But in the number of telegrams even they — not to mention the others — surpassed the Russians. They did so too in the number of communities with telephone networks, of which Russia had a mere 29, Italy 51, Britain 213, France 194, and the United States 1,351. In another set of figures the Russian statistician presented the difference between western and Russian agricultural production as measured by the output per *desiatina* (2.7 acres) of the chief crops: wheat, rye, and potato. And in each case the Russians stood below all the others, except the Italians in their rye crop. Conversely, they consumed less of the chief grains *per capita* than all the others. And taking the *per capita* value of each country's foreign trade, Italy scored double the Russian amount, Germany six times, and Britain over 13 times. In short, whichever way this statistician looked, Russia always appeared at the bottom of the scale. There was no denying the obvious conclusion: Russia was hopelessly behind on every count by which at the end of the nineteenth century the wealth of nations was measured. Here lay statistical proof for the complaint which a foreigner could so often hear from fellow passengers on the trains: "Yes, you in Europe have *Kultur*, but here in Russia. . . ." Here in Russia people who had the ambition to be cultured were condemned, to use a harsh term of Gorki's, to live in a pigsty.

Of course, as any outsider looking into Russia could abundantly observe, they tried to escape from the pigsty as best they could. They bought all tokens of *Kultur* which they could afford (and more) from the West. What a plentiful variety of foreign goods there was admitted into Russia over her European border during that January of 1897![10] The biggest item was cotton, the raw material of the Russian textile industry, her largest, to the tune of nearly nine million rubles. The next most valuable item was machinery and technical apparatus, priced at around 4½ million rubles. Another two million were spent on various qualities of iron, and half a million on steels. These imports, plus the dyes, paints, chemicals, and pharmaceuticals made possible whatever modern industries Russia possessed and indirectly also the various consumer goods which her factories produced. But so many goods were simply not made in Russia. One notices among the imports of that month also 35,000 rubles worth of grand pianos and 58,000 of uprights, 17,000 of spectacles, 9,000 of cameras, and 384 bicycles (worth 38,000 rubles). Books and pictures cost the importers another 192,000 rubles; clocks, watches, and the parts for them 366,000 rubles, *galanterie* items almost as much as books and pictures, not to mention ostrich feathers, hats and caps, umbrellas, and foreign clothes of all sorts. Imported delicacies for the tables of the rich piled up even larger amounts: 630,000 rubles went for wines and liquors, half that much for oranges and lemons, or for coffee. Tea naturally was one of the largest imports from the West, to the

---

[10] From *Svedeniia o vneshnei torgovle po evropeiskoi granitse za Ianvaria 1897 goda* in *Vneshnaia torgovlia Rossii v 1897 godu* (St. Petersburg, 1898).

value of 1½ million rubles (yet only one-third of what came over the Asiatic boundaries). All these imports were part of the fructifying lava that poured down from western Europe into the hinterlands of civilization, and from the United States too through the Bell Telephone Company, the Singer sewing machines, and McCormack reapers, Baldwin locomotives, and American type-writers, cash registers, adding machines, or life insurance policies. Together with the foreign goods also arrived foreign gold. In January 1897 Russia formally adopted the gold standard and thus joined the international monetary system over which foreign credit could flow freely into her growing industries, the golden rain that would modernize Russia's stagnating industry and Europeanize the country.

Material goods, however, were only a small part of the foreign influx. More important still were the imported experts who disseminated their ideas, skills, and concepts among the Russian population. During January 1897, the arriving foreigners outnumbered the departing Russians, and fewer foreigners left than arrived. Thus there was a net gain of foreigners (as there was on a smaller scale a net loss of Russians). The exchange in January 1897 was typical of the traffic across the European boundaries during these years.[11] But even more important than foreign governesses, engineers, salesmen, and purveyors of know-how were the books and magazines bringing from Europe an image of "the cultured life."

A perusal of an arbitrary collection of Russian newspapers and periodicals published in January 1897 will permit an insight into the nature and force of that impact. Picking up the pile of the *Novoe Vremia (New Times)*, the most influential daily of St. Petersburg, and glancing at the issue of January 2nd, one finds as the first item at the top of the front page the theater news announcing a musical drama *The New World* translated from the English, next a play *Le Comte de Risour*, and Gounod's *Faust* given at the Italian Opera. Further down one reads that P. D. Boborykin, a popular Russian novelist of the day, was giving a public lecture on Zola. Then skimming over two book notices (one being a text on railway affairs), tarrying briefly over an advertisement for the Central Hotel ("opposite Bahnhof Friedrichstrasse") in Berlin and finally look-ing over the Imperial *ukazes*, one comes to the news. The first topic stemmed from France: the French reaction to the appointment of the new Russian for-eign minister Muraviev; the next from London, dealing with the plague in Bombay; and the third (and minor one) from near-by Kronstadt. Thereafter one reads the latest cables datelined New York, Paris, Rome, Suez, Yokohama, Constantinople, Berlin, Colombo, Paderborn, Buenos Aires, Washington, Lon-don, Sofia, and finally three Russian cities, Odessa, Iuriev, and Kharkov. The stockmarket news issued from Paris. Next followed a lengthy column datelined St. Petersburg [!] but reporting a session of the Chambre in Paris. On the second page, at last, we come to the Russian news, official announcements, ap-pointments, and the full text of the budget for 1897 just approved by the State Council. On the third page Russian and western items again mingled, and on the fourth a column entitled "News of Foreign Literature" invited subscrip-tions. The next day's paper repeated the pattern, *Faust* and *Romeo and Juliet*

[11] *Ibid.*

at the opera, Joseph Hofmann giving a piano recital, a Rheims firm advertising its champagne, or an engineering firm a steam injector patented by Davis and Metcalf. The stockmarket report this time came from Berlin, and the news under the St. Petersburg dateline dealt with the Anglo-American arbitration treaty. Again half of the other items were of foreign origin. On the inside of the paper the reader finds an interesting article by P. P. Leroy-Beaulieu on the industrial progress of Germany. In the issue for January 5th his eyes were attracted by an unusually rich mixture of advertisements on the front page, a *cinématograph lumière* (in French), then (in Russian) Viennese furniture, life insurance by L'Urbains, Benedictine liqueur from Bordeaux, and again the Central Hotel in Berlin; book news of three new editions of philosophical works, two of Kant, one of Schopenhauer, and also a new treatise by W. Wundt on female psychology. Lower down on the page it was Verdi, Gounod, and Joseph Hofmann, plus *eau de sauveur*. The latest correspondence was again mostly concerned with foreign news, the feature story from St. Petersburg again discussing the western reaction to the appointment of Muraviev and then going on to a report from the Caucasus. On the inside a column on "Foreign Life and Literature" contained two anecdotes about the Emperor William II and the writer Ibsen; the other columns dealt with Russian items except for an article on the Austrian oil industry. The theater section, however, proved revealing again. The Mikhailovskii Theater offered *Villa Gaby, Les amants, Les viveurs, Tartuffe,* and *Les erreurs de marriage;* the Mariinskii Theater *Tannhäuser, Barbe Bleu, Romeo and Juliet, Manon, Samson and Delila, Carmen,* and *Faust.* To cite one last item, the "positions wanted" column on page five in the issue of the 21st of January. Here one reads, in French, of a *jeune homme* of good education with a knowledge of German sought for the household of a southern industrialist, and, in the same language, of lessons in French and German offered by a musical *Polonaise* educated in Austria in return for room and board; and after her of *une jéune Française* giving conversation lessons, then of *ein junges Mädchen* wishing to take care of children or sew for a shop, followed by *eine Revalenserin* to serve at table, and *une Parisienne bien recommendée.* And after that one's eyes run over *on offre, on cherche, à louer,* till they finally meet with the Russian language again in a few requests for a *frantsuzhenka* or a *niemka,* a French bonne or a German girl.

To advance next to the *St. Petersburg News.*[12] The *News* of January 4th offered an even ampler treatment of European affairs, with articles on the condition of the Poles in Germany, a congress of socialists in London, the state of Denmark in 1896, Christmas shopping in Berlin, the importance of oaths in England, and a spate of foreign news items, topped by an account of the French census of 1896, the German *Kolonialverein* and the spreading use of telephones in Berlin. An intruding column entitled "Our Press" was quickly succeeded by further telegrams from London, Paris (Loubet elected to the presidency of the Senate), Cetinje, Budapest, Vienna, and Constantinople; only the two last bits concerned Russian events. The bibliographical section listed a volume on *The Practical Electrician* translated from the German, a *Russian History of Music,*

[12] *S-Peterburgskiia vedomosti.*

another translation from the German under the title *Women in Science and Ethnology*, a practical guide for making potash out of salt (in Russian) and finally *zemstvo* reports. As for musical attractions in town, the paper announced also a chamber music concert at the Imperial Russian Music Society with pieces by Borodin, Brahms, and Beethoven. Turning to the issue of January 7th and feeling bored with the familiar pattern the visitor becomes engrossed in a well-done piece on the Goethe Gymnasium in Frankfurt and detailed information on the internal affairs of France. In the column "Our Press" his attention is arrested by a curious passage in an article on "the proper organization of agricultural statistics in western Europe and America." It emphasized the importance of good statistics for the development of agriculture and lamented in conclusion: "With us, unfortunately, statistics are in a very unsatisfactory state."

To shift next to the Moscow papers, first the *Russian News*.[13] Anyone expecting a greater concentration upon Russian affairs in the old capital would be quickly disillusioned. The advertisements at the head of the January 1st issue featured Jules Verne, Hammond typewriters, Lavisse-Rambaud's *Histoire Universelle*, Beloch's *Griechische Geschichte*, and English bicycles. The *News*, to be sure, gave more prominence if not to the affairs of Russia at least to those of St. Petersburg, for reasons which the issue of January 3rd accidentally revealed. The unusual hesitation of the Moscow stockmarket on the previous day, it reported, was caused by the fact that the telegraph from St. Petersburg had broken down. And so in general, Moscow took its clues and much of its European news from St. Petersburg. On the inside pages, however, Europe reappeared in full immediacy, for instance in a column entitled "News of Science, Art, and Literature," which announced the *Cambridge Modern History*, an English volume on the German social-democrats, a *Petite bibliothèque économique française et étrangère*, *L'œuvre complet de Rembrandt*, and a new work by Benjamin Kidd (also frequently mentioned in other papers). And to judge by the theater and opera section, Moscow hardly boasted a less brilliant season than St. Petersburg, with Gounod's *Romeo and Juliet* at the Bolshoi, a play by Sudermann at the Malyi, and *La dame aux camélias* at the Paradise Theater. What a strange kaleidoscopic view of European culture this paper conveyed, associating in its pages the great artists like Eleanora Duse or Joseph Hofmann with a new cheap edition of John Stuart Mill, Francis-Joseph mineral waters from Budapest with an exhibition of French art, French mademoiselles with the great industrial firms in Germany or the German shopkeepers of Moscow advertising musical instruments or printing presses. The Latin script of three European languages carelessly mingled with the cyrillic alphabet of the native tongue.

The patent western orientation of the *Russian News* was not due entirely to its well-known liberal convictions, for the *Moscow News*,[14] a stalwart conservative paper, hardly lagged behind. The very first item on the front page of the January 1st issue was a very large obituary notice in English saying that

13 *Russkiia vedomosti.*
14 *Moskovskiia vedomosti.*

Elizabeth B. Gibson had departed this life. Yet there could be no question of the Russian views of the editor Gringmut who greeted the New Year with an editorial on the political ideals of Alexander III. "Western state doctrines contradict not only the interests of the Russian government, but also every simple healthy thought. Even in the West their shortlived fame is paling and the sober minds of European politicians see the deceptiveness of these doctrines and look with involuntary envy upon Russia, which has kept free from that deception and all its consequences. . . ." Of all the Russian papers, in this random sample, this one, to be sure, gave the most space to Russian affairs, yet as Gringmut's editorial shows, not without constant reference to the West. And *unter dem Strich*, in the feulleton section, Europe made its reappearance unashamedly with a story "Why they love Nice," an advertisement of a new brand of German beer, a report on "Shakespeare on the London stage," news of Professor Bilroth's international language, and advice on "the bicycle, its use and its harm." Conservatism apparently, was conferring no immunity to the lure of the good things of Europe.

The same could be said of Prince Meshcherskii's *Grazhdanin* ("The Citizen"), appearing twice a week in St. Petersburg, and reported to be the only paper read by the Emperor. Its foreign news, favoring the doings of European conservatives (with a special weakness for the French anti-semitic journalist Drumont) ranked a close second to domestic news; and in its advertising section the New York Life Insurance Company, *Wiener Chic* (in Latin characters) and Harrach glass (from Bohemia) rubbed elbows with jewelry from Schubert's in St. Petersburg and watches from Watkey's. More representative perhaps of the mentality of the St. Petersburg public was a slick paper weekly called *Niva*, a family magazine making its way without imperial subsidy. In its extensive advertising columns it conducted a motley fair of European merchandise, Dutch bulbs, *Leichners Fettpuder, Eau de Cologne,* Parisian dentifrice, Hungarian bitters, seeds from Erfurt, Viennese fashion journals, gramophones, and various makes of typewriters. Special notices were inserted by a German firm setting up starch factories, a Russian firm acting as agent for American machine builders, or a Baden-Baden sanitorium for morphine addicts. Every issue also carried an article on French fashions. The richly illustrated feature articles skillfully alternated Russian and foreign topics of a wide variety. In No. Two of 1897, for instance, it offered first an installment of a novel by Nemirovich-Danchenko, next a story about Cossack life, then two illustrations from the French art exhibit in St. Petersburg, followed by an article on how children learn to think and speak, translated from the German. Among the subsequent smaller topics the reader could choose from Russia and abroad, including items on the historian Kliuchevskii or the new "gadget" of the German aviator Lilienthal. Obviously this magazine catered to a well-educated clientele that knew their Europe and wanted to keep up with its accomplishments.

Taking up next the "fat" periodicals — the subject is of such significance as to warrant belaboring the point to the utmost — one discovers that most of the articles in the *Scientific Review* [15] were either reporting the work of foreign

[15] *Nauchnoe obozrenie.*

scientists or constantly referring (and deferring) to them. The January issue, for instance, printed papers on d'Holbach, the sociological teachings of Karl Marx, and Lester Ward's *Psychological Factors of Civilization*. The review section listed a critique of Marx by Leo Buch, a survey of new chemical elements by P. Barère, an Italian author on epilepsy, a German one on tropical rain and another one on the temperature of the earth, a Frenchman on the respiration of fish, and after listing several more pages of foreign books, ended with an American treatise on child psychology. In the section called "News of Foreign Literature" the American read about a German review article on "Tolstoy and the Russian Theater," but afterwards about more foreign works, including Jevon's *Introduction to the History of Religion*. In the section of "The History of Science" one encounters Pascal's *Lettres* as the chief piece. Could there have been any better evidence of how the intellectual accomplishments of Europe were penetrating into Russia? The title of one famous periodical indeed epitomized the entire process; it was called *The Messenger of Europe*.[16] This influential liberal magazine conveyed amidst its account of the presidential campaign of McKinley or of contemporary Alaska, a translation of a novel by Spielhagen, and an appeal for contributions to the Louis Pasteur Fund, surprisingly much information about Russian events — "ah, Russian events," so a conservative Russian might sigh, "seen through the eyes of a western liberal." Proceeding from the *European Messenger* to *The World of God*,[17] one finds as the first piece an installment from a novel by Potapenko, the second selections from the poems by Walter Scott translated into Russian, and the third referring to England as the classical land of modern feminism. And in the subsequent pages Europe again came spilling over into the eager Russian minds as richly as ever.

But to vary the selections. *The Mining Journal*,[18] edited by the Mining Science Commission in St. Petersburg, contained an article entitled "The contemporary condition of technology in the southern mines and smelteries." Here one reads: "By placing a high tariff on iron and coal our government obviously intended to develop our mining industry with the help of the Russian people." But these hopes, the author continued, had not been realized. With the exception of a few outstanding Russian engineers and industrialists, the Russian people had let these southern industries fall into the hands of foreign capitalists. "Because of their inertia the Russian people did not only stand aside in the development of their mines but lightheartedly gave them away to the foreigners, one after the other. . . ." There was nothing to be done about this, the author concluded, but to accept the inevitable and to make sure that "the economic interests of Russia are not violated and Russian self-esteem not offended."

The advertisers' announcements readily indicated to what extent Russian mines depended upon foreign equipment. The first advertiser in *The Engineer*,[19] published in Kiev, to give another example, was the German firm AEG,

16 *Vestnik evropy.*
17 *Mir bozhii.*
18 *Gornyi zhurnal.*
19 *Inzhener.*

and the names of the subsequent ones were predominantly German, although Portland Cement and one John Sumner selling American and Swiss machinery provided some variety. An article on the rolling stock of Russian railroads in this magazine made the following statements: "Our railroad network is considerably poorer than foreign ones in regard to rolling stock," and in another article one finds Philadelphia's Reading Terminal praised as a model for Russian railroad terminals, but with the advice that the Russian ones be built on a more modest scale. Turning then to *Technical Education*,[20] published by the Imperial Russian Technological Society in St. Petersburg, we find the leading article concerned with technical and professional education in Switzerland. Scanning the table of contents of *Education*,[21] another St. Petersburg "fat" magazine, reveals that three out of eight articles dealt with foreign subjects or were translated from the English. In the section "From the world of knowledge" two out of three articles were imports; in the following section "From the West" — why even bother to read the titles? The next section, "News of foreign literature," was succeeded by one "From foreign journals," by which time the reader has leafed through more than two-thirds of the volume. Analysis, finally, of *Russian Wealth* and three Moscow periodicals, *The Russian Messenger, Russian Thought*, and *The Messenger of Education*,[22] would hardly change the emerging conclusions. *Russian Thought* — one cannot help noticing the irony — began with a poem by Shelley in a Balmont translation, then offered a story by Ostrovskii, thereafter one by Paul Hervé. Next came a brief Russian poem succeeded by a story by Marie von Ebner-Eschenbach, followed in turn by a story by Nemirovich-Danchenko on San Marino. Was all this Russian thought or European thought? Or was Russian thought European thought?

Granted that the preceding analysis of the Russian press during January 1897 may have overstressed the habit of instinctive comparison with the West. But who would dare judge the foreign impact by a mere quantitative analysis? So many of the Russian items were presented in a manner borrowed from the West, footnoted with western titles and buttressed by references to western authors. How can one draw a clear line between Russian and western material? Needless to say, the proportion between Russian and western topics varied somewhat according to the outlook of the editors, the conservative or *narodnik* ones being somewhat more impervious, at least on the surface, to the western influence. But everything considered, the presence of the West was an overwhelming reality wherever one looked. It vastly exceeded in strength the foreign influence which any western European or American would observe in his own country.

Every day, a host of European messengers, goods, ideas, images, and impressions descended upon the Russian mind, or at least the minds of those who read these papers and periodicals. They also descended upon those who bought foreign goods or Russian goods patterned after them, or those who associated

[20] *Tekhnicheskoe obrazovanie.*
[21] *Obrazovanie.*
[22] *Russkoe bogatstvo, Russkii vestnik, Russkaia mysl, Vestnik vospitaniia.*

with foreigners (not to speak of those who travelled abroad). Each of these seemingly minute and harmless messengers — not to mention here all the illegal carriers of the prohibited ideas of democracy, constitutional government, or socialism — attacked in his own tiny way the validity of the Russian ways of doing things, daubing them with the reproach of insufficiency. "There is nothing either good or bad but thinking makes it so," and thus the Russians, their thinking wrought in western Europe, transformed their country. They despised it merely because they looked at it with eyes and minds made disloyal by the constant squint-eyed reference to Europe. Was there anything at all that could stand up under the withering comparison?

A small item in the reactionary *Moscow News* summed up the Russian condition in the prophetic clarity which sometimes attaches to a casual remark.[23] That paper, early in 1897, had quoted the prospectus of a new publication named *World Echoes* — one of the many which were started only to run afoul of the censorship. It called itself "a Russian organ, yet at the same time not exclusively national." And then came the amazing admission: "Under nationality one understands, for the most part, the sum total of peculiarities lodged since times immemorial in the popular mind and presumably forever distinguishing the Russians from all other people. However, under the influence of historical conditions and of progress many phenomena which distinguished Russian nationality are now changing and therefore prove to be no longer genuine and unchangeable (excepting, of course, the rooted principles of Russian autocracy and social organization)." Under the influence of "progress," so one might rephrase that sentence in order to savor it still more, what had been considered an essential part of Russian nationality was suddenly melting away, dissolved by the contempt of the multitude of nimble and insinuating European messengers. Whether autocracy and the peasant commune were really exempt from this subversion one might doubt. The editor of the *World Echoes* may have stated the exception merely as an obligatory bow to the authorities.

The historian trying to work his way beneath the surface of Russian events in the mid-nineties is thus driven to his first major conclusion. There was no blending of old and new, as the American minister to Russia had written. The old was being ruthlessly subverted by the new; both were bitterly at war. There was going on in Imperial Russia, he begins to realize, a vast revolution from without, a revolution pressed forward by almost all members of Russian society, by the conservatives and reactionaries as well as by the Marxists and *narodniks* in their secret circles, and advancing on a level far deeper than government policy or even human awareness. The Grand Dukes and retired generals were in rebellion against backwardness. They showed it by their preference for living in Nice, Paris, or the German spas. They could afford to live like human beings by quitting Russia. And all the wealthy Russians who travelled to Europe once a year or as often and for a long a stay as they could manage were disloyal too. The poorer people, or the intelligentsia, who were chained by their poverty to

[23] *Moskovskiia vedomosti*, No. 3 (1897), 3rd January, in the column "dnevnik pechati."

the "pigsty," could not thus easily withdraw. Their escape lay in a mental absenteeism, induced by immersion into western literature and the image of the West conveyed by their press. Or, if they wanted action as well, they ran away into the revolutionary dream of "the real Russia" which was going to replace the present "Asiatic" Russia. And since they had no chance of enjoying the good life abroad (or perhaps were better patriots than the Grand Dukes), they had to give their lifeblood to remodelling their fatherland by revolutionary action. At any rate, if there was going to be a revolution from within, its way had long been prepared by a greater revolution from without.

The first reaction of any westerner who had observed the backwardness of Imperial Russia at close quarters could only be sympathetic to the universal revolt against the "pigsty." The "new" was of his own civilization: he had no reason to doubt its mission. Yet could he speak for all the Russians as well? A look at the third edition of K. P. Pobedonostsev's book *Moscow Reflections*, found in the St. Petersburg bookstores in January 1897,[24] might make a westerner pause. It is easy, to be sure, to misread this volume; on first acquaintance it repels by its vehemence. Yet in the light of the conclusions just stated it suddenly gains a tragic depth. For what the author was trying to express, in the ill-suited language of western conservatism — alas, he too had to resort to a western model! — was a justified protest against the subversion by the ubiquitous messengers of Europe. "The faculty of seizing and assimilating on faith these abstract ideas," so one reads there, "has spread among the masses and becomes infectious, more especially to men insufficiently or superficially educated, who constitute the great majority everywhere." [25] As a result the people were made unhappy. "In our time discontent is universal. . . . We grow up with infinite expectations, begotten of immeasurable vanity and innumerable artificial needs," [26] taught, so it would seem from the foregoing, by the western advertisements and incapable of being satisfied under Russian conditions. Another passage pointed to the spiritual malaise produced by the inchoate mixture of the old and the new. "Life has become deformed, false, and meaningless beyond belief . . . all discipline of thought, of sentiment, and of morale has disappeared. Corruption and disintegration have destroyed the simple organic relations of public and family life; their place has been usurped by institutions and abstract principles for the most part false in themselves or in false relation to life and actuality. The simple needs of the soul and body have been expelled by a multitude of artificial requirements, and the simplest sentiments have given way to sentiments complex and artificial which seduce and irritate the soul. . . ." [27]

The crowning lament in Pobedonostsev's book was the maxim "Things not absolute are unstable." [28] How true! In Russia "historic conditions and progress" (as the *World Echoes* had put it euphemistically) undermined all the

[24] Cited here from K. P. Pobedonostsev, *Reflections of a Russian Statesman* (London: G. Richards, 1898), tr. R. C. Long.

[25] *Ibid.*, p. 30.
[26] *Ibid.*, p. 90.
[27] *Ibid.*, p. 94.
[28] *Ibid.*, p. 139.

absolutes of Russian tradition; everything was giving way. But how could any society survive without absolutes? In western Europe and even the United States, the rate of change had been slow, and the new originated always from within the old; there was no drastic break. In England, for instance, the monarchy had been preserved as an historic absolute, likewise the Church, Parliament, and the common law. And the United States had taken over many of the absolutes of Britain and evolved its own, the Constitution. In Russia, on the other hand, all the foundations were crumbling. She was a profoundly sick country by the standards of the western model, uprooted, drifting, unable to set her own course.

Those who find it repulsive to agree with the hated reactionary might listen more readily to one of his greatest antagonists and one deeply venerated in the West, Leo Tolstoy. Tolstoy, like other Russians had been very much attracted by an imported western innovation, the bicycle, and had enthusiastically taken up the sport himself. Suddenly his moral instinct had caught up with him, and he had entered into his diary in May 1896: "I have stopped riding the bicycle. *I wonder how I could have been so infatuated!*" [29] Russia, like Tolstoy, was carried beyond her depths by the new gadgets of western Europe, by the bicycle, the *cinematograph lumière*, the *Fettpuder*, the typewriter, the dynamo, the gold standard, and all the other subversive messengers. Would she have sense enough to stop the mad rush? Or, to put the question more realistically, in view of her backward position in Europe could she afford not to accelerate it?

It was Russia's tragedy — and that of many underdeveloped countries after her — that the bases of her society and tradition, the pillars of a sound polity, were being irresistibly undermined at the very time when the ambitions of both government and the people required the utmost effort to catch up to the western model. When state and society should have been exceptionally strong to cope with an exceptional emergency, they were progressively weakened by the disloyalty created by that very model. Much of Russia's subsequent development has been conditioned by an understandable desire to escape from the worst effects of such subversion.

Revolution from Without? (A COMMENTARY ON "IMPERIAL RUSSIA AT THE TURN OF THE CENTURY: THE CULTURAL SLOPE AND THE REVOLUTION FROM WITHOUT," BY THEODORE H. VON LAUE.)[30]

MARY C. WRIGHT

The fundamental processes leading to the collapse of Imperial Russia, so vividly described by Mr. Von Laue, seem to me in sharp contrast to the

[29] *The Journal of Leo Tolstoy (1895–1899)* (New York, 1917), entry for 2 May 1896 (italics my own).

[30] From *Comparative Studies in Society and History*, Vol. IV, No. 2 (January 1962), pp. 247–252. Copyright by the Society for the Comparative Study of Society and History. Reprinted by permission of the author and publisher.

processes leading to the collapse of Imperial China. Since Mr. Von Laue suggests that the pattern he discerns for Russia at the turn of the century has been the tragic pattern for many other countries that have since tried to catch up with the West quickly, it may be useful to examine his major theses with reference to China, since the obvious similarities in the histories of the two countries may easily obscure the fundamental differences. Such a comparison may add to our comprehension of the re-formation of both civilizations and suggest somewhat different questions about the process of "modernization" in general.

If I understand him correctly, the gist of Mr. Von Laue's argument is, first, that the Russian revolution, in the broad sense, was a "revolution from without" and not in any significant way the product of Russian history; and second, that among the influences from without, political, economic, and intellectual influences — ideas, battleships, and bonds — were merely the "surface aspects of power." The real destroyers of Russia, "the termites of Western influence," were the luxuries and gadgets of the West.

On the first point, the Chinese revolution, in the same broad sense, was certainly a "revolution from without," so strikingly so that a comparison suggests that the Russian revolution, in the perspective of the global changes precipitated by the concomitants of the scientific and industrial revolutions in Western Europe, was, by contrast, revolution from within. In this light, Mr. Von Laue's impressive list of indices of the cultural slope of Russia from its high points in the North and West down to the South and East, as Western European influences faded, indicates that Russia was in fact part of the West. In the non-Western world, cultural slopes follow no such pattern. In nineteenth century China, for example, there was no single general slope, and however the arguments may go about regional contours, one thing is certain: there was no descent from high points of greatest European influence near the Treaty Ports to low points in the interior. My point here is not the obvious one that Russia had had far more extensive contact with Western Europe than China had had — although it should be remembered that there were Western European Jesuits at the court of the K'ang-hsi Emperor before Peter the Great went West — but that the existence of this slope means that Western influences were of an internal rather than an external character. Was the Russian culture on which Mr. Von Laue quotes Pobedonostev so eloquently any more different from the nineteenth century upper class culture of Western Europe than were the cultures of Ireland, Southern Italy, or Greece? Are not these all European sub-cultures?

No one would argue with Mr. Von Laue's point that the union of old and new in Russia was strained. The point at issue here is whether the old and new were not both Russian; whether at least from the time of the late eighteenth century cultural flowering, a true national style, as a part of Western civilization, had not developed. Let me illustrate with two examples which Mr. Von Laue takes as evidence that Russia was not Western. First, he points to the "fluid conditions of employment in Russia," which invalidated the neat categories of the new census forms. "The modern design did not fit the Russian realities." But was the same thing not true of much of what I would call the rest of the West? Second, he points to the lack of statistical skills among the chinovniks, and to the fact that the Ministry of the Interior none the less failed to make use of trained Russian statisticians. To an historian of China, the striking points are that professional Russian statisticians existed and took part in international conferences, and that even the chinovniks saw the need for a modern census. The failure of entrenched bureaucrats to ask the professional advice of outside specialists can scarcely be called un-Western.

In sum, on the basis of the interesting material presented by Mr. Von Laue, I suggest that it is more useful to think of Russia as the last of the major Western countries to struggle with the problems of modernization, rather than as the first of the non-Western countries to make the attempt. The latter have faced different and more difficult problems.

With reference to Mr. Von Laue's second major thesis: that the true destroyers of Russian traditional culture at the turn of the century were imported gadgets and habits that corrupted manners and mores, the picture is very different for the last decades of the Chinese Empire. In China, where imports of consumers' goods were predominant, there are no signs that these imports reflected an undermining taste for foreign luxuries or any desire to ape foreign ways. According to Mr. Von Laue's figures, Russian imports of raw cotton, machinery, and iron and steel dwarfed all the corrupting imports of grand pianos, wines and liquors, and the like. Trade statistics do not therefore seem relevant to the discussion. No one would say of the Chinese upper classes, as Mr. Von Laue says of the Russian: "Of course as any outsider looking into Russia could abundantly observe, they tried to escape from the pigsty as best they could. They bought all the tokens of Kultur which they could afford (and more) from the West." The Chinese upper classes, being non-Western, serenely preferred the tokens of their own culture, the Empress Dowager's clock collecting notwithstanding. A reformer might occasionally take an interest in surveying instruments, for example, and try to explain to the public that these were not necessarily espionage devices. But on the whole, if we except the special problem of imported opium, China imported plain cotton cloth and coarse yarns, which could be produced more cheaply in Manchester. On arrival, these were used to clothe the poor in Chinese style.

More important than material goods in undermining Russian tradition, according to Mr. Von Laue, was the flow of Western experts, from engineers to governesses, into Russia, and the flow of Russians to Western Europe. There were substantial numbers of foreign missionaries and businessmen in China too by the turn of the century, and Chinese emigration had been massive. The numbers involved in both Russia and China were tiny in proportion to the total populations of the two countries, but each foreign and each emigrant group exerted an influence greatly disproportionate to its size. The point I would make is that these influences were strikingly different in the two societies. Evidently, in the Russian case, the foreigners were invited, esteemed, and emulated. In the Chinese case, the foreign movment into the country was wholly foreign inspired. The difference in attitude is clear from the beginning of the contact of the two countries with modern Western Europe. Peter the Great ordered his officials to shave, to wear Western clothes, and to study new subjects. The Jesuits at the Court of Peking donned Chinese dress, studied Chinese civilization, and wrote of it with great admiration. The Chinese set a very Chinese tone of intercourse, and were interested only in a few Western skills that reinforced the Chinese imperial system: improved astronomy, cannon-casting, and cartography. It is symbolic as well as true that the Chinese insisted that in the map of the world prepared by the Jesuits, China be shifted to the center, Western Europe to the periphery. Only in the second half of the nineteenth century and by the slowest steps did the Chinese bring themselves to the view that Westerners were not all barbaric. Even then, they were to be tolerated, not emulated. One of the most enlightened statesmen of the 1890's, compelled by circumstances to attend official receptions, noted privately that the members of the Diplomatic Corps in formal dress reminded him of nothing so much as a scurrying flock of squawking geese.

The difference between emigrants from China and Russia is as marked as the difference between foreign groups within the two countries. Paris and London were not magnets to upper-class Chinese, who went abroad only with reluctance and for limited assignments. When a reformer and pioneer journalist visited Edinburgh, his momento was a self-portrait in Chinese dress, with the hills of the city transformed into a classic Chinese landscape. When he came home, he wrote not about Great Britain but about strengthening China's basic institutions. There was a massive lower class emigration, under pressure of dire necessity, but the dream of the coolie was not to rise in the Western world, or in a Western way, but to make money to send home, and to retire, or at least to be buried, in China. The Chinatowns of the West were closed social corporations, apart from the life of the host country.

More deadly even than goods and people in undermining Russian culture, according to Mr. Von Laue, was the Russian periodical press, with its foreign advertisements, announcements of Western plays and concerts, disquisitions of French writers, and the like. Here again the Chinese case was quite different. The missionary publications, with their occasional articles on useful Western knowledge, did not represent a Chinese search for Western learning. Chinese-language newspapers, generally regarded as foreign business enterprises, were issued only in a few hundred copies and were widely resisted. Even in these two types of essentially external periodicals, there is nothing resembling the Western penetration that Mr. Von Laue has described so vividly for the Russian press of the time.

The truly Chinese press was completely disinterested in Western products, entertainment, or art. The gazette-type papers continued to give very Chinese official pronouncements. The fly-by-night gossip sheets remained very Chinese entertainment. There was in the very year from which Mr. Von Laue has taken his sampling of the Russian press, 1897, a burst of the new reform periodicals in China, with a sharp increase in interest in the world outside China. But the character of the interest was the reverse of that attributed to the Russian press. These journals were put out by reform clubs, whipped into action by the fear of national extinction at the hands of the great powers. They discussed the great issues of politics, economics, and morals from a firm Chinese base. The editors and writers were literati, steeped in Chinese tradition, who were trying to understand the West in order to save *China*. The clubs had names like "Protect the Nation Society." Even the underground revolutionary organization was called the "Revive China Society." Their slogans were such phrases as "provide for the common people and strengthen the state." If there was a lead article on the Western custom of mixed social gatherings, its clear purpose was to dispel the lingering Chinese notion that such gatherings were lusty brawls and thus promote a more rational attitude toward the foreigners who were inevitably in China. No one except their own hangers-on wanted them there, or wanted to emulate them. Increased knowledge of the West led no Chinese to call China a pigsty.

In short, the outside influences exerted by imported goods, the movement of people, and the periodical press worked very differently in late Imperial Russia and late Imperial China. The difference, I suggest, results from the fact that Russians, themselves Western, wanted to become part of the most advanced West and so let a regional tradition wither. The Chinese, not in the least attracted by the West but compelled to deal with it on all fronts and on very uneven terms, struggled to strengthen and preserve their civilization in new circumstances. They failed because of what Mr. Von Laue calls the mere surface aspects of power — political, economic, military, and intellectual pressures.

I have commented on Mr. Von Laue's paper in the light of Chinese experience in the late nineteenth century not because of simultaneity of period but because it is the only plausible comparison to make. For later periods, after the founding of the republic and years of civil war, when Chinese traditions were already ineffective and there was no central authority, the "termites of Western influence" that began to appear in the form of ballroom dancing and bobbed hair were clearly symptoms of a collapse that had already occurred. During the first World War, the imperial powers being pre-occupied, some sectors of Chinese commerce boomed and the Chinese dollar was high on the world market. In consequence, in some strata of urban society of the 1920's one finds traces of the picture Mr. Von Laue has drawn of Russia in the 1890's. But the real impact of the West in the 1920's was in the ferment of ideas stimulated by study of the West, including Russia, for the creation of a new China, ideas that were frustrated by international politics and domestic institutional weakness. Generalissimo Chiang Kai-shek was one of a small minority who attached real importance to these fripperies from abroad, and considered them a cause and not a symptom of the explosive situation in China.

In his concluding paragraph, Mr. Von Laue remarks: "It was Russia's tragedy — and that of many underdeveloped countries after her — that the bases of her society and tradition, the pillars of a sound polity, were being irresistibly undermined at the very time when the ambitions of both government and the people required the utmost effort to catch up. When state and society should have been exceptionally strong to cope with an exceptional emergency, they were progressively weakened by the subversive Western model."

If one looks around the globe, recalling the history of the past two centuries, can one find a single country whose institutions were "exceptionally strong" at the time of the "exceptional emergency" presented by the post-mercantilist expansion of Europe? Were not virtually all of them in a period of exceptional institutional weakness, a weakness of greatly varied origins and kinds, but in no case the result of the subversive Western model? The real problem for each of these countries has been nothing less than the creation of a new civilization — for survival. In each country, there has been a traditionalistic faction crying for a program of breathing life back into already moribund national institutions, of bringing a few of the finest fruits of the industrial revolution in for the use of the state and the dominant class, while at the same time preventing these from having any substantial effect on society. Japan succeeded for a time, but paid heavily in the end. Elsewhere these efforts have hindered more than they have helped the painful process of modernization.

Ideology and Organization
in Communist China:
Prologue

FRANZ SCHURMANN

The Chinese Revolution is for the latter half of the twentieth century what the Russian Revolution was for the first half. By transforming Chinese society, it has brought a great power into being which proclaims itself the revolutionary and developmental model for the poor countries of the world.

From the eighteenth century to the present, the world has been caught in a wave of revolutions. The industrial revolution in England started a process of economic transformation that has now reached to the farthest corners of the globe. The French Revolution sowed the seeds of a process of political revolution that has given rise to the modern nation-state. The results of these two revolutions have become the goals of the world's new countries: economic development and political integration. Above all, the new countries desire a national economy resting on an industrial-technological basis capable of creating wealth and power, and a national unity which arises from effective political institutions. It is symbolic that these two processes should have different points of origin, for most new countries have discovered that it is difficult to attain both goals simultaneously.

Economic development takes time; we may speak of it as a process of revolution. The British Empire and the world market were brought into being by a long series of developments which finally led to an economic system of great power and creativity. The present world market system, which grew out of the industrial revolution and became global in the nineteenth century, has shown the new countries a road to economic development: linkage to that world market system which will allow them to share in the wealth already created by the old countries. In so doing, they launch their own economic revolutions by becoming a part of a world-wide process of economic revolution.

However, the choice of such a road often prevents the new countries from achieving their other great goal, national unity. Though modern cities, factories, schools, and communications networks arise within their borders, they are usually restricted to a few areas, frequently on their coastlines where they are in close relation to the world's trade routes. The regions of the interior, vital for the creation and maintenance of national unity, benefit little from these developments. Moreover, all the wealth and power of economic development do not give the new countries a sense of national identity through which po-

From Franz Schurmann, *Ideology and Organization in Communist China* (Berkeley: University of California Press, 1966), pp. xxix–xlvi. Reprinted by permission of the author and publisher.

FRANZ SCHURMANN is Professor of Sociology and of History, University of California, Berkeley. An authority on China, he has written numerous articles on that country in scholarly journals. His major work is *Ideology and Organization in Communist China* (1966). Recently he has edited *The China Reader* (3 vols., 1967) with Orville Schell. He has also written *The Politics of Escalation in Vietnam* (1966) with Peter Scott and Reginald Zelnick.

litical integration can be achieved. Thus they are often faced with the choice of ignoring the peoples of the interior and the poor of the cities in order to develop economically within the world-wide context or seeking their support for political integration but thereby sacrificing easily available economic gains.

Though France's history as a nation-state began long before the French Revolution, that revolution gave the people of France a sense of national identity, expressed in the words *patrie, citoyen,* and *français.* The political revolutions that have brought new countries into being in the nineteenth and twentieth centuries have almost without exception sought to create the same sense of national identity in their peoples as the French Revolution did for the people of France. In this sense, many of the political revolutions have succeeded, for they have been able to create unity where earlier it did not exist. However, unity has often been acquired at the cost of economic development, a price which France also paid with its belated industrialization and modernization.

Modern France came into being, not by a process, but an act of revolution which swept away more than an ancient political system; it destroyed an entire social class. The French Revolution was, in effect, a social revolution. De Tocqueville, in describing the conditions leading to the French Revolution, makes clear what may be the essence of all social revolutions: an act of destruction willed against a whole ruling class.

Though all new countries of the preceding and the present centuries have participated in the processes of economic and political revolution, not all have undergone social revolution. Germany and Japan, for example, were able to combine the processes of economic development and political integration without social revolution. Many new countries of this century, however, face the possibility of social revolution as a consequence of their inability to achieve sufficient economic development and political integration. They may have some wealth and power and a sense of national identity, but not enough to still the forces of social revolution.

Revolutionary France is the world's first example of a modern social revolution. In 1917, Russia underwent its social revolution. And, in the late 1940's, it became clear that China had come through its social revolution, marked by the revolutionary struggle of the land reform. China's social revolution had causes deeper than its inability to develop economically and politically, but the shallowness of its economic and political revolutions made the social revolution inevitable.

A series of rebellions began in China toward the end of the eighteenth century, and continued until the advent and final triumph of Chinese communism. In retrospect, we can say that these rebellions began the process of revolution. Generally Buddhist or Taoist in ideology, they combined a revolutionary chiliasm with a hatred of secular authority. They occurred in certain inland areas of the country, many of which took on an endemic rebellious character. The greatest of these rebellions was that of the Taipings (1848–1864). There was much in the Taiping cry *ta-kuan,* smash the officials, which was reminiscent of the murderous hatred of the aristocracy during the French Revolution. The Taipings were crushed, but the process of social revolution did not end. Revolts continued to break out in the inland regions. The Communists succeeded in combining these forces of revolt into a mighty revolutionary movement. The military victories of Chinese communism took place at the same time that a revolutionary struggle was waged on the land against the rural gentry. A whole class was destroyed, not only physically but psychologically. Every act of land reform was climaxed by a drama where the landlord literally "lowered his head" (*tit'ou*) and so symbolically expressed his acceptance of defeat by the people.

All social revolutions are directed against elites, ruling classes. There has been a contemporary revival of interest in elites, for modernization and industrialization are seen as requiring leadership. But the elite concept involves more than leadership. An elite must not only be able to lead men in the organizational structures that criss-cross society, but must have legitimate status at the top levels of a social system. When an elite loses its capacity to lead and the legitimacy of its status, it reaps contempt and hatred from the people. The histories of social revolutions indicate that where an elite constitutes an entire ruling class, hatred can reach intense levels of collective fury.

Why the collective fury should have broken out with such ferocity during the Taiping Rebellion is not clear. The eighteenth century was a period of stability in China, for which it was widely admired in Europe. Toward the end of that century, extreme misery reappeared, but, as De Tocqueville indicates, misery is not the cause of revolution. During the Opium War of the early 1840's, China had sustained a stinging defeat at the hands of England. Not only was China as a country humiliated, but, moi: specifically, those who exercised authority in its name in Kwangtung, an area not far from where the Taiping Rebellion broke out. Whether the defeat China suffered in the Opium War had anything to do with the outbreak of the Taiping Rebellion is a subject for historical inquiry. However, humiliation at the hands of an external enemy who proclaims his moral superiority is particularly subversive to the authority of an elite. If this is paired with ineptness in domestic leadership, the conditions exist for social revolution. The stage is set for the act of class destruction.

China had its political revolution in 1911 and thus became a modern nation-state. The urban bourgeoisie eventually found a role in the emerging republic. But the landed gentry found no real role in the new government. Whether it would have if Chiang Kai-shek had been able to achieve political unity is a matter of dispute. Probably not. Few members of the gentry had much modern education, nor much understanding of the great things of the modern world which had an increasing attraction for the people of the country. The outcries of anger against "corrupt officials and lewd politicians, local landlords and inferior literati" began to erupt again. It was inevitable that the Communists, taught to look for revolutionary seeds in the cities, sooner or later would perceive the potential for social revolution in the rural areas. By the 1930's it was clear that China was moving toward a revolution similar to those of France and Russia. Chiang Kai-shek's dream of emulating the German and Japanese examples of nation-building was being gradually shattered. Nevertheless, by 1936 it appeared for a while that Chiang could succeed. The Communists had been reduced to a small band of stragglers holed up in the caves of remote Shensi, and the country enjoyed relative stability and prosperity.

One can argue *ad infinitum* whether the Chinese Revolution would have broken out if the Sino-Japanese war had not started. Even granting the wisdom of retrospection, it seems unlikely that a powerful Japan could have long coexisted with a reunited China, particularly with the mounting demands within China to recover Manchuria and the foreign concessions in China's most advanced regions. There was a growing student movement and a deep dissatisfaction within the corps of younger army officers. The Sino-Japanese war and the United Front between Kuomintang and Communists deflected revolutionary energies in the cities, but created conditions for a new revolutionary outburst on the land. If there had been no war, the revolutionary process would probably have started again within the cities and the Kuomintang. But there *was* war, and it sparked the dormant social revolution in China's rural regions.

France emerged from the revolution as one of the most highly organized countries in the world. The beginnings of political centralization antedate 1789, but the revolution and the first empire completed the process. Revolution followed by political centralization is a phenomenon repeated time after time in the wake of the French Revolution. It has been true of all Communist countries ever since the Russian Revolution. One can see it today in the newly emerging countries. Revolutions are followed by the creation of networks of organization.

Social system and organization must be viewed as two different things; a true elite is solidly imbedded in both. When a revolution destroys a social system, it also annihilates its elites. The new revolutionary regime can only pull society together again through organization. Political centralization is one of the forms that postrevolutionary organization has taken.

When a society has experienced political revolution and moves to resurrect organization, it looks for leadership, and naturally turns to its elites. But if its ruling class has lost the capacity to lead, that is, the capacity to strike out in new directions and to get men to follow them on the new road, then organization remains an empty shell. Nothing reveals the nakedness of a ruling class so starkly as its impotence in organization. When a social revolution destroys a social system, it is no longer possible for society to reach out toward its erstwhile elites for leadership, for they have ceased to exist. But the destruction of the social system makes organization more necessary than ever, for otherwise society would disintegrate into chaos. New leaders arise, whose primary qualification is their ability to lead. In time they may turn into a new elite by adding social status to their political positions. The system is reconstituted, but this time on a new basis. Both France and Russia have their elites today, though they are far different from the classes they replaced in the wake of social revolution.

The Manchus, when threatened by the West, did what all rulers do when facing the need to create and staff new organization: they turned to their traditional elite. The tide of social revolution which had erupted with the Taipings had subsided. There was no reason to suspect that the bureaucrats had lost their leadership abilities. The attempt failed. The Kuomintang tried a different approach. The destruction of the monarchy cleared the road for setting up all kinds of new organizational structures. The Kuomintang acquired a strong military streak during the 1920's, and military men have a keen sense of organization. But the Kuomintang persisted in staffing organization with old elites. What was left of the rural gentry moved into inland government positions. The urban bourgeoisie acquired powerful positions in the central government. Chiang Kai-shek, impressed with Germany and Japan, felt that strong military-political organization imposed from the top down, combined with civil government staffed by old and new elites, could accomplish the task of unification. It failed because of the inability of the elites to make civil government work. When the forces of social revolution revived, in the rural areas and within the Kuomintang itself (young army officers and intellectuals), Chiang attempted to suppress them. It was clear by the 1930's that the social revolution had eroded the social system. China needed organization to pull it together again. Chiang realized this, but he never understood that organization needs leaders.

The Communists, however, understood this very well. They recognized the forces of social revolution and made use of them. They not only saw revolution destroying a social system, but actively aided the process. While the revolution was still in the making, they already began to build new structures of military and civil organization. But, in great contrast to the Kuomintang, they knew that new organization needed new leaders. From the beginning of the Yenan period (1935–1946), their main organizational effort concentrated on recruiting and training new leaders. These became the cadres of the revolution and of organization.

The series of rebellions that broke out in China toward the end of the eighteenth century started a process of social revolution that, in some respects, has not yet ended. De Tocqueville's suggestion that economic factors were not major causative elements in the French Revolution could be generalized: the immediate factors that lead to acts of class destruction are not economic. Thus, when a country faces social revolution, economic countermeasures alone cannot prevent it. But in a more fundamental sense, the matrix from which revolutionary processes arise is economic. In China, it was not Western imperialism with its new business and industry which created the economic matrix of revolution, because Western enterprise did not come until the latter part of the nineteenth century. Moreover, the impact of Western imperialism was largely confined to the coast and a few select inland regions, whereas the social revolution was an inland phenomenon. Although there was a brief period of revolutionary ferment in the cities during the second and third decades of the twentieth century, which clearly was linked to the economic changes produced by imperialism, the great continuing revolution took place in remote inland regions.

The Communist party was born in Shanghai, but its destiny was in the interior. Ping-ti Ho in his *Studies on the Population of China, 1368–1953* (Harvard University Press, 1959) indicates that far-reaching changes had occurred in China's economic and demographic situation toward the end of the eighteenth century: "The over-all opportunities for gainful employment in the nation began to be reduced amidst continual population increase and technological stagnation" (p. 226). This suggests that the traditional economic fabric had started to disintegrate. But "technological stagnation" is not a phenomenon of nature. It is a manifestation of incapacity on the part of those who hold economic responsibility. In China, the accusation of economic responsibility falls on the shoulders of the gentry. The rebellions that broke out late in the eighteenth century were ferocious, and they were repressed with equal ferocity. That thread of ferocity created a social and psychological climate which ultimately led to the revolutionary terror of the late 1940's. However, it was the ever more evident impotence of the gentry in the face of economic challenges that marked its fall from elite position.

The economic elements that played a part in the genesis of the French Revolution arose from the transformation of post-feudal society, not from the industrial revolution which had just occurred in England. So it was in China. Ping-ti Ho's explanations of the growing tide of misery as due to population increase amidst technological stagnation sketches the terrible problem that has faced all Chinese governments since the end of the eighteenth century. No one has ever been more sensitive to this problem than the present leaders of China who have been trying to create a technological and economic base for Chinese society adequate for its population.

The period of peace and stability which China enjoyed during much of the eighteenth century was very different from a similar period of prosperity a thousand years before during the Sung dynasty. Then a new gentry had appeared on the scene; cities were growing; new ideas came into society. But the eighteenth century was different. The Manchus had allied themselves with an old ruling class that had strong local roots. Cities were mostly stagnant. And, except for a few new political ideas of the early Ch'ing, China's intellectuals had turned into tedious and plodding academics. Rebellion and internal migration in the late eighteenth century were warning signals that something was wrong with the social fabric. Western imperialism led to the rise of new great cities and thus provided new economic opportunities for the rural masses. But the rent in the social fabric had already taken place and could not be healed. The counter-revolutionary ferocity of General Tseng Kuo-fan in combatting the revolutionary ferocity of the Taipings created an atmosphere that made the final act of class destruction inevitable. Just as economic improvement in pre-1789 France and pre-1917 Russia failed to stem the tide of revolution, so periodic economic recovery and even progress in pre-1949 China failed to halt the social revolution.

The 1911 upheaval in China destroyed the monarchy and was succeeded by a republic which, in form, was quite modern. But by the 1930's it was evident that more had crumbled than the political system alone. The social fabric had disintegrated in much of rural China, yet the new patterns in the cities were too weak to exercise a commanding force over the country. The disintegration of the traditional economic system which began in the eighteenth century continued without interruption, yet the modern sector could not constitute an effective substitute. In the world of ideas and values, Confucianism was dying. The sharp cry of the intellectuals during the May-Fourth Movement, *fan li-chiao*, an untranslatable slogan which in effect announced that the old elite of the country had lost its moral charisma in the eyes of the young, signaled the disintegration of the value system. The Communists saw the trends of history and fought to complete the revolution. In the course of their long struggle, they looked to the future, and began to prepare for it with ideology and organization. When they triumphed, they replaced system by organization, and ethos by ideology.

The French and Russian revolutions were characterized by a seizure of state power which opened the floodgates of the social revolution. The waves of revolution spread outward from Paris and Petrograd to the provinces. Class warfare broke out and sent counterwaves back to the capital which pressed the leaders of the revolution into ever more radical directions. The Chinese Revolution was different. The seizure of state power was the climax of a revolution which began deep in the provinces. The social revolution had been burning for a century and a half. It remained relatively dormant during much of the early twentieth century, but broke out again in the late 1920's. The peasant jacqueries of the Kiangsi period were still reminiscent of the classical rebellions, despite the veneer of Bolshevist ideology. But in Yenan, the Communists began to use the dynamics of revolution and war to build organization. A dual process began to emerge. On the one hand, the drama of class destruction continued, reaching its culmination in the revolutionary terror of the land reform of the late 1940's. On the other hand, the Communists began to create the building blocks of their organizational network, which was to become the basis for their rule over the Chinese Mainland after final victory.

The French and Russian Revolutions went from the top down. The apex of the political system was smashed with one blow, actually and symbolically, and this led to a disintegration of the social fabric at all points of the system. There were other revolutions from the top down which did not have this effect, because the revolutionary pressures within the social system were not as great. One of them was the Meiji Restoration. The shogunate was overthrown by a basically conservative cabal of feudatories, but soon thereafter leadership passed into the hands of a radical group. One can see the pace of radicalization moving fast during the first years of the Meiji era. A system of social stratification and political order that had taken centuries to construct was obliterated. But there was neither a revolutionary bourgeoisie nor a revolutionary peasantry. The transformation of the political apex did not open the floodgates of social revolution, despite the unsettling rapidity of change.

Why were forces of social revolution, comparable to those of France, Russia, and China not present in Japan? There was no absence of peasant discontent during the Tokugawa; there was discontent among a new group of inland merchants who fought against the entrenched privilege of the city bourgeoisie; there was a highly dissatisfied and highly educated body of minor nobility seeking a new role in society. But Japan was yet too feudal, an argument that De Tocqueville also invokes to explain the absence of revolutionary pressures in Germany at the end of the eighteenth century. But the French Revolution, like the Russian, was directed against the state and a ruling class closely identified with it. Feudalism had imposed a complex of patchwork of social and political relationships on society. Processes of rationalization in France had long before the revolution done away with these patterns, leaving them only as vestiges of an earlier age. Russia and China never knew feudalism in its West European and Japanese senses.

Though China's social revolution was similar to that of France and Russia, it was also different. In the former countries, the ruling classes had lost that intimate involvement with local regions that remained so important in China. The French and Russian aristocracies became court aristocracies, living in cities and drawing their sinecures from their local possessions. The Chinese gentry did not live in the villages, but neither did it live in Peking. The court aristocracy, in the nineteenth century was Manchu, an alien race. The 1911 revolution did away with the aristocracy, but left the gentry undisturbed. Thus one of the aims of the Taiping Rebellion had been accomplished. But not the other, the destruction of the traditional gentry. In France and Russia, the ruling aristocracies were destroyed by revolutions that seized state power. It was not possible to destroy the Chinese gentry in a similar way. One might say that the Chinese gentry had strong linkages to both state and society. After 1911, it lost its linkages to the state, and, to compensate for this, held on more firmly to its particular interests in society.

This was not the first time that an alien group had come to power leading to a temporary retreat of the gentry from the scene. Most gentry undoubtedly thought that sooner or later the state would require its services again. Indeed, it was not disappointed, for that is precisely what the Kuomintang did. The weakened tie to the state had its advantages, for it immunized the gentry from the constant political changes in Peking and Nanking. On the other hand, heightened commitment to its landed possessions made it more vulnerable to the pressures of social revolution. Revolutions are profoundly influenced by the character of ruling classes. The entrenched localism of gentry power made it inevitable that the Chinese Revolution, in contrast to the revolutions of France and Russia, would come from the outlying areas to the center rather than the reverse, and, moreover, that it would take a long time. The gentry was widely distributed throughout China, and could not be destroyed with one blow. The peculiar conditions of the social situation in China gave the Chinese Revolution a populist character, one which neither Trotsky nor Stalin understood. It retains that character to the present day.

The Chinese Communists claim that their revolution is prototypical for the revolutionary process now burning in the countries of Asia, Africa, and Latin America. They argue that revolution cannot be won by sudden seizures of state power, by occupation of a capital city; they preach the "building-blocks" approach; they argue for revolution as a long-term process; they see capture of state power as the last act in a long drama.

Are they right in their assessment of the world revolutionary situation? Our analysis of revolution suggests that the seeds of social revolution are present when a traditional elite is incapable of exercising leadership in organization and when its status disappears as the result of disintegration of the social system. Thus it loses power and authority. In traditional peasant societies, the elite derives power and authority both from state and society. By society I here mean a localized social system which operates in a district or a region rather than in the country as a whole. The ownership of land usually is an important element in the localized social system. The Chinese Communist doctrine of revolution states that the revolutionaries must strike against such local systems — that it is here where the revolution will be won.

Every old elite tries desperately to maintain its positions in state and society. It will try to staff government with its people, and it will hold tenaciously to its local interests. The lessons of history suggest that it cannot do both. The pressures for land reform force the elite to hold on even more tightly to the reins of government. If a liberal government accedes to demands for land reform, as did Alexander II in Russia, the elite demands in return control of decision-making positions. It is not accidental that the most liberal of bureaucratic administrators often come from the old elite, like Count Witte. On the other hand, if strange people move into government, then the elite must preserve its interests in society. Benito Juarez became president of Mexico, but the caciques maintained a tight grip on the land. The one part of the world that appears to constitute a testing ground of the Chinese thesis is Latin America. Most Latin American countries have old Hispano-Portuguese elites with strong roots on the land and close association with government. Social and economic reform alone will not resolve the problem, for the dispossessed elite will simply move into the cities and into government. This is exactly what emancipation in Russia did. No matter how liberal and reformist the old elite becomes, historical example suggests that revolutionary pressures will rise against it. Land reform may ease revolutionary pressures in the villages, but the presence of a discredited elite in the cities and in the structure of government creates revolutionary pressures in the cities. This would portend a revolution of the French or Russian type. On the other hand, if the elites rather surrender their hold on government than their grip on the land, a revolution of the Chinese type threatens. The Chinese Communists believe that this will be the pattern of revolution in the coming years.

The Sino-Soviet dispute is not only a conflict between two powers, but one between two different revolutionary models. These two approaches to revolution are reflected in the split that has appeared in revolutionary groups in Latin America. On the one hand, there are the old-line Communists who maintain their tightly disciplined, centrally organized parties, waiting for the day that a February Revolution will break out. On the other hand, there are the Castroites, spiritually akin to the Chinese, working for a guerrilla war of social revolution on the land.

Can social revolution with all its bloodshed be avoided in Latin America? Marx said that no ruling class departs willingly from the stage of history. Perhaps he is right: the chances of avoiding revolution would appear to be slim. However, the rapid emergence of a liberated peasantry on the land, and a new class of technocratic administrators and entrepreneurial managers in the cities could furnish a chance of avoiding social revolution. The old elite, tainted irreparably with ineptness and loss of charisma, would be replaced by younger men of ability, of mixed race reflecting the character of Latin America, and by men who can produce as well as consume. The new men would not only have to have real power, but would have to be visible, to stand out as the true leaders of the country.

After a social revolution has taken place in a country, there no longer exists a ruling class to constitute a source of recruitment for the leadership roles that organization requires. To survive, the revolutionaries need organization. China went through a social revolution in the third century B.C., which led to the disappearance of an old feudal aristocracy. The Ch'in empire emerged from that struggle as the most highly organized political entity known to that time in Chinese history, and armed with an ideology called legalism, which was in fact an ideology of organization. Triumphant revolutionary movements often tend to be military, not only because of the importance of armed struggle, but because armies are by their nature pure organization. The successful revolutionary movement has desperate need for leadership to direct the organization it creates. It recruits leaders from where it can find them. But the type of organization which a revolutionary movement creates in its formative phases, and the kinds of leaders which it recruits, have a decisive influence on the kind of society it builds up after victory.

In Russia, the tight conspiratorial organization of the Bolsheviks, and its direction almost entirely from outside of the Russian social context, influenced the type of organization and leadership that arose after the Russian Revolution. The revolutionary process in Russia had developed for a long time before the October Revolution. However, the Bolshevik party, because of its inability to operate openly in the country, could not become a true mass organization until the eve of the revolution itself. It was a highly centralized organization with a straight-line chain of command. Though the top leaders were intellectuals (as in China), the Party fighters were men of the working class. Despite the rapid regrowth of bureaucracy during the early 1920's, the new Party men were more managerially than bureaucratically minded. In the early 1920's, workers were put in positions of power to make certain that the proletariat ruled in organization. Subsequently, Stalin made great efforts to create a "workers' intelligentsia." Russia moved in the direction of great organizational centralization. Stalin wanted a phalanx of trained working-class managers to run that organization. Thus revolutionary Russia embarked on a process of political centralization, comparable to that of revolutionary France, but far more thorough. In contrast to the bourgeoisie that came to be the new elite in nineteenth-century France, in Russia organization was increasingly staffed by sons of workers.

The organization and the leaders that came out of the Chinese Revolution were different. Not since 1927 was the Chinese Communist party simply a conspiratorial group aiming to seize state power. In Kiangsi, it was mainly an army riding to power on the waves of a jacquerie. During the Yenan period, it turned into a political-military organization that sought systematically to use the forces of social revolution. The ideal nucleus of that organization was a small armed band that at times fought but at other times tended to agricultural production. The leaders of Communist organization during the Yenan period were the poor young peasants of the villages who centuries earlier had been recruited into defense brigades or roamed the hills as rebels. Out of this group emerged the cadres who led the revolution, fought the battles, took control of the production teams, and finally launched the acts of revolutionary land reform in the later 1940's. The Chinese Communists during the Yenan period wanted leaders first and foremost, and they sought them out wherever they could find them. The young peasant cadres had a military bent; for centuries their predecessors had gone forth to fight. War against the hated Japanese provided fertile ground for organizing. The village elders could not quarrel with the patriotic cause. But, as the land reform shows, the real target was the rural elite. The peasant jacquerie of the early 1930's broke out before the Sino-Japanese war. The revolutionary terror of the late 1940's burst forth after the Japanese had been defeated.

If any group in society is not an elite, it is the poor and the young. They have neither wealth, nor power, nor prestige. In China, the poor and the young peasants became the leaders of the revolution. But leadership could only be actualized in organization. Thus by destroying the social system and replacing it with organization, they created a role for themselves in the new society. What they sought was leadership and power, not status and authority.

The one great organizational product of the Chinese Revolution has been the Chinese Communist party. It is an organization made up of leaders whose one great purpose in life is to lead — at all levels of the structure. In its early years, it was a party of youth. Today, though older, it is still made up largely of workers and peasants. The Party has created an organizational context which gives them a continuing role in society.

Organization, in contrast to a social system, needs conscious efforts to survive. This is all the more so when organization cannot rely on a social system, such as recruiting its leaders from a solidly based status group. In wars, armies survive through the challenges of battle. The end of the war often has a demoralizing effect on military organization, as was the case with the American army after World War II. The Chinese Communists have understood this well, and thus "struggle" (toucheng) has become the watchword of the Party. This was not an abstraction, for the constant reappearance of "rectification" keeps the atmosphere of struggle alive, particularly when the leadership role of the Party diminishes. Ideology provides the moral cement that not only arouses commitment but creates the cohesive forces which prevent struggle from turning into disintegration. Cohesion through conflict is a problem with which both Western sociologists and the Chinese Communists have concerned themselves. For the latter, it has been a life and death matter.

When the Chinese Communists triumphed in 1949, there no longer was a social system to which they could turn for support, even if they had wanted to. There was no gentry left, and they distrusted the bourgeoisie. But there was a choice of directions. Should they construct organization along the lines they had developed during the ten years of Yenan or should they emulate the one model they respected above all: the Soviet Union? They chose the latter course, and thus for the first five years of the 1950's, China began rapidly turning into a second Soviet Union. The imposition of bureaucratic organization from the top down proceeded rapidly, symbolized by the elaboration of a vast planning structure. China appeared to be following the road to bureaucratic centralization. If centralization meant the emergence of a new professional elite, the changes in Communist party recruitment in the early 1950's followed the model perfectly. Large numbers of old and new intellectuals were recruited into the Party. Expertise became a prime qualification for Party membership. Untrained rural cadres were dropped from Party rolls. Managers were coming into their own again. A "new class" was in the process of coming into being. But the process was stopped in 1955. The purge of oppositional elements in Manchuria and Shanghai led to the elimination of large numbers of budding apparatchiks. In the summer of 1955 the Party struck against the bureaucracy. And finally collectivization led once again to radicalization.

The evidence indicates that there was a social core to this process. The demobilization of the army in 1955 saw millions of war veterans return to the countryside where they became leaders of the collectivization drive and rural Party cadres. The enormous jump in Party membership went hand in hand with political radicalization and collectivization. Despite the consolidation of 1956 and 1957, the rural Party organization continued to grow. Late in 1957, rectification once again struck the Party and the professionals. While the "regionalization of the Party" was opposed, decentralization nevertheless gave the local Party apparatus great power. When communization was introduced, a great ground swell of enthusiasm came precisely from the young rural cadres. Today, in the declining years of his life, Mao Tse-tung calls for the recruitment of a new generation of Party members from among young workers and peasants. These are the cadres with whom he made the revolution, and these are the young leaders who tried to implement his programs of rural reconstruction. China in the mid-1950's thus veered sharply from the Soviet model of organization which it so assiduously followed during the early 1950's.

China's social revolution has been long. The type of organization that has emerged from it has been much more directly involved with the masses of society than in the Soviet Union. The Chinese peasant, even in remote inland areas, has been drawn into political life. Mao's dream is the transformation of the Chinese peasant into a modern producer. Land reform destroyed the old rural elite. Collectivization deprived the peasant of his ownership over the soil. Communization changed the whole pattern of work organization. Was this the final act of liberation from which a new peasant will emerge? It seems almost inevitable that the forces of bureaucratic centralization will once again make themselves felt in China. It does not seem likely that a political semi-elite of worker and peasant cadres and a social semi-elite of professionals can long coexist in peace. Neither is it likely that the professionals will long be content to do staff work for their red executives nor that the red cadres will forego the chances of acquiring social status through education and professionalization. The lure of education is powerful. If, however, the "new class" emerges after society has been truly transformed, and if the peasant has been brought into the modern world, then Mao's dream will have been realized. Then institutionalization can set in once again. The revolution will then be over. A new society will begin to emerge.

The great challenge of the modern world is the transformation of masses who are outside of that world into individuals who become a part of it. Western capitalism and imperialism have brought about remarkable economic and social development in far-flung parts of the world, but only in a few select locations. Great cities have arisen, but often separated by a deep chasm from their hinterlands. The processes of transformation have not been completed in the Soviet Union, as indicated by Khrushchev's hope for a new Soviet man. Mao Tse-tung preaches that social revolution is a reality in the poor countries, and that political organization must reach out to the most distant and poorest of the masses. From them it will derive the strength to win, and in the course of struggle will transform them. What China offers to the world is a new model of revolution. In France and Russia, the fermenting social revolution gave impetus to the revolutionary parties, but the social revolution itself was not well organized. China preaches the organization of the social revolution itself, and specifically that of the revolution on the land. It also provides a model of postrevolutionary organization based on a cadre led Party. There already is evidence that the Chinese model, whether by emulation or the force of historical circumstances, is being repeated, notably in Cuba and Algeria.

Despite failures in many areas, the over-all record of Communist China's performance in the past decade and a half has been one of great success. A country wracked by chaos has been transformed into a powerful nation-state. The Chinese have already gone a long way on the road to industrialization and modernization. The Chinese Communist organizational model clearly is not without its demonstration effect. It offers an approach to organization quite different from that of the West or even of the Soviet Union. Its attractions are not so much in the industrial field, where its greatest successes have been achieved with essentially Soviet type methods, but in organizing a poor backward country, holding it together, preventing bureaucratization, and achieving basic social changes.

It is no coincidence that the origins of Chinese Communist organization have been essentially military, arising from guerrilla-type struggle. All civilized societies have armies, but normally they remain dichotomous to society. Devices are fashioned to keep the wall standing between military organization and civil society. There have been periods in world history when attempts have been made to militarize society, but never with the means available to contemporary society. The old separation of military organization and civil society is breaking down in many parts of the world. This means that a new form of civil organization is challenging both traditional and modern bureaucratic organizations. Political parties in many one-party countries are increasingly taking on a military cast, and are operating according to organizational principles different from those of the Max-Weber-model. Perhaps the Chinese model of organization is transitional, perhaps it serves a purpose which, once achieved, will lead to bureaucratization. On the other hand, there is enough evidence from stable Western societies to indicate that total routinization is not the fate of all organization. Innovative managerial leaders sometimes suddenly appear again in a context of extreme routinization, and a dormant institution turns back again into active organization. The Chinese have constructed a powerful and effective organization, but one that has in-built deterrents against bureaucratization. In theoretical terms, it constitutes a non-Weberian model of organization.

In the West, there has been an increasing stress on organizational integration during the past decades. Present-day managerial ideologies stress cooperation and human relations. Bureaucratization has emerged as a major stabilizing factor in industry. Despite the teachings of Max Weber, there is as yet no certitude that bureaucratization will inevitably lead to stabilization and integration. What appears to me much more plausible is that organization remains Janus-faced, that its rational and integrative aspects remain inherent in it and in contradiction to each other. In China, the Party has evolved as a mechanism to keep contradictions in organization alive, to prevent routinization and excessive bureaucratization. The institutionalization of organization has progressed much farther in the advanced Western countries than in China, but I doubt that one can say that organization has made a decisive transition to institution. Economic competition, for example, demands managerial leadership in contrast to mere bureaucratic expertise. Organization will survive if it retains its leadership capacities and yet rests on a basis of continuity for which bureaucratization can serve as an indicator. As with a true elite, effective organization must perform adequately and also be supported by the social system. This is not a static, but a constantly shifting, conflict-ridden situation. Organization is made up of many parts. There are the tendencies toward routinization and integration that come from the administrative bureaucracy. But there are also countertendencies toward active leadership that come from managers who sense the challenge coming from the outside, and countertendencies of protest that come from below where there is unwillingness to accept routinization on the terms offered.

Even a cursory glance at the writings of the Chinese Communists will reveal their acute concern with problems of organization. In earlier decades, Chinese intellectuals wrote about socialism, anarchism, and the nature of the world and society. This made for an intellectual liveliness that has since disappeared. But few of the intellectual great men of that time had the slightest notion about the true problems of organization. By the time of Yenan, "theory" had been canonized, and the Chinese Communists turned their attention to "practice," namely organization and action. One might say that almost the entire literature of Chinese communism since Yenan has revolved around these two questions.

There is little in the traditional literature of China that prepares the researcher for grappling with Communist China. One can look far and wide in the traditional literature for discussions on leadership, whereas the literature of Communist China often consists of nothing else. In preparing the manuscript of this book, I was repeatedly impressed how little "Chinese" it appears to be. Where is China in all these processes? Chinese culture has not disappeared, but China's traditional social system has. Revolutionary changes, which began more than a century ago and were brought to completion by the Communists, have profoundly altered the substance and form of Chinese society.

There is indeed a new China — a China of organization. This complex struggle, to create and impose structures of organization on the country, is the subject of this book.

The Political Economy of the
Tropical Far East

J. S. FURNIVALL

A meeting of the Society was held on May 6, 1942, the Right Hon. Lord Hailey, G.C.S.I., G.C.M.G., G.C.I.E., in the Chair.

In introducing the speaker, the Chairman said: I would like to welcome on your behalf Mr. Furnivall, who after some twenty years' service in Burma has retired and given himself largely to the study of economic questions in the Far East. I have had the pleasure of reviewing his book on the Netherlands East Indies. A knowledge of development in the Dutch colonies is of fundamental importance to all students of colonial

From *Journal of the Royal Central Asian Society*, Vol. 29 (1942). Reprinted by permission of Kraus Reprint Limited. Footnotes taken from J. S. Furnivall, *Netherlands India* (Cambridge, Eng.: The University Press, 1944; New York: The Macmillan Co., 1944), pp. 446–464.

J. S. FURNIVALL (1878–1960) was a civil servant in Burma from 1902 until his retirement in 1931. After 1931, he continued his scholarly work on South-East Asia, and especially on Burma. He taught at Cambridge University between 1935 and 1942. His principal works are *An Introduction to the Political Economy of Burma* (1931), *Netherlands India: A Study of Plural Economy* (1939), *Educational Progress in South East Asia* (1943), *Colonial Policy and Practice: A Comparative Study of Burma* (1956), and *The Governance of Modern Burma* (1959).

affairs. Mr. Furnivall's work deserves the most careful study; the reader will obtain from it a much clearer impression of the modern situation and modern economics of the Dutch Netherlands East Indies than from any other source I know.

You have kindly asked me to talk to you this afternoon about the Tropical Far East — the region extending from Burma through Thailand (Siam) and French Indo-China to the Philippines, and from Formosa in the north to Netherlands India in the south. That is a wide survey. In Netherlands India alone there are over 200 peoples speaking different tongues, and in Burma nearly 150; altogether there must be well over a thousand peoples, and if I am to deal with all of them I can allow no more than about two seconds to each. Obviously the task would be impossible if there were not something common to all these countries, and it is only because they have, in my opinion, a fundamental similarity that I have ventured on so wide a theme. That common link, I would suggest, may be found in the political and economic structure of their society; in other words, in their political economy. The term "political economy" is out of fashion; nowadays one talks of economics. But it is so far out of fashion that we can perhaps use it in a new sense, or rather in the original sense. I quite agree that certain economic principles are independent of social and political forms, yet, when dealing with the wealth of certain nations rather than with general principles, it would seem well to insist that their political economy is what concerns us, and I know no other term so apt.

The theme is wide, and I would like therefore to define somewhat closely the general purpose of this paper. First, I wish to establish that, common to all these countries of the Tropical Far East, there is a distinctive form of society with a characteristic political and economic constitution — a characteristic political economy; then, to trace the evolution and essential properties of this economy; and, finally, and very briefly, to examine its bearing on some urgent problems. But I must deal with the whole theme very briefly. . . .

SOCIAL CONSTITUTION

The outstanding feature of the social constitution of the Tropical Far East is that everywhere Western Powers have come to exercise dominion over Eastern peoples, or, at least, as in Thailand, a large measure of economic control. I propose to examine first the native element, then the Western element, and then the effect of contact between East and West.

(a) *The Native Element.* Over the whole region there is a similarity of tropical climate; the common racial stock is Indonesian, overlaid with Mongol elements; and rice and fish are the staple foods. Under native rule the basis of the social order was the family, supporting itself by domestic agriculture, and living in a small hamlet where most of the people were akin; the land was a family affair, and the women played a larger part in family affairs than in either India or China. Above the hamlet social relations were personal, based on the matrilineal or patrilineal stem rather than on the village; the political organization was genealogical rather than geographical, tribal rather than territorial.

From the beginning of the Christian era this common pattern of social life was enriched, except in the remoter tracts, by strands of culture from the ancient civilizations of India and China, and everywhere it followed a similar course of evolution. In general, the main lines of political development seem to have been due to the influence of Indian colonists, who for many centuries were founding settlements all along the coast from Burma to Annam and also in the archipelago. In all the more advanced societies there evolved a dual political organization, comprising distinct central and local elements. The central administrative system was purely official, radiating out from the person of the ruler. This was linked up with the people through a local organization in which an hereditary official was at once a servant of the central government and a chieftain among his own people. That was the typical system of administration everywhere, and it lasted up to, and for some time after, the introduction of Western rule.

Despite, however, the strong Indian influence, not on political organization only but on religion and general culture, there are certain features of Indian life that everywhere were obstinately rejected. Everywhere the women have great freedom; in Java, where three centuries of Islam have succeeded a thousand years or more of Hinduism, the women are freer in some ways than in Buddhist Burma. Everywhere the people rejected the central institution of Hinduism — caste; even in Bali, which is Hindu to the present day, the caste system is merely nominal. And everywhere the people held to their own traditions of land tenure; even where Indian influence worked so strongly as in Java it is still possible to recognize the general characters of Indonesian land tenure, and the main features of Indonesian tenures are exactly described in the technical terms of land tenure in Burma. The social organization was not, as in India, built on caste and land, but on personal relations, often — though inaccurately — termed quasi-feudal. It would be easy to site many other features common to the whole region in letters, architecture, sculpture, music, drama, but we may pass over these more superficial characters; the status of women, land tenure, and class relations go to the root of social life, and the resemblance in these matters argues sufficiently a fundamental similarity.

One matter deserves close attention: the preference for personal relations rather than caste as the basis of social organization. This had grave consequences. In India, caste has to some extent protected the Hindu social system against the solvent influence of Western individualism; in the Tropical Far East, society has no such protection. Again, with a social organization based on personal relations, differences of race or religion tended to give society a plural character, reflected in its political constitution. Everywhere social and political relations were personal, not legal, and authority was personal, based on will and not on law. King and people had privileges and duties, resting on custom and sanctioned by religion; but no one had any legal rights and there were no legal restrictions on obligations; both person and property, land and people, were equally at the disposal of the ruler. The whole social organization rested on religion, personal custom, and duties. That, in brief, was the general character of the Tropical Far East on its first contact with the West in the morning of the modern world.

(b) *The Western Element.* It is, I suppose, superfluous to argue that the Western Powers which have come to exercise dominion in the Tropical Far East likewise had a fundamental unity. I do not suggest that Portuguese and Spaniard, Dutch, English, French, and American are all alike. All had their distinctive national character which was an invisible export on every ship from Europe. Saigon, Batavia, Rangoon, though all Western towns in Eastern lands, are as different as French, Dutch, and English. Similarly, each ruling Power has stamped its own imprint on its system of administration in the tropics. But the West has — or had — much in common in a civilization derived from Greece and Rome under the vitalizing force of Christianity. On its first contact with the East, the rebirth of reason had newly liberated fresh sources of material power by the rationalization of economic life; from that time onwards there has been a growing tendency to base economic relations on reason, impersonal law, and rights. This much the West has had in common, despite national diversity.

(c) *The Effect of Contact.* Wherever a Western Power has gained dominion in the Tropical Far East, or even, as in Thailand, has gained a large measure of economic control without actual political sovereignty, contact has been established between these two contrary principles of social life: between the Eastern system, resting on religion, personal custom, and duties, and the Western system, resting on reason, impersonal law, and rights. Contact has been established with different objects and in different ways, but everywhere with very similar results.

The mode of contact has been determined by the Western Powers, mainly with reference to their economic advantage. But the conception of economic advantage has changed with time and circumstances. Two alternative lines of policy were open: one was to build on the Eastern principle of authority or will, the other was to substitute the Western principle of law. The Dutch, in the days of the Company and later under the Culture System, aimed at tribute chiefly in the form of export crops. They could obtain these only by help of the native chieftains, and this required a system of indirect rule based on the Eastern principle of personal authority. The British, after the Industrial Revolution, aimed at trade, at selling British manufactures. They could sell them only if the cultivators had money to spend on British goods; it was to their interest, therefore, to substitute paid service for compulsion, to leave the cultivator free to grow what paid him best, and to encourage the use of money both in commerce and taxation. The native chieftains were no longer required as agents of compulsion, and the exercise of their authority on Eastern lines prejudiced the new Western system of economic freedom and the rule of law; they were not only useless but a hindrance, and, during the nineteenth century, direct rule came to be accepted as the normal type of colonial government. But, towards the end of the century, economic relations between East and West took a new turn; the West acquired a new interest in the production of tropical commodities — in rubber, oil, tin, and so on — and indirect rule once again came into favour under the style of the dual mandate.

Yet, in spite of this diversity of aims and of administrative systems, everywhere the result was pretty much the same. Everywhere the organic structure of Eastern society has been drained of vital force and, in place of it, there has been set up the complex economic and administrative machinery of the modern West. And everywhere this double process of disintegration and reconstruction has stamped the Tropical Far East with its most striking feature: a medley of various peoples — European, Chinese, Indian, and Native. It is in the strictest sense a medley, a mixture; for they mix but do not combine. Each group holds by its own religion, its own culture and language, its own ideas and way of life. As individuals they meet together; but only in the market-place, in buying and selling. Under native rule the social organization had a plural character; under Western rule it has been transformed into what may be termed a plural society, with different sections of the community living side by side but separately within the same political unit. Everywhere in the Tropical Far East — under Spanish, Dutch, British, French, or American rule; among Filipinos, Annamese, Javanese, Malays, or Burmans; whether the objective of the ruling power has been tribute, trade, or production; under direct rule as under indirect — the outstanding and obvious result of contact between East and West has been the evolution of a plural society.[1]

EVOLUTION OF THE PLURAL SOCIETY

It should, I think, throw light on the nature of the plural society if we examine the circumstances of its evolution. It is important, in the first place, to notice that it has evolved and not been planned; only in a very small degree is it a product of design, but it has come about by the play of quasi-natural forces.

When Europeans took over the government in the Tropical Far East, whether they aimed at tribute or trade, they wanted to increase production; and Western intervention created a demand for certain forms of economic

[1] In *Netherlands India* (Cambridge, Eng.: The University Press, 1944), p. 446, Furnivall defines a plural society as "a society . . . comprising two or more elements or social orders which live side by side, yet without mingling, in one political unit," and comments: "In this matter Netherlands India is typical of tropical dependencies where the rulers and the ruled are of different races: but one finds a plural society also in independent states, such as Siam, where Natives, Chinese and Europeans have distinct economic functions, and live apart as separate social orders. Nor is the plural society confined to the tropics; it may be found also in temperate regions where, as in South Africa and the United States, there are both white and coloured populations. Again, one finds a plural society in the French provinces of Canada, where two peoples are separated by race, language and religion, and an English lad, brought up in an English school, has no contact with French life; and in countries such as Ireland where, with little or no difference of race or language, the people are sharply divided in their religious allegiance. Even where there is no difference of creed or colour, a community may still have a plural character, as in Western Canada, where people of different racial origin tend to live in distinct settlements and, for example, a Northern European cannot find work on the railway, because this is reserved for 'Dagoes' or 'Wops.' And in lands where a strong Jewish element is regarded as alien, there is to that extent a plural society. Thus Netherlands India is merely an extreme type of a large class of political organizations." [Ed.]

activity in which foreigners — Europeans, Chinese, Indians — had advantages over the natives. Naturally, one may say, foreigners, attracted by the prospect of good money, came in to meet the demand. Let us look at one or two examples of the working of this process in Burma. Burma was conquered with troops from India, and, when the troops first occupied the country, there was a demand for roads and buildings. The engineers came with the troops from Madras; they did not know Burmese, and the Burmans did not know what was wanted. It was much less trouble to employ Indian contractors and coolies than to learn Burmese and train Burmans; also the Indian, with a lower standard of living, was cheaper in actual money than the Burman. Later, it was found still cheaper to import Indian convicts instead of coolies. There was only one urban occupation in which Burmans could compete with Indians; almost every Burman was literate, and it was much less trouble to teach Burmans how to print than to teach Indians Burmese, so that, up to the present day, much of the printing trade is in Burmese hands. Otherwise, in urban occupations, the Indian had an advantage over the Burman; on the other hand, the Burman had the advantage in cultivation. Thus, by the ordinary working of the economic process of natural selection by the survival of the cheapest, the Burman was pushed out into the rice land and the jungle, while the towns, in more direct contact with the modern world, were crowded with a medley of foreigners.

The course of events was similar throughout the Tropical Far East, and everywhere there is a division of labour along racial lines. The typical native is a cultivator or a clerk; the Chinaman or Indian is an artisan or else, as moneylender, broker, or retailer, acts as middleman between the native and the European capitalist. Even within the major groups there are subsections with particular functions. Wherever Indians are numerous, one class will be engaged in money-lending, another in coffee shops, another in tailoring, one or more distinct classes in the police, and even among the coolies some classes specialize on earthwork, others as coolies in the mills. That is not merely an expansion of Indian caste tradition, for among the Chinese one finds a similar correlation between class and function. It has come about merely through the economic process of the survival of the cheapest. That is at work always, everywhere, and in many respects there is nothing unusual in the conditions of the Tropical Far East. At different times America, Africa, Australia have been flooded with immigrants, and among these immigrants there has been a tendency towards a racial differentiation of function. But elsewhere immigration has been brought under control; where it was of such a character, or on such a scale, that the immigrants could not by appropriate measures be absorbed into the general community it has been restricted or stopped. Thus it is no sufficient explanation of the plural society in the Tropical Far East to say that it has come into existence by the working of economic forces; we must examine why these forces were not controlled. The course of social evolution will, I think, suggest an answer.

Native rule was, on the whole, the kind of government that the people liked, and did what they wanted in a way they understood. It was neither very strong nor very stable, but it stood on its own feet, deriving its authority from its subjects, and was an organic expression of native social life that lived in virtue of its inherent vitality. But it did not do what Europeans wanted, and, to get what they wanted, they had to take over the government. In the first instance, they tried to get what they wanted through native chieftains who would comply with their requirements. Outwardly there seemed little change; but, in fact, the whole native political organization was subverted; the chieftains no longer stood on their own feet deriving their authority from below, but hung down from above, deriving their authority from their European overlords. That in itself drained the vitality of native social life. But the process did not stop there. It was not sufficient for Europeans to get what they wanted; they wanted to get it in their own way, and only in their own way could they get all they wanted. Often the units of native rule were illogical, inconvenient. It is absurd, for example, to have one county the size of Yorkshire and another the size of Rutland. Efficiency, common sense, still more, economy, demanded uniformity, and the territorial limits of traditional organic communities were readjusted to suit administrative convenience. Moreover, the system of governing through native chieftains had its disadvantages; and, either alongside, or in place of, the hereditary chieftains, a new administrative system was built up on Western lines. Thus, by degrees, but more or less completely, the whole edifice of native society collapsed, leaving no organic unit higher than the village. That was the first, or political, stage in the disintegration of society: the country was broken up into villages. Above the village there was a vast Western superstructure of administrative and economic machinery, continually growing more elaborate. It gave, on the whole, the kind of government that Europeans liked, and did what they wanted in a way they understood. But it did not do what the natives wanted or work in a way they understood; it had no roots in the soil of native life.

This process of political disintegration, the break-up of the organic social structure into isolated villages, led further to a process of social dissolution, the break-up of the village into individuals. This also was due in part to quasi-rational principles of administration. At very much the same time, and for very similar reasons, the Dutch in Java and the British in Burma were readjusting village boundaries to promote administrative efficiency. In both countries efficiency declined and the policy was reversed, but the attempt to put Humpty Dumpty together again had very little success. It is easy to cut down a tree; time and nature are required for it to grow. But that is only one example of the manner in which the village was converted from an organic unit of society into an instrument of foreign rule; sometimes merely for administrative convenience in the collection of revenue or the suppression of crime, sometimes with the best intentions of enhancing welfare, but with no less deplorable results.

But at the same time that the village was being tinkered with from outside, corporate life within the village was being sapped by the victory of individual demand over social demand. Perhaps I should explain what I mean by the term "social demand." One might perhaps define it as the economic aspect of social will. Take, for example, sanitation. If any town or village in England wants better sanitation, it can spend more on conservancy, either by putting a farthing on the rates or by spending less on roads or street lighting. There is a collective demand that the economist can measure with his supply and demand curves and schedules. Between collective and individual demand there is a conflict, and at periodical elections people can decide whether they would rather have better conservancy or more money in their pocket. Collective demand is only one form of social demand. In the East, social demand often reserves a patch of jungle close to the village as a public convenience; it would cost less to cut fuel there rather than further off, but social demand, enforced by village custom, forbids; or one might say rather that the idea of cutting fuel there does not occur to anyone.

Not so very long ago these primitive arrangements sufficed, or were suffered, in Rangoon. But timber was scarce, fuel was costly, in a mixed population there was no barrier of public opinion, and it occurred to someone that a valuable source of fuel was being left unworked; individual demand prevailed over social demand and the scrub jungle began to disappear. Some Europeans thought they had suffered long enough and agitated for modern sanitation. After long consideration of various costly schemes, the Commissioner passed orders that no one should cut fuel near the town. But law is no substitute for social demand. The orders were ineffective, and before long improved conservancy arrangements had to be introduced. But because a social demand for them has not been fostered they are costly and unsatisfactory.

Let me take one more instance of the failure of social demand. So far as I know, there is no law against the use of rickshaws in England. It is not necessary. Rickshaws might be cheaper than taxis, but we would rather walk than use them. The individual demand for cheap conveyances is overborne by the social demand for human decency. When I first went out to the East there were no rickshaws in Burma or in Java. Now there are hundreds of them in Rangoon, drawn by Madrasi coolies. A rickshaw is a flimsy thing, but, apparently, it lives longer than a rickshaw coolie. The life of a rickshaw coolie is put at four to five years — unless it is cut short when he jerks like a snipe in front of an approaching motor-car. He is, in fact, a nuisance to car owners, and many Europeans in Rangoon, partly on humanitarian grounds, would gladly see rickshaws abolished. But they are owned by Chinamen, used by Burmans, and drawn by Indians. Even in the old days, when Government could tread on people's toes with fewer apologies, any proposal to abolish rickshaws would have raised a hubbub in the press. Now such a proposal is quite impracticable. All classes alike have an economic interest in the retention of rickshaws, but there is no common standard of social decency, no social demand that can be mobilized against them. One could not get rid of rickshaws from Rangoon. Yet there are none in Java. The Dutch, partly on political grounds — they wanted no more Chinamen — partly on humanitarian grounds — they disliked this method of reducing the surplus Javanese population — refused to admit the rickshaw. And one result is now one can travel all over Batavia in excellent native-driven taxis, even more cheaply than one can travel by rickshaw in Rangoon.

These are merely isolated instances of a process that has been acting everywhere and always, and I would like to discuss it in more general terms. In all human affairs, so far at least as they are rational, we can trace the working of one process — the economic process of natural selection by the survival of the cheapest. Ordinarily, everyone would pay twopence rather than threepence for the same thing; that is a matter of universal common sense, irrespective of race or creed. There may, in particular circumstances, be reasons to the contrary; people may willingly pay more for home products or for goods free of sweated labour.[2] But such arguments rest on national or moral grounds and are valid only for people of the same nation or with the same moral standards; the economic process works without regard to such considerations. Within limits it is a powerful instrument of progress; but it tends to eliminate from human intercourse all values that are not purely material, and even in material affairs it responds only to immediate advantage. It seemed cheaper to employ Indian coolies and convicts on road-making in Burma, but twenty years later the Commissioner had to report that "there are no roads, canals, tanks, or other works in the interior," and even after a hundred years conditions in that part of the country were very much the same. It seemed cheaper to employ Indians (and, again, convicts) in the printing of English in Burma, but printing has remained so costly and unsatisfactory that even to-day much of the English printing and some of the Burmese printing is done in India. The cutting of fuel near Rangoon and the introduction of rickshaws exemplify the working of the economic process without regard to public health or human life, and in both cases the final result was unsatisfactory even on economic criteria. The economic process, unless controlled, leads finally not to progress but to degeneration.

In actual life the working of the economic process is controlled in one of two ways. One is by the operation of the economic motive, the desire for individual material advantage. But this, usually, is anti-social. Within recent years there have been many illustrations of control exercised in the interests of individuals. The justification alleged for the successive restrictions imposed on rubber, sugar, tin, and tea was that, if the industries were left uncontrolled, they would be ruined by "cut-throat competition." Such restrictions may conceivably be in the general interest, but they are not conceived in the general interest; their object, formally and directly, is to keep up prices in the interests of producers. Moreover, the economic motive, as such, disregards non-economic values, and is therefore in the long run an agent of degeneration. Powerful interests have been concerned to protect existing stocks of rubber, tin, oil, and sugar from the competition of additional supplies, but there have been no such interests at work to protect native society against the "cut-throat competition" of foreign immigrants, or to maintain moral standards against attrition by economic forces.

The other check on the economic process is social will, insisting that man

---

[2] "In a unitary society, the working of the economic process is controlled by social will, and if the cheaper vender cuts the price by methods which offend the social conscience, he will incur moral and perhaps legal penalties" (*Netherlands India*, p. 449). [Ed.]

does not live by bread alone. This restrains economic forces by appealing to some principle of social welfare transcending the domain of economics. Formerly in the Tropical Far East, when rule was based on personal relations, the social will, taking effect through custom sanctioned by religion, provided adequately according to local standards for the general well-being; it reserved, for example, the patch of jungle that we have mentioned. But in protecting society against harmful change it tended to prevent *all* change, and became a barrier against economic progress. That is largely why these countries were unable to resist Western Powers, representing a social order based on more secure foundations, and able therefore to allow greater scope to reason in the direction of affairs. Western society could run the risk of individualism. But even in Western society economic forces are still controlled by social will.

This may be embodied in the form of law, or, as a collective demand, can be measured in the form of rates and taxes. But it also acts, as in the East, subconsciously, more often and more strongly than we are apt to recognize. It might, for instance, pay to start a rickshaw service in London, but, among other things, the social demand for decent life forbids; no one would even think of doing so, any more than formerly the oriental villager thought of encroaching on common land. But in the East, social demand has been unable to prevail against individual demand, and there has been no effective barrier against the working of the economic process. Everywhere economic forces, working through individual demand, tend to create a mixture of races; ordinarily these forces are kept under control by social demand. But in the Tropical Far East the social organization has broken down, individual demand has prevailed over social demand, economic forces have had free play, and the result is the plural society. Let us attempt, then, to analyse the distinctive characters, political and economic, of such a society.

Political Aspect. Looking at the political aspect of a plural society, we find three characteristic features: taking the society as a whole, it comprises separate racial groups; taking each section as a whole, it is an aggregate of individuals rather than a corporate unit; and looking at each individual we see that his social life is incomplete. Let me briefly develop these three points. The social life of everyone is incomplete. The European, for example, looks at social problems in the East, political and economic, from the standpoint of a capitalist and employer of labour and not from the standpoint of a citizen. At the other extreme, the native, so far as political and economic problems impinge upon his consciousness, looks on them from the standpoint of the peasant. Under native rule the people lived within a narrow world, but they had the freedom of their world, and their cultural horizon was co-extensive with its limits; Western rule brought them into economic contact with a wider world, but closed down their horizon to the limits of their immediate interests as cultivators; in a wider world their life was narrower than before.

Again, each section or group is not a social unit but an aggregate of individuals. To Europeans this may be most obvious in the European section: people are continually on the move; there are no children in the home; the club and not the home is the centre of social life; and everyone looks forward, more or less eagerly, to returning "home." They work in the East but do not live there. In the other foreign groups conditions are very similar; among Indians, for example, caste loses its validity, and census officers in Burma have found it impossible to compile useful returns of caste. And in all accounts of native society we read of the breakdown of corporate village life. In Indo-China, it has been said, there is nothing but the Government and twenty-three million individuals. The same is true, in greater or less degree, of all these countries.

Looking at the society as a whole, as a collocation of separate communities, the closest analogy is with a confederation of allied states, united by treaty or within the limits of a formal constitution, merely for certain common ends, but otherwise, in matters outside the terms of union, each living its own life. Yet there are notable points of difference. In a confederation the component elements are segregated each within its own territorial limits; there is contact between the states but not between individual members of different states; the union is voluntary and the terms of union are definite and limited; finally, if the yoke of union should become intolerable, a remedy is open in secession. But in a plural society the sections are not segregated; the members of the different sections are intermingled and meet as individuals; the union is not voluntary but imposed by the ruling power and the working of economic circumstances; and the union cannot be dissolved without the whole society relapsing into anarchy.

Like a confederation, a plural society is a business partnership rather than a family concern, and the social will common to all groups and holding them together is restricted to their common interests. It might seem that the common interest should be strong; for a dissolution of the partnership means the bankruptcy of all the partners. But it is strong only in so far as this common interest is recognized. The only example known to me of a stable plural society is Hindu society in India. Here, as in the Tropical Far East, separate groups or classes have come to exercise distinct economic functions. But in India, caste has a religious sanction in the Hindu religion; in the Tropical Far East, there is no immediate prospect of Europeans, Chinese, and others being turned into Hindus. There are castes without the cement of a religious sanction; few recognize that in fact they have common material interests, but most see that on many points their material interests are opposed, and on these points economic forces are always tending to create friction.

Economic Aspect. Let us turn, then, to consider the plural society in its economic aspect; rather, perhaps one should say, in its economic aspects. For in economic affairs everything has two aspects, according as it is seen from the standpoint of the consumer or the standpoint of the producer.

The economic constitution naturally reflects the political constitution, and the defect of social will finds expression in the weakness of social demand. Social demand, like social will, is partial. The European demands cheap labour and cheap produce without regard to the welfare of the community as a whole; the native demands well-paid jobs without reference to efficiency. Neither can envisage social problems as a whole. Again, within each section individual demand prevails over social demand. And, thirdly, taking the society as a whole, there is no common standard of welfare, and therefore no social demand for general welfare.

If, on the other hand, we look at the plural society from the standpoint of production, we find that here also it has a distinctive character. Everywhere the working of economic forces makes for tension between groups with contrary economic interests: between town and country, industry and agriculture, capital and labour. But in the Tropical Far East this tension is aggravated by a corresponding cleavage along racial lines.[3] Thus, not only are the relations between the sections confined to the economic sphere, but, even within that sphere, there is no common standard of conduct other than the standards that are prescribed by law. The European has his own standard of decency of what, even in business, "is not done"; so also has the Chinaman, the Indian, and the native. They all have their own ideas as to what is right and proper; but on most points they have different ideas. Yet they are all subject to the working of the economic process, and all, in greater or less degree, respond to the economic motive. Thus, in the plural society of the Tropical Far East the economic motive is the highest factor common to all groups, and tends to prevail in its crudest form. This is emphasized by Dr. Boeke, Professor of Tropical Economy in Leiden. In the East, he says, "there is materialism, rationalism, individualism, and a concentration on economic ends far more complete and absolute than in homogeneous Western lands; a total absorption in the exchange and market; a capitalist structure with the business concern as subject, far more typical of capitalism than one can imagine in the so-called 'capitalist' countries, which have grown slowly out of the past and are still bound to it by a hundred roots." He was speaking with especial reference to the European group, but his remarks are true of all sections, so far as they come into contact, directly or indirectly, with the economic forces newly liberated under Western rule. In the first half of the last century economists praised the Economic Man; during the latter half they explained that he did not exist. Unfortunately, they were mistaken. He was cast out of Europe, but found refuge in the East; now, I fear, we see him returning, with seven devils worse than himself.

This emphasis on the material aspect of life in the Tropical Far East has political reactions. For it is strongest in those sections that are most closely associated with capitalist interests. The native, on the other hand, is especially

---

[3] "This distribution of production among racial castes aggravates the inherent sectionalism of demand; for a community which is confined to certain economic functions finds it more difficult to apprehend the social needs of the country as a whole. In a homogeneous society the soldier looks at social problems from the standpoint of the soldier, the merchant looks at them as a merchant and the cultivator as a cultivator; yet at the same time they regard such problems from the standpoint of a common citizenship, and the soldier, merchant, or cultivator cannot wholly disregard the views and interests of other classes. In every community there is a conflict of interest between town and country, industry and agriculture, capital and labour; but the asperity of conflict is softened by a common citizenship. In a tropical dependency, however, the conflict between rival economic interests tends to be exacerbated by racial diversity. Thus, in British India, one finds Europeans in the towns, directing industry and owning capital, and Natives up-country, engaged in agriculture and owning little but their labour" (*Netherlands India*, p. 451). [Ed.]

identified with labour. Hence the common tendency of capitalists to regard labour merely as an instrument of production encourages them to regard the native merely as an instrument of production. Native labour is ignorant and unorganized, economic forces are paramount, and the power which ordinarily accrues to capital through the working of economic forces is enhanced. Capital is far stronger in the Tropical Far East than in the West. And because the maintenance of capitalist control is, or seems to be and — this is important — is believed to be the peculiar interest of the ruling power, no remedy is possible except by dissociating political and capitalist control.[4]

Here then, I suggest, are the essential features of the political economy of the Tropical Far East. There is a plural society in which, on the one hand, economic forces are more active than in Europe; and, on the other hand, demand is more feeble. Under native rule the social organization was weak and unstable; the machinery of Western rule is stronger and — to outward view — more stable; but the organization of the community for social life has been transformed, more or less completely, into an economic system, organized like a factory for production. As Professor Boeke says, "there is a capitalist structure, with the business concern as subject." So long as the structure holds together it is stronger than the old social organization. But it can be held together only by external forces; without external support it must collapse and the whole system crumble into dust.

So far as this analysis is valid, it has, I venture to suggest, important consequences; it implies that in the Tropical Far East political and economic problems are quite different, different in kind, from those to which we are accustomed in the West. Here, in Europe, we can take social will for granted, and the central problem of applied political science is how best to ascertain and give effect to it; but in the Tropical Far East political science starts at an earlier stage, and the central problem is to organize a common social will. In the West we can take demand for granted, and the central problem of applied economic science is how best to organize supply; but in the Tropical Far East the central problem is to organize demand.

Current Problems.[5] These considerations may seem remote, academic, theoretical. Let me try very briefly to apply them to some problems due for solution, and long overdue. We may assume, perhaps, that the object of modern colonial policy is to make these countries of the Tropical Far East capable of independence; various formulas are used to describe — disguise — the object, but all will

---

[4] In *Netherlands India*, Furnivall summarizes as follows: "Plural economy differs then from a homogeneous economy firstly because, in place of a social demand common to the whole society, there are two or more distinct and rival complexes of social demand proper to each constituent element; secondly, by the grouping of production into castes; and, thirdly, by the further sectionalization of demand which follows when the social demand, proper to each constituent element, ceases to embrace the whole scope of social life and becomes concentrated on those aspects of social life falling within its separate province" (p. 452). [Ed.]

[5] Furnivall's suggestions for action, written in 1942, are in many respects dated. Yet we retain this section because it gives, in preview, many of the problems confronting, and policies followed by, an independent government. [Ed.]

be found on analysis to mean the same thing. It seems to be taken for granted that there are recognized stages on the path to independence: representative government, partly responsible government, and wholly responsible government. But this attractive programme shirks the difficulty inherent in the nature of a plural society. What is the representative government to represent — the people or foreign capital? And who constitutes the people? Are we to take into account only the natives, or should we include the foreign elements — European Indian, and Chinese? On any system that involves the counting of heads the natives will usually have a majority of votes. But how far *can* interests in mines, plantations, commerce be entrusted to a majority representing people who know nothing of industry, commerce, and the modern world? And how far *will* such interests consent to such a plan? An orderly progress towards independence through recognized stages assumes a common social will; in a plural society with no common social will these "recognized stages" will mark only a disorderly progress towards anarchy. The plan has no relation to the facts.

Turn now to the economic problems. Everyone agrees that economic progress is desirable, that it needs technicians, and that native technicians will be cheapest. So the usual policy is to *supply* technicians — cautiously, expensively, and with great care not to create a surplus in excess of the demand. You will never do anything in that way. Create or organize a *demand* for technicians, and lads — and lasses — will tumble over one another to be trained. India is often cited as a horrible example of the divorce between education and practical affairs. But it supplied the best instance that I know of successful vocational education. Nearly a hundred years ago the foundations of the modern educational system were laid down in the great Despatch of 1854. Among its recommendations was one for vocational instruction to remedy the lack of lawyers. Well, no one in India complains now of a lack of lawyers; not because we created a supply, but because we encouraged trade and therefore multiplied law courts, which created a demand for lawyers.

Or look at the other aspect of economic life, at welfare. It is generally assumed that instruction is an instrument of welfare. Yet, so long as Western education was merely an instrument of welfare, it spread very slowly in the East; teachers had to go out into the by-ways and hedges to get pupils. But as soon as it was realized that Western education might be profitable, there arose a demand for schools and teachers. And this demand created a supply. Or compare Java and Burma in respect of primary instruction. In Java the people do not want to have their children taught to read and the village schools can be filled only by "gentle pressure"; in Burma the people, already under native rule, as Buddhists, wanted their children to be taught, and in response to the demand there was a network of monastic schools over the whole country.

Here, then, is what I feel about many projects of Utopia in the Tropical Far East and elsewhere: that they have no relation to the facts. We do not arrive at the right answers because we do not ask the right questions. We are playing the old game of cross-questions and crooked answers. The examination candidate who does not answer the questions put to him is ploughed, however brilliantly he may write on things that the examiner does not want to know. We are now facing a practical examination in political economy, and unless we read the questions rightly we shall fail.

These, as I see it, are the questions: How can we organize a common social will? And how can we organize demand? [6] There is a Burmese proverb, "The cattle herd can ask questions that the Buddha alone can answer." Prudence would confine me to the rôle of cattle herd, but I will be rash enough to make a few suggestions, venturing only to plead that even foolish suggestions have their use as leading by a process of exclusion to wise ones.

The plural society, I say, has the nature of a confederation. Let us aim first at turning it into a closer union, into a federal society, by multiplying and strengthening the links between the several groups. Take just one example. In Java the Government fostered a commercial textile industry among the natives. Thus, during the depression, the flood of Japanese imports threatened not only Dutch but native manufacturers; both had a common interest in protecting the local market. That is only one instance of what might be attempted towards building a federal society. Again, the depression, and subsequently the present war, did much in Netherlands India towards turning capitalists into nationalists. And the history of rubber suggests what might be done towards turning nationalists into capitalists. Along some such lines it might not be impossible to create a common social will embracing all the sections in a federal society, leading finally perhaps to a unified society.

The second problem is how to organize demand. Take, for example, the demand for technicians. Require all Western enterprises to take out licenses, renewable only on condition of satisfactory progress in replacing management, staff, and employees with men of local origin. For the more difficult task of organizing a demand for welfare we might get useful hints from Dutch practice and experience in the use of civil service as social engineers and welfare officers.

All aspects of all these problems, however, require far greater knowledge than we now possess. We do not even know what we want to know. We need, then, some machinery by which all countries of the Tropical Far East could pool their knowledge and experience. This need might be met in part by constituting a local branch of a newly reconstituted League of Nations, in which all these countries, and the various interests and groups in all these countries, would be represented.

And the constitution of such a body should go far towards fostering goodwill, and would serve also as a guarantee of good faith. It might, I think, help to solve the problem of dissociating political and capitalist control. . . .

[6] "In a homogeneous society the basic problem of applied political science is how to provide most adequately for the expression of social will; in some circumstances this may best be achieved by the machinery of a representative assembly, in other circumstances by submission to a benevolent autocrat or to a dictator. But in a plural society the basic problem of political science is far more elemental; it is impossible to provide a vehicle for the expression of social will until there is a society capable of will, and the basic problem of political science in such a community is the integration of society. Dr. de Kat Angelino hints at this when he remarks that in normal conditions Society is the parent of the State, whereas in Netherlands India the pressing burden on the State is the creation of Society" (*Netherlands India*, pp. 462–463). [Ed.]

Political Myths of Colonization
and Decolonization in Africa

GEORGES BALANDIER

In Africa south of the Sahara, colonization was superimposed on societies that some anthropologists have described, and still describe, as being subject to the sovereignty of myth. For that reason many of these societies — for example, the Dogon of Western Sudan — are better known to us through the image projected by their myths than by an objective and direct study of their social organization and their social structures. In this case, indeed, myth appears to be the condition of all "profound understanding" — using an expression of Marcel Griaule and those who continue his work. Myth is considered to be the source of all knowledge, the model that successive generations refer to for the maintenance of the established order of things, a certain state of social relations, a certain blending of cultural themes. If we look at this from a different angle, we can say that, from this perspective, myth seems to incarnate or materialize itself at a certain time to constitute society and culture, while the continuing reference to myth, from generation to generation, makes it possible to keep things as they are. According to this viewpoint, myth imposes its rigid constraint to keep society and culture free from the vicissitudes of history.

It is also interesting to note that the interpretations that most frequently allude to the teachings of mythologies to explain social relationships are those that neglect the vicissitudes undergone by societies frequently and lazily described as "having no history." If, right from the outset, I refer to such a perspective, it is because it manifests a real devotion to myth, an attachment that distorts the facts and is incapable of grasping what is essential.

In societies that have only an oral tradition, as is the case for most pre-colonial African societies, myth undoubtedly has a conservative function. It contains, along with its particular symbolic trappings, a certain amount of knowledge. It is the equivalent of a Genesis; it more or less implies a theory of nature; it accounts for the appearance of man and for the emergence of culture, etc. All this is generally recognized. Myth, with its extensions into legend, is also a substitute for archives. It can recall the migrations and the distant adventures, evoke the primordial clans and their alleged founders. It can also suggest the conditions under which a system of political authority emerged. This is commonly acknowledged; but it seems to me (and this is useful for our purpose) that myth is much more than that. It comprises, even in these African societies, even before colonization, *an element of ide-*

Translated by Jean-Guy Vaillancourt from "Les Mythes politiques de colonisation et de décolonisation en Afrique," *Cahiers Internationaux de Sociologie*, Vol. XXXIII (July–December, 1962), pp. 85–96. Reprinted by permission of the author and Presses Universitaires de France éditeurs.

GEORGES BALANDIER is Professor at the Sorbonne and Director of Studies at L'Ecole Pratique des Hautes-Etudes. He is the author of *Le Tiers-Monde* (1957), *Sociologie actuelle de l'Afrique noire*, 2nd ed. (1963), and *La vie quotidienne au royaume de Kongo du XVIe au XVIIIe siecle* (1965). Among the translated works of this political anthropologist is *Ambiguous Africa: Cultures in Collision* (1966).

ology. It has a legitimizing function which the guardians of traditions, the holders and beneficiaries of authority, know very well how to utilize. This is precisely what B. Malinowski saw and recalled in a neglected study, *The Foundations of Faith and Morality.* There he suggests that myth must be viewed "as a social charter concerning the existing form of society with its system of distribution of power, privilege and property." This point of view, then, is not only my own; it is shared also by Malinowski. If one accepts it, one can understand how myth and political ideology are internally related; this permits an explanation of the change in the meaning of myth, from the classical sense of the term to the sense given it by G. Sorel.

After this brief summary, we must now consider the effects of colonization. Colonial intervention, with its various manifestations and in its different phases, has had important consequences for the life of African myths and legends. There are transformations and modifications which manifest, in mythical language, the vicissitudes and the problems posed to men and their society by the colonial situation. To facilitate the analysis of this we must distinguish various phases. I shall describe three phases which involve highly differentiated processes and illustrate various uses of myths.

The first phase is the recognition of the colonial situation: its interpretation and acknowledgment. Colonialism is experienced, and it must be faced and more or less put in its place. The second phase is the reaction to colonial domination. The third phase is the demand for independence and the transition from myth to political ideology and then to political doctrine. Having presented my outline, I must add the two following remarks. Every colonial administration has aimed at establishing a depoliticized regime or has emphasized maximum depolitization of all the expressions of native life. This effort to suppress political activity at the level at which it existed before colonization resulted in a genuine *phenomenon of transfer.* Consequently, political reactions against the colonial situation were expressed indirectly at first, for example, through new syncretist religious movements loaded with revolutionary implications. Surely, this is a transfer. The political reaction does not occur at the level at which it is expected, because the colonial administration has had as its goal, in every colonial regime, the freezing of the native political life. If this is so, it is understandable that the modern political efforts resulting from the colonial situation were first expressed through myths and that they protected themselves, in a sense, behind the veil of myths. This is a process of concealment which it is useful to uncover. I wanted to make these two points because they help the reader understand the choice of my examples and the mode of analysis that I intend to use.

I

Let us now look at the first stage: *myth and recognition of the colonial situation.* At first, colonization appears as an intrusion. It introduces people, goods, and values that are not only of foreign origin but in certain regards alien. So the colonized must "locate" these new agents and elements in his mental world; he must also "master" them as much as possible, to diminish the disorder and the perturbations that can result from this irruption. In this case, the transformed and adapted myth makes intelligible these disturbing factors, values, goods, and people that were ushered in by colonization. Besides, the ritual associated with the myth, or the imitation of ritual, in many ways gives the impression of a sure grasp over these alien and perturbing elements.

I would like to go beyond this very general statement by giving a few simple examples. Syncretism becomes a means of controlling and integrating values, and especially religious values. The Bwiti cult, which I studied among the Fang in Gabon, is one example among many others. This cult linked Christian themes to the mythical themes on which the main traditional cults are based. It has, on the other hand, attempted to compete for supremacy with missionary Christianity by presenting itself as a "major religion." This case illustrates how syncretism allows the natives to "capture," in a sense, the colonizer's values and eventually to compete with him.

As for the first material goods introduced by trading, we notice that their use was, by and large, in the first period of colonization, *symbolic*. These imported and highly valued goods were linked to the material symbols that guaranteed matrimonial exchanges. They became signs of authority and prestige for the chiefs and notables who in a way capitalized on them. These goods sometimes were exchanged in the struggle for prestige — struggles that could evoke the antagonistic dualism inherent in some of the myths. I have described this phenomenon in a recent issue of the *Cahiers Internationaux de Sociologie* in which I showed how, among the *Bilaba* of the people of Southern Cameroon, trading goods were used in a struggle for prestige and also in a "struggle for wealth" (using the expression of M. Mauss) that evoked the symbolism linked with the dualistic thought of the people of Southern Cameroon.

The partners introduced by colonization must be examined with greater care because they touch our subject more directly. The effigy, or image, of types of colonizers — the administrator, the merchant, in certain cases the missionary and even the anthropologist — was sometimes assimilated into the characters composing the society of masks. And here I can give as an example one of my colleagues who was doing research in Sudan, studying the productions of the society of masks of the Dogon; he was surprised to find that a recently made mask, whose meaning was not obvious, simply represented the anthropologist at work. In a certain way, a ritual control is thus exercised over esteemed personalities that are representative of the colonial society. This ritual control reverses in imagination the relations of subordination that exist in real life. The missionary, administrator, and trader who are represented as characters in such and such a society of masks are manipulated by those in charge of the association, while in everyday life, as long as the colonial situation is not abolished, the opposite occurs.

Still more significant: In the areas that have been more deeply affected by colonization — certain African cities — semi-ritual associations have often been created which are rough copies of the colonial society and its hierarchical functions. The literature devoted to these institutions is now rather abundant. It has revealed this imitation of colonial hierarchies. The will to parody is not absent from such innovation, but neither is the desire completely absent to compete with the colonizer by using his own methods. In certain cases — and that is the reason I report these facts here — this capture of white society, of its order and hierarchies, is accomplished through myth and ritual. I shall refer here to a well-known anthropological film by Jean Rouch entitled "Les maitres fous" ("The Mad Masters"). This document illustrates in a very precise manner this phenomenon to which I have just alluded. It describes the Haouka sect, which appeared in Niger after 1920 and then spread to Ghana in the thirties. The cult emphasizes the state of being possessed. This state appears as a game, at once tragic and burlesque, during which the members identify with the most diverse and most representative persons of rank in colonial society: the governor, the general, the guardsman, the locomotive engineer, etc. — as a matter of fact, with a whole series of characters who seem to be particularly typical of the social universe of the whites and of the civilization ushered in by the colonizers. In a sense, the members of the sect, through these practices, domesticate the powers unleashed by the colonizers and benefit, at the same time, from a real and effective therapy. I do not want to dwell any longer on this example since it is well known; I only wanted to report it, because it has some direct bearing on our subject.

For this first period, which is connected with what I have called the acknowledgment and acceptance of the colonial reality, it is advisable to point out some other processes. These are steps that reveal a crude understanding of the colonial situation; and this is what interests us in the phenomenon.

First, I shall mention the acknowledgment of the poverty of the colonized, in comparison with the colonizer. In certain cases a depressing awareness of material powerlessness and of poverty is expressed, at the level of myths, by themes presenting the colonized as *victims of an actual curse*. Let me give an example with which I am directly acquainted: that of the Fang of Gabon. These people have a legend of the Nsas, which was recorded during the last decades of the 19th century. This legend is interesting because one of its parts ascribes the poverty of the black man and the wealth of the white man to a genuine divine intervention. Allow me briefly to present a few of the expressions that help us understand the deep meaning of this text.

At one point, God (Nzame) is speaking to the black man and to the white man, and he tells them: "You, black man, get up and return to your wives and populate the earth, and you shall always remain nude. You, white man, you shall be rich, richer than you have ever been in your dreams." The meaning is not veiled. On one side is he who accumulates demographic capital only; on the other side, he who hoards all the material goods. As I have noted, this text was recorded near the end of the last century, at a time when the colonial situation was asserting itself with its constraints, its technological strength, its coveted manufactured goods. Later, the feeling of malediction will be attenuated, but the world of the colonizers will continue to be seen, and with an increased clearness, as the world of money and of material wealth. The Fang of Gabon, to whom I have just referred, will suggest, fifty years after having conceived the modern version of the Nsas legend, that they want to follow the "European way." That is their expression. And why? They answer: "To earn money and become powerful like the Europeans."

The Bakongo are another people that I have had the opportunity of studying in the field. The Bakongo around Brazzaville and Leopoldville, when they sing modern poems, express feelings identical to those of the Fang. One of these poems, used in their songs and dances, starts with the following words: "The white man has left Europe to make money, the white man came to Africa to get money." Behind these themes we can uncover the admission of material inferiority, the acknowledgment of the inequality of wealth, the recognition of the relationship that exists between the colonial situation and the seizure of money. It appears to be a crude understanding, as I have said before, of the reality of the colonial situation. And thus, slowly, the popular consciousness of the system of colonization advances.

II

We must now look at a more crucial stage; we come then to the second point mentioned: the *relationship between myth* and the *reaction against colonial domination*. Before the modern nationalist movements and independence movements were organized, the reactions against colonial constraints took various forms. In spite of their diversity, it is nevertheless possible to group them into a limited number of types, each one representing a particular mode of myth. Consequently, I would now like to look at certain types of reactions and to show their specific link with myth.

a) The first type, the first group of phenomena, is the process of *rehabilitation* of African cultures and style of life. By rehabilitation, we mean reinstating what has been challenged by the colonizer — a certain style of life, a certain cultural order, a certain organization of African societies. In this regard, it seems to me that the example of a few Christianized societies is the most revealing, the most striking. As a matter of fact, the Bible, which is considered to be the written myth of the white man, of the European colonizer, becomes the reference book for which Africans indoctrinated in Christian teachings find the *justification* of aspects of culture and social organization that are attributed to their state of "savagery." The Bible exhibits a certain number of customs — polygamy, taboos, sacrifices — that are highly valued by Africans but are nevertheless challenged by the missionaries and colonizers who have imposed their laws. By consulting the Bible, the written myth of the white man, the Africans discover some kinship with the people of the Book — a noble, undeniable kinship, which reinstates in their eyes their culture and their society.

Thus the Africans transform missionary teachings into an instrument of emancipation. The arguments of the missionary are turned not only against him but also against the entire colonial society. Jomo Kenyatta, the prestigious nationalist leader of Kenya, has referred to this reversal in *Facing Mount Kenya*, a book about the Kikuyu people. We could find many other examples, because this occurrence is commonplace; it is very widespread over a large portion of the black continent, from the equator to the cape. Another point must be made. In these popular movements, the reference to the biblical type of society plays the same role for the lowest stratum of slightly Christianized masses as the reference to ancient Egypt in certain intellectual circles of Africa. . . . We must realize that this position is the starting point of a militant mythology which develops gradually. This then is a first type of reaction.

b) A second type comprises *religious innovations with revolutionary goals*. These innovations, born of the colonial situation, can give rise to violent, short-term movements, which contain in embryo form some millennial themes. For example, from 1928 to 1929, a revolt took place in Upper-Sanaga in the Congo. It was fomented by a religious leader named Karinu, who predicted the expulsion of the Europeans, saying — and here I quote him — that he "had eaten their hearts." This expulsion would be followed by an unending era of abundance and wealth.

These religious innovations have often led to the creation of prophetic and messianic movements which have compelled recognition by their persistence. Some of them have existed in Africa south of the Sahara since the second half of the 19th century; others have persisted and flourished in central Africa, and especially in Congolese Africa, from 1920 right up to these last few years. These movements have developed a doctrine which is halfway between myth and ideology, a doctrine which is both militant and syncretic. I do not have the leisure to present here the texts which would justify this assertion. When a content analysis of these texts is made, the observation that I have just reported is strikingly confirmed. These religious innovations in Africa south of the Sahara, represent the *prehistory* of African nationalism. To understand the latter, it is necessary to consider phenomena in their entirety, before as well as after 1945, and at a level lower than that of modern leadership.

c) A third type of phenomena is the *popular revolts* which are directed against the colonizers and their indigenous allies, those who have been called the "collaborators" of colonialism. Here a few examples are necessary. We can point in particular to the revolt of the Bamikele in the Cameroon. It had some of the aspects of a *jacquerie* in the sense that it was directed against the chiefs who had misused their authority during the colonial period and who had taken advantage for many years of the opportunities offered them by the colonial economy. On the other hand, this Bamikele rebellion, aimed at the collaborators of colonization, occurred simultaneously with the most violent demonstrations of the most radical Cameroon nationalism. Thus it was both a peasant revolt, aimed at the "compromised" authorities, and a nationalist outburst that occurred in the midst of the most revolutionary nationalist activity.

But it seems to me that, in this third subdivision, the most significant example is that of the Mau-Mau movement, which spread in Kenya from May 1952 to the beginning of 1954. For one of my colleagues, the British anthropologist Max Gluckman, the Mau-Mau movement is a nihilistic enterprise born of despair. In the words of Gluckman, "It is a question of killing and of getting killed"; it is necessary to accept being destroyed, but one must first destroy the order that is no longer accepted and which cannot be changed. Nevertheless, it does not seem as if this subversive activity can be interpreted solely as an ultimate act of revolt, a suicidal revolt. It seems to me that in many respects this movement is also, and much more so, a revolution created by black peasants whose entire culture and hope had been taken away by the colonial system. In this case, the united weapons of myth, ritual, and magic are not superfluous. The tribal land is extolled, along with the ancestors that are buried in it; it is in the name of the tribal land of the ancestors that one agrees to sacrifice his life. The oath which was widely used by the Mau-Mau organizers — a traditional form of oath — binds irrevocably those who are inside the movement. Magic intervenes here, like in Madagascar, to lead the Mau-Maus to believe that the bullets from the guns of the colonizers will be changed to water; magic offers a remedy to material weakness by guaranteeing invulnerability. This insurrection failed, not only because of its material weakness, but also because it had not been conceived in terms of modern political subversion. It remained a force oriented towards an idealized past, the pre-colonization period, rather than a force oriented towards a precisely defined future. In a way, and this explains their failure, the Mau-Maus' revolt remained enclosed in mythical time and did not take place in consciously accepted and assumed historical time.

III

The Mau-Mau movement serves as a good introduction to my last point, which I shall be forced to present very briefly, *independence and transition from myth to political ideology*. One first fact is compelling. The political ideology, or the ideology with political implications, appears as soon as the demand for autonomy and then independence is organized. As soon as the national movements take form and are directed by a certain number of leaders, the political ideology begins to be constructed. It is articulated, for better or worse, more or less successfully, around the mythical themes of revolt or resistance which I have already commented upon.

At first, the initiative belongs to a minority with a so-called Western education, a minority preoccupied with the development of a cultural as well as a political liberation. Better still, in the case of African countries, for a certain period, the emphasis was on the first of these requirements, the cultural liberation, rather than on the second, the political liberation.

The most representative of these ideologies is the ideology of negritude. It was conceived by French-speaking Africans; it was, as a matter of fact, formulated theoretically by J. P. Sartre in a study entitled: *Orphée noir* (*Orpheus Negro*), which is the Introduction to an anthology of African poetry written in French. The theory of negritude is presented by Sartre as a myth, in the sense given to that word here. It is viewed as a means of negating white supremacy. It is recognized as a phase, a negative phase which must be superseded. Myth as "negative phase" — this is the expression that we find in J. P. Sartre's Introduction, this is the notion that we find in most of the articles that attempt to interpret negritude. The theory, although it is presented as a negative phase to be superseded, remains even today a deep source of inspiration for some of the African political leaders, particularly for the political theoreticians who see in it the essence of African culture. This is the case of Leopold-Sedar Senghor who, in a book published recently on Teilhard de Chardin, emphasizes the notion of negritude and its implications. In this book Senghor presents negritude as a way of adhering to the world, as a certain way that the black man has of being in the world; he describes it as being "spontaneous and vital" rather than "intellectual." Thus this theory of negritude has its place in the long tradition of the irrational. Senghor nevertheless attributes to negritude the mission of universalizing the values of the Negro race. The reader will realize that this ideology, to which I have made a brief reference, was the object of harsh controversies, particularly among young Marxist-educated African intellectuals. It was simple for them to recall the falseness of all racial interpretations, it was easy to criticize the exaltation of irrationality that accompanied the theory, and it was even easier to show its political deficiencies. The most severe criticisms came from a Senegalese writer, who is also a brilliant university professor, Abdoulaye Ly.

Yet, in spite of the criticisms, this ideology, it must be said, is still influential. The theory of negritude contributes heavily to the presently widespread trend towards a "remaking of the African personality." When the heads of states recognize as one of their main tasks this obligation to rebuild the African personality, they pay homage to the theory of negritude. This is the case of Mr. Sékou Touré.

Apart from this theory of negritude, there is also the effort on the part of some writers to give, or to try to give, to African history an aura of glorious accomplishments. They exhalt or reconstruct the past to assure the rehabilitation of African civilizations and of Negro peoples. They reverse the relation of dependence, they transform the great civilizations — those that we have called the great civilizations — into debtors to African civilization. This is the case for a very popular Senegalese writer, Cheikh Anta Diop. In various works, he claims that the Egyptian pharaonic civilization was a Negro civilization. Thus Egypt and what comes from Egypt is in a direct relation of filiation, of historical dependence, on the black African civilizations. I must point out that Cheikh Anta Diop was only reviving a thesis already formulated by Volney in his Voyage en Egypte et en Syrie (Journey in Egypt and in Syria), published in 1787. This can also be illustrated by another, lesser-known example: I refer to the Bureau of the National Archives of Ghana which has edited an illustrated documentation attributing to black people the major inventions of humanity. This documentation, consisting of a series of postcards which illustrate the great human inventions, claims that Africans discovered them, using for that purpose quotations from Volney's book which I have just cited.

I would add finally that the appeal to history is not the monopoly of a few writers. African political leaders have also had recourse to history, with intentions very similar to those of the authors I have just alluded to. For example, Mr. Sékou Touré, in an address delivered just after the independence of Guinea, opposed the weakness of Capetian France to the vigor of the great Sudanese empires which were its contemporaries. Dr. Kwame Nkrumah, similarly opposed an England, not yet constituted as a nation and consequently very weak, to a brilliant Empire of Ghana, which served as a center towards which Moslem scholars converged.

I would like to make a final comment, to show that certain modern political doctrines contain a messianic accent that represents an elaborate theoretical counterpart to the popular messianisms that have expressed the first resistance against the situation of dependence. I shall refer to the work of the Senegalese writer whom I have already mentioned, Mr. Abdoulaye Ly. This author, who is also a man active in politics, published a few years ago a stimulating book entitled *Les masses africaines et l'actuelle condition humaine* (*The African Masses and the Present Human Condition*). It is a sociological, political, and economic essay on Africa south of the Sahara and the so-called underdeveloped countries. In this book, A. Ly presents, naturally, a critique of imperialism. Furthermore he proposes a radical critique of what he calls the two imperialisms: colonial imperialism and, in his own words, "Soviet imperialism." Beyond that, he projects a view of the near future, based on his interpretation of the African situation and of the situation of developing countries. In this analysis, he extols the "indomitable dialectical ability" possessed by masses kept dependent for a long time and exposed to very diversified cultural influences. It is not only the historical mission of these masses that is presented but also their intellectual capacity to renew our theories and our ways of thinking, to shake up our conformist positions — whatever this conformity may be. On the other hand, Abdoulaye Ly sees in the revolt of the underdeveloped peasantries the only "revolution" worthy of its name; according to him, no total revolution has yet been achieved; none yet has changed the human condition in a decisive way and for everyone. The only historical transformation that will count will be the one now being prepared among underdeveloped peasantries. Along with this evocation of a stimulating if not irrefutable theory, I shall also mention a similar thesis defined in the passionate work of a deceased writer and activist, F. Fanon, who participated in the Algerian independence movement. In his posthumous book, published recently, *The Wretched of the Earth*, we find the same lyrical inspiration, the same passion, the same exaltation of the historical mission of the masses of the Third World. I must add, speaking this time on the level of political action and no longer on the level of doctrine or ideology, that the supporters of *African socialism* are not just concerned with adapting socialism to Africa but are also certain that they are making a *crucial contribution* to socialism. If we study their interpretations, we will see that beyond what might appear to be an opportunistic justification, an ad hoc argument, the conviction exists that they are building a new kind of socialism. Nor are messianic undertones absent here.

I cannot dwell on this issue of African socialism, but we may come back to it in the discussion. Indeed, a full account would have to be presented if we were to make a useful study of the topic. With these last remarks, we have gone all the way from the traditional myth, which implies some ideology, to the modern political doctrine, which contains some mythical aspects. This process, this transition from myth with ideological implications to political doctrine with mythical implications, has shown us *the* problem of contemporary Africa, the problem that Africa is awakening to. This problem is the dialectic of tradition and revolution.

SECTION G

POLITICS OF MODERNIZATION:
SEARCH FOR A NEW ORDER

Introduction

"Social groups considered politically" in non-Western countries can be compared and contrasted with the same subject in modern industrial societies (Section E1). Our analytical dimensions here reveal new and urgent empirical problems. What seems typical for these new nations is the greater intensity of cleavages within the social order as well as between society and the state. These states are divided not only by economic interests but also by racial, religious, and cultural factors to a much greater extent than Europe and North America, partly because colonial rule exacerbated rather than diminished existing divisions. Hence the problem of accommodating protest and integrating divisive groups into a national community, discussed by Bendix in regard to European working classes, becomes much greater. Similarly, the state that provides the political framework for the interaction of these groups sometimes has the character of an alien imposition, a creation of Western imperialism which retains some of its foreign quality even after independence has been achieved. The issue here is one of bringing people and political institutions into a satisfactory relationship in a process of modernizing traditional social orders and democratizing the political structure. Finally, these societies are not only "underdeveloped" economically but "underpowered" in their relations with the industrialized nations. Accordingly, their political structures are likely to be influenced by external "organized interests" — not only foreign states, but in some cases the same corporations and interest groups which Ehrmann considers a threat even to Western political structures. The working out of this last issue, whose study has often been neglected by social scientists,[1] affects the future of Western and non-Western nations alike.

[1] Charles C. Moskos and Wendell Bell, in "Emerging Nations and Ideologies of American Social Scientists" (*The American Sociologist*, Vol. II, May 1967, p. 71), note that "one of the most outstanding features in the writings of American social scientists [is] the failure to explore the contingencies on political and social development resulting from the growing gap between the rich and the poor nations. . . . It is assumed that if the new states would settle down, then their interests would correspond to those of the United States. The possibility is seldom broached that

Merle Kling, by taking such external influences as the major cause of political instability in Latin America, exemplifies the observation made by Collins (Section A) that recognition of the international context can be essential for an understanding of domestic events. The governments of these countries are relatively powerless to change the pattern of resource control held by large landowners and foreign investors. Hence, they can neither protect the "public interest" of the society nor provide a satisfactory political arena for a peaceful contention among indigenous interest groups. Instead, governmental positions appear as a prize of economic competition and as a means of attaining social mobility. The resulting turnover of personnel has little effect on the structure of these societies or on their relations with other states.

Despres, in contrast, focuses on the indigenous structure of these societies in a commentary on the controversy concerning plural societies which began with the work of J. D. Boeke and J. S. Furnivall. His test case, British Guiana, is in some respects atypical because it is so completely a product of colonialism — 96% of its population migrated under colonial rule, principally from India and Africa. Nevertheless, the role played by European ideas and institutions, the dominating position of European or Westernized groups, and the existence of potentially conflicting cultural sections is paralleled to some degree in the great majority of non-Western countries.

Despres discusses two theoretical models, taking as his criterion their success in describing the situation accurately and in predicting the nature of social conflict. The "plural model" postulates separated cultural sections and suggests that the society is held together primarily by the dominant minority section. Since force in open or disguised form is almost inevitably present, the society is threatened by serious and potentially violent conflict. The "reticulated model," on the other hand, assumes that stratification by color and class is mitigated by the participation of members of various groups in common institutional structures. Common values emerging from this institutional system and a process of assimilation should make it unlikely that conflicts will arise which are serious enough to threaten the political framework. Despres concludes that both models are only partially adequate descriptively; he finds the plural model more correct in its prediction of conflict, although it fails to specify under what conditions violence will occur. Lacking in both models, he argues, is the dimension of organized action, the conscious attempts by political leaders to manipulate the interactions of potentially conflicting groups.

In the face of efforts to provide determinate systems models, this final point of Despres is a useful reminder that while social structures and political "rules of the game" may provide the conditions and frameworks of human action, they never completely determine these actions. Like other models, the plural-society concept has its empirical shortcomings, as Despres notes. Nevertheless, the concept allows us to distinguish between cases, such as British Guiana, where many traditional cultural orders coexist under a single political frame-

the national interests of the United States, *as presently constituted*, and its role in the economic division of the world, may not be compatible with the future political progress of the underdeveloped areas."

work, and cases where members of a single traditional and originally fragmented social order respond to new economic and political conditions. Rudolph
leads us to a consideration of the latter case, since India, except perhaps for
its Hindu-Muslim divisions, is not really a plural society. Rather, it is a caste
society in the process of transformation.[2] Caste associations, although they
represent appeals to traditional ties, often in traditional language, are by no
means traditional in their orientation to the new social and political order and
in their ability to unite once fragmented local caste groups (in some cases
groups widely separated in the traditional hierarchy). Rudolph therefore suggests that, in modified form, primordial ties can become a basis for democratic
politics. Such ties may promote a social pluralism which allows individuals to
enter into contact with the state, while at the same time be protected from it.[3]

A final note of caution is in order. The "plural society" as used here must
be distinguished from the "pluralism" of modern political theory. A plural
society, in its ideal-typical form, has no common values, and conflict potentially
involves entire cultural sections opposed to one another radically and perhaps
violently. "Pluralism," on the other hand, emphasizes the importance of a multitude of overlapping associations and group memberships that protect the
individual from the state. Pluralism is compatible with the "class society" of
the modern nation-state, in which members of a single socio-economic category
might unite for common purposes within the basic cultural or political framework of the society. The compatibility of a "plural society" and the nation-state
is at least problematic.

[2] The differences between the caste model and the plural-society model are significant and should be emphasized, particularly since the term "caste" is often applied to
race relations. If used in its concrete historical sense, "caste" refers to a society (such as
India) where stratified groups exist under a system of accepted values (those of purity
and pollution) and where conflict typically takes the form of factionalism: members
of the same "caste" did not traditionally unite for the purposes of conflict. Caste
thus differs from a racially divided plural society both in its structuring of conflict and
in the existence of a social-value system, rather than just a political framework, to
unify groups.
[3] For a contrary argument, to the effect that the caste structure is not only changing
but weakening, see André Beteille, "Closed and Open Stratification" (*European
Journal of Sociology*, Vol. VII, 1966, pp. 224–248), especially pp. 240–244. Evidence
that caste associations and caste movements are becoming less significant politically
may indicate that these phenomena are transitional.

Towards a Theory of Power and Political Instability in Latin America

MERLE KLING

I

"One may consider science," James B. Conant has observed, "as an attempt
. . . to lower the degree of empiricism or to extend the range of theory. . . .
Almost all significant work of scientists today, I believe, comes under the heading of attempts to reduce the degree of empiricism." [1]

Despite the conception of science and theory prevalent in the natural sciences
and reflected in the formulation of Conant, the discipline of political science
has yet to reject decisively the notion of theory as an aggregation of metaphysical speculations unrelated to experience and practice. Academically, in fact,
the field of political theory, within the discipline of political science, traditionally has defined its role as recording, with varied degrees of interpretation,
the history of metaphysical speculations in the area of politics and the state.[2]
But "theorizing, even about politics," as Lasswell and Kaplan correctly assert,
"is not to be confused with metaphysical speculation in terms of abstractions
hopelessly removed from empirical observation and control." [3]

Within a scientific framework, consequently, a theory of power and instability in Latin America must attempt to discharge at least four functions. (1)
An adequate theory must serve "to reduce the degree of empiricism"; that is,
it must place in a broad and meaningful context the apparently disconnected
manifestations of instability in Latin America. (2) It must offer generalizations
regarding the exercise of power and the prevalence of instability in Latin
America which are compatible with the available evidence. (3) It must offer
a guide and provide a framework for relevant research. A scientific theory
neither anticipates every future event nor solves every practical problem. A
theory with scientific pretensions, however, does provide directions for the
investigation and solution of subsequent problems. (4) A theory of Latin
American instability, if it is to endure, must not be rooted in relatively static
elements in the Latin American environment; it must take account of dynamic
forces which are subject to change. For example, a "theory" which "explains"

From *Western Political Quarterly*, Vol. IX (March 1956), pp. 21–35. Reprinted
by permission of the author and the University of Utah, copyright owners.

MERLE KLING is Professor of Political Science, Washington University, St. Louis. A
specialist on Latin America, he is also an expert on international organizations. He is
the author of *The Soviet Theory of Internationalism* (1952) and *A Mexican Interest
Group in Action* (1961).

[1] James B. Conant, *Science and Common Sense* (New Haven: Yale University Press,
1951), pp. 58–59. "Only by the introduction of a theoretical element can the degree
of empiricism be reduced." James B. Conant, *Modern Science and Modern Man*
(New York: Columbia University Press, 1952), p. 28.

[2] For a systematic expression of dissatisfaction with the contemporary state of
theory in American political science, particularly its "decline into historicism," see
David Easton, *The Political System: An Inquiry into the State of Political Science*
(New York: Alfred A. Knopf, 1953).

[3] Harold D. Lasswell and Abraham Kaplan, *Power and Society: A framework for
Political Inquiry* (New Haven: Yale University Press, 1950), p. x.

instability in Latin America on the basis of the "hot blood" of the "Spanish temperament" is vulnerable on at least two grounds: the biological laboratory cannot sustain the assumption of peculiar heat in the blood of persons of Spanish descent; and the ultimate development of political stability in Latin America can be rationalized only by the projection of fantastic concepts of biological mutation.[4] Similarly, a "theory" of Latin American instability rooted in geographical factors is not reconcilable with probable changes of a significant order; for the Andes mountains are not likely to lose important elevation and the Amazon River is not likely to contract in length appreciably in the relevant future. By ignoring the dynamic aspects of Latin American society, however, such a "theory" postulates major geographical transformations if political stability is achieved.[5] To attribute political instability in Latin America, finally, to "history" and the heterogeneous cultures of Spaniards and Indians buries any viable theory in an inextricable maze of historical and cultural determinism. This arbitrarily excludes the possibility of rapid developments in the direction of political stability.

A theory of power and political instability in Latin America, therefore, is not a substitute for empirical research. But, while subject to verification by experience, the theory must reach beyond the scope of analysis of isolated and superficially haphazard political episodes; and the theory should provide a guide for fruitful and detailed investigations.

II

Political instability in Latin America is distinguished by three characteristics: (1) it is chronic; (2) it frequently is accompanied by limited violence; (3) it produces no basic shifts in economic, social or political policies.

Political instability in a Latin American country cannot be evaluated as a temporary deviation in a pattern of peaceful rotation in office. In many Latin American republics, despite prescriptions of written constitutions, an abrupt change of governmental personnel through violence is a regular and recurrent phenomenon. In Honduras, "from 1824 to 1950, a period of 126 years, the

---

[4] Reflecting a "racist" emphasis, William Lytle Schurz — two years before the *coup d'état* which brought Peron's group to power in Argentina — wrote: "Conditions in Argentina are unusually favorable to the development of political democracy. It is peopled by a predominantly white race. It is free from the dead weight of a heavy Indian population, the too mercurial influence of the Negro, and the disturbing leaven of mixed peoples, who move in an uncertain world between the fixed status of the pure bloods." *Latin America: A Descriptive Survey* (New York: E. P. Dutton & Co., 1941), p. 140. In a new and revised edition (1949), Schurz, while retaining his descriptive comments on the "races" of Argentina, rephrases his opening conclusion in a more cautious vocabulary: "Basic conditions in Argentina would appear to be unusually favorable to the development of political democracy" (p. 135).

[5] ". . . policy consists of decisions about the future. The scientist who wishes to contribute to such decisions therefore focuses his research on problems which bear upon the relevant future. . . ." Ernest R. Hilgard and Daniel Lerner, "The Person: Subject and Object of Science and Policy," in Daniel Lerner and Harold D. Lasswell, *The Policy Sciences: Recent Developments in Scope and Method* (Stanford: Stanford University Press, 1951), pp. 42–43.

executive office changed hands 116 times." [6] "During the nine-year interval ending in 1940, Ecuador had no less than fourteen presidents, [and had] four of them during the single month which ended on September 17, 1947. Instability is likewise dramatized on the cabinet level: twenty-seven different ministers occupying eight cabinet posts between May 29, 1944, and August 23, 1947. Twelve foreign ministers attempted to administer Ecuadoran foreign policy in the two-month period between August and October 1933." [7] And the observations of a member of a United Nations mission to Bolivia in 1951 would not be inapplicable in substance to many Latin American states: "In the past ten years, Bolivia has had nine major revolutions. None of its Presidents has served out his constitutional term of office during the last twenty-five years. There have been eighteen Ministers of Labor in four years; eight Ministers of Finance in eighteen months." [8]

Reflecting the persistence of political instability since World War II, governing personnel, including presidents, have been displaced by "irregular" methods on at least the following occasions:

October 1945. Venezuela	June 1950. Peru
October 1945. Brazil	May 1951. Bolivia
January 1946. Haiti	May 1951. Panama
July 1946. Bolivia	March 1952. Cuba
January 1947. Paraguay	April 1952. Bolivia
May 1947. Nicaragua	December 1952. Venezuela
August 1947. Ecuador	June 1953. Colombia
September 1947. Ecuador	May 1954. Paraguay
March 1948. Costa Rica	July 1954. Guatemala
June 1948. Paraguay	August 1954. Brazil
October 1948. Peru	December 1954. Honduras
November 1948. Venezuela	January 1955. Panama
December 1948. El Salvador	September 1955. Argentina
January 1949. Paraguay	November 1955. Argentina
November 1949. Panama	November 1955. Brazil
May 1950. Haiti	

Occupancy of key governmental positions, consequently, has been secured at least 31 times in disregard of formal procedures since the Second World War. Nor does the above list take into account the numerous "unsuccessful" plots, suppressed uprisings, arrests, deportations, declarations of state of siege, boycotts, riots and fraudulent "elections" which have punctuated Latin American politics in the last decade.[9] And the list, of course, does not include

[6] William S. Stokes, *Honduras: An Area Study in Government* (Madison: University of Wisconsin Press, 1950), p. 181.

[7] George I. Blanksten, *Ecuador: Constitutions and Caudillos* (Berkeley: University of California Press, 1951), p. 181.

[8] Albert Lepawsky, "The Bolivian Operation," *International Conciliation*, No. 479 (March, 1952), 106.

[9] Evidence of recent political instability, particularly for the year 1952, is summarized in a pamphlet by Miguel Jorrín, *Political Instability in Latin America* (Albuquerque: University of New Mexico, 1953).

references to political irregularities in non-sovereign areas such as British Guiana.

Revolts, uprisings and *coups d'état*, moreover, constitute incomplete evidence of the range of political instability in Latin America. For obscured by data of these kinds is the presence of "concealed" instability. The protracted tenure of a Vargas in Brazil (1930–1945), of an Ubico in Guatemala (1930–1944), the single candidate (*candidato único*) "elections" of Paraguay, Honduras, the Dominican Republic, Nicaragua and Colombia, the abortive "elections" of 1952 in Venezuela are not to be construed, of course, as symptomatic of political stability. For these also constitute instances in which governmental authority has been retained by the exercise of force in disregard of formal requirements. *Continuismo*, prolonged office-holding by a strong *caudillo*, in its essence represents the reverse side of the shield of political instability. *Continuismo* signifies not the absence of political instability, but the effective suppression of potential and incipient rebellions by competing *caudillos*. *Continuismo*, in fact, may be regarded as perpetuation in office by means of a series of successful *anticipatory* revolts.

Unlike cabinet instability in France, political instability in the Latin American states is neither sanctioned by the written constitution nor dictated by the rigidity of domestic party alignments. Latin American instability, in contrast with the French version, occurs in an environment of amorphous political parties and involves the limited employment of violence. It is not the withdrawal of votes by a doctrinaire bloc of deputies which precipitates the collapse of a Latin American regime; rather, it is the personal military following of an opportunistic *caudillo* which impresses a Latin American president with the timeliness of seeking asylum in a foreign embassy. The pervasiveness of violence justifies the conclusion of Stokes: "Violence seems to be institutionalized in the organization, maintenance, and changing of governments in Latin America." [10]

Although violence provides a continuing strand in the fabric of Latin American politics, revolution, in the sense of a fundamental transformation of society, "is rare in Latin America, and even mass participation in violence is only occasionally found." [11] A leader may be assassinated or exiled, a new junta may assume the posts of political authority, but control of the economic bases of power is not shifted and the hierarchy of social classes is not affected; in short, there is no restructuring of society. The label "palace revolution," as

[10] William S. Stokes, "Violence as a Power Factor in Latin-American Politics," *Western Political Quarterly*, V (1952), 445.

"One of the most typical aspects of Latin American life is the tendency to settle political issues by force. Government by revolution might almost be said to be the rule. Since the turn of the present century the governments of the nations to the south have been overthrown by revolt seventy-six times — an average of nearly four successful uprisings per country. No one knows how many unsuccessful rebellions have occurred during these years because no one has ever taken the trouble to count them, but they certainly run into the hundreds."

Austin F. Macdonald, *Latin American Politics and Government*, 2d ed. (New York: Thomas Y. Crowell Co., 1954), pp. 11–12.

[11] Stokes, *op. cit.*, p. 461.

defined by Lasswell and Kaplan, can be appropriately applied to the pattern of political change in Latin America; for political instability in Latin America, like a palace revolution, involves "a change in governors contrary to the political formula but retaining it." Again violence in Latin America, in conformity with the characteristics of a palace revolution, produces a "change in government without corresponding changes in governmental policy." [12] General Gustavo Rojas Pinilla may be a party to a successful revolt in Colombia, and General Zenón Noriega may be a party to an unsuccessful revolt in Peru; but the basic economic, social and political policies of Colombia and Peru are not altered by either the successful or the unsuccessful general. Violence is virtually always present; fundamental change is virtually always absent.

III

"In the general course of human nature," wrote Alexander Hamilton in *The Federalist* (No. 79), "a power over a man's subsistence amounts to a power over his will." And research in Latin American studies suggests that the distinguishing characteristics of the Latin American economy, despite the influence exerted by the Church and other institutions, are of primary importance in determining conditions for the retention and transfer of power.

Traditionally, ownership of land has been regarded as a major economic base for the exercise of power in Latin America. Despite the continued dependence today of more than two-thirds of the Latin American population on agriculture as a chief source of income, the system of land tenure operates to prevent the widespread diffusion of economic power. Concentration of land ownership in the hands of a tiny minority — whether symbolized by the *latifundio, hacienda, estancia, fazenda,* or *finca* — represents the prevailing, as well as historic, agrarian pattern of Latin America. "In many countries in Latin America," concludes a recent analysis by the United Nations Department of Economic Affairs, "the main feature of the agrarian structure is the high degree of inequality in land ownership." [13]

Although they can be introduced only with qualifications as to reliability, statistical estimates offer striking evidence of the narrow agrarian base of power. In Chile, whereas 43.4 per cent of all land holdings are under five hectares, they account for only 0.5 per cent of the farm area; large holdings (1000 hectares and over), on the other hand, constitute only 1.4 per cent of all holdings, but they incorporate 68.2 per cent of the farm area. Acknowledging that "the agrarian structure of Chile is characterized in the main by an abundance of very small holdings and a large concentration of large estates in the hands of a small number of proprietors," the government of Chile, in reply to a United Nations questionnaire, emphasized the difficulty of modifying the pattern of land ownership:

---

[12] Lasswell and Kaplan, *op. cit.*, p. 270. For striking evidence of the equanimity with which economically dominant groups view rivalries among military cliques in El Salvador, see *New York Times*, February 6, 1955, p. 12.

[13] United Nations, Department of Economic Affairs, *Progress in Land Reform* (New York, 1954), p. 37.

Owing to the economic and political structure of the country, land reform in Chile is difficult to carry out. Landholders who would be affected by any action of an economic, political, administrative, legal or social nature will vigorously oppose its implementation, and their political and economic influence is very powerful.[14]

In Brazil, 1.5 per cent of all land holdings account for 48.4 per cent of the farm area.[15] According to the 1950 census of Bolivia, 4.5 per cent of the rural landowners possess 70 per cent of the private landed property.[16] In the province of Pichincha in Ecuador, 1.5 per cent of all holdings incorporate 65.3 per cent of the farm area, and the government reports that "Ecuador has not developed a policy of land reform." [17] In Cuba, 1.4 per cent of all holdings comprise 47 per cent of the farm area.[18] Even in Mexico, where the government claims that about 23 per cent of the total area in holdings was distributed to *éjido* farmers between 1916 and 1940, in lands not under the *éjido* system 0.8 per cent of all holdings constitute 79.5 per cent of the farm area.[19] And patterns of highly concentrated land ownership persist in Argentina, Peru, and Venezuela.

This monopolization of agrarian wealth injects an element of rigidity into the power relations of Latin American groups; for the effect of the land tenure system is to establish relatively fixed economic boundaries between the landowners and the peon, since "the relationships growing out of the large estates have. matured into deep inflexibility." [20] Indeed, the authors of a very carefully documented study of Latin America have concluded: "Monopolization of land has been and still is both the source and the technique of political power in Latin America." [21]

Yet it is possible to exaggerate the independence, the freedom from restraint, of the landowner in Latin American society. Viewed solely in terms of domestic Latin American patterns of land tenure, the landowner appears almost to personify the classical definition of sovereignty. He seems to possess virtually absolute power. But an analysis of the nature of agricultural production reveals important inhibitions on the discretionary power of the landowner, and he

[14] *Ibid.*, pp. 42–43.

[15] *Ibid.*, p. 41.

[16] *Ibid.*, p. 40. In Bolivia, "the most usual model, surviving with little change from colonial times, is the large estate with absentee owner and cultivated by native labour." Harold Osborne, *Bolivia: A Land Divided* (London: Royal Institute of International Affairs, 1954), p. 111.

[17] United Nations, Department of Economic Affairs, *op. cit.*, pp. 43–44. "An Ecuadorian economist recently called attention to the fact that, according to the register on real-estate tax paid in the greater part of the Sierra between 1943–8, 486 landowners, i.e., less than 2 per cent of the persons subject to the tax, owned three-quarters of the land, while the remaining quarter was distributed among over 23,000 small owners. Many properties were no larger than one-tenth of an acre, while others extended over more than 15,000 acres." Lilo Lanke, *Ecuador, Country of Contrasts* (London: Royal Institute of International Affairs, 1954), p. 118.

[18] United Nations, Department of Economic Affairs, *op. cit.*, p. 46.

[19] *Ibid.*, p. 39.

[20] Simon G. Hanson, *Economic Development in Latin America* (Washington: Inter-American Affairs Press, 1951), p. 67.

[21] George Soule, David Efron, and Norman T. Ness, *Latin America in the Future World* (New York: Farrar and Rinehart, 1945), p. 63.

fails to qualify as an economic sovereign. For as a producer of crops peculiarly dependent on foreign markets, in an agrarian economy characterized by monoculture, the landowner finds his economic base of independence subject to severe limitations. When 50 per cent to 60 per cent of Brazilian exports consists of coffee,[22] when normally 80 per cent of the total value of exports of El Salvador consists of coffee,[23] when "coffee cultivation . . . contributes more than 70 per cent of total exports and is the basic cash crop on which nearly everything else depends" in Guatemala (according to a Mission sponsored by the International Bank for Reconstruction and Development),[24] when coffee represents 73.2 per cent of the value of all exports in Colombia for 1953,[25] when coffee is the predominant export of the Central American Republics (representing 56.4 per cent of all exports in 1953) [26] — when the Western Hemisphere produces about 85 per cent of the world's exportable coffee and the United States consumes 65 per cent to 75 per cent of all the coffee shipped [27] — the domestic proprietors of coffee plantations cannot be immune to the pressures (regardless of the indirection, diplomacy and circumspection with which they may be exerted) that emanate from their principal export market. When over half of the total value of exports of the Dominican Republic [28] and about three-fourths of the total value of Cuban exports [29] consist of sugar, the domestic owner of sugar plantations cannot be indifferent to the influence of international markets. "Sugar," reported an Economic and Technical Mission organized by the International Bank for Reconstruction and Development, "is not only Cuba's principal source of livelihood. It dominates the economy — and the outlook of the people — in various ways. Sugar plays an even greater part in the exports of Cuba today than it did in the past." [30] Hence the fundamentally colonial and monocultural nature of the Latin American economies, as evidenced by the role of coffee and sugar exports, constricts the economic base even of the apparently omnipotent landowner.[31]

[22] United Nations, Department of Economic Affairs, *Economic Survey of Latin America 1953* (New York, 1954), p. 54; Pan American Union, Division of Economic Research, *Economic Developments in Brazil 1949–50* (Washington, D.C., 1950), p. 37.

[23] United States, Department of Commerce, *Foreign Commerce Yearbook 1949* (Washington, 1951), p. 402.

[24] International Bank for Reconstruction and Development, *The Economic Development of Guatemala* (Washington, D.C., 1951), p. 24.

[25] United Nations, Department of Economic Affairs, *Economic Survey of Latin America 1953* (New York, 1954), p. 56.

[26] *Ibid.*, p. 64.

[27] *Americas*, II (January, 1950), 2.

[28] Pan American Union, *Foreign Commerce of Dominican Republic 1941–1947* (Washington, D.C., June 1950), p. 17.

[29] United Nations, Department of Economic Affairs, *Economic Survey of Latin America 1953* (New York, 1954), p. 57.

[30] International Bank for Reconstruction and Development, *Report on Cuba* (Washington, D.C., 1951), p. 7. In 1954, the United States absorbed 60.1 per cent of Cuban sugar exports. United Nations, Department of Economic and Social Affairs, *Economic Survey of Latin America 1954* (New York, 1955), p. 59.

[31] In certain conspicuous instances, of course, the landowner is not a native of a Latin American state. The United Fruit Company, for example, is reported to own

The main characteristics of the ownership of mineral wealth and the conduct of the mining industries in Latin America further accentuate the colonial nature of the economies and add to the obstacles in the path of discovering native, local command over decisive economic elements of power. Foreign ownership of mineral resources and foreign utilization of mineral products imply that an important economic base of power in Latin America is not indigenously controlled. Thus over 90 per cent of Chilean copper is regularly produced by United States–owned enterprises; of 351,000 tons of copper mined in 1953, in excess of 325,000 tons were produced by large mining companies financed by United States capital.[32] The United States–owned Cerro de Pasco Corporation of Peru accounts for about two-thirds of the Peruvian copper output.[33] In the case of Bolivia, despite the nationalization of the principal tin mines, the virtually complete reliance on exports of the mining industry as a source of indispensable foreign exchange perpetuates a political climate which is subject to foreign pressures. For "the products of the mining industry account for some 98 per cent of the country's total exports. And tin concentrates account for some 75 per cent of the total mineral exports." Consequently, "the financial position of Bolivia is always peculiarly sensitive to — is indeed dangerously dependent upon — fluctuations of price and demand in the world markets for non-ferrous metals." [34] Control of petroleum production in Latin America resides almost exclusively in the hands of foreign-owned corporations. A United States company produces more than 70 per cent of Peru's crude petroleum; in Venezuela, which accounts for almost 80 per cent of the crude petroleum output of Latin America, a subsidiary of a United States company ranks as the largest oil company in the country.[35]

Venezuela and its oil industry perhaps may be cited as a case study in the predominant role of foreign capital with respect to the control of the mineral bases of power in Latin America. Petroleum, which is exploited almost exclusively by foreign-owned companies, operating under government concession, occupies a crucial position in Venezuelan exports.[36] In one fashion or another, more than 60 per cent of the revenue of the Treasury in Venezuela is contributed by the oil companies; during the budget year 1949–1950, about one-third of the total budget receipts consisted of petroleum *royalties* alone.[37]

---

about 3,000,000 acres, mainly in Colombia, Costa Rica, Cuba, the Dominican Republic, Ecuador, Guatemala, Honduras and Panama. *New York Times*, July 4, 1954, p. 4E.

[32] United Nations, Department of Economic Affairs, *Economic Survey of Latin America 1953* (New York, 1954), p. 185.

[33] *Ibid.*, p. 187. The Cerro de Pasco Corporation "accounted for 84 per cent of the copper, 36 per cent of the gold, and 55 per cent of the silver produced in Peru between 1906 and 1938." Division of Economic Research, Pan American Union, *The Peruvian Economy* (Washington, D.C., 1950), p. 104.

[34] Osborne, *op. cit.*, p. 107.

[35] United Nations, Department of Economic Affairs, *Economic Survey of Latin America 1953* (New York, 1954), pp. 233–238.

[36] *Ibid.*, p. 62: United States Tariff Commission, *Mining and Manufacturing Industries in Venezuela* (Washington, 1945), p. 47.

[37] United Nations, Department of Economic Affairs, *Public Finance Surveys: Venezuela* (New York, January, 1951), p. 47.

Unlike other mineral industries, moreover, petroleum has continued to attract new capital investment from the United States. Since 74 per cent of United States private direct-investment in the period following the Second World War (1947–1949) was channeled to the petroleum industry, a considerable share has been invested in Venezuela as a country with exploitable petroleum resources.[38] Clearly the foreign-owned oil companies constitute factors which cannot be ignored in the power structure of Venezuela. But a precise description of the manner in which power is exercised by the petroleum industry cannot be documented. It would be valuable, for purposes of a study of power, to have accessible a public record of the specific reactions of the oil companies to the seizure of governmental authority by a revolutionary junta led by Romulo Betancourt in 1945. It would be valuable, for purposes of a study of power, to have available an accurate record of the policies and decisions of the oil companies in so far as they affected the deposition of President Romulo Gallegos and his supporters, including Betancourt, in 1948. But details of this type are unavailable not only to academic investigators of power in Latin America; they elude public detection and identification in most systems of power. The obscure nature of certain details, however, cannot serve to justify the rejection of an inference that a correlation exists between the economic dominance of the oil companies and the pattern of political behavior in Venezuela. While the exact techniques of the exercise of power are not easily demonstrated, obviously a substantial economic base of power in Venezuela is controlled by economic institutions beyond the geographical boundaries of the country. The control of mineral wealth, consequently, within the framework of colonial economies, introduces an external element of restraint on the exercise of power by domestic forces and movements within Latin America.

Industrialization would appear to represent a significant challenge to the economic forces of colonialism in Latin America. Undoubtedly a successful program of industrialization could alter radically the distribution of power in the Latin American area. Tangible fragments of evidence, in fact, suggest that the present level of industrialization has stimulated modifications in the established patterns of economic power. Consumer goods industries, particularly textiles, have expanded rapidly. Reflecting the influence of domestic manufacturing interests, Latin American governments have been anxious to maintain protective tariff policies. With industrialization, labor organizations have evolved and have made it possible for new leaders, drawing upon fresh sources of support, to compete for the possession of power. The well-publicized role of Lombardo Toledano in Mexican politics, the prolix constitutional and statutory provisions for social security, the turbulent strikes in some of the Latin American states, the ostentatious, if demagogic, manifestations of solicitude for labor on the part of Juan Domingo Perón, testify to the enhanced prestige of labor and labor unions in a society experiencing the initial tensions and strains of industrialization in the twentieth century.

But the position of manufacturing as an economic base of power in Latin

[38] Gordon Gray, *Report to the President on Foreign Economic Policies* (Washington, November 10, 1950), pp. 61, 121.

America can be overstated. Hitherto a level of industrialization has not been achieved which would make possible the displacement of the conventional economic bases of power. By United States standards, the Latin American consumer continues to absorb only a small amount of manufactured goods. The Latin American countries continue to be dependent on imports for many items utilized in manufacturing, as well as for much of their machinery, transportation facilities and factory equipment. And "the most significant economic trend in 1953," according to the Secretariat of the Economic Commission for Latin America, "was, without doubt, the clear indication of a slackening in the rate of industrialization. . . . As a consequence, the industrial share of the gross product in 1953 was only 25.6 per cent, no greater than in 1945." The fact, moreover, that the industrial labor force, compared with total manpower, has not increased since 1950 constitutes evidence of a "fundamental decline in industrialization" in Latin America.[39] A decline of 21 per cent in total Latin American imports of capital goods in 1953, in relation to 1952, also emphasizes the limited potentialities of industrialization in the immediate future.[40]

Notwithstanding the somewhat spectacular construction of the Volta Redonda steel plant in Brazil and the opening of the earthquake-proof Huachipato steel works in Chile, heavy industries remain in an embryonic stage of evolution. By 1954, for example, Brazilian industry produced only 1,100,000 tons of steel ingots annually, and total Chilean production of steel ingots in 1954 amounted to 320,000 tons.[41] "Such industrialization as exists," Gordon concludes with ample evidence, "is either an undernourished image of the Great Society or else a highly specialized form, such as in mining, which exists by grace of foreign ownership and foreign markets." [42]

From the point of view of locating the economic sites of power, the current program of industrialization in Latin America presents an apparent paradox. The desire for industrialization evidently originates with leaders who seek to transfer economic bases of power from foreign to domestic jurisdiction; and the economic nationalism which normally has accompanied the drive for industrialization would seem to substantiate this assumption. But the financial techniques utilized have not hastened the transfer of power, based on control of industry, to native groups in Latin America. For, lacking huge reservoirs of local capital to finance heavy industry, unwilling (and perhaps unable) to compel modifications in the investment practices of landowners, the Latin Americans, in their attempt to move toward the goal of industrialization, once again have sought foreign capital. Prominent among the suppliers of new capital

[39] United Nations, Department of Economic Affairs, *Economic Survey of Latin America 1953* (New York, 1954), pp. 10–11.

[40] *Ibid.*, p. 68.

[41] United Nations, Department of Economic and Social Affairs, *Economic Survey of Latin America 1954* (New York, 1955), p. 96. For data regarding the share of manufacturing in Latin American national incomes, see: George Wythe, *Industry in Latin America*, 2d ed. (New York: Columbia University Press, 1949), p. 13; and the United Nations, Secretariat of the Economic Commission for Latin America, *Economic Survey of Latin America 1948* (New York, 1949), p. 2.

[42] Wendell C. Gordon, *The Economy of Latin America* (New York: Columbia University Press, 1950), p. 20.

to Latin America has been the Export-Import Bank of Washington. Every sovereign state in Latin America except Guatemala has received funds from this Bank. By 1954, the Export-Import Bank, which supplied more than half of the investment capital required by the Volta Redonda and Huachipato steel plants,[43] had authorized credits of $2,152,023,000 to the Latin American countries.[44] In addition, half of the states in the Latin American region have received loans from the International Bank for Reconstruction and Development. By 1954 this specialized agency of the United Nations had authorized loans of $426,000,000 to Latin American countries.[45] Since voting power in the International Bank for Reconstruction and Development is based on the proportion of capital subscribed by each member, the United States speaks with a dominant voice in the affairs of the Bank.

Potentially, then, industrialization may prove of large consequence in creating new economic bases of power in Latin America. At some future date, it may modify drastically the position of the conventional economic bases of power. But industrialization on such a scale as yet has failed to materialize. Promise, hope, and aspiration must be distinguished from performance and accomplishment. Accordingly, at the present time, industrialization in Latin America, realistically appraised, is taking place within the context of an environment which in its economic content remains basically colonial.[46]

IV

An analysis of the distinguishing characteristics of the economic bases of power in Latin America suggests that the conventional economic sources of power constitute relatively static elements of power. Since ownership of land or mines does not pass readily from the hands of one group to another, control of conventional bases of power cannot be secured by the ambitious mestizo,

[43] *New York Times*, November 26, 1950.

[44] Export-Import Bank of Washington, *Seventeenth Semiannual Report to Congress for the period July–December 1953*, p. 22. At least one member of the Chilean Senate has argued that President Gabriel Gonzalez Videla was forced to revise his internal policies in order to qualify for an Export-Import Bank loan designed to encourage industrialization. Salvadore Ocampo, "You Have Invaded My Country," *New Republic*, CXVII (December 1, 1947), 10–12. Also see Roger S. Abbott, "The Role of Contemporary Political Parties in Chile," *American Political Science Review*, XLV (1951), 454, 457.

[45] United Nations, Department of Economic and Social Affairs, *Foreign Capital in Latin America* (New York, 1955), p. 13.
". . . one of the most noteworthy developments in the field of foreign investment during 1954 was the marked increase in the loan activity of the International Bank for Reconstruction and Development and of the Export-Import Bank. After authorizing development-type credits to Latin America to a value of 90 million and 57 million dollars in 1953 and in the first half of 1954, respectively, they approved total credits for 196 million dollars during the second half of the year and over 100 millions in the first quarter of 1955." United Nations, Department of Economic and Social Affairs, *Economic Survey of Latin America 1954* (New York, 1955), p. 51.

[46] Fourteen Latin American states are classified as "underdeveloped" and none as "highly developed" by Eugene Staley, *The Future of Underdeveloped Countries: Political Implications of Economic Development* (New York: Harper, 1954), pp. 16–17.

mulatto or Indian without a major social upheaval. The system of land tenure dooms to frustration ambitious individuals in search of a new agrarian base of power. Foreign exploitation of mineral resources effectively blocks the possibilities of shifts in the possession of mineral bases of power. And at its current pace of development, industrialization has failed to expand into a broad, substantial base of power.

But while the conventional economic bases of power, landownership and control of mineral resources represent essentially economic constants in the contemporary equation of power in Latin America, government and the army — often indistinguishable in Latin American society — represent notable variables. For in Latin America, government does not merely constitute the stakes of a struggle among rival economic interests; in Latin America, government itself is a unique base of economic power which, unlike the conventional economic bases of power, is subject to fluctuations in possession. Whereas direct profits from oil fields or copper mines may not be within the grasp of the Latin American, the legal sovereignty of the Latin American states demands that the governmental personnel who serve as intermediaries between the foreign-owned company and the domestic concession shall be of native origin. Thus the discrepancy between the political independence and the economic colonialism of the Latin American states permits government, in the power system of Latin America, to occupy an unusual position as a shifting base of economic power. With the number of lucrative governmental and army posts necessarily limited, the competition understandably is keen. As political office provides a uniquely dynamic opportunity to acquire an economic base of power, however, sufficiently large segments of the population are prepared to take the ultimate risk, the risk of life, in a revolt, in a *coup d'état*, to perpetuate a characteristic feature of Latin American politics — chronic political instability. In the distinctive power structure of Latin America, government serves as a special transformer through which pass the currents of economic ambition.

The pattern of political instability, significantly, has not evolved as a challenge to the conventional economic bases of power, for irregular shifts in control of government take place without disturbing the established economic bases of power. Although widespread industrialization, accompanied by an intensification of economic nationalism, could alter the existing pattern of power, although an extensive program of land reform could not help but affect the distribution of power, seizure of government by a new *caudillo*, on the contrary, does not provoke profound social and economic repercussions in Latin America. Thus chronic political instability serves as an avenue of socio-economic mobility, but it does not pose a genuine danger to the control of the conventional economic bases of power. When a "revolutionary" junta replaced Federico Chaves as President of Paraguay in May 1954 with Tómas Romero Pereira and subsequently, in July, arranged for the election of General Alfredo Stroessner without opposition, the pattern was a familiar one: the cast of political characters was shuffled, and the colonial economy of Paraguay remained intact. Indeed, such events can be evaluated adequately only in terms of the French aphorism, "Plus ça change, plus c'ést la même chose."

The interpretation of power and political instability in Latin America developed by this study may be summarized in a series of generalized propositions. A decisive correlation exists between the control of the economic bases of power and the real exercise of political power in Latin America. Control of the conventional economic bases of power remains relatively static. Because of the colonial nature of the Latin American economies, an exceptional economic premium attaches to control of the apparatus of government as a dynamic base of power. Whereas the conventional bases of power effectively restrict mobility in economic status, control of government provides an unusually dynamic route to wealth and power. Thus the contrast between the stable character of the conventional economic bases of power and the shifting, unconventional position of government provokes intense and violent competition for control of government as a means of acquiring and expanding a base of wealth and power. In the vocabulary of mathematics, *chronic political instability is a function of the contradiction between the realities of a colonial economy and the political requirements of legal sovereignty among the Latin American states.*

V

Significant implications for both public policy and research appear inherent in the interpretation of Latin American politics here formulated. In the field of public policy, this interpretation implies that it is not possible for the United States to have powerful allies in Latin America so long as present economic patterns persist. Contemporary economic patterns of colonialism are conducive to the maintenance of reliable *diplomatic* allies for the United States in Latin America; and the *diplomatic* reliability of the Latin American states is faithfully registered, on many issues, in the voting records of the General Assembly of the United Nations. But the same economic conditions which ensure diplomatic reliability weaken the *power* position of the Latin American states. For, as Hans Morgenthau recognizes in the second (and not the first) edition of his *Politics among Nations*, the quality of government itself is a factor of power in international politics.[47] Hence economic colonialism promotes political instability, which detracts from the power of reliable diplomatic allies of the United States; but, while the achievement of political stability would augment the power of the Latin American states, the elimination of a status of economic colonialism may diminish the diplomatic reliability of their governments! And the dilemma thus brought to the surface by the interpretation of Latin American politics offered in this study has never been publicly acknowledged by the United States Department of State.

For research, the implications of this interpretation of Latin American politics are rather obvious. If political studies of the Latin American area are to rest on more than superficial foundations, they can rest neither on formal analyses of constitutions nor on the diplomatic exchanges between the United States and various Latin American countries. Nor, in the light of this interpretation, can a study nourish the illusion that it has penetrated to the realities

[47] Hans J. Morgenthau, *Politics Among Nations* (New York: Alfred A. Knopf, 1954), p. viii.

of Latin American politics when it has applied the label "dictator" to a particular holder of governmental office in Latin America. The Latin American
caudillo, according to the implications of the interpretation presented here,
operates within a narrowly-circumscribed range of power, since he may not
tamper with the traditional economic bases of power. Serious attempts to
analyze the nature of politics in Latin America, therefore, must seek to identify
the ambits of political maneuverability within which power may be exercised
by those who occupy posts of governmental authority in sovereign states with
colonial economies. The successful conclusion of such attempts should result in
a new awareness of the limitations on the nature of the power actually exercised
by presidents and junta members in the politically unstable environment of
Latin America.

The Implications
of Nationalist Politics
in British Guiana
for the Development
of Cultural Theory [1]

LEO A. DESPRES

This paper has a threefold purpose. First, I want to discuss some of the theoretical developments that have emerged from anthropological studies in the
Caribbean. These developments have reached the stage where they are beginning to crystallize around two theoretical points of view. Neither of these, it
seems to me, offers much by way of a very fruitful approach to the study of
sociocultural change in national societies. Second, to illustrate my position, I
want to examine these theories in light of data collected in a study of culture
and nationalist politics in British Guiana. Finally, I want to suggest what may
be a more realistic approach to the study of sociocultural changes in emerging
nations that contain different cultural sections.

THEORETICAL DEVELOPMENTS

The accumulation of acculturation and ethnohistorical studies of Caribbean
cultures over the past 30 years has provided fructuous circumstances for the

Reproduced by permission of the American Anthropological Association and the
author from the *American Anthropologist*, Vol. 66, No. 5 (October 1964), pp.
1051–1077.

Leo A. Despres is Associate Professor of Anthropology, Western Reserve University,
Ohio. He is an expert on African and Caribbean ethnology and political anthropology,
and has published numerous articles in professional journals.

[1] The data used in this paper were collected in a study of culture and nationalist
politics in British Guiana in 1960–61.

formulation and evaluation of cultural theory. In response to these circumstances, several publications have appeared which deal with theoretical issues.[2] In order to bring the problem with which I am concerned into sharper focus, it is useful to briefly summarize some of the issues and theoretical points of view that have resulted from research in the Caribbean.

Herskovits pioneered anthropological research in the Caribbean. His work among the bush Negroes in Surinam and his studies in Haiti and Trinidad [3] have had a profound influence on subsequent investigators. In all of these works Herskovits' major concern was to account for the patterns of Negro culture in the New World in terms of their African origins. Although the "Africanism" thesis has been questioned very seriously by some investigators [4] it has managed to entangle almost every major commentator on the Caribbean since the nineteen thirties.[5] This controversy has served to focus Caribbean studies on the problem of cultural continuity and change. Variations in different aspects of culture have been related to factors which have brought them about or to factors which seem to explain their persistence.[6]

[2] M. G. Smith, *A Framework for Caribbean Studies* (Extra Mural Department, University College of the West Indies, 1955); J. Steward, *Theory of Culture Change* (Urbana: University of Illinois Press, 1955) and *People of Puerto Rico* (Urbana: University of Illinois Press, 1956); V. Rubin (ed.), *Caribbean Studies: A Symposium* (Institute of Social and Economic Research and the Program for the Study of Man in the Tropics, 1957); V. Rubin (ed.), *Social and Cultural Pluralism in the Caribbean* (Annals of the New York Academy of Sciences, 1960), pp. 761–916.

[3] M. J. Herskovits and F. S. Herskovits, *Rebel Destiny* (New York: McGraw-Hill Book Co., 1934); M. J. Herskovits, *Life in a Haitian Valley* (New York: Alfred A. Knopf, 1937); M. J. and F. S. Herskovits, *Trinidad Village* (New York: Alfred A. Knopf, 1947).

[4] E. Franklin Frazier, *The Negro Family in the United States* (Chicago: Chicago University Press, 1939); T. S. Simey, *Welfare and Planning in the West Indies* (London: Oxford University Press, 1946); F. Henriques, *Family and Colour in Jamaica* (London: Eyre and Spottiswood, 1953); Raymond T. Smith, *The Negro Family in British Guiana* (London: Routledge and Kegan Paul, 1956); and M. G. Smith, "The African Heritage in the Caribbean," in V. Rubin (ed.), *Social and Cultural Pluralism . . .* , pp. 34–46, and *West Indian Family Structure* (Seattle: University of Washington Press, 1962).

[5] For example, V. Rubin (ed.), *Social and Cultural Pluralism. . . .*

[6] The problem of cultural persistence and change emerges in a number of studies dealing with Negro kinship patterns (R. Smith, *The Negro Family*; M. Freilich, "Serial Polygyny, Negro Peasants, and Model Analysis," *American Anthropologist*, Vol. 63, 1961, pp. 955–975; M. G. Smith, *West Indian Family Structure*). Simpson has dealt with similar problems in his research on religious cults; see "Political Cultism in West Kingston, Jamaica," in *Social and Economic Studies*, Vol. 4 (1955), pp. 133–149, and "Jamaican Revivalist Cults," *Social and Economic Studies*, Vol. 5 (1956), pp. 321–342. Braithwaite has considered the problem of cultural stability and change with reference to social stratification in Trinidad ("Social Stratification and Cultural Pluralism," in V. Rubin (ed.), *Social and Cultural Pluralism . . .* , pp. 816–31). Several investigators have analyzed the relationships between cultural sections in the context of cultural change; see E. P. Skinner, "Ethnic Interaction in a British Guiana Rural Community," unpublished doctoral dissertation, Columbia University; 1955; D. J. Crowley, "Plural and Differential Acculturation in Trinidad," *American Anthropologist*, Vol. 59 (1957), pp. 817–824; E. Williams, "Race Relations in Caribbean Society," in V. Rubin (ed.), *Caribbean Studies*, pp. 54–60; R. T. Smith, *British Guiana* (London: Oxford University Press, 1962). Also, a number of studies have appeared which give almost exclusive attention to the persisting or changing

Investigators in the tradition of Herskovits have generally approached this problem from an ethnohistorical point of view.[7] The functional articulation of cultural forms with the existing social system may be recognized,[8] but concern with this articulation is submerged frequently by preoccupation with problems of acculturation process or problems involving the origin of cultural forms. It is not surprising that T. S. Simey, a sociologist primarily interested in social welfare and planning, was one of the first to seriously question the utility of the ethnohistorical approach in the analysis of Caribbean cultures.

In addressing himself to problems of welfare and planning, Simey found that the "Africanism" thesis, particularly with respect to family organization and its relationship to a variety of social ills, provided little insight into the dynamics of the situation.[9] Simey suggests that the problems of West Indian society should be understood not only in terms of their historical roots, but also in terms of the prevailing conditions that affect the different subcultural groups as they now exist. Implicitly, then, Simey perceives deeply-rooted subcultural patterns as modes of adaptation to existing social and economic conditions.

The idea of adaptive cultural change and persistence is expanded and interpolated within the framework of cultural evolution by Julian Steward and his co-workers in their Puerto Rican studies.[10] Subsequent investigators in the British Caribbean, however, have preferred to develop this idea in the framework of structural-functional analysis. It is the theoretical issues that have emerged from the studies of this latter group with which I am primarily concerned. These issues are outlined in two important summaries edited by Vera Rubin.[11] For the sake of brevity, I will confine my discussion to the theoretical debate that appears to have developed between Raymond Smith and M. G. Smith.[12]

---

characteristics of cultural sections; see M. Fried, "The Chinese in British Guiana," *Social and Economic Studies*, Vol. 5 (1956), pp. 54–73; D. J. Crowley, "Plural and Differential Acculturation in Trinidad"; M. Freilich, "Cultural Diversity among Trinidadian Peasants," unpublished doctoral dissertation, Columbia University, 1960; M. Klass, *East Indians in Trinidad* (New York: Columbia University Press, 1961); V. Rubin, "Culture, Politics and Race Relations," *Social and Economic Studies*, Vol. 11 (1962), pp. 433–455.

[7] For example, W. R. Bascom, "Two Forms of Afro-Cuban Divination" in Sol Tax (ed.), *Acculturation in the Americas* (Chicago: University of Chicago Press, 1952); E. Clarke, "Land Tenure and the Family in Four Communities in Jamaica," *Social and Economic Studies*, Vol. 1 (1953), pp. 81–118; M. Deren, *Divine Horsemen: The Living Gods of Haiti* (New York: The Vanguard Press, 1953); G. E. Simpson, "Political Cultism . . ." and "Jamaican Revivalist Cults."

[8] For example, Clarke, "Land Tenure . . ."; Simpson, "Jamaican Revivalist Cults."

[9] Simey, *Welfare and Planning*. . . .

[10] J. H. Steward *et al.*, *People of Puerto Rico* (Urbana: University of Illinois Press, 1956).

[11] Rubin (ed.), *Caribbean Studies* . . . , and *Social and Cultural Pluralism*. . . . In the first of these two summaries, almost every paper and accompanying critical comment concerned itself, explicitly or implicitly, with the disagreements between ethnohistorical and structural-functional interpretation of data reported in studies of Caribbean cultures.

[12] I feel justified in focussing on this debate because Raymond Smith and M. G. Smith clearly subscribe to the theoretical positions with which I am concerned. Moreover, as a result of the very fine field work of these two anthropologists, their

In a Malinowskian vein, M. G. Smith has revised J. S. Furnivall's conception of pluralism [13] and suggested its application to the study of Caribbean societies. He takes the position that the "basic" institutional system (that which embraces kinship, education, religion, property, economy, etc.) forms an integral whole.[14] A population that shares such a system tends to be a closed sociocultural unit. When a society (society being defined as a territorially distinct unit with its own governmental institutions) contains two or more populations with distinct institutional systems, it is culturally and socially pluralistic. The groups within such a society form separate cultural sections.[15] M. G. Smith maintains that this concept not only helps us to avoid the error of analyzing the problems of pluralism in terms of race relations, but it is also essential "for comparative sociology." [16]

Raymond Smith, among others, has taken direct issue with M. G. Smith's theory of pluralism.[17] He suggests that the concept of "cultural pluralism" has little value other than summarizing in two words some very complex problems.[18] What he seems to reject most is M. G. Smith's view that, at the societal level, there is no necessary functional integration of subsystems or sections.[19]

Raymond Smith's own theoretical approach is in the tradition of Radcliffe-Brown. He adheres to the principle that the unit of study is the total social system and that culture is relevant only as a system of shared "symbolic meanings which make communication possible in an ordered social life." [20] From an analytical point of view, the differentiation of cultural sections in the Caribbean is a structural problem resulting from the color/class divisions within the

---

theoretical postures have increasingly assumed the status of models for subsequent studies.

[13] J. S. Furnivall, *Colonial Policy and Practice* (London: Cambridge University Press, 1948), p. 304.

[14] M. G. Smith, "Social and Cultural Pluralism" in Rubin (ed.), *Social and Cultural Pluralism* . . . , p. 767.

[15] *Ibid.*, p. 77.

[16] *Ibid.*, p. 763. Included among the anthropologists who appear to subscribe to the point of view expressed by M. G. Smith are M. Nash, "The Multiple Society in Economic Development: Mexico and Guatemala," *American Anthropologist*, Vol. 59 (1957), pp. 825–832; C. Wagley and M. Harris, *Minorities in the New World* (New York: Columbia University Press, 1958); C. Wagley, "Discussion of M. G. Smith's Social and Cultural Pluralism," in Rubin (ed.), *Social and Cultural Pluralism* . . . , p. 777–780; M. Klass, *East Indians in Trinidad*; and M. Freilich, "Serial Polygyny, Negro Peasants, and Model Analysis."

[17] Anthropologists who appear to agree with Raymond Smith's position include Crowley, "Plural and Differential Acculturation in Trinidad"; V. Rubin, "Discussion of M. G. Smith's Social and Cultural Pluralism," in *Social and Cultural Pluralism* . . . , pp. 780–785; Braithwaite, "Social Stratification and Cultural Pluralism"; E. P. Skinner, "Group Dynamics and Social Stratification in British Guiana" in Rubin (ed.), *Social and Cultural Pluralism* . . . , pp. 904–912; and B. Benedict, "Stratification in Plural Societies," *American Anthropologist*, Vol. 64 (1962), pp. 1235–1246.

[18] R. Smith, "Review of Social and Cultural Pluralism in the Caribbean," *American Anthropologist*, Vol. 63, 1961, p. 155.

[19] *Ibid.*, p. 156.

[20] R. Smith, *The Negro Family in British Guiana*, p. 253.

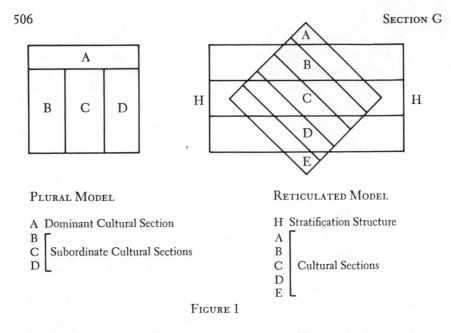

PLURAL MODEL

A Dominant Cultural Section
B ⎡
C ⎢ Subordinate Cultural Sections
D ⎣

RETICULATED MODEL

H Stratification Structure
A ⎡
B ⎢
C ⎢ Cultural Sections
D ⎢
E ⎣

FIGURE 1

total social system.[21] These divisions are hierarchically arranged in terms of social statuses, different degrees of political power, and different social functions.[22] In other words, as far as Raymond Smith is concerned, cultural sections are structurally and functionally integrated in the total system and to consider them as separate entities is "misleading." [23]

Briefly, then, these are the theoretical frameworks that have been used recently in the study of cultural sections in Caribbean societies. Both frameworks employ the "systems" approach. They differ essentially in that one considers cultural sections as integrated and separate units while the other treats them as reticulated sub-units of the total system. These two models are not unrelated to the disagreements between structural-functional and ethnohistorical interpretations in earlier theoretical discussions.[24] Raymond Smith's reticulated model rejects the theoretical significance of historically deep-rooted subcultures in favor of the point of view that the total system has so modified these subcultures that they no longer retain an independent identity. M. G. Smith's pluralistic model, on the other hand, allows for the persistence and residuality of relatively independent cultural traditions. This difference may be seen more concretely in terms of graphic representations.

The contrasts between these two models are extremely important to those anthropologists who are interested in the sociocultural changes resulting from the transformation of colonial and/or tribal societies into nation-states. Plural societies depend for their maintenance on the regulation of intersectional rela-

21 *Ibid.*, p. 255.
22 *Ibid.*, p. 255.
23 Skinner, "Group Dynamics and Social Stratification . . . ," p. 911.
24 For example, Rubin (ed.), *Caribbean Studies.* . . .

tions by one or another of the component cultural sections.[25] From the plural model we would predict that when the dominant section is a minority, political order is secured primarily by force or the threat of force. The reticulated model, on the other hand, presupposes that the cultural sections are enmeshed in an overall institutional system. Political order, it seems, would emerge from the value consensus which the system produces. Value consensus is necessary because the system must be capable of containing the cultural diversity that exists within it.

Apart from these considerations, attempts to conceptualize social and cultural pluralism and to define, precisely, what it is that constitutes a cultural section have involved numerous ambiguities.[26] Part of the conceptual difficulty arises from the elusive distinction between society and culture. Also related to the problem is the difficulty of differentiating between social and cultural pluralism on the one hand, and social and cultural heterogeneity on the other. For example, are ethnic diversities to be considered cultural sections? It is not possible to deal here with all the ramifications of this particular problem. For clarity, however, it will be useful if I briefly state my own views.

First, I fundamentally agree with M. G. Smith's contention that culture and society are not always conterminous or interdependent.[27] I also consider sound his position that institutional differences serve to distinguish differing cultures and social units: how else are we able to make such distinctions? The question as to how different these basic institutional systems have to be in order to consider them independent cultural sections implies a continuum for which anthropologists have not yet devised appropriate measures. In the absence of such measures, I find Steward's concept of levels of cultural integration suggestive for making qualitative evaluations. Inasmuch as the basic institutional system of a population serves to integrate it, socially and psychologically, into the total society in a manner quite different from the institutional system of another population, to that degree the two populations may be said to constitute cultural sections.

In these terms, an ethnic group (normally identified with reference to national origin, or religious practice, or some other one or two institutional dimensions) might be thought of as a "minimal" cultural section. The ethnic group is no different from other groups in a society with reference to most institutional dimensions (e.g., family system, occupational status, social class membership, etc.). A "maximal" cultural section, however, differs from other groups by virtue of its total institutional pattern. Moreover, because of this difference, a "maximal" cultural section is usually integrated into the total society in a distinguishable manner. For example, contrast Polish Americans with the Hopi Indians; the latter constitute a "maximal" cultural section.[28]

---

[25] M. G. Smith, "Social and Cultural Pluralism," p. 774.

[26] For example, *ibid.*; C. Wagley, "Discussion of M. G. Smith's Social and Cultural Pluralism"; Rubin, "Discussion of M. G. Smith's Social and Cultural Pluralism."

[27] J. W. Bennett and L. A. Despres, "Kinship and Instrumental Activities: A Theoretical Inquiry," *American Anthropologist*, Vol. 65 (1960), pp. 254–267.

[28] I find the distinction between "minimal" and "maximal" cultural sections useful particularly with reference to marginal groups that do not display a clearly independent

Lévi-Strauss tells us that a structural model should be so constructed as to make immediately intelligible all the observed facts.[29] Unfortunately, Lévi-Strauss does not tell us how we are to judge when a structural model has achieved this objective. One possibility, according to Redfield,[30] is to ascertain the degree to which the model fits the phenomena reported within its conceptual framework. I now turn to an examination of these models in light of the data collected on the cultural aspects of nationalist politics in British Guiana.

CULTURAL SECTIONS IN BRITISH GUIANA

The population of British Guiana is a product of its colonial history. According to census classifications it includes Amerindians (4.0 percent); Europeans (.9 percent); Portuguese (1.4 percent); Chinese (.6 percent); "Mixed" (11.3 percent); Africans (33.5 percent); and East Indians (48.2 percent). Amerindians represent the only indigenous peoples; all others resulted from European colonial expansion in the Caribbean.

1. In terms of the definition given above, Amerindians may be called a maximal cultural section. Their traditional way of life has been modified by more than 150 years of European contact. Nevertheless, almost all of the Amerindians live in isolated villages in the interior. They are connected to coastal settlements by airlines or by difficult water and overland routes. Mission schools exist in these villages and many of the villages are loosely integrated into the structure of local government which is centralized in Georgetown, the capital. A few Amerindians work for government agencies helping with geological surveys and similar projects conducted in the interior. Some also work on cattle ranches, in lumber mills, in the balata fields, or in the diamond and gold fields. Otherwise, Amerindians have a subsistence economy and follow a way of life not much different from their traditional way of life. Government efforts to integrate the Amerindians more thoroughly into the national life of the country have met with limited success as a result of their isolation.

2. The Europeans probably would also constitute a maximal cultural section. Not many individuals classified as European are native to British Guiana. While Europeans are dispersed throughout the country, they do tend to

---

pattern of cultural integration. In the United States, for example, it makes sense to talk about the Irish vote, or the Catholic vote. Members of these groups may well have enough in common to respond similarly to certain kinds of situations. We would not conclude from this, however, that these individuals share a common culture. The members of a maximal cultural section share a way of life. We would expect them to respond similarly to many different kinds of situations. I believe that it is because of this high level of cultural integration that maximal cultural sections are more easily manipulated, politically, than minimal cultural sections. This distinction appears to shed light upon the ambiguous position of the "Colored" in Guianese national politics.

[29] C. Lévi-Strauss, "Social Structure" in A. L. Kroeber (ed.), *Anthropology Today* (Chicago: University of Chicago Press, 1953), pp. 525.

[30] R. Redfield, "Relations of Anthropology to the Social Sciences and to the Humanities" in A. L. Kroeber (ed.), *Anthropology Today*, pp. 730–731.

cluster in Georgetown where they occupy the command posts of colonial government, high positions in the civil service, or managerial positions in the European commercial and industrial complex. On the sugar estates Europeans form the administrative elite. They live in compounds which segregate them from most non-Europeans. By Guianese standards, life in these compounds is very affluent. Georgetown has its counterpart to the compound on the sugar estates but for political and commercial reasons :t is relatively less segregated. Some non-European Guianese, usually business and professional people or politicians, have access to the European cocktail set in Georgetown but it would seem more appropriate to describe the nature of this access as instrumental rather than affective.

3. The Portuguese came to British Guiana as indentured workers. Finding life too harsh on the sugar estates they migrated to the urban areas where they became shopkeepers and businessmen. Over the years, they have achieved important positions in British Guiana's commercial economy. With reference to European institutional patterns, the Portuguese would probably constitute a minimal cultural section. They are identified by their national origin. They occupy a lower status than Europeans in the class structure by virtue of their indentured past. They also differ from Europeans in that most of them are now native to British Guiana. Probably because of their status aspirations, they segregate themselves more completely from Africans and East Indians than do many of the Europeans. With reference to other institutional dimensions, however, it is difficult to differentiate the Portuguese from the Europeans.

4. The Chinese also came to British Guiana as indentured workers. Like the Portuguese, they moved from the sugar estates into the urban areas where they became shopkeepers. Because of their numbers and the size of their enterprises, they are not as important to the economy as the Portuguese. Thus, the Chinese occupy a somewhat lower socioeconomic status. Fried has shown us that they have lost most of their traditional culture.[31] However, they have managed to maintain their ethnic identity through endogamous marriages and also through the organization of an ethnic association. In these respects, they would seem to constitute a minimal cultural section.

5. The Colored or Mixed population is a relatively large group (11.3 percent) and it presents a difficult problem of classification. Most of the Colored are mulattoes. Until very recently they have been the most educated of the non-European populations. As a result, they have occupied positions of relatively high status in the professions and the civil service. With their favored position, the Colored have adopted many patterns of European behavior. Family patterns, for example, are European (an absence of serial polygyny). Consumption patterns (particularly with reference to dress, the purchase and use of automobiles, housing and house furnishings, etc.) reflect European norms. Recreational patterns (e.g., cocktail parties, eating out, etc.) also tend to be

[31] Fried, "The Chinese in British Guiana."

European. However, the social status of the Colored today is relative to one's point of view and political perspective.

In terms of the traditional colonial perspective, from a European point of view, the Colored are considered to be middle class. In terms of the same perspective, from an African point of view, the Colored represent an African elite or upper class. The new nationalist perspective is different from the traditional colonial perspective. In terms of the new nationalist perspective the Colored perceive themselves and are perceived to be Afro-Guianese. Thus, they frequently emphasize institutional patterns which they share with Africans. These include responses to racial identity, recognition of an African heritage, deep-rooted frustrations in response to colonial experiences and, most important, values pertaining to political aspirations. On the personal level of interaction, nationalist politics has alienated the Colored from European society and brought them closer to African society than they have ever been before.

It would seem to make sense, therefore, to consider the Colored as a minimal cultural section with reference to two institutional patterns. They are the most European of the Afro-Guianese at a time when it is no longer fashionable to be European. The contradictory pressures exerted by these two patterns, I believe, help to explain the rather ambiguous role which the Colored play in nationalist politics.

6. Africans and East Indians: The Africans, when compared to the East Indians, clearly constitute a maximal cultural section in British Guiana. First evidence of this derives from census figures. In 1946, 39.3 percent of the African population lived in urban areas compared to 9.9 percent of the East Indian population. If the Colored are included with the Africans, 43.2 percent of the total population of the two groups lived in urban areas. A more effective way of looking at these figures is to calculate the percentage of Africans in the urban population. In 1946, 54.4 percent of the population of Georgetown and New Amsterdam was African and 15.6 percent was East Indian. Again, if the Colored are counted with the Africans, 73.9 percent of the total urban population could be called African.

Regardless of how one chooses to look at the figures, the Africans are considerably more urban than the East Indians.[32] These figures exclude the urban oriented Mackenzie City area where over 90 percent of the bauxite workers are Africans. In the urban areas, the Africans make up the vast majority of the skilled and semi-skilled workers. Until recently they, with the Colored, dominated the teaching profession, the legal profession, the constabulary and other civil service departments such as Transport and Harbors, Local Government, Post Office, and Communications.

This description, however, does not take into account the fact that large numbers of Africans reside in rural areas. How do rural Africans relate to urban Africans? How do the cultural forms which integrate them differ from those which integrate rural and urban Indians?

[32] West Indian Census, A Census of the Population of the Colony of British Guiana (Kingston, Jamaica: Government Printer, 1946), p. xx.

AFRO-GUIANESE PATTERNS OF CULTURAL INTEGRATION

Following Emancipation, a relatively strong African peasantry emerged in British Guiana. The acquisition of land was made possible by the savings slaves had accumulated during the apprenticeship period and by the rapidly declining value of plantations. Depending upon the method used to purchase land, two types of villages were established. Young has called these "proprietary villages" and "communal villages." [33] In the proprietary villages each villager held a separate title for the land he purchased. Land titles in the communal villages were vested, by way of a single deed, in the names of representatives of a group of purchasers who had pooled their resources. Individual members of the group were listed as owning undivided shares of land. The communal village came to be the dominant form of African rural settlement.

I mention these types of settlement patterns because they are related to the fact that the African peasantry, as a cultural form, lacked survival value. In the communal villages land fragmentation almost immediately became a serious obstacle to economic viability. When "shares" were divided in the communal villages, care was taken to provide each shareholder with a proportionate amount of good and bad land. As a result, agricultural lands were divided into widely separated plots or parallel strips 20 to 40 feet wide and four to five miles long. This physical fragmentation made cultivation difficult. It also complicated the problem of maintaining the drainage and irrigation system upon which agriculture depended.

African land in the communal villages was also socially fragmented. When the central government took over the maintenance of roads and sea dams, it became necessary to partition shares of undivided land for tax purposes. Under Roman-Dutch law, the code that still exists in British Guiana with respect to property rights, in the event of intestacy, the widow and children inherited specific but undivided shares of a deceased proprietor's land. The Guianese call this "children's property" because it belongs to all the descendants as a group. As land passed from one generation to another, all the descendants of an original proprietor inherited proprietary rights to his land. These rights could not be alienated unless all the members of the group agreed to alienate them. Meanwhile, each member of the group could use the land as he or she saw fit.

The problem of "children's property" was further complicated by the African pattern of kinship. Under slavery the traditional patterns of African kinship were destroyed. These were replaced by a bilateral structure partly extended through the practice of serial polygyny.[34] With respect to inheritance, the principle of equal division among offspring transformed the bilateral structure into one that is multilineal. In other words, in each generation, ego's legitimate children inherited along with his illegitimate children. His sons inherited as

---

[33] A. Young, *The Approaches to Local Self-Government in British Guiana* (London: Longmans, Green and Co., 1958), pp. 10–13.
[34] R. Smith, "The Negro Family in British Guiana."

well as his daughters. The same applied to the second generation of children: all of them inherited equal rights to whatever land ego owned unless he specified otherwise by making out a will and he could not afford to do this unless he, through the death of relatives, had acquired clear title to the "children's property" of his father and/or his mother.

The accumulated effect of these cultural-ecological patterns are important with respect to the cultural integration of rural and urban Africans in British Guiana today. Over the past hundred years, the progressive fragmentation of African land has forced increasing numbers to seek a livelihood outside of the village, usually in the urban environment. The urban movement was further facilitated by the spread of primary education to rural Africans as a result of the compulsory education bill of 1877.[35] At the same time, the African who migrated in search of urban employment continued to retain his rights to "children's property" in the village. Furthermore, "children's property" was just as important to the urban African as it was to the rural African. It represented a source of economic security at the subsistence level during periods of unemployment or in old age, when the urban African was forced to retire with a very small government pension.

What effect has this pattern upon the rural African village? In the two villages studied in 1960, the data revealed quite conclusively that African villages tend to be inhabited by women, children, and elderly men. Most of the men interviewed had worked for years, sometimes as much as 30 or 40 years, in the bauxite mines, in the balata fields, in the diamond or gold fields, or in Georgetown. It was not uncommon to encounter individuals who had worked outside of the country during most of their lives. The absent husbands of women living in the villages worked in similar places. In MacKenzie City, for example, over 150 African workers were interviewed. When asked where they lived, regardless of how long they had been living in MacKenzie with or without their families, two out of three responded by naming a village in which they owned "children's property." When possible, these individuals send money to village relatives. When unemployed, they return to the village where they use "children's property" to practice a form of subsistence agriculture that makes a relatively insignificant contribution to the cash crop economy. Thus, urban Africans and rural Africans are integrated by virtue of family ties and "children's property."

The values that pervade this pattern of integration, however, are largely urban in character. They derive from the experience of urban employment. In rural areas Africans are not very much interested in agricultural innovations, land development schemes, or agricultural cooperatives. They join savings cooperatives, educational societies, and a wide variety of church-sponsored clubs and organizations. Agriculture is not their way of life except in retirement, and it is very doubtful if even this would persist very long with adequate urban employment, housing, and retirement pensions. To a considerable degree, rural Africans are urban Africans out of place. In this manner, the Afro-

[35] N. W. Cameron, *The Evolution of the Negro*, 2 vols. (Georgetown, B. G.: The Argosy Co., 1929), pp. 73–74.

Guianese are integrated into the total society in a way that is very different, in terms of institutional patterns, from that found among East Indians.

EAST INDIAN PATTERNS OF CULTURAL INTEGRATION

In contrast to Africans, Indians came to British Guiana as indentured workers on the sugar estates. They came in successive waves between 1840 and 1917. The indenture system, unlike the slave system, favored a continuity in East Indian cultural patterns. For one thing, the indentures were relatively confined to the estates where they were placed and this prevented them from mixing with other groups. Also, new migrants mingled with those that came earlier and this served to reinforce many traditional habits and customs. In addition, the law prevented planters from imposing their customs on Indian workers. Continuity in culture was favored also by the attitude of Indians toward sending their children to school. Indian parents did not want to send their daughters to Christian schools where they might take up with Africans. This would make it difficult for them to arrange marriages with suitable husbands. At the same time, Indian parents preferred their sons to work in boys' gangs on the estates in order to supplement family income. The planters, of course, found these attitudes profitable and the Indians were exempted from the compulsory education law of 1877. Thus, many avenues of Western influence were not completely available to Indians until the indenture system was terminated in 1917 by the government of India.

The effects of these conditions are very much in evidence today in British Guiana. In 1946, for example, 90 percent of the Indian population was classified as non-Christian.[36] In the same year, more than 44 percent of the Indians over the age of ten were illiterate in English. Illiteracy as well as Christian prejudice served to keep Indians in rural areas by preventing access to the professions, to civil service positions, and to other types of white collar employment. In 1931, for example, less than 16 percent of the professionals in British Guiana were Indians and only 8 percent of those employed in public service were Indians.[37] As late as 1943, Indians comprised only 11 percent of the fixed establishment of the civil service.[38] Meanwhile, on the sugar estates, Indians were given inferior jobs. The emancipated African with a primary education looked upon the Indian as an individual of inferior status, as a "coolie-man."

Today, East Indians constitute a peasantry as well as a rural proletarian class. In 1956, for example, approximately 75 percent of all farm operators were East Indians.[39] Most of these peasant farmers cultivate rice, the only cash crop of any significance in British Guiana other than sugar. As a matter of fact, rice agriculture represents the second largest source of employment in the

[36] West Indian Census, pp. 38–40.

[37] D. Nath, A *History of Indians in British Guiana* (London: Thomas Nelson and Sons, 1950), p. 216.

[38] *Ibid.*, p. 216.

[39] S. K. Fitzgerald, *Some Population and Land Aspects of British Guiana*, unpublished I.C.A. Report, University of Maryland, 1956, Table 14.

country. Also, in 1956, nearly 80,000 people lived on sugar estates. It is estimated that 70 percent or more of these people are East Indians. Many of the Indians who live and work on the sugar estates also cultivate rice. Data collected at Plantation Skeldon in 1960 revealed that one out of every five Indian families living in estate housing both cultivated rice and had one or more of its members working in the sugar industry.

Rice cultivation, beginning with World War I, represents a major avenue of economic mobility for Indians. Perhaps as much as any other single factor, it has contributed to the persistence of a peasant way of life in Indian communities. Rice farms operate on the basis of family labor except for certain periods when some outside help is needed. Over half of these farms are less than five acres in size. However, these small family farms are frequently more profitable, for those lacking in educational advantage, than employment on the sugar estates. Data collected in 1960 show that a typical farmer who cultivates five acres of rice with family labor on drained land can earn and save more money than by working an average year as a fieldhand on a sugar estate. Under the same conditions, ten acres of land will bring enough profit to finance a tractor. The tractor, in turn, will increase family income. If the family continues to work together, and if additional income is used to rent or purchase additional land, enough capital may be accumulated to open a small rum or dry goods shop. This is the way that many wealthy Indian families in British Guiana have acquired rice mills and Georgetown businesses. Its possibilities are sufficiently recognized that it has created a condition of land hunger among the East Indians.

The problems of land fragmentation that prevented many Africans from full participation in a cash crop economy have not existed for most of the Indians in the two villages studied in 1960–1. There are several reasons for this. For one thing, many Indians originally obtained their land in government settlement schemes in exchange for return passage to India when their period of indenture ended. The last of these settlement schemes was established in the late 1940's. These schemes were not always successful, but those who refused to become discouraged acquired most of the land given up by those who left the schemes to work on the estates. In any event, land in the schemes was divided into uniform lots and these, in turn, were not allowed to be subdivided into less than half-acre plots. Tenure was secured by individual title, and Indians learned from Africans the difficulties encountered by allowing their titles to lapse into "children's property."

In the villages studied, kinship patterns also functioned to prevent land fragmentation. Much of the traditional Indian kinship system has been retained. Inheritance is patrilineal and it follows the principle of ultimogeniture. Marriages are arranged with traditional ceremony.[40] In the marriage of daughters, the rule of village exogamy is normally followed. The dowery received by

[40] R. T. Smith and C. Jayawardena, "Hindu Marriage Customs in British Guiana," *Social and Economic Studies*, Vol. 7 (1958), pp. 178–194; "Marriage and the Family Amongst East Indians in British Guiana," *Social and Economic Studies*, Vol. 8 (1959), pp. 321–375.

the daughter's husband is considered to be her inheritance and, unless the father is very wealthy, it never consists of land.

Following the marriage of sons, residence tends to be patrilocal from a few months to a few years, the time depending upon the number of sons, their ages, and how rapidly they marry. Patrilocal residence provides a basis for the family functioning as a corporate economic group. The father and sons work together. When the oldest son marries, he lives with his father who, as head of the household, continues to manage the family income. When money is available extra land is rented or purchased by the group. The new land becomes the special responsibility of the oldest son and when the next son marries, if no room is available in the father's house, the oldest son will move his family into a house nearby. If enough land is not available to support the extended group, some sons will be encouraged to seek wage employment until additional land can be obtained. Eventually, however, the original land owned by the father becomes the special responsibility of the youngest son, the last to marry and the last to take up residence in the father's house. When the father dies, the sons continue to work all the land together until their own sons begin to marry, whereupon the land is divided and the youngest son claims his father's land and house. In the villages studied, a significant relationship was observed between a family's economic success and the extent to which it followed this pattern and functioned as a corporate economic group.

The kinship group lies at the center of Indian cultural integration. Its stability is reinforced by religious beliefs, traditional marriage forms, economic functions, and, to a limited extent, vestiges of caste. Relatives are bound together in ever-widening circles of diminishing strength. Village exogamy creates affinal ties between one village and another. At the periphery of these circles of relationships economic ties and ceremonial responsibilities shade off into friendships and social connections which have no economic base. Ultimately, this pattern of integration involves a value system which supports a cultural identity that serves to bind the Indian population together as a maximal cultural section. In terms of this pattern of integration, the Indian population is a national community with a national, but non-Western, way of life.[41]

Thus, East Indians and Africans exist as separate cultural sections in British Guiana. Africans, rural and urban, are integrated by structures that are quite different from those that integrate the Indian section. The values that sustain these structures are also different. While both sections are integrated at the societal level by virtue of their involvement in a common economic and political system, it must be kept in mind that this level of integration is one imposed by a cultural minority, the Europeans.

---

[41] This paragraph should not be interpreted to mean that hostility, disputes, and fractions do not occur among East Indians; they do, and quite frequently. Family disputes over land can often lead to physical violence. Families are often jealous of one another's prosperity. Villages frequently split into factions over issues that appear to be relatively insignificant to outsiders. In many villages Moslems and Hindus do not get along very well. However, these differences tend to disappear in the presence of an outside threat and the Africans are perceived to represent such a threat by most Indians.

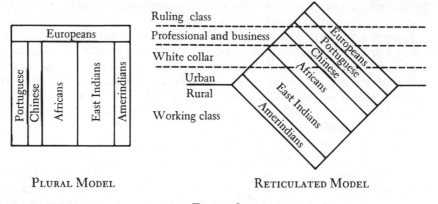

PLURAL MODEL   RETICULATED MODEL

FIGURE 2

Moreover, the national level of integration has not grown out of reticulated structures that functionally relate Africans and Indians at lower levels of integration. This is not to suggest that some common structures do not exist at lower levels of integration. For example, Africans as well as Indians belong to the sugar union, the Man Power Citizens Association. However, the membership and the leadership of this organization has always been dominated by East Indians. The reverse is the case with the British Guiana Mine Workers Union, the British Guiana Teachers' Association, the Post Office Workers' Union, and many others.

Similarly, the vast majority of villages in British Guiana contain Africans as well as Indians. This was true of the four villages studied in 1960–1. However, in each village one group or the other represented a considerable majority. Participation of the minority in village activities, including local government, was either nonexistent or limited to token representation. In some villages, where the two groups were represented in equal numbers, the Department of Local Government has had to segment the village into two separate and independent local authorities in order to preserve local government institutions.

Interaction between Africans and Indians in mixed villages tends to be instrumental. If they must, Africans will buy from Indian shops or Indians will buy from African shops. When they participate in games, they do so to compete with one another. They do not mix at dances. They almost never eat in one another's homes. At the level of family structure there is practically no integration of the two groups. Both groups are endogamous as far as marriage is concerned. The individual who marries outside of his group, particularly in rural areas, is ostracized by both groups. Skinner has pointed out that sexual contacts exist between the two groups in Canalville,[42] but such relationships are not institutionalized and they hardly serve as a basis for cultural integration.

The above description of the cultural sections existing in British Guiana provides the basis for considering these sections in light of the models discussed

[42] Skinner, "Group Dynamics and Social Stratification . . . ," p. 909.

earlier. Graphic representations are shown in Figure 2 for purposes of illustration.

That the substitution of data into these structural models presents certain difficulties can be perceived almost immediately. To a certain extent, the data are distorted by both models. Consider the plural model first. It exaggerates distinctions between Europeans, Portuguese, and Chinese. Distinctions in power exist between these groups, as the model suggests, but distinctions in culture are not as evident. In terms of European institutional patterns, the Portuguese and Chinese are minimal cultural sections. Without modification of the model, the Colored are not easily dealt with. Politically, the Colored population is identified with the African population. In terms of most institutional dimensions, however, the Colored practice a way of life not unlike that of the Europeans. The Colored may be more accurately considered as a minimal cultural section with reference to both African and European institutional patterns. And, most important to those interested in the cultural aspects of nationalist politics, the plural model does not show the extent to which members of different cultural sections have been able to achieve positions of power by penetrating the European section. This penetration has created a "native" elite, and it is from this elite that nationalist leaders have emerged.

The reticulated model presents other difficulties. As far as power is concerned, it characterizes the situation more accurately by directing our attention to the small segments of each group that have entered the upper levels of power. The reticulated model also suggests that various groups have been affected by adopting or adjusting to certain European patterns. In emphasizing these points, however, this model obscures some very real cultural distinctions that do exist between certain groups. Especially overlooked in applying this model to the data are the patterns of cultural integration which differentiate Africans and East Indians, the two most politically viable groups because of their numbers.

Another difficulty with the reticulated model concerns the problem of stratification and the color/class continuum. In substituting data into this model an attempt was made to follow, as closely as possible, the color/class structure described by Raymond Smith.[43] At best, the color/class structure is extremely ambiguous. It confuses a multitude of variables — racial, social, cultural, economic, and demographic. For example, Raymond Smith suggests that the Arya Samaj, an unorthodox Hindu religious association, is indicative of the fact that many Indians have turned from the "barbarism" and "superstition" of traditional Brahmanical Hinduism in favor of Western values while, at the same time, they insist upon the glories of Indian culture.[44] Whether Brahmanical Hinduism is "barbaric" and "superstitious" is a matter of values, to be sure. However, in the villages studied in 1960–1, less than 10 percent of the Indians had joined the Arya Samaj and most of those who had joined were among the most conservative in all respects except religion. How the adoption of Western values articulates with the color spectrum is purely a matter of speculation.

[43] R. Smith, *British Guiana* (London: Oxford University Press, 1962), pp. 98–117.
[44] *Ibid.*, p. 110.

The difficulty with the color/class continuum, it seems, is that it presents an analysis of social stratification exclusively in terms of a European frame of reference that associates skin color and the adoption of European values with social status.

Still another difficulty associated with the reticulated model pertains to the levels of cultural integration. Africans are integrated with one another at various levels as a result of their kinship system, "children's property," village patterns, the occupations they pursue, the organizations they join, their Western values (compared to Indians), and race. These levels of integration are parallel to but different from those characteristic of East Indians. Thus, East Indians tend to enter the professional and business class (see Figure 2) as businessmen; Africans tend to enter as professionals. Indian businessmen retain their rural interests, African professionals do not. In rural areas East Indians are rice farmers and sugar workers; Africans may be sugar workers but they are primarily subsistence farmers. In urban areas Indians who are not businessmen tend to be gardeners and unskilled laborers. Africans who are not professionals tend to be civil servants, skilled laborers, or domestics. The patterns of mobility are different for the two groups and these differences, as will be shown, are important in nationalist politics. The plural model directs our attention to these levels of integration; the reticulated model tends to ignore them.

THEORETICAL MODELS AND PREDICTION

The degree to which a model "fits" the data is one test of validity. Prediction is another. What predictions may be deduced from these two models and how accurate have they been with respect to changes resulting from nationalist movements in British Guiana?

Those who employ the reticulated model have emphasized the concept of the unified society. Raymond Smith, for example, has stated that British Guiana constitutes a "unitary whole capable of containing such social and cultural diversity as exists within it and that it is still in the process of developing new forms for the expression of that unity." [45] More recently, Raymond Smith has stated that the whole trend of change has been "in the direction of creating a unified society within which there is a high degree of religious and cultural freedom and racial tolerance." [46] From these statements it would be logical to deduce a transformation hypothesis which would predict that cultural sections are being assimilated into the main political framework of the society. Consequently, serious conflict — conflict which threatens the political framework of the society, should not be expected.[47]

The plural model suggests that society depends for its structural form and continuity on the regulation of intersectional relations by a minority that domi-

[45] R. Smith, "British Guiana" in *Sunday Guardian of Trinidad, West Indies Federation Supplement*, April 20, 1958. Also, as quoted by Skinner, "Group Dynamics and Social Stratification . . . ," p. 911.

[46] R. Smith, *British Guiana*, pp. 182–3.

[47] Raymond Smith is not very precise about this prediction. In fact, it would be more accurate to say that he avoids making a prediction as to what form political change will take in British Guiana (*Ibid.*, pp. 163–83).

nates the government. Changes in this structural form presuppose political changes. M. G. Smith states that political changes of this order "usually have a violent form." [48]

After the 1957 elections in British Guiana it became increasingly evident that the major nationalist fronts were being organized in terms of cultural sections. Under the leadership of Cheddi Jagan, the Peoples Progressive Party organized the East Indian cultural section. The Peoples National Congress, led by L. F. S. Burnham, organized the African cultural section. In opposition to both of these groups a third party, the United Force, was organized in 1960 by Peter D'Augiar, a prominent Portuguese businessman.

Considerable data were collected on the election campaigns of these political parties. As the 1961 elections approached, "apanjaht" became the election cry of Indians throughout the country. It means "vote for your own kind." "Apanjaht" and the P.P.P. became synonymous and to be anti-Jagan was tantamount to being a traitor to the Indian people. In Indian areas, particularly along the Courantyne Coast, individuals who voiced opposition to the P.P.P. were ostracized and, in several cases, severely beaten. In order to stem the tide of "apanjaht" politics, the P.N.C. intensified its efforts to create a solid African racial front. The U.F., on the other hand, spent large sums of money in an attempt to create a united front dominated by business interests.

The 1961 elections conclusively demonstrate how tight nationalist lines were drawn around cultural sections. The P.P.P. won large majorities in all constituencies where East Indians constituted large majorities. All 20 of the constituencies won by the P.P.P. were rural. The U.F. won three seats in those Georgetown constituencies in which the Portuguese lived. As a result of church influences, the U.F. also won an Amerindian seat in the interior. The P.N.C. won large majorities in all constituencies where Africans or Colored constituted large majorities. All 11 of the constituencies won by the P.N.C. were located in urban or suburban areas. Close races developed between the P.N.C. and the P.P.P. only in those areas where the distribution of Africans and Indians was close. The P.P.P. polled 46.7 percent of the total number of votes cast for all three parties compared to 44.7 percent for the P.N.C. These figures are almost identical to the ratio of Indians and Africans in British Guiana when the Colored are counted with the Africans. Thus, very few voters appear to have crossed the lines drawn around cultural sections.

Voting behavior is an index of the competition for power between the two major cultural sections: it is not an index of conflict. However, violent conflict emerged between the two major cultural sections in February of 1962, less than six months following the elections. The Trades Union Council, dominated by African trade unions, called a general strike, ostensibly in opposition to Jagan's 1962 tax proposals. I use the word "ostensibly" because interview data collected in 1961 revealed that if the P.P.P. remained in power a strategy of opposition was to be drafted that would utilize every means available to bring down the government. The protest strike led to violence and mob riots. Indian shops in Georgetown were gutted as seven blocks of the business district were destroyed.

[48] M. G. Smith, "Social and Cultural Pluralism," p. 776.

The government was forced to call in British troops to restore law and order. Similar disturbances erupted in April, May, and June of 1963. Reports in Guianese newspapers, including those published by the political parties, indicate that confrontations have been most direct between Africans and Indians in both urban and rural areas.

The events described above indicate that the plural model has more predictive value than the reticulated model, at least with respect to nationalist politics in British Guiana. Yet, the plural model fails to meet the test of making all the data intelligible in spite of its predictive value. For example, it was noted previously that political changes of the order described above "usually have a violent form." This implies that such changes need not be violent and it raises the question: what circumstances or conditions are necessary in order that political competition between cultural sections be transformed into violent confrontations?

The answer to this question, it seems to me, lies in a dimension of social phenomena which the plural model, because of its structural focus, fails to take into account. I refer to what Raymond Firth has called the dimension of organizational activity.[49] Cultural sections, having different structures and different levels of integration, are not in themselves politically functional. They become politically functional only when individuals and groups make them so. Therefore, in order to understand the functional role of cultural sections in nationalist politics, we must look at the organizational activities of specific individuals and groups. In the case of British Guiana, we must look at the organizational activities of political parties.

ORGANIZATIONAL ACTIVITIES AND NATIONAL POLITICS

In British Guiana there are people who profess ideologies that reflect capitalist, socialist, and Marxist postures. All three are off-spring of the colonial experience. Each has served to create a faction among the new nationalist elite. These factions have become the nuclei of political parties. At the same time, however, none of these ideologies make much sense to the Guianese masses who are not accustomed to thinking about their relatively concrete needs in terms of abstract political ideas and values. Therefore, important as ideologies may be in comprehending the posture of political factions, ideological issues are not the fundamental context of political struggle.

The most immediate context of political struggle is the constitutional system which Guiana has inherited from the British. It provides for free and periodic elections. Because of this the politician, before he can impose his ideological values on the nation, must capture the positions of power that are being vacated by the European minority. Short of a revolution, the only way this can be done is at the polls. Thus, the major problem confronting the politician is that of getting himself elected. Since the masses neither understand nor concern themselves with ideological issues, in order to get elected, the politician must

---

[49] I am employing here the distinction between social structure and social organization made by R. Firth, *Elements of Social Organization* (London: Watts, 1951), pp. 35–40. For a discussion of these concepts see Bennett and Depres, "Kinship and Instrumental Activities . . ."

resort to means other than that of political debate. The alternative to political debate is the organization of mass support.

A year before the 1946 elections, Cheddi Jagan and a number of young Georgetown intellectuals, conservatives as well as liberals, organized the Political Affairs Committee. Its purpose was mainly educational. It published a news-sheet which contained numerous articles that presented a Marxist view of the British Guiana situation. In 1950 L. F. S. Burnham, a dynamic young lawyer with considerable influence among African workers, joined the group. In preparation for constitutional advancement, Jagan and Burnham transformed the Public Affairs Committee into the Peoples Progressive Party, the first political party with real credentials to exist in British Guiana.

By 1953, when the elections were held under an advanced constitution, the P.P.P. had party cells operating throughout the country. The major responsibilities of these cells were to create a political consciousness among the masses, to discuss issues and disseminate political information, and to see to it that party supporters got to the polls and voted as they had been instructed to vote. When the 1953 elections were held the P.P.P. represented a nationalist front that united Africans and Indians in a single movement. It contested 24 seats against four splinter parties and 130 candidates of whom no less than 79 were independents. The opposition lacked organization. P.P.P. candidates won 18 of 24 seats in the legislature.[50] The new government lasted 133 days before the constitution was suspended by the governor and an Interim Government was appointed. The suspension is not relevant to this paper, and it is mentioned here only to maintain the sequence of events leading to the split which occurred between Jagan and Burnham during the period when British Guiana was under the rule of an Interim Government.

The split I refer to occurred in 1955. The belief is widely held that the split was caused by a struggle for party leadership and a clash of personalities. While these may have been factors in the situation, they were neither crucial nor decisive. Data collected in 1960–1 reveal that the left wing members of the party, led by Cheddi Jagan, were in the process of engineering the split even before the 1953 elections. It is necessary to consider the split in some detail because it helps to explain why the organizational activity of the two major political parties came to be designed in terms of cultural sections.[51]

Immediately preceding and following the 1953 elections, before the new ministers had been selected, the Jaganites held a number of secret meetings. During these meetings it was decided that whoever controlled the P.P.P. would also control British Guiana for the next 20 to 30 years, time enough to secure

[50] *Report of the British Guiana Constitutional Commission,* Sir James Robertson, Chairman (London: H. M. S. O., 1954), 9274, pp. 23–24.

[51] The data collected in 1960–61 force me to take issue with Raymond Smith concerning the Jagan-Burnham split. Smith's interpretation (*British Guiana,* pp. 178–181) seems to be based largely on news reports and popular opinion. My data were collected mainly from individuals who belonged to the left wing of the P.P.P. in 1953 and who participated in the decisions that were made at that time with respect to Burnham. Informants included Indians as well as Africans, members of the P.P.P., and ex-members of the P.P.P.

a complete social revolution. The Jaganites concluded that Burnham could not be allowed to occupy this position of power. A number of considerations led to this decision:

First, the Jaganites felt that Burnham was a deviationist. He did not accept, completely and unreservedly, Marxist doctrines, or, if he did, he was too much of a nationalist to be of use to the Communist international movement in so far as it would involve British Guiana.

Second, Burnham could not be trusted. He was under considerable pressure from middle class African intellectuals (many of whom are Colored). Some of these intellectuals broke with the P.P.P. before the elections because they rejected its extremist policies and its Marxist point of view. Others broke with the party because they feared that Jagan, an East Indian, subordinated African interests to Indian interests. In any event, the Jaganites felt that Burnham, the son of an African schoolteacher, would eventually give in to middle class pressure and join forces with the imperialists. These considerations reflect the ambiguous position of the Colored as a minimal cultural section. As Africans, the Colored displayed a nationalist pose; but, at the same time, their style disclosed a European heritage which Indians, as well as some Africans, distrusted.

A third consideration involved the Federation issue. Burnham favored British Guiana joining the Caribbean Federation. Jagan was against it. Jagan felt that Federation membership would make Guiana's independence movement a domestic rather than an international issue. He also believed that the power of the P.P.P., as a working class movement, would be submerged in the Federation by the forceful leadership of Williams of Trinidad and Bustamante of Jamaica, both of whom he regarded as "capitalist stooges." Finally, Jagan believed that Federation membership would alienate too many Indian supporters who interpreted it to mean "black domination."

For these reasons, a plan was devised to oust Burnham from the P.P.P. and, at the same time, to leave him with as little African support as possible. The plan provided that popular Africans loyal to Jagan would circulate among the African masses and accuse Burnham of being a racist as well as a "stooge" for sugar interests. It also called for creating a superficial alliance between Burnham and two Indian leaders, Dr. Lachmansingh and Jai Naraine Singh, in order to give Burnham the impression that he possibly could secure the support of Indian sugar workers. Finally, the plan provided that a party election would be staged at a time when Jagan and other left wing leaders could not attend in order to give Burnham the occasion to assert his leadership and take over the party without opposition. Later, a second congress would be called by the Jaganites. The first election would be declared null and void and Burnham would be expelled from the party for holding an "illegal election."

By 1955 this plan was fully implemented. When the split came, it appeared that Burnham had managed it on his own initiative for the purpose of securing personal power. That the Jaganite strategy was successful may be illustrated by the 1957 elections. Under a revised constitution, several political parties contested 14 seats in the new legislature. Important among these were the United Democratic Party, the political arm of the African middle class; the P.P.P.

under Jagan's leadership; and the P.P.P. under Burnham's leadership. Burnham's faction was able to win only three seats, all of them in Georgetown districts where Burnham had a personal following among African workers. Jagan's faction, on the other hand, won nine seats with 48 percent of the popular vote.

Therefore, as a result of the strategy described above, Jagan's faction was able to oust Burnham from the P.P.P., prevent a serious split in the African vote in 1957, and maintain a relatively integrated national front. However, not long after the 1957 elections several of the Africans who had plotted against Burnham in 1953 broke with Jagan and joined Burnham. Mainly, they did this because they also began to fear Indian domination within the P.P.P. Also, shortly after the 1957 elections, the African middle class party dissolved and joined forces with Burnham to form the Peoples National Congress. Thus, the stage was set for organizing the nationalist movements in terms of cultural sections.

The strategy to be used by the P.P.P. to make the Indian cultural section politically functional was outlined in a speech Jagan delivered to the 1956 Party Congress. Noting the racial, cultural, and economic differences existing between various groups in British Guiana, Jagan compared the Portuguese native capitalist with the emerging Indian capitalist: "Whereas the Indian capitalist poses a threat to Portuguese native capitalism (mainly in commerce), he suffers from a feeling of cultural, political, and economic oppression and, consequently, is further removed from, in fact, opposed to imperialism. . . . The Indian capitalist up to this stage puts his 'national' interests before his 'class' interests. Consequently, he can be a resolute ally against imperialism within these considerations." [52]

Jagan also observed that the Indian capitalist had a dual personality. As a land owner and a rice miller "he combined the functions of feudalism with the functions of capitalism." Therefore, he played a "reactionary-progressive" role: reactionary because he exploited Indian peasants; progressive because his national interests were anti-imperialist. Jagan outlined what the P.P.P. was to do in regard to these structural conditions: " . . . it is our duty to split this personality, to carry out an uncompromising struggle against his reactionary, feudal, landlord tendencies in the interest of peasant farmers while, at the same time, winning him over in our struggle against our common enemy, imperialism. This requires tact and careful handling." [53]

There are several reasons why it was important for the P.P.P. to win the support of Indian capitalists. First, if the Indian capitalist could be weaned from his rural enterprises and made to concentrate on his urban affairs, the P.P.P. could remove an obstacle to the communization of the agricultural sector of the economy. At the same time, this would increase support among Indian peasants who are hostile toward the Indian landowners and rice millers that exploit them. Second, by motivating the Indian capitalist to concentrate upon their urban affairs, the P.P.P. could pit them in competition against the European

[52] C. Jagan, "Address to the Congress of the Peoples' Progressive Party," in the December 22, 1956 issue of *The Daily Chronicle*, Georgetown, B.G.
[53] *Ibid.*

and Portuguese capitalists who controlled too much of the country's commerce. Finally, Indian capitalists were important to the P.P.P. because they represented a major source of financial support for party activity as long as the British controlled foreign policy and restricted outside sources of financial support.

The organizational suggestions provided a focus for the collection of data on the organizational activities of the P.P.P. The data reveal that after the 1957 elections Jagan proceeded to mobilize the Indian cultural section on several fronts. Two of them will be dealt with here. The first involves legislation which was passed when the party organized the government after the 1957 elections.

During the war a commodity control commission was established by the Colonial Government to regulate import quotas in British Guiana in keeping with the war effort. After the war, this commission became an informal arm of the Chamber of Commerce. It functioned to protect the interests of European business houses. The Jagan Government initiated legislation to do away with commodity control and, thereby, make it possible for Indian businessmen to import goods that enabled them to tap the mass market in competition with European firms. These new sources of income served to detract Indian capitalists from their rural enterprises to some extent and, at the same time, the impression was created that the P.P.P. was loyal to the interests of Indian businessmen. In gratitude, Indian businessmen organized a Junior Chamber of Commerce. The Junior Chamber supported Jagan on important issues and several of its members were appointed to Jagan's economic development committee. In return, prominent members of this group contributed substantial sums of money to the P.P.P. for the purpose of purchasing a new printing press.

Meanwhile, the P.P.P. did not lose sight of the sugar workers and the rice farmers. With respect to the former, the party became an unofficial union in opposition to the anti-Jagan Man Power Citizens' Association. Party workers fomented unrest on the estates, a task that was not too difficult, and took advantage of every occasion that afforded an opportunity to undermine the M.P.C.A. or worker confidence in the sugar industry. Dissatisfied workers were encouraged to travel to Georgetown and register their individual complaints with P.P.P. officials. Whenever possible, the P.P.P. interfered with disputes or strikes on behalf of the workers.

Attention was given to rice farmers mainly by diverting the major portion of Guiana's $110 million development program to land development schemes and other projects designed to improve conditions in the rice industry. For example, between 1957 and 1960, 90 thousand acres of newly developed land were distributed primarily to Indian peasants on a leasehold basis. Rice production more than doubled during this period.[54] That these schemes were designed, in part, to consolidate Indian support is substantiated by data collected in one of the schemes in 1960.

In the particular scheme under study, seventeen-acre plots were leased to ap-

[54] *Paper of the Second Legislative Council on British Guiana's 1960–64 Development Programme* (Georgetown, B.G.: The British Guiana Lithographic Co., 1959).

plicants selected on the basis of need. The selection committee consisted of representatives from several government departments. The Minister of Natural Resources, also Chairman of the P.P.P., passed final judgment on all applicants. Five of the committee's seven members had connections with the P.P.P. At the time data were collected only 150 families had been settled in the scheme. Of these, 147 were East Indian families. It was argued by some officials that Africans did not apply for land. This was partly true. However, many did not apply because they were not directed into the channels of application by party organizers. Another reason they did not apply was because successful applicants, to qualify, had to sell their homes in the villages and move into the scheme's housing development. In other words, individuals had to alienate transported property or unproductive "children's property" in order to receive land by lease from the government. Regardless of the reasons one wishes to emphasize, Africans were not receiving many benefits from the development money that was being spent. This was true of land development schemes and it applied to many other types of development programs which the government supported between 1957 and 1960.

"Apanjaht" politics held out a variety of promises to the East Indian population. It promised them more land on which they could cultivate rice. It promised them better representation in the sugar industry. It promised them better opportunities in business. It also promised them positions of power that, in the past, could be achieved only by Europeans, Portuguese, Chinese, or Africans (particularly the Colored). Above all, "apanjaht" politics gave the Indian way of life a political identity which it had never had before. "Apanjaht" politics also held out promises to the P.P.P. By virtue of their high birth rates, East Indians could give the P.P.P. a substantial majority and uncompromising control over the nationalist movement in British Guiana for years to come.

Africans, as a group, shared the threat of Indian domination on several fronts. In rural areas Indian expansion threatened the existence of villages in which urban African workers retired. African workers also felt threatened because industrial development lagged at the expense of agricultural programs. Because of Jagan's efforts to "Indianize" the civil service, African civil servants also displayed considerable anxiety. When the Jagan Government mounted a program to take charge of all denominational schools that had been built with government money, African schoolteachers and headmasters also were threatened by "apanjaht" politics. It was along these lines, therefore, that the organizational activity of the P.N.C. was focussed.

In rural areas P.N.C. politicians, in private meetings as well as public, emphasized the threat of Indian expansion and what Jagan's agricultural program could do to their "ancestral" land. They pointed to villages in the Courantyne area where Indians were already squatting on African land, apparently with P.P.P. encouragement. Also in the Courantyne area, some African land had been taken over by the government in the development schemes. P.N.C. officials explained how the leasehold system in these schemes would force Africans to give up what little they had accumulated since their fathers were emancipated. Even the rural health centers constructed by the government were being located in Indian villages. All of these things represented sources of fear which the P.N.C. exploited to consolidate an African front.

In the urban areas, in addition to the usual campaign programs designed for African tastes (e.g. dances, souse parties, excursions, etc.), the P.N.C. made a special effort to secure the support of African-dominated labor unions. Particularly important were the various civil service unions (e.g., teachers, postal workers, government clerks, transportation, communications, etc.) and the various industrial unions (e.g., building and trade, mine workers, printers, etc.). In the event of a P.P.P. victory these unions, being critical to the economy as well as the normal administrative operations of government, represented major sources of power that could be used most effectively to oppose the government. Almost without exception, these unions were brought into the P.N.C. organization. Even the British Guiana Mine Workers Union, a group that had opposed Burnham in two previous elections, joined the P.N.C. camp to stem the tide of "apanjaht" politics. Thus, the P.N.C. organized the African cultural section in opposition to the P.P.P. and Indian nationalism.

The Colored, as a minimal cultural section, were not easily cemented to this African racial front. One month before the 1961 elections, for example, members of this group could not agree upon the economic policy statement supported by other members of the P.N.C. executive. The statement was too "radical." Within a fortnight of the elections, Colored pressure forced the executive to expel the extreme racial element from the party in the person of Sidney King. Nevertheless, the organization of the African cultural section was at least partially successful. Although the P.N.C. captured only 11 of the 35 seats contested in the 1961 elections, it did emerge with a popular vote of 89,000, just 3,000 short of that received by the Peoples Progressive Party.

CONCLUSIONS

In this paper I have tried to delineate two theoretical models that have been employed by a number of anthropologists studying Caribbean societies. The plural model presupposes the existence of cultural sections which constitute separate and possibly incompatible systems. At the societal (nation-state) level, political order is maintained by a dominant section primarily through the use of force or the threat of force. The plural model predicts that changes in the power relationships between cultural sections usually, but not always, have a violent form. The reticulated model, on the other hand, suggests that the cultural sections of a society are integrated by an overall institutional system which is capable of containing the differences between them within the framework of its political order. The relationships between cultural sections are structured, in the Caribbean, in terms of the color/class continuum or, more specifically, the power dimension of the total system. This kind of political order ultimately depends upon consensus. Therefore, the reticulated model predicts that changes in the relationships between cultural sections will be transformational rather than violent.

The application of these two models in the analysis of data dealing with nationalist politics in British Guiana reveals that both are inadequate in the study of cultural changes of this type. To a certain extent, both models distort the data. The plural model, for example, directs our attention to the manner in which cultural sections are integrated differently. However, it fails to show the degree to which these patterns of integration serve to maximize or minimize the separateness between cultural sections. This consideration would seem to be important. In British Guiana, minimal cultural sections have not lent themselves to political manipulation as readily as maximal cultural sections. In a similar fashion, the plural model fails to show that certain members of different cultural sections have formed a new elite by penetrating the dominant European section.

The reticulated model directs our attention to this new elite by emphasizing the integration of the total social system. In doing so, however, it obscures some very important differences existing between the various cultural sections. Particularly, it obscures the fact that different cultural sections are integrated into the total system in parallel but distinct ways. Also, the reticulated model deals with the problem of power in terms of the "color/class continuum." The "color/class continuum" is not only vague and ambiguous, but it seems to represent a European frame of reference which may not be relevant to the context of nationalist politics in an emerging nation.

In applying these two models to the data collected, the test of prediction was also considered. Recent events in British Guiana indicate that the reticulated model has very low predictive value. The plural model more accurately predicts the violent form political changes have taken. However, violence is not a necessary consequence of the competition between cultural sections, not even when the cultural sections are incompatible. What form political competition may take is, at least in part, a function of the organizational strategy in terms of which different structures become politically viable. Although the plural model has more predictive value than the reticulated model, it fails to specify those conditions under which violence becomes a necessary consequence of competition between cultural sections.

These specific findings have more general implications with respect to anthropological research dealing with problems of culture change. Both models discussed in this paper share a very strong structural point of view. As such, they tend to construct social systems in two-dimensional terms. Individuals or groups are described as being related to one another either vertically or horizontally. As a result of these relationships certain structures come into existence. This represents one dimension, a spatial dimension. These structures, in turn, either reticulate with one another or they do not. Reticulation, or the lack of it, is explained either in terms of cultural-historical variables or by invoking certain functions which the structures serve vis-à-vis one another. This represents a second dimension, a time dimension. From these two dimensions vectorial projections are deduced with respect to how individuals and groups will behave. These projections are normative and deviations from them are deviations and nothing else.

This conceptual framework, which characterizes both models, omits what I would like to think of as a third dimension, an action or organizational dimension. In the action dimension individuals are more than units related to one another in time and space. They may be this, but they are also conscious agents capable of calculated action with respect to themselves as well as the universe around them. Thus, individuals weigh the alternative available, plan strategy, and select the means to implement strategy.

In the third dimension, spatial and temporal arrangements are manipulated to become functional in some ways rather than others. I recall, for example, an informant in British Guiana, an important political leader, telling me quite explicitly that regardless of the outcome of the 1961 elections, there would be trouble within six months and his party would be prepared for it. Thus, in the action or organizational dimension in British Guiana, certain politicians had made decisions, and certain events would follow from these decisions as night follows day. It is true that these politicians occupied structural positions which permitted them to make and implement decisions, but it is also true that they could have made alternative decisions leading to very different effects. Structural positions, in other words, tell us very little about the kinds of decisions individuals will make and the ways in which they will implement these decisions.

No two-dimensional model permits us to systematically investigate organizational activity. In the past, the dimension of organizational activity may not have been particularly relevant in studies of culture change. However, this is an age of planned change, political as well as technological. Nationalist politicians with advanced degrees, working with experts at their sides, weigh facts, devise programs on the basis of five and ten year projections, calculate strategy, and elect what appears to be the most efficient means available to achieve their objectives. Cultural sections no longer clash by chance or because they have incompatible structures: they clash because certain individuals and groups have decided that something can be achieved by making them clash. Anthropologists interested in the problems of culture change, it seems to me, will have to devise models that take this third dimension into account.

The Modernity of Tradition:
The Democratic Incarnation
of Caste in India

LLOYD I. RUDOLPH

Marx's century-old socio-political analysis of peasant nations and of India's traditional village and caste society, because it captures so much of contemporary social and political analysis, provides a convenient framework for critical discussion and evaluation of the relationship between traditional society and modern politics in India. Peasant nations such as mid-nineteenth century France, Marx observed in *The Eighteenth Brumaire of Louis Napoleon,* are formed "by simple addition of homologous magnitudes, much as potatoes in a sack form a sackful of potatoes." [1] Objectively, peasants form a class; the mode of life, interests and culture which flow from their productive circumstances separate peasants from other classes and place their class in opposition to other classes. But subjectively and practically, peasants form a vast mass, "the members of which live in similar conditions, but without entering into manifold relations with one another." They are isolated from each other by their mode of production, poor communications and poverty. The small holding, because it cannot support division of labor or the application of science, lacks multiplicity of development, diversity of talents and a variety of social relationships. Peasant society consists of self-sufficient peasant families; ". . . a few score of these make up a village, and a few score villages a Department." [2]

Peasants do not form a class, Marx argued, because their relations are "strictly local." They know each other only parochially. Because the "identity of their interests begets no unity, no national union and no political organization," they "cannot represent themselves, they must be represented." "Their representative," he continued, "must at the same time appear as their master, as an authority over them, as an unlimited governmental power that protects them against other classes and sends them the rain and the sunshine from above. The political influence of the small peasants, therefore," he concludes, "finds its final expression in the executive power subordinating society to itself." [3]

Many contemporary social scientists would agree with Marx that in the early stages of economic development, social change and political modernization in peasant societies will produce popular authoritarian or revolutionary ideological regimes which subordinate society to themselves. The circumstances of mid-twentieth century India bring these possibilities into sharp focus and provide

From the *American Political Science Review,* Vol. LIX, No. 4 (December 1965), pp. 975–989. Reprinted by permission of the author and publisher.

LLOYD I. RUDOLPH is Associate Professor of Political Science, University of Chicago. He is a specialist in Indian studies, and has published numerous articles in professional journals. He has just written a book entitled *The Modernity of Tradition,* in collaboration with Suzanne Hoeber Rudolph.

[1] Karl Marx, *Selected Works,* 2 vols. (New York: International Publishers, n.d.), II, 415.
[2] *Ibid.,* pp. 414–415.
[3] *Ibid.*

the basis for an assessment of Marx's view of the politics of peasant nations in the course of modernization.

At Independence, Indian society encompassed active but receding feudal classes; a growing, vigorous but divided bourgeoisie; a visible, important but still immature industrial economy; and a massive peasantry.[4] Despite increasing fragmentation and debt, Indian peasants — like peasants elsewhere [5] — have not, as Marx thought they would, parted with their attachment to the small holding nor provided that "chorus without which the solo song [of the urban proletariat] in all peasant nations becomes a swan song." [6] Instead of surrendering themselves to a political master in the hope of protection and benefits or recognizing their "natural ally and leader" in the industrial proletariat, Indian peasants have found the means in traditional social arrangements to represent and rule themselves.

Indian peasants through self-transformation have begun to realize in their consciousness and organization a modern society and a democratic polity. In Britain, aristocracy saved itself by timely reform; in India, caste is doing so. The leading and most pervasive natural association of the old regime — caste — is transforming itself from below and within. From an expression of the hierarchy, privilege and moral parochialism of the old order, caste has become the means to level the order's inequalities by destroying its moral basis and social structure. In doing so, caste, in its new form, the caste association, has served to attach the peasantry to the ideas, processes and institutions of political democracy.

I

India's old regime was — and is — diffuse and decentralized, dominated by micro- rather than macro-institutions. The traditional society of villages, castes

---

[4] See Howard L. Erdman, "India's Swatantra Party," *Pacific Affairs*, Vol. 36 (Winter, 1963–64), pp. 394–410, for the political role of India's feudal classes. For its business classes see Helen B. Lamb, "Indian Business Communities and the Evolution of an Industrial Class," *Pacific Affairs*, Vol. 28 (June, 1955), pp. 101–116 and D. R. Gadgil, *Origins of the Modern Indian Business Class* (New York: Institute of Pacific Relations, 1959). For India's social and political development see B. B. Misra, *The Indian Middle Classes: Their Growth in Modern Times* (London: Oxford University Press, 1961); Charles Heimsath, *Indian Nationalism and Hindu Social Reform* (Princeton: Princeton University Press, 1964) and Bruce T. McCully, *English Education and the Origins of Indian Nationalism* (New York: Columbia University Press, 1940). For industrial development see Vera Anstey, *The Economic Development of India*, 4th ed. (London: Longmans, Green, 1952); H. Venkatasubbiah, *Indian Economy Since Independence* (Bombay: Asia Publishing House, 1961); and Charles A. Myers, *Labor Problems in the Industrialization of India* (Cambridge, Mass.: Harvard University Press, 1958). Myron Weiner's *The Politics of Scarcity* (Chicago: University of Chicago Press, 1962), provides a useful analysis of interest groups in Indian politics.

See the Government of India, Central Statistical Organization, Department of Statistics, *Statistical Abstract of the Indian Union, 1961* (Delhi: Manager of Publications, 1961), for particulars on the distribution of national income among sectors of the economy. Agriculture, not including Forestry and Fishing, accounted for 46.8 per cent of National Income in 1959–60. See p. 21.

[5] See, for example, David Mitrany, *Marx Against the Peasant: A Study in Social Dogmatism* (New York: Collier Books, 1961).

[6] Marx, II, "Brumaire," p. 419.

and families had been in considerable measure self-regulating; social integration and control were given form and substance by the high culture, by Hindu metaphysics, morals and social organization. But the high culture was widely varied in its practical expression and increasingly dilute as it approached the lower reaches of society and its little traditions.[7] The weakness and failure of revolution and reaction, the strength and persistence of traditional values and social forms and the fact that social and political change has come from within and below as well as from without and above — all are closely related to the relative weight of micro- as against macro-institutions in traditional Indian society. The predominance of micro-institutions deflected and contained the extremes of organized change through political action. India's traditional macro-institutions were difficult to attack or defend nationally: Hinduism had no church, no ecclesiastical hierarchy, no doctrinal orthodoxy; the nobility of the sword, like that of the robe, lacked institutional means to give it political standing or effectiveness as an estate of the realm; nor was India's third estate organized or represented as such.[8]

The strength and importance of macro-institutions in Indian society and government also affected the quality of imperial rule. Imperial rule, like that of a revolutionary ideological regime in a new nation, manufactures and induces change from outside and above.

Imperialism, at least as it was practiced in India, was not so sweeping in its concern to create a modern economy and to realize new values, nor so eager for quick results, nor so coercive and total in its methods as revolutionary ideological regimes like those in Russia or China. Yet it remains true that the imperialism of the British *raj* in its task of destruction and reconstruction was restrained and hindered by the strength and predominance in traditional society of diffuse and decentralized micro-institutions.

"England," Marx wrote in 1853, *"has broken down the entire framework of Indian society, without any symptoms of reconstitution yet appearing."*[9] It has, however, "a double mission to fulfill . . . one destructive, and the other regenerative — the annihilation of old Asiatic society [or despotism] — and the laying of the material foundations of Western society in Asia."[10] It had begun the latter[11] by imposing political unity, now [1853] to be strengthened and perpetuated by the electric telegraph; by introducing the first free press in Asia, "a new and powerful agent of reconstruction"; by creating private property in land;

---

[7] For a discussion of the structures, processes and roles which link the society and culture of the locality in India with that of its civilization, see Milton Singer, "The Social Organization of Indian Civilization," *Diogenes*, 45 (Spring, 1964), pp. 84–119. It surveys and integrates the relevant monographic literature, particularly the work of Singer himself, M. N. Srinivas, Bernard S. Cohn and McKim Marriott.

[8] For India's modern constitutional history see Reginald Coupland, *The Indian Problem, Report on the Constitutional Problem in India* (London: Oxford University Press, 1944).

[9] Karl Marx, *Selected Works*, II, "The British Rule in India," p. 652 (underlining mine).

[10] *Ibid.*, p. 658.

[11] "The work of regeneration hardly transpires through a heap of ruins," he observes. "Nevertheless it has begun." *Ibid.*

by educating Indians and thereby producing "a fresh class . . . endowed with the requirements for government and imbued with European science"; by connecting India through steam navigation with itself and the world, thereby breaking the isolation "which was the prime law of its stagnation"; and by gifting India "with the means of irrigation and of internal communication [railroads] which will, when completed, liberate her productive powers by revitalizing agriculture and enabling her to exchange what she produces." [12]

The railroads, along with the multiplication of roads, he predicted, would destroy village isolation and its accompanying "self-sufficient inertia" by supplying that intercourse with other villages without which *the desires and efforts indispensable to social advance*" are absent. By introducing foreign and domestic manufactured goods, modern transportation and communication would "put the hereditary and stipendiary village artisanship of India to full proof of its capacity, and then supply its defects." [13] Because the railway system requires industrial processes for its support and because Indians had the aptitude and were getting the requisite training to man it, the railway system "will become the forerunner of modern industry." Modern industry in turn "will dissolve the hereditary divisions of labour, upon which rest the Indian castes, those decisive impediments to Indian progress. . . ." [14] When the people have appropriated all the English bourgeoisie has created, they will be able to emancipate themselves and mend their social condition by using the material civilization it brought forth. For Marx, the India of tomorrow was both western and socialist.

England's mission of destruction, "the annihilation of old Asiatic society," was not yet complete in 1853. "We know," he wrote, "that the municipal organization [village and caste *panchayats* or councils] and the economical basis of the village communities have been broken up, but their worst feature, the dissolution of society into stereotype and disconnected atoms [*i.e.*, the India of villages and castes], has survived . . ." [15] the revolutionary impact of British imperialism. The *raj* did indeed undermine the "self-sufficient inertia" of village and caste, and release "the desires and efforts indispensable to social advance." [16] Improved communication, particularly the railroads, did further this process. But what form and purpose did these desires and efforts for social advance assume? Marx left this question unanswered because unnoticed, concentrating his attention instead on the development of the material bases for a modern economy and society which he expected would be appropriated by the people for their emancipation and well-being. Caste, that most pervasive and, for most students of Indian society — Marxian and non-Marxian alike — most retrograde of India's social institutions, has not only survived the impact of British imperialism but also transformed and transvalued itself. In doing so, it

[12] *Ibid.*, pp. 658–660.

[13] Marx quoting Chapman, *The Cotton and Commerce of India, ibid.* at page 661 (underlining mine).

[14] *Ibid.*, pp. 661–662.

[15] *Ibid.*, p. 660.

[16] *Ibid.*, p. 661.

has helped dissolve what Marx called the "village system," [17] including a caste-based social hierarchy, and contributed to the success of political democracy.[18] Change in India has come from within and below as well as from above and outside.

II

Kamaraj Nadar, formerly the Chief Minister of Madras State, now President of the ruling Congress Party and, along with Prime Minister Lal Bahadur Shastri, the dominant figure in Indian public life after the death of Jawaharlal Nehru, is the descendant of a caste whose recent history illustrates the process of social change and modernization from within and below. At the time Marx wrote, Shanans were toddy tappers, an occupation considered polluting by Brah-manical Hinduism. Over the past century, the caste has transformed itself by creating new units of consciousness, organization and action. Today, by success-fully changing its caste culture and getting this change recognized by the state and by Madras society, it — like other castes which have participated in the same process [18a] — occupies a new and higher place in a changed social order.

One of the first evidences of Shanan aspirations for greater equality and dignity is found in the homely story of the "bosom" controversy. Shanan women had for a generation clothed themselves above the waist even though caste custom dictated that dressing in such a manner was reserved for higher

[17] *Ibid.*, pp. 654–655.

[18] See Lloyd I. Rudolph and Susanne Hoeber Rudolph, "The Political Role of India's Caste Associations," *Pacific Affairs*, Vol. 33 (March, 1960), pp. 5–22.

[18a] See below, section IV, for the Vanniyars. Although the Nadars and the Vanniyars are Madras (southern India) castes, developments similar to those detailed here can be found in other states and regions of India. Some indication of them in Gujarat (western India) is given in the discussion of the Gujarat Kshatriya Sabha, also in section IV, below. Nirmal Kumar Bose deals with two Bengali (eastern India) caste asso-ciations, of the Yogi and the Namasudra, in "Some Aspects of Caste in Bengal," in Milton Singer (ed.), *Traditional India* (Philadelphia: American Folklore Society, 1959), pp. 199–200. William Rowe has explored the history of caste associations among two castes distributed throughout northern India, the Noniya and the Kayastha, in "The New Cauhans: A Caste Mobility Movement in North India," in J. Silverberg (ed.), *Social Mobility in Caste in India* (forthcoming) and "Mobility in the Caste System," a paper delivered at the Conference on Social Structure and Social Change, University of Chicago, June 3–5, 1965. For social and cultural change at the local level among the Chamars, an extensive "untouchable" caste found primarily in Uttar Pradesh, see Bernard S. Cohn, "The Changing Status of a Depressed Caste," in McKim Marriott (ed.), *Village India* (Chicago: University of Chicago Press, 1955) and "Changing Traditions of a Low Caste," in Milton Singer, *op. cit.*, above. Owen M. Lynch, "The Politics of Untouchable," another paper at the University of Chicago Conference, June 1965, above, describes the origin and changing ideology and func-tions of Chamar caste association in Uttar Pradesh. Robert J. Miller dealt with the Mahars, a numerous "untouchable" caste of Maharashtra (western India), in "Button, Button . . . Great Tradition, Little Tradition, Whose Tradition," mimeo., University of Wisconsin, 1 March 1965.

Returning to the South, two well established and powerful caste associations represent the Nairs and the Ezhavas in Kerala, while in Mysore the Lingyats and the Okaligas are well organized and highly influential.

castes only. Threats and disturbances provoked by this practice culminated in the Travancore Riot of 1858. The question of whether Shanan women would or would not give " . . . up the practice of going about without an upper cloth" [19] had become sufficiently serious to require state intervention. The next year, Sir Charles Trevelyan, the Governor of Madras, granted them permission to wear a cloth over the breasts and shoulders; and the Maharaja of Travancore, in whose princely state the riot had occurred, found no objection to Shanan women putting on a jacket, tying themselves round with coarse cloth or "to their covering their bosoms in any manner whatever, but not like the women of higher castes." [20]

Soon after these events, pamphlets setting out the caste's claims to *kshatriya* (warrior-ruler) status appeared. Members began to claim the right to wear the sacred thread, symbol of the spiritually twice-born Brahman, Kshatriya and Vaisya *varnas*, and to be carried on palanquins at their wedding ceremonies — also a custom previously confined to the highest castes. "Kshatriya" academies, open to all, but designed particularly for the education of Shanan boys, were started, marriage rules tightened, Brahmans "of a less particular kind" induced to act as priests and "a sort of incomplete parody of the ceremony of investiture with the sacred thread" symbolizing twice-born status practiced.[21] "We humbly beg," a group of Shanan petitioners addressed the Census Commissioner in 1901, "that we are the descendants of the Pandya or Dravida Xatra race who . . . first disafforested and colonized this land of South India" and presented him with an historical volume entitled *Short Account of the . . . Tamil Xatras, the Original but Downtrodden Royal Race of Southern India*." [22] Shanans claimed that ancient coins called Shanans proved that they long ago had the authority to strike coinage and that the honorific, Nadar, by which leaders of the caste were addressed, proved they were *kshatriyas* because it meant ruler of a locality. In 1891 the Census Commissioner observed that the Shanans were " . . . usually placed a little above the Pallas and Paraiyans, and are considered to be one of the polluting castes, but of late many have put forward the claim to be considered Kshatriyas, and at least 24,000 of them appear [*i.e.*, gave their caste to the census enumerator] as Kshatriyas in the caste tables." To the learned commissioner, this was "of course, absurd as there is no such thing as a Dravidian Kshatriya" although he conceded that the Shanans may have been "at one time a war-like tribe. . . ." [23]

Leading Shanans saw matters differently; through a new associational life [24] which organized and gave expression to their changing consciousness, culture

[19] Edgar Thurston, *Castes and Tribes of Southern India*, 7 vols. (Madras: Government Press, 1909), VI, 365.

[20] *Ibid.*

[21] *Ibid.*, pp. 365–366.

[22] *Ibid.*, p. 367.

[23] *Ibid.*, p. 369.

[24] There are two Nadar Caste Associations, the Nadar Maha Jana Sangam of Madurai and the Dakshina Mara Nadar Sangam of Tirunelveli. The Nadar Maha Jana Sangam, the larger and more influential of the two, has organized annual Nadar conferences since 1910.

and identity, they pressed for recognition and legitimation from orthodox Hindu society. At its moral and ritual center lay religion and its most visible and accessible target, the temple. In 1874, the Shanans pressed unsuccessfully to establish their right to enter the great Minakshi Temple at Madurai.[25] In the *Kamudi Temple* case of 1899 [26] the Shanans through the legal system of the British Raj made a major effort to cross the pollution barrier of orthodox Hindu society and establish their claim within it to be a twice-born caste. They hoped to win through the legal processes and sanctions of the alien and secular political order what they had been denied by the religious macro-institutions of traditional society, sacred legitimacy for their claims to a greater measure of equality.

Their hopes were cruelly dashed by the courts. The District Court at Madura, and, on appeal, the High Court of Madras and the Privy Council agreed, in the face of Nadar claims that it was their immemorial right to enter the temple at Kamudi, that neither custom nor *sastras* (sacred texts) sanctioned their doing so.

"There is no sort of proof," the High Court held, "that even suggests a probability that the Shanans are descendants from Kshatriya or warrior castes of Hindus, or from Pandiya, Chola, or Chera race of kings." Nor did the honorific appellation Nadar entitle them to claim higher status or greater rights; it in no way changed their ritual status. From time immemorial, the Shanans had cultivated the Palmya palm and collected and distilled its juice, an occupation that placed them in general social estimation "just above that of . . . Pariahs . . . who are on all hands regarded as unclean, prohibited from the use of Hindu temples and below that of the . . . Maravans [one of the caste directly concerned] and other classes admittedly free to worship in Hindu temples." Further, the court held, there were no grounds whatsoever for regarding them as of Aryan origin; their worship, said the court, was a form of demonology.

The court was not unaware of the radical changes in Shanan circumstances:

> No doubt many Shanans have abandoned their hereditary occupation, and have won for themselves by education, industry and frugality respectable positions. . . . In the process of time, many Shanans took to cultivating, trade, and money lending, and today there is a numerous and prosperous body of Shanans who have no immediate concern with the immemorial calling of their caste. In many villages they own much of the land, and monopolize the bulk of trade and wealth.

The Court recognized that these *de facto* changes created difficulties: the Shanans have "not unnaturally sought for social recognition, and to be treated on an equal footing in religious matters." It was also "natural to feel sympathy for their efforts . . . but such sympathy," the court warned, "will not be increased by unreasonable and unfounded pretensions, and, in the effort to rise, the Shanans must not invade the *established rights* of other castes."

[25] Thurston, *op. cit.*, VI, 355.

[26] Sankaralinga Nadan v. Rajeswara Dorai, Indian Law Reports, 31 Madras 236 (1908). The quotations below are all drawn from this report of the case.

The Court invoked Brahman written and edited law and the testimony of Brahman witnesses concerning local custom to sustain its interpretation:

> According to the Agama Shastras which are received as authoritative by worshippers of Siva in the Madura district, entry into a temple, where the ritual prescribed by these Shastras is observed; is prohibited to all those whose profession is the manufacture of intoxicating liquor and the climbing of palmyra and cocoanut trees.

Plaintiffs' thirty-four witnesses were unanimous in testifying that Shanans did not enter the temple at Kamudi. "Most of them are Brahmans," the Court observed, "who, being in a position of acknowledged superiority to both contending parties, Shanans and Maravans, are less likely than others to be swayed by personal bias or self-interest." [27] Although some among the Shanans' twenty-eight witnesses were Brahmans, they were generally "men of much lower standing and respectability, and are to large extent in the pay or under the control of the Nadars . . ." The Court's allegations were confirmed but seemed to cut both ways when the Rajah of Ramnad, the trustee of the temple and the original plaintiff, agreed — after he had won the case in the district court — to "compromise" in the face of the Shanans' appeal to the High Court, by allowing them to enter the Kamudi temple and worship there. "A very sordid motive for this surrender," their Lordships of the Privy Council observed, "was specifically asserted and has not been disproved." When the High Court joined other plaintiffs to the original plaintiff so that the suit could be heard on appeal, the Rajah's confidence in the justice of his suit "convalesced."

In the Court's judgment, birth, not achievement, defined social identity. Rights were rooted in Brahmanically defined custom and Brahmanically edited sacred texts, not in treating equals equally or in "right reason." Only Aryans, not Dravidians, could be *kshatriyas;* the pollution of the fathers followed the sons into commerce, the professions and agriculture. The Court advised the Shanans, in phrases reminiscent of the United States Supreme Court's doctrine in *Plessy v. Ferguson* with respect to Negro claims to equality,[28] to be separate but equal by using their own temples. Shanans were "numerous and strong enough in wealth and education to rise along their own lines . . . without appropriating the institutions or infringing the rights of others."

A minor civil war in the form of the Tinnevelly Riots of 1899 followed close

[27] For a discussion of the critiques of the Madras High Court, particularly its Brahmanic bias, see Lloyd I. Rudolph and Susanne Hoeber Rudolph, "Barristers and Brahmans; Legal Cultures and Social Change," *Comparative Studies in Society and History,* Vol. 8, No. 1 (December, 1965).

[28] 163 U.S. 537 (1896). "If one race," the Court observed, "be inferior to the other socially, the Constitution of the United States cannot put them on the same plane." "We consider the underlying fallacy of the plaintiff's argument [that by enforcing segregation between whites and negroes the states were denying the equal protection of the laws assured by the Fourteenth Amendment] to consist in the assumption that the enforced separation of the two races stamps the colored race with a badge of inferiority. If this be so, it is not by reason of anything found in the act, but solely because the colored race chooses to put that construction upon it" (p. 551).

on the heels of the *Kamudi Temple* case. "The pretensions of the Shanans to a much higher position in the religio-social scale than the other castes are willing to allow," the Inspector-General of Police wrote in his *Administration Report* for that year, was the cause of extensive civil disorder and violence.[29] High on the list of Shanan "pretensions" was their claim to entry of temples. When the manager of the Visvanatheswara Temple at Sivakasi closed it rather than give in to the pressure of a massive Shanan agitation for entry — an act again reminiscent of American events in the struggle for integration — Shanans and their enemies agreed that they had gained at least a partial victory. Most opposed to Shanan mobility were the Maravans, their near neighbors in space and status. A "clean" caste, the Maravans could enter the temple at Sivakasi. To share it with the Shanans, a polluting caste according to the ritual definitions of traditional society, seemed intolerable. The Maravans struck back by organized attacks on Shanan villages and sections, burning, looting and sometimes killing. The Shanans violently resisted five thousand Maravans who marched on Sivakasi to enforce their demands. The police summed up the struggle in the following statistics: 23 murders; 102 robberies; many cases of arson; 1958 arrests; and 552 convictions; including seven death sentences.

By 1921, the Shanans had gained sufficient social esteem and political influence so that they alone, among the many castes making the attempt, succeeded in changing their name and shedding officially their traditional occupation. Their metamorphosis was wrought neither by the macro- or micro-institutions of traditional society nor by the legal system of the British state finding in the custom or the sacred texts of traditional society grounds to justify Shanan claims. Instead it was the Government of Madras, responding to the determined representations of the organized "Nadar" community, that did so. "The Shanar of 1911," Census Commissioner G. T. Boag wrote in 1921, "now appears as a Nadar; this is done under orders of the Government of Madras, that the word Shanar should cease to be used in official records." [30]

The Shanans' secular and official social transformation extended to occupation as well as name when the Government decided to list in the census actual rather than traditional ones. The Census Superintendent observed that neither common names nor common traditional occupations were "safe guides" to the definition of caste or the identification of a particular caste. The Nadars, for example, who were in earlier censuses shown as toddy-drawers, ". . . now claim that they are by tradition and inheritance lords of the soil and that

---

[29] Thurston, *op. cit.*, VI, 364.

[30] Census of India, 1921, Vol. XIII, *Madras* (Part I) *Report* (Madras: Superintendent, Government Press, 1922), p. 153, note. The relevant Government Orders are: Government of Madras, Law (General) Department, G.O. No. 56, dated 8 April 1921, and G.O. 785, 7 July 1921. Circulars No. 4 and No. 5 of the Nadar Maha Jana Sangam contain the instructions of the caste association to its followers concerning the responses to be given to census enumerators. Census Commissioner Boag's description and analysis of changes in caste names generally on pp. 153–155 of Vol. XIII is particularly instructive for the shift from Shanan to Nadar. I wish to thank Robert L. Hardgrave, Jr. for his help in obtaining the texts of the relevant G.O.s and the Sangams circulars and the Nadar Maha Jana Sangam for its courtesy in making its archives available to him.

toddy-drawing was the occupation only of comparatively few degenerate members of the caste." In deference to the wishes of the representatives of the Nadar community," he continues, "the Madras Government have decided on this occasion not to show traditional occupations in the census tables. . . ." [31]

Today only those relatively few who live in more remote villages and engage in toddy tapping know themselves and are known to others as Shanans; for a number of generations Shanans have increasingly shared the public identity, Nadar. The community has breached the pollution barrier, changed its rank within traditional society and now occupies an important place in the modern society of Madras and India.[32]

The story of the Shanans illustrates in some measure the general processes of social change and political modernization which have affected traditional Indian society. Castes, "the stereotype and disconnected units" which Marx, over a century ago, described as having survived the break-up of the village economy and government, but which were to be dissolved by the effects of industrialization, have not yet been so. Instead, they seem, in good Hindu fashion, to have been reincarnated in a modern form as the caste association.[33] This has become a vehicle for internal cultural reform and external social change. It enables middle and lower castes to establish self-esteem under circumstances in which they had begun to feel the inferiority rather than the inevitability of their condition and to win social esteem, first from the state, then from society at large and last and most slowly from the village and locality. A vehicle of consciousness and organization, it enabled lower castes to emulate twice-born castes' norms and practices, and by doing so to appropriate some of their charisma and prestige for themselves. The result has been to level the

[31] Census of India, 1921, Vol. XIII, *Madras*, p. 154.

[32] See *Man in India*, Vol. 39, No. 2 (April–June 1959), particularly McKim Marriott's "Interactional and Attributional Theories of Caste Ranking," for discussions of the relationship between caste mobility and caste ranking. Marriott is critical of Srinivas' for being too "attributional." For Srinivas' views see his *Caste in Modern India and Other Essays* (Bombay: Asia Publishing House, 1962). Milton Singer in his ". . . Indian Civilization . . . ," *Diogenes*, tries to accommodate both views but suggests that Marriott may have overstated the case against attributional ranking. See particularly the sections on "Sanskritization and Cultural Mobility," ". . . Attributes vs. Interactions in Caste Mobility" and "Westernization and Sanskritization," pp. 99–108.

The case of the Shanans who became Nadars seems to suggest that the study of caste ranking, like the study of social change generally, has not paid enough attention to middle sector analysis, which examines change as it occurs in the social space between village and *jati* on the one hand and society and *varna* on the other and takes several generations as its relevant time span. It is less (narrowly) behavioral and philosophical, more historical and sociological, in its ideas and methods.

How much and in what ways the Shanans' changing social standing was reflected over time in village consciousness and behavior is not yet entirely clear. Because their rise was accompanied by increasing wealth and education, decreasing pollution and the emulation and appropriation of high caste behavior and symbols, it seems reasonable to assume that locally the Shanans' change of name and status was in considerable measure recognized *over time* by appropriate changes in the evaluations and behavior of non-Shanans of all ranks and castes.

[33] See L. Rudolph and S. H. Rudolph, "Caste Associations," *op. cit., passim.*

ritually based social hierarchy of the caste-ordered society. Uniting similar but dispersed and isolated *jatis* (subcastes) of village and locality in larger organizations with common identities, the caste association has contributed significantly to the success of political democracy by providing bases for communication, representation and leadership. It taught and enabled illiterate peasants to participate meaningfully and effectively in politics. Lower castes whose large numbers gave them an advantage in competitive democratic politics, gained influence, access and power in state and society. With these at their command, they have changed in their favor the allocation of resources, privilege and honor.

III

If India, a peasant nation, is not what Marx thought such nations must be — a "sackful of potatoes," the result of the "simple addition of homologous magnitudes," a society of stereotype and disconnected atoms — if it does not need a political master to which its peasants may subordinate themselves, as he thought they would, and has not developed revolutionary consciousness, it is because India's peasants can represent and rule themselves; and caste helps them to do so. This is not to underestimate the problems caste poses for the creation of a modern society and the realization of individuality but is to place caste in its incarnation as caste association in an analytic context and there assess its meaning.

The caste association has contributed to the decompression and deparochialization of the *jati* and the locality, particularly the village, which is the *jati*'s historical and natural home. By reaching out toward the state and national legislative constituency, to the Community Development Block and District and their recently created parallel organs of local government, to legislative, administrative and executive arms of the State Government, and even to the government in Delhi and the politics of the nation, the caste association has educated and elevated caste consciousness, interest and purpose and given caste a voice in decisions at these levels. Doing so has helped inform the *jati*, aroused its imagination along with its ambition, and led it to larger and more inclusive identities and loyalties. As the block and district headquarters, the market town, local school and nearby cinema become increasingly relevant to village lives, as they energize and shape identities, they create alternative environments for prestige and self-esteem. The expansion of horizons and the growth of empathy have reduced the concentration of affect, power and economic dependence at the local level.[34] The caste association both independ-

---

[34] The caste association can be viewed as both an independent and dependent variable in the processes of decompression and deparochialization. A few studies that highlight these processes are F. G. Bailey, who describes how the extension of the economic and political frontier (by which he means primarily the State administration) has liberated several castes, particularly the Boad Outcastes, from the social, cultural and governmental authority of the village of Bisipara: *Caste and the Economic Frontier* (Manchester: Manchester University Press, 1957); T. Scarlett Epstein, who shows how in the "dry" village of Dalena (but not in the wet one of Wangala) in Mysore, radical economic change led to its integration into the regional economy, undermined the principle on which its society was organized (p. 325) and displaced ritual by economic aspects of prestige (p. 334): *Economic Development and Social*

ently and as the carrier of other forces and institutions contributes to the
reduction of the affect and interest invested in the face-to-face communities
of caste and village. A unit of consciousness and organization which transcends
both, it leads its members to new symbols, models and reference groups and
to contexts of action which are structurally less diffuse but affectively more so.
The drift of power, profit and honor away from the locality has not yet made
Indian villages into bedroom suburbs but it has broken their ancient monopoly
on all aspects of life.

Membership in a caste association is based on both birth and choice. One
must be born into a particular *jati* to qualify, but then one must choose to join
the association. The ascriptive element strongly suggests that there is a natural
limit to the caste association's capacity to approximate a wholly voluntary
association. However far it may lead those who identify with it from the narrow
confines of the traditional face-to-face community, it can not, so it is argued,
lead them beyond ascriptive boundaries. The individual can never be fully free
to define himself, to make his own destiny, and as a consequence he is unable
to act politically in ways that are untainted by group parochialism and selfishness.

Several recent developments have challenged this view. First, in so far as it
is possible in India to "leave" traditional and "join" modern society by, for
example, being educated in the English medium and "western" ideas, being
trained in a modern profession and practicing it, marrying out of caste, and
associating with people who, at least ostensibly, do not take caste into account
in their friendships — and this is possible up to a point in India today — the
modernization of Indian society and politics through the transformation of
caste becomes only one of two ways to achieve modernity. But the kind of
westernization that Marx was talking about and the kind that Srinivas hypothe-
sizes,[34a] that is, an alternative process of change that results in the formation of
society in western terms, is more an analytic construct than a description of
reality. Westernization has created a "shadow" society, like the opposition's
cabinet in British politics, ready to take power but for the moment serving as a
critic of those in power and an innovator or catalyst of change. Like a shadow
cabinet, it can change the existing regime's direction without ever replacing
it. Modernity has entered into Indian character and society but it has done so
through assimilation not replacement.[35] The changes that now appear on the
horizon with respect to the further evolution of the caste association and its

---

Change in South India (Manchester: Manchester University Press, 1962); and William
S. Rowe, who has shown how the Noniyas, an aggressively upward mobile caste of
Senapur, loosened the hold of the village's dominant caste by building a school with
tiles purchased outright from a potter's village adjacent to Banaras twenty-five miles
away: "Changing Rural Class Structure and the Jajmani System," *Human Organization*, Vol. 22 (Spring, 1963). For the concept of empathy, its role in modernization
and its relation to communication, see Daniel Lerner, *Modernizing the Middle East;
The Passing of Traditional Society* (Glencoe, 1958), esp. chs. 1 and 2.

[34a] M. N. Srinivas, *op. cit.*, chs. 1–3.

[35] The burden of Edward Shils' argument in *The Intellectual Between Tradition and
Modernity; The Indian Case* (The Hague: Mouton, 1961), seems to me to be consistent with these thoughts.

transcendence of ascription have to do with internal differentiation (fission) and the operation of integrative institutions upon it and federation or consolidation of caste associations into larger groupings (fusion).

IV

In 1952, the Vanniyars, largest single caste in Madras state, capped a history of internal reform (Sanskritization) and organizational modernization not unlike that of the Nadars (formerly Shanans) by contesting the first General Election under the standards of the Tamil Nad Toilers (hereafter TNT) and Commonweal Party, the first strongest in South Arcot District but reaching into Salem and Tiruchirapalli Districts, and the second strongest in North Arcot. The two were virtually caste parties. The TNT captured nineteen and the Commonweal Party six seats in the Madras Assembly, or 13 per cent of the total. After S. S. Ramaswami Padayachi, head of the TNT, in 1954 joined N. A. Manickkavelu Naicker, leader of the Commonweal Party, in the reorganized Congress Government of Kamaraj Nadar, the Vanniyars, who represent ten per cent of the state's population, occupied two of the eight (25 per cent) cabinet seats. Their slogan in the 1952 election had been "Vanniyar Vottu Anniyarukku Illai" (Vanniyar votes are for non-Vanniyars). In 1957, at the time of the second General Election, the Vanniyars, now solidly entrenched in Kamaraj's Congress Party, seemed to have perfected the technique of *caste* representation. Nominated in large numbers by the Congress, they helped it gain an impressive victory that year.

By 1962, however, radical changes had taken place in the Vanniyars' social and political circumstances. Internal differentiation along economic, cultural and social lines and personal ambition were articulated and reinforced outside the Vanniyar community by parties competing for support. The result shattered Vanniyar corporate power. They were subsumed to an even greater degree than had been the case when they had moved from their own parties into Congress by the leadership and policy of a voluntary association and integrative institution, the political party. This effect is most sharply etched in South Arcot District, over half of whose 2.5 million population are Vanniyars and where the TNT in 1952 had captured thirteen of the District's nineteen MLA seats.[36] In 1954, when that party's chief had led his followers into Kamaraj Nadar's Government and he had become a Minister, the first crack in Vanniyar solidarity had appeared. A splinter TNT group under A. Govindaswami, MLA, opposed the merger and joined what has come to be Madras's leading opposition party, the Dravida Munnetra Kazagam (Dravidian Progressive Federation, hereafter DMK).[37]

---

[36] *Express* (Chittoor), March 7, 1962. I should like to acknowledge the very helpful extensive and detailed articles of the *Express*'s Special Correspondent, M. Mohan Ram, on the 1962 election in North Arcot, Salem, Tiruchirapalli, Tanjore and South Arcot Districts; see the *Express* (Chittoor) for March 7, 15, 17, 20 and 21, 1962, upon which much of the analysis below is based.

[37] For an analysis of it and Dravidian politics generally, see Lloyd I. Rudolph, "Urban Life and Populist Radicalism; Dravidian Politics in Madras," *Journal of Asian Studies*, Vol. 20 (May, 1961), pp. 283–297.

In 1957, when the Congress Party gave tickets to (nominated) former TNT members in preference to old-time Congressmen, K. S. Venkatakrishna Reddiar, along with other higher caste landowning notables from his own (Reddiar), Naidu, Vellala and Mudaliar castes and with the support of dissident or still dependent sections of the Vanniyars, helped form the Congress Reform Committee (hereafter CRC; later the Indian National Democratic Congress, hereafter INDC). Despite the fact that the leadership of the CRC was drawn from a class which had been and in some measure still was the master and sometimes the oppressor and exploiter of its Vanniyar tenants and laborers, it was able to rally considerable numbers to its electoral cause and gain a modest electoral success. By 1962, however, the INDC, some members having made their peace with the Congress, others having joined the DMK or the Swatantra Party, had evaporated. In 1960, a year after the Swatantra Party was created, S. S. Ramaswami Padayachi, the creator and leader of the TNT, began to move in its direction; by 1961, he had joined it and become its head in South Arcot District.

The once monolithic Vanniyar political front in 1962 was "divided into three contending groups — one supporting the Congress under Mr. Srinivasa Padayachi, the second owing allegiance to the DMK, led by Mr. Govindaswami, and the third under Swatantra influence, loyal to Mr. Ramaswami Padayachi." [38] The effect was to place all three major parties in South Arcot District under Vanniyar leadership. And of the District's fifteen non-reserved seats (four seats were reserved for Harijan candidates) in the 1962 General Election, thirteen were won by Vanniyars — eight as Congress and five as DMK candidates. S. S. Ramaswami Padayachi and a number of other Swatantra candidates lost, however, some by close margins.

The external boundaries of the caste association began to collapse under pressure from outside as the internal forces and strategic calculations which maintained the caste association's solidarity were weakened by differentiation, the absorption of more modern ideas and political calculations designed to express both. A modern aggregative and integrative institution, the political party, by capitalizing on internal differences, destroyed its monolithic solidarity, further weakened the caste's ascriptive and particularistic hold on social identity and behavior, divided and diffused the association's political power and brought it into closer approximation with the assumptions and behavior of modern society and democratic politics (i.e., more universal and functionally specific norms).

The ascriptive and particularistic qualities of caste associations are being affected by higher levels of integration (fusion) as well as by disintegration (fission). The Kallan, Maravar and Agamudiar castes [39] of central and southern

---

[38] *Express* (Chittoor), March 21, 1962.

[39] For the Parumali-nadu Kallans see Louis Dumont's *Une Sous-Caste de L'Inde du Sud; Organisation Sociale et Religieuse des Pramalai Kallar* (Paris: Mouton, 1957); for Kallans generally see Thurston, *Castes*, III, 53–91; for Maravans, Thurston, *Castes*, V, 22–48; and for the Agamudiar, Thurston, *Castes*, I, 5–16. The link among these castes is older than the present beginnings of political federation. They share common mythological ancestors (see Thurston, *Castes*, I, 7 for two versions of the Agamudiar

Madras have been defined and separated historically by ritual rank, social distance and endogamy. Recently their caste associations and leaders, under the interacting influences of democratic institutions and processes and those of traditional society,[40] have begun to create new and larger forms of consciousness, organization and action.[41] Experience in the Madras Assembly, the lessons of party and electoral politics, a growing sense of common purpose and the importance of numbers for realizing political objectives contributed to this result. The three castes have styled themselves Mukkulator (literally "three castes") and have begun to represent themselves in terms of this common name; and the organization and leadership which brought it into being contribute to its growing importance and strength. The basis of Mukkulator social and political identity remains that of an ascriptive social and cultural group with a given geographic location. But just as the caste association attenuated the importance of these factors by upgrading and extending the *jati*, so this federation of caste associations has further attenuated them by again diluting birth and particularism with choice. The self and public definition of the Mukkulators and their organization and political role approach even more closely than the caste association the qualities, form and functions of voluntary associations with political objectives. By further blurring the line between natural and voluntary association, the caste federation seems to break down the dichotomy between ascription and choice which helps to distinguish traditional from modern societies. What appeared to be an absolute division in theory if not in practice has become, in the Indian context, an increasingly relative one suggesting that a continuum which bridges the two rather than a dichotomy may be a more appropriate statement of both the practical and theoretical issues involved.

A recent study by Rajni Kothari and R. M. Maru, "Caste and Secularism in India; A Case Study of the Gujarat Kshatriya Sabha," [42] confirms and deepens these observations. The Sabha is a federation of many economically depressed cultivators and landless laborers. Over time it has helped them to become "kshatriyas" in their own and society's eyes, by articulating their "common economic interests and a growing secular identity born partly out of past folk-

---

creation myth) and a common mobility pattern in traditional society. "There is a Tamil proverb," Thurston writes, "to the effect that a Kallan may become a Maravan. By respectability he may develop into an Agamudiyan, and, by slow degrees, become a Vellala, from which he may rise to be a Mudaliar." *Ibid.* Vellala and Mudaliar are traditionally ranked above Agamudiyan.

[40] W. H. Morris-Jones' analysis of the "languages of politics" and of the "dialogue" between government and political forces have been very helpful for the formulation and statement of the argument here. See his *The Government and Politics of India* (London, 1964), ch. 2, "Politics and Society" and ch. 6, "The Ordering Framework" for these two ideas.

[41] The discussion below is based in part on an interview with Mr. Ramanchandran, MLA, Chief Whip of the Congress Party in the Madras Assembly. He is in no way responsible for my judgments.

[42] *Journal of Asian Studies* (forthcoming). Myron Weiner's excellent study "Segmentation and Political Participation: Kaira District, which came into my hands too late to be taken into account in this text, also deals with the [Gujarat] Kshatriya Sabha. His analysis complements and sharpens that of Kothari and Maru.

lore but more out of a common resentment against well-to-do castes. . . ." [43] The caste federation's break with the ascriptive and particularistic features of traditional society and its assumption of a modern social and politically democratic character is found, Kothari and Maru argue, in the motivation "that lies behind such a process of group assertion." Caste consciousness plays a part but it is no longer geared, they believe, to the preservation of caste traditions and customs but rather to "the acquisition of power and the transformation of traditional positions." This process, including its accompanying transformation of consciousness, the authors call "secularization." They relate it to the simultaneous sanskritization (the emulation of high caste norms and practice) of lower castes and the westernization (acculturation and social organization based on western values and forms) of higher; [44] sanskritization narrows the gap between lower and higher castes and westernization widens it. Secularization, however, joins lower and higher castes in a common experience of social levelling and articulation of group purposes. Although both higher and lower castes are concerned respectively to preserve or improve their status through political action, political considerations fuse them together: the upper castes need numerical strength to sustain their power and status, the lower need access to resources and opportunities which support from the higher can yield. Lower castes may agree to be led and even governed by upper castes but their agreement to do so is ". . . increasingly conditioned by norms of accountability and notions of 'interest' and 'right.' " [45]

V

Political man in democratic India has been wrought out of traditional materials; he is not a new man. Acting through caste associations and federations he is capable at various levels and contexts of the pursuit of countervailing power and the calculation of political advantage. Parties seeking to integrate group purposes while differentiating themselves from their competitors have in most instances harnessed and subsumed India's transformed associational life. The result has been to make representative democracy meaningful and effective in a peasant nation and caste society.

The role of caste in Indian politics has nevertheless been subjected to severe and often uncomprehending criticism. Its ascriptive and particularistic features and the parochial selfishness and chauvinism which they support deeply trouble those committed to the progressive realization of a liberal democratic or socialist society and state. The individual must precede the group in time and importance for the contractual civil society or the ideological collective to have meaning and validity. Yet the blurring of the line between natural and voluntary associations in India has placed her associational life in a situation not too different from that of modern western nations. Natural associations based

[43] The new identity and organization brings within its fold a fairly broad social spectrum ranging "from *Rajputs* who are highest in the Kshatriya hierarchy to *Bhils* who are semi-tribal, with Barijas middle on the way." Kothari and Maru, "Secularism," pp. 7–8.

[44] See Srinivas, *op. cit.*, ch. 2, "A Note on Sanskritization and Westernization."

[45] Kothari and Maru, "Secularism," p. 55.

on language, religion, ethnicity and locality have not been assimilated or dissolved and continue to play a crucial, sometimes decisive, part, in their politics.[46] Nor is it true, despite the cross-cutting pressures of structural, economic and cultural pluralism in a democratic society and state, that formally voluntary associations are free from the characteristics and behavior attributed to natural associations.[47] Efforts to distinguish traditional from modern society, in terms of a natural versus a voluntary basis for their associational life, run the risk of confusing structure and formal requirements with a more indeterminate reality in which one blends into the other and is affected over time by contextual forces. Other ways may have to be found for distinguishing natural associations that find benign ways of merging the concerns for individuality and for achievement in modern society from those which are disruptive.

Massive natural associations based on religion led to the partition of the Indian sub-continent in 1947; the tribal associations in Ruanda led the Watusi

[46] For America, see Will Herberg, *Protestant, Catholic, Jew: An Essay in American Religious Sociology* (Garden City, N.Y.: Doubleday Anchor Books, 1960); Nathan Glazer and Daniel Patrick Moynihan, *Beyond the Melting Pot: The Negroes, Puerto Ricans, Jews, Italians, and Irish of New York City* (Cambridge: M.I.T. and Harvard University Press, 1963); and Milton M. Gordon, *Assimilation in American Life; The Role of Race, Religion and National Origins* (New York: Oxford University Press, 1964).

[47] For a recent critical view of social pluralism as it has hardened and subordinated itself to bureaucratic leadership, see Henry Kariel, *The Decline of American Pluralism* (Stanford: Stanford University Press, 1961). Kariel is so concerned that he "would have us move . . . from the much celebrated ideal of Tocqueville toward the still unfashionable one of Rousseau."

Milton Gordon in *Assimilation in American Life* (New York: Oxford University Press, 1964), mounts an impressive case for the rigid compartmentalization of American communal life at the rank and file level. S. M. Lipset, Martin Trow and James Coleman in *Union Democracy; The Inside Politics of the International Typographical Union* (Glencoe: The Free Press, 1956), examine the rigidities and bureaucratic domination of union and professional associations by analysing the exceptional case. Everett C. Hughes in *Men and Their Work* (Glencoe: The Free Press, 1958), suggests how occupational associations in America, like castes in India, upgrade themselves by changing their names and histories and purify themselves and their rituals by emulating "higher" occupational groups in the matter of educational requirements, licensing standards and ceremonial niceties. John R. Murphy's "Professional and Occupational Licensing: A National Problem with State Control," a term paper in Government 155a, Government Regulation of Industry, Harvard University, 1959–1960, along with Hughes' analyses, suggested these comparisons with caste mobility in India.

For social and political statements of the viability and benefits of social pluralism based on individuality, voluntarism and liberty, see William Kornhauser, *The Politics of Mass Society* (London: Routledge and Kegan Paul, 1960) and David B. Truman, *The Governmental Process; Political Interests and Public Opinion* (New York: Alfred A. Knopf, 1951).

Kariel and Lipset, Trow and Coleman emphasize the inability of members of formally voluntary associations, like peasants in Marx's analysis, to represent and rule themselves; therefore they fall victim to the executive power (the bureaucracy). William H. Whyte, Jr., in *The Organization Man* (New York: Simon & Schuster, 1956), while not ignoring structural factors, emphasizes the ways in which formally voluntary organizations absorb and tend to monopolize the affective life and identities of their members and their families.

to bring charges of genocide against the Bahutu; [48] and tribal politics in the Congo fuelled chronic political instability and supported rebellion and civil war. When natural associations are too few, when they are socially and morally independent of each other, and when they lack a limited but critical identification with leaders, ideas and institutions capable of sustaining a national politics and modern state, they destroy the possibility or validity of a civil society that transcends them. Natural associations — including caste associations — in India in a few contexts such as Kerala, where society has become divided into five (Ezhavas, Harijans, Nairs, Christians and Muslims) large, roughly equal and relatively rigid groups, have contributed more to political instability than to political modernization. As the state's political parties have become increasingly congruent with these social differences, their integrative capacities have declined. Instead of subsuming, combining or disintegrating social differences based on birth, they have in considerable measure begun to re-enforce them. But the situation in Kerala is more the exception than the rule. The difficulties being experienced in Belgium, and Canada in recent years [49] derive from natural associations which have resisted or absorbed strong modern pluralistic forces, values antithetical to ascription and particularism and integrative institutions, particularly the political party. The caste association has created less severe strains in modern Indian politics than have religion and language in these modern societies even while it has contributed to political socialization, modernization and meaningful participation in a society whose economic and social underdevelopment stands in marked contrast to these.[50]

---

[48] See Jacques J. Maquet, *The Premise of Inequality in Ruanda* (London: Oxford University Press, 1961). For the genocide charge see *Keesing's Contemporary Archives*, Vol. 14 (1963–1964), pp. 20085–86.

[49] For Walloon-Flemish differences in Belgium see Ernest Mandel, "The Dialectic of Class and Region in Belgium," *New Left Review*, No. 20 (Summer, 1963), pp. 2–31; *Keesing's Contemporary Archives*, Vol. 13 (1961–1962), pp. 17968, 18391, 18623 and 18941 and Vol. 14 (1963–1964), p. 19601. For the differences in Canada between the French Catholics and English Protestants see the *Preliminary Report* of the Royal Commission on Bilingualism and Biculturalism (Ottawa, 1965). The Commission warned that Canada was undergoing "the greatest crisis in its history" (p. 13). See also Edmund Wilson, *O Canada* (New York: Farrar, Straus & Giroux, 1965).

[50] See S. M. Lipset, "Some Social Requisites of Democracy: Economic Development and Political Legitimacy," *American Political Science Review*, Vol. 53 (March, 1959) for a proposition and supporting evidence which strongly suggest that democracy should be an utter failure in India. On almost every statistical measure of the "requisites of democracy" (per capita income, literacy, industrialization and urbanization) India stands at or near the bottom, yet it is a democracy. Lipset derides those who use a deviant case to challenge the validity of the notion that there are "social conditions which are regularly associated with a given complex political system" (p. 70) such as democracy. Theoretical propositions "must be subject to test by a systematic comparison of *all* available cases. . . ." A deviant case, according to Lipset, is properly treated as one out of many. Only woolly minded and unscientific political philosophers would argue that "a given situation clearly violates [a] thesis . . ." (p. 70). Yet Lipset, in selecting his cases on the basis of "whether a country had had a history of more or less free elections for most of the post-World War I period" (pp. 73–74) does not consider India, although she meets the test. It seems reasonable to question, therefore, whether *all* available cases have been considered. It also seems reasonable to inquire whether it is valid to treat this deviant case "as one case out of many."

Because caste in most instances continues to divide society horizontally and not (like religion and language) vertically, and because the horizontal divisions continue to be many rather than few, it remains primarily an instrument of political representation capable of being aggregated, integrated and led. Its closest functional equivalent now may be the ethnic and religious groups in American politics which, contrary to "official" ideology, retain great influence particularly at the local and state level.

If this is so or is proving to be so, the situation is paradoxical and ironical. Indians, unlike Americans, were not, as Tocqueville put it, born equal. They have had or will have to become so. In so far as they have achieved equality, they have done so by transforming the most rigidly hierarchical and compartmentalized system of social stratification, the caste system. The measure of equality that has been realized is in part the result of a marriage between the transplanted and assimilated liberalism of the British *raj* and traditional Indian culture. The offspring of this union is a political culture with characteristics that embrace not only political democracy and parliamentary government but also caste associations. It is a political culture that includes, in Morris-Jones' terms,[51] traditional, modern and "saintly" languages. Those who know and love one parent often ignore or reject the displeasing features of the other. Yet Indian political culture is surely a product of this union, a "genetic" fusion which

---

In the name of aggregative characteristics of systems and multivariate analysis of causality, we are asked to treat the experience of India's almost 500,000,000 people as equivalent to that of the smallest Latin American "nation."

Lipset himself, drawing upon Weber, suggests an alternative theory of cumulative causation (see below) to explain the existence and persistence of democracy, but unfortunately abandons it in favor of aggregative social characteristics, on the basis of what seems at best a marginal and at worst a meaningless distinction between the "social conditions" which "support" democracy and the "internal mechanisms" which "maintain" it. It would seem that both theories deserve a place in the sun: the theory of cumulative causation explains better the supports for and the continued existence of democracy in India, while the aggregative social conditions theory, which Lipset advances as a *general* theory, does not. This suggests that the Indian case may very well be a "universe" unto itself rather than "one case out of many." A general theory would then have to "explain" the Indian case *and* the cases with which Lipset deals. Instead, Lipset claims to deal with all cases but does not do so and treats, by implication, "universe" differences as "deviant" cases.

The theory of cumulative causation would explain the support and maintenance of democracy by proposing that "unique events may account for *either* the persistence *or* the failure of democracy in any particular society . . . key historical events . . . set one process in motion in one country, and a second process in another . . . once established, a democratic political system gathers momentum . . ." (p. 72). Lipset warns us, in the light of this line of analysis, not to "overstress" the high correlations he displays between democracy and his measures for requisites. He also allows that what he calls "premature" democracies which survive will do so by "facilitating the growth of conditions conducive to democracy. . . ." But his choice of examples here, universal literacy and autonomous private associations — presumably not ones based on caste — highlight his bias toward certain "modern" aggregative social characteristics as the requisites of democracy. The Indian "universe" radically contradicts Lipset's view (as it does Marx's) but supports the abandoned theory of cumulative causation.

[51] Morris-Jones, *op. cit.*, ch. 2.

some may think impossible, others immoral, but which its vigor and viability over the years is hard to deny or ignore.

Changes in the internal arrangements and public function of caste and in political culture and structure are necessary but not sufficient if caste is to be made compatible with democracy. A profound change in the nature of human sensibility is also required but to a lesser extent realized. Tocqueville contrasted the state of human sensibility in aristocratic and democratic nations by observing that "real sympathy can exist only between those who are alike, and in aristocratic ages men acknowledge none but the members of their own caste to be like themselves. . . . When all the ranks of a community are nearly equal, as all men think and feel in nearly the same manner, each of them may judge in a moment of the sensations of all the others; he casts a rapid glance upon himself and that is enough." [52] Yet Indians have been profoundly separated by their traditional social arrangements. "The survival of the caste system," Edward Shils observes, "cuts human beings off from each other. It inhibits the growth of sensibilities which are required for the perception of the moral quality of other human beings. . . . It is the caste system which helps deaden the imagination to the state of mind of other human beings." [53]

Democratic ideas and the equality of conditions, Tocqueville argues, turn superiors and inferiors into "new beings and place them in new relative positions." In hierarchical societies as yet unaffected by these influences, inferiority does not degrade the character of those who are inferior because they neither know nor imagine any other self-definition.

> But while the transition from one social condition to another is going on, there is almost always a time when men's minds fluctuate between the aristocratic notion of subjection and the democratic notion of obedience. Obedience then loses its moral importance in the eyes of him who obeys . . . he does not yet view it under its purely human aspect; it has to him neither the character of sanctity or justice. The lines that divide authority from oppression, liberty from license, and right from might are . . . jumbled together and confused [so] that no one knows exactly what he is or what he may be or what he ought to be. Such a condition is not democracy but revolution.[54]

India may have been spared such a revolutionary situation by the transformation of caste over more than a century. But because it is still identified with ritual rank and sacred duty rather than social levelling and democratic representation, the degree to which Indians have put aside the aristocratic notion of subjection and accepted as moral and just the democratic one of obedience remains obscure.

Rajputs who ruled the former princely states which comprise contemporary Rajasthan, for example, saw their Congress opponents in the 1952 General Election as "no-account," no longer guided by duty and loyalty, trouble makers and riff-raff, not so much because they resented them as because their

[52] *Democracy in America* (Garden City, N.Y.: Anchor ed.), II, 173, 175–6.
[53] *Op. cit.*, note 35 above, p. 70.
[54] *Democracy in America, ibid.*

social circumstances prevented them from knowing or imagining what Congress-men were like as human beings. Ten years later their human and highly dif-ferentiated view of the Rajasthan Congress leadership was in part the result of the attention that power commands. Those Shanans a century ago who thought they were entitled to be known and treated as *Kshatriyas* (warrior-rulers) became in time Nadars; one of their descendants now sits in the Con-gress *gaddi* (royal cushion). What Edward Shils has called the democratization of charisma [55] has come about in part from the successful emulation of higher by lower castes and the greater homogeneity of society that it produced, in part through the use of caste in a secular form to achieve influence and power and through them self-esteem and public respect. The Nadar who sits on the Congress *gaddi* symbolizes a massive historical change. Castes no longer live as races apart, capable of fellow feeling for their caste brothers only. A deepening sense of universal citizenship and a broadly shared political culture may have made Indians, in Locke's phrase, "capable of a majority," and in Aristotle's, of ruling and being ruled in turn. Tocqueville's tests for the transi-tion from aristocratic subjection to democratic obedience — the capacity to be governed by authority rather than oppression, to practice liberty rather than license and to maintain order through right rather than might — may be passed successfully.[56]

[55] "Concentration and Dispersion of Charisma; Their Bearing on Economic Policy in Underdeveloped Countries," *World Politics*, Vol. 11 (October, 1958), pp. 1–19.

[56] This is more apparent at the national and state than at the local level of govern-ment. The literature on village factionalism and the failures of *panchyati raj* suggest that oppression, license and might in some localities are stronger than authority, liberty and right. But much of this literature reflects an administrative not a political view. A recent study by Adrian C. Mayer sees the problem rather differently. He finds that "caste ties help a leader to gain power in the rural committee system; but that his allocation of development funds does not unduly favor supporters of his own caste. . . . His favours may stem from the influence he has with officials and poli-ticians as a leader of the rural system; but the favours do not form part of that system, while his allocation of development funds does. Hence, the rural leader controls the committee system and the attached development allocation as much to attain the external benefits (for which the system provides the springboard) as to hold power within the system.

"Community development *is* therefore a factor in rural politics; but its role is part of a much wider process, in which rural leaders are asserting themselves in a changing balance of general political power. For rural leaders are using the influence which they are gaining as brokers outside the rural system to compete for power with the incum-bent, mainly urban-oriented, politicians of the national parties." "Some Political Im-plications of Community Development in India," *Arch. Europ. Social.* Vol 4 (1963), p. 106.

This headline from the *Statesman* of June 19, 1961, CASTE HIERARCHY DE-CLINES, AS CASTEISM RISES, sums up some of the case for the modernity of tradition through the democratic incarnation of caste.

G 2 / Structure of Authority

Introduction

According to Max Weber, a legal-rational authority structure is one of the hallmarks of a modern nation-state. Obedience is owed to a legally established impersonal order in which the officeholder possesses a legally defined authority.[1] Yet, though bureaucratic standards and concepts are often applied to non-Western countries, the history of state administration in these countries is quite different from the gradual bureaucratization of European states by which the governments of the territorially delimited nations developed stabilized and centrally controlled administrations.[2]

Colonial rulers had a tendency to set up rational-legal administrations quite different from the patrimonial-bureaucratic regimes or the more localized and diffuse forms of rule that these societies had previously known. In earlier periods and in some parts of the colonial empires a policy of "indirect rule"[3] was followed, in an attempt to work through indigenous authority structures. Yet almost everywhere by the end of the 19th century a different pattern had become prevalent: native elites were employed within the bureaucratic state of the colonial power. The process was a slow one; tendencies towards localized rule plagued the colonial rulers for long periods and were brought under control only with difficulty.

Broomfield's article is set within this context of an imposed colonial bureaucracy. The British in India had to use indigenous elites in ruling their far-flung territories, but except for the Indian native states this rule was a directly imposed bureaucratic one. Broomfield shows that Indian elites made use of their new opportunities as caste groups have always taken advantage of various regimes (see Frykenberg, Section C). Nevertheless, the system they used was

[1] Max Weber, *The Theory of Social and Economic Organization*, trans. A. W. Henderson and T. Parsons (New York: The Free Press, 1947), pp. 328 ff.

[2] See Reinhard Bendix, "Bureaucracy," in *The Encyclopedia of Social Sciences*, 2nd ed.

[3] The doctrine of indirect rule was most fully developed by Lord Lugard in *The Dual Mandate in British Tropical Africa* (Edinburgh and London: Wm. Blackwood and Sons, 1922).

a rational-legal administration, and these particular caste groups — the original Westernized elites in Bombay, Bengal, and Madras — could use it because their traditions and skills enabled them to meet the educational standards imposed by the West. Other native groups (for instance, Muslims and high-caste non-Brahmins in Madras) had based their power on military dominance; originally they missed out on the opportunities provided by colonial rule and only later challenged the position of the Westernized elites, in this way aiding the rise of "counter-elites." Thus, Broomfield describes the growth of Indian nationalism in terms of the differential response of such traditional groups to the new demands and opportunities created by colonial domination.

Unlike the Western national bureaucracies, imperial bureaucracies involved the rule of non-contiguous territories from a distant "metropolis." Upon achieving independence, the new states broke this connection but attempted to maintain the formal structures that had been set up. Now these structures are staffed by natives of the area and hence come into close contact with the indigenous social order and its many internal divisions. In this context, charges of "corruption" indicate the extent to which both the Westernized members of these countries and social scientists continue to apply the bench mark of rational-legal bureaucracy.

Questions concerning this intellectual framework are raised by Wertheim, who represents an important tradition of research by the Dutch in South-East Asia. His discussion illustrates how time- and culture-bound a widely accepted and relatively unambiguous concept like "corruption" can be. There is a close historical connection between this concept and the emergence of a distinction between the private and public spheres in the life of the official. In that sense, "corruption" can only exist within a rational-legal order, even though, as Wertheim points out, there were generally effective customary limits to exploitations by the officials, regents, or nobles who had to live off proceeds collected from their subjects. Wertheim draws attention to a new value "breakthrough" particularly evident in some Communist countries, which "might be summed up in the adage that private right is public duty" and which parallels the gradual acceptance of the principle in 18th-century Europe that public right is public duty. Thus the sharp distinction between public servant and "private citizen," which was so hard to establish in some countries, is already being challenged in others. In fact, it seems that some parts of the world may move into a post-bureaucratic era before having known well-developed bureaucracies in the Weberian sense.

The fact that Weber's historically derived types allow for the appearance of previously unanticipated configurations is more fully brought out in Roth's contribution. In some of the newly independent nations personal rulership may represent the growth of a new type of authority structure in the sense that rulership of this kind has not before appeared under these historical conditions. Here we find a specific kind of alliance among individuals in high places rather than impartially recruited officeholders bound by formally and contractually defined obligations. At the same time, Roth emphasizes that the identification of this type of authority points to cognate elements in modern rationalized bureaucracies which previously went unrecognized. On a more substantive level this article points to the fundamental instability of personal rulerships in contrast to the relative stability of traditional regimes, although otherwise personal rule and traditional authority have much in common.

The Regional Elites:
A Theory of
Modern Indian History

J. H. BROOMFIELD

This paper will have served its purpose if it simply raises doubts as to the validity of some of the generally accepted assumptions underlying the interpretation of modern Indian history. It tries to expose a few of the current cliches, and if, in the reader's opinion, it merely trades old cliches for new, then I hope the resulting dissatisfaction will stimulate someone to offer fresh ideas to vary the rather stale fare of Indian historiography. The paper is full of grand sub-continental generalisations, but where I have paused to illustrate my argument I have chosen evidence from Bengal, which is my field of research.

1. One of the great social significances of the eighteenth century in the Indian international sub-system, with its internal political disorder and emerging power of the Europeans, was the destruction of the power of existing ruling groups. This was effected not simply by military and political means, but also through radical changes in such areas as trade, law, and land-revenue assessment. It was accomplished for many of the displaced ruling groups by a loss of control over land.

2. At the same time large opportunities opened up in various places in the international sub-system for those able to take advantage of them. There were special opportunities in the three initial areas of British intrusion, Bengal, Madras, and Maharashtra, and the groups which grasped those opportunities became the elites in these societies in the nineteenth century.

3. The development of each of these elite groups was determined by the following factors:

    A. *The Group's Experience before the British Intrusion and Its Situation at*

From the *Indian Economic and Social History Review*, Vol. III, No. 3 (October 1966), pp. 279–291. Reprinted by permission of the author and publisher.

J. H. BROOMFIELD is Assistant Professor of History, University of Michigan, where he teaches courses in the history of modern India. An authority on Bengal, he is preparing a book on his area of interest entitled *Elite Conflict in a Plural Society: 20th Century Bengal* (1968).

That Time. This largely determined what "cultural baggage" the group carried with it into the new situation.

At this point I would question the utility of the commonly-used metaphor of a British impact on India, with its implication of a dynamic force — expansive Europe — hitting a static object — Indian society. I believe that we are better able to understand the effects of the British intrusion if we take account of the fact that the pattern of relationships among Indian elites was subject to constant change in periods before the European arrival, as much as in the period of European dominance. We must recognise that in many areas, and certainly in the peripheral areas with which I am primarily concerned, there was considerable social mobility in pre-European times. Certainly the British presence affected the direction and possibly also the speed of movement, most directly by providing new opportunities for economic gain, but it is significant that the groups which took advantage of these new opportunities did so very largely in terms of their old methods of action.

To illustrate this let us look at Bengal. In that area before the British arrival there was fairly extensive international trade, considerable manufacturing in inland centres, and developed administrative and judicial organisation in the Mughal province and in the Hindu rajadoms, which occupied extensive areas of Bakarganj and Chittagong districts in the east, and Bankura and Burdwan districts in the west. Thus there were opportunities for enterprise in administration, law or commerce which parallelled those which were to be available after the British arrival, and it appears to have been the same group which took advantage of the opportunities in both periods. One sees in particular the movement of Brahmins, Baidyas, and Kayasthas into the service of the East India Company from similar service under the Hindu rajas or in the Mughal system. They were able to move in to the new system because they already possessed certain skills: experience in administration and law; entrepreneurial techniques and an accustomed readiness to work in an alien *lingua franca* (the talents of the *dubash:* the go-between); literacy, and experience in using that literacy in the service of organisation. The group's experience before the British intrusion and its situation at that time, I said earlier, largely determined what "cultural baggage" it carried with it into the new situation. In the Bengal case, these skills were part of that baggage.

B. *The Nature of the New Opportunities Offered.* Just as the experience and situation of the groups in the various regions differed, so did the opportunities of which they were able to take advantage.

For Bengal I would point to two in particular: the development of Calcutta as the British capital in India; and the opportunity for those who prospered in service to invest in landed property. Access to land for the new administrative elite was provided by the inequitable land revenue settlements of the period 1770 to 1790, the recognition by the law courts of the principle that land was saleable to realize debt, and the command of the legal system by the same group which had capital free for investment as a result of its success in service. By investing in land in preference to commerce, the elite revealed another piece of its cultural baggage: its belief in the superior prestige and security resulting from the possession of landed property.

C. *The Manner in Which the Group Came to Terms with the New Situation.* There are a number of points to be noted here:

    i. some *modus vivendi* had to be reached with things European, whether through total acceptance, a synthesis, or rejection. I lump these three together for although they appear to be fundamentally different they were all possible responses to the European intrusion, and even among those elite groups which were to benefit from the new opportunities almost the whole range of response was to be found from individual members, or, perhaps more significantly, from the group as a whole towards different items of the intruders' values. The range from total acceptance at one end to rejection at the other should be seen as a continuum. It is one of the unfortunate consequences of the impact on India metaphor that we have generally concentrated our attention on one end of that scale, where we have isolated a phenomenon which we have labelled "westernisation," and in doing so have lost sight of its integral relationship to the whole range of actual response.

    ii. the fact is important that the groups which had been able to grasp the opportunities and become elites were high caste, with pride in their roles as guardians of great cultural traditions.

    As a consequence we see in all three regions — Bengal, Madras, and Maharashtra — an articulate reconsideration of the local cultural tradition and a concern with its adaptation to the new intellectual situation. Each of the elites developed a new and distinct cultural synthesis, drawing in part upon European ideas but drawing as well upon their past experience.

    iii. the elite had not only to look upward to the Europeans and European culture, it had also to look downward to the lower strata of its own society, and work out for the new situation new relationships with them. Again the proud caste status of the elites was important. In Bengal, where there was a running discussion throughout the nineteenth century on the proper ordering of society, the elites justified their social dominance, at least to their own satisfaction, by a definition of their position which nicely combined their ascriptive caste ascendancy with their achievement. They called themselves *bhadralok:* the respectable people. Bhadralok was almost synonymous with high caste — Brahmin, Baidya, and Kayastha — but not quite, for this was an open not a closed status group.[1] A British government report of 1915 correctly, if rather tactlessly, described Bengali society "a despotism of caste, tempered by matriculation." [2] "The school," wrote the Government of Bengal on another occasion, "is the one gate to the society of

[1] I have accepted here Max Weber's definition of status group, and his distinction between open and closed status groups. See H. H. Gerth and C. Wright Mills (eds.), *From Max Weber: Essays in Sociology* (New York: Oxford University Press, 1958), p. 405.

[2] *Bengal District Administration Committee,* 1913–1914, Report, 1915, p. 176.

bhadralok." [3] Education, especially English-language education, the professional and clerical employment, and the literate culture to which that education gave access, as well as the acceptance of high-caste proscriptions, were the measures of bhadralok status.

The bhadralok's role was to lead. In their eyes it was proper that they should be the political class, that they should dominate the learned professions, that they should control the institutions of education, and that they should provide Bengal with its music, art and literature, as that they should be accorded honour in village and town as the respectable people. They were benevolent in their attitude to the lower orders, but it was as often a benevolent disdain as a benevolent paternalism.

4. Involved for each group in the process of coming to terms with the new situation was the process of forming a new identity.[4] This new identity found its expression in distinct interpretations of the past, in distinct cultural values, in distinct styles of life, in distinct attitudes as to the proper organisation of society, in distinct institutions, and in the distinct use of language. Distinct that is to say, from other groups within the regional societies and also from the elites in other regions.

My last point, the distinct use of language needs no labouring. A moment's reflection will remind you of the role which the elites played in the nineteenth-century development of Bengali, Tamil, and Maharathi, and the immense significance to them of these achievements. I will select one other item from the Bengal experience further to illustrate my point: the bhadralok's distinct view of the past. By the 1880's and certainly by the time of Vivekananda's evangelism, the bhadralok had a generally accepted interpretation of their history which not only explained the foreign conquest of Bengal, but gave a sanction to the cultural division between elite and non-elite in the society, and provided direction for future bhadralok action. Bengal once strong in the classical age, it was said, had been emasculated by the quietist doctrines of Buddhism and the emotional popular cults of medieval Hinduism. The "true Brahmanical virtues" of intellectual initiative and rational self-assertion had been neglected, and the degradation of the Muslim conquest was a natural consequence. "Let us think for a moment of the fatal and universal weakness which had beset our people when the English first came to this land," Chittaranjan Das exhorted his fellow Bengal Congressmen in 1917. "Our Religion of Power — the Gospel of 'Sakti' — had become a mockery of its former self; it had lost its soul of beneficence in the repetition of empty formulas and the observance of meaningless mummeries. . . . The Hindus of Bengal had lost strength and vigour

---

[3] *Report of the Indian Statutory Commission*, 1930, Vol. VIII, "Memorandum of the Government of Bengal," p. 24.

[4] I define group identity in this way: A group with identity has agreed values, understood internal relationships, accepted roles for various members at developing stages of life, a language and channels of communication, a shared interpretation of the past and hopes for the future, common heroes, common symbols, and common myths. The members of such a group are aware of their membership, and the group is identifiable by other groups and individuals in the society.

alike in Religion, Science, and Life." [5] To Das, as to other bhadralok of his own and the preceding generation, it was self-evident that it was their ordained mission, as Bengal's culture elite, to restore the glory of Bengal through strength in action. This interpretation of the past, with its implicit doctrine of elite action, as effectually separated the bhadralok from the mass of their fellow Bengalis, whether Muslims or Vaishava Hindus, as it did from the Madrasi and Maharashtrian elites, whose historical reinterpretations were concerned with other places and directed to other problems.

Taking a general view of this process of identity formation it is important to note:

    a. the intense emotional attachment of the elite to each of the channels of expression of their new identity.

    b. the complexity and sophistication of these forms of expression. This fact has been badly played down, largely it seems as a consequence of that concept "westernisation," which implies cultural borrowing or copying. Certainly these new Indian cultures were indebted to Europe, just as Europe in an earlier age had been indebted to western Islam, but they were not carbon copies — black, smudged, imperfect reproductions of an exotic original. They were themselves originals; distinct cultures with fairly complex institutional structures by the end of the nineteenth century.

    c. that they were regionally developed and regionally distinct.

5. The elites had social power but as subject people of a foreign imperialism they did not have satisfactory political power.

As a qualification to this statement, it is important to realise (as neither of the "classical" schools of modern Indian history — British or nationalist — appears to have done) that the Indian elites did have *some* political power under the British. The major reason for the common failure to recognise this fact is that "politics" appears to have been defined too narrowly. As a consequence of the classical schools' exclusive concern with the struggle between the nationalists and the British for control of the state, "politics" and "nationalism" have usually been equated, and "non-nationalist" politics, if not totally disregarded, have been seen as "anti-nationalist." The failure to take account of the elites' political power has been a source of misinterpretation in a number of areas:

    a. the British are incorrectly represented as having been free agents in constitutional reconstruction.

    b. British attempts to use constitutional reform as a way to change the power relationships between elites and counter-elites have been largely under-estimated and the consequent grave dangers to order have been overlooked.

    c. the leaders of the political elites have not been given due credit for the self-restraint and concern for the maintenance of order which they usually displayed in the exercise of their power. Nor conversely have

[5] "Bengal and the Bengalees," Presidential Address, Bengal Provincial Conference, Calcutta, April 1917. Rajen Sen: *Deshbandhu Chittaranjan Das. Life and Speeches*, 1926, p. 11.

d. the limitations imposed upon them by the responsibilities of power been recognised.

d. the contest between elites and counter-elites has normally been seen as a contest for future power, not for the control of present power.

With these qualifications in mind, we can return to the primary point that the elites did not have *satisfactory* political power. Seeking to be master of its own political future and as a further expression of its identity, each elite developed a nationalism. For this the inspiration was European, most directly the struggles for unity in Italy and Germany, and according to the European ideal the nation to which it aspired was universal: the Indian nation. The existence under British control of a centrally-organised state called India was of equal importance in giving the elites a supra-regional nationalist vision. In the process of establishing hegemony over the sub-continent, the British had widened the horizons of ambition for the coastal elites, making it feasible for them to attempt an extension of their elite dominance beyond the confines of their regions. India was an exciting concept for them in the 1860s, and it was equally exciting for them in the eighties to discover that this concept gave them common ground for discussion with men elsewhere on the sub-continent, a discussion facilitated by the same alien *lingua franca* which had enabled them to work effectively outside their home region.

They defined their nationalism universally but they acted exclusively. Each elite, I have said, developed a nationalism as a means of political fulfilment and as a further expression of its identity. As with the other forms of expression many of the manifestations of this nationalism were in practice local and exclusive: regional institutions, regional leaders, regional languages, regional symbols, regional heroes and myths, and regional patriotism. In each case there was a passionate attachment to the particular nationalism, and, where the elites met as at the Indian National Congress sessions, the confident belief by each group that it supplied the initiative and the leadership for Indian nationalism.

This leads me to some general observations on our perception of Indian nationalism. Most historians have now rejected the concept of Indian nationalism as a "monolith" — a solid, homogeneous bloc in opposition to the British, committed unquestioningly to one doctrine — but they have replaced that concept with another which is almost as misleading. Many of them have depicted Indian nationalism as some sort of "container" in which were mixed more or less satisfactorily a variety of divergent views and aspirations. So may Indian nationalism appear to the detached observer floating above the affairs of the sub-continent on the magic carpet of historical research. So too it has appeared even to those involved on some occasions when the proponents of divergent views and aspirations have stood toe to toe to fight out points of disagreement.

Where the "container" concept is misleading is that it distracts attention from the essential fact that for most of the time, for most of the groups and individuals to whom nationalism was important, it was and could be only one thing: that they perceived it to be. Most saw it as a "monolith" not as a "container." Many would be offended at the suggestion that it was or should be a "container." This explains why on many of the occasions when events brought the proponents of divergent views face to face, they regarded one another with amazement, disbelief, and incomprehension, and sometimes angrily rejected the other's claim even to rank as a nationalist. Discomfort and anger in this situation are understandable, for each individual concept of nationalism had been formed in the image of a particular interpretation of the Indian past, and this particular view of history was the core of each group's sense of identity. It is this intimate connection between identity and perception of nationalism which explains the emotional involvement of groups — their emotional vested interest — in the maintenance of their particular "monolithic" nationalism.

Because of these factors myths have assumed extraordinary importance. To talk as many do of stripping away the mythology surrounding Indian national-ism to uncover the realities, is to overlook the fact that the myths are part of the reality, frequently the most passionately defended part. Without a healthy respect for the potency of mythology and a willingness to give sympathetic at-tention to myth formation, the observer of the tension between the Indian elites and their rivals will find himself with little ability to comprehend what he sees. Much of the action before him must appear to be shadow play, for much of it will be the conflict of irreconcilable myths.

6. There are two points to be noted about timing in the development of the elites:

    a. the coastal elites did not develop at equal pace, for example in politics the Tamil Brahmins lagged 20 odd years behind the Bengal bhadralok; nor were the elites which developed on the first beachheads of the British invasion to remain the only elite groups.

    b. the situation for the elites was never static. For instance, their initial opportunities were extended as the British marched up-country con-quering more territory, and members of the elites could follow with the baggage train: Tamil Brahmins through southern and eastern India; Maharashtrian Brahmins throughout the Deccan and into northern India; the Bengal bhadralok into Orissa and Assam, and right up the Gangetic valley. The result was the establishment by each of the elites of colonies beyond their regional frontiers, colonies of English-speaking men who dominated the new professional life of the up-country towns. Then came the contraction of these opportunities with the growth of new regional elites in the hinterland, and with challenges from aspiring counter-elites beneath the old elites in their home regions. Changes in the economy of the sub-continent had opened opportunities for groups in new areas and for new groups in the old areas. Again the timing was not uniform for all three old elite groups, but each was faced at some stage by attacks on its position at home and in its colonies up-country.

    The result in Bengal was that by the 1890's the bhadralok were faced with growing economic difficulties. What was already a serious situa-tion as a result of population growth which had reduced the per capita income from landed rent holdings and increased the pressure on that limited areas of "white-collar" employment which the bhadralok considered respectable, was aggravated by job-competition from local Muslims and low-caste Hindus, who were now acquiring English-language education in small but significant numbers, and by the emergence throughout the towns of north India of new indigenous educated groups, who demanded of the local Governments the exclusion of "outsiders" from administrative employment. The very fact that they now distinguished the Bengalis as "outsiders" is in itself significant, indicating the development, or at least a new expression, or regional consciousness.

7. For the old elites these challenges from without and within were both part of one crisis and the appearance of their inter-relation was enhanced by the fact that both the new up-country elites and the aspiring counter-elites at home repudiated the leadership of the old elites in the nationalist movement, scornfully pointing out the disparity between their universal protestations and their exclusive actions, and declaring that they had lost touch with the "Indian nation" because of their "Anglicisation." They had gained their dominance through association with the British, it was said, and were irrevocably committed to the maintenance of the imperial structure, whether under British control or their own. New leaders from newly emerging groups were produced by the up-country areas, with new concepts of nationalism and an appeal aimed at all the new aspiring groups. Thus Gandhi, a *banya* from Gujarat, attempting to influence Bengal politics in 1920 directed his appeal for a mass movement to the Muslims and low-caste Hindus, the aspiring counter-elite in Bengal.

The vulnerability of the old elites to criticism and the difficulty which they had in countering the influence of the new nationalists points to a significant fact: that those administrative and entrepreneurial skills which had carried them so successfully into the British system, and which had become formal measures of elite achievement as the new cultures were given structure in the nineteenth century, were no longer of great advantage — if indeed they were not of positive disadvantage — in the changed political conditions of the twentieth century. The skills which political leaders had to command if they were to be effective in the new situations were those of brokerage and communication. They had to be capable of articulating and aggregating interests, of manipulating popular symbols and imagery to give expression to wider political identities. The old elites were ill-fitted and ill-inclined to perform these roles.

8. The connection between the two challenges to the old elites' dominance — the challenges from up-country and at home — was not in fact as close as it appeared to be, for the aspiring counter-elites in the old areas did not readily accept the preferred leadership from outside or the preferred redefinition of nationalism. They had their own definitions, and, as with the elites they were trying to displace, the context of these definitions was regional. The aspiring counter-elites valued the home ground as much as did the old elites and were determined to battle with them for its possession. In each of these areas, elite and counter-elite became engaged in bitter in-fighting, and they were left struggling on the periphery of a nationalist movement which was hence-forth di-

rected from the new areas by a leadership which had far less regional commitment.

This suggests two points:

a. that in the old areas there were strong regional identifications by the second decade of the twentieth century, resulting from the development of complex social structures with internal centres of power, status and wealth, the control of which was keenly contested.
b. that similar regional identifications had not developed in what I have called the new areas, and apparently as a consequence the new nationalist leadership could act as well as talk universally.

9. Looked at from one angle, the "universalist" nationalism of the post-1920 leadership can be understood as a result of the development of nationalist sentiment among more sections of society in widespread areas of the subcontinent, who could respond to attacks on the regional and exclusive disposition of the old elites. This does not, however, explain how the new leadership could define their nationalism universally, nor how they could escape primary involvement in regional affairs. For that explanation I believe we must look at the character of the three areas which supplied most of the nationalist leadership from the twenties into the early sixties: the U.P., Bihar and Gujarat.

I see four reasons for *Gujarat's* production of "universalist" nationalists:

a. the Maharashtrian elite had previously dominated the institutions of this area of Bombay province, as they had all other areas outside Bombay city.
b. Gujarati families with political ambitions in the service of the native states which were thick on the ground in this area. It is significant, I think, that Gandhi's family was in this line of business.
c. the splintering of Gujarat between the native states and a conglomerate British Indian province like Bombay, with its cosmopolitan coastal capital, discouraged the development of regional consciousness.
d. the *banyas* who became so prominent in the Gujarati Congress had a supra-regional culture (Vaisnavism-Jainism) and most had family connections throughout India's trading centres.

Bihar is a comparable case:

a. this was a "colonial" area for the Bengal bhadralok into the first decade of this century and an indigenous elite had difficulty raising its head as a consequence.
b. Bihar was but one part of a wider cultural and linguistic region, embracing the U.P., Delhi and sections of the Punjab, Rajputana and Central India. Most important, for the U.P. as well as Bihar, this was the seat of the classical Indian imperial tradition. If the idea of a universal India had any historic home this was surely it.

There are special and particularly interesting features in the *U.P.* case. Here, it appears, the continued dominance of the great landholders from the Mughal period into the British period, as a result of the protective policy of the "Oudh School," prevented the rise of an elite of the Bengal Maharashtrian variety. The great landholders, with their Indo-Persian "husk culture" (as

Anthony Low has called it), their social dominance, and their control of political institutions, were in fact the elite at least until the 1920s, and those who then challenged them could best do so through that universalist and "anti-dominant" nationalism of the new elites and counter-elites. The Nehrus, Tandon, Kidwai and their ilk, in shaking themselves off the coattails of the great landholders could use local discontents to advantage (viz. their use of the *kisans*) but they were not embarrassed by detailed regional commitments.

10. The effect of this extra-regional stance on the part of the nationalist opponents of the great landholders was to leave the U.P. without one clearly dominant group as the power of those landholders declined in the 1930s. The regional struggles from the late thirties to the present have been concerned as much with the contest between rival caste and class groups over the redistribution of power, as with the task of wresting that power from the great landholders.

In Maharashtra and Tamilnad new, relatively stable counter-elites were firmly in power by the 50s. In West Bengal the partition had allowed the bhadralok to reassert themselves in a remnant of their former domain. But in the U.P. no one clearly dominant elite has yet emerged. The struggle goes on and the political bosses of Congress balance dexterously but dangerously on the rolling balls of the struggle.

Sociological Aspects
of Corruption in Southeast Asia

W. F. WERTHEIM

There is often a considerable discrepancy between the significance of a social phenomenon and the attention paid to it by sociology. One greatly neglected phenomenon is that of corruption. Though a favourite subject for club conversation and newspaper headlines, it has so far received remarkably little attention from professional sociologists. As a result, the current concept of "corruption" is still enmeshed in emotional reactions and popular notions; it hardly reflects any real understanding of the historical roots and social significance of the phenomenon. This explains how it was possible for an experienced

From W. F. Wertheim, *East-West Parallels* (The Hague: W. van Hoeve, Ltd., 1964), pp. 103–131. Reprinted by permission of the author and publisher.

W. F. WERTHEIM is Professor of Sociology at the University of Amsterdam, the Netherlands. He is the author of *Indonesian Society in Transition* (1956) and *East-West Parallels: Sociological Approaches to Modern Asia* (1964), and the co-editor (with J. M. Romein) of *A World on the Move: A History of Colonialism and Nationalism in Asia and North Africa from the Turn of the Century to the Bandung Conference* (1956).

sociologist like Raymond Aron to consider corruption in the state apparatus to be one of the most important causes of revolution.[1] He could have asked himself whether the argument should not run the other way. The truth is, rather, that in a revolutionary situation the accusation of corruption is raised because it has always proved to be an effective weapon. Clearly Aron still takes his point of departure from the popular notion that there must be a necessary and logical connection between corruption and the fall of a regime or dynasty. However, as early as 25 years ago Van Leur wrote that corruption does not necessarily impair the efficiency of an administration. A corrupt regime can be quite viable and function smoothly, says Van Leur — leaving aside its "right of existence": that is not an historical question, but a political and ethical one, a value judgement.[2] Indeed, world history has known many regimes which have enjoyed periods of stability, and even of prosperity, in spite of practices that would nowadays be called corrupt — or should one even say, because of such practices? One example is the United States at the end of the nineteenth century: the army that waged the "Comic Opera War" against Cuba exhibited a "record in bureaucratic corruption, inefficiency and bungling." [3] But if corruption flourished, so did the United States where the Americans were in the process of realizing Adam Smith's prediction, made as early as 1776, that they would create "one of the greatest and most formidable (empires) that ever was in the world." [4]

When therefore corruption in many newly independent non-Western countries hits the headlines, at home and abroad, sociologists should not be content with the shallow judgement that it is a portent of the imminent collapse of these countries, even though the prediction as such may be right. Rather should we analyse the phenomenon within its own historical setting, taking into account the social forces which brand as corruption practices which in the past may not have been experienced as such.

This brings us to the crucial question: What do we mean by corruption? In present-day language we usually associate this concept first and foremost with the readiness of officials to accept bribes. "In everyday life corruption is taken to mean that a public servant abuses his official power in order to procure for himself an extra income from the public." [5] It is true that the concept also implies bribery of persons other than public servants, e.g. politicians, trade-union leaders, journalists, members of the liberal professions, electors, and, most important, employees of private industry; it was largely to counteract this last form of corruption that the British "Bribery and Secret Commissions Preven-

[1] In discussing the problem of rebellion and revolution at the Fourth World Congress of Sociology, Milan-Stresa, 1959.

[2] J. C. van Leur, *Indonesian Trade and Society: Essays in Asian Social and Economic History* (The Hague/Bandung: W. van Hoeve, Ltd., 1955), pp. 287–288.

[3] Jacob Presser, *Amerika: Van kolonie tot wereldmacht* (America: From colony to world power; Amsterdam: Elsevier, 1949), pp. 399–400.

[4] Adam Smith, *An Inquiry into the Nature and Causes of the Wealth of Nations* (London, 1884), p. 257.

[5] Jacob van Klaveren, "Die historische Erscheinung der Korruption, in ihrem Zusammenhang mit der Staats- und Gesellschaftsstruktur betrachtet," *Vierteljahrschrift für Sozial- und Wirtschaftsgeschichte*, Vol. 44 (1957), p. 289.

tion League" was set up. But here I shall for the most part limit myself to a study of corruption of public servants in the countries of Southeast Asia. There, owing to the rapid growth of the administrative apparatus, which sharply contrasts with the under-developed state of private industry, corruption of public officials is of far greater significance than any other form. With the rapid increase of limited liability companies in Western Europe, corruption in private industry became a problem of alarming proportions only from the second half of the nineteenth century onward. Administrative corruption, on the other hand, is an age-old problem which has cropped up wherever an extensive bureaucratic structure of public services has existed. Therefore, although outside the official sphere the problem is not essentially different, corruption can best be studied in its official form, which has its roots in centuries-old traditions.

According to the common usage of the term "corruption" of officials, we call corrupt a public servant who accepts gifts bestowed by a private person with the object of inducing him to give special consideration to the interests of the donor. Sometimes also the act of offering such gifts or other tempting favours is implied in the concept. Extortion, *i.e.* demanding such gifts or favours in the execution of public duties, too, may be regarded as "corruption." Indeed, the term is sometimes also applied to officials who use the public funds they administer for their own benefit; who, in other words, are guilty of embezzlement at the expense of a public body. This problem I prefer to leave outside the scope of the present paper. The specific feature of corruption in its most usual sense is that it involves two or more parties. This is also the fundamental reason why concrete cases of corruption are so difficult to trace; for there is as a rule no sign of it in the accounts of those concerned, and both parties are interested in keeping the transaction secret. Perhaps one might even see in such secrecy — as the Dutch sociologist H. J. Brasz has suggested [6] — a criterion for the "corrupt" nature of a certain transaction: secrecy shows awareness on the part of those concerned that they are doing something which in the eyes of the society in which they live seems objectionable, a "corruption" of morals.

Favours from third parties accepted or demanded by an official on behalf of members of his family or party, or of other personal connections, may be referred to as forms of corruption even if he does not directly benefit either financially or otherwise. In all these cases the crucial point is the conduct of officials who infringe the principle of keeping their public and private concerns and accounts strictly separate.

At the same time, however, this definition shows that what is nowadays meant by corruption cannot possibly serve as a universal sociological concept. For it presupposes a social structure in which the separation between these two kinds of account-keeping has either been carried through in actual fact, or else has been generally accepted by society as a criterion for proper conduct on the part of civil servants. Only then can the acceptance, or demanding, of gifts as a precondition for the bestowal of favours be regarded as a "corruption" of the prevailing standards of morality. Therefore a sociological analysis of corruption

[6] H. J. Brasz, "Some Notes on the Sociology of Corruption," *Sociologia Neerlandica*, Vol. 1, no. 2 (Autumn, 1963), pp. 117 ff.

ought to be preceded by an historical treatment of the social awareness which brands certain type of conduct as corrupt.

In the above study Van Leur also wrote: "A modern, strict officialdom was only created with the Napoleonic state. Criticism of the integrity of eighteenth-century officials is thus *ex post facto* criticism." [7] Indeed, before the time of Napoleon public and private revenues were not kept separate as a matter of principle either in Europe or anywhere else in the world.

In the pre-Napoleonic period the predominant type of state, which in Asia dates back even before the Christian era, was what Max Weber has called the patrimonial-bureaucratic state.

> Patrimonial relationships as the basis of political structures have been extraordinarily widespread. . . . Princely possessions directly administered as territorial domains have always only constituted part of the ruler's political realm, which in addition embraces other territories which are not regarded as domains proper, but merely as subject to his political authority. . . . Whenever, then, a prince organizes his political authority . . . on the basic principles that apply to the exercise of his rule over his own domains, we speak of a patrimonial state structure. Up to the very threshold of the modern era and indeed in the modern era itself, the majority of large continental empires bear a rather pronounced patrimonial character.[8]

A particular feature of these patrimonial-bureaucratic empires is their broad agrarian basis. The peasantry produces primarily for its own needs, but part of the harvest is claimed by the rulers for the upkeep of the court and the maintenance of the urban population living in the environs of the palace. Besides this the agrarian population is required to render all kinds of services. In the process of further differentiation of functions and more rational organization involving increased clerical work and a growing hierarchy, the patrimonial administrative apparatus may take on certain bureaucratic features.[9] All the same, positions in the patrimonial structure continue to lack the bureaucratic separation between a "private" and a "public" sphere, which distinguishes them from modern bureaucracy as a conceptual type. In a predominantly rural society dominated by a barter economy officials are not remunerated in money, but with a share in the produce of the land. This goes together with a far-reaching decentralization of the patrimonial rule, as the administrative pattern of the crown domains is copied in the more distant territories. Whereas the domains are subject to the direct control of the prince, the latter territories are merely under his political authority. Essentially what is found there is but a repetition of the same pattern in which the local lord maintains a court of his own by means of the tithes levied from the peasants and the services rendered by them. The peasants are not *taillables et corvéables à merci*: their tributary obligation is always largely governed by custom.[10] The local lord, for his part, in recogni-

---

[7] Van Leur, *op. cit.*, p. 287.

[8] Max Weber, *Wirtschaft und Gesellschaft*, Second Ed. (Tübingen: J. C. B. Mohr, 1925), p. 684.

[9] Weber, *op. cit.*, p. 695.

[10] *Ibidem*, p. 685.

tion of the prince's supreme authority, is obliged to pay a tribute to the latter's court, which has usually to be delivered once a year. At the same time he is required to supply the prince, on request, with manpower for large building operations or for wars. This call for agrarian manpower is usually confined to seasons in which it can be withdrawn from agriculture without much damage. Sultan Agung of Mataram (Java) used to conduct his wars, year after year, during the dry East monsoon. And in all probability the huge temples of Java were also built during a succession of post-harvest periods, as were the Chinese Great Wall and the Egyptian pyramids.

> Among the large continental empires this type of conglomerative political structure was as of old the most widely adopted form; though its individual manifestations understandably exhibit a great many variations, there is nonetheless remarkable consistency in basic determinants. Even the Chinese empire, in spite of the uniformity of its officialdom displayed, well into the modern era, these characteristics of a conglomeration of satrapies, some of them only nominally dependent, grouped around the directly governed central provinces. As in the Persian satrapies, also here the local authorities kept the revenues from their provinces in their own hands, defraying local expenditures in advance out of such revenues. The central government received nothing but its lawful tribute, any increase in which could only be effected with great difficulty and in the face of passionate opposition on the part of provincial interest groups.[11]

If the above picture of the early Asian empires, which is largely derived from Max Weber's works, is correct — and its correctness is confirmed not only by Duyvendak's study of China but also by such writers as Vella on Thailand, Schrieke on Java and Leach on Ceylon [12] — then Wittfogel's representation of these ancient Asian empires as strongly centralized units over which the prince exercised "total power" would appear to be far removed from historical reality. Insofar as the rulers tried time and again to keep the local lords under control by force, this is not a sign of absolute power, but rather of weakness. Among the means tried to prevent imperial disintegration and to ensure the regular payment of tribute, Weber mentions the following: periodic royal tours; dispatch of confidential agents; demands for "personal guarantees" (in the form either of hostages or of regular appearances at the court); attaching sons of officials to the court as pages; putting relatives in important positions (which usually proved to be a double-edged sword), or just the reverse:

[11] *Ibidem*, pp. 710–711.

[12] J. J. L. Duyvendak, *China tegen de Westerkim* (China against the Western Horizon, Third Ed., Haarlem: De Erven F. Bohn, 1948), pp. 205–206; Walter F. Vella, "The Impact of the West on Government in Thailand," *University of California Publications in Political Science*, Vol. 4 (1955), pp. 317–410; B. Schrieke, *Indonesian Sociological Studies: Selected Writings*, Part One (The Hague/Bandung: W. van Hoeve Ltd., 1955), pp. 184 ff.; Schrieke, *Indonesian Sociological Studies: Selected Writings*, Part Two: *Ruler and Realm in Early Java* (The Hague/Bandung: W. van Hoeve Ltd., 1957), pp. 217 ff.; E. R. Leach, "Hydraulic Society in Ceylon," *Past and Present*, no. 15 (April, 1959), pp. 2 ff., containing a thorough criticism of Wittfogel's theory; see e.g. on p. 5: "The investigator looks only for positive evidence which will support his thesis; the negative instance is either evaded or ignored."

appointing people of inferior class or foreigners as *ministeriales*; brief terms of office; exclusion of public servants from seigniorages over territories where they have landed property or family connections; attaching celibates or eunuchs to the court; having officials supervised by spies or censors.[13] None of these expedients proved to be a panacea, and imperial unity was continually threatened from within by decentralizing tendencies.

This system leaves no room for corruption in the present sense of the term. In principle the local lord collects taxes and levies in kind on behalf of his own court. He does not have to render account of his income or expenditure to anybody. So long as he fulfils his tributary obligation to the satisfaction of the prince and shows no sign of rebelliousness, he is free to dispose of the assets he has collected. The limit to these is determined by tradition, which brands any increase in the charges as abuse. Transgression moreover gives rise to the danger of active resistance from the peasants. Therefore the prince arrogates to himself the right to call the local lord to account whenever he has reason to fear that the latter is becoming too independent or is endangering the continued obedience of the population by too heavy levies. In that case he will punish as "abuse" conduct which in the past may have been generally accepted as ancient custom. "Anyone who enriched himself too much and too quickly aroused the envy and hostility of these overlords. What was considered too much or too quickly is not always clear. In any case "too much" was simply what others with sufficient influence regarded as such." [14] Thus, although in the absence of any clear distinction between the private and the public spheres no accurate dividing line between custom and abuse could be drawn, accusations of corruption were nevertheless conceivable within this structure.

This links up with the fact that even long before the Napoleonic period certain trends came to the fore which eventually led to the emergence of new social norms. As early as the fourteenth century, Philippus of Leiden had tried, in his *Tractatus de cura rei publicae et sorte principantis*, to impress upon his prince the doctrine that he held the power bestowed upon him for the benefit of the community, and that he was obliged to exercise this power himself and not to delegate it arbitrarily to any other persons or groups. To the practice of exercising seigniorial rights for private purposes Philippus opposed a theory which boils down to the maxim: "public right is public duty." Since then the development of various European empires has proceeded gradually in the direction of increasing bureaucratization, though in the *ancien régime* bureaucratic features in the modern sense did not yet predominate.

Similarly, in some Asian empires remarkable experiments were made in the direction of bureaucratization and defeudalization. For example, the introduction of the examination system in China, combined with the practice of temporary appointments of mandarins in the function of magistrate, were steps which strike us at present as surprisingly advanced. But even the examination system could not fundamentally alter the patrimonial character of the Chinese administration. Many officials still derived their income primarily from those under

[13] Weber, *op. cit.*, pp. 704–705, 708.
[14] Van Klaveren, *loc. cit.*, p. 322.

their control. In an economic system largely based on barter, with a poorly developed transport system, payment of officials in cash from the imperial treasury was difficult to realize.[15]

However, in the eighteenth century new norms were coming to the fore, particularly in the European world. Increasing complaints of corruption — in France, in the United Dutch Republic, in the Indies of the Dutch East India Company — do in themselves not necessarily imply that the phenomena we call corruption were becoming more widespread. They could equally well indicate that a kind of public conduct hitherto considered normal was now looked at with other, more critical eyes.

The patrimonial-bureaucratic type of state was clearly represented by the eighteenth-century Java of the Dutch East India Company. Though formally a commercial body, the Company bore in its main structure a close resemblance to a state organization. Its Java can in some respects be regarded as the successor to the seventeenth-century Mataramese empire, in which patrimonial-bureaucratic features were also apparent.[16]

In the eighteenth century the patrimonial-bureaucratic character of the Company's rule found a typical expression in the letters of the "transitional figure," Dirk van Hogendorp to his brother Gijsbert Karel.[17] We owe to Mme Elisabeth du Perron-de Roos both the publication of this correspondence and the term "transitional figure," which stresses the fact that Dirk van Hogendorp, though himself still fully taking part in the patrimonial-bureaucratic system in the Indies, nevertheless in the course of his career developed a new sense of values, a "new conscience" which gradually made conditions from which he and others profited seem abuses.[18]

The nominal salary drawn by the employees of the Company was of merely symbolic significance. In the case of Dirk van Hogendorp it was such a trifle

[15] Still, from E. A. Krache, Jr., *Civil Service in Early Sung China, 960–1067* (Cambridge, Mass.: Harvard University Press, 1953), one might deduce that in the period discussed by the author there have been serious attempts to introduce a system of salaried officials paid from the treasury (see *e.g.* p. 83). On the other hand, even at that time "among the most conspicuous complaints concerning officials of this period were low morale and venality, particularly in the lower ranks, traceable in large measure to inadequate pay" (p. 196). The author also admits that "Many of the duties of local administration in the rural areas were carried out, under the guidance of these officials, by local functionaries who served without pay and who undertook such tasks as tax assessment, police duties, the management of storehouses, local public works, and the settlement of minor litigations" (p. 47). At any rate, it should be noted that according to Kracke, China at an early stage "pioneered . . . in applying techniques to maintain honesty, discipline, and initiative — in other words administrative responsibility — among government personnel" (p. 1).

[16] Schrieke, *op. cit.*, Part One, pp. 184 ff.; Part Two, pp. 217 ff.

[17] Gijsbert Karel van Hogendorp became one of the outstanding Dutch statesmen. He played an important role in paving the way for the return of the prince of Orange as King William I of the Netherlands after Napoleon's defeat. His brother Dirk, on the other hand, served as a general under Napoleon, and died in exile.

[18] E. du Perron-de Roos, "Correspondentie van Dirk van Hogendorp met zijn broeder Gijsbert Karel" (Correspondence between Dirk van Hogendorp and his brother Gijsbert Karel), *Bijdragen tot de Taal-, Land-en Volkenkunde van Nederlandsch Indië*, Vol. 102 (1943), pp. 125–273, see pp. 133, 170–171.

(80 guilders per month) that he made it over to his two unmarried sisters in The Hague, by way of pin-money. According to the Company's system employees obtained their rewards in a different way. Dirk's father had perished in a shipwreck on the way from Java to the Netherlands; probably his ship capsized as a result of being overloaded with contraband. According to Dirk's memoirs, this was quite a regular occurrence thanks to "the corruption common to all branches of the Batavia administration and well-nigh legitimated by the detestable system of the Company to pay its employees badly, thus fostering unlimited cupidity. . . ." Dirk's revenues as Commissioner for the extreme East of Java were also of a dubious nature. He excuses himself for them with the argument that he "could not live on the wind. . . . Moreover such Charges had been imposed upon me that without Revenues I could not possibly meet them." Towards the end of the eighteenth century these perquisites of office were considered so normal that instead of receiving a nominal salary, an annual "office charge" had to be paid to the Company (in Van Hogendorp's case this amounted to more than four thousand rixdollars). In addition he had to pay two thousand rixdollars to the Governor of the Northeast Coast of Java "in accordance with ancient custom," apart from other, similar payments. Legal and police expenditure were chargeable to his own account. All this, including his own upkeep, had to be paid for out of the same revenues that his predecessors had enjoyed, such as proceeds from "overweight" in the levies of rice, profit from the sale of opium, gifts and fines from Natives and Chinese.

Elsewhere Van Hogendorp mentions the frequency with which such gifts are demanded from the native regents: on the arrival of the new commissioner; on each New Year's day; every time the commissioner's wife expects a baby; upon his periodical embassy to the governor general in Batavia; upon his periodical embassy to the governor in Semarang; on his departure; from each new regent he appoints. No need to ask who in the last resort had to bring in these gifts. No one could contract out of this system. Therefore, when on the basis of his new sense of values the militant "transitional figure" Van Hogendorp criticized the overlords in Batavia sharply in his "Address to the Dutch People," they were able to accuse him of the very abuses which under the prevailing system were unavoidable. This power of the central ruler to brand at will a custom as abuse fits in with the patrimonial-bureaucratic system.

After the century of growing awareness the Napoleonic reforms came as a revolutionary innovation. The French act of 17 February, 1800 created the administrative foundation of the great political edifice designed in the stern and symmetrical Empire style. "With this act," according to Presser,[19] "Bonaparte threw a solid block of granite into the shifting sands of post-revolutionary France — not the only one, but one of the most lasting pieces. It was the well-known division into departments, *arrondissements* and municipalities headed by prefects, sub-prefects, and mayors." Though certainly not biased in favour of Napoleon, Presser nonetheless speaks appreciatively of the dutiful and sober conduct of the first draft of prefects. "Corruption under a dictatorship like

[19] Jacob Presser, *Napoleon: Historie en legende* (Napoleon: History and myth; Amsterdam: Elsevier, 1946), p. 143.

that of Napoleon," again according to Presser, "is especially to be found at the top, within the leadership. It is centralized. It may easily go together with a high degree of devotion and disinterestedness among the lower ranks of the hierarchy" [20] — at any rate in the early days, before the rot had also penetrated further down.

The Napoleonic structure was of course not entirely new. It borrowed elements both from the Prussian state and from the reforms which immediately followed the Revolution of 1789. But the Napoleonic reforms were in any case the first to create the prototype of a state structure which Weber has called the "modern bureaucratic state." According to him, its main features are: a distribution of authority arranged systematically in accordance with generally applicable rules; a hierarchy of offices with a corresponding fixed order of procedural affairs dealt with in writing and with minutes being kept; special qualifications for offices that presuppose a certain amount of training; the principle that an official's normal daily task should be the fulfilment of his duties, and that these various functions should be exercised according to more or less strict, exhaustive regulations that can be learnt.

As a result of this system tenure of office becomes a profession; the position of a civil servant bestows a certain social distinction; the civil servant is appointed by a higher authority, normally for life; he is remunerated in money, with a fixed salary and the right to a pension; the civil servant counts on a civil-service career with a prospect of promotion according to rules of seniority, subject to the specialized qualifications required for a particular office.[21]

The bureaucratic structure, Weber holds, is everywhere a late development. It is possible only in an advanced money economy; technically it is more perfect than any other form of organization. The system aims at accuracy, quickness, written records, continuity, discretion, uniformity, strict hierarchy. One of its principles is that all cases are dealt with objectively, according to calculable rules and without respect of persons. Public and private matters are kept strictly apart, Philippus of Leiden's principle that public right is public duty, being carried to its logical conclusion.

It is obvious that the preceding features are characteristic of the ideal-type of a modern bureaucratic state, to which reality corresponds only in very rough outline. Thus the prefects of Napoleon's time were not entitled to a pension; and affairs were dealt with very sluggishly, since the various spheres of authority were not clearly defined, and unimportant matters had to wait for decisions at the highest level. Furthermore, the bureaucratic structure long continued to show a weakness in that the apparatus could function properly only with the safeguard of regular supervision. In the Napoleonic apparatus supervision from above was provided for, but the highest levels themselves were not subject to any supervision, and were thus exposed to the temptation of unbridled pursuit of gain. Even the institution of a supervisory body such as the Audit Chamber

---

[20] Presser, *op. cit.*, p. 154.
[21] Weber, *op. cit.*, pp. 650 ff. (translated in H. H. Gerth and C. Wright Mills, eds., *From Max Weber: Essays in Sociology*, London: K. Paul, Trench, Trubner, 1948, pp. 196 ff.).

was no safeguard in itself, for who should keep the keepers? Not until late in the nineteenth century did the trend toward publicity in state affairs and government responsibility to representative bodies create the necessary preconditions for a serious application of the adage public right is public duty.

Still, the nineteenth century atmosphere of modern bureaucratic government allowed the present concept of "corruption," as defined in the foregoing, gradually to take shape.

Historical reality, however, never conforms to "pure types" — it always presents itself, as Max Weber put it, in mixed forms. The Netherlands East Indies government apparatus in the middle of the nineteenth century is a good example of such a mixed form, and an analysis of the situation there is the more interesting as it may lay bare the roots of present-day developments in many Asian countries. In that period once again a "transitional figure" played a part: Eduard Douwes Dekker, better known as Multatuli, the author of that famous *document humain, Max Havelaar*.[22] His difficulties and clashes with the official apparatus were partly due to the tension between a still predominantly patrimonial-bureaucratic indigenous substructure and a modern-bureaucratic European superstructure imbued with a new sense of values which was only slowly beginning to permeate that substructure.

Daendels had tried in vain to introduce the Napoleonic concept of government in Java. The Javanese princes and regents were not prepared to be demoted to the position of civil servants on the Western model, and to surrender their traditional privileges as landed aristocrats. A major rebellion, commonly called the Java War (1825–1830), compelled the colonial government partly to restore the regent aristocracy to its old glory. Once more their offices became hereditary in principle and they retained the right to all sorts of personal services from the population. Moreover they were rewarded, as were other groups of civil servants — including Europeans — by emoluments over and above their salaries. This extra income took the shape of a percentage of the yield of the crops, grown under a system of forced cultivation on government plantations in their districts — a typical patrimonial-bureaucratic form of remuneration. In the Priangan regencies (Western Java) the so-called Priangan System was even maintained up to 1871; this system allowed the regents to keep their traditional revenues instead of receiving a salary paid by the government.

Only in an infertile area like Douwes Dekker's Lebak (Southwestern Java) where government plantations were practically non-existent, did the regents and the lower-echelon indigenous civil servants have to make do with their salaries; but this was impossible if they wanted to live "in accordance with their social status." To secure the required income they stepped up the tributes and services demanded from the population to a level far above the latter's capacity. No wonder that an idealistic civil servant with a modern outlook like Douwes Dekker, who wanted to take a stand against such "abuses," could not help hurling himself against the powerful, traditional state apparatus — only to be crushed by it.

---

22 The best-known English translation is the one to which D. H. Lawrence wrote an introduction; it was published in New York, 1927. A new translation is forthcoming.

Towards the end of the nineteenth century, however, attempts were made gradually to bring the Javanese administrative infrastructure into closer accord with modern Western conceptions of government. The so-called *panchen* duties (domestic services due to native civil servants) were abolished. Henceforth the regents, and the chiefs of districts and sub-districts, were expected to live on their salaries. But this modernization failed to reach down to the foundation of the whole administrative structure, the village: the *desa* [23] headmen received no pay from the treasury and were rewarded for their services with a fixed percentage of the land tax collected by them, and with the proceeds of "official fields" which were specially allotted to them and worked by the villagers on a rotating basis. No wonder that the principles of modern administration had hardly begun to penetrate the sphere of the village economy, and that nothing was easier for a Chinese *batik* [24] manufacturer or the owner of a cigarette factory than to induce *desa* headmen and *desa* police to round up female workers who had stayed away from work and to return them to the factory — although they had no right to do so and the women often stayed away or absconded because of the abominable treatment they received.[25]

What was the state of affairs as regards corruption in the Netherlands East Indies administration? Towards the end of the nineteenth century in many areas conditions still prevailed which to Dutch ways of thinking were quite shocking, and which various publications have brought to light. Thus for example Opheffer mentions in one of his letters the Augean stable in the area of Rembang (Central Java).[26] Dijkstra, himself clearly a somewhat odd character, wrote a pamphlet on the basis of his experiences in the Lampongs (Southern Sumatra), denouncing "The Corruption among Netherlands East Indies Officials." [27] In 1902 Van den Brand published a sensational pamphlet with the title *The Millions from Deli*, which dealt with the methods used by the tobacco planters of the East Coast of Sumatra to secure the benevolent co-operation of civil servants. In general, the system was an indirect one:

> When Satan sets out to tempt, he hides his horns and carefully disguises his hooves and tail. A direct attempt at bribery is therefore rare. In the first place such an attempt is risky in itself, but what is more, it's stupid, down-right stupid. The money has to reach the party concerned, but he must be able to give a plausible reason for its acceptance. . . . It is the general custom for a junior European administrative official who is transferred to another post to put up his belongings for auction. And the proceeds are largely determined by his relationship with the local planter

[23] *Desa* — Javanese village.

[24] *Batik* — cotton prints made by a special technique, developed in Java.

[25] P. de Kat Angelino, *Batikrapport: Rapport betreffende eene gehouden enquête naar de arbeidstoestanden in de batikkerijen op Java en Madoera* (Batik report: on an inquiry into working conditions in the *batik* workshops in Java and Madura, Vol. 2, Central Java, 1931), pp. 28 ff., 310 ff.

[26] *Brieven van Opheffer* (Uplifter's letters, Third Ed., Maastricht, 1944), pp. 339 ff. Opheffer (Uplifter) was a pseudonym of a well-known civil servant, G. L. Gonggrijp.

[27] J. F. Dijkstra, *De corruptie in de Nederlandsch-Indische ambtenaarswereld, of: Mr. Rhemrev als regeerings-commissaris* (Corruption among Netherlands East Indies officials, or: Mr. Rhemrev as Government Commissioner, Rotterdam, 1906).

during his — the official's — term of office. Obviously a magistrate who punishes the coolies severely at the slightest provocation, and at the same time deals extremely mildly with any offence committed by a European, is held in high esteem by his white compatriots. To express this esteem and prove his appreciation of the administrator as a person, the wealthy planter gladly pays a hundred or more guilders for the pen with which the harsh sentence of his coolie was entered in the register. A pleasant keepsake, for sure. . . . Look at some of the amounts that were spent some three years ago [*i.e.* in 1899] at the auction held by a civil servant who was leaving government service with a decent pension: five hundred and ten guilders for an ink stand, purchaser the chief manager of the Royal Company for the Exploitation of Oil Wells in the Netherlands East Indies; . . . three hundred and fifty guilders for a cigar-cutter, purchaser the chief manager of the Deli-Batavia Company; . . . six hundred guilders for a globe, purchaser the chief manager of the British Deli and Langkat Tobacco Company.

The Indonesian princes and Chinese headmen also offered incredible prices at these auctions — the princes, according to Van den Brand, "so as to be able to continue their oppression and extortion of the people"; the Chinese headmen because they controlled "the farming out of opium, pawnshops, and gambling leases, not to mention the fact that they owned nearly all the brothels." [28]

However, the *indirect* form that "bribery" takes in this case — the high prices paid at such auctions were especially intended to show the successor what he might expect if he took good care of the business interests in his locality [29] — is quite significant in itself. For in the course of the years the incorruptibility of the Indies civil service had come to be regarded as an indisputable fact. In this respect the Netherlands East Indies administration as a whole gained a reputation which closely approached that of the Western European democracies. J. S. Furnivall, a noted authority on the pre-war Indies, wrote that in Java corruption was "practically unknown." [30]

He contrasted this with Burma, where during the same period corruption thrived so profusely that he devoted nearly eight pages to it. . . .[31] His facts were primarily derived from a report published on the eve of the Second World War. The commission of inquiry doubted if among the civil servants of the two lower grades more than thirty per cent were honest. It was suggested that no less than two thirds of all police inspectors were corrupt; the excise officers were "by general consent the most universally corrupt." In the prisons "a prisoner could have anything he wanted except women; some said he could even have women." In the medical department false reports could be obtained for a consideration; ward servants deliberately treated their patients roughly

[28] J. van den Brand, *De millioenen uit Deli* (The millions from Deli; Amsterdam/ Pretoria, n.y.), pp. 15–19.

[29] Van den Brand, *Nog eens: de millioenen uit Deli* (Once more: the millions from Deli; Amsterdam/Pretoria, n.y.), p. 41.

[30] J. S. Furnivall, *Colonial Policy and Practice: A Comparative Study of Burma and Netherlands India* (New York: New York University Press, 1956), p. 269.

[31] Furnivall, *op. cit.*, pp. 170–178.

if they were not paid. And so on throughout his survey of the various public services.

The most important source of corruption was stated to be the multiplication of all sorts of "welfare" measures which were disliked by the public. People readily made small gifts in order to escape such bothersome measures as vaccination, slaughter of diseased cattle, and building restrictions. The extension of the administrative apparatus created new opportunities for corruption. The general public was still unfamiliar with the difference between private and public interests: "Even to this day the rural public frequently draws no distinction between payments to government officers which go into the Treasury, and those which do not. . . ."

One may well ask what was the reason for the difference between Furnivall's estimate of the situation in Burma and his opinion of conditions in Java. Was there a real difference? Or was it largely due to the fact that in Burma an official inquiry had been held, whereas in Java there had been none? One should keep in mind that in general not only those who have been corrupted, but also those who do the corrupting have little cause for revealing their practices.

On the other hand it might be argued that such inquiries are the product of pressure on the part of a public that is convinced of the existence of large-scale bribery. In Burma this pressure came from nationalist politicians. No doubt Indonesian nationalists, too, would have used accusations of corruption if there had been the slightest chance of backing them up. The absence of such accusations in the, often violent, publications of the nationalists therefore argues in a certain sense against the existence of corruption on a large scale. Moreover corruption is furthered by a public opinion which takes it for granted that it is ubiquitous. For it is very risky to offer bribes to an official if the chances are that he will refuse them.

All the same there is enough evidence to justify the contention that Furnivall, in describing corruption as "practically unknown," idealized the actual conditions prevailing in the pre-war Netherlands East Indies. Patrimonial relationships were not confined to the *desa* economy: in the official apparatus, too, there were plenty of remnants of the traditional political structure. Thus the loyalties of Indonesian officials were still divided between state and family. To refuse a request from a member of one's family, whether for financial aid or for a job, was contrary to the moral code which still held good in Indonesian society. Hence Indonesian officials got into financial difficulties because, owing to their traditional family obligations, they lived beyond the means provided by their official salaries. The colonial government often had to overlook financial irregularities in its efforts to maintain its aristocratic props in their posts. Hence also the recurring complaints about "nepotism" among the regents.[32] The traditional Javanese custom of presenting those in high office with small gifts — a basket of fruit, a few chickens — also made it difficult to draw any sharp dividing lines. More serious abuses, judged by the standards of the public ethics of a

---

[32] See for an attempt to justify the system P. A. A. Djajadiningrat, *Herinneringen* (Memoirs; Amsterdam: G. Kolff/Batavia, 1936), pp. 213–214.

modern bureaucracy, were not lacking either. They were found especially in the Outer Regions, where the Indonesian officials were less well trained and, more than in Java, entangled in *adat* [33] and family relations; where, moreover, the European officials, often far removed from the central authority, had to carry extremely heavy responsibilities. Particularly in the twenties serious complaints were raised in the *Volksraad* (People's Council) about the acceptance of secret commissions — mainly in connection with contractor's agreements, for example by the State Railways. I quote from an article by D. M. G. Koch:

> Governor General Dirk Fock, who had gained the impression that corruption had deeply corroded the Netherlands East Indies administration usually so much praised for its integrity, had started a hunt for fraudulent officials and ordered a relentless prosecution of those who accepted secret commissions or committed embezzlement at the expense of the treasury. Sensacional cases of dismissal from the service occurred, which created the impression that untrustworthiness had attained vast proportions and that it was creditable to take part in this hunt and to denounce people. [34]

Nevertheless Koch's statement in the same passage to the effect that the administration had a reputation for integrity is true, provided it is taken in a comparative sense by relating it to an Asian, colonial environment. Public morality was moving in a Western-bureaucratic direction, but many remnants of the traditional political structure were still there; and most important of all: insofar as the civil administration was incorruptible, this was due not so much to its Indonesian branch having been imbued with a new morality of complete loyalty to the colonial government, as to a strict supervision exercised by the European authorities.

But perhaps there was also another reason why, during the first decades of this century, the phenomenon of corruption tended to disappear into the background. In the early days it was still very important for a private person to win the favour of a local administrator. Hence the collusion between planter and official to which Van den Brand drew attention — partly the outcome of solidarity among the whites, partly of the great power of the local authorities.

But the period prior to the Second World War saw an increasing concentration of business interests within large concerns whose claims could better be pressed in Batavia or in The Hague than on the spot. At the same time the influence of these concerns in government circles steadily increased. There was no longer any need for businessmen of importance to have recourse to the tricky method of bribery: they could achieve their ends equally well by legal means. When therefore in the "twenties critics of Governor General Fock's regime complained that high finance was unduly favoured — the cancellation of a proposal to levy export duty on oil meant an annual loss to the treasury of well over fifty million guilders [35] — this criticism implied that businessmen

---

[33] *Adat* — custom, customary law.

[34] D. M. G. Koch, "De zaak-Baljet" (The Baljet affair), *De Nieuwe Stem*, Vol. 11 (1956), p. 484.

[35] Koch, *Om de vrijheid: De nationalistische beweging in Indonesië* (For freedom: The nationalist movement in Indonesia; Jakarta: Jajasan Pembangunar, 1950), p. 76.

managed to obtain their ends by perfectly legal means. The rubber policy during the period of the great depression, which was gravely attacked by Governor Van Suchtelen, also favoured the Western estate owners by "legal" means.[36]

At most one might speak — or rather whisper — of bribery by indirect means. But this no longer occurred on a small scale, as had been the case with the auctions on the East Coast of Sumatra at the beginning of the century. During the period of the growing power of the big concerns high officials who had served the business world well were rewarded by profitable directorships when they were pensioned off. In the public debates on the so-called Jambi affair, for example, the charge was made that a governor general and certain ministers had, in return for service rendered, been awarded with prominent positions in the Royal Dutch Petroleum Company. In this case Minister De Waal Malefijt denied the imputation of corruption, but added:

> Allow me to say that in general I emphatically disapprove of civil servants, who in their former posts were able to render services to a company, being offered high-salaried positions, and accepting them, even though in fact there is nothing wrong. Such offers create the impression that they are intended as a reward for services rendered, and might encourage slackness in officials who are still on active duty.[37]

So the situation began to develop along the lines described recently by an American sociologist: "Nobody any longer needs to be bribed. Every member of Eisenhower's cabinet has been a director of large corporations, with the exception of the Secretary of Labor." [38]

In the pre-war Netherlands East Indies a development could thus be noted which lagged behind nineteenth-century standards insofar as certain traditional elements continued to feature in the administrative structure; on the other hand we also saw a typically twentieth-century development as a result of which nineteenth-century ethical standards ceased to be entirely adequate in the changing circumstances.

Against this historical background the problem of present-day corruption can now be analysed in further detail. Again I will confine myself mainly to conditions in Southeast Asia. There the world-wide phenomenon of corruption can be observed in its purest form as it were.

Smith tells us that under President Quirino in the Philippines corruption extended from the lowest level of the civil service to the top, excepting the president himself. One could not enter government service without paying for it — small sums in the lower regions, considerable ones higher up. Criticism became so sharp that the president was forced to call a meeting to start a "clean-up campaign." But much of its effect was lost because a reporter had been listening under an open window and had overheard one of the president's

36 B. C. C. M. M. van Suchtelen, *Nederlands nieuwe Eereschuld aan Indië* (The Netherlands' new debt of honour to the Indies; Hilversum, 1939).
37 *De waarheid over Djambi* (The truth about Jambi; pamphlet, n.p., 1921), p. 78.
38 Edwin B. Burgum, "American Sociology in Transition," *Science and Society*, Vol. 24 (1959), p. 322.

closest advisers exclaim: "But what's the use of being the majority party if we can't have a little honest graft?" [39] This of course was promptly printed in the papers.

In Burma the political tensions within the large government party, which eventually led to military rule, predominantly centered around the question of corruption. Furnivall writes: "U Nu held that without drastic action to purge the party it would die a shameful if lingering death from the cancer of corruption. Others held that the remedy was more dangerous than the disease; it would entail a major operation and the patient would die under the surgeon's knife." [40] About Thailand we read: "The chief problems of the civil service at the present time are low salaries and corrupt practices," and "Corruption is probably more highly organized in the Police Department than in any other department." [41]

So if in a certain period of the history of post-war Indonesia corruption occupied the centre of attention, this was by no means exceptional in Southeast Asia. At most one might say that the country's pre-war reputation of being a favourable exception had been lost. But the situation in Indonesia during that period — covering the years from 1951 to 1957 — also makes possible a closer study of the nature of post-war corruption and the form in which it appears. I am not sufficiently familiar with local developments after 1957 (the year in which I visited many parts of Indonesia) to determine to what extent the situation in this respect has been remedied since.

First of all we have to take into account that the post-war forms of so-called corruption still frequently conceal relics of the traditional social structure. Village headmen for example are still unpaid, so that they have to maintain themselves by partly legal, partly illegal levies on the population. The patrimonial-bureaucratic substructure still influences all other sections of society, while traditional family ties continue to clash with modern cencepts of morality in public affairs. Even as late as 1957 in several public services in Western Sumatra it could be observed that all the personnel in one particular office belonged to a single family group: that of the office chief.

Besides these relics from an ancient past, however, post-independence corruption in Indonesia also had many typical post-war features. In the first place, under the direct influence of war, Japanese occupation, and revolution, the borderline between legal and illegal had become extremely vague and shifting. But even apart from the direct influence of war and revolution, new factors have been operating since the creation of the Indonesian Republic which promote corruption, or give it a new aspect.

One of these is the continuous extension of the duties of the public au-

[39] Robert A. Smith, *Philippine Freedom, 1946–1958* (New York, 1958), p. 137. See further for an enlightening discussion of the corruption problem in the Philippines: Onofre D. Corpuz, *The Bureaucracy in the Philippines* (Manila: Institute of Public Administration, University of the Philippines, 1957), especially pp. 221 ff.

[40] Furnivall, *The Governance of Modern Burma*, Second Ed. (New York: Institute of Pacific Relations, 1960), p. 117.

[41] Wendell Blanchard and others, *Thailand: Its People, Its Society, Its Culture* (New Haven: HRAF Press, 1958), pp. 184, 198.

thorities. In the crisis years before the war a beginning was made with economic controls. During and after the war this process continued, as nearly everywhere else in the world, at ever-increasing speed. This gave rise to a new official apparatus exerting considerable power over the most varied sectors of the economy. Many of these services are manned by personnel without any schooling in the pre-war civil service ethics. As in other Southeast Asian countries, the number of officials in Indonesia has multiplied: this is one of the many aspects of disguised unemployment. This leads, in turn, to serious underpayment of civil servants, which makes it not only a temptation but for most of them even a necessity to seek all sorts of supplementary remuneration.

In contrast with the extremely low level of living imposed by the salaries paid to officials is the demonstration effect emanating from the luxurious way of life of certain groups, such as foreigners and the new class of Indonesian traders and industrialists. Before the war the Indonesian officials and politicians considered the way of life of the European elite as beyond their reach. But since the Revolution much larger sections have come to regard a life with private cars and weekend bungalows as no more than their due.

Another factor which lends a new aspect to the phenomenon of corruption is that of party politics. During elections officials charged with the issue of numerous licences and permits took it upon themselves to make such favours dependent upon a donation to their party funds. The introduction of party politics has led to a spoils system — as was also shown by that conversation overheard in Manila.

Intervention by the army was regarded by many — in Burma, Pakistan, and Indonesia — as a means of putting an end to the political corruption. But experience soon taught that unlimited power in the hands of the army leadership, after an initial period of improvement, only tended to make matters worse. The regional commanders often start off with the best intensions, their actions being provoked by the fact that the central government does not provide them with sufficient funds for properly discharging their duties. Thus for example it is known that the regional commander in Celebes conducted a large-scale contraband trade in copra with the Philippines in order to obtain the necessary foreign exchange. In 1957, I heard the following story: A Chinese trader from Menado (Northern Celebes) told a friend in Jakarta of his intention to return to Menado. "But why, I thought you left there after the Revolution because you could do better business over here?" "Yes, in those days. But you know how it is. . . . Here in Jakarta I have to tip five high officials to get a licence, but in Menado I only have to bribe one lieutenant."

Besides, in the countries of Southeast Asia business affairs are getting so much tangled up with the state apparatus that many transactions smelling of corruption are conducted by strictly "legal" methods. When representatives of foreign interests use part of aid funds for the benefit of high officials, for example by offering them expensive trips abroad, this could certainly rate as an attempt at "corrupting" these officials, though the action does not come strictly under the technical heading of "corruption."

The foregoing, mainly historical, survey was necessary because history and sociology, if they can ever be separated at all, are certainly inseparable in this case. We may now attempt to draw from it a number of theoretical conclusions.

In post-war conditions we find various factors which clearly foster the phenomenon of corruption, such as the moral disruption caused by war and revolution, the extension of government intervention in economic life, the low remuneration of officials, and the lure of the way of life of certain groups. Moreover the great publicity given to corruption tends in itself to promote corruption.

However, there are also factors which point in the direction of changing social views and which may be regarded as indications that a new sense of values is breaking through. In the colonial era there could be no question of complete loyalty among indigenous officials in Java to a government which embodied the Western concept of the state. Under certain circumstances obligations towards relatives weighed at least as heavily. And the peasantry knew loyalty only towards their regent, hardly at all towards a central state apparatus of foreign origin.

The nationalist revolution was symptomatic of a new type of solidarity on a national basis. But this sense of unity has not penetrated deeply enough to guarantee strict loyalty from civil servants and citizens also in times of peaceful construction. The traditional particularistic loyalties are now seen to be too narrow; but an extended "quasi-universalistic" loyalty towards the Indonesian Republic is for many still too wide. Party politics make it possible for an intermediate loyalty to arise, loyalty towards a political party, which frequently overrides loyalty towards the state as a whole. Hence making the grant of licences conditional on the receipt of donations to one's party is not felt as an infringement of public-service morals. In the absence of a fully matured national conscience, loyalties also frequently attach themselves to ethnic entities: one is faithful not primarily to one's national leaders, but rather to those of one's own area or island. This lay at the root of the Nadjamuddin affair, a sensational case in what was the State of East Indonesia during the few years of federal government under Dutch control, when an ex-premier was tried for corruption without losing his prestige among his followers.

Such intermediate loyalty in conflict with loyalty to the Republic can also be due to faithfulness to a military leader under whom one has fought during the Revolution. The regional commander who maintains his own troops on the proceeds of so-called smuggling may be completely accepted by his followers. The way in which he demands levies and services from the population in his area often still bears pronounced patrimonial-bureaucratic features — a relic from the past.

In contrast to these more or less particularistic loyalties a growing national consciousness condemns as "corruption" actions which those concerned do not feel to be reprehensible. As in Western Europe in the eighteenth century, present-day Southeast Asia is in a period of transition, during which value systems are gradually shifting. Moreover, along with the new set of values that is breaking through, much higher demands are made on the government than formerly. True, in the past many activities which in the Western world were left to private initiative, in the East were performed by the government. But this was largely done on traditional lines. The present world situation requires from the public authorities a dynamic and imaginative activity which is possible only if all loyalties are concentrated on this all-embracing social task. This new sense of values brands as corruption many formally legal instances of collusion between private persons and government officials, so that those most deeply impregnated with the new norms are even inclined to style the whole of Southeast Asian society as "corrupted."

It is this discrepancy between norm and reality, between expectations and shortcomings, which draws so much public attention to the phenomenon of corruption. The attempt to inculcate nineteenth-century standards of public behaviour into the civil administration founders on the one hand on the immature sense of loyalty of the public servant himself, and on the other on the multitude of demands made on him, which in a growing welfare state far exceed those which the nineteenth-century bureaucracy had to meet. Thus the lack of stability of the new Asian regimes is due primarily, not to the frequency of corruption, but to the discrepancy between social norm and reality — a permanent tension with a dysfunctional and disintegrating effect.

The foregoing also makes it clear why the fight against corruption in the new Asian states is such a labour of Sisyphus. In 1953 a high Indonesian official saw three possibilities: first, to shoot all corrupt officials — but that he thought too radical a measure; second, to imprison them, but that (and I quote literally) "would cause work to come to a standstill, as it is mostly minor officials that are involved" (it is interesting to learn that minor officials are more indispensable than higher ones); the third way, according to this "expert," was the best: "to introduce a new tax only payable by corrupt people. . . ." [42] Apparently it did not occur to him that this would merely lead to higher tariffs . . . quite apart from the fact that most corrupt people are not in the habit of advertising their bad practices. But more intelligent experts, seeking a solution for example in stricter supervision are also faced with insurmountable difficulties. Who should keep the keepers? And, as we have seen above, to have recourse to a military dictatorship in the long run only makes matters worse by withdrawing government activities from public control.

All such measures fail because of their negative approach: they merely combat undesirable symptoms. The root of the evil is the lack of a more positive attachment to the government and of a spiritual involvement in its task in society, on the part both of the officials and of the whole community.

That is why the Chinese example is so instructive, for there a serious attempt has been made to encourage such a positive approach in all public servants — through education and propaganda accompanied by sharp measures against any deviations. In 1951 a mass movement was started from above, popularly known as the "Three Anti's" and directed against the following evils in the public services: corruption, waste, and a bureaucratic outlook. But it is interesting that this action was soon followed by a new mass action, this time among the popu-

[42] *Indische Courant voor Nederland*, 24 November, 1953.

lation and directed against similar activities regarded as harmful to the state: the so-called "Five Anti's" movement against bribery, tax evasion, fraud, theft of state assets, and leakage of state economic secrets.[43] These mass movements were accompanied by pressure on every citizen, from highest to lowest, to denounce any instance of corruption or similar abuse that had come to his knowledge — criticism and self-criticism in official terms, spying and brainwashing according to Western terminology. These campaigns moreover were conducted in an atmosphere in which Spartan simplicity, thrift, and discipline in private life were being stressed. The breaking off of practically all contact with the outside world and the expulsion of many wealthy foreign traders helped to eliminate the possible demonstration effect emanating from the way of life among social groups living in luxury.

The Chinese example also teaches us, however, that in an atmosphere of dynamic reconstruction the sharp distinction between public servant and citizen is in the process of disappearing. In the welfare state the public servant is required not only to keep public and private concerns strictly separate, dealing with the first in accordance with the prevailing legal regulations; a positive attitude and a dynamic activity in the interest of the community are also demanded of him. But the private employee, too, is no longer expected to be merely a faithful "organization man": he has to be conscious all the time of his social task in the community in which he lives, and conflicts may arise between these two loyalties.

This trend, though in many countries still quite weak, is of the utmost importance for the development of the concept of corruption. Just as in the eighteenth century a new sense of values broke through in keeping with the maxim public right is public duty, so now a new sense of value is developing that might be summed up in the adage private right is public duty. The idea of trusteeship which has recently been incorporated in all world religions and which implies that the owner in effect administers his property for the public benefit, is a clear indication that this new sense of values is not confined to Asia alone.

But in this light the situation in these Southeast Asian states, which have so recently won their independence might be summarized as a tension between a past in which patrimonial-bureaucratic and particularist features strongly predominated and a universalist future aimed at socialization of the means of production. In their present condition of tension, these states cannot possibly find a secure foothold in a nineteenth-century official morality which is becoming obsolete.

[43] Theodore Hsi-en Chen and Wen-hui C. Chen, "The 'Three-Anti' and 'Five-Anti' Movements in Communist China," *Pacific Affairs*, Vol. 26 (1953), pp. 31 ff.

Personal Rulership, Patrimonialism, and Empire-Building in the New States

GUENTHER ROTH

The concrete lessons of recent history have helped us to appreciate the paramount importance of the political preconditions of social and economic development in the new states. The basic problem of political stability must be solved before all others — or everything else may be in vain. For this reason, some of the scholarly attention that used to be focused on social and economic development has shifted to political organization and has given prominence to terms such as "nation-building," "political culture," and "democratization." At the same time efforts have been made to modify the usual evolutionary and dichotomous conceptions of social and political development. The two-faced nature of tradition and modernity has come under scrutiny again.

Two basic theoretical choices have been made in the face of the complexity of the subject matter: one choice has been to resort to a relatively novel terminology that is intended to transcend Western historical connotations — witness the attempt by Gabriel Almond and his collaborators to adapt the Parsonian scheme; the other has been to re-examine older terms for their contemporary usefulness and to work with historically more specific concepts — an approach prominently pursued by Reinhard Bendix.[1]

I shall follow the latter path because I should like to reconsider a neglected part of Max Weber's typology of *Herrschaft*, the notion of patrimonial rule, for it seems to me that many of the features of legal-rational modernity may not appear in the new states and that certain basic modes of administration persist, even though traditionalist legitimacy has disintegrated in most cases. From the beginning, it should be clearly understood that Weber's sociology of *Herrschaft* deals not only with beliefs in legitimacy but also with the actual operating modes and administrative arrangements by which rulers "govern," not just "rule" (to paraphrase Adolphe Thiers's constitutional theory). This is made abundantly clear in his historical analyses of patrimonialism, sultanism, feudalism, the routinization of charismatic rule, hierocracy, and the city-state. If you wish, Weber tried to find out "how systems really work." It is true that he organized his great opus *Economy and Society* around a typology of social

From *World Politics*, Vol. XX, No. 2 (January 1968), pp. 194–206. Reprinted by permission of the author and publisher.

GUENTHER ROTH is Associate Professor of Sociology, University of California, Davis. He is the author of *The Social Democrats in Imperial Germany* (1963). He is translator and editor (together with Claus Wittich) of Max Weber, *Economy and Society* (1968, 3 vols.). A number of his articles have appeared in professional journals.

[1] See, for example, Gabriel Almond and Bingham Powell, *Comparative Politics* (Boston: Little, Brown and Co., 1966). For Bendix, see his *Nation-Building and Citizenship* (New York: John Wiley & Sons, 1964), 2, and "Modernization and Inequality," a paper prepared for Session I, Sixth World Congress of Sociology, ISA, mimeographed, 52 ff.

action and of legitimacy, but both in the terminological exposition (in Part I) and in the more descriptive analyses (in the older Part II) he always dealt with *Herrschaft* in terms of both legitimacy and the typical staff arrangements of the various kinds of rulers.[2] Here lies the great difficulty of translating *Herrschaft*, which in English is usually rendered either as "authority" (Parsons) or "domination" (Bendix, Rheinstein, Shils). Patrimonial rulers, for example, endeavor to maximize their personal control. Like all rulers, they are continually engaged in a struggle with their staff over ultimate control. In this regard, traditionalist legitimacy may be a burden as well as a help for them (as both Weber and Eisenstadt have shown).[3] Such legitimation may fetter them and prevent them from mobilizing the resources needed for empire-building, a handicap that Eisenstadt has considered the fatal flaw of the "historical bureaucratic societies." Rulers, then, avail themselves of various political and administrative devices that transcend the bases of their legitimacy. Patrimonial rulers resort to "extrapatrimonial" recruitment, which may retain the fiction of patriarchal subordination but may in fact be based on a feudal-contractual, bureaucratic-contractual, or merely personal relationship.

TRADITIONALIST PATRIMONIALISM AND PERSONAL RULERSHIP

Lately, some attempts, primarily in the field of African studies, have been made to remember the meaning of patrimonialism, yet by and large Weber's broad typology of *Herrschaft* has been underutilized and, in fact, reduced to the dichotomy of bureaucracy and charisma. Not only patrimonialism but also collegial government and rule by notables have been disregarded.

I wish to distinguish two kinds of patrimonialism. One is the historical survival of traditionalist patrimonial regimes; the foremost example is Ethiopia, where the researcher, if he gains access at all, can almost perform the feat of travelling into the past.[4] The second type of patrimonialism is personal rulership on the basis of loyalties that do not require any belief in the ruler's unique personal qualification, but are inextricably linked to material incentives and rewards. This second variant has been submerged in much of the literature

---

[2] See Part I, chap. 3, and Part II, chaps. 10–16, of my forthcoming variorum edition of *Economy and Society* (Totowa, N.J.: Bedminster Press, 1968).

[3] See S. N. Eisenstadt, *The Political Systems of Empires: The Rise and Fall of the Historical Bureaucratic Societies* (New York: The Free Press, 1963).

[4] See Donald N. Levine, "Ethiopia: Identity, Authority, and Realism," in Lucian W. Pye and Sidney Verba (eds.), *Political Culture and Political Development* (Princeton: Princeton University Press, 1965), 245–81; also Levine, *Wax and Gold: Tradition and Innovation in Ethiopian Culture* (Chicago: University of Chicago Press, 1965). Levine's fascinating accounts disregard the literature on patrimonialism. For a detailed description of personal rulership and palace intrigues, see Richard Greenfield, *Ethiopia* (London: Pall Mall Press, 1965). On the much more precarious Iranian case, see Leonard Binder, *Iran: Political Development in a Changing Society* (Berkeley and Los Angeles: University of California Press, 1962); and now also Norman Jacobs, *The Sociology of Development: Iran as an Asian Case Study* (New York: Frederick A. Praeger, 1966).

through the indiscriminate use of the term "charismatic." As long as patrimonialism is considered to rest exclusively on traditionalist legitimation and hereditary succession, the category obviously loses applicability to the extent that these phenomena decline. Personal rulership, however, is an ineradicable component of the public and private bureaucracies of highly industrialized countries; some of the newer states lack the institutional matrix (whether pluralist or totalitarian) of these countries to such an extent that personal rulership becomes the dominant form of government. In terms of traditional political theory, some of these new states may not be states at all but merely private governments of those powerful enough to rule; however, this only enhances the applicability of the notion of personal rulership (in the sense of detraditionalized, personalized patrimonialism). Such personal governance easily evokes notions of opportunism and corruption from the perspective of charismatic or legal-rational legitimation.[5] Traditionalist as well as personal patrimonial regimes differ from charismatic rulership in that the patrimonial ruler need have neither personal charismatic appeal nor a sense of mission; they differ from legal-rational bureaucracies in that neither constitutionally regulated legislation nor advancement on the basis of training and efficiency need be predominant in public administration.

Also, personal rulership should not be mistaken for "authoritarianism," which has little to do with "authority" as such. After the First World War, the doctrine of authoritarianism was developed by right-wing nationalists, who championed the autonomy of the state apparatus as against parliament with its parties and interest groups and even as against the dynastic families and their loyalist supporters. Nowadays, however, the term is usually applied to the many political regimes that lie between democratic and totalitarian ones. These regimes base themselves on a limited structural pluralism, which admits of some interest-group articulation; strategies of *divide et impera* are usually more important than legitimation or ideological integration, and for that reason authoritarian regimes may be less stable and have less "authority" than democratic and totalitarian states.

Many authoritarian regimes have features of traditional and personal patrimonialism, which may be more important than charismatic appeals, the belief in legal rationality, and bureaucratic practices. Typologically, however, it would be inadvisable to equate "patrimonial" with "authoritarian." The latter term has been useful in establishing a continuum ranging from pluralist democracy to totalitarianism; the former category properly belongs to a typology of beliefs *and* organizational practices that can be found at any point of such a continuum.[6]

[5] For one of the latest examples, see Conor Cruise O'Brien, former member of the Irish delegation to the United Nations and vice-chancellor of the University of Ghana from 1962 to 1965, "The Counter-revolutionary Reflex," *The Columbia Forum*, IX (Spring 1966), 21f.

[6] For an excellent discussion of authoritarianism, see Juan J. Linz, "An Authoritarian Regime: Spain," in E. Allardt and Y. Littunen (eds.), *Cleavages, Ideologies and Party*

PERSONAL RULERSHIP IN
INDUSTRIALIZED COUNTRIES

In order to emphasize that personal rulership transcends the dichotomy of tradition and modernity, I shall first illustrate its continued functioning in industrialized countries, before turning to some African and Asian regimes. In the older political science literature the phenomenon has been subsumed under terms such as "machine" and "apparatus," or even "clique" and "faction"; organization analysts have rediscovered some aspects under the names "primary groups" and "informal relations," and they customarily contrast these with the formal structure of bureaucracy, which is usually and misleadingly called the Weberian model (as if Weber had not scrutinized patrimonial bureaucracies and modern higher civil servants as status groups and vested interests).

The old urban machines are a familiar example. They had, of course, some kind of traditionalist legitimation because of the immigrants' Old World ties, but they functioned primarily on the basis of personal loyalty — plebeian, not feudal — material reward; offices were distributed by a noncharismatic and nonbureaucratic ruler, and occupying them amounted to holding a benefice. The boss might have had great power, but his legitimacy was precarious; thus he had little authority and had to envelop his "clients" in an intricate web of reciprocities.[7]

The old machines have largely disappeared, but personal rulership has not. Instead of the Irish bosses of yesteryear there is the Kennedy "clan" with its charismatic appeals to the electorate. However, the organizational power of the Kennedys has been based on an apparatus that only recently brought its

---

Systems (Helsinki: Transactions of the Westermarck Society, 1964), 291–341. Linz argues that "Max Weber's categories can and should be used independently of the distinction between democracy, authoritarianism, and totalitarianism. Within each of these systems the legitimacy of the ruler, for the population or his staff, can be based on one or another of these types of belief. . . . While we want to stress the conceptual difference between authoritarian regimes and traditional rule, we also want to suggest that they sometimes have elements in common and that the students of such regimes could gain as many insights from Weber's analysis of patrimonial rule and bureaucracy as those of totalitarianism have gained from his thinking about charisma" (pp. 319, 321). My approach differs from Linz's suggestion in that it treats patrimonialism not only as a type of traditional belief but also as a strategy of rulership.

For another treatment of authoritarianism, which does not emphasize the issue of personal rulership, see Lewis A. Coser, "Prospects for the New Nations: Totalitarianism, Authoritarianism, or Democracy?" in Coser (ed.), *Political Sociology* (New York: Harper Torchbook, 1967), 247–71.

[7] In his discussion of patriarchalism and patrimonialism, Weber pointed out that traditionalist authority is not sufficient to ensure conformity with the directives of a patriarchal head; the ruler must be particularly responsive to his group as long as he does not have an efficient staff; once he has it, he must be responsive to his staff, lest he risk his power or even his position. In the language of the pattern variables, patrimonial organizations are particularist, but I shall show below that this is not necessarily so; on the other hand, Parsons himself long ago stressed the inherent instability of universalist orientation within legal-rational bureaucracy (*The Social System* [New York: The Free Press, 1951], 268).

patrimonial character to public attention during the Judge Morrissey affair in Boston.[8] For that matter, every American President, in order to be effective, cannot merely rely on his constitutional (legal-rational) powers, the institutionalized charismatic aura of his office, or any personal charismatic appeals to the public, but must build his own personal apparatus out of the so-called in-and-outers, who efficiently take the place of a permanent civil service of the British kind (as Richard E. Neustadt showed in his comparison of cabinet and presidential government, much of which reads like a description of personal governance).[9] Even the authority of the presidential office does not suffice to hold this apparatus together, and "authoritarian" imposition easily misfires.

The phenomenon of personal rulership is no less important in a totalitarian state than in a pluralist one. Nikita Khrushchev's fabled personal apparatus, which he took from Moscow to the Ukraine and back, served him well until defection eroded it. In the spring of 1966, his successor, Leonid I. Brezhnev, managed to enlarge to thirteen full members and seven candidates the number of Central Committee members who hailed from, or had connections with, the Ukrainian Dnepropetrovsk region, where he was born and began his career. Some of these are said to have been old friends from before World War II. At the same time, Kremlinologists identified another ascending group made up of Byelorussians and headed by Politburo member Kirill T. Mazurov, which is alleged to have made unusual gains on the Central Committee and to have taken over important positions.[10]

Far from being a vanishing phenomenon, personal rulership in public bureaucracies is apparently enlarged by the extension of government functions in industrialized countries. Both in Western Europe and in the United States, there are an increasing number of semipublic agencies and corporations in which such patrimonial relationships emerge and officials tend to become "benefice-holders." In the literature on industrial bureaucracies, this development is referred to by the wholly imprecise term of "industrial feudalism," which indicates the appropriation of managerial functions and prerogatives. Such prerogatives include the use of expense accounts, representation funds, official residences, limousines, and first-class tickets. The contractual character of the civil-service relationship may be changed because some officials cannot be dismissed *de jure* or *de facto*. Such officials may also be able to co-opt candidates and thus displace universalist criteria of formalized recruitment. However, along another universalist dimension, the hiring of highly qualified friends (from law school or graduate school days) can be very efficient. Finally, such patrimonial organizations may even be able to levy indirect taxes.

---

[8] Almost forgotten are the charges of liberal Democrats in 1960 that J. F. Kennedy "bought" the nomination of his party, meaning that he had such great financial resources that he could build an overpowering nationwide machine.

[9] "White House and Whitehall," *The Public Interest*, 1 (Winter 1966), 55–69. [See also this volume, pp. 308–20. (Ed.)]

[10] See Harry Schwartz, "Brezhnev Favors Old Colleagues," *New York Times*, July 15, 1966.

REVOLUTIONARY LEGITIMACY
AND PATRIMONIAL PRACTICE

It is my contention that in some of the new states patrimonial features in the detraditionalized, personalized sense are more important than bureaucratic and charismatic ones, and hence that it is too simplified a typology to contrast, for example, "the charisma of party" with "the bureaucracy of the military." [11] Neglect of the patrimonial dimension of government has also led to a tendency to interpret all political leadership as charismatic. Both analytical trends usually ignore Weber's point that bureaucracy and charisma are not necessarily exclusive of each other and that, in fact, bureaucracies can be superior instruments for charismatic leaders.[12] Moreover, the treatment of almost all political leaders in the new states as "charismatic" has been misleading on at least two counts: it has obscured the difference between "charismatic authority" and "charismatic leadership," [13] and it has taken at face value the international propaganda claims of some of the new leaders. Most heads of government in the new states do not have the magic of personal charisma for many groups in the society, nor do they have the kind of impersonal, institutional charisma that Edward Shils has stressed as a basic requirement for organizational stability.[14] The political situation in many African and Asian countries is so fluid exactly because leadership is merely personal and lacking in both charismatic qualities, that is, personal as well as office charisma.

For an outside observer it is very hard to gauge to what extent the international charismatic imagery of men like Nkrumah, Sukarno, Ben Bella, and Nasser has had substance for the various strata in their countries. At any rate, the sudden downfall of such men or slow attrition of their leadership shows that they lose power in the same way in which patrimonial rulers have often lost it: by a palace coup, especially by intervention of the army.[15] For reasons of legitimation some of them may be retained as figureheads; this is perhaps a good measure of charismatic efficacy, although in the case of Sukarno in 1966 the military's calculated "neutralization" of the head of state may have been as

[11] See Irving Louis Horowitz, *Three Worlds of Development* (New York: Oxford University Press, 1966), 263.

[12] Weber's example was Gladstone and Chamberlain's Liberal party machine, to which he gave much attention. See Weber, "Politics as a Vocation," in H. H. Gerth and C. Wright Mills (eds.), *From Max Weber* (New York: Oxford University Press, 1958), 106; on the relation of Weber's position to Michels' "Iron Law of Oligarchy," see Guenther Roth, *The Social Democrats in Imperial Germany* (Totowa, N.J.: Bedminster Press, 1963), 255 f.

[13] The distinction between charismatic authority and leadership is embedded in Weber's work, but was made explicit in Reinhard Bendix, *Max Weber* (New York: Doubleday & Co., 1960), 301, and was elaborated independently in Robert Bierstedt, "The Problem of Authority," in Morroe Berger and others (eds.), *Freedom and Control in Modern Society* (New York: D. Van Nostrand Co., 1954), 71 f.

[14] "Charisma, Order, and Status," *American Sociological Review*, xxx (April 1965), 199–213.

[15] For the first major study of Nkrumah's downfall, see Henry L. Bretton, *The Rise and Fall of Kwame Nkrumah: A Study of Personal Rule in Africa* (New York: Frederick A. Praeger, 1966).

important a motive for his retention as his charismatic halo in the eyes of millions of Indonesians. At any rate, the successors of these charismatic leaders tend to have a more pragmatic bent — another patrimonial feature.

Much has been written about armies in underdeveloped countries as a major, and sometimes the only, modern bureaucracy and force for modernization. They certainly are hierarchical organizations, and some of them indeed approach the bureaucratic realities of a Western army, but most of them have personal patrimonial traits that facilitate the takeover of government; that is, the troops are more loyal to their immediate commanders than to the governmental leaders. Significantly, some of the more stable countries (Morocco, Iran, Ethiopia, Thailand) still have armies in which the belief in traditionalist legitimacy is alive. However, such legitimation has never been sufficient insurance against the overthrow of the ruler, partly because of the administrative strategies of patrimonial regimes. One such strategy has been the creation of a military force that differed in social, ethnic, or tribal composition from the population, so that the social distance between apparatus and subjects would be maximized. However, this strategy could easily put the ruler at the mercy of his troops. (Weber took his major historical examples for this double-edged role from the Near Eastern armies, particularly the Mamelukes and Janissaries.) [16]

There seems to be a parallel here to the dilemma of present-day nationalist leaders, who want to have a "national" army free from regional and tribal ties. The course of events has proved that they can quickly lose control over their own instrument, either because regional or tribal elements in the army resist or because a "nationalized" army becomes the only nationally effective force in an otherwise fragmented state. In the Near East as well as in Africa the pattern of military takeover that was typical of traditional regimes is repeating itself. Some sub-Sahara kingdoms, for example, used to be unstable because army units tended to be more loyal to their immediate commanders (princes or other members of the ruling families) than to the king. In some of these areas political instability is part of the precolonial tradition, not just a phenomenon of transition and modernization.

It should be clearly understood that such patrimonial loyalties are compatible with universalist components. Among the Bantu, where interregnum wars and princely usurpations were frequent, patrons selected their clients among commoners according to administrative and military ability. Conversely, under British control the modern Bantu bureaucracy, which had been modeled after the British civil service, at times had to be "corrupt" (i.e., particularist) in order to reconcile conflicting values.[17]

Once in power, army leaders tend to become personal rulers: we can think of the extremely precarious position of the South Vietnamese corps commanders ("Baby Turks"), with their practices of appointment by loyalty and taxa-

[16] *Economy and Society*, Part II, chap. 12:5.
[17] See Lloyd Fallers, *Bantu Bureaucracy* (Chicago: University of Chicago Press, 1965, first published 1956), 241 f., 248 f. In spite of his recognition of universalist elements in traditional relationships, Fallers continues to think in terms of the dichotomy of bureaucracy and charisma (p. 250).

tion by discretion, or of their much more entrenched neighbors in Thailand.[18] Several years ago Edgar L. Shor considered Thailand an unusual case, but actually the overall pattern he pictured has frequently been repeated. Shor perceived a transitional corruption of the civil service model, which had been borrowed from England in the 1880's, a corruption that would eventually be overcome. Like many others, his standard was the "classic Weberian model"; however, his description of the "aberrations" in the administrative realities of Thailand amounted to what I mean here by "personal governance": Deprived of the traditional deference accorded the morally legitimized monarchy, governments have relied upon the disposition of offices and shared material rewards to obtain the support of key leaders. . . . In the Thai bureaucracy, patterns of authority relationship are habitually hierarchical, predominantly personal, and inherently unstable. . . . The personal clique, based on a feudal-like system of personal obligation, provides the principal focus of bureaucratic loyalty and identification. Bonds of reciprocal obligation, reminiscent of earlier patron-client structures in the traditional social system, informally align a number of dependent subordinates with individual political and administrative leaders in more or less cohesive informal structures. In contrast to primary group ties in some other Asian countries, the clique groupings in Thailand are substantially independent of family or kinship relations. . . . Since the clique generally consists of a ranking superior and his subordinates within the organization, it usually coincides with the legal structures. . . . The dependence of careers on political and personal favor apparently dictates an entrepreneurial career strategy for the ambitious.[19]

The importance of personal loyalties and of material rewards does not exclude a peculiar mixture of reform-mindedness and "corruption" in such regimes. In his vivid description of the Young Turks' patrimonialism — which he never called by this name — Dankwart Rustow pointed to the "uninterrupted chain that links the Kemalists to the Young Turks, to the men of the Tanzimat, and to the classical Ottoman Empire — the sponsors of modernity in the twentieth century with the founders of tradition in the thirteenth." If the Ottoman Empire was "in essence a military camp and an educational institution," it is still true that "the sentiments persist among younger military officers that only an authoritarian regime under military aegis can accomplish the necessary tasks of social, cultural, and economic reform." [20] Rustow's portrayal of Turkish bureaucracy reveals a patrimonial administration that has not changed much since the Ottoman Empire adopted a formal French pattern; then as now there exists what is imprecisely known as "corruption": "connections" count, favoritism prevails, and for the few there is abundant profit in real-estate dealings. Corruption in the conventional sense varies with the strength of puritanical sentiment among reformist or revolutionary functionaries — office-holders or

[18] See Denis Warner's account of the practices of the South Vietnamese commanders in *The Reporter* (May 5, 1966), 11 f.

[19] "The Thai Bureaucracy," *Administrative Science Quarterly,* V (June 1960), 70, 77, 80. See also Fred W. Riggs, *Thailand: The Modernization of a Bureaucratic Polity* (Honolulu: East-West Press Center, 1966).

[20] "Turkey: The Modernity of Tradition," in Pye and Verba, 172 f., 187.

aspirants. However, reforms do not seem to change the largely personal character of loyalty patterns.

In sum, nowadays the nationalist leaders of the new state claim revolutionary legitimacy. Most of them embrace some variation of national socialism, which in the 1930's often came close to Nazism and Japanese fascism and later moved toward communism. Frequently, the same men have made the switch without drastically changing their outlook, whether they were Indonesian or Arab nationalists. Behind the ideological veneer lie goals and means that are closer to native traditions of government than tends to be apparent to the leaders themselves and to many an outside observer. Europeanization, Americanization, Westernization, and simply modernization — there is no similarly accepted term for the influence of Russian or Chinese communism — provide so many influential ideological and institutional models, but are not necessarily dominant in administrative practice.

PERSONAL RULERSHIP AND EMPIRE-BUILDING

One of the major reasons for the predominance of personal rulership over legal-rational legislation and administration in the new states seems to lie in a social, cultural, and political heterogeneity of such magnitude that a more or less viable complementary and countervailing pluralism of the Western type, with its strong but not exclusive components of universality, does not appear feasible. Even the total victory of a totalitarian minority merely leads to a highly centralized variant of personal governance under which the ruler has maximum discretion (what Weber called "sultanism"). The foremost task of these states is the political integration of greatly disparate elements — ethnic, tribal, religious, linguistic, or even economic. Structurally, much of what is today called nation-building should perhaps be called, more precisely, empire-building, if the political connotations of the term do not make it too difficult to use it in a strictly sociological, value-neutral sense. The problem of empire is the problem of establishing political order in the face of social and cultural heterogeneity. By contrast, nation-building finds its historical matrix in the European nation-state, which aimed at the integration of a population with a common culture, especially a common language and common historical legacies shared by various strata. It is no accident that pluralist democracy has been successful, on a larger scale, only in fairly homogeneous countries.[21]

An empire in the sense meant here was the Austro-Hungarian Double Monarchy, which introduced parliamentary government only for each of its halves and not for the whole realm. Even Imperial Germany faced a substantial problem of integrating diverse cultural and political elements, but because of com-

---

[21] The term "state-building" can perhaps substitute for "empire-building," but it does not imply equally well the integration of disparate elements. In Weber's terminology, which is applied here, the state is defined as a group that asserts an effective monopoly of legitimate force over a given territory; this definition does not specify the cultural and social aspects of the problem of political integration. The United States and the Soviet Union, which face tasks of international integration, can be called great or global empires (*Weltreiche*); expansionist states may be called "imperialist" in the conventional sense.

pensating homogeneous forces this task was ideologically perceived as that of building a nation.[22]

The problem of empire is not one of bigness as such, and the absolute number of people is not decisive. China is commonly called an empire by virtue of a combination of sheer size, historical longevity, military power, and expansionist ideology, but smaller African countries, for instance, face "empire problems" similar to those of India and Indonesia, because they have more tribal fragmentation on a smaller geographical scale and perhaps because they have a smaller "critical mass" of elites. In fact, Weber used his model of patrimonialism for African petty kingdoms as well as for the great empires of history.[23]

Despite technological progress — in particular, vastly increased communication facilities — many of the problems that troubled the patrimonial states of the past persist or recur. The agonies of Indonesia provide a stark example: Sukarno adhered to a rhetoric of the nation-state and of racial unity that simply denied the facts of an exceedingly complex pluralism and particularism. In a well-focused community study of social change and economic modernization in Indonesia, Clifford Geertz recognized several years ago what I call the problem of empire and stated it succinctly: "The ideologies of modern nationalism, arising as they do out of intense concern with massive social reconstruction, show a strong tendency toward a neglect, even an outright denial, of important variations in domestic cultural patterns and of internal social discontinuities. . . . With regard to national economic planning this leads to a failure to cast proposals in a form which attempts to take maximum advantage of the peculiarities of various local traditions, to an unwillingness even to consider differentiated plans for different cultural and social groups. . . . In the over-concern with national integration, conceived in a wholly monistic sense, the very construction of such integration . . . may be undermined." [24]

Personal rulerships can be more responsive to cultural and social diversity than intensely ideological leaders are willing to be. But this does not imply that such regimes are much more likely to solve the "problem of empire" in

[22] It should not be forgotten, however, that Imperial Germany remained a federation of states under the hegemony of Prussian constitutional monarchism (or monarchic constitutionalism), which combined dominant features of traditionalist patrimonialism with subordinate legal-rational (constitutional and bureaucratic) arrangements.

[23] Weber and Eisenstadt have been almost alone among sociologists in giving systematic attention to the phenomenon of empire. Weber dealt with it throughout his career: in his book *Roman Agrarian History and Its Importance for Public and Civil Law* (1891), in his essay "The Social Causes of the Decline of Ancient Civilization" (1896), in his book *The Agrarian Conditions of Antiquity* (1909), in the major body of *Economy and Society* (1911–1913), and in the collected *Essays in the Sociology of Religion*. Eisenstadt applied structural-functionalism to the great "patrimonial-bureaucratic" empires, as Weber called them. Both writers have been particularly concerned with the reasons for the empires' ultimate failure, the causes of stagnation and disintegration.

[24] *Peddlers and Princes* (Chicago: University of Chicago Press, 1963), 155 f. For an informative analysis of neotraditionalism in Indonesia, see Ann Ruth Willner, *The Neotraditional Accommodation to Political Independence: The Case of Indonesia*, Center of International Studies, Princeton University, Research Monograph No. 26 (Princeton: Princeton University Press, 1966).

the direction of faster economic growth and modernization. A country's diversity may amount to an inflexible pluralism that is not amenable to integration through the compromise strategies of personal rulers. Moreover, radical intellectuals deny legitimacy to ideologically uninspiring forms of personal rulership and in the long run can undermine them in both domestic and international politics. Since such intellectuals have taken over from traditional ones the role of legitimizers, personal rulerships are likely to have precarious legitimacy, and this is one reason for the pattern of frequent coups and countercoups. If self-proclaimed charismatic leadership with its ideological preoccupations fails to achieve the necessary amount of economic growth, personal rulership may fail to sustain political stability despite its pragmatic tendencies, and hence may also retard economic growth. This vicious circle may make it impossible for many of the new states to solve urgent problems of modernization, not to speak of catching up with the highly industrialized countries in the foreseeable future.

This skeptical conclusion is intentionally set in opposition to the predictions of those who, like Clark Kerr, envisage "the age of total industrialization" and anticipate that "by the middle of the twenty-first century, industrialization will have swept away most pre-industrial forms of society, except possibly a few odd backwaters." [25] It is equally possible to foresee a century in which the past will repeat itself and issues of personal rulership and empire-building will persist.

[25] Clark Kerr and others, *Industrialism and Industrial Man* (New York: Oxford University Press, 1964), 3, 221.

G 3 / Aspects of Legitimacy

Introduction

The great majority of newly established states have not yet succeeded in attaining political stability. Only in a few of them is there agreement among the various social groups concerning the rules that are to govern the resolution of conflicts. In many cases, effective government is prevented by dissension and internal conflicts; and regimes in power are threatened, not only by legal opposition, but also by various types of insurrection and coups d'état by competing groups who try, very often unsuccessfully, to establish their own position as rulers, both by force and in some measure by the consent of the ruled. In most cases the shared understanding between rulers and ruled concerning the exchange of demanded subordination, on the one hand, and acknowledgment of rights, on the other, is not sufficient for the establishment of a "political community." Thus, rulers and officials cannot rely on the existence of good will on the part of the majority of citizens, on their readiness to respond positively to commands and rules, or on their loyalty.

A central problem facing political elites in developing countries is how to develop legitimacy — an accepted "title to rule" [1] — while their society is undergoing social transition. This transition includes in most cases a continuous process of political activation of great masses of people, who before often did not share common political institutions. In this situation the establishment of the legitimacy of rulers may be impeded by two related factors: one is the possible intensification of struggles among competing elites and among sections of the population; the other is the growing commitment of the rulers to initiate policies of social mobilization in the political, economic, and educational spheres — commitments which they often cannot fulfill at the expected scope and pace. National political leaders in most of the newly independent states of Africa and Asia thus face the problem of winning the loyalties of newly activated masses whose expectations, aroused by nationalist and social movements, by formal education and mass communications, remain unfulfilled.

[1] See S. M. Lipset, "Political Sociology" in N. J. Smelser, *Sociology* (New York: John Wiley & Sons, 1967), p. 442.

The selections in this section present various aspects of these problems of legitimacy, with a common analysis of situations in terms of the historical roots of social factors relevant to the establishment of a political community. Their emphasis is on the legitimation process, that is, on the state of "becoming" rather than "being," on the process of creating national identity and on successful performance of administration.

Many discussions claim that charismatic authority is prevalent in the new states. Both Lipset and Bendix discuss this phenomenon, but with a different focus. Lipset concentrates on the task which can be fulfilled by a charismatic leader in the process of social transition; Bendix challenges the widespread use of the term and reanalyzes various aspects of charismatic leadership in terms of the Weberian conceptualization.

Lipset examines the early period of America's history with an effort to elucidate through comparative analysis three problems that are common to all new nations.[2] (1) He suggests that charismatic justification for authority can be the effective mechanism of transition between *the abolition of an old authority and the establishment of a new one.* However, charismatic leadership is characteristically unstable due to its highly personalized nature. Since it provides not distinction between the agent and the source of authority, the inclinations of the leader determine, to a large extent, the kinds of political patterns that become institutionalized. (2) *The lack of national unity and consensus* is a function of the internal fragmentation of the new states. In many cases their boundaries do not coincide with the existing social groups but delineate artificially determined political units established by the foreign colonial powers (see Sections F and G 2, as well as Eberhard, Section B). (3) In regard to *the position of the opposition*, many of the rulers of the new states do not allow an effective and organized political opposition to function. Both in early America and in the new states of the present, the ruling groups try to repress the rights of their political opponents; they do not accept criticism as proper, viewing it as an attack on the state itself.

Bendix' discussion is essentially a conceptual-methodological one. After restating Weber's original formulation of "charismatic leadership" — according to which both the followers' recognition and the leader's own claims and actions are crucial — he suggests that the concept should not be loosely applied but rather should refer specifically to a pattern of interactions between a leader and his followers which can be investigated empirically. Genuine charisma is a rare event, but charisma *appears* to occur frequently because both the leaders and the led search for it. A number of analytical problems which arise when the term is applied to four contemporary Asiatic leaders exemplify the difficulty of relating ideal types to concrete social phenomena. In the cases of both Nehru and Mao Tse-tung the focal problem is the most difficult one for charismatic leadership — the problem of succession. The case of Prince

[2] One should keep in mind that Lipset is aware of, and catalogues, the limits of comparability of the early United States and the contemporary new states. His argument for the function of charisma in the new states is made by analogy alone. For a criticism of this approach, however, see Huntington (Section D).

Sihanouk is presented as an attempt to transfer the charisma of royalty to the leader of a political party and a modern state. Kim Il-sŏng of North Korea and China's Mao Tse-tung are presented as examples of charisma-by-publicity; in their regimes all channels of communication are utilized for the buildup of the leader's image.

An attempt to analyze the political situation in a newly independent state from the perspective of Western democratic political arrangements is presented in the third selection. Weiner analyzes obstacles to the growth of stable democratic institutions in India in terms of several pre-independence attitudes that persist among political leaders into the present. Ambivalent feelings towards political power and the readiness to go outside the legal framework of the political system to achieve political goals reflect both traditional Indian values and attitudes developed during the struggle for independence. Side by side with these are other elements which tend to ease the adjustment to Western democracy. Weiner mentions among these the great Western impact on India as well as the successful operation of the parliamentary system, which is likely in his opinion to bring about a change in India's attitudes toward political power and the acceptance of the system by opposition groups.

In this analysis Weiner is typical of many social scientists who take democratic stability as the norm and then locate negative factors in terms of non-Western traditions and positive factors in terms of the impact of the West. Perhaps the most severe limitation of this approach is its neglect of the changes in the relations among social groups occurring during the colonial period and continuing after independence. It should be emphasized that while "attitudes" are certainly an aspect of the rules of the game that define legitimacy, their analysis depends also on the ideal and material interests of these changing social groupings.

Leaders in modern and in developing states attempt to legitimate their positions. The leader in a modern state attempts to maintain his power and satisfy the citizens' expectations within a framework of established legal, economic, and educational institutions. By contrast, the leader in a new state is typically faced with the problem of building such institutions. This is a more hazardous task.

The United States —
The First New Nation

SEYMOUR M. LIPSET

THE CRISIS OF LEGITIMACY
AND THE ROLE OF THE CHARISMATIC LEADER

A core problem faced by new nations and post-revolutionary societies is the crisis of legitimacy. The old order has been abolished and with it the set of beliefs that justified its system of authority. The imperialist ogre upon whom all ills were blamed has now disappeared, and with it the great unifying force, nationalism, under whose banner private, ethnic, sectional, and other differences were submerged, has been weakened. The new system is in the process of being formed and so the question arises, to whom is loyalty owed? What kinds of values will legitimize the exercise of power? For the essence of legitimacy, be it traditional, charismatic, or rational-legal, is derived from shared beliefs, that is, feelings among the members as to what constitutes allegiance. In new states, the government finds that it cannot assume loyalty among the majority of its citizens, for such feelings, or even the experiences that give rise to them, develop slowly. Ernest Renan in a lecture in 1882 pointed to *consent* as the essential factor. He said, that if the people do not believe in the government's right to act, if they question its basis of authority, then the very essence of a stable policy is under attack.[1] Particularly in new states the governing authority faces situations in which significant segments of the society feel that it is ineffective or directly hostile to their interests. In such situations the question as to why such groups should obey, why they should accept a decision that works against their values and interests, may arise.

As Max Weber pointed out, there are essentially three ways in which an authority system may gain legitimacy. (1) It may gain this right through *tradition*, through "always" having possessed it and by reinforcing the belief in its rightness through various symbolic acts. The title held by monarchical societies is essentially of this type. (2) *Rational-legal* domination exists when those in authority are obeyed because of a general acceptance of the appropriateness of the system of rules under which they hold office. (3) *Charismatic* authority, a concept introduced by Max Weber into sociology, "rests upon the uncommon and extraordinary devotion to the sacredness or the heroic force of the exemplariness of an individual and the order revealed or created by him." [2]

Old states possess traditional legitimacy, and new states may sometimes be in a position to enhance their own legitimacy by incorporating the already existing legitimacy of heads of subordinate authority centers. Thus, nation states

From *Transactions of the Fifth World Congress of Sociology* (Washington, D.C., September 2–8, 1962), pp. 310–332, 357–361. Reprinted by permission of the author.

[1] Cited in Frank H. Underhill, "A United Nation Is Not Enough," *The Globe Magazine*, March 24, 1962, p. 5. For a more detailed discussion of the relationship of legitimacy to democracy see S. M. Lipset, *Political Man* (Garden City: Doubleday & Co., 1960), pp. 77–90.

[2] Max Rheinstein (ed.), *Max Weber on Law in Economy and Society* (Cambridge, Mass.: Harvard University Press, 1954), p. xi.

which retain local rulers, for example dukes, counts, chiefs, clan heads, and create a larger national authority system based on them, may be more stable than those which seek to destroy local centers of authority. For instance the national legitimacy of Europe's most stable republican government, Switzerland, may be the consequence of the preserved legitimacy of cantonal government and power. Contemporary Malaya is a recent example of an effort to foster national legitimacy by retaining traditional symbols of local rule.

But where traditional legitimacy is absent, as it was in post-Revolutionary United States or France and much of contemporary Asia and Africa, it can be developed only through reliance on legal and/or charismatic authority. Legal domination, resting on the assumption that the created legal structure is an effective means of attaining group ends, is necessarily a weak source of authority in societies in which the law has been identified with the interests of the colonial exploiter.

Charismatic authority is well suited to the needs of newly developing nations. It requires neither time nor a rational set of rules, and is highly flexible. Such a leader plays several roles. He is first of all the symbol of the new nation, its hero who embodies in his person its values and aspirations. But more than merely symbolizing the new nation, he legitimizes the state, the new secular government, by endowing it with his "gift of grace." Apter shows the ways in which the government of Ghana gained diffuse legitimacy from the charisma of Nkrumah. The institutionalization of a legal-rational order, of parliamentarian- ism, of due process and the like were made possible because of Nkrumah's sanction.[3]

Charismatic justification for authority can be seen as a mechanism of transi- tion, an interim measure, which gets people to observe the requirements of the nation out of loyalty to the leader until they eventually learn to do it for its own sake. In short, the hero helps to bridge the gap to a modern state. The citizens can feel an affection for the hero which they may not for the abstract entity nation.[4]

Charismatic leadership, however, because it is so personalized is extremely unstable. Unlike the situations of traditional or rational-legal authority where it is possible to remove subordinates without undermining the source of au- thority, be it the monarch or the constitution, in a charismatic system the source of authority is never separated from its agent of implementation.[5] Given the inability to separate the sources from the agencies of authority, the charis- matic leader must either place himself in a situation where he is not subject to criticism, e.g., a strong one-party system, or he must transcend partisan con- flict. And, as long as the charismatic leader is present, there may be opposition

[3] David Apter, *The Gold Coast in Transition* (Princeton: Princeton University Press, 1955), p. 303.
[4] See Edward Shils, "The Concentration and Dispersion of Charisma," *World Politics*, 11, 1958, pp. 2–3; and Immanuel Wallerstein, *Africa, Politics of Independence* (New York: Vintage Books, 1961), pp. 85–102.
[5] For a discussion of this point see W. G. Runciman, "Charismatic Legitimacy and One-Party Rule in Ghana," *European Journal of Sociology*, IV, 1963, pp. 148–165.

on an individual or even informal factional basis but not an Opposition that is organized into a formal party with its own leader.

A consequence of this personalized leadership is that the kinds of patterns that become institutionalized are determined to a considerable extent by the inclinations of the particular leader. He may gather around himself a staunch group of disciples, men who feel a personal loyalty to him as their chief, and concentrate both the symbols and the practice of power in his own person. Or, by playing a role comparable to that of a constitutional monarch, who possesses both a government and a loyal opposition, but stands above partisan struggles, he may encourage the development of political parties and the evolution of a bureaucratic system. Thus the framework for the eventual development of either democratic or dictatorial institutions may be established.

The early American Republic, like many of the new nations, was legitimized by *charisma*. We tend to forget today that George Washington was idolized as much as many of the contemporary leaders of new states.

> In the well-worn phrase of Henry Lee, he was *first in war, first in peace and first in the hearts of his countrymen*. . . . He was the prime native hero, a necessary creation for a new country. For America, he was origi-nator and vindicator, both patron saint *and* defender of the faith, in a curiously timeless fashion, as if he were Charlemagne. Saint Joan and Napoleon Bonaparte telescoped into one person. . . . Babies were being christened after him as early as 1775, and while he was still President, his countrymen paid to see him in waxwork effigy. To his admirers he was "godlike Washington." [6]

Washington's role as the charismatic leader under whose guidance democratic political institutions could grow was not an unwitting one. He self-consciously recognized that he alone could help the new nation gain stable legitimate insti-tutions.

> "With me . . . a predominant motive has been, to endeavor to gain time for our country to settle and mature its yet recent institutions, and to progress without interruption to that degree of strength and consist-ency, which is necessary to give it, humanly speaking, the command of its own fortunes." [7]

The charismatic legitimacy which Washington conveyed upon the new political institutions was clearly necessary. Like latter-day leaders of new states, he was under pressure from those close to him to actually become a monarch. However, he recognized that his most important contribution to the new state was to give it time to establish what we now call a rational-legal system, a gov-ernment of men under law. He permitted the members of his cabinet to form factions under the leadership of Hamilton and Jefferson and to fight over issues, even though he personally disliked the views of the Jeffersonians.

Washington wished to retire after one term in office, but the conflict between

[6] Marcus Cunliffe, *George Washington, Man and Monument* (New York: Mentor Books, 1960), pp. 20–21, 15–16, 22.
[7] *Ibid.*, pp. 149–150.

his two principal collaborators would not permit it. And on the urging of many, including Hamilton and Jefferson, he agreed to serve another term, thereby unwittingly permitting the further peaceful intensification of the conflict and the gradual formation of opposition parties to occur while he was still President, though, of course, he bitterly regretted the emergence of opposition politics. This turned out to be a crucial decision since, during the second administration, the country was torn apart by diverse sympathies for the French Revolution, and between Britain and France as military opponents.

Although there seems little question that Washington was treated like a charismatic leader, it may be argued that he was not one, since, unlike the ideal-typical example, he sought to retire from leadership. His ultimate success in refusing to accede to the demand that he act out his potential charisma — he withdrew from the presidency while seemingly in good health — may have pushed the society faster toward a legal-rational system of authority than would have evolved had he taken over the charismatic role *in toto* and identified the laws and the spirit of the nation with himself. This particular halfway type of charismatic leadership probably had a critical stabilizing effect on the society's evolution, for had Washington taken full advantage of his godlike position, the transition to a more stable form of authority would have been much more difficult. Of particular importance in this regard is the fact that the first succession conflict between John Adams and Jefferson took place while he still held office, enabling him to set a precedent as the first head of a modern state to turn over office to a duly elected successor. If he had continued in office until his death, it is quite possible that subsequent Presidential successions would not have occurred as easily.

The importance of Washington's role to the institutionalization of legal-rational authority in the early United States is best expressed in the role's four most pertinent dimensions: 1) His prestige was so great that he commanded the loyalty of the leaders of the different factions as well as the general populace. Thus, in a political entity marked by much cleavage he, in the person of himself, provided a basis for unity. 2) He was strongly committed to constitutional rules of the game and exercised a paternal guidance upon those involved in developing the machinery of government. 3) He stayed in power long enough to permit the crystallization of factions into embryonic parties. 4) He set a precedent as to how succession should be managed by voluntarily retiring from office.

In most new nations the charismatic leader has tended to fulfill the first dimension only, acting as a symbol which represents and prolongs the feeling of unity developed prior to the achievement of independence.[8] Thus, following the Revolution, the charismatic personality is invaluable as a force continuing to bind together otherwise diverse private, ethnic and sectional groups formerly held together by a common antagonism to the "imperialist ogre." However the neglect of the other three important dimensions of Washington's role results in "charismatic personalities . . . not ordinarily build[ing] the institu-

[8] See Donald S. Rothchild, *Toward Unity in Africa* (Washington, D.C., Public Affairs Press, 1960), p. 2.

tions which are indispensable for carrying on the life of a political society."
Thus, the disappearance of charismatic personalities raises again, as did the
achievement of independence, the difficult problem of maintaining national
unity among a conglomeration of groups and interests.

THE PROBLEM OF NATIONAL UNITY
AND THE ROLE OF THE INTELLECTUALS

In new states, it is the young revolutionary intellectuals who have been the
contenders "for the nation's right to exist, even to the extent of promulgating
the very idea of the nation." [9] They have realized that the creation of a feeling
of national unity among diverse elements, being necessary for the achievement
of nationhood, is one of the most important problems of their new nations. The
intellectuals have recognized "the parochialism of the constituent segments of
the societies of the new states . . . [and that] the sense of membership in the
nation, which is more or less coterminous with the population residing within
the boundaries of the new states, is still very rudimentary and very frail." [10]
This tendency toward parochialism is common because the boundaries of new
national communities are artificial in the sense that they follow those "established by the imperial power rather than those coincident with pre-colonial
socio-political groups." [11] Myron Weiner suggests the urgency of this problem
when he reports with specific reference to South Asia that "the maintenance of
national unity in the countries of South Asia is perhaps their most severe
political problem." [12] In Africa also the "issues and problems of national unification are at the center of politics in the new and emergent societies." [13]

The problems of national unity and consensus alluded to by the various
writers cited above are clearly more complex than those faced by the United
States when it broke with Britain. Many African and Asian states are separated
internally because of numerous linguistic groups and tribal units,[14] many of
which have histories of bitter antagonism. India has been unable to resist
demands that its internal state boundaries are drawn along linguistic lines, a
development which places severe strains on its ultimate national unity.[15]

[9] Edward Shils, "The Intellectual in The Political Development of The New States"
(mimeographed, 1962), pp. 3–4.

[10] Edward Shils, "Political Development in the New States," *Comparative Studies
in Society and History*, 2, 1960, p. 283.

[11] James S. Coleman, "Nationalism in Tropical Africa," in John H. Kautsky (ed.),
Political Change in Underdeveloped Countries. (New York: John Wiley & Sons, 1962),
p. 189. See also Thomas Hodgkin, *Nationalism in Colonial Africa* (New York: New
York University Press, 1957), pp. 22–23.

[12] Myron Weiner, "The Politics of South Asia," in Gabriel Almond and James S.
Coleman (eds.), *The Politics of Developing Areas* (Princeton: Princeton University
Press, 1960), p. 239.

[13] Coleman, "Nationalism in Tropical . . . ," *op. cit.*, p. 367. See also Max F.
Millikan and Donald L. M. Blackmer (eds.), *The Emerging Nations* (Boston: Little,
Brown and Co., 1961), pp. 76, 77–78.

[14] See Kautsky, *op. cit.*, p. 34.

[15] For an analysis of the relationship between variations in knowledge of different
languages and the statistical chances for the triumph of a language as the national
one, see Karl Deutsch, *Nationalism and Social Communication* (New York: John Wiley
& Sons, 1953), esp. pp. 97–126, 170–213.

Pakistan is divided into two sections, which vary in language and in level of economic development. Indonesia has faced the difficulty of resolving differences between the Javanese and those living in the outer islands, as well as ethnic and religious cleavages. Burma has had at least five different separatist movements struggling for autonomy or independence. The West Indian Federation, in spite of a similar language background, has broken up. The various efforts to create a federated structure out of the successor states of the French African Empire have failed. This has been true also with respect to attempts to unite any two or more of the Arab nations. And the tragic story of the Congo presents the most extreme example of the difficulties inherent in winning the loyalty of areas and groups with diverse cultures and histories to a new political authority system which is dominated by others.

Early American history presented similar problems and reactions even though the oldest new nation was relatively unified in cultural terms. Its Western European heritage "established certain common traditions in advance, facilitating the task of harmonizing differences of language, culture, religion and politics." [16] Nevertheless, "throughout the colonial period, Americans had tended to assume that these differences of language, culture, and religion would prevent the growth of a common loyalty." [17]

Deutsch and his associates point out that one of the essential conditions for the amalgamation of small political units into a larger one is the growth of "compatibility of the main values held by the politically relevant strata of all participating units." They observe that values current in the colonies underwent "accelerated change and development in the course of the American Revolution and its aftermath." [18] "During the Revolutionary era the need to stress national unity sometimes induced Americans to become forgetful of their diverse ethnic origins and to overlook the persistence of cultural differences. Particularly was this so among men who were anxious that the young republic should be fatally weakened by a denial of adequate powers to the federal government." [19]

One of the processes by which the integration of political units often proceeds is by the decline of "party divisions which reinforce the boundaries between political units eligible for amalgamation, and the rise in their stead of party divisions cutting across them." [20] Early America possessed social bases for political cleavage which cut across the established political units: the states. In many of them demands emerged for broader voting rights and for proportionate representation in the legislatures for rural and western counties as against the richer or more urbanized seaboard. These cleavages provided one basis for trans-state parties.

[16] Rothchild, op. cit., p. 6.

[17] Maldwyn Allen Jones, American Immigration. (Chicago: The University of Chicago Press, 1960), p. 40.

[18] Karl W. Deutsch, S. A. Burrell, R. A. Kann, M. Lee, Jr., M. Lichterman, R. E. Lindgren, F. A. L. Loewenheim, R. W. Van Wagenen, Political Community and the North Atlantic Area (Princeton: Princeton University Press, 1957), p. 48.

[19] Jones, op. cit., p. 39.

[20] Deutsch et al., op. cit., p. 76.

However, before parties based upon these cleavages could play a role in unifying portions of the polity across state lines, interest groups in the different states had to learn to see beyond the particular issues with which they were concerned. They had to recognize that they had something in common with other groups advocating different forms of equality. And a political arena in which the individual rather than the state was the political unit had to be created.[21]

In spite of working and fighting together in a seven-year struggle for independence, the best governmental structure which the Americans could devise was a loose federal union under the Articles of Confederation. This union lacked any national executive, and in effect, preserved most of the sovereignty and autonomy of each state. This effort at a supra-national state was concerned with limiting any central authority.

The pressure to establish a unified central authority structure in the contemporary new states comes mainly from the nationalist intellectual elite who are concerned with creating an important arena of effective operation through which the new nation, and they, can demonstrate the competence. Currently, the main instrument for such action has been the revolutionary party.

After 1783, a national party that unified interests across state lines was approximated by "the advocates of central authority, who set up the plans for a convention on federal authority, to be held in Philadelphia. . . . A small group of political leaders with a Continental vision and essentially a consciousness of the United States' *international* impotence, provided the matrix of the movement. . . . Indeed, an argument with great force — particularly since Washington was its incarnation — urged that our very survival in the Hobbesian jungle of world politics depended upon a reordering and strengthening of our national sovereignty." [22] Many of those served as delegates in what became the Constitutional Convention had served in the Revolutionary Continental Congress. "If there is any one feature that most unites the future leading supporters of the Constitution, it was their close engagement with this continental aspect of the Revolution. . . . All of them had been united in an experience, and had formed commitments, which dissolved provincial boundaries. . . . The future of this generation's careers were staked upon the national quality of the experience which had formed them. In a number of outstanding cases energy, initiative, talent, and ambition had combined with a conception of affairs which had grown immense in scope and promise by the close of the Revolution. There is every reason to think that a contraction of this scope, in the years that immediately followed, operated as a powerful challenge." [23] Shils points to an analogous situation in a discussion of the nationalist movements in Asia and Africa when he states that young intellectuals "drew inspiration and

[21] See William N. Chambers, *Parties in a New Nation* (New York: Oxford University Press, 1963), Chapter 1, p. 11 (in manuscript).

[22] John P. Roche, "The Founding Fathers: A Reform Caucus in Action," *The American Political Science Review*, 60, 1961, p. 801. (Emphasis in the original.)

[23] Stanley Elkins and Eric McKitrick, "The Founding Fathers: Young Men of The Revolution," *Political Science Quarterly*, 76, 1961, pp. 202–3, 205–6.

comfort from abroad [and] felt that their actions were one with a mighty surge all over the world. . . . *This sense of being a part of the larger world infused into the politics of the second [younger] generation the permanently bedeviling tension between province and metropolis. . . .*" [24]

Deutsch and his associates discovered that the growth of a new political generation is common in the growth of a new political community from several smaller ones. It breaks habits of thinking in terms of the older political units. "The younger men were usually more committed to new ways of doing things and more willing to accept the new size of political units than their predecessors had been." [25]

The Constitutional Convention being composed mainly of these young ambitious "Continentalists," was relatively free of ideological clashes, and therefore much like a political party convention of unitary-state advocates, meeting to create a political platform acceptable to the public.

John P. Roche has argued that there was no biological rift within the Constitutional Convention because almost all the delegates belonged to the central government party. He suggests that the differences of opinion which did emerge were structural or tactical rather than ideological. That is, there was no conflict between "nationalists" versus "states-rightists" but rather an argument over representation, the small states versus the big states. "The Virginia Plan [which] envisioned a unitary national government effectively free from and dominant over the states . . . may . . . be considered, in ideological terms as the delegates' Utopia. . . ." [26] However, "the delegates from the small states . . . apparently realizing that under the Virginia Plan, Massachusetts, Virginia and Pennsylvania could virtually dominate the national government — and probably appreciating that to sell this program to the 'folks back home' would be impossible . . . dug in their heels and demanded time for a consideration of alternatives." Out of this consideration came the New Jersey Plan, which according to standard analyses was an expression of "states-righter's" "reversion to the *status-quo* under the Articles of Confederation. . . ." However, Roche suggests this was a political maneuver designed to gain support from those not represented at the Convention, rather than a defense of states' rights among the delegates.

> It is true that the New Jersey Plan put the states back into the institutional picture, but [Roche] argues that to do so was a recognition of political reality rather than an affirmation of states' rights. A serious case can be made that the advocates of the New Jersey Plan, far from being ideological addicts of states' rights, intended to substitute for the Virginia Plan a system which would both retain strong national power and have a chance of adoption in the states. . . . In other words, the advocates of the New Jersey Plan concentrated their fire on what they held to be the political liabilities of the Virginia Plan — which were mat-

[24] Shils, *op. cit.*, p. 277 (emphasis mine).
[25] Deutsch *et al.*, *op. cit.*, p. 86.
[26] Roche, *op. cit.*, p. 805.

ters of institutional structure — rather than on the proposed scope of national authority.[27]

This "group of extremely talented democratic politicians" were not "rhapsodic" about the final form of the Constitution, but they had "refused to attempt the establishment of a strong, centralized sovereignty on the principle of legislative supremacy for the excellent reason that the people would not accept it . . . *political realities* forced them to water down their objectives and they settled, like the good politicians they were, for half a loaf. . . . The result was a Constitution which the people, in fact, by democratic processes, did accept, and a new and far better national government was established." [28]

Thus the energy behind the "nationalistic" aims of the Constitutional Convention came from leaders who were mainly a young generation whose careers, having been launched in the Continental war effort of the Revolution depended upon the continuance of a nationalistic outlook provided by a centralized government. In age and aspiration, they resembled the leadership of many contemporary new states which usually consists of young revolutionary intellectuals, often antagonistic toward the older generation, who do not share their nationalistic vision because they are better established in local social hierarchies. Similarly, those opposed to a strong central American government, who had little, if any, representation at the Constitutional Convention, came from an older generation whose careers were not only state-centered but had been formed prior to the Revolutionary war effort.[29]

The young intellectuals in contemporary new nations experience political antagonism to the powers that be. This often comes from a sense of frustration because they have no place in the old society. Their new values do not coincide with those that would place them in honored positions in the old local hierarchies. Opportunism more than economic or class differences accounts for the conflict between the old and the new "generations."

> Unlike the "old" predominantly sacred intellectuals most of whom represented or spoke for the powers-that-were, . . . non-western intelligentsias do not, sociologically speaking, as a rule represent anyone but themselves. It is the exception rather than the rule that the young aristocrat, the landowner's son or for that matter even the scion of a newly-established bourgeois class, once he has acquired a western education . . . becomes the defender and spokesman of the class of his social origin. . . .
>
> In short, non-western intelligentsias, in so far as they are politically active . . . tend to be social revolutionaries whose ideological aims as often as not militate against the *status quo*.[30]

Following the American revolutionary war "the spirit of unity generated by the struggle for independence . . . lapsed" and the older generation reverted

[27] *Ibid.*, p. 806.
[28] *Ibid.*, pp. 813, 815, 816.
[29] Elkins and McKitrick, *op. cit.*, pp. 203–4.
[30] See Kautsky, *op. cit.*, p. 240.

to its old provincial ways, the particularism and inertia of local authority.[31]
With the exception of Pennsylvania this meant primarily that men far more
than measures, personal connections rather than party machines played the
most significant role in the conduct of politics.[32]

In this respect, the difference between the anti-Federalists and the "Continental" Federalists is suggestive of Hodgkin's classification of the structure
of African parties into primitive and modern.

> Parties of the former type [primitive] are dominated by "personalities,"
> who enjoy a superior social status, either as traditional rulers or members
> of ruling families, or as belonging to the higher ranks of the urban, pro-
> fessional elite (lawyers, doctors, etc.). . . . Their political machinery,
> central and local, is of a rudimentary kind. . . . They have little, if any-
> thing, in the way of a secretariat or fulltime officials. . . . They depend
> for popular support less upon organization and propaganda than on
> habits of respect for traditional authority, or wealth and reputation. . . .
> Parties of the second type [modern] aim at . . . a much more elaborate
> structure. Since their chief claim and function is to represent the mass,
> they are committed to a form of organization that is (certainly on
> paper and to some extent in practice) highly democratic. . . . Parties of
> this type are able to achieve a much higher level of efficiency than the
> "parties of personalities"; . . . because they possess a continuously func-
> tioning central office. . . . Indeed, dependence upon professional poli-
> ticians — *permanents* — "who naturally tend to form a class and assume
> a certain authority" for the running of the machine is one of the most
> distinctive features of the "mass" party. . . . It depends for its strength
> not on the backing of traditional authority but upon propaganda, de-
> signed to appeal particularly to the imagination of the young, to women,
> to the semi-urbanized and discontented; to those who are outside the
> local hierarchies, and interested in reform and change.[33]

"Modern" national parties are serving to unite the varying ethnic divisions
in emerging African states. However, early America differed from the nations
in Africa in that it did not have "modern" parties after which to model its own
attempts to unify the country. These emerged as a result of needs in the American situation, some of which, nevertheless tend to parallel those which stimulate "modern" party organization in Africa and Asia today.

The continental "caucus" at the Constitutional convention did not represent a full transition to a modern party. Such a transition implies the growth
of an organization that is rationally calculated toward vote getting. It also implies that this organization is connected with a social base whose ideological
interests are common. The struggle for ratification was particular to each state.
In some the upper classes were for it while in others they were against it according to the peculiarities of politics in each. The "Constitutionalists" relied
on old political techniques, including the manipulation of notables, cliques
and coteries to get ratification through.

[31] Elkins and McKitrick, *op. cit.*, p. 206.
[32] Chambers, *op. cit.*, Chapter I, p. 5.
[33] Hodgkin, *op. cit.*, pp. 156–159.

However, in so far as the transition to modern parties implies the rational calculation of what policies are necessary to get votes, the Constitutional convention marked a step in this direction. First, it created an organ in which policies touching on the interests of persons in all of the states were to be debated. Secondly, it marked a movement away from the politics of notables and coteries who were deeply tied to the old political structure of state supremacy. By establishing the principle of rationally calculating how to marshall public support, it opened the door for policies that circumvented state politics and addressed themselves directly to specific interest groups in all states. As such it cast the die (to use Weber's analogy) in the direction of popular based parties that could unify the polity across state lines.[34]

This is similar in some respects to the policies of nationalist intellectuals in new states who espouse populism as a consequence of their opportunistic politics. Where they are not connected to the existing power hierarchies, their only source of power lies in the people. It becomes a way of legitimating their leadership, be it democratic or oligarchical, because the people constitute the substance to be served by governmental policy. However, their populism is derived from their ambivalence toward more developed nations. In attempting to establish a national identity that will make their nation one among many, they feel they need to play up those elements that make their nation unique. They may try to overcome their own feeling of cultural inferiority by rejecting the premises of "culture" in the more developed countries and lauding the values in their own culture on some other grounds. The cult of populism, the "belief in the creativity and in the superior moral worth of the ordinary people, of the uneducated and the unintellectual" [35] enables the intellectuals to have faith that the culture of their embryonic states will quickly far surpass those of the decadent imperialist nations.

The Federalist party organization could be described as parallel to those patron parties in Africa that are national but which represent a linking of local notables rather than an organization designed to mobilize the common people.[36] The first "modern" party in the sense that there was a "coordination in activity between leaders at the capital, and leaders, activities and popular following in the states, counties, and towns" [37] was to come with the crystallization of the Jeffersonian Democratic Republican party.

The Democratic Republicans developed party organizations for some of the same reasons that leaders develop such organizations in Africa today. They were opposed to the established authorities whose policies largely dominated politics through the Federalist organization.[38] When the Jay treaty caused popular indignation and concern on the part of some merchants that the

---

[34] Max Weber, *The Methodology of the Social Sciences* (Glencoe, Ill.: The Free Press, 1949), pp. 182–185.

[35] Edward Shils, "The Intellectuals and the Powers: Some Perspectives for Comparative Analysis," *Comparative Studies in Society and History*, 1, 1958, p. 20.

[36] Ruth Schacter, "Single-party systems in West Africa," *American Political Science Review*, 55, 1961, p. 297.

[37] Chambers, *op. cit.*, Chapter 4, p. 8.

[38] Schacter, *op. cit.*, p. 295.

British would not pay their war debts, the Republicans took advantage of these disaffected elements to organize an opposition based on popular support. They appealed to social categories that cross-cut existing political boundaries just as the African mass-based parties do.[39] In so doing, the Democratic-Republican party served as a means of uniting the citizens of the several states in national citizenship by mobilizing their common interests in the national power arena.

However, as is well known, the evolution of national political parties could not erase differences in regional interests. Nor did the ratification of the Constitution serve to legitimate the new governmental structure, even though it provided a basis for national unity. Only with time, and after many attempts to thwart its powers, was the federal government finally able to achieve a high degree of political legitimacy.

A number of Southern apologists after the Civil War, and more recently Arthur Schlesinger, Sr. (who definitely doesn't fall in that category), have documented the proposition that almost every state in the country and every major political faction and interest group attempted, at one time or other between 1790 and 1860, to eliminate the power of the national government or to break up the Union directly.[40]

There were many threats to secede in the first decade of national existence coming from both northern and southern states.[41] In 1798 two future Presidents, Jefferson and Madison, sought the passage of nullification ordinances by state legislatures which proclaimed the right of each state to decide on national authority within its boundaries.

After leaving national office in 1801, various Federalist leaders sought in 1804, 1808, and 1812 to take the New England or northern states out of the Union or to push the western ones out. Aaron Burr, Democratic-Republican Vice-President from 1801–1805, tried to organize a secession by the West. The New England Federalists opposed the War of 1812 and many of them, including elected state officials, sought to sabotage the war effort.

Secessionist threats are characteristic in contemporary new nations. For example Rothchild states that one of the basic problem[s] which Nigerians must be prepared to face is secession [for] during the last decade politicians from every area in the country have threatened secession. . . ."[42] However, he feels that "the growth of national parties will do a great deal to make the federal government a dynamic and unifying force in Nigerian life."[43]

In the United States, when the slavery issue became important, both abolitionists and defenders of slavery talked of destroying the Constitution and the Union. In the early period of the struggle when the abolitionists de-

---

[39] See *ibid.*, p. 301 for a description of the unifying functions of the African mass parties.

[40] See Arthur Schlesinger [Sr.], *New Viewpoints in American History* (New York: The Macmillan Company, 1922), pp. 220–240; Jefferson Davis, *The Rise and Fall of the Confederate Government* (New York: Collier Books, 1961), pp. 56–60.

[41] See Marshall Smelser, "The Federalist Period as an Age of Passion," *The American Quarterly*, 10, 1958, p. 393.

[42] Rothchild, *op. cit.*, pp. 174–175.

[43] *Ibid.*, p. 176.

spaired of eliminating slavery because of guarantees in the Constitution, it was described by some as a "slave-holder's" document and Garrison called it "a covenant with death and an argument with hell." [44]

Because of opposition to slavery, some northern states argued non-cooperation with the government during the Mexican War, perceived by them as a struggle to extend slave territory.[45] There were, in fact, many deserters from the American Army during this war. It is "apparently the only case known in which a body of United States soldiers after deserting subsequently formed a distinct corps in the enemy's army. . . ." [46]

Various northern states passed laws during the 1850's, the so-called Personal Liberty Laws, which were designed to prevent the enforcement of federal legislation, the Fugitive Slave Law.[47]

Thus, in the early United States, as in contemporary new states, the achievement of national unity, in part based upon the development of respect for a national authority, was no easy task.

The possibilities of secession remain one of the basic problems facing many new states. Their unity immediately after gaining independence "is largely explained by the negative, anti-Western, anti-colonial content of non-Western nationalism. One need not be a prophet of doom to anticipate that this negative unity may in time, and perhaps before long, weaken, and that the newly independent non-Western nation-states may then find themselves confronted by some of the dissensions and antagonisms which nationalist aspirations have so often brought in their wake elsewhere." [48]

OPPOSITION RIGHTS AND THE ESTABLISHMENT OF NEW POLITIES

The issues involved in the emergence of legitimate national authority and of the creation of national unity and those which pertain to the establishment of democratic procedures are clearly separate problems, although they are sometimes confused in discussing the politics of new nations. Democracy may be conceived of as a system of institutionalized opposition in which the people choose among alternative contenders for public office.[49] To create a stable representative decision-making process which provides a legitimate place for those without power to advocate "error" and the overthrow of those in office, is extremely difficult in any polity, and is particularly problematic in new states which must be concerned also with the sheer problem of national authority itself.

[44] W. L. Garrison, *The Words of Garrison* (Boston: Houghton Mifflin Co., 1905), p. 25.

[45] See Schlesinger, *op. cit.*, pp. 230–231.

[46] Edward S. Wallace, "Notes and Comment — Deserters in the Mexican War," *The Hispanic American Historical Review*, 15, 1935, p. 374.

[47] Schlesinger, *op. cit.*, p. 231.

[48] Benda, *op. cit.*, pp. 40–1. See also Coleman, *op. cit.*, pp. 167–194.

[49] I have elaborated the concept of democracy in other writings. See my *Political Man*, *op. cit.*, pp. 45–47; "Introduction" to Robert Michels, *Political Parties* (New York: Collier Books, 1962), pp. 33–35; and S. M. Lipset, M. Trow, and J. S. Coleman, *Union Democracy* (Glencoe, Ill.: The Free Press, 1956), pp. 405–412.

In a recent Ghanese White Paper seeking to justify legislation and police actions which involved restrictions against and actual imprisonment of opposition politicians, the Ghana government suggested that these actions were necessary because of plots, saboteurs, subversion, and threats of foreign intervention. The White Paper argues that "[T]he strains experienced by an emergent country immediately after independence are certainly as great as, if not greater than, the strains experienced by a developed country in wartime." [50] According to Nkrumah, a new state "is still weakly expressed as a national unity," and its frail structure must be protected by "identifying the emergent nation with the party," that is, by denying the possibility of a legitimate opposition since the latter would endanger the stability of the nation.[51]

Restrictions on democratic rights and opposition parties are, of course, not unique to Ghana among the contemporary new states. In Africa, the only new state with more than one significant party is Nigeria, "and this is true only because it is a federal . . . [system] reflecting one-party domination in the regions." [52]

Essentially the establishment of democratic rights requires the institutionalization of the rules of the political game. In the absence of such institutionalization, the participants are involved in situations where the rules are not clearly defined, at least there are no formal guarantees, and hence they have no assurance that their sense of morality, what they believe should or should not be done, is shared by others. Their status is insecure and is easily threatened by the presence of opposing groups who may press for "evil" measures and personal power. The desire to foster one set of goals, or to protect prestige and power, press those involved to ignore weak rules designed to protect opposition rights. An examination of history provides the argument that tolerance or protection of "error" usually emerged as a result of conflict among diverse factions. Sometimes it occurred because opposing groups found they could not destroy each other, and, after a long conflict came to accept each other. On other occasions, opposition groups, denied democratic rights by power-holders, have advanced a democratic ideology as part of their criticism of the incumbents, and upon succeeding to office enacted juridical protections of freedom. The history of efforts to institutionalize such rights in voluntary associations and in new states and post-revolutionary societies, indicates how fragile is a simple intellectual commitment to democratic rights, when placed against the conviction that truth will vanish with the opposition's triumph, or that present office holders will lose all claim to significant status.

The early history of the United States reveals many of the same problems and pressures to eliminate democratic rights as do those of contemporary new states. During Washington's first administration, all important differences of opinion could be expressed within the government since both Jefferson and Hamilton, the leaders of what were to become the two major parties, were the

[50] Discussed and cited in Dennis Austin, "Strong Rule in Ghana," *The Listener*, 67, 1962, p. 156.
[51] *Loc. cit.*
[52] Runciman, *op. cit.*

most influential members of the Cabinet. After Jefferson's withdrawal at the end of Washington's first term, and the subsequent formation of an opposition party around 1797, tactics such as subversion and defiance on both sides increased greatly.[53]

In many respects, even though early America had no "modern" type parties on which to model its political organization, the evolution of a "government" party and then an "opposition" party parallels developments in contemporary new states. Hamilton, the political genius behind the first incumbents, organized the first party to insure popular support for governmental policies. It was a national "government party" as opposed to the previous state politicking. It was "a party of stability, dedicated in effect to the idea that the first imperative of government in a new nation was that it must govern and sustain itself." [54] As such, organized opposition to it was contrary to its conception.

Opposition to the government's policies did not grow initially as a party but as individual protest both on the popular level and within the political elite. The idea of political organization was itself new. However, opposition gradually crystallized into a political movement around the leadership of Madison and Jefferson. Its adherents were asserting "that the new polity should also [in addition to maintaining its stability] provide room for counter action. . . ." So "the emerging republicans were 'going to the people' in a virtually unprecedented attempt not only to represent popular interests and concerns, but to monopolize popular opposition to those who held power. . . . [I]f their appeal to planters, farmers, and 'mechanics' was broadened sufficiently to succeed, it would end by displacing the Federalists in power and substituting a new set of governors." [55]

The Federalists viewed such organized opposition in much the same light as many leaders of the contemporary new states view their rivals.

> [T]he Federalists took an intolerant position regarding the opposition party, which seemed to be a race of marplots characterized by excessive ambition, unwholesome partisanship and a dangerous reliance upon the judgment of the voters. . . . Federalist private correspondence was peppered with references to Republican disloyalty, insincerity, intrigue and demagoguery. . . . The conclusion almost forced upon the reader . . . is that the *two-party system is immoral. . . . It became almost normal to consider opposition as seditious and, in extraordinary cases, as treasonable.*[56]

In a sense, Madison and Jefferson were feeling their way. They were loyal to the nation they had helped to create but they felt that the principles, such as equality, which justified its creation were being undermined. Madison evolved a novel solution to the problem of discontent. It involved acceptance of organized opposition within the system, one that would permit the displacement of the present holders of power "not only by intrigue or

---

[53] Joseph Charles, *The Origins of the American Party System* (New York: Harper Torch Books, 1961), p. 42.
[54] Chambers, *op. cit.*, Chapter 3, p. 15.
[55] *Ibid.*, Chapter 3, p. 16.
[56] Smelser, *op. cit.*, pp. 394–395 (emphasis mine).

violence but by peaceful means, by the weight of votes in elections, by popular choice or decision." [57] Thus there were provided ways for the political
system sketched in the Constitution to continue gaining legitimacy among
those portions of the public and politicians who opposed the policies of office
holders at any given time.

The strains endemic in the establishment of a new structure of authority
were enhanced by the fact that the nation and the embryonic parties were
divided in their sympathies for the two major contestants in the European war,
Revolutionary France and Great Britain. Each side was convinced that the
other had secret intentions to take the country to war in support of the forces
of evil. The French terror was a particular evil to the Federalists, and they,
like conservatives in other countries, were convinced that French agents were
conspiring with sympathetic Americans to overthrow the government here.[58]

The Federalists, frightened by the French Revolution and by various examples of domestic violence, were opposed to any form of organized opposition.
They were much more violent in their denunciations of the treasonable activities of the Republicans than were the Jeffersonians in return.[59] The Alien and
Sedition Acts passed in 1798 gave the President "the power to order out of
the country any alien whom he thought dangerous to the public peace or whom
he had reasonable grounds to suspect of plotting against the government" and
left such aliens without recourse to the courts.[60] The Sedition Act "was intended to deal with citizens or aliens who too severely criticized the government. . . . In its final form it was made a high misdemeanor 'unlawfully to
combine and conspire' in order to oppose the legal measures of the government
. . . [t]o publish a false or malicious writing against the government of the
United States, the President, or Congress with the purpose of stirring up
hatred or resistance against them. . . ." [61]

The fact that the law was designed for partisan purposes was obvious.
All those arrested and convicted under it by the Federalist officials and juries,
were Republicans.[62] These efforts to undermine democratic rights gave Jefferson
and Madison a major issue which historians believe played an important
role in defeating the Federalists in 1800.

Once defeated for the Presidency in 1880, the Federalists never were able
to regain office on a national scale and virtually disappeared after 1814. The
causes for the downfall of the Federalists are many and complex. Among
them are the extension of the suffrage, and their unwillingness or inability
to learn how to perform as an opposition party in a democracy, particularly one
which emphasized equality. Some historians suggest they failed basically be-

[57] Chambers, op. cit., Chapter 3, p. 16.

[58] John C. Miller, Crisis in Freedom. The Alien and Sedition Acts (Boston: Little,
Brown and Company, 1951), p. 14.

[59] Smelser, op. cit., pp. 397–398.

[60] See Miller, op. cit., and James M. Smith, Freedom's Fetters, The Alien and
Sedition Laws and American Civil Liberties (Ithaca, N.Y.: Cornell University Press,
1956).

[61] John Spencer Bassett, The Federalist System (New York: Harper and Bros.,
1960), pp. 258–259.

[62] Ibid., pp. 263–264.

cause they did not believe in parties which appealed to the people, and particularly as men convinced of the propriety of their right to rule, they did not believe in an opposition party.[63]

The civil liberties record of the Jeffersonians, in office, is a better one than that of the Federalists. Their years of opposition had led them to make many statements in favor of democratic rights, but oppositionists in other lands have forgotten such programs once in power when faced with "unscrupulous criticism." Perhaps more important is the fact that the Democratic-Republicans did believe in states rights and did oppose using federal courts to try common law crimes. Also, the federal judiciary remained for some time in the hands of Federalist judges, who presumably were loath to permit convictions of their political co-thinkers. Finally, there was the difference in the nature of the opposition. The Federalists were dealing with a growing party that could realistically hope for eventual victory; while the Democratic-Republicans, when in office, were faced by a rapidly declining party, whose very lack of faith in the extension of democratic processes was to undermine any chance it had of returning to office. Since the Federalists were committing political suicide, there was no urgent need for the administration to find extreme means to repress them. The existence of a real but declining opposition may, therefore, be regarded as a contribution to the institutionalization of democratic rights.

Yet it should be noted that on the level of state government, Democratic-Republicans did use their power to crack down on Federalist opinion. "Jefferson was no advocate of a 'licentious' press; like Hamilton and Adams, he believed that the press ought to be restrained 'within the legal and wholesome limits of truth.' He differed from the Federalists chiefly in favoring that this restraint be imposed by the states rather than by the Federal government. . . ." [64] In 1803, Jefferson wrote to Governor McKean of Pennsylvania in the following terms:

> The Federalists, he noted, having failed to destroy the freedom of the press "by their gag law, seem to have attacked it in an opposite form, that is by pushing its licentiousness and its lying to such a degree of prostitution as to deprive it of all credit. . . . I have long thought that a few prosecutions of the most eminent offenders would have a wholesome effect in restoring the integrity of the presses." [65]

Where the Federalists controlled a state government, as in the case of Connecticut, and hence prevented the application of the Democratic doctrine that seditious libel was a state offense, Jefferson was not loath to inaugurate prosecutions in the federal courts. In 1806, six indictments were drawn against four Connecticut Federalist editors and two ministers on the charge of seditious libel of the President. The ministers were charged with committing the libel in *sermons*.[66]

---

[63] William O. Lynch, *Fifty Years of Party Warfare* (1789–1837) (Indianapolis: Bobbs-Merrill, 1931), pp. 122–123.
[64] Miller, *op. cit.*, p. 231.
[65] *Ibid.*, p. 300. The state did indict a Federalist editor shortly thereafter.
[66] *Ibid.*, pp. 302–305.

Leonard Levy concludes his survey of freedom of speech and press in early American history by arguing that the Democrats, no more than the Federalists, believed in these freedoms when confronted with serious opposition. Each was prepared to use principled libertarian arguments when his "ox was being gored."

The various efforts by both Federalists and Democratic-Republicans to repress the rights of their opponents clearly indicate that in many ways our early political officials resembled those heads of modern new states who view criticism of themselves as tantamount to an attack on the nation itself. Such behavior characterizes leaders of polities in which the concept of democratic turnover in office has not been institutionalized. To accept criticism as proper, demands the belief that men may be loyal to the polity and yet disapprove of the particular set of incumbents. The defeat of the Federalists in the elections of 1800 represented *the first occasion in modern politics in which an incumbent political party suffered an electoral defeat and simply turned over power to its opponents.* This acceptance of the rules of the electoral game has not occurred in many new states, and even in some of the old states which have had democratic elections for many years.

The decline of the Federalists after 1800 meant that the United States did not experience a real succession problem again until 1829 with the inauguration of Andrew Jackson. The Virginia Dynasty of Jefferson, Madison, and Monroe, governed the country for 24 years, one succeeding the other without difficulty. A national two-party system did not emerge anew until the 1830's, when President Jackson's opponents united in the Whig party.

The almost unchallenged rule of the Virginia Dynasty and the Democratic-Republican Party served to legitimate national authority and democratic rights. By the time the nation divided again into two broad warring factions which appealed for mass support, the country had existed for 40 years, the Constitution had been glorified, and the authority of the courts had been accepted as definitive.

.   .   .

CONCLUSION

All states that have recently gained independence are faced with two interrelated problems, legitimating the use of political power and establishing national identity. If they seek to establish a democratic polity, they must develop institutional and normative constraints against efforts to inhibit organized opposition or to deny civil liberties to critics.

This paper has explored several development processes, as they emerged in the early United States. National identity was formed under the aegis first of a charismatic authority figure, and later under the leadership of a dominant "left wing" or revolutionary party led successively by three Founding Fathers. The pressures in new nations to repress opposition movements which exacerbate the strains in such societies were reduced in America by the rapid decline of conservative opposition. The revolutionary, democratic values, which thus became part of its national self-image and the basis for its authority structure, gained legitimacy as they proved effective. Under them the general standard of living improved and the nation came closer to equalling the nations of Europe economically.

The need to establish stable authority and a sense of identity led the leaders of the United States to resist efforts by "old states" to involve the young nation in their quarrels. But at the same time that Americans rejected "foreign entanglements," they clearly used the Old World as both a negative and a positive reference group, rejecting its political and class structures as backward, but nevertheless viewing its cultural and economic achievements as worthy of emulation. The intellectuals, particularly, expressed this ambivalence since they played a major role in establishing and defining the state, but then found that the task of operating and living in it required them to conform to vulgar populist and provincial values.

In specifying the processes in the evolution of the first nation that are comparable to those in contemporary societies of Asia and Africa, I am arguing by analogy. "We cannot assume that because conditions in one century led to certain effects, even roughly parallel conditions in another century would lead to similar effects. Neither can we be sure, of course, that the conditions were even roughly parallel." [67] It is fairly obvious that conditions in the early United States were quite different; as compared with most of the new nations of today, it had a simpler set of problems.

America grew up in a world that was very different from the one that the new nations face today. Although internal conflicts stemming from attitudes toward the French Revolution disrupted the young American polity, there was no world-wide totalitarian conspiracy seeking to upset political and economic development from within, and holding up an alternative model of seemingly successful economic growth through the use of authoritarian methods. Also the absence of rapid mass communication systems meant that early Americans were relatively isolated, and hence did not compare their conditions with those in the more developed countries. The United States did not face a "revolution of rising expectations" based on the knowledge that life is much better elsewhere. The accepted concepts of natural or appropriate rights did not include a justification of the lower classes' organized participation in the polity to gain higher income, welfare support from the state, and the like. And whatever the effects attributed to the existence of an open land frontier, there can be little doubt that it contributed to social stability.

America possessed a number of other advantages that made its birth, as a democratic nation, easier. Internal value cleavages, which frustrate contemporary new nations' efforts to establish a national identity and which plagued many European nations' efforts to establish a stable democratic polity, were comparatively less significant in young America. The United States was formed by a relatively homogeneous population, most of whom came from Britain. There was a common language, a relatively similar religious background (although denominational differences did cause some problems), and a common

[67] Deutsch *et al., op. cit.,* p. 11.

cultural and political tradition. And, the class structure of America, even before the establishment of the new nation, came closer to meeting the conditions for a stable democracy than those of the Old World. Writing shortly before Independence was finally attained, Crèvecœur, though sympathetic to the Tory cause, pointed up the egalitarianism of American society:

> The rich and the poor are not so far removed from each other as they are in Europe. . . . A pleasing uniformity of decent competence appears throughout our habitations. . . . It must take some time ere he [the foreign traveler] can reconcile himself to our dictionary, which is but short in words of dignity, and names of honor. . . . Here man is free as he ought to be; nor is this pleasing equality so transitory as many others are.[68]

The ability to work the institutions of a democratic nation requires sophistication both at the elite level and the level of the citizenry at large. And as Carl Bridenbaugh has well demonstrated, the America of revolutionary times was not a colonial backwater.[69] Philadelphia was the second largest English city, only London surpassed it in numbers. Philadelphia and other colonial capitals were centers of relatively high culture at this time. They had universities and learned societies, and their elite was in touch with, and contributed to, the intellectual and scientific ideas of Britain.

In this respect, the common political traditions that the American colonists held were of particular importance since they included the concept of the rule of law, and even of constitutionalism. Each colony operated under a charter which defined and limited governmental powers. Although colonial subjects, Americans were also Englishmen and thus accustomed to the rights and privileges of Englishmen. Through their local governments they actually possessed more rights than did most of the residents of Britain, itself. In a sense, even before independence, Americans met a basic condition for democratic government, the ability to work its fundamental institutions.[70]

Unlike many contemporary new states, the United States was not bedeviled in its first decades of existence by a potentially politically powerful military class who could use the army to seize power. The entire army in 1789 consisted of 672 men.[71]

However, of prime importance in facilitating America's development as a nation, both politically and economically, was the fact that the weight of ancient tradition which is present in almost all the contemporary new states was largely absent in early America. It was not only a new nation, it was a new society, much less bound to the customs and values of the past than any

[68] J. Hector St. John Crèvecœur, *Letters from an American Farmer* (New York: Dolphin Books, n.d.), pp. 46–47.

[69] Carl Bridenbaugh, *Rebels and Gentlemen, Philadelphia in the Age of Franklin* (New York: Reynal and Hitchcock, 1942).

[70] See John Plamenatz, *On Alien Rule and Self Government* (London: Longmans, Green and Co., 1960), pp. 47–8.

[71] James R. Jacobs, *The Beginning of the U.S. Army, 1783–1812* (Princeton: Princeton University Press, 1947); see also Deutsch *et al.*, *op. cit.*, p. 26.

nation of Europe. Crèvecœur has well described the American as a "new man," the likes of which had never been seen before.[72]

Religion, of course, may be viewed as a "traditional" institution which played an important role in the United States. The separation of Church and State is particularly crucial in new nations which are by definition committed to change. In the first half-century of the American Republic, as we have seen, the defenders of religious traditionalism were seriously weakened. Following Independence, the various state churches were gradually disestablished.

On the other hand, the new United States was particularly fortunate in the religious traditions which it did inherit. The special religious tradition of Calvinistic Puritanism, which was stronger in the colonies than in the mother country, contributed greatly to making the new nation work. A positive orientation toward savings and hard work, and the strong motivation to achieve high positions which derive from this religious tradition, have been seen as elements which make it one of the principal causes of the remarkable economic expansion that made possible the legitimation of equalitarian values and democratic government. Max Weber, the most prominent exponent of the thesis that ascetic Protestantism played a major role in the development of capitalism in the Western world, stated "The whole typically bourgeois ethic . . . is identical with the ethic practiced by the sects in America. . . . The survivals in contemporary America are the derivation of a religious regulation of life which once worked with penetrating efficiency." [73] Their "insistence that ones' works were signs of eternal grace or damnation" has been transformed into a secular emphasis upon achievement.[74]

The Puritan tradition may also have made it easier to legitimize American democracy by the rule of law. Tocqueville saw that an egalitarian and democratic society has a special need for self-restraining value system in order to inhibit the tyranny of the majority.[75]

The Calvinistic-Puritan tradition was particularly valuable in training men to the sort of self-restraint that Tocqueville felt was necessary for democracy. By making every man God's agent, ascetic Protestantism made each individual responsible for the state of morality in the society, while making the congregation a disciplinary agent helped to prevent any one individual from assuming his brand of morality was better than others.[76]

Despite all these advantages in the United States which have been discussed above, the evidence suggests that this new nation came very close to failing in its effort to establish an unified legitimate authority. The first attempt to do so in 1783, following on Independence, was a failure. The second and successful

[72] Crèvecœur, *op. cit.*, pp. 49–50.
[73] Max Weber, "The Protestant Sects and the Spirit of Capitalism," in *Essays in Sociology*, translated by Hans Gerth and C. W. Mills (New York: Oxford University Press, 1946), pp. 309, 313.
[74] Robin Williams, *American Society* (New York: Alfred A. Knopf, 1957), p. 313.
[75] Alexis de Tocqueville, *Democracy in America* (New York: Vintage Books, 1959), I, p. 316.
[76] Williams, *op. cit.*, p. 312.

effort was endangered by frequent threats of secession and the open flaunting of central authority until the Civil War. Thus the advantages, which the early United States possessed, compared to most of the contemporary new states, only show more strongly how significant are the similar reactions experienced by developing states of the present and the past.

Reflections on Charismatic Leadership

REINHARD BENDIX

"The term 'charismatic leader' has recently attained widespread and almost debased currency. In the past, it was occasionally applied to Gandhi, Lenin, Hitler, and Roosevelt. Now nearly every leader with marked popular appeal, especially those of new states, is indiscriminately tagged as charismatic." [1] Difficulties in the use of this term arise not only from indiscriminate labeling but also from conflicting theories of societies. Two recent discussions are especially instructive in this respect.

In an assessment of Max Weber's political writings Karl Loewenstein has raised the question of whether or not the term "charisma" can properly be applied in contemporary politics. Charismatic leadership depends upon a widespread belief in the existence of extraordinary or supernatural capacities, but such beliefs are at a discount in secular contexts. Though democratization has increased the plebiscitarian component of modern politics, the qualities of personality which attract voters indicate the popularity, but not necessarily the charisma, of a successful political leader. Accordingly, Loewenstein feels that today "charisma" in the proper sense is likely to be found in those areas of the world in which a popular belief in supernatural powers is still widespread, as in some parts of Africa or Asia.[2]

Quite the opposite position has been formulated by E. A. Shils, who sees a charismatic element in all societies. Shils notes Weber's distinction between

This paper originated in a symposium organized by the Association of Asian Studies, which met in New York, 1966, under the chairmanship of Professor Rupert Emerson. Subsequently the editors of *Asian Survey* arranged for the publication of papers on four Asian leaders with this essay serving as an introduction (*Asian Survey*, Vol. VII, June 1967, pp. 341–352). In the republication of the essay in this volume, I have made several revisions as well as included factual materials which originally appeared in separate essays by Professor Roger M. Smith, Dr. Margaret Fisher, Professor Chongsik Lee, and Dr. Stuart R. Schram. I wish to thank the authors and the editors of *Asian Survey* for their permission to use materials from the articles in this revised form.

[1] Ann Ruth and Dorothy Willner, "The Rise and Role of Charismatic Leaders," *Annals of the American Academy of Political and Social Studies*, Vol. 358 (March 1965), p. 78.

[2] Karl Loewenstein, *Max Weber Staatspolitische Auffassungen in der Sicht unserer Zeit* (Frankfurt: Athenaum Verlag, 1965), pp. 74–85.

the disruptive or innovative effects of charisma and the continuous and routine character of tradition or the legal order; this parallels Loewenstein's distinction between the magico-religious contexts that encourage and the secular contexts that discourage charisma. As Shils points out, Weber himself did not confine his use of the term to magical or religious beliefs, and he analyzed the institutionalization of charisma through kinship, heredity, and office. But he also believed that the opportunities for genuine charisma had diminished in the course of an increasing rationalization and bureaucratization of Western society. Shils takes issue with this last point. He maintains that men in all societies confront exigencies of life which demand a comprehensive solution. Man's position in the cosmos, birth, death, marriage, basic ideas of equity are among these central concerns. The need for establishing some order with reference to these concerns may vary among men, but the point is that charisma attaches itself to those individuals or institutions which satisfy that need or promise to do so. Such ordering may involve philosophical or artistic representations, religious doctrines, interpretations of the law, or the authority of government. Charisma has necessarily a protean character, since it may become a focus of belief whenever ultimate concerns are given an authoritative ordering.[3]

This is not the place to discuss these larger questions substantively, but it is appropriate to refer briefly to one rather topical application of the term "charisma." The new nations provide a setting of rapid change in which charismatic leaders may achieve new forms of political integration. In his analysis of *Ghana in Transition* David Apter has suggested that charismatic leadership helps to undermine tribal authority and thus helps to make way for the creation of secular, legal institutions in a nation-state. He notes, however, that charismatic leadership is not easily reconciled with secular systems of authority. Perhaps a charismatic leader like Nkrumah can transfer some of the loyalty, traditionally accorded to tribal chiefs, to the agents and symbols of a secular government — as long as he is the leader. But then the problem is: How can the loyalties of a personal following be transferred to the institutions of government ("routinized" in Weber's terminology)? Without such transfer governmental stability is not assured.[4]

In a critique of writings on Ghanaian and African politics Claude Ake has raised the basic question whether or not in the new nations charismatic leaders can fulfill any such constructive functions. They often command a large percentage of the vote, but this may involve a fleeting acclamation and an engineered consent rather than widespread public support. Since in the new nations political instability is rife and integration difficult to achieve, any leader may at times obtain considerable political power, if he can command a certain degree of loyalty. Modern means of publicity can give such leadership all the appearance of charisma: the singular gifts of the leader and the unques-

[3] E. A. Shils, "Charisma, Order and Status," *American Sociological Review*, Vol. XXX (April 1965), pp. 199–213.
[4] See David Apter, *Ghana in Transition* (New York: Atheneum, 1966), pp. 303–306. See also pp. 168, 173–174, 233, 296–297, and 323.

tioning devotion of his followers. But such appearances can be misleading. The popular celebrations at Nkrumah's overthrow (in 1966) suggest either that his charisma had disappeared by then, or that it had been on the wane for some time past, or indeed that there had been little of it in the first place. Such uncertainties only point up the evanescent qualities of "charisma," which may come to the fore in times of rapid change but which are neither a substitute for regular leadership nor easily reconciled with enduring political institutions.[5]

These contemporary uncertainties in the use of the term suggest that there are special hazards in drawing analogies between new nations, then and now. In his analysis of *The First New Nation* S. M. Lipset has noted that George Washington was a source of unity in the early years of the United States and that his commanding military success inspired widespread veneration of his person. But Lipset also notes that Washington was oriented to the rule of law, permitted the growth of an embryonic party system, and established a precedent for succession to office by voluntarily stepping down in favor of President-elect Adams. Genuine as Washington's charisma probably was, it was acted out in a framework of received political and legal institutions — and it is just the absence of such a framework which jeopardizes analogies between this early American and the contemporary experience in the new nations.[6]

I have cited the large interpretative questions raised by Loewenstein and Shils and the uncertainties of the contemporary application of the term because I believe that the proper definition and use of the concept "charisma" must be clarified, before these larger issues can be addressed. My purpose in this paper is, therefore, to restate Weber's original formulation of the concept and emphasize its dynamic implications. Secondly, I shall comment briefly on some analytic problems which arise when the term "charismatic leadership" is applied to four Asiatic leaders, whose careers illustrate different facets of the problem.

In referring now to Weber's specification of the term "charisma" I confine myself to the concept of "charismatic leadership," leaving out the "routinization of charisma" (through its association with kinship, heredity, and office) as well as the positive or negative relations between charisma and social structure. An analysis of individual political leaders need not be concerned with routinization, except in so far as it bears on the problem of succession. Also, the leaders under consideration are politically active in societies

[5] See Claude Ake, "Charismatic Legitimation and Political Integration," *Comparative Studies in Society and History*, Vol. IX (October 1966), pp. 1–13. Mr. Ake raises many appropriate questions but does not seem aware that it is inappropriate to expect a legitimation of regular political institutions from charismatic leadership — these institutions exist already.

[6] S. M. Lipset, *The First New Nation* (New York: Basic Books, 1963), pp. 16–45. Cf. the contrasting interpretation by S. P. Huntington, "Political Modernization: America vs. Europe," *World Politics*, Vol. XVIII (April 1966), especially pp. 408–414 (reprinted in this volume, pp. 170–200).

undergoing rapid change, i.e., in contexts presumably favorable to charismatic appeals.[7]

Weber defines "charisma" as

> a certain quality of an individual personality by virtue of which he is set apart from ordinary men and treated as endowed with supernatural, superhuman, or at least specifically exceptional powers or qualities. These are such as are not accessible to the ordinary person, but are regarded as of divine origin or as exemplary, and on the basis of them the individual concerned is treated as a leader.[8]

Five specifications are added to this basic definition. Weber notes first that "charisma" is probably the greatest revolutionary power in periods of established tradition, and second that it typically neglects considerations of economic efficiency and rationality.[9] Thirdly, he emphasizes that the charismatic leader and his followers constitute a congregation (*Gemeinde*); he has no officials assisting him but rather disciples or confidants, who have no career or qualifications in the bureaucratic sense and no privileges. They are personally called by their leader based on his peremptory judgment of their own charismatic gifts; they may be as summarily dismissed when he judges that they have failed his trust in them.

Weber's fourth and fifth specifications are of special interest to us here. For that reason it may be best to quote him verbatim:

> It is *recognition* on the part of those subject to authority which is decisive for the validity of charisma. This is freely given and guaranteed by what is held to be a "sign" or proof (*Bewährung*), originally always a miracle, and consists in devotion to the corresponding revelation, hero worship, or absolute trust in the leader. But where charisma is genuine, it is not this which is the basis of legitimacy. This basis lies rather in the conception that it is the *duty* of those who have been called to a charismatic mission to recognize its quality and to act accordingly. Psychologically

[7] Weber's discussion tends to obscure the distinction between leadership and authority (*Herrschaft*), since he always analyzes the latter in terms of the chance that a command will be obeyed, and this criterion can be applied to leadership as well. In Weber's terminology charismatic authority in the sense of routinized charisma can be distinguished from charismatic authority in the sense of personal leadership, but that appears to leave no room for personal leadership that is not charismatic. I return to this question briefly at the end of this paper. At any rate, the present discussion is confined to charismatic authority in the sense of personal leadership, or what I call charismatic leadership. For an illuminating discussion of this point cf. Robert Bierstedt, "The Problem of Authority," in Morroe Berger, Theodore Abel, and Charles Page (eds.), *Freedom and Control in Modern Society* (New York: D. Van Nostrand Co., 1954), pp. 71–72.

[8] Max Weber, *The Theory of Social and Economic Organization* (New York: Oxford University Press, 1947), pp. 358–359.

[9] The first of these points relates to the discussion by Loewenstein and Shils; Weber's statement is obviously conditional. Not the presence of "charisma" but its power to revolutionize the social order is judged to be greatest, where traditions are well established. Weber also makes clear that "pure" charisma is incompatible with economic routine, not with material gain or possessions as such. *Ibid.*, pp. 363–364.

this "recognition" is a matter of complete personal devotion to the possessor of the quality, arising out of enthusiasm, or of despair and hope.

No prophet has ever regarded his quality as dependent on the attitudes of the masses toward him. No elective king or military leader has ever treated those who have resisted him or tried to ignore him otherwise than as delinquent in duty. . . .

If proof of his charismatic qualification fails him for long, the leader endowed with charisma tends to think his god or his magical or heroic powers have deserted him. If he is for long unsuccessful, above all *if his leadership fails to benefit his followers*, it is likely that his charismatic authority will disappear. This is the genuine charismatic meaning of the phrase "by the grace of God" (*Gottesgnadentum*).[10]

A first reading of this passage might suggest that a leader is charismatic when his followers recognize him as such, because they see "powerful results achieved in the absence of power." [11] But closer examination suggests that both the recognition by followers and the leader's own claims and actions are fundamentally ambivalent.

For the charisma of a leader to be present, it must be recognized by his followers, and in the ideal typical case this recognition is a matter of *duty*. But a personal devotion arising from enthusiasm, despair, or hope is easily contaminated by the *desire for a "sign"* which will confirm the existence of charisma. In turn, the leader demands *unconditional devotion* from his followers, and he will construe any demand for a sign or proof of his gift of grace as a lack of faith and a dereliction of duty. Yet his "charismatic authority will disappear, . . . if *proof of charismatic qualifications* fails him for too long." It appears then that charismatic leadership is not a label that can be applied but refers rather to a problematic relation between a leader and his followers which must be investigated. For it is in each case a question of fact: To what extent and in what ways has the followers' desire for a sign — born out of their enthusiasm, despair, or hope — interfered with, modified, or even jeopardized their unconditional devotion to duty? And similarly it is a question of fact: To what extent and in what ways has the leader's unconditional claim to exceptional powers or qualities been interfered with, modified, or even jeopardized by the actions which he construes as proof of his charismatic qualifications?

The following sketches of four political leaders in Asia may be considered with these questions in mind.

1. PRINCE NORODOM SIHANOUK, CAMBODIA (1923———)

Prince Sihanouk exemplifies in his own person the transition from prince to plebiscitarian leader. He was called to the throne in 1941, at the age of eighteen, presumably because the French colonial rulers considered him submis-

---

[10] *Ibid.*, pp. 359–360. The translation has been modified slightly. I have also rearranged the sequence of Weber's specifications.

[11] The phrase in quotation marks has been suggested by Dankwart Rustow, *The World of Nations* (Washington, D.C.: The Brookings Institution, 1967), p. 165. It is a succinct paraphrase of the miraculous element in the followers' perception of charisma.

sive. Yet at an early time, Sihanouk faced up to the problem of procuring Cambodia's independence from French rule, while dealing with the leading political party, which was not only nationalist and anti-French but also opposed to the monarchy. The Prince recognized the difficulties which would surround the emerging state and did not want to foreclose the possibility of appealing to France for assistance. Therefore he chose to negotiate the achievement of independence rather than win it through open revolt. But by winning independence as a monarch in 1953, Sihanouk also succeeded in countering anti-monarchical sentiments. Because the throne was customarily above national politics, Sihanouk recognized that in an independent Cambodia he had to choose between his monarchical position and an active political role. Accordingly, he abdicated in favor of his father in 1955 and founded a party, the *Sangkum*, in order to arouse greater public interest in political affairs. Originally, the party was not intended to be "political"; however, the people responded enthusiastically, and eventually all other parties were dissolved, and their leaders and followers joined the *Sangkum*. In 1960, upon the death of his father, Sihanouk was requested to ascend the throne once again, but he refused. Instead, his mother became Queen, while the Prince suggested that the National Assembly amend the Constitution and create the position of Chief of State. The amendment was passed, and Prince Sihanouk was elected to the newly created position.

In this way the charisma of the royal family was transferred in good part to the position of a plebiscitarian political leader. The concept of the *Sangkum* party as a loyal following of the entire people may be considered similarly: a transmutation of subjects into citizens with the ideology of the people's loyalty to the king virtually intact. The subsequent dissolution of all competing parties may have the same significance; while pressure was no doubt exerted, it may have involved to a great extent an appeal to loyalty which even the opponents of the Prince could not ignore. The same populist approach is evidenced in the National Congress. Originally designed to provide a forum for the people to voice their opinions and complaints, the agenda of the Congress are arranged in practice by the *Sangkum*. Prince Sihanouk presides over the meetings of the Congress, while the people in attendance are a largely passive audience. The Prince is generally able to influence the course of the meeting which becomes in effect a royal audience in plebiscitarian disguise.

In his new role of plebiscitarian leadership the Prince has reenacted the attributes of a benevolent ruler with a strong emphasis on good works and modernity. The populist stance, the jokes to get people relaxed, human warmth and personal solicitude, the appeal to the people at large and to the grandeur of the country's traditions, even the Prince's exemplary actions such as the design of textiles or well-publicized acts of manual labor — all these are instances of symbolic identification with the people in a context of popular affection and deference. Reactions are not unequivocal, however. There are signs of discontent among competing groups within the *Sangkum*, which are critical of the Prince's foreign and domestic policies; there is also unrest among the educated youths who cannot find the opportunities for which they feel themselves qualified. Nevertheless, the Prince apparently uses his protean talents to show his solidarity with the people rather than to manifest his exceptional powers as a leader. And accounts of popular reactions present the people as, on the whole, content and deferential rather than devoted or eager for signs and miracles. In sum, this is a case of institutionalized charisma, with the aura and potential terror of royalty mellowed by populist appeals and an adaptation of plebiscitarian methods of government.

This classification is suggested also by Prince Sihanouk's personnel policy. The men he has employed are not disciples but rather men distinguished by their experience and independent judgment. His present advisors include men who formerly opposed him but whom he appointed apparently because he valued their talents. However, two of the chief advisors are relatives of the Prince. It is speculated that the future leaders of Cambodia will be recruited from this group of advisors, perhaps under the direction of Prince Monireth, Sihanouk's uncle. But the question is whether or not any successor can achieve anything like Prince Sihanouk's very personal combination of royalist tradition and plebiscitarian methods. As long as Sihanouk is still "King" to the people at large, no one is likely to question his right to name his successor; indeed some years ago the Prince designated one of his sons as the future head of the *Sangkum* party. But how long will this belief in the institutionalized charisma of royalty remain intact? The Prince's son, for example, would succeed not to the throne but to the position of party leader. And unless he is quite as successful as his father in holding the warring party factions at bay by an appeal to the people and by successful actions in their behalf, his image will get tarnished more quickly than it would in the presence of comparable intrigues at a royal court with its base in the sacred blood ties of the royal family.

The strength of institutionalized charisma (as in royalty) is that succession is solved through inheritance; its weakness is that personal qualification for office is a matter of chance. In the case of charismatic leadership proper the assets and liabilities are reversed: there is no rule for succession, while personal qualifications can be decisive. The relation between Gandhi and Nehru is a case in point.

2. JAWAHARLAL NEHRU, INDIA (1889–1964)

Among the four leaders considered here, Nehru is the only one who is clearly a disciple and a publicly designated successor. Since in the eyes of his followers at least, Nehru's charisma was derived from Gandhi, we are obliged to examine the transfer of charisma from teacher to disciple, in order to assess the latter's charismatic appeal. Weber discusses the transfer of charisma as an aspect of "routinization." Since by definition charisma is out of the ordinary and dependent upon manifestations of strictly personal qualities, it exists in pure form only in the person in whom it originates. Yet the disciples of the leader and his followers at large share a strong desire to perpetuate that "gift of grace" and its real or presumed benefits, and efforts at such perpetuation come to the fore when the problem of succession must be solved. In this respect Weber distinguishes six typical alternatives; the one of interest here is that the original charismatic leader designates his own successor, who is then accorded recognition by the community.

Nehru's long schooling in England had prepared him to become a junior member in his father's legal firm, but he found this prospect dull. In 1919, at the age of thirty, he became actively involved in the Indian independence movement. The designation of Nehru as a successor to Gandhi took place over a number of years. During this early period, Nehru emerged as a young, conspicuously Western, relatively wealthy, and intensely theoretical member of the inner circle of disciples. All the disciples were held together by their faith in Gandhi's political and moral leadership. Yet there were divisions among them, for the specific goals of Hindu-Moslem harmony, the elimination of untouchability, and the improvement of village life were broad enough to allow considerable variation with regard to means and ends. In the context of the movement for independence the most noteworthy division concerned nonviolence, which was a creed to some and a tactic to others. This tells us something about Gandhi's tolerance for diversity among his immediate followers, suggesting the permissive preaching of the *exemplary prophet* which "says nothing about a divine mission or an ethical duty of obedience, but rather directs itself to the self-interest of those who crave salvation, recommending to them the same path as he himself traversed." [12]

Nehru's tie to Gandhi was based on deep respect and acceptance of Gandhi's tactical skill, but these sentiments did not affect Nehru's own wide-ranging ideological and political explorations and commitments. Such world-political preoccupations separated Nehru from things Indian even in the midst of intense political activities. Gandhi commented in 1924 that Nehru was one of "the loneliest young men of my acquaintance in India." [13] This personal and cultural isolation was directly related to the articulation of Nehru's political position. His views on international affairs sharpened his conflict with the older Congress leaders including his father, but these views also enabled Nehru to appeal effectively to labor groups and radical youth, among whom some had lost faith in Gandhi. In this setting Gandhi, choosing to withdraw from the Congress presidency in favor of Nehru (1930), used Nehru to keep the young rebels in line. Gandhi also induced his chosen disciple to accept policies that bewildered him so that Nehru was forced for the sake of party unity to represent as his own a position in which he did not believe. This pattern recurred during the long years of discipleship, from Gandhi's reconciliation between Nehru and his father in 1919 to his formal designation of Nehru as his political heir in 1942. For Nehru these were also years during which he was pulled in

---

[12] Max Weber, *The Sociology of Religion* (Boston: The Beacon Press, 1963), p. 55.

[13] In a letter to Motilal Nehru, September 2, 1924. Quoted from B. R. Nanda, *The Nehrus: Motilal and Jawaharlal* (New York: The John Day Co., 1963), p. 247, in Margaret Fisher, "India's Jawaharlal Nehru," *Asian Survey*, Vol. VII (June 1967), p. 367.

several directions, dedicated to the man in whose charisma he believed, but at odds with him in his style and judgments. Yet Nehru served him and the cause of independence with complete devotion despite the false positions and humiliating experiences into which Gandhi's tactics forced him from time to time.

A lesser man might have succumbed to the strain of that relationship, compounded as it was by Gandhi's cooperative and antagonistic relations with Nehru's father. But Nehru was an intense and ebullient man, who apparently overcame the ambiguities of his position and his own ambivalence. He was aided not only by his courage and idealism for India but also by Gandhi's patient trust in his qualities of mind and character despite outbursts of temper, doctrinaire views, and repeated clashes with other Congress leaders. Nehru's relationship with Gandhi reflected his ambivalence to India as a whole. Admiring Gandhi's tactical "magic" and his uniquely Indian means of achieving independence, Nehru still saw non-violence only as a tactic to achieve a political purpose; thus at the same time he identified with, and dissociated himself from, this symbol of India. While he enjoyed Gandhi's trust during the long years of his discipleship, Gandhi still mixed expressions of confidence with fatherly admonitions, giving Nehru his blessing but withholding his mandate. There is some suggestion in this context that Nehru's successful campaigns among the Indian masses were an escape from an enervating tutelage as well as a discovery of India. Contacts with the Indian people were a means of attaining confidence in his mission, for he witnessed the unconditional devotion with which they viewed him as the embodiment of Gandhi's charisma and the charisma of his own sacrifices for independence. There is an almost tragic irony in the paradox that what his personality represented to the people was largely independent of what he said to them. Nehru's effect on the masses inspired his confidence in India while increasing the scepticism of his colleagues. Yet this mass enthusiasm and Nehru's continued isolation among the disciples provided Gandhi again and again with the opportunity to weld the factions of the Congress together. And then, at the age of fifty-three, once more in jail, Nehru learned from the book of an Englishman what it was that distinguished him from Gandhi. The book distinguished between the prophet, who pursues the truth relentlessly, and the leader, who strikes a compromise between truth and the views of the average man. Nehru thought his own role to be that of the leader but believed Gandhi had confused the two roles. Apparently Nehru did not recognize Gandhi's unique fusion of prophesy and teaching, which was a part of that specific charisma of India's holy men that was beyond his own grasp. By separating the teacher's role from the educative function of exemplary conduct, Nehru revealed his own Western acculturation as well as the discrepancy between his self-image and the Indian people's recognition of his charismatic gift. He wanted to be their teacher, while they sought in him the exemplary prophet.

In this all too brief consideration I have emphasized the problem of succession, highlighted by the great charisma of Nehru's mentor. It may be noted that the charismatic appeal of Gandhi and of Nehru is entirely the by-product of their personal gifts in the context of the Indian independence movement. In turning now to a discussion of two leaders in Communist countries, we must attempt to disentangle the relationship between the leader and his people from the manipulated representation of that relationship by the mass media.

3. KIM IL-SŎNG, NORTH KOREA (1919———)

It is difficult to separate the fact from fiction in the life history of Kim Il-sŏng. Kim has concentrated in his hands all power of decision-making in the party, the government, and the army. To account for this fact, and to celebrate it, North Korean historians have written hagiological accounts which twist the story of Kim's childhood, his role as a guerilla leader, and the first phase of his party leadership into so many anticipations of his present preeminence. For that reason it becomes difficult to assess the rather meagre descriptions of Kim's leadership. The Korean party appears to model its mobilization of the people after a shock-troop pattern, giving its civilian appeals and organizational efforts the appearance of simulated combat under conditions of guerilla warfare. For example, Kim approaches production problems in the manner of a self-confident guerilla leader who himself masters whatever he asks of his soldiers and by his example encourages them to greater effort. He reportedly learns the technicalities of the factories or collectives he will visit, thus living up to the reputation of the omniscient leader. In this way he emphasizes by his example the Party's mission as the teacher of the people. Organized propaganda shows this leadership in action and seeks to enhance its exemplary effects by the testimony of "awed witnesses." But this inevitably raises questions, as does Kim's power to divert resources to those farms and enterprises which have been selected for exemplary success in their production efforts. Propagandistic manipulation of this kind can give a hollow ring to the claim of exceptional powers on behalf of the leader, and a mere joke or derisive comment aimed at such manipulation can turn a follower's devotion into a sceptic's "withdrawal of efficiency" (Veblen).[14]

Here we come to a lacuna in Weber's approach to charisma, due to the time at which his analysis was written (1913–14). He did not foresee that it would be possible to *simulate* publicly all aspects of charismatic leadership — the manifestations of the leader's extraordinary gift, the unconditional devotion of his disciples, and the awed veneration of his large following — saturating all channels of communication so that no one could escape the message. Modern dictatorships have used such centrally organized, public hagiology exten-

[14] According to Chong-sik Lee biographical data detrimental to Kim's official image have been suppressed, such as his flight to Siberia to escape the Japanese invasion, which makes his subsequent political prominence largely the result of Russian or Chinese influence. There is some question, of course, whether the manipulation of such biographical details enters into people's awareness; but even in the absence of knowledge, suspicions and rumors can spread quickly if they project people's feelings.

sively; and, given the possibilities of the "great lie" and the "will to believe," a widespread belief in charisma can be created under favorable conditions. Yet the built-in limitations of "charisma by publicity" should not be overlooked. All hagiological writings contain paeans to the virtues of the saints; in the eyes of the believers the credibility of these writings is enhanced, rather than diminished, by stories showing "powerful results achieved in the absence of power," and such stories are also a regular feature of dictatorial propaganda. But then the authors of conventional hagiology were true believers themselves, who expressed their own sense of the miraculous for the edification of their readers, in the absence of any claim to be believed other than the authenticity of their own religious experience. In this respect, a manipulated hagiology differs. Where all media are saturated with news of the leader's great deeds and the devotion of his followers, ordinary people may begin to resist the message by various strategies which help them escape the din and the drive to mobilize them. For the saturation of the media *means* manipulation and can suggest even to the unlettered that "powerful results are 'achieved' in the presence of power" and hence in the absence of miracles.

Nevertheless, it would be mistaken to infer that charismatic leadership cannot occur under these conditions. First of all, central manipulation of news is still compatible with credibility. All totalitarian regimes have an interest, for example, in obtaining testimonials to the leader by prominent individuals with a reputation for probity and independent judgment. Whether or not pressure is used to obtain such testimonials, they can be turned to good account by the mass media — at least for quite a time. Again, the leader himself may use the media to project his supreme confidence in his mission, while pomp and circumstance can enhance the effect of that message. In this respect it is quite wrong to suppose that charismatic leadership implies the absence of deliberate manipulation on the part of the leader. On the contrary, a sense of personal mission will justify the manipulative enhancement of the charismatic appeal, so long as this does not conflict with the appeal itself.[15] Secondly, the leader's career may exemplify his charisma in the eyes of the people, and the mere fact of media manipulation will not necessarily undermine their belief in him. Indeed, a people's recognition of that charisma — born of "the will to believe" and manifest in their devotion to duty — may endure long after they have begun to discount the credibility of the leader's entourage and of the whole apparatus of media manipulation. This consideration may have some bearing on the case of Mao Tse-tung.

4. MAO TSE-TUNG, CHINA (1893————)

The evidence of Mao Tse-tung's leadership is overwhelming, and there is little doubt that this leadership deserves the attribute "charismatic." Stuart Schram points out that Mao gives the appearance of an "average Chinese

---

[15] It is probably more difficult to make testimonials to the leader appear genuine, when these are given by his direct collaborators, because the secular context militates against the image of the disciple who is moved by unselfish devotion to duty and who partakes of the leader's charisma.

peasant." [16] The peasant is traditionally a symbol of weakness; Mao's success has made him a symbol of strength. For great power to develop out of universal weakness is indeed a miracle in the literal sense. Since in this case identification with the peasant also symbolizes the nation, Mao personifies the whole transformation of his country. His grand and remote appearance only intensifies the impression of mystery associated with miracles — whether or not this appearance is a personal trait, a manner acquired during a dramatic life spent in revolutionary politics, an impression created by party propaganda, or a sign of old age, or some combination of these.

Three main aspects of Mao's thought are directly related to his rise to power. His nationalism is exemplified in the mobilization of the Chinese against Japanese aggression. His concern with military action is related to his long experience in guerilla warfare with its combination of militancy and populism. And his emphasis on voluntarism and conscious action (though related to Leninist ideas) reflects the special importance he has attributed throughout his career to moral and psychological preparedness as the principal basis of revolution. These themes were articulated in Mao's early writings, and his continued adherence to these basic ideas conveys an impression of extraordinary consistency. In his own mind and those of his devoted followers these ideas are directly related to the success of the Chinese revolution. Accordingly, Mao's outlook is seen as the cause of "powerful results achieved in the absence of power." It is not surprising that an aging leader relies on this inspiration of his successful achievements of the past, when his revolutionary regime begins to encounter the resistance of men and the complications of circumstance, as all established revolutionary regimes do.

A number of factors have been cited to explain the excesses of the Mao cult in recent years: a struggle for power within the highest ranks of the party, senile vanity, echoes of traditional emperor worship, Mao's penchant for a personalist approach to problems of leadership despite his awareness of the importance of organization, and last but not least his conscious manipulation of his own personality-cult as a political weapon. To this plethora of causes an outsider hesitates to add further possibilities. But if the evidence for Mao's charisma is as strong as has been suggested, then it is probable that mounting complexities bring out both the supreme leader's fear of losing his extraordinary powers and that mixture of hope and fear of despair with which the young generation reacts to a charisma placed in jeopardy. As the difficulties of the regime mount, the populist desire for a "sign" or proof of charisma is increasing, just at the time when the leader who embodies that charisma is visibly aging. After all, the paradox is that a personality cult centering on a seventy-four-year-old man comes to a crescendo at a time when he must solve the most difficult problem of charismatic leadership — the problem of succession. The more the cult centers on him personally, the more insoluble that problem becomes, and Mao appears to be quite aware of this fact. Referring to

[16] See Stuart R. Schram, "Mao Tse-tung as a Charismatic Leader," *Asian Survey*, Vol. VII (June 1967), pp. 383–384.

organizational changes involving the delegation of his power to Liu Shao-ch'i and Teng Hsiao-p'ing in 1956, Mao stated in October 1966:

> When I retreated into the second line by not conducting the daily work and by letting others execute it, my purpose was to cultivate their prestige so that when I have to see God, the country can avoid great chaos.[17]

In now reversing that earlier decision according to his own interpretation, Mao is apparently attempting to transform the people's recognition of his personal charisma into a cult of sacred objects. It remains to be seen whether such a transformation can capture the imagination of the people and also preserve their devotion to duty — in the absence of visible miracles and eventually in the absence of the charismatic leader himself.

All this is without precedent in the history of Communist movements only in the sense that a career of leadership which spans the entire period from the beginning of the revolutionary movement until eighteen years after the seizure of power is also without precedent. This factor must be recognized in making comparisons between Mao and either Lenin or Stalin. Lenin's early death removed him from the contentions arising later so that the deification of his person and the canonization of his writings became weapons for his immediate followers in their struggle over the succession and in subsequent policy disputes. Mao's position is quite different. Still being alive, he has become the leading participant in struggles in which he uses his own deification and canonization in order to resolve the problem of succession and the policy disputes associated with that problem. Again, Stalin was the disciple who won out in the struggles for the succession following Lenin's death and in the absence of any clear settlement of that succession by Lenin himself. The purges instigated by Stalin in the 1930's were well removed from that question; they could be compared to Mao's present situation only if instead Lenin had lived and had instigated these purges in order to designate his successor and make certain basic policy decisions binding upon him and the Party leadership.

There is reason to anticipate some deification of Mao after his death, as old and young followers alike seek to preserve the power of his charisma for themselves and the community at large.[18] At present Mao appears to anticipate just such a development. By laying the ground work not only for the choice of his successor but for the terms in which that successor will be obliged to implement the legacy of Maoist revolutionary achievements, he may be attempting to foreclose the gross misuse of his charisma by followers whose interest in institutionalization is greater than his own. It is an arresting thought that Mao's effort to replace the party elite with new men and to employ the Red Guards as an instrument of "permanent revolution" is in part an old man's

[17] Quoted in Gene T. Hsiao, "The Background and Development of 'The Proletarian Cultural Revolution,'" *Asian Survey*, Vol. VII (June 1967), p. 392. Mr. Hsiao has suggested to me that the reference to "God" is meant ironically, and the statement itself is clearly polemical. But these considerations do not, I think, affect the interpretation suggested here.

[18] Cf. Weber's discussion of the impulse behind the routinization of charisma in *Theory of Social and Economic Organization*, pp. 364–366.

struggle over the use that is to be made of his work and his person by those who will live after he is gone.

In conclusion it is appropriate to consider the distinction between charismatic leadership and leadership *sans phrase*, to which I alluded earlier. The term "charisma" is used indiscriminately, because this distinction is difficult to make in practice, though not in theory. All types of leadership are alike in that they involve an ambivalent interaction between leaders and led. A leader demands unconditional obedience, because he does not want his performance to be tested against criteria over which he has no control. Such tests jeopardize his authoritative right to command. On the other hand, the led withhold an ultimate surrender of their will (if only in the form of mental reservations), because they do not want to forego their last chance for a quid pro quo, i.e., for a gain through effective leadership in exchange for the obedience shown. Yet to withhold unconditional obedience in this way always runs the risk that leadership will fail us, because we have not shown our ultimate devotion to duty. The interactions between leaders and led probably trace an erratic path between this Scylla and Charybdis. The hazards of cumulative causation (as actions and reactions reenforce each other) and the reluctance of most men to face the ultimate consequences of their acts frequently lead to a tempering of demands and expectations on both sides. By not claiming ultimate authority and demanding unconditional obedience leaders can avoid being challenged and yet hope to accomplish a modicum of success. And the led are ready to obey when no ultimate commitment is demanded of them, because a mixture of acquiescence and performance leaves them free to hope for benefits with only a moderate inconvenience to themselves. In theory it is easy to see that "charisma" makes its appearance when leaders and led are convinced that these easy accommodations are no longer enough, when consummate belief, on one side, and the promptings of enthusiasm, despair, or hope, on the other, imperatively call for unconditional authority and obedience. In theory it is even easy to see that "charisma" appears to be present and yet is in jeopardy, when such convictions animate the leader *or* the led, but not both simultaneously. There are many historical examples of a leader who feels the call but cannot find a following, or of people at large searching in vain for a leader who will satisfy their longing for a miracle. Thus, charisma appears to occur frequently because the search for it continues. But genuine charisma is a rare event, born as it is of a belief in the mysterious gift of one man which that man shares with those who follow him.

Struggle against Power:
Notes on Indian Political Behavior

MYRON WEINER

India's experiment with democratic institutions is still only an experiment. Although India adopted a parliamentary system when she achieved independence in 1947 and has thus far been able to maintain her democratic institutions with much more success than some other newly independent Asian nations, no observer can have complete confidence in their stability. Indians have had to adjust from the role of natives in a country occupied by an imperialist power to that of citizens in a democracy, and the adjustment has not been easy. Traditional attitudes have a way of persisting and are not always readily accommodated to a parliamentary system of government.

This article will examine several pre-independence attitudes that persist in India today as obstacles to the growth of stable democratic institutions and will conclude with a brief discussion of the extent to which some of these attitudes have been weakened. Such traditional attitudes are not the only elements which affect India's democratic prospects and current political behavior; nevertheless, they are essential factors which are frequently overlooked. They center on the problems of political power, civil disobedience, and the use of violence.

At the core of any democratic system is an acceptance of certain basic attitudes toward law, authority, political power, violence, and the like which in the long run may have a greater influence than the formal legal structure in shaping the development of the political system. In the absence of agreement on these attitudes, the legal structure becomes a façade behind which the system really operates; the gap between law and practice grows wide and democracy flourishes in name only. For an example we have only to look at prewar Japan, where a semblance of parliamentary government existed although government was actually authoritarian.

In attempting, therefore, to discover the prospects for the success of democratic institutions in India, it is important not only to understand the country's rate of economic development, the political strength of the ruling party, and the kind of constitutional structure that has evolved; one must also understand those traditional attitudes which affect current political behavior, and their impact upon the democratic system.

1. POLITICAL CALCULATIONS
AND RENUNCIATION OF POWER

One prerequisite for a viable democratic system is the existence of a willingness on the part of political groups to make political calculations. That is to

From World Politics, Vol. VIII (April 1956), pp. 392–403. Reprinted by permission of the author and publisher.

MYRON WEINER is Professor of Political Science, Massachusetts Institute of Technology. He is the author of Indian Political Behavior (1955), Party Politics in India (1957), The Politics of Scarcity (1962), Political Change in South Asia (1963), and Party Building in a New Nation (1967). He has co-authored, edited, and co-edited several other books in recent years.

say, political parties must be concerned with their electoral prospects and must be willing to make compromises and join or work with other groups in order to increase their own strength. A viable democratic system has little room for party sectarianism. In India, as in nearly all the other nations of South and Southeast Asia which recently won independence, there has been a marked unwillingness on the part of political parties and interest groups to make compromises and merge with one another. As a result, there are in India today some fifty political parties with seats in either Parliament or the state assemblies.

The phenomenon of party splintering is a rather complicated one and cannot be dealt with exhaustively here. Needless to say, it is a phenomenon which may have a profound effect on the growth of stable government. One reason for such splintering is the absence of a basic consensus on the nature of the state. A number of India's fifty parties are Hindu communal parties that reject the secular order. Others are provincial and linguistic parties that have strong allegiances to local caste or language groups. Still others, like the Communist and Marxist left parties, reject the democratic parliamentary framework.

But even among political parties which agree on basic values, political splintering is widespread in India. Underlying this fragmentation is a lack of concern on the part of the political leaders and their followers for the electoral consequences of their actions. When the Socialists broke from the Congress Party in 1948 and when a group of Gandhians broke from it in 1951, the rank and file of both these groups cared little about the effect of their actions on their electoral prospects. Similarly, when the Rashtriya Swayamsevak Sangh (RSS), a Hindu organization of young people, decided to form a political party, its members were more concerned with maintaining their individuality than with finding some existing party in which they could work effectively. Again, when a few of the leaders of the Hindu Mahasabha and Jan Sangh, the two largest Hindu communal parties, tried to arrange a merger, the rank and file and the other party leaders were more interested in maintaining their own organizations than in increasing their political effectiveness.

An Indian Aneurin Bevan would hardly have fought for long to maintain his position within his party. He would most likely have resigned the moment there was talk of expulsion: he would have condemned the party, its leaders, and its program and proceeded with his own followers to form a new party. He might have given some thought to his electoral chances, but that would have been a secondary consideration. And if he considered his electoral prospects at all, his assessment probably would have been unrealistic.

Why do political consequences or calculations (in the sense of taking electoral prospects into account) play such a small part in the splits that have occurred in Indian political parties? To some extent, this absence of political calculations can be traced to the ambivalent feeling of many Indian politicians and of the party rank and file toward political power as an objective. Perhaps this appears to be a contradiction in terms, since political parties are by nature instruments for achieving power. But it is possible for a political party to exist, to have an ideology, to make demands upon the government, to organize demonstrations and strikes, and yet to be unwilling to assume the responsibility of running a government, and to feel at heart that there is something "dirty" and unpleasant about the whole business of politics.

How widespread such anti-political power feelings are can be easily illustrated. For instance, there are the many members of the Rashtriya Swayamsevak Sangh in the Jan Sangh Party [1] who believe that their objective of changing Indian society and revitalizing Hinduism will come about not through the attainment of political power but through propaganda and example. There are sections of the Praja Socialist Party which view the entire political process skeptically. Many of the party members are Gandhians who want to devote their lives to constructive work in the villages or to *bhoodan* work (voluntary land-collecting) and hope thereby to bring about a change in society without governmental intervention. There are Socialist followers of the late M. N. Roy who advocate a society in which there are no political parties and where change would be brought about by activity in villages and factories. And then there are those Socialists who, without being articulate ideological anarchists, nevertheless feel general contempt for the political process and for political power itself. Similarly, anti-power feelings can even be found in the Marxist left parties, many of whose members have abandoned politics to become *sannyasis* (monks) at the famous Aurobindo *ashram* in Pondicherry.

These anti-power feelings, which exist in nearly every opposition party in India,[2] are in large part the product of certain traditional values. Traditionally, high status in India has not been associated with political power. Status was traditionally a function of one's position in a caste hierarchy in which the *Brahman* priest rather than the *Kshatriya*, or ruler-warrior, was at the top.[3] Special status was, however, accorded to those persons, almost irrespective of their caste position, who strove for *maksha* (salvation), an ideal achieved through renunciation, sacrifice and, above all, detachment from this world. The key notion is "detachment." One should not have any desire for wealth or power, nor any strong attachments to friends, or one's wife, or children. There may be love, but it must be for all creatures or for God, and for no one more than others.[4] One must be detached from all worldly desires.[5]

"Renunciation," "sacrifice," and "detachment" are not the ideals by which

[1] Jan Sangh is the largest Hindu communal party and the fourth largest party in India. The other three are the Congress Party, the Praja Socialist Party, and the Communist Party of India.

[2] The one exception being the Communist Party, perhaps the most Westernized of all the Indian parties and one which is completely concerned with the objective of winning power.

[3] D. Mackenzie Brown, *The White Umbrella: Indian Political Thought from Manu to Gandhi* (Berkeley, Calif.: University of California Press, 1953), p. 17.

[4] See, for example, M. K. Gandhi, *Gandhi's Autobiography — The Story of My Experiments with Truth* (Washington, D.C.: Public Affairs Press, 1948), pp. 31–32, in which Gandhi says, "He who would be friends with God must remain alone, or make the whole world his friends."

[5] A disciple of Gandhi wrote that a central teaching of the *Bhagavad Gita* which played a major part in Gandhi's thinking was the ideal of *mishkamakarma* (action without the desire for result). Gopinath Dhawan, *The Political Philosophy of Mahatma Gandhi* (Ahmedabad: Navajivan Publishing House, 1946), p. 13.

all men live; only a few can choose this path. For the rest, each man must live in accordance with the duty assigned to him by his caste. In the West, too, the religious life of withdrawal has been confined to a relative few; what makes this notion noteworthy in India is, first, the number of people who leave established positions to devote themselves to the search for salvation; and second, the fact that these ideals are still widely accepted in modern India and have considerable impact even on the lives of those who do not withdraw.

It is also interesting to note that Hindu tradition, while it accords high status to the *Kshatriya* ruler, holds it important that others should not strive for positions of authority. Each man must accept his own *dharma* (duty) and perform his duty well. Better to perform one's own duty poorly, say the scriptures, than to perform someone else's duty well. Authority is acceptable, but to struggle for a position of authority is not.

As an aside, it might be mentioned here that the Indian tradition of asceticism (which is an extension of the notion of detachment) has posed a dilemma for Gandhian constructive workers who, while they live an ascetic life themselves, advocate the betterment of the villagers' lot. How can one accept the goal of a higher standard of living, but continue to believe in the principles of asceticism? One possible reconciliation — perhaps an unconscious one — seems to be for the Gandhian constructive worker to help the villager without encouraging him to want to improve his lot. Perhaps this is why some of the Gandhian constructive projects have possessed overtones of paternalism in spite of the Gandhian principle of teaching the villagers to help themselves.

The ascetic ideal does, however, have the beneficial effect of discouraging conspicuous displays of wealth. By emphasizing asceticism and village constructive work, Gandhi made one of his great contributions to Indian political and social development: he helped to narrow the gap between the educated classes and the villagers, a gap which in other countries has been much wider and has constituted a major obstacle to economic development and social welfare.

Under British rule, Indian feelings toward government were ambivalent. On the one hand, politics grew in importance as the state took on more functions. But on the other hand, cooperation with the alien British rulers became anathema as the nationalist movement grew. Indians who accepted office were looked upon with some opprobrium. Even after 1936 when the Congress Party agreed to assume office in a number of provinces, virtually the entire leftist section of the party denounced the move. And while one section of the Congress Party talked of the uses to which an Indian national government could be put when independence came, another section under Gandhi continued to emphasize the need to change society by non-governmental activities. With this in mind, Gandhi created a large number of village constructive work organizations. Gandhi's own attitude toward power is illustrated by the story of his reply to a proposal by some of his friends that he become the first Governor-General of India after the achievement of independence. Gandhi is reported to have said that were he to accept office for even one minute, he would negate all of the principles for which he stood.

Today, even with a nationalist government, there are widespread feelings against the "scramble for ministerial posts," especially among those in opposition. Many Indian intellectuals are prone to feel a certain contempt for those in political office, and to question their motives. These feelings, however, are not so widespread within the Congress Party, since most of those who felt this way, including many Gandhian constructive workers, have left the party. For those who have remained in it, a government post now confers considerable prestige. But this feeling is not generally shared by those outside the Congress Party. Any mention of a "deal" which would result in the award of ministerial posts is likely to be looked upon not as shrewd politics but as dirty politics. This no doubt motivated part of the criticism of the Socialists — which was voiced by many of the Socialists themselves — when the Praja Socialist Party accepted power in the southern state of Travancore-Cochin and formed a minority government with the support of the Congress Party.

These anti-political power feelings not only influence Indian attitudes toward government, but also affect attitudes toward leadership. Politically active Indians, particularly those in the non-Marxist parties, prefer their leaders to be detached even from formal power within their own organizations. The leaders, too, prefer to be outside the formal structure. Gandhi, for example, was not even a dues-paying member of the Congress Party. The leader of the Praja Socialist Party, Jayaprakash Narayan, no longer holds any office in the party. The founder-leader of the Hindu communal party, Ram Rajya Parishad, is Swami Karapatri, a religious leader who is not a member of the party he leads. Golwakar (usually called "Guruji," or "Reverend Teacher") is the recognized leader of the RSS and the ideological leader of Jan Sangh, but he holds no position in the latter. Savarkar is the accepted leader of the Hindu Mahasabha but likewise has no official position. All of these men have reputations for "sacrifice" and "detachment," and by virtue of their very lack of political attachments are effective in settling the factional disputes that constantly plague every Indian party.

II. STRUGGLE FOR POWER

In a society whose members have been wielding political power for only a short time, one can expect few rules about the just and unjust ways of using power. In India, this situation is compounded by the absence in tradition of any notion of a universal system of ethics. There are no Ten Commandments: each man has his own *dharma*, and if he wants to achieve a better position in his next life, he must act in accordance with his prescribed role. Each *dharma* prescribes its own ethical rules. While on the one hand, for example, there is a tradition of non-violence among some sects of Hinduism, on the other hand, in the *Bhagavad Gita*, one of the most famous and popular religious texts, Krishna tells the warrior Arjuna that he must kill because it is his duty to do so. Another famous work, the *Arthasastra*, describes the ways of winning, keeping, and using power in a manner which outdoes Machiavelli's *Prince* in its apparent disregard for moral principles. But these seemingly non-religious attitudes are nonetheless part of the religious tradition. The ethical rules for the behavior of a *Kshatriya* ruler are different from those of a *Brahman* priest, just as their *dharma* differs.

When power does become a goal in a society in which an ideal is the renunciation of power, and where no system of ethical rules has developed concerning its uses, it is frequently sought in chaotic fashion and used in "unethical" ways (in the conventional Western sense of the word). This may help to explain why in the 1952 elections nearly six thousand independents contested seats for the various state legislatures — averaging nearly two independent candidates per seat — and why the Congress Party was flooded with office-seekers shortly after independence. This may also help to explain why before the 1952 elections state governments were frequently handicapped by politicians who used their government posts to make money and aid relatives and friends, and why corruption and nepotism have often been practiced openly and in rather crude ways.

The struggle *against* power therefore has its converse in the struggle *for* power. Each reinforces the other. The views of the anti-power personality, especially, are reinforced by observation of the behavior of those who struggle for power. Lack of familiarity with democratic rules breeds irresponsibility and, in turn, irresponsibility breeds a greater contempt for the democratic system.

III. LAW AND CIVIL DISOBEDIENCE

In pre-independence India, civil disobedience, or what Gandhi called *satyagraha* (truth force), was a major weapon against the British rulers. So long as this refusal to obey government law was directed against an alien ruler, law-breaking was accepted as a weapon by virtually all politically active Indians. But the British emphasis on the rule of law had a profound effect on Indian intellectuals, especially those who entered the legal profession. Gandhi himself was a lawyer and although he urged civil disobedience against the British, he emphasized respect for the law. Civil disobedience was frequently, although not always, directed against administrative rulings rather than the law, and it was often paralleled by legal action in the courts by Indian barristers. But whatever Gandhi's intentions, the over-all effect of *satyagraha* could only be a receptivity to the violation of law on the part of the Indian masses. So long as law was the product of an alien rule, British attempts at making law legitimate through reference to democratic notions could hardly be convincing to most Indians.

But with the achievement of freedom, the use of *satyagraha* came into question. Does organized law-breaking, even when it is non-violent, have a place in a democratic society? The Socialists, who during the past few years have accepted many of Gandhi's principles, conducted *satyagrahas* on several occasions in Uttar Pradesh, Bombay, and elsewhere against what they considered to be injustices on the part of the government. Eviction of tenants and high taxes — especially high land or irrigation taxes — have frequently been the targets of Socialist civil disobedience movements. While Gandhians have criticized the misuse of *satyagraha*, in principle they continue to support it.

Harijan, the official Gandhian weekly, published a note by its late editor, K. G. Mashruwala, in defense of *satyagraha:* "Satyagraha — insistence on truth — does not depend upon the form of Government. . . . Even if it needs to take the form of individual or organized non-violent civil resistance of an unjust law or order, or of non-cooperation with a general or particular evil, or of a resort to fast, a *satyagrahi* [one who takes part in a *satyagraha*] cannot avoid it even in a democracy . . . it has to be taken after attempts of bringing about conversion through arguments and discussion and other legal remedies have failed . . . in a well-governed democracy, there should be few occasions for resorting to it. But it cannot be entirely ruled out in a proper case."

The same issue of *Harijan* published a reply by Pandit Pant, then Chief Minister of Uttar Pradesh and now Home Minister in Nehru's cabinet: ". . . in matters of conscience — on spiritual issues — one is always entitled to offer Satyagraha. But, for a democratic set-up, I had always stressed the importance of settling political differences by argument and persuasion. . . . If Satyagraha is to be resorted to or threatened every time there is a difference of opinion, then public opinion does not receive the respect that is due to it. . . . It would, no doubt, be a matter of conscience if one were forced to offer Satyagraha in a case where the issues are clear, and the Government's stand is patently untenable, and where before any recourse to Satyagraha the pros and cons have been examined in an impersonal, detached and dispassionate manner, and all other remedies have been exhausted. He who decides on Satyagraha should have a clear conscience and an open mind: his judgment should be detached and his decision should be unbiased. But in the midst of political partisanship, how many are there who can, or will, act in this manner? Democracy would lose much of its significance if, in the name of Satyagraha, everyone were to take it as his unfettered right to incite the masses, as much as possible, against the system of Government established by the people's elected representatives in a democratic State, in order to belittle and resist the law of the land in a concerted manner. . . ." [6]

In spite of the protests of the Indian government and of most Congress Party leaders, *satyagraha* has been applied on a number of occasions by several political parties since independence. The *satyagraha* in Andhra, culminating in the fast-unto-death by a Telugu leader, was a major factor in the government's decision to sanction the formation of the state of Andhra out of the Telugu-speaking areas of Madras.

Non-violent law-breaking likewise played a large part in the Jammu and Kashmir agitation in early 1953. The major Hindu communal organizations, the Jamma Praja Parishad, Bharatiya Jan Sangh, the Hindu Mahasabha, and Ram Rajya Parishad joined together to agitate for "full and unqualified" accession of Jammu and Kashmir to India. Jan Sangh and the Hindu Mahasabha

---

[6] This and the preceding quotation are taken from *Indian Press Digests* (Berkeley, Calif.: Bureau of International Relations of the Department of Political Science, University of California), II, No. 1 (October 1953), p. 81; reprinted from *Harijan*, September 20, 1952, pp. 253–55.

were particularly active in Delhi, where they organized demonstrations in defiance of police orders. Syama Prasad Mookerjee, the Jan Sangh leader, defied the government by entering Kashmir without the necessary government permit. He was subsequently arrested, as were a large number of leaders and party members who took part in the *satyagraha*.

Civil disobedience movements have occurred throughout India since independence, and the Indian government has in virtually every instance used the power of state to suppress them. In spite of the fact that India is no longer subject to foreign rule, most organizations outside the government or the Congress Party still believe that *satyagraha* is a legitimate technique for achieving one's objectives. Their feeling is that when they fail to achieve their objectives through regular channels — petitions, elections, delegations to the government, and the other devices for exerting influence within a democratic society — non-legal devices ought to be employed. Those who think this way do not accept the notion of the sanctity of law which underlies the power of most Western democratic governments, where legal rules legitimize the authority of government.

In India, political power has not yet been made legitimate. The justification for power by reference to *dharma*, whatever role it once may have played, ceased to be a justification with the arrival of the British. Instead, the British introduced the concept of "justice under law." Although this idea made considerable inroads on Indian thinking during the nineteenth century, so long as the national government was under foreign rule, the bulk of the nationalist movement — as we have already noted — saw no "justice under law." Thus at the time of independence, India was not, to use Max Weber's term, a society based on "rational-legal authority," that is, a society in which authority is made legitimate by reference to law. Opposition party members and apparently large numbers of peasants and workers do not yet feel the restraints of law. Injustice, whether it be by act of government or of landlords, is greeted by a readiness to violate law or contract.[7]

---

[7] Although Gandhi personally rejected the use of government to achieve the kind of society he envisaged, he did contribute a device for channeling resentment against government. While he was apparently prepared, *under any kind of government* (even in a democracy), to violate laws he considered unjust, violations were to be accomplished in a non-violent way. In a society such as India, where there are few self-restraints to prevent violation of law and where the population is becoming increasingly aware of the existence of "injustice," the choice is not merely between abiding by or violating law, but is frequently between non-violent and violent law-breaking. Gandhi's contribution was a special set of non-violent, albeit non-democratic, rules by which laws could be violated. The degree of violence might be far greater in India today had not Gandhi provided such a set of rules. As Lois Murphy noted in a recent study (Chapter 4 in Gardner Murphy, *In the Minds of Men*, New York, Basic Books, 1953), in a society in which there is a tradition of little violence and where consequently there are no rules that put some restraint on its employment (rules such as "Fight like a man," "Don't hit below the belt," and other canons of "fair play" and "sportsmanship"), when violence is committed, it may be even more extreme and cruel than in a society where its use is customary.

IV. LEARNING THE RULES

It is not surprising to find that Asian countries, having suddenly adopted political structures of a Western type, are struggling to accommodate their traditions to the new institutions. As this article has indicated, despite India's success thus far with democratic institutions, there still persist traditional attitudes which do not always facilitate adjustments. India's problem is the same as that of many other Asian countries: how to adapt traditional attitudes to a rational-legal democratic political system.

There are, however, a number of elements at work in India that tend to ease her adjustment to democracy and make the prospects for her political future more hopeful than those of many other Asian countries.

First of all, the intensity and duration of the Western impact have been greater in India than in nearly any other Asian country. Traditional Indian attitudes and institutions have been profoundly affected. A large, Westernized university system has been established, and English has become the language of the educated community. The administrative and military services, among the most efficient in Asia, are Westernized. The number of lawyers inculcated with Western legal notions is very large, probably considerably larger than one finds, for instance, in Japan. Furthermore, even before 1947, many Indians had gained considerable experience in the state legislatures and in high government posts.

It is not possible here to analyze exhaustively the extensive impact which the West has had on India and the remarkable modifications which have been made not only in social and political practices, but in religious and political theory as well. What is important to note, however, is that Hinduism has shown a remarkable capacity to assimilate and integrate Western notions. In large part, traditions are being modified rather than supplanted.

Secondly, those traditional attitudes which are not consistent with democratic rules are beginning to break down as Indian politicians and the party rank and file grow accustomed to a parliamentary system. It takes time to learn new rules, and only since the 1952 elections have most Indians begun to feel that they are living under a new political system. For example, minor parties are increasingly recognizing the necessity to make compromises and merge with other parties to augment their strength.

In the 1952 elections, the splintering of the opposition allowed the Congress Party to win a clear majority of the seats in Parliament with only 45 per cent of the popular vote. But the absence of proportional representation, and the presence of a system in which a plurality vote means victory, may eventually force some of the smaller groups either to merge or to resort to extra-legal, extra-parliamentary devices to avoid extinction. In the long run, the successful operation of the parliamentary system is likely to bring about a change in Indian attitudes toward political power, especially as government successfully meets the needs of the community. Likewise, if the gap between expectations and fulfillment is narrowed, and if discontented groups discover that they can achieve results through the regular channels of a parliamentary system, there is likely to be a decrease in civil disobedience. Even now, although civil disobedience is practiced, there is considerable criticism of it and those who have violated the law have found it necessary to explain publicly why in a parliamentary system they must resort to civil disobedience.

The essential point is that the sheer survival and operation of stable democratic government in India are in themselves perhaps the major factors that will contribute toward the breakdown of traditional obstacles to the democratic system and toward persuading opposition groups to accept the system. Political stability is a function of many complex factors, but underlying them all is the simple matter of survival for a substantial period of time. "Nothing succeeds like success" still makes a good political axiom. If the present democratic institutions of India continue to function effectively, if law and order are maintained and stable government continues in the various states as well as in the central government, faith in the system is likely to grow. If Indians come to recognize that their aspirations can be fulfilled within the democratic system, then they are likely to operate within the rules.

BIBLIOGRAPHICAL GUIDE

Rather than give an extensive listing of titles, which would be self-defeating, we make the following suggestions for further readings in the hope that students will explore one or another of the areas touched on in this volume. The suggestions are ordered in keeping with the outline of the Reader, and they are confined to English titles. Each of the selections, of course, contains numerous references to the literature as well.

A. *Introduction* and B. *Perspectives*

The problems touched on in Sections A and B are old. One of the most lucid and comprehensive discussions of "state and society" that combines an institutional emphasis with intellectual history is contained in Ernest Barker, *Principles of Social and Political Theory* (Oxford: Clarendon Press, 1951), Books 1 and 2.

As yet, no comprehensive account of "comparative political sociology" is available, but some problems in this area are explored in Stanislav Andreski, *The Uses of Comparative Sociology* (Berkeley: University of California Press, 1965). The most complete introduction to problems of historical sociology is still contained in Max Weber's posthumous work *Wirtschaft und Gesellschaft*. An English translation of the whole text by Guenther Roth and Claus Wittich, *Economy and Society*, has been published in 1968 by the Bedminister Press and the Macmillan Company. For an analysis of Weber's approach to political sociology, see Reinhard Bendix, *Max Weber: An Intellectual Portrait* (Garden City, N.Y.: Doubleday Anchor Books, 1962), especially pp. 285–494; developments of this approach in relation to the work of Tocqueville are found in Reinhard Bendix, *Nation-Building and Citizenship* (New York: John Wiley & Sons, 1964).

The functional approach to comparative politics is best represented in the writings of Gabriel Almond. Following his introduction to Almond and Coleman (eds.), *The Politics of the Developing Areas* (Princeton, N.J.: Princeton University Press, 1960), he has reformulated his position in "A Developmental Approach to Political Systems," *World Politics*, Vol. XVI (1965), pp. 183–214. A variety of contributions from a largely functionalist standpoint are contained in Jason L. Finkle and Richard W. Gable (eds.), *Political Development and Social Change* (New York: John Wiley & Sons, 1966).

For a general review of political sociology see Scott Greer and Peter Orleans, "Political Sociology," in R. E. L. Faris (ed.), *Handbook of Modern Sociology* (Chicago: Rand McNally & Co., 1964). This review points up the lack of theoretically oriented comparative studies in this area and the resulting deficiency of general explanations of political behavior and institutions. Note, however, the book by Ernest Gellner, *Thought and Change* (London: Weiden-feld & Nicolson, 1964; Chicago: University of Chicago Press, 1965), which contains a probing comparative analysis of industrialization and its political consequences.

C. Pre-Modern Politics

A brief, illuminating introduction to politics in the absence of the nation-state is contained in Clifford Geertz, "Politics Past, Politics Present," *European Journal of Sociology*, Vol. VIII (1967), pp. 1–14. This contribution by an anthropologist may be related to the comprehensive survey of anthropological materials by Lucy Mair, *Primitive Government* (Baltimore: Penguin Books, 1962). Both may be compared with two analyses of pre-modern politics which were precursors of the modern state; namely, Marc Bloch, *Feudal Society* (Chicago: University of Chicago Press, 1961), Part VII, and Max Weber, *Economy and Society* (Totowa, N.J.: The Bedminster Press, 1968), chapters on patrimonialism and feudalism. Other related works are S. N. Eisenstadt, *The Political Systems of Empires* (New York: Free Press of Glencoe, 1963), and C. H. McIlwain, "Medieval Estates," *The Cambridge Medieval History* (New York: The Macmillan Co.; Cambridge, Eng.: The University Press, 1932), Vol. 7, Chap. 23, written by a sociologist and a constitutional historian, respectively.

The selections and references for Asian, African, and ancient as well as medieval European conditions might well be supplemented by references to Latin America. See, for example, Richard N. Morse, "Toward a Theory of Spanish American Government," *Journal of the History of Ideas*, Vol. 15; Frank Tannenbaum, *Ten Keys to Latin America* (New York: Alfred A. Knopf, 1962); and Eric Wolf and E. C. Hansen, "Caudillo Politics: A Struc-tural Analysis," *Comparative Studies in Society and History*, Vol. IX (1967), pp. 168–179. Two neglected older works are also worth mentioning: Cecil Jane, *Liberty and Despotism in Spanish America* (Oxford: The Clarendon Press, 1929), and Duncan Aikman, *The All-American Front* (New York: Doubleday, Doran & Co., 1940). This last book contains a striking description and analysis of Latin-American politics by a perceptive journalist, albeit hidden under a meaningless and misleading title.

D. The Western Experience: Politics of Transition

The selections in this section may be supplemented by a reading of Ernest Barker, *The Development of Public Services in Western Europe 1660–1930* (London; New York: Oxford University Press, 1945), which compares the growth of the state in England, France, and Prussia in the fields of administra-tion, conscription, education, and taxation. The same theme is treated with special emphasis on the social implications of bureaucratization in a case study of one of these countries, Prussia, by Hans Rosenberg, *Bureaucracy, Aristocracy and Autocracy* (Cambridge, Mass.: Harvard University Press, 1958). The wider political and cultural context of these developments in the important European countries as well as overseas receives comprehensive treatment in the several contributions to J. O. Lindsay (ed.), *The New Cambridge Modern History*, VII. *The Old Regime, 1713–1763* (Cambridge, Eng.: The University Press, 1957). A briefer comparative account of many of the same materials is contained in Walter Dorn, *Competition for Empire, 1740–1763* (New York: Harper Torchbooks, 1963).

On the rise of democratic institutions the classic work is Tocqueville's *The Old Regime and the French Revolution* (Garden City, N.Y.: Doubleday Anchor Books, 1955). The case of England is particularly crucial in view of its influence as a model for other nations. There is considerable controversy among historians in interpreting the developments that led to the "politics of notables" of the 18th century. For an introduction to the main themes see Lawrence Stone (ed.), *Social Change and Revolution in England 1540–1640* (London: Longmans, Green & Co., 1965); the volume includes a useful bibliography. An interesting interpretation of the consequences of these developments is contained in J. H. Plumb, *The Origins of Political Stability: England 1675–1725* (London: The Macmillan Co., 1967). Mention should also be made of the comparative study of revolutions. Among older works the major contribution is still Crane Brinton's *The Anatomy of Revolution* (New York: Vintage Books, 1952); among recent works note William Kornhauser, "Rebellion and Political Development," in Harry Eckstein (ed.), *Internal War: Problems and Approaches* (New York: Free Press of Glencoe, 1964), pp. 142–156. The outstanding contribution by a comparative historian is R. R. Palmer, *The Age of the Democratic Revolution* (Princeton, N.J.: Princeton University Press, 1959, 1964), 2 vols.

E. *The Western Experience: Politics of the Modern State*

E1. *Social Groups Considered Politically*. The three selections in this section go back to previous work that should be mentioned. Bendix' essay is a comparative application of an analysis first developed with reference to England by T. H. Marshall, "Citizenship and Social Class," *Class, Citizenship, and Social Development* (Garden City, N.Y.: Doubleday & Co., 1964). Ehrmann's contribution is based on studies of interest groups in selected countries, published previously in Henry Ehrmann (ed.), *Interest Groups on Four Continents* (Pittsburgh: University of Pittsburgh Press, 1960). A very illuminating case study of the changing relations between interest groups and government in American society is contained in Henry Ehrmann, "Functional Changes of Democratic Institutions in the United States," in Ehrmann (ed.), *Democracy in a Changing Society* (New York: Frederick A. Praeger, 1964), pp. 24–52. Finally, Lipset's essay may be compared with his own earlier discussion of related problems in *Political Man* (Garden City, N.Y.: Doubleday & Co., 1960) as well as with two quite divergent treatments of problems of representation in Alfred de Grazia, *Public and Republic* (New York: Alfred A. Knopf, 1951), and William Kornhauser, *The Politics of Mass Society* (New York: Free Press of Glencoe, 1959). Cf. also Kornhauser's essay " 'Power Elite' or 'Veto Groups'?" in Reinhard Bendix and S. M. Lipset (eds.), *Class, Status and Power*, 2nd ed. (New York: The Free Press, 1966), pp. 210–218. On the mobilization of social groups into political participation in a modern society, see Karl Deutsch, *Nationalism and Social Communication* (Cambridge, Mass.: The M.I.T. Press; New York: John Wiley & Sons, 1953), and more recently Seymour M. Lipset (ed.), *Student Politics* (New York: Basic Books, 1967).

E2. *Structure of Authority*. Not many detailed, comparative case studies are available which go beyond the conventional treatments of comparative government. Therefore, it is worth singling out for special attention the excellent analysis by Z. Brzezinski and S. P. Huntington, *Political Power: USA/USSR* (New York: Viking Press, 1964), which deals not only with the structure of authority but also with problems of legitimacy and hence is relevant for the next section as well. A comparative study of bureaucracy with an emphasis on the Western experience is contained in Fritz Morstein Marx, *The Administrative State* (Chicago: University of Chicago Press, 1957); this book supplements the material covered in Barker's *Development of Public Services* (London; New York: Oxford University Press, 1945), mentioned above. The distinctiveness of the French bureaucratic culture pattern against this general background is the subject of Part IV of Michel Crozier, *The Bureaucratic Phenomenon* (Chicago: University of Chicago Press, 1964). Cf. also Bruce Hackett, *Higher Civil Servants in California* (Institute of Governmental Studies, University of California, Berkeley, 1967), which relates studies of the social recruitment of administrators to changing trends in modern government.

Special attention should be called to comparative works dealing with the relation between the state and economic development. Note particularly Alexander Gerschenkron, *Economic Backwardness in Historical Perspective* (Cambridge, Mass.: Belknap Press of Harvard University, 1962); Hugh G. J. Aitken (ed.), *The State and Economic Growth* (New York: Social Science Research Council, 1959); and Eli Heckscher, *Mercantilism* (London: Allen & Unwin; New York: The Macmillan Co., 1955), 2 vols.

A useful collection of articles on other aspects of authority is available in Harry Eckstein and David E. Apter (eds.), *Comparative Politics* (New York: Free Press of Glencoe, 1963).

E3. *Aspects of Legitimacy*. One comprehensive discussion of problems of legitimacy is contained in R. M. MacIver, *The Web of Government* (New York: The Macmillan Co., 1965). The student can also profit from examining side by side three such different treatments of the same problem as Joseph Tussman, *Obligation and the Body Politic* (New York: Oxford University Press, 1960); Morton Grodzins, *The Loyal and the Disloyal* (Chicago: University of Chicago Press, 1956); and Gabriel Almond and Sidney Verba, *The Civic Culture* (Princeton, N.J.: Princeton University Press, 1963).

The several selections in this section raise questions which can be explored further by reference to some of the following writings. One of the most important comparative legal studies in recent years which follows lines of inquiry similar to the studies by Pekelis, is Otto Kirchheimer, *Political Justice* (Princeton, N.J.: Princeton University Press, 1961). An earlier work by the same writer (together with G. Rusche), *Punishment and Social Structure* (New York: Columbia University Press, 1939), is also relevant. Dahrendorf's essay can now be read together with his own more sustained treatment of related problems in *Society and Democracy in Germany* (Garden City, N.Y.: Doubleday & Co., 1967); the book is written from the standpoint of a comparative analysis of democracy. Since Germany and Japan have repeatedly been compared, it is instructive to relate Dahrendorf's work to that of Masao Maruyama, *Thought and Behavior in Modern Japanese Politics*, ed. by Ivan Morris (London; New York: Oxford University Press, 1963). Rimlinger's analysis may be followed up by reference to Brzezinski and Huntington, *Political Power: USA/USSR* (New York: Viking Press, 1964), cited above; Z. Brzezinski, *Ideology and Power in Soviet Politics* (New York: Frederick A. Praeger, 1962); Yehoshua Arieli, *Individualism and Nationalism in American Ideology* (Cambridge, Mass.: Harvard University Press, 1964); and R. Bendix, *Work and Authority in Industry* (New York: John Wiley & Sons, 1956). In relation to the essay by Ben-David and Collins cf. *Student Politics* (New York: Basic Books, 1967), edited by Seymour M. Lipset, in which the article appeared, and Edward A. Shils, *The Intellectual between Tradition and Modernity: The Indian Situation* (The Hague: Mouton, 1961).

F. *Politics of Modernization: Western Impact and Native Response*

In an era of declining colonial regimes and independence movements it is easy to think of the origins and repercussions of the "Western impact" in too simple a fashion. From the "side of the West" it is also easy to guard against this deception. Hans Kohn's *The Idea of Nationalism* (New York: The Macmillan Co., 1944) provides a comprehensive comparative description of the background; and two studies of the 19th century, Eric Stokes, *The English Utilitarians and India* (Oxford: The Clarendon Press, 1959), and Ronald Robinson and John Gallagher, *Africa and the Victorians* (New York: St. Martin's Press, 1961), give a more detailed picture of British expansion. In this context mention should be made of a brilliant case study of the Western impact on India by Duncan M. Derrett, "The Administration of Hindu Law by the British," *Comparative Studies in Society and History*, Vol. IV (1961), pp. 10–52. Reference may also be made to a useful compilation of "theories of imperialism" by Harrison M. Wright (ed.), *The "New Imperialism"* (Boston: D. C. Heath & Co., 1961), which also has a good bibliography.

The perspective from "the other side" is also well represented. A comprehensive comparative survey is contained in Jan Romein, *The Asian Century* (Berkeley: University of California Press, 1965). A brief but telling juxtaposition of Western and Asian aspects of the Western impact is contained in Joseph Levenson (ed.), *European Expansion and the Counter-Example of Asia, 1300–1600* (Englewood Cliffs, N.J.: Spectrum Books, 1967). Levenson's own work, *Confucian China and Its Modern Fate* (Berkeley: University of California Press, 1958, 1964, 1965), 3 vols., is a major contribution to an understanding of the "crises of legitimacy" following the Western impact, as is Franco Venturi's *Roots of Revolution* (New York: Alfred A. Knopf, 1960) dealing with revolutionary movements in 19th-century Russia. Venturi's book and Von Laue's article may be supplemented by Theodore H. Von Laue, *Why Lenin,*

Why Stalin? (Philadelphia: J. B. Lippincott Co., 1964). For a dramatic expression of the African reaction to colonialism, drawing especially on the Algerian revolution, see Frantz Fanon, *The Wretched of the Earth* (New York: Grove Press, 1963, 1965); and a collection of materials on colonialism and its aftermath may be found in Immanuel Wallerstein (ed.), *Social Change, The Colonial Situation* (New York: John Wiley & Sons, 1966).

Other supplementations can be suggested. Furnivall's article is a very brief statement which derives from his own comprehensive studies, especially *Colonial Policy and Practice* (New York: New York University Press, 1948), in which he compares colonial policies in Indonesia and Burma. Furnivall's work reflects the writings of the Dutch economist, J. H. Boeke, especially *The Structure of Netherlands Indian Economy* (New York: Institute of Pacific Relations, 1942) and the brief, generalizing account in *The Interests of the Voiceless Far East* (Leiden: Universitaire Pers Leiden, 1948).

Several attempts at a comprehensive assessment on a comparative basis are also available. See, among others, John Plamenatz, *On Alien Rule and Self-Government* (London: Longmans, Green & Co., 1960); David Apter, *The Politics of Modernization* (Chicago: University of Chicago Press, 1965); Rupert Emerson, *From Empire to Nation* (Cambridge, Mass.: Harvard University Press, 1960); Cyril Black, *The Dynamics of Modernization* (New York: Harper & Row, 1966); Dankwart Rustow, *A World of Nations* (Washington, D.C.: The Brookings Institution, 1967); S. N. Eisenstadt, *Modernization: Protest and Change* (Englewood Cliffs, N.J.: Prentice-Hall, 1966); and the many other works cited in these studies. For a theoretical critique and an analysis of modernization as a process of international emulation, see Reinhard Bendix, "Tradition and Modernity Reconsidered," *Comparative Studies in Society and History*, Vol. IX (April 1967), pp. 292–346.

G. *Politics of Modernization: Search for a New Order*

G1. *Social Groups Considered Politically*. Since all modern societies have been "modernizing" at one time, there is a vast historical literature that appropriately belongs under this heading. Volumes 8–12 of *The New Cambridge Modern History* (Cambridge, Eng.: The University Press) provide ample factual and bibliographical information.

Considered in the more restricted context of the so-called developing countries, the relevant literature is still vast, though it may be useful to single out a few titles which will enable the student to explore further, starting with the selections we have chosen. Merle Kling's contribution may be followed up by a reading of the work of John J. Johnson, *Political Change in Latin America* (Stanford, Calif.: Stanford University Press, 1958) and *The Military and Society in Latin America* (Stanford, Calif.: Stanford University Press, 1964). See also the several contributions to John J. Johnson (ed.), *Continuity and Change in Latin America* (Stanford, Calif.: Stanford University Press, 1964). In relation to the article by Despres the reader will find it useful to examine one of the writings by M. G. Smith, for example, *The Plural Society in the*

British West Indies (Berkeley: University of California Press, 1965), which directly challenges the assumption of a consensual basis of all societies. Note in this connection the important essay by Clifford Geertz, "The Integrative Revolution, Primordial Sentiments and Civil Politics in the New States," in Geertz (ed.), *Old Societies and New States* (New York: Free Press of Glencoe, 1963). Rudolph's contribution may be related to the study by Myron Weiner, *The Politics of Scarcity* (Chicago: University of Chicago Press, 1962), with its "interest group" analysis of Indian politics. Cf. in the same context the various publications of F. G. Bailey, especially his *Politics and Social Change* (Berkeley: University of California Press, 1963).

G2. *Structure of Authority.* Here again a few titles are singled out to suggest further exploration along the lines suggested in our selections. Broomfield poses the whole question of socially and politically dominant groups in countries that have become economically or politically dependent. Levenson's study of *Confucian China and Its Modern Fate* (Berkeley: University of California Press, 1958, 1964, 1965), referred to earlier, may be examined in this context. For related materials on Africa the reader should consult the writings by Max Gluckman, for example, his *Order and Rebellion in Tribal Africa* (New York: Free Press of Glencoe, 1963), as well as Lloyd A. Fallers, *Bantu Bureaucracy* (Chicago: University of Chicago Press, 1965) and *The King's Men* (London; New York: Oxford University Press, 1964).

One meaning of "political development" is that the structure of authority in a "developing" country is in flux. This suggestion is contained in Wertheim's and Roth's essays, and may be followed up most easily by reading the literature on comparative administration and the role of the military. On the first topic cf. Joseph LaPalombara (ed.), *Bureaucracy and Political Development* (Princeton, N.J.: Princeton University Press, 1963), and Fred W. Riggs, *Administration in Developing Countries* (Boston: Houghton Mifflin Co., 1964); on the second cf. S. Andrzejewski, *Military Organization and Society* (London: Routledge & Kegan Paul, 1954), S. E. Finer, *The Man on Horseback* (New York: Frederick A. Praeger, 1962), and Morris Janowitz, *The Military in the Political Development of New Nations* (Chicago: University of Chicago Press, 1964).

G3. *Aspects of Legitimacy.* As our selections make clear, "legitimacy" is not an attribute which governments possess once and for all but one which they may gain or lose; and concentration on this important aspect necessarily neglects governments which lack legitimacy, difficult as it may be to assess this condition. Accordingly it may be useful for the reader to follow up our selections by reading some of the attempts to diagnose the structure of "illegitimate" regimes. An important contribution in this respect is Samuel Huntington's "Political Development and Political Decay," *World Politics*, Vol. XVII (1965), pp. 386–430, which — but for reasons of space — we would have included in this volume. Of similar relevance are the two contributions by Huntington and David Rapoport in S. P. Huntington (ed.), *Changing Patterns of Military Politics* (New York: Free Press of Glencoe, 1962). Regarding the analysis of legitimacy itself see the several contributions and appended Bibliography in David Apter (ed.), *Ideology and Discontent* (New York: Free Press of Glencoe, 1964).

A comprehensive analysis of social groups, authority, and problems of legitimacy in the "developing countries" is contained in Edward A. Shils, *Political Development in the New States* (The Hague: Mouton, 1962).

SECOND EDITION REPRINTED

1